BARRON'S

CIVIL SERVICE CLERICAL EXAMS

MAY 2010

6TH EDITION

by

JERRY BOBROW, Ph.D.
Founder
Bobrow Test Preparation Services
Programs at major universities, colleges,
and law schools throughout California

PETER Z ORTON, Ph.D.
IBM Center for
Advanced Learning
Author and lecturer

WILLIAM COVINO, Ph.D.
Provost
California State
University, Stanislaus

Contributing Authors
Kyle Marion
Jeramie Orton
Barbara Swovelin, M.A.
Jerry Swovelin, M.A.

BARRON'S

Acknowledgments

I would like to thank the following people for their contributions to this work:

Dianne Young, M.S., professor of Typing and Office Skills, Santa Monica Community College

Joy Mondragon-Gilmore, M.S., for organization and proofreading

Contributing authors for this edition: Kyle Marion, Jeramie Orton, Barbara Swovelin, M.A., and Jerry Swovelin, M.A.

My special thanks for permission to use excerpts from existing works to:

Gregg Publishing Division, McGraw-Hill Book Company, Inc., Student's Transcript of *Gregg Shorthand Simplified for Colleges*, Volume Two, Second Edition, pages 12, 19, 26–27, 34, 81. Authors Louis A. Leslie, Charles E. Zoubek, and Russell J. Hosier. Copyright 1958, for transcription material beginning on page 393.

South-Western Publishing Company, *College Typewriting*, Tenth Edition, pages 310, 312, 313, 315, 345, 368, 370, 371. Authors Wanous, Duncan, Warner, Langford. Copyright 1980, for typing passages beginning on page 368.

And finally, appreciation to Susan Bobrow and her children, Jennifer Lynn, Adam Michael, and Jonathan Matthew, for their patience and moral support.

All inquiries should be addressed to:
Barron's Educational Series, Inc.
250 Wireless Boulevard
Hauppauge, New York 11788
www.barronseduc.com

Library of Congress Catalog Card No. 2009033315
ISBN-13: 978-0-7641-4302-1
ISBN-10: 0-7641-4302-6

3 9082 10110 7608

Library of Congress Cataloging-in-Publication Data

Bobrow, Jerry.
    Barron's Civil Service clerical examinations / by Jerry Bobrow, Peter Z. Orton, William Covino.—6th ed.
        p. cm.
    Includes index.
    ISBN-13: 978-0-7641-4302-1
    ISBN-10: 0-7641-4302-6
    1. Civil service—United States—Examinations—Study guides. 2. Clerical ability and aptitude tests—Study guides. I. Orton, Peter Z. II. Covino, William A. III. Title. IV. Title: Civil Service clerical examinations.
    JK717.C54B63 2010
    651.3′741076—dc22

2009033315

PRINTED IN THE UNITED STATES OF AMERICA
9 8 7 6 5 4 3 2 1

Contents

Will Studying Help Me?

The most common questions involving exams are "Will studying help me?" and "If so, how should I study?"

Proper preparation can significantly improve your chances of doing your best on an exam. An exam gives you the opportunity to display your skills, knowledge, and ability to apply information. Your chances of doing your best and getting your best possible score will increase tremendously if you take the time to

1. become aware of the types of questions on the exam;
2. understand the techniques and strategies that will help you on these questions; and
3. practice applying your skills by using the techniques and strategies at home before the exam.

Once you learn what is on your exam, you can focus your study on specific types of material. You can review the basic skills that you need in order to do well on the exam.

But how you study is also important. Make sure that your study time is "quality" study time. This time should be uninterrupted blocks of one to two hours, but usually not more than that. Many study periods of one to two hours are usually much more effective than fewer, very long study periods. These study and practice times must be in a quiet, distraction-free setting that will make the study time more effective. This is important, as concentration is a key to good studying.

Make sure to have all the proper materials and supplies with you as you begin to study. It is easy to waste time and break concentration if you have to stop to find the proper materials.

An effective study plan will help you review in an organized manner. Take some time to set up a study schedule. Then stick to it. Once you've completed your study regimen, you should go in to take the test with a positive attitude because you've now prepared and are ready. Going in with this positive attitude will help you to apply what you know and will help you to do your best.

Will studying help you? If you study properly, it can give you the opportunity and the edge to do your best.

Why should you study? Because these exams are competitive and you want every advantage to do your best.

Getting Started: Four Steps to Success

---

1. Awareness
2. Understanding Question Types
3. Using Your Test Preparation Checklist
4. Practice

AWARENESS

This book is designed to provide you with necessary information to help you plan and organize a comprehensive preparation for your Civil Service exam. The Verbal Abilities and Clerical Abilities sections of the Civil Service Clerical Examinations differ greatly from the test sections given a few years ago. Tests are no longer identical for one job across different states or even within the same state at different office levels (city, county, state). Different jurisdictions may now have different tests for the same job title and same job responsibilities. What does that mean for you? It's simple! To prepare for your examination, you must first learn which question types will be on the test you are planning to take.

UNDERSTANDING QUESTION TYPES

You do not want to spend time studying areas that won't be on your exam. Information about test questions appearing on your test should be available from your government agency or its web site. Prepare for only those question types that will appear on your exam. **A word of caution: Question types may appear with different names.** Be aware that a question type may have different names depending upon the jurisdiction in which the test is given. A question type may also be given a new name not indicated in the checklist on the following page. Therefore it's essential that you take care in identifying questions that will be on your test and use the corresponding page numbers in this book to prepare for those questions.

USING YOUR TEST PREPARATION CHECKLIST

The following checklist will enable you to plan your study. As soon as you learn which questions will be on your test, check them off in the left-hand column of the checklist. Use the checklist to **study only** those page numbers corresponding to the areas on your test. **Ignore** other question types which will not appear on your test.

PRACTICE

In addition to the sample practice problems at the beginning of each section, this book offers you hundreds of practice problems to help you apply your knowledge to specific question types. Practice, practice, practice is the key to your success on your Civil Service exam.

Introduction

This book is designed to serve three purposes:

1. To provide information about the experience and training requirements for a variety of office occupations in government agencies, namely, stenographers, typists, word processors, clerks, and office machine operators.
2. To acquaint applicants with the step-by-step approach to getting a federal job and the question types for the tests required for these positions.
3. To *prepare applicants to do their best on the civil service clerical exams*. This final purpose is the major emphasis of this book and includes
   —careful analysis of the test question types
   —important test-taking techniques
   —effective strategies for attacking each question type
   —basic skill review
   —extensive sample tests for practice and review

This introductory section will discuss How to Get a Federal Government Job, Career Opportunities, and Additional Information About These Civil Service Positions and Tests. The rest of the book focuses squarely on preparing for these important tests.

HOW TO GET A FEDERAL GOVERNMENT JOB

STEP 1: Obtain an official announcement and application form from the federal government personnel office, whose local address and phone number are listed in your telephone directory. You can also get valuable information including "resume building" on the Internet at *www.usajobs.gov.*

STEP 2: Complete the application form, as instructed by the announcement. Send it to the address printed on the application and/or announcement.

STEP 3: If a clerical exam is required, become familiar with the test, the question types, its required basic skills, and effective test-taking strategies. The information contained in this book, Barron's *Civil Service Clerical Examinations*, will help you improve your basic skills as well as test-taking skills. Spend as much time as necessary for a thorough preparation.

STEP 4: Many agencies send by mail or email an admission blank and instructions for taking a civil service test, if required. The instructions will list the location and time of the test, and the proper materials for you to bring to the exam (such as sharpened #2 pencils, a photo I.D., and more).

STEP 5: Become familiar with the location of the test site.

STEP 6: On the day of the exam, arrive early and prepared to do your best.

STEP 7: After your exam, the government agency evaluates your qualifications and places your application in its working files.

STEP 8: The government agency interviews candidates and makes selections based upon candidate qualifications and interviews.

CAREER OPPORTUNITIES

Clerk-Typist and Clerk-Stenographer

The positions filled from these examinations are paid under the General Schedule, in which there are a number of grades that indicate the difficulty and responsibility of the work and the necessary qualifications requirements. Normal entrance levels are for Clerk-Typist positions and Clerk-Stenographer positions. This difference in grade reflects the greater difficulty of the stenographic work and the additional skill required.

Where there are concentrations of government employees, the opportunities for well-qualified typists and stenographers are very favorable. The demand for Clerk-Stenographers and Clerk-Typists continues to be steady. There is also a need for persons with extra qualifications required for higher-level Clerk-Stenographers and higher-level Clerk-Typists.

Vacancies in government agencies are constantly occurring in clerical positions as employees are promoted to higher-grade positions, transfer to other jobs, or leave for personal reasons. Career development and promotion programs make Clerk-Stenographer and Clerk-Typist positions a good training ground and an avenue of promotion to higher-grade positions of these types and to secretarial positions. There are also opportunities for promotion to other kinds of positions, such as Administrative Assistant and related occupations.

Clerk

The title "Clerk" covers many specialized fields. While some positions call for specialized experience or training, most of the specialized work is at higher levels. In the government service, clerks have many opportunities to advance to higher-level clerical, supervisory, and administrative positions. Descriptions of some of the major groups of jobs follow.

There are clerical and clerical-administrative positions in *accounting, payroll,* and *fiscal* work, exclusive of those in professional accounting. Accounts Maintenance Clerks perform accounting clerical work that requires ability to learn and to apply specific instructions, rules, regulations, and procedures, but does not require technical knowledge of bookkeeping or accounting. Other clerks in this area work in the general accounting field; some of these positions provide experience in almost the full range of accounting duties and, when supplemented by appropriate education, help prepare employees for professional accounting careers. Related large occupational groups include Military Pay Clerks and Leave and Payroll Clerks.

A very important group comprises Voucher Examiners. These jobs begin at higher levels because of the responsible and difficult nature of the work.

A distinct job is Cash Processing Clerk. These clerks handle and watch for irregularities in cash items; they also learn and apply requirements for accepting documents that are the basis for the transactions of commercial, federal, and other financial institutions in processing cash items.

A very large group of clerical positions is in the *general clerical* and *administrative* field. This includes Mail and File Clerks, a much smaller group of Correspondence Clerks, and several thousand other clerical jobs of types too numerous to list here.

In the *personnel* field, clerks have an opportunity to advance to a variety of administrative and technical positions in support of professional personnel work.

The movement of people and material makes up a large part of the business of the federal government. In particular, the movement of military personnel and supplies and the movement of agricultural and other shipments offer additional opportunities for clerks. These clerical positions are in a range of grade levels. Many of the positions provide opportunities for promotion to freight or passenger rate work or other higher-level assignments.

The huge problems of supply for the Department of Defense, Veterans Administration, and other agencies call for thousands of clerks in *general supply, stock control,* and *storekeeping.* Most of these positions are in the two agencies just mentioned, but there are sizable numbers in the Treasury Department and in the General Services Administration, the agency in charge of procurement, supply, and maintenance of property for the federal government.

Finally, the extensive statistical programs of the government agencies utilize skilled Statistical Assistants. Their work includes the collection and analysis of data from census and other surveys, crop prediction reports, work measurement studies, and many other functions. While the entry level into these jobs is usually lower, many opportunities for advancement exist, and specialized training courses in statistics and in data processing are available to employees.

Office Machine Operator

Data Transcribers operate numeric and alphabetic machines, using skills similar to those required in typewriting and word processing. There is a considerably smaller number of Electric Accounting Machine Operators, who operate a variety of tabulating equipment. In these groups most employees are at the entry levels.

These jobs provide an opportunity to work with and learn various data processing systems. With additional specialized training or experience, employees are able to prepare for careers in computer system operations, programming, and planning.

There are several thousand other Office Machine Operators, whose duties include the operation of one or more types of office imprinting (including embossing), duplicating, or reproducing machines, or the operation of miscellaneous office machines or equipment. Most of these positions are at the GS-2 level.

Bookkeeping Machine Operator and Calculating Machine Operator positions require special skills and training. Most of the positions in this group are entry level.

THE TESTS

The tests normally taken for the positions just described include

1. The Clerical Exam: Verbal Abilities and Clerical Abilities Parts

2. The Dictation Test

3. The Typing (Word Processing) Test

There are also some special tests for certain Office Machine Operator positions, including a simplified typing test for Teletypists and other operators of machines with alphabetic keyboards, and a test of abstract reasoning for Electric Accounting Machine Operators (Tabulating Machine Operators) and Cryptographic Equipment Operators.

With the diagnostic and model tests included in this book, candidates can determine if they have sufficient ability to meet the standards of the federal government, or if they need to build their skills and, if so, to what degree. These tests can also help candidates in identifying their shortcomings while there is time to focus their training accordingly. Applicants can thus diagnose areas needing improvement and then practice to strengthen their weak areas.

ADDITIONAL INFORMATION ABOUT THESE CIVIL SERVICE POSITIONS AND TESTS

The following paragraphs summarize current information concerning office positions, including stenographer and typist positions. (For the sake of brevity, in this book positions are often referred to as stenographer and typist positions rather than by the official titles of Clerk-Stenographer and Clerk-Typist.) For more information, contact the office of Personnel Management at *www.usajobs.gov.*

Salaries and Other Benefits

Appointments to stenographer positions are usually made at higher grade levels. For example, GS-3 and GS-4 for federal employment. For the latter grade, 1 year of appropriate experience or education above the high school level is required. Appointments to typist, dictating machine transcriber, clerk, and office machine operator positions are usually made at intermediate grade levels. For example, GS-2 and GS-3 for federal employment. Appointments are also made at higher levels to specialized clerk positions. Always consult your local announcement for current salary rates.

General Federal Schedule Pay

The current General Schedule (GS) pay scale for federal employees can be obtained through the U.S. Office of Personnel Management at *www.opm.gov/oca* (click on "salaries and wages"). Please note that this pay scale is adjusted geographically and pertains only to federal civil service positions. Locality payments in the continental United States range from 10.09 percent to 22.23 percent. Pay rates outside the continental United States are 10 percent to 25 percent higher. Also, certain hard-to-fill jobs, usually in the scientific, technical, and medical fields, may have higher starting salaries. Exact pay information can be found on position vacancy announcements and through different city, county, and state government agencies.

Test and Experience Requirements

Tables 1 and 2 indicate the federal tests that are usually taken and the education and experience requirement for the positions. Similar requirements are expected from other agencies.

Final numerical rating in the examination is typically based on the written Clerical Exam: Verbal Abilities and Clerical Abilities Parts. Typing and dictation tests are qualifying only and are not added into the final rating. Higher scores are generally required for the higher grades.

The latest information regarding applying for Clerical and Administrative Support Positions is available on the web at *www.usajobs.gov*. The agencies now have several options to use in filling a position. The Clerical and Administrative Support Exam is no longer administered on a regular basis, only as requested by the hiring agency to fill a position. Carefully review each job announcement to see if and when a written test will be given. Note the type of exam given and the areas covered. Sample exam problems are sometimes included.

SAMPLE FEDERAL CLERICAL REQUIREMENTS

TABLE 1

Clerk, Typist, and Stenographer

| | Typical Tests Used*** | | | | |
| | The Clerical Exam | | | | |
	Verbal Abilities Part	Clerical Abilities Part	Typing*	Stenography*	Education Experience**
Clerk GS-2	Yes	Yes	No	No	High school
Typist GS-2	Yes	Yes	Yes	No	graduate 3–6
Stenographer GS-3	Yes	Yes	Yes	Yes	months of appropriate experience
Clerk GS-3	Yes	Yes	No	No	1 year of
Typist GS-3	Yes	Yes	Yes	No	appropriate
Stenographer GS-4	Yes	Yes	Yes	Yes	experience or 1 academic year of post-high school education

*An acceptable proficiency certificate can be substituted for these tests—see section "Proficiency Certificates."
**The appropriate experience for clerk is progressively responsible clerical or office work. Appropriate experience for typist and stenographer is either (1) experience that included, as a significant part of the work, application of the required skill (i.e., typing, dictating machine transcribing, or stenography) or (2) any type of clerical work that demonstrates the ability to perform the duties of the position to be filled, provided that the applicant demonstrates an adequate degree of proficiency in the required skills(s).
***Agencies may use other exams or assessments.

(For qualification standards for general administrative, clerical, and office services, go to www.opm.gov/qualifications/standards/indexes/0300=ndx.asp.)

TABLE 2

Office Machine Operator

	Tests	Education/Experience*
GS-2	The Clerical Exam Verbal and clerical parts for all applicants. For additional tests for certain positions, see section "The Office Machine Operator Special Test," page 419.	a) 6 months specialized experience, or b) specialized course of instruction in operation of appropriate machine and 3 months of experience, or c) successful completion of a federally financed course of instruction (e.g., Work Incentive Program, Job Corps, Comprehensive Employment Training Act Program, etc.) of appropriate content, intensity, and duration, or d) high school graduation. Education must have included training in operation of appropriate machine, unless a performance test is available for the particular occupation.
GS-3		a) 1 year of office-type experience of which at least 6 months is specialized, or b) 1 academic year of post-high school education, which included training in the operation of appropriate machine, unless a performance test is available for the particular occupation.

Different requirements may be in effect in some localities. If so, these different requirements will be stated in the examination announcements for those localities. Be sure to check specific government agencies.

Proficiency Certificates

Arrangements have been made with many schools and other authorized training organizations to accept from the applicants a teacher's certificate of proficiency in typing and shorthand. Submission of such a certificate will excuse the applicant from taking the typing and/or shorthand tests. A teacher may certify that the student has demonstrated proficiency in typing and/or shorthand on unfamiliar and continuous material at a standard at least high enough to meet the agency's requirements. Certificates are valid for only a limited period and are usually issued only to those persons who are still in school. Applicants with satisfactory certificates will still have to take the verbal and clerical abilities tests. If you have any questions concerning the use of proficiency certificates, contact the area office of the agency servicing your area.

Physically Handicapped Applicants

Although applicants for federal employment must be able to perform the duties of a position, this does not prevent physically handicapped persons from being hired. Physically handicapped persons are encouraged to apply for positions in the federal government. Each area office has a Selective Placement Specialist who is responsible for assuring that all handicapped applicants are able to take advantage of the available employment opportunities for which they apply. Government agencies also have coordinators for selective placement to assist in job placements. In addition to regular competitive placements, severely handicapped persons may be able to secure excepted appointments in some positions.

Most clerical, typing, stenographer, and office machine operator jobs require good distance vision in one eye and the ability to read, without strain, material the size of typewritten characters. Glasses may be used. However, blind typists can fill many positions, such as dictating machine transcribers. Blind applicants should state on their application cards that they are blind, since special arrangements must be made for their examination.

Ability to hear the conversational voice is required for most positions; however, some positions are suitable for deaf applicants.

Be sure to tell the examiner ahead of time if you need special assistance in taking a civil service test. Often you can be accommodated by having more time to complete non-speeded portions of tests. Also, parts of tests may be waived for you.

If you have a disability and are interested in a civil service job with the federal government, another avenue for assistance is the federal Selective Placement Coordinator of the federal agency where you would like to work. Every agency and location has a personnel official who serves as a Selective Placement Coordinator. This person can place you directly in a position without the use of ability and aptitude tests. The appointment is a noncompetitive, excepted service appointment. If you perform the job successfully for two years, you can be converted noncompetitively to the competitive service. You will be treated the same as competitive service hires in terms of health benefits, life insurance, and retirement eligibility. Also, you will have the same leave benefits. In the case of an invisible disability, other employees will never know that you were hired under an excepted appointment. In any case, you will be treated with the same respect given anyone else. The main disadvantage to an excepted service appointment is that you are in a separate reduction-in-force category from competitive service appointments. (However, reductions in force are fairly rare.) There are no formal documentation requirements to enter these programs and a statement from a professional in a health field may be sufficient documentation. States also have special appointing authorities for hiring people with disabilities; these should be explored.

Your rehabilitation counselor can work with you in making contacts with the federal Selective Placement Coordinator or with the comparable state official.

Veterans

If you are a veteran of the military services, the Department of Labor's Employment Services have excellent specialized services available to you; you need to mention that you are a veteran and ask for help as a veteran. There are excellent employment resources listed at *www.usajobs.gov*.

Equipment Needed for Tests

In some localities, competitors taking the typing test must furnish a typewriter and a typing table for use in the examination. Applicants who wish to use an electric typewriter should ask the examining office, in advance of the examination date, whether there is an electric outlet in the examining room.

Stenographer applicants may use any system of taking and transcribing dictation provided it does not interfere with the dictation or with other competitors. Any system of manually written shorthand notes or any noiseless shorthand writing machine may be used provided the notes are given to the examiner after they have been transcribed. Blind persons may be required to furnish a transcribing machine for use in the examining room.

How and Where to Apply

Civil Service examinations for typists and stenographers are usually announced together and given at the same time at individual agencies. Examinations for Clerk and for various types of Office Machine Operator, such as Data Transcriber, may be announced separately. However, some or all of these examinations may be combined in a single Office Assistant Examination. There may also be some training positions in these occupations. Check with your local government agency for details on positions, locations, and grade levels for which the examination is being held, and specific instructions on how to apply. Applicants are usually provided with samples of the tests to be given in the examination.

Full information about applying for these and other federal, state, county, and city jobs is provided by *www.USAJOBS.gov*. Local offices are usually listed in local telephone directories under "U.S. Government."

Internet Job Search

The Internet is the best source for government jobs, both locally and nationally. It can be both time-consuming and fun. Working with a friend, you can do some very fascinating searches. However, you can work alone and have fun doing it as well. The following sources will aid in your search.

USA Jobs: *www.usajobs.gov*. This is the official government web site for Civil Service employment. It is maintained by the United States Office of Personnel Management and should answer many of your questions about government employment. It lists job opportunities by government agency, job category, and job location. Job postings are updated on a 24-hour basis. If you register with USAJOBS and create an account, you receive help to build and post your resume and you will be notified by email when new job listings are posted.

United States Department of Labor: *www.dol.gov*. This is an excellent resource providing a variety of information about employee rights, wages, benefits, disability resources, and employment statistics. For links to other government agencies, click "audience (job seekers)" and look under "job and training information."

America's Career Information Net: *www.acinet.org/acinet/* or *www.careeronestop.org*. If you're looking for information about job searches, exploring careers, training, or general employment information, this web site can help you explore alternatives.

Career Voyages: *www.careervoyages.gov*. This is a web site co-sponsored by the U.S. Department of Labor and the U.S. Department of Education. It will help you explore and prepare for a career in Civil Service. It offers information and guidance for "in-demand" job opportunities, education and training, and projected popular careers.

Local Newspapers. Many newspapers list all job openings on the Internet. The employer is charged for both the written newspaper advertisement and the Internet advertisement. For example, *The Washington Post* provides job advertisements on the Internet. The Post's site is: *www.washingtonpost.com.* You can use such a site and go to other sites through links provided. You will find all of the jobs listed in *The Washington Post.* Also, you will find help in writing resumes and cover letters as well as other assistance.

Career Path: www.careerpath.com. This web site is one of the most used job search sites. It is very user-friendly. You can conduct a job search. You can put your resume online.

Online Career Center: www.monster.com. You can search for jobs and company profiles here. Also, you can put your resume online.

Other Government Internet Systems. To go into all of the federal government's Internet systems, I suggest using the White House links as an entry source: http:// whitehouse.gov

Google and Other Browsers. If you are looking into areas to find information about companies, or information about jobs, use a web browser. After you go into the web page, you will be asked for key words for your search. Google is widely used and provides links for other browsers: *www.google.com.*

Internet Availability. You can use the Internet at public libraries in most cities. Usually, you would be given 30 to 40 minutes of terminal time each time you request it. The librarian will show you how to do a search, if you are unfamiliar with the Internet. Also, many cities have large job-search collections in some libraries. Ask the reference librarian where these collections are held. There are extensive job search manuals and books to help in a job search for specific occupations and occupations in general. Also, there are many reference books that can be used for job searches.

Wherever you go, you will find the Internet easy to use. The Internet is extensively cross-referenced with links to other sites so that you can go from one site to another in your job search. Also, if you are using library facilities in your job search, you may want to explore with the librarian how to set up an E-mail account through various free E-mail systems that will not interfere with the library's account, so that you can hear back from employers. (Do not be concerned if you cannot set up such an account; the prospective employer will call or write to you, if you do not have such an account.)

Temporary Appointments

If you are offered a temporary position, you should consider taking it. This is particularly true if it is for one year or longer. Temporary positions of one year or longer usually offer most of the same benefits as permanent positions offer. Also, temporary positions often are converted to permanent positions. The process for this conversion may require you to recompete. However, if you retain a copy of your notice of rating, normally you will not need to retake a civil service examination.

Completion of Answer Sheet

Most test answer sheets are machine scored. Therefore, it is very important that they be filled out properly. Most tests allow only one answer for each question; if there is more than one answer, the scoring machine is programmed to score the answer as incorrect. Therefore, an applicant must be careful to erase an answer completely if he or she changes it.

Great care must be taken to insure that an applicant's name and Social Security account number are recorded properly.

Veterans' Preference Provisions

The following information regarding Veterans' Preference is available on the USAJOBS web site *www.usajobs.gov*.

Veterans' Preference

Since the time of the Civil War, Veterans of the Armed Forces have been given some degree of preference in appointments to Federal jobs. Recognizing that sacrifices are made by those serving in the Armed Forces, Congress enacted laws to prevent veterans seeking Federal employment from being penalized because of the time spent in military service.

By law, veterans who are disabled or who served on active duty in the Armed Forces during certain specified time periods or in military campaigns are entitled to preference over nonveterans both in hiring from competitive lists of eligibles and in retention during reductions in force.

Preference does not have as its goal the placement of a veteran in every vacant Federal job; this would be incompatible with the merit principle of public employment. Nor does it apply to promotions or other in-service actions. However, preference does provide a uniform method by which special consideration is given to qualified veterans seeking Federal employment.

Preference applies in hiring from civil service examinations, conducted by the Office of Personnel Management (OPM) and agencies under delegated examining authority for most excepted service jobs, and when agencies make temporary appointments or use direct hire and delegated examining authorities from the U. S. Office of Personnel Management.

General Requirements for Preference

To be entitled to preference, a veteran must meet the eligibility requirements in section 2101(2) of title 5, United States Code. This means that:

- An honorable or general discharge is necessary.
- Military retirees at the rank of major, lieutenant commander, or higher are not eligible for preference unless they are disabled veterans. (This does not

apply to Reservists who will not begin drawing military retired pay until age 60.)

- For non-disabled users, National Guard or Reserve active duty does *not* qualify for preference.
- When applying for Federal jobs, eligible veterans should claim preference on their application or resume. Applicants claiming 10-point preference must complete form SF-15, Application for 10-Point Veteran Preference.

Note: The National Defense Authorization Act for Fiscal Year 2006 clarified the scope of the term "veteran" for the purposes of determining who is entitled to veterans' preference. OPM is in the process of revising its regulations to conform to this clarification. In the interim, agencies should rely upon the statute and this guidance in determining who is entitled to veterans' preference.

Types of Preference

5-POINT PREFERENCE (TP)

Five points are added to the passing examination score or rating of a veteran who served:

- During a war; or
- During the period April 28, 1952, through July 1, 1955; or
- For more than 180 consecutive days, other than for training, any part of which occurred after January 31, 1955, and before October 15, 1976; or
- During the Gulf War from August 2, 1990, through January 2, 1992; or
- For more than 180 consecutive days, other than for training, any part of which occurred during the period beginning September 11, 2001, and ending on the date prescribed by presidential proclamation or by law as the last day of Operation Iraqi Freedom; or
- In a campaign or expedition for which a campaign medal has been authorized. Any Armed Forces Expeditionary medal or campaign badge, including El Salvador, Lebanon, Grenada, Panama, Southwest Asia, Somalia, and Haiti qualifies for preference.

Medal holders and Gulf War veterans who enlisted after September 7, 1980, or entered on active duty on or after October 14, 1982, must have served continuously for 24 months or the full period called or ordered to active duty. The service requirement does not apply to veterans with compensable service-connected disabilities, or to veterans separated for disability in the line of duty, or for hardship or for other reasons under 10 U.S.C. 1171 or 1173.

10-POINT PREFERENCE

Ten points are added to the passing examination score of:

- A veteran who served any time and who (1) has a present service-connected disability of at least 10 percent but less than 30 percent or (2) is receiving compensation, disability retirement benefits, or pension from the military or the Department of Veterans Affairs. Individuals who received a Purple Heart qualify as disabled veterans.

- An unmarried spouse of certain deceased veterans, a spouse of a veteran unable to work because of a service-connected disability, and
- A mother of a veteran who died in service or who is permanently and totally disabled.

Preference in Examination

Veterans meeting the criteria for preference and who are found eligible have 5 or 10 points added to their numerical ratings depending on the nature of their preference. For scientific and professional positions in grade GS-9 or higher, names of all eligibles are listed in order of ratings, augmented by veteran preference, if any. For all other positions, the names of 10-point preference eligibles who have a compensable, service-connected disability of 10 percent or more are placed ahead of the names of all other eligibles on a given register. The names of other 10-point preference eligibles, 5-point preference eligibles, and non-veterans are listed in order of their numerical ratings.

Entitlement to veterans' preference does not guarantee a job. There are many ways an agency can fill a vacancy other than by appointment from a list of eligibles.

Positions for Preference Eligibles Only

Certain *examinations* are open only to preference eligibles as long as such applicants are available. These are custodian, guard, elevator operator, and messenger.

Special Complaint Procedures for Veterans

Veterans who believe that they have not been accorded the preference to which they are entitled may file a complaint with the U.S. Department of Labor's Veterans Employment and Training Service (VETS).

The Department of Labor's Office of the Assistant Secretary for Policy and Veterans' Employment and Training Service developed an "expert system" to help veterans receive the preferences to which they are entitled. Two versions of this system are currently available, both of which, help the veterans determine the type of preference to which they are entitled, the benefits associated with the preference, and the steps necessary to file a complaint due to the failure of a Federal Agency to provide those benefits. The Internet address for the veterans' preference program is *www.dol.gov/elaws/vetspref.htm*. (State Employment Service Offices have veteran representatives available to assist veterans in gaining access to this information.)

PART I

THE CLERICAL EXAM: VERBAL ABILITIES PART

Verbal Abilities General Strategies: A Diagnostic Test

with Answers and Explanations/ Analysis of Strengths and Weaknesses

THE VERBAL ABILITIES PART

The Verbal Abilities Part includes questions that measure such language skills as knowledge of the meaning and relationship of words, ability to spell common words, and skill in recognizing sentences that are grammatically correct in contrast to others that are not acceptable. The test also includes questions that measure the ability to read and understand written material. Possible question types include:

- Word meaning (vocabulary)
- Analogies (word relationships)
- Grammar (language usage)
- Spelling
- Reading (understanding and interpreting written material)
- Punctuation

Procedure

You will have time to study the directions and sample questions on the front of your test booklet and to mark the answers to these sample questions in the space provided. You will then be told when to begin the actual test.

General Strategies

Because there is a limited amount of time to answer the questions, some very important considerations regarding speed, marking, eliminating choices, and guessing come into play. We recommend you become familiar with the following strategies:

MARKING IN THE TEST BOOKLET

Many test takers are allowed to mark in the test booklet. Take full advantage of opportunities to mark key words and cross out wrong choices *in the test booklet.* Remember that writing in your test booklet (as explained later) can significantly help you stay focused, as well as help you isolate the correct answer choices. It will also enable you to successfully use the following strategy.

THE ONE-CHECK, TWO-CHECK SYSTEM

Many people score lower than they should on the Verbal Abilities Part simply because they do not get to many of the easier problems. They puzzle over difficult questions and use up the time that could be spent answering easy ones. In fact, the difficult questions are worth exactly the same as the easy ones, so it makes sense not to do the hard problems until you have answered all the easy ones.

To maximize your correct answers by focusing on the easier problems, use the following system:

1. Attempt the first question. If it is answerable quickly and easily, work the problem, circle the answer in the question booklet, and then mark that answer on the answer sheet. The mark on the answer sheet should be a complete mark, not merely a dot, because you may not be given time at the end of the test to darken marks.

2. If a question seems impossible, place two checks (✔✔) on or next to the question number in the question booklet and mark the answer you guess on the answer sheet. *(On most exams, there is no penalty for a wrong guess.)* The mark on the answer sheet should be a complete mark, not merely a dot, because you may not be given time at the end of the test to darken marks,

3. If you're in the midst of a question that seems to be taking too much time, or if you immediately spot that a question is answerable but time-consuming (that is, it will require a minute or more to answer), place one check (✔) next to the question number, mark an answer you guess on the answer sheet, and continue with the next question.

NOTE THAT NO QUESTIONS ARE LEFT BLANK. AN ANSWER CHOICE IS *ALWAYS* FILLED IN BEFORE LEAVING THAT QUESTION, SINCE ON MOST EXAMS THERE IS NO PENALTY FOR GUESSING.

4. When all the problems in a section have been attempted in this manner, there may still be time left. If so, return to the single-check (✔) questions, working as many as possible, changing each guessed answer to a worked-out answer, if necessary.

5. If time remains after all the single-check (✔) questions are completed, you can choose between

   a. attempting those "impossible" double-check (✔✔) questions (sometimes a question later on in the test may trigger your memory to allow once-impossible questions to be solved);

or

   b. spending time checking and reworking the easier questions to eliminate any careless errors.

6. You should try to use *all* the allotted time as effectively as possible.

Use this system as you work through the Verbal Ability diagnostic and practice test questions in this book; such practice will allow you to make "one-check, two-check" judgments quickly when you actually take your exam. As our extensive research has shown, use of this system results in less wasted time.

THE ELIMINATION STRATEGY

Faced with four or five answer choices, you will work more efficiently and effectively if you immediately *eliminate* unreasonable or obviously wrong choices. In many cases, several of the choices will immediately appear to be incorrect, and these should be crossed out *on your test booklet* immediately. Then, if a guess is necessary among the remaining choices, you will not reconsider these obvious wrong choices, but will choose from the remaining choices.

Consider the following reading question:

> According to the theory of aerodynamics, the bumblebee is unable to fly. This is because the size, weight, and shape of his body in relationship to his total wingspan make flying impossible. The bumblebee, being ignorant of this "scientific truth," flies anyway

> *The paragraph best supports the statement that* bumblebees
> A) cannot fly in strong winds
> B) are ignorant of other things but can't do all of them
> C do not actually fly but glide instead
> D) may contradict the theory of aerodynamics

Test takers who do not immediately eliminate the unreasonable choices here, and instead try to analyze every choice, will find themselves becoming confused and anxious as they try to decide how even unreasonable choices might be correct. Their thinking might go something like this:

> "Hmmmm, I've never seen a bumblebee in a strong wind. I'm not sure what (B) means. I wonder if bumblebees do glide;
> I've never looked at them *that* closely. Hmmmm, (D) could be right, but what about the other three? I had better took at them again in case I missed something."

On and on they go, sometimes rereading choices three or four times. In a test of this nature, they cannot afford to spend so much time on one question!

Using the elimination strategy, a confident test taker proceeds as follows:

"A)? Ridiculous and irrelevant. Cross it out.
B)? I don't understand this. Put a question mark after it.
C)? That sounds ridiculous. Cross it out.
D)? That's possible. in fact, that's a much better choice than (B), which I'm not sure I even understand. The answer I'll mark is (D)."

This test taker, aware that most answer choices can be easily eliminated, does so without complicating the process by considering unreasonable possibilities.

To summarize this strategy:

—Look for incorrect answer choices. Cross them out in the test booklet.
—Put question marks after choices that could be possible.
—Never reconsider choices you have eliminated.

Eliminating incorrect choices will lead you to correct choices more quickly and will increase your chances when you make a guess.

GUESSING

As previously mentioned, on most exams there is no penalty for an incorrect answer, even if it is a guess. So *never* leave a blank on the Verbal Abilities Part. (This rule does not apply to the other tests, however.)

Whenever you are faced with a difficult, seemingly impossible, or time-consuming question, never leave it until you have *at least registered a guess on the answer sheet.*

CHANGING ANSWERS AND STRAY MARKS

If you find it necessary to change an answer on your answer sheet, make sure to erase the incorrect answer *completely*. Any partial marks in the answer spaces may be picked up by the scoring machine as a "second answer choice marked" on one question, and that question will be marked incorrect. Therefore take great care to erase completely, and not to make stray marks on your answer sheet.

A DIAGNOSTIC TEST WITH ANSWER EXPLANATIONS

The purpose of this diagnostic test is to familiarize you with selected question types on the Verbal Abilities Part. It is designed to introduce you to some of the testing areas and to assist you in evaluating your strengths and weaknesses. This will help you focus your review. Chapter 2 will give you a more complete range of problem types and specific strategies for each section. After correcting the diagnostic test and assessing your strengths and weaknesses, you should start your area reviews and practice in the next chapter.

The diagnostic test should be taken under strict test conditions.

First take a few minutes to review the sample questions given here before starting the exam. (NOTE: Sample questions are usually distributed with the announcement and if so may not be given in the official examination.) Now tear out your answer sheet from this book, turn to the next page, and begin the exam.

REVIEWING THE KEY STRATEGIES

Remember to:

1. Answer easy questions first.
2. Skip "impossible" questions, marking them with the double check (✔✔).
3. Skip "time-consuming" questions, marking them with the single check (✔), coming back to these later, if possible.
4. Answer every question. Fill in a guess, if necessary.
5. Use *all* the allotted time.

Answer Sheet

VERBAL ABILITIES GENERAL STRATEGIES

1 Ⓐ Ⓑ Ⓒ Ⓓ	23 Ⓐ Ⓑ Ⓒ Ⓓ	45 Ⓐ Ⓑ Ⓒ Ⓓ	67 Ⓐ Ⓑ Ⓒ Ⓓ
2 Ⓐ Ⓑ Ⓒ Ⓓ	24 Ⓐ Ⓑ Ⓒ Ⓓ	46 Ⓐ Ⓑ Ⓒ Ⓓ	68 Ⓐ Ⓑ Ⓒ Ⓓ
3 Ⓐ Ⓑ Ⓒ Ⓓ	25 Ⓐ Ⓑ Ⓒ Ⓓ	47 Ⓐ Ⓑ Ⓒ Ⓓ	69 Ⓐ Ⓑ Ⓒ Ⓓ
4 Ⓐ Ⓑ Ⓒ Ⓓ	26 Ⓐ Ⓑ Ⓒ Ⓓ	48 Ⓐ Ⓑ Ⓒ Ⓓ	70 Ⓐ Ⓑ Ⓒ Ⓓ
5 Ⓐ Ⓑ Ⓒ Ⓓ	27 Ⓐ Ⓑ Ⓒ Ⓓ	49 Ⓐ Ⓑ Ⓒ Ⓓ	71 Ⓐ Ⓑ Ⓒ Ⓓ
6 Ⓐ Ⓑ Ⓒ Ⓓ	28 Ⓐ Ⓑ Ⓒ Ⓓ	50 Ⓐ Ⓑ Ⓒ Ⓓ	72 Ⓐ Ⓑ Ⓒ Ⓓ
7 Ⓐ Ⓑ Ⓒ Ⓓ	29 Ⓐ Ⓑ Ⓒ Ⓓ	51 Ⓐ Ⓑ Ⓒ Ⓓ	73 Ⓐ Ⓑ Ⓒ Ⓓ
8 Ⓐ Ⓑ Ⓒ Ⓓ	30 Ⓐ Ⓑ Ⓒ Ⓓ	52 Ⓐ Ⓑ Ⓒ Ⓓ	74 Ⓐ Ⓑ Ⓒ Ⓓ
9 Ⓐ Ⓑ Ⓒ Ⓓ	31 Ⓐ Ⓑ Ⓒ Ⓓ	53 Ⓐ Ⓑ Ⓒ Ⓓ	75 Ⓐ Ⓑ Ⓒ Ⓓ
10 Ⓐ Ⓑ Ⓒ Ⓓ	32 Ⓐ Ⓑ Ⓒ Ⓓ	54 Ⓐ Ⓑ Ⓒ Ⓓ	76 Ⓐ Ⓑ Ⓒ Ⓓ
11 Ⓐ Ⓑ Ⓒ Ⓓ	33 Ⓐ Ⓑ Ⓒ Ⓓ	55 Ⓐ Ⓑ Ⓒ Ⓓ	77 Ⓐ Ⓑ Ⓒ Ⓓ
12 Ⓐ Ⓑ Ⓒ Ⓓ	34 Ⓐ Ⓑ Ⓒ Ⓓ	56 Ⓐ Ⓑ Ⓒ Ⓓ	78 Ⓐ Ⓑ Ⓒ Ⓓ
13 Ⓐ Ⓑ Ⓒ Ⓓ	35 Ⓐ Ⓑ Ⓒ Ⓓ	57 Ⓐ Ⓑ Ⓒ Ⓓ	79 Ⓐ Ⓑ Ⓒ Ⓓ
14 Ⓐ Ⓑ Ⓒ Ⓓ	36 Ⓐ Ⓑ Ⓒ Ⓓ	58 Ⓐ Ⓑ Ⓒ Ⓓ	80 Ⓐ Ⓑ Ⓒ Ⓓ
15 Ⓐ Ⓑ Ⓒ Ⓓ	37 Ⓐ Ⓑ Ⓒ Ⓓ	59 Ⓐ Ⓑ Ⓒ Ⓓ	81 Ⓐ Ⓑ Ⓒ Ⓓ
16 Ⓐ Ⓑ Ⓒ Ⓓ	38 Ⓐ Ⓑ Ⓒ Ⓓ	60 Ⓐ Ⓑ Ⓒ Ⓓ	82 Ⓐ Ⓑ Ⓒ Ⓓ
17 Ⓐ Ⓑ Ⓒ Ⓓ	39 Ⓐ Ⓑ Ⓒ Ⓓ	61 Ⓐ Ⓑ Ⓒ Ⓓ	83 Ⓐ Ⓑ Ⓒ Ⓓ
18 Ⓐ Ⓑ Ⓒ Ⓓ	40 Ⓐ Ⓑ Ⓒ Ⓓ	62 Ⓐ Ⓑ Ⓒ Ⓓ	84 Ⓐ Ⓑ Ⓒ Ⓓ
19 Ⓐ Ⓑ Ⓒ Ⓓ	41 Ⓐ Ⓑ Ⓒ Ⓓ	63 Ⓐ Ⓑ Ⓒ Ⓓ	85 Ⓐ Ⓑ Ⓒ Ⓓ
20 Ⓐ Ⓑ Ⓒ Ⓓ	42 Ⓐ Ⓑ Ⓒ Ⓓ	64 Ⓐ Ⓑ Ⓒ Ⓓ	
21 Ⓐ Ⓑ Ⓒ Ⓓ	43 Ⓐ Ⓑ Ⓒ Ⓓ	65 Ⓐ Ⓑ Ⓒ Ⓓ	
22 Ⓐ Ⓑ Ⓒ Ⓓ	44 Ⓐ Ⓑ Ⓒ Ⓓ	66 Ⓐ Ⓑ Ⓒ Ⓓ	

Answer Sheet

Verbal Abilities Diagnostic Test

Time allotted—35 minutes

Directions and Sample Questions

Study the sample questions carefully. Each question has four suggested answers. Decide which one is the best answer. Find the question number on the Sample Answer Sheet. Show your answer to the question by darkening completely the space corresponding to the letter that is the same as the letter of your answer. Keep your mark within the space. If you have to erase a mark, be sure to erase it completely. Mark only one answer for each question. Do NOT mark space E for any question.

Sample Questions

1. *Previous* means most nearly

   A) abandoned   C) timely
   B) former   D) younger

2. Just as the procedure of a collection department must be clear cut and definite, the steps being taken with the sureness of a skilled chess player, so the various paragraphs of a collection letter must show clear organization, giving evidence of a mind that, from the beginning, has had a specific end in view.

   The paragraph best supports the statement that a collection letter should always

   A) show a spirit of sportsmanship
   B) be divided into several paragraphs
   C) be brief, but courteous
   D) be carefully planned

   Decide which sentence is preferable with respect to grammar and usage suitable for a formal letter or report.

3. A) They do not ordinarily present these kind of reports in detail like this.
   B) A report of this kind is not hardly ever given in such detail as this one.
   C) This report is more detailed than what such reports ordinarily are.
   D) A report of this kind is not ordinarily presented in as much detail as this one is.

   Find the correct spelling of the word and darken the proper answer space. If no suggested spelling is correct, darken space D.

4. A) athalete   C) athlete
   B) athelete   D) none of these

5. SPEEDOMETER is related to POINTER as WATCH is related to

   A) case   C) dial
   B) hands   D) numerals

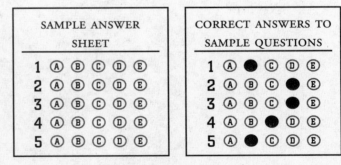

SAMPLE ANSWER SHEET	CORRECT ANSWERS TO SAMPLE QUESTIONS
1 Ⓐ Ⓑ Ⓒ Ⓓ Ⓔ	1 Ⓐ ● Ⓒ Ⓓ Ⓔ
2 Ⓐ Ⓑ Ⓒ Ⓓ Ⓔ	2 Ⓐ Ⓑ Ⓒ ● Ⓔ
3 Ⓐ Ⓑ Ⓒ Ⓓ Ⓔ	3 Ⓐ Ⓑ Ⓒ ● Ⓔ
4 Ⓐ Ⓑ Ⓒ Ⓓ Ⓔ	4 Ⓐ Ⓑ ● Ⓓ Ⓔ
5 Ⓐ Ⓑ Ⓒ Ⓓ Ⓔ	5 Ⓐ ● Ⓒ Ⓓ Ⓔ

Answer Explanations for Sample Questions

1. **(B)** *Previous* means came before, or *former*.
2. **(D)** "A specific end in view" indicates a careful plan in mind.
3. **(D)** In (A), "these kind" is incorrect; it should be "this kind." In (B), "not hardly ever" is incorrect; it should be "hardly ever." in (C), "than what such reports" is incorrect; the "what" should be deleted.
4. **(C)** The correct spelling is *athlete*.
5. **(B)** The second word is the "indicator" on the first word.

The Test

Read each question carefully. Select the best answer and darken the proper space on the answer sheet.

Word Meaning (Vocabulary)

1. *Flexible* means most nearly

   A) breakable   C) pliable
   B) flammable   D) weak

2. *Option* means most nearly

   A) use   C) value
   B) choice   D) blame

3. To *verify* means most nearly to

   A) examine   C) confirm
   B) explain   D) guarantee

4. *Indolent* means most nearly

   A) moderate   C) selfish
   B) hopeless   D) lazy

5. *Respiration* means most nearly

   A) recovery   C) pulsation
   B) breathing   D) sweating

Analogies (Word Relationships)

6. PLUMBER is related to WRENCH as PAINTER is related to

   A) brush   C) shop
   B) pipe   D) hammer

7. LETTER is related to MESSAGE as PACKAGE is related to

   A) sender   C) insurance
   B) merchandise   D) business

8. FOOD is related to HUNGER as SLEEP is related to

   A) night   C) weariness
   B) dream   D) rest

9. KEY is related to TYPEWRITER as DIAL is related to

   A) sun   C) circle
   B) number   D) telephone

Grammar (Language Usage)

10. A) I think that they will promote whoever has the best record.
    B) The firm would have liked to have promoted all employees with good records.
    C) Such of them that have the best records have excellent prospects of promotion.
    D) I feel sure they will give the promotion to whomever has the best record.

11. A) The receptionist must answer courteously the questions of all them callers.
    B) The receptionist must answer courteously the questions what are asked by the callers.
    C) There would have been no trouble if the receptionist had have always answered courteously.
    D) The receptionist should answer courteously the questions of all callers.

Spelling

12. A) collapsible   C) collapseble
    B) collapseable   D) none of these

13. A) ambigeuous   C) ambiguous
    B) ambigeous   D) none of these

14. A) predesessor   C) predecesser
    B) predecesar   D) none of these

15. A) sanctioned   C) sanctionned
    B) sancktioned   D) none of these

Reading (Understanding Written Material)

16. The secretarial profession is a very old one and has increased in importance with the passage of time. In modern times, the vast expansion of business and industry has greatly increased the need and opportunities for secretaries, and for the first time in history their number has become large.

    The paragraph best supports the statement that the secretarial profession

    A) is older than business and industry
    B) did not exist in ancient times
    C) has greatly increased in size
    D) demands higher training than it did formerly

17. Civilization started to move ahead more rapidly when people freed themselves of the shackles that restricted their search for the truth.

    The paragraph best supports the statement that the progress of civilization

    A) came as a result of people's dislike for obstacles
    B) did not begin until restrictions on learning were removed
    C) has been aided by people's efforts to find the truth
    D) is based on continually increasing efforts

18. *Vigilant* means most nearly

    A) sensible   C) suspicious
    B) watchful   D) restless

19. *Incidental* means most nearly

    A) independent   C) infrequent
    B) needless   D) casual

20. *Conciliatory* means most nearly

    A) pacific   C) obligatory
    B) contentious   D) offensive

21. *Altercation* means most nearly

    A) defeat   C) controversy
    B) concurrence   D) vexation

22. *Irresolute* means most nearly

    A) wavering   C) impudent
    B) insubordinate   D) unobservant

23. DARKNESS is related to SUNLIGHT as STILLNESS is related to

    A) quiet   C) sound
    B) moonlight   D) dark

24. DESIGNED is related to INTENTION as ACCIDENTAL is related to

    A) purpose   C) damage
    B) caution   D) chance

25. ERROR is related to PRACTICE as SOUND is related to

    A) deafness   C) muffler
    B) noise   D) horn

26. RESEARCH is related to FINDINGS as TRAINING is related to

    A) skill   C) supervision
    B) tests   D) teaching

27. A) If properly addressed, the letter will reach my mother and I.
    B) The letter had been addressed to myself and my mother.
    C) I believe the letter was addressed to either my mother or I.
    D) My mother's name, as well as mine, was on the letter.

28. A) The supervisors reprimanded the typists, whom she believed had made careless errors.
    B) The typists would have corrected the errors had they of known that the supervisor would see the report.
    C) The errors in the typed reports were so numerous that they could hardly be overlooked.
    D) Many errors were found in the reports which they typed and could not disregard them.

29. A) minieture   C) mineature
    B) minneature   D) none of these

30. A) extemporaneous   C) extemperaneous
    B) extempuraneus   D) none of these

31. A) problemmatical   C) problematicle
    B) problematical   D) none of these

32. A) descendant   C) desendant
    B) decendant   D) none of these

33. The likelihood of America's exhausting her natural resources seems to be growing less. All kinds of waste are being reworked and new uses are constantly being found for almost everything. We are getting more use out of our goods and are making many new by-products out of what was formerly thrown away.

    The paragraph best supports the statement that we seem to be in less danger of exhausting our resources because

    A) economy is found to lie in the use of substitutes
    B) more service is obtained from a given amount of material
    C) we are allowing time for nature to restore them
    D) supply and demand are better controlled

34. Telegrams should be clear, concise, and brief. Omit all unnecessary words. The parts of speech most often used in telegrams are nouns, verbs, adjectives, and adverbs. If possible, do without pronouns, prepositions, articles, and copulative verbs. Use simple sentences rather than complex or compound ones.

    The paragraph best supports the statement that in writing telegrams one should always use

    A) common and simple words
    B) only nouns, verbs, adjectives, and adverbs
    C) incomplete sentences
    D) only the words essential to the meaning

35. To *counteract* means most nearly to

    A) undermine   C) preserve
    B) censure   D) neutralize

36. *Deferred* means most nearly

    A) reversed   C) considered
    B) delayed   D) forbidden

37. *Feasible* means most nearly

    A) capable   C) practicable
    B) justifiable   D) beneficial

38. To *encounter* means most nearly to

    A) meet   C) overcome
    B) recall   D) retreat

39. *Innate* means most nearly

    A) eternal   C) native
    B) well-developed   D) prospective

40. STUDENT is related to TEACHER as DISCIPLE is related to

    A) follower   C) principal
    B) master   D) pupil

41. LECTURE is related to AUDITORIUM as EXPERIMENT is related to

    A) scientist   C) laboratory
    B) chemistry   D) discovery

42. BODY is related to FOOD as ENGINE is related to

    A) wheels   C) motion
    B) fuel   D) smoke

43. SCHOOL is related to EDUCATION as THEATER is related to

    A) management   C) recreation
    B) stage   D) preparation

44. A) Most all these statements have been supported by persons who are reliable and can be depended upon.
    B) The persons which have guaranteed these statements are reliable.
    C) Reliable persons guarantee the facts with regards to the truth of these statements.
    D) These statements can be depended on, for their truth has been guaranteed by reliable persons.

45. A) The success of the book pleased both the publisher and authors.
    B) Both the publisher and they was pleased with the success of the book.
    C) Neither they or their publisher was disappointed with the success of the book.
    D) Their publisher was as pleased as they with the success of the book.

46. A) extercate   C) extricate
    B) extracate   D) none of these

47. A) hereditory   C) hereditairy
    B) hereditary   D) none of these

48. A) auspiceous   C) auspicious
    B) auspiseous   D) none of these

49. A) sequance   C) sequense
    B) sequence   D) none of these

50. The prevention of accidents makes it necessary not only that safety devices be used to guard exposed machinery but also that mechanics be instructed in safety rules which they must follow for their own protection, and that the lighting in the plant be adequate.

    The paragraph best supports the statement that industrial accidents

    A) may be due to ignorance
    B) are always avoidable
    C) usually result from inadequate machinery
    D) cannot be entirely overcome

51. The English language is peculiarly rich in synonyms, and there is scarcely a language spoken that has not some representative in English speech. The spirit of the Anglo-Saxon race has subjugated these various elements to one idiom, making not a patchwork, but a composite language.

The paragraph best supports the statement that the English language

A) has few idiomatic expressions
B) is difficult to translate
C) is used universally
D) has absorbed words from other languages

52. To *acquiesce* means most nearly to

A) assent   C) complete
B) acquire   D) participate

53. *Unanimity* means most nearly

A) emphasis   C) harmony
B) namelessness   D) impartiality

54. *Precedent* means most nearly

A) example   C) law
B) theory   D) conformity

55. *Versatile* means most nearly

A) broad-minded   C) up-to-date
B) well-known   D) many-sided

56. *Authentic* means most nearly

A) detailed   C) valuable
B) reliable   D) practical

57. BIOGRAPHY is related to FACT as NOVEL is related to

A) fiction   C) narration
B) literature   D) book

58. COPY is related to CARBON PAPER as MOTION PICTURE is related to

A) theater   C) duplicate
B) film   D) television

59. EFFICIENCY is related to REWARD as CARELESSNESS is related to

A) improvement   C) reprimand
B) disobedience   D) repetition

60. ABUNDANT is related to CHEAP as SCARCE is related to

A) ample   C) inexpensive
B) costly   D) unobtainable

61. A) Brown's & Company employees have recently received increases in salary.
B) Brown & Company recently increased the salaries of all its employees.
C) Recently Brown & Company has increased their employees' salaries.
D) Brown & Company have recently increased the salaries of all its employees.

62. A) In reviewing the typists' work reports, the job analyst found records of unusual typing speeds.
B) It says in the job analyst's report that some employees type with great speed.
C) The job analyst found that, in reviewing the typists' work reports, that some unusual typing speeds had been made.
D) In the reports of typists' speeds, the job analyst found some records that are kind of unusual.

63. A) oblitorate   C) obbliterate
B) oblitterat   D) none of these

64. A) diagnoesis   C) diagnosis
    B) diagnossis   D) none of these

65. A) contenance   C) countinance
    B) countenance   D) none of these

66. A) conceivably   C) conceiveably
    B) concieveably   D) none of these

67. Through advertising, manufacturers exercise a high degree of control over consumers' desires. However, the manufacturer assumes enormous risks in attempting to predict what consumers will want and in producing goods in quantity and distributing them in advance of final selection by the consumers.

    The paragraph best supports the statement that manufacturers

    A) can eliminate the risk of overproduction by advertising
    B) distribute goods directly to the consumers
    C) must depend upon the final consumers for the success of their undertakings
    D) can predict with great accuracy the success of any product they put on the market

68. In the relations of humans to nature, the procuring of food and shelter is fundamental. With the migration of humans to various climates, ever new adjustments to the food supply and to the climate became necessary.

    The paragraph best supports the statement that the means by which humans supply their material needs are

    A) accidental
    B) varied
    C) limited
    D) inadequate

69. *Strident* means most nearly

    A) swaggering   C) angry
    B) domineering   D) harsh

70. To *confine* means most nearly to

    A) bide   C) eliminate
    B) restrict   D) punish

71. To *accentuate* means most nearly to

    A) modify   C) sustain
    B) hasten   D) intensify

72. *Banal* means most nearly

    A) commonplace   C) tranquil
    B) forceful   D) indifferent

73. *Incorrigible* means most nearly

    A) intolerable   C) irreformable
    B) retarded   D) brazen

74. POLICE OFFICER is related to ORDER as DOCTOR is related to

    A) physician   C) sickness
    B) hospital   D) health

75. ARTIST is related to EASEL as WEAVER is related to

    A) loom   C) threads
    B) cloth   D) spinner

76. CROWD is related to PERSONS as FLEET is related to

    A) expedition   C) navy
    B) officers   D) ships

77. CALENDAR is related to DATE as MAP is related to

    A) geography   C) mileage
    B) trip   D) vacation

78. A) Since the report lacked the needed information, it was of no use to them.
    B) This report was useless to them because there were no needed information in it.
    C) Since the report did not contain the needed information, it was not real useful to them.
    D) Being that the report lacked the needed information, they could not use it.

79. A) The company had hardly declared the dividend till the notices were prepared for mailing.
    B) They had no sooner declared the dividend when they sent the notices to the stockholders.
    C) No sooner had the dividend been declared than the notices were prepared for mailing.
    D) Scarcely had the dividend been declared than the notices were sent out.

80. A) compitition   C) competetion
    B) competition   D) none of these

81. A) occassion   C) ocassion
    B) occasion   D) none of these

82. A) knowlege   C) knowledge
    B) knolledge   D) none of these

83. A) deliborate   C) delibrate
    B) deliberate   D) none of these

84. What constitutes skill in any line of work is not always easy to determine; economy of time must be carefully distinguished from economy of energy, as the quickest method may require the greatest expenditure of muscular effort, and may not be essential or at all desirable.

The paragraph best supports the statement that

A) the most efficiently executed task is not always the one done in the shortest time
B) energy and time cannot both be conserved in performing a single task
C) a task is well done when it is performed in the shortest time
D) skill in performing a task should not be acquired at the expense of time

85. It is difficult to distinguish between bookkeeping and accounting. In attempts to do so, bookkeeping is called the art, and accounting the science, of recording business transactions. Bookkeeping gives the history of the business in a systematic manner; and accounting classifies, analyzes, and interprets the facts thus recorded.

The paragraph best supports the statement that

A) accounting is less systematic than bookkeeping
B) accounting and bookkeeping are closely related
C) bookkeeping and accounting cannot be distinguished from one another
D) bookkeeping has been superseded by accounting

Answer Key

Word Meaning (Vocabulary)

1. **C**	18. **B**	35. **D**	52. **A**	69. **D**
2. **B**	19. **D**	36. **B**	53. **C**	70. **B**
3. **C**	20. **A**	37. **C**	54. **A**	71. **D**
4. **D**	21. **C**	38. **A**	55. **D**	72. **A**
5. **B**	22. **A**	39. **C**	56. **B**	73. **C**

Analogies (Word Relationships)

6. **A**	23. **C**	40. **B**	57. **A**	74. **D**
7. **B**	24. **D**	41. **C**	58. **B**	75. **A**
8. **C**	25. **C**	42. **B**	59. **C**	76. **D**
9. **D**	26. **A**	43. **C**	60. **B**	77. **C**

Grammar (Language Usage)

10. **A**	27. **D**	44. **D**	61. **B**	78. **A**
11. **D**	28. **C**	45. **D**	62. **A**	79. **C**

Spelling

12. **A**	29. **D**	46. **C**	63. **D**	80. **B**
13. **C**	30. **A**	47. **B**	64. **C**	81. **B**
14. **D**	31. **B**	48. **C**	65. **B**	82. **C**
15. **A**	32. **A**	49. **B**	66. **A**	83. **B**

Reading (Understanding Written Material)

16. **C**	33. **B**	50. **A**	67. **C**	84. **A**
17. **C**	34. **D**	51. **D**	68. **B**	85. **B**

Analysis Chart

Now that you've corrected your exam, use the following chart to analyze your results and spot your strengths and weaknesses. This analysis should help you focus your study and review efforts.

Section	Total Number of Questions	Number Correct	Number Incorrect	Number Unanswered*
Word Meaning (Vocabulary)	25			
Analogies (Word Relationships)	20			
Grammar (Language Usage)	10			
Spelling	20			
Reading Comprehension (Understanding Written Material)	10			
TOTAL	85			

*Since there is no penalty for incorrect answers on most of the Verbal Abilities Part, you should have left no question unanswered. Even if you didn't have time to answer a question, at least you should have filled in the answer space with a guess.

Answer Explanations

1. **(C)** Flexible means bendable, or *pliable*. *Flex* means bend.
2. **(B)** *Option* means selection or alternative, or *choice*.
3. **(C)** To *verify* means to prove, or to *confirm*.
4. **(D)** *Indolent* means not inclined to work, or *lazy*.
5. **(B)** *Respiration* means inhaling and exhaling, or *breathing*.
6. **(A)** The second word is a tool of the first word.

7. **(B)** The second word is sent or delivered in the first word.

8. **(C)** The first word eliminates the second word.

9. **(D)** The first word is the operative mechanism on the second word.

10. **(A)** In (B), the verb tenses should be "would like to have promoted." "Such of them" in (C) is incorrect. (D) should read: "whoever has the best record."

11. **(D)** In (A), "all them callers" is incorrect; it should be "all callers," In (B), "what are asked" is incorrect; it should be "asked." In (C), "had have" should be "had."

12. **(A)** collapsible

13. **(C)** ambiguous

14. **(D)** Correct spelling; predecessor.

15. **(A)** sanctioned

16. **(C)** "Their number has become large" indicates that the number of secretaries has greatly increased in size.

17. **(C)** "When people freed themselves of the shackles that restricted their search for the truth," civilization moved ahead. This indicates that civilization's progress was aided by people's efforts to find the truth.

18. **(B)** *Vigilant* means on guard, or *watchful*. Note the root word, *vigil*.

19. **(D)** *Incidental* means of minor event or circumstance, or *casual*.

20. **(A)** *Conciliatory* means to bring together or make peaceful. *Pacific* is the best synonym. Note the root word, *pacify*.

21. **(C)** *Altercation* is a quarrel, or *controversy*.

22. **(A)** *Resolute* means firm; *irresolute* means wavering.

23. **(C)** The first word is the absence of the second word.

24. **(D)** *Designed* means by *intention. Accidental* means *by chance*. The first word occurs through the action of the second word.

25. **(C)** The second word eliminates or lessens the first word.

26. **(A)** The second word is the intended result of the first word.

27. **(D)** In (A), (B), and (C), the phrase should be "my mother and me."

28. **(C)** in (A), "Whom" should be "who." In (B), "of known" is incorrect; it should be simply "known." In (D), "they" is vague, and "and could not disregard them" is awkward.

29. **(D)** Correct spelling: miniature

30. **(A)** extemporaneous

31. **(B)** problematical

32. **(A)** descendant

33. **(B)** "Getting more use out of our goods" indicates that more service is obtained from a given amount of material.

34. **(D)** "Concise" and "brief" indicate that, in telegrams, one should use only words essential to the meaning.

35. **(D)** To *counteract* means to check the effects of an action, or to *neutralize*. Note the prefix, *counter,* meaning against, and the root word, act.

36. **(B)** *Deferred* means put off, or *delayed*.

37. **(C)** *Feasible* means possible, able to be done, or *practicable*.

38. **(A)** To *encounter* means to come in contact with, or to *meet*.

39. **(C)** *Innate* means inborn, or *native*.

40. **(B)** The first word learns from the second word.

41. **(C)** The first word takes place in the second word.

42. **(B)** The first word consumes the second word for energy.

43. **(C)** The first word is a place for the purpose of the second word.

44. **(D)** In (A), "reliable and can be depended upon" is repetitious. In (B), "which" should he "who." In (C), "the facts with regards to the truth" is repetitious and awkward.

45. **(D)** In (A), "both" indicates two people, whereas "publisher and authors" must mean a minimum of three people. In (B), "was" should be "were," among other errors. (C) should be "Neither they *nor . . .*"

46. **(C)** extricate

47. **(B)** hereditary

48. **(C)** auspicious

49. **(B)** sequence

50. **(A)** The necessity that "mechanics be instructed in safety rules" indicates that accidents may be due to ignorance.
51. **(D)** "There is scarcely a language spoken that has not some representative in English speech" indicates that the English language has absorbed words from other languages.
52. **(A)** To *acquiesce* means to give in, or to *assent*.
53. **(C)** *Unanimity* means total agreement, or *harmony*. Notice the root, *unanimous*.
54. **(A)** *Precedent* means a standard, or *example*.
55. **(D)** *Versatile* means multiskilled, or *many-sided*.
56. **(B)** *Authentic* means worthy of trust or reliance, or *reliable*.
57. **(A)** The first word is a book using the second word.
58. **(B)** The first word is made by means of the second word.
59. **(C)** The first word results in the second word.
60. **(B)** The second word is the price of the first word.
61. **(B)** In (A), the 's should be on *Company*, not *Brown*. In (C), "has" and "their" must agree; the correct form is "its employees." In (D), "have" should be "has" to agree with "its."
62. **(A)** The error in (B) is the vague use of "it." The error in (C) is awkward sentence structure, not as direct or clear as it could be. The error in (D) is the informal phrase "kind of" unusual.
63. **(D)** Correct spelling: obliterate
64. **(C)** diagnosis
65. **(B)** countenance
66. **(A)** conceivably
67. **(C)** That "the manufacturer assumes enormous risks in attempting to predict what consumers will want" indicates that manufacturers must depend upon the final consumers for the success of their undertakings.
68. **(B)** "*New adjustments* to the food supply and to the climate" indicates that the means by which humans supply their material needs are varied.
69. **(D)** *Strident* means grating, or *harsh*.
70. **(B)** To *confine* means to keep within bounds, or to *restrict*.
71. **(D)** To *accentuate* means to increase, or to *intensify*.
72. **(A)** *Banal* means worn-out and predictable, or *commonplace*.
73. **(C)** *Incorrigible* means uncorrectable, or *irreformable*.
74. **(D)** The first word is the person who restores the second word.
75. **(A)** The second word is a tool of the first word.
76. **(D)** The first word is a collection or group of the second word.
77. **(C)** The second word is a unit comprising the first word.
78. **(A)** The main error in (B) is "were"; it should be "was." The main error in (C) is "real useful"; it should be "really useful," or simply "useful." The main error in (D) is a nonstandard phrase, "being that"; it should be "because."
79. **(C)** Each of the incorrect choices here is unclear about the relationship between declaring the dividend and sending the notices.
80. **(B)** competition
81. **(B)** occasion
82. **(C)** knowledge
83. **(B)** deliberate
84. **(A)** That "economy of time must be carefully distinguished from economy of energy" indicates that the most efficiently executed task is not always the one done in the shortest time.
85. **(B)** "It is difficult to distinguish between bookkeeping and accounting," as they are closely related.

Understanding the Verbal Abilities Sections: Key Strategies

CHAPTER 2

Practice, Practice, Practice

WORD MEANING (VOCABULARY)

This question type tests your vocabulary. You are given words and must decide which choice means the same or most nearly the same as the given word. For example:

To *terminate* means most nearly

A) schedule   C) finish
B) begin   D) disallow

Since to *terminate* means to cease or to *put an end to*, the best choice is (C) *finish*.

Helpful Techniques and Strategies

1. Choose the most nearly correct word from among the choices given. Sometimes the best choice may not be perfect or convey exactly the same meaning you would use yourself, but if it is the best of the choices, it is the correct answer.
2. Work as quickly as you can. Scan the possible answers and decide immediately on the correct one. Take time out to study each individual choice only if the words are unfamiliar or especially difficult for you.
3. Although the words used should not be technical or obscure, they maybe long and/or difficult. Break these words up into prefixes, suffixes, and roots to help in understanding the meaning. Item 6 contains a list of prefixes, suffixes, and roots.
4. If possible, use the given word in a short, clear sentence. This may help give you a context to work from and increase your understanding of the word's meaning. Then substitute the choices into your sentence to see if the sentence retains the same meaning.

5. Many words carry a strong connotation. If, for example, a word sounds "positive" or "good," then choose a word that has a positive connotation. If a word sounds "negative" or "bad," then your choice should reflect this negative connotation. Sometimes you may not know the exact meaning of a certain word, but it will just sound "positive" or "negative" to you. Trust your instincts and select the answer choice that reflects this connotation. Example:

Noxious means most nearly

A) clean   C) famous
B) luminous   D) poisonous

Since *noxious* has a strong negative connotation, you can eliminate all choices except (D) *poisonous*, which also is negative, and is the correct answer.

6. Review the list that follows.

Some Common Prefixes, Suffixes, and Roots

Prefix	Meaning	Examples
ad-	to; at; near	*adhere* stick to
anti-	in opposition; against	*antislavery* against slavery
auto-	self; by self; of one's self	*automatic* self-acting
bene-	good; well	*benevolence* disposed to do good
bi-	two; twice; double	*bisect* cut into two equal parts
circum-	around; all around	*circumnavigate* sail around (the globe)
co-		*cooperate* perform together
com-; con-	with; together; altogether	*combine* merge with
		connect join together
contra-	against; contrary	*contradict* assert the contrary of
de-	down; from; away	*descend* travel down
dia-	through; between; across	*diagonal* across a figure
dis-	not; apart	*disapprove* not approve
ex-	out of; out; from	*expel* drive out
extra-	beyond; without	*extraordinary* beyond the ordinary
fer-	wild; untamed	*ferocity* wildness
fore-	beforehand; in front	*foresee* see beforehand
geo-	earth	*geography* the study of the earth and its inhabitants
hemi-	half	*hemisphere* one-half a sphere or globe
hyper-	too much; beyond; over	*hypersensitive* oversensitive
hypo-	beneath; too little	*hypodermic* beneath the skin
inter-	between; among	*interfere* enter between or among others
intro-	within; in; into	*introduce* bring or lead in
mal-, male-	bad; ill; badly	*malfunction* function badly
mis-	wrongly; badly	*misinformed* badly informed
mon-, mono-	single; having only one	*monomania* obsessed by one idea
non-	not	*nonprofessional* not belonging to a profession
omni-	all; everywhere	*omnipotent* all-powerful
per-	through; throughout; thoroughly	*perforate* pierce through

Some Common Prefixes, Suffixes, and Roots (continued)

Prefix	Meaning	Examples
poly-	many	*polygamy* having many husbands or wives at one time
post-	after; behind	*postnatal* after birth
pre-	before; prior to	*preview* see beforehand
pro-	before; forth; forward	*produce* bring forth
re-	back; again	*recall* call back
sal-	health	*salutory* healthful
semi-	half	*semicircle* half circle
sub-	under; beneath; inferior	*subordinate* inferior in rank
super-	above; greater; more than	*superhuman* greater than human
trans-	across: through; beyond	*transport* carry across
un-	not	*uncommon* not common
-able	able to; capable of being	*lovable* capable of being loved
-acity	character; quality	*veracity* the quality of truth
-ence, -ance	a state of being	*abundance* the state of being abundant
-ful	full of	*grateful* full of gratitude
-fy	to make	*beautify* to make beautiful
-ion, -sion. -tion	the act or condition of	*reaction* the act of reacting
-ism	belief in; practice of; condition of	*activism* the practice of being actively involved
-less	free from; without	*penniless* without money
-logy	doctrine or science; the study of	*geology* the study of the earth
-ness	state of being	*emptiness* state of being empty
-some	abounding in; full of	*troublesome* full of trouble
-wise	in the manner of; in the direction of	*lengthwise* in the direction of length

Root	Meaning	Examples
acr	sharp; bitter	*acrimonious* bitter
ag, act	to do; to act	*agent* doer
		retroactive having a reverse action
agog	leader	*demagogue* false leader
agri, agrari	fields	*agrarian* farmer; one who works on fields
ali	another	*alias* another name
alt	high	*altitude* height
anim	mind; soul	*unanimous* of one mind
ann	year	*annually* yearly payment
		biennial every two years
aqua	water	*aquatic* living in water
arch	ruler, government	*anarchy* no government
aud	to hear	*audible* can be heard
belli	war	*belligerent* carrying on war or aggression
ben, bene	good; well	*benefactor* one who does good
biblio	book	*bibliograph* list of books
bio	life	*biography* story of a person's life
breve	short	*brevity* briefness; shortness
cap	head; to take	*captain* chief; headwaiter
		capture seize; to take captive

Some Common Prefixes, Suffixes, and Roots (continued)

Root	Meaning	Examples
cede; cess	to go; to yield	*precede* to go before
		concession the act of yielding
chron; chrono	time	*chronicle* a register of events arranged in order of time
		chronology the time order of events
cid, cis	to kill; to cut	*homicide* killing of a person by another
		incision a cut
civi	citizen	*civil* relating to citizens
clos, clud	to close; to shut	*enclose* to close in
		exclude to shut out
dic. dict	to say; to speak	*diction* speech
domin	to rule	*dominate* to rule or have power over
due	to lead	*induce* to lead or bring on
ego	I; self	*egocentric* self-centered
gani	marriage	*bigamy* marriage to two people at once
gen, gener	class; race; kind	*general* applying to a whole class or race
geo	earth	*geochemistry* the chemical study of the earth
greg	flock; herd; group	*gregarious* grouping together
jac, jact, ject	to throw	*projectile* something thrown forward
labor, laborat	to work	*laboratory* workplace
liber	book; free	*library* collection of books
		liberty freedom
man, mani, manu	hand	*manufacture* create; make by hand
mar	sea	*submarine* under the sea
mit, miss	to send	*transmit* send across
		dismiss to send away
mov, mot, mob	to move	*remove* to move away
		emotion "moving" feelings
		mobile movable
nav	ship	*navigate* sail a ship
pac	peace	*pacific* peaceful
port, portat	carry	*portable* able to be carried
put, putat	to calculate; to cut	*compute* to calculate
		amputate to cut off
quer, quisit	to ask	*query* to ask a question
		inquisitive questioning
quies	quiet	*acquiesce* to agree quietly without protest
radi	ray	*irradiate* to shine light on
rap, rapt	to seize	*rapine* the act of seizing others' property by force
		rapture the state of being seized or carried away by emotion
rid, ris	to laugh	*deride* to laugh at scornfully
		risible capable of laughing
rog, rogate	to ask	*interrogate* to ask questions of
rupt	break	*rupture* to break
sag	wisdom	*sage* a wise person
		sagacity wisdom

Some Common Prefixes, Suffixes, and Roots (continued)

Root	Meaning	Examples
sat, satis	enough	*satiate* to provide with enough or more than enough
		satisfy to meet the need of
schis; schiz	to cut; to split	*schism* a split or division
		schizophrenia a mental disorder characterized by separation of the thoughts and emotions
sci	to know	*science* knowledge
scop	to watch; to view	*telescope* an instrument for viewing things from a distance
scrib, script	to write	*prescribe* to write a medical prescription
		transcript a written copy
sec, sect	to cut	*section* to cut into parts
		bisect to cut in two
sed, sess, sid	to sit	*sedentary* doing much sitting
		session a meeting
		preside to sit in position of authority
sent, sens	to feel; to perceive	*resent* to feel annoyance
		sensible perceiving through the senses
sequ, secu, secut	to follow	*sequel* that which follows
		consecutive one following another
solv, solut	to loosen; to solve	*absolve* to free (loosen) from guilt
		solution act of solving a problem
soph	wise; wisdom	*sophisticate* a worldly, wise person
spec, spect, spic	to watch; to look; to appear	*spectator* observer
		inspect to look over
		perspicacious having sharp judgment
spir, spirit	to breathe	*expire* to exhale; to die
		spirit life
sta, stat	to stand	*stable* steady
		stationary fixed; unmoving
stru, struct	to build	*construe* to explain or deduce the meaning
		structure a building
suas, suad	to urge; to advise	*persuasive* having the power to cause something to change
		dissuade to advise someone against something
sum, sumpt	to take	*assume* to take on
		resumption taking up again
tact, tang	to touch	*tactile* perceptible through touch
		intangible unable to be touched
tempor	time	*contemporary* at the same time
ten, tent, tain	to hold	*tenure* holding of office
		retentive capable of holding
		retain to hold onto
tend, tens	to stretch	*extend* to stretch out or draw out
		tense to stretch tight
terr	land; earth	*terrestrial* pertaining to the earth
the, theo	god	*atheist* one who believes there is no God
		theocracy rule by God or by persons claiming to represent Him

Some common prefixes, suffixes, and roots (continued)

Root	Meaning	Examples
thermo	heat	*thermal* relating to heat
tract	to draw	*attract* to draw
trud, trus	to thrust; to push	*protrude* to stick out
		intrusive pushing into or upon something
tum, tumi	to swell	*tumor* swelling
		tumify to cause to swell
un, uni	one	*unanimous* of one opinion
		uniform of one form
urb	city	*suburban* outside the city
ut, util	to use; useful	*utility* the quality of being useful
vac	empty	*vacuum* empty space
ven, vent	to come	*intervene* come between
		advent an arrival
ver	true	*verify* to prove to be true
verb	words	*verbalize* using words
		verbatim word for word
verd	green	*verdant* green
vert, vers	to turn	*avert* to turn away
vi, via	way	*deviate* to turn from the prescribed way
		via by way of
vid, vis	to see	*evident* easily seen
		invisible unable to be seen
vinc, vict	to conquer; to win	*invincible* unconquerable
		victorious winning
vit, viv	to live	*vital* alive
		vivacious lively
voc, voke, vocat	to call	*revocable* capable of being called back
		invoke to call on
		vocation a calling
void	empty	*devoid* empty of (feeling)
volv, volut	to roll or turn around	*evolve* to develop by stages; to unfold
		revolution movement around
vol	to fly	*volatile* vaporizing quickly

Practice Set 1

Select the best answer to each question and write the letter of your choice in the space provided.

1. To *amend* means most nearly to _____

   A) pass   C) legislate
   B) correct   D) finish

2. *Respite* means most nearly _____

   A) rest   C) despite
   B) dine   D) few

3. *Mammoth* means most nearly _____

   A) mammal   C) gigantic
   B) extinct   D) dead

4. *Iota* means most nearly _____

   A) tiny bit   C) speedster
   B) group   D) friend

5. *Latitude* means most nearly _____

   A) freedom   C) emotion
   B) style   D) worth

6. *Jargon* means most nearly _____

   A) puzzle   C) language
   B) lizard   D) container

7. *Knoll* means most nearly _____

   A) bell   C) hill
   B) instrument   D) harmony

8. *Liaison* means most nearly _____

   A) go-between   C) rifle
   B) foreigner   D) gallop

9. *Proximity* means most nearly _____

   A) closeness   C) prurient
   B) cleanliness   D) fitness

10. To *saturate* means most nearly to _____

   A) enjoy   C) construct
   B) soak   D) disturb

11. *Stamina* means most nearly _____

   A) strength   C) dye
   B) root   D) limb

12. To *tantalize* means most nearly to _____

   A) please   C) tease
   B) seize   D) freeze

13. *Toxic* means most nearly _____

   A) waste   C) poisonous
   B) smelly   D) growing

14. *Lesion* means most nearly _____

   A) league   C) army
   B) injury   D) ridicule

15. *Clandestine* means most nearly _____

   A) friendly   C) secret
   B) remorseful   D) pensive

16. *Combustible* means most nearly _____

   A) eatable   C) burnable
   B) breakable   D) thinkable

17. To *condone* means most nearly to _____

   A) condemn   C) forgive
   B) require   D) praise

18. *Frailty* means most nearly _____

   A) weakness   C) real estate
   B) frenzy   D) purpose

19. *Mandatory* means most nearly _____

   A) required   C) masculine
   B) able   D) separate

20. *Medley* means most nearly _____

   A) half-note   C) mixture
   B) interruption   D) snoop

21. *Lustrous* means most nearly _____

   A) lawsuit   C) willowy
   B) shining   D) fortunate

22. *Benevolent* means most nearly _____

   A) warlike   C) angry
   B) generous   D) rebellious

23. *Emaciated* means most nearly _____

   A) content   C) wasted
   B) strong   D) lofty

24. *Glossy* means most nearly _____

   A) free   C) stealthy
   B) shiny   D) refurbished

25. To *maim* means most nearly to _____

   A) defoliate   C) issue
   B) beg   D) injure

Answers for Practice Set 1

1. **(B)** correct
2. **(A)** rest
3. **(C)** gigantic
4. **(A)** tiny bit
5. **(A)** freedom
6. **(C)** language
7. **(C)** hill
8. **(A)** go-between
9. **(A)** closeness
10. **(B)** soak
11. **(A)** strength
12. **(C)** tease
13. **(C)** poisonous
14. **(B)** injury
15. **(C)** secret
16. **(C)** burnable
17. **(C)** forgive
18. **(A)** weakness
19. **(A)** required
20. **(C)** mixture
21. **(B)** shining
22. **(B)** generous
23. **(C)** wasted
24. **(B)** shiny
25. **(D)** injure

Practice Set 2

Select the best answer to each question and write the letter of your choice in the space provided.

1. *Plagiarism* means most nearly _____

   A) theft   C) illness
   B) anarchism   D) evilness

2. To *reiterate* means most nearly to _____

   A) compound   C) affect
   B) repeat   D) retreat

3. *Monotonous* means most nearly _____

   A) large   C) uninteresting
   B) growing   D) jagged

4. *Futile* means most nearly _____

   A) engine   C) useless
   B) missile   D) decorative

5. *Pensive* means most nearly _____

   A) wealthy   C) thoughtful
   B) tense   D) idle

6. *Utilitarian* means most nearly _____

   A) useful   C) rich
   B) despondent   D) indolent

7. *Trepidation* means most nearly _____

   A) tearfulness   C) hard work
   B) anxiety   D) cleverness

8. *Labyrinth* means most nearly _____

   A) infantile   C) maze
   B) hardship   D) welcome

9. *Defection* means most nearly _____

   A) sickness   C) bad temper
   B) problem   D) desertion

10. *Cumbersome* means most nearly _____

    A) clumsy   C) vegetation
    B) remarkable   D) encompass

11. *Intimidation* means most nearly _____

    A) memory   C) fear
    B) secret   D) expectation

12. *Dais* means most nearly _____

    A) platform   C) prejudice
    B) waste   D) dress

13. *Candid* means most nearly _____

    A) hidden   C) frank
    B) peeping   D) funny

14. *Ambiguous* means most nearly _____

    A) long   C) reliable
    B) uncertain   D) aloof

15. *Chassis* means most nearly _____

    A) engine   C) framework
    B) classic   D) reliable

16. *Carmine* means most nearly _____

    A) model   C) sweet
    B) red   D) speedy

17. *Complacent* means most nearly _____

    A) self-satisfied   C) quiet
    B) ordered   D) natural

18. *Audible* means most nearly _____

    A) profitable   C) hearable
    B) knowledgeable   D) greedy

19. *Affluent* means most nearly _____

    A) proud   C) wealthy
    B) keen   D) understanding

20. To *loathe* means most nearly to _____

    A) bake   C) clean
    B) detest   D) limp

21. *Levity* means most nearly _____

    A) air   C) gaiety
    B) measurement   D) judgment

22. *Lethal* means most nearly _____

    A) ancient   C) deadly
    B) gas   D) formal

23. To *ferret* means most nearly to _____

    A) search out   C) wander
    B) cut   D) whip

24. *Genial* means most nearly _____

    A) scientific   C) kindly
    B) wizardly   D) superficial

25. *Vacuum* means most nearly _____

    A) utensil   C) blower
    B) cleaning   D) empty

Answers for Practice Set 2

1. **(A)** theft
2. **(B)** repeat
3. **(C)** uninteresting
4. **(C)** useless
5. **(C)** thoughtful
6. **(A)** useful
7. **(B)** anxiety
8. **(C)** maze
9. **(D)** desertion
10. **(A)** clumsy
11. **(C)** fear
12. **(A)** platform
13. **(C)** frank

14. **(B)** uncertain
15. **(C)** framework
16. **(B)** red
17. **(A)** self-satisfied
18. **(C)** hearable
19. **(C)** wealthy
20. **(B)** detest
21. **(C)** gaiety
22. **(C)** deadly
23. **(A)** search out
24. **(C)** kindly
25. **(D)** empty

Practice Set 3

Select the best answer to each question and write the letter of your choice in the space provided.

1. *Oaf* means most nearly _____

   A) tree   C) stupid person
   B) rest   D) model

2. *Mobile* means most nearly _____

   A) fixed   C) movable
   B) gasoline   D) car

3. *Migratory* means most nearly _____

   A) protected   C) unhappy
   B) wandering   D) fickle

4. *Gusty* means most nearly _____

   A) enjoyable   C) windy
   B) throaty   D) happy

5. *Hapless* means most nearly _____

   A) unfortunate   C) disappointed
   B) sad   D) reliant

6. *Arcade* means most nearly _____

   A) passageway   C) games
   B) shipwreck   D) curvature

7. *Fraudulent* means most nearly _____

   A) perfect   C) deceitful
   B) friction   D) dangerous

8. To *goad* means most nearly to _____

   A) urge   C) bark
   B) punish   D) gather

9. *Homogenous* means most nearly _____

   A) pasteurized   C) similar
   B) blended   D) healthy

10. *Hubbub* means most nearly _____

    A) uproar   C) comedy
    B) friend   D) sidekick

11. *Omnipotent* means most nearly _____

    A) odorous   C) all-powerful
    B) obsolete   D) homesick

12. *Placid* means most nearly _____

    A) peaceful   C) perfunctory
    B) straight   D) foremost

13. *Tirade* means most nearly _____

    A) carnival   C) scolding
    B) fuselage   D) parade

14. *Stagnant* means most nearly _____

    A) smelling   C) playful
    B) motionless   D) ancient

15. *Succinct* means most nearly _____

    A) brief   C) loving
    B) achieving   D) tarnished

16. *Disgruntled* means most nearly _____

    A) belittled   C) discontent
    B) prudent   D) injured

17. To *amputate* means most nearly to _____

    A) hospitalize   C) prune
    B) dissolve   D) electrocute

18. *Apothecary* means most nearly _____

    A) talisman   C) curse
    B) druggist   D) opening

19. *Intermittent* means most nearly _____

    A) periodic   C) winterized
    B) settled   D) joking

20. To *aspire* means most nearly to _____

    A) sweat   C) seek
    B) hurry   D) allow

21. *Tenacious* means most nearly _____

    A) sportsmanlike   C) steadfast
    B) boring   D) angry

22. *Haphazard* means most nearly _____

    A) deliberate   C) unfortunate
    B) accidental   D) hairy

23. *Infamous* means most nearly _____

    A) notorious   C) expensive
    B) heroic   D) unknown

24. *Inept* means most nearly _____

    A) worrisome   C) incompetent
    B) relentless   D) lazy

25. *Increment* means most nearly _____

    A) increase   C) infirmity
    B) prohibition   D) insufficient

Answers for Practice Set 3

1. **(C)** stupid person
2. **(C)** movable
3. **(B)** wandering
4. **(C)** windy
5. **(A)** unfortunate
6. **(A)** passageway
7. **(C)** deceitful
8. **(A)** urge
9. **(C)** similar
10. **(A)** uproar
11. **(C)** all-powerful
12. **(A)** peaceful
13. **(C)** scolding
14. **(B)** motionless
15. **(A)** brief
16. **(C)** discontent
17. **(C)** prune
18. **(B)** druggist
19. **(A)** periodic
20. **(C)** seek
21. **(C)** steadfast
22. **(B)** accidental
23. **(A)** notorious
24. **(C)** incompetent
25. **(A)** increase

Practice Set 4

Select the best answer to each question and write the letter of your choice in the space provided.

1. *Murkiness* means most nearly _____

    A) mud   C) gloom
    B) cheer   D) accident

2. *Perimeter* means most nearly _____

    A) area   C) boundary
    B) machine   D) yardstick

3. *Haughty* means most nearly _____

    A) dour   C) flabby
    B) proud   D) quick

4. *Forte* means most nearly _____

    A) strength   C) score
    B) battalion   D) barracks

5. To *engross* means most nearly to _____

   A) outnumber   C) absorb
   B) revile   D) dislike

6. To *deduce* means most nearly to _____

   A) reason   C) remain
   B) subtract   D) forbid

7. *Contorted* means most nearly _____

   A) aborted   C) twisted
   B) playful   D) harbored

8. To *cauterize* means most nearly to _____

   A) mix   C) burn
   B) count   D) dissuade

9. *Berserk* means most nearly _____

   A) frenzied   C) friend
   B) ornate   D) sheltered

10. To *rectify* means most nearly to _____

    A) make right   C) destruct
    B) turn away   D) build

11. *Pugnacious* means most nearly _____

    A) small   C) quarrelsome
    B) queasy   D) foreboding

12. *Mediocre* means most nearly _____

    A) brownish   C) ordinary
    B) healthful   D) small-minded

13. To *hone* means most nearly to _____

    A) sharpen   C) return
    B) possess   D) rank

14. To *reminisce* means most nearly to _____

    A) publish   C) answer
    B) remember   D) lessen

15. *Frivolous* means most nearly _____

    A) obstinate   C) trivial
    B) patient   D) ornate

16. To *flaunt* means most nearly to _____

    A) bury   C) praise
    B) allow   D) display

17. *Precarious* means most nearly _____

    A) not reckless C) risky
    B) prepared   D) formidable

18. *Mishap* means most nearly _____

    A) sadness   C) strange looking
    B) accident   D) beggar

19. *Fiasco* means most nearly _____

    A) celebration C) failure
    B) pottery   D) artwork

20. *Crony* means most nearly _____

    A) companion   C) retiree
    B) money   D) polish

21. *Scrutiny* means most nearly _____

    A) deceit   C) inspection
    B) wicked   D) fear

22. *Robust* means most nearly _____

    A) automaton   C) healthy
    B) decaying   D) stealing

23. To *relinquish* means most nearly to _____

    A) tie up   C) give up
    B) sum up   D) pick up

24. *Gnarled* means most nearly _____

    A) eaten   C) twisted
    B) fused   D) flabby

25. To *debilitate* means most nearly to _____

    A) ease   C) weaken
    B) pay back   D) show off

Answers for Practice Set 4

1. **(C)** gloom
2. **(C)** boundary
3. **(B)** proud
4. **(A)** strength
5. **(C)** absorb
6. **(A)** reason
7. **(C)** twisted
8. **(C)** burn
9. **(A)** frenzied
10. **(A)** make right
11. **(C)** quarrelsome
12. **(C)** ordinary
13. **(A)** sharpen
14. **(B)** remember
15. **(C)** trivial
16. **(D)** display
17. **(C)** risky
18. **(B)** accident
19. **(C)** failure
20. **(A)** companion
21. **(C)** inspection
22. **(C)** healthy
23. **(C)** give up
24. **(C)** twisted
25. **(C)** weaken

Practice Set 5

Select the best answer to each question and write the letter of your choice in the space provided.

1. *Benediction* means most nearly _____

   A) argument   C) blessing
   B) retirement   D) treason

2. To *acquiesce* means most nearly to _____

   A) yield   C) understand
   B) familiarize   D) resolve

3. To *abhor* means most nearly to _____

   A) yell   C) dissolve
   B) force   D) detest

4. *Unwitting* means most nearly _____

   A) unconscious   C) droll
   B) ill-humored   D) stupid

5. To *recant* means most nearly to _____

   A) take back   C) allow
   B) deceive   D) forbid

6. *Morbid* means most nearly _____

   A) gruesome   C) allowable
   B) stiff   D) enthusiastic

7. *Occult* means most nearly _____

   A) mysterious   C) cold
   B) silent   D) oily

8. *Preposterous* means most nearly _____

   A) commonplace   C) profound
   B) skilled   D) absurd

9. To *resuscitate* means most nearly to _____

   A) revive   C) remind
   B) reneg   D) reproach

10. *Subtle* means most nearly _____

    A) soft   C) not obvious
    B) dirty   D) careless

11. *Uncanny* means most nearly _____

    A) pure   C) moldy
    B) strange   D) open

12. *Vigilant* means most nearly _____

    A) angry   C) forceful
    B) watchful   D) unknowledgeable

13. *Environs* means most nearly _____

   A) vicinity   C) chains
   B) forest   D) prison

14. *Entrepreneur* means most nearly _____

   A) roughneck   C) foreigner
   B) businessman   D) deceiver

15. To *poach* means most nearly to _____

   A) trespass   C) instruct
   B) model   D) hang

16. *Revelry* means most nearly _____

   A) merrymaking   C) anger
   B) reminder   D) overthrow

17. *Shoddy* means most nearly _____

   A) doubting   C) cheap
   B) intermittent   D) ghostly

18. *Virile* means most nearly _____

   A) sick   C) manly
   B) deadly   D) watchful

19. *Mutinous* means most nearly _____

   A) silent   C) ponderous
   B) rebellious   D) changeable

20. *Profound* means most nearly _____

   A) discovered   C) very deep
   B) receptive   D) absurd

21. To *fabricate* means most nearly to _____

   A) enhance   C) lie
   B) free   D) urge

22. To *falter* means most nearly to _____

   A) blame   C) stumble
   B) draw out   D) decree

23. *Coy* means most nearly _____

   A) bashful   C) cowardly
   B) brief   D) aware

24. *Bland* means most nearly _____

   A) musical   C) mild
   B) friendly   D) happy

25. *Calligraphy* means most nearly _____

   A) measurement   C) penmanship
   B) profession   D) communication

Answers for Practice Set 5

1. **(C)** blessing
2. **(A)** yield
3. **(D)** detest
4. **(A)** unconscious
5. **(A)** take back
6. **(A)** gruesome
7. **(A)** mysterious
8. **(D)** absurd
9. **(A)** revive
10. **(C)** not obvious
11. **(B)** strange
12. **(B)** watchful
13. **(A)** vicinity
14. **(B)** businessman
15. **(A)** trespass
16. **(A)** merrymaking
17. **(C)** cheap
18. **(C)** manly
19. **(B)** rebellious
20. **(C)** very deep
21. **(C)** lie
22. **(C)** stumble
23. **(A)** bashful
24. **(C)** mild
25. **(C)** penmanship

Practice Set 6

Select the best answer to each question and write the letter of your choice in the space provided.

1. To *haggle* means most nearly to _____

   A) show off   C) bargain
   B) rob   D) raid

2. *Boisterous* means most nearly _____

   A) masculine   C) sentimental
   B) rowdy   D) trite

3. *Molten* means most nearly _____

   A) melted   C) lost
   B) furry   D) evil

4. *Mentor* means most nearly _____

   A) teacher   C) temperature
   B) salesperson   D) adage

5. To *avow* means most nearly to _____

   A) marry   C) acknowledge
   B) adapt   D) help

6. *Mercenary* means most nearly _____

   A) greedy   C) murderous
   B) quick   D) reliable

7. To *reimburse* means most nearly to _____

   A) profit   C) pay back
   B) require   D) foretell

8. *Paltry* means most nearly _____

   A) chicken   C) insignificant
   B) friendship   D) white

9. *Mandatory* means most nearly _____

   A) masculine   C) required
   B) foolish   D) perceptive

10. To *petrify* means most nearly to _____

    A) harden   C) frighten
    B) kiss   D) embezzle

11. *Interim* means most nearly _____

    A) upset   C) meantime
    B) boundary   D) subject

12. To *desist* means most nearly to _____

    A) punish   C) stop
    B) forgive   D) allow

13. *Component* means most nearly _____

    A) part   C) circle
    B) conduct   D) conspiracy

14. *Avocation* means most nearly _____

    A) job   C) hobby
    B) trip   D) decoration

15. *Apathetic* means most nearly _____

    A) important   C) calm
    B) horrified   D) indifferent

16. *Compliant* means most nearly _____

    A) submissive   C) argument
    B) unhappy   D) restrictive

17. *Soothsayer* means most nearly _____

    A) dentist   C) predictor
    B) sleepwalker D) debater

18. *Sinister* means most nearly _____

    A) winding   C) evil
    B) smiling   D) truthful

19. *Redundant* means most nearly _____

   A) bouncing   C) self-reliant
   B) repetitious   D) hardy

20. To *mimic* means most nearly to _____

   A) pander   C) imitate
   B) mumble   D) threaten

21. *Impeccable* means most nearly _____

   A) faultless   C) encouraging
   B) hairy   D) religious

22. *Idiosyncrasy* means most nearly _____

   A) peculiarity   C) rhythm
   B) weirdness   D) reliability

23. *Furtive* means most nearly _____

   A) sneaky   C) powerful
   B) sterile   D) limited

24. To *gorge* means most nearly to _____

   A) blast   C) cut short
   B) stuff   D) corrupt

25. *Dank* means most nearly _____

   A) dark   C) damp
   B) dim   D) dear

Answers for Practice Set 6

1. **(C)** bargain
2. **(B)** rowdy
3. **(A)** melted
4. **(A)** teacher
5. **(C)** acknowledge
6. **(A)** greedy
7. **(C)** pay back
8. **(C)** insignificant
9. **(C)** required
10. **(A)** harden
11. **(C)** meantime
12. **(C)** stop
13. **(A)** part
14. **(C)** hobby
15. **(D)** indifferent
16. **(A)** submissive
17. **(C)** predictor
18. **(C)** evil
19. **(B)** repetitious
20. **(C)** imitate
21. **(A)** faultless
22. **(A)** peculiarity
23. **(A)** sneaky
24. **(B)** stuff
25. **(C)** damp

Practice Set 7

Select the best answer to each question and write the letter of your choice in the space provided.

1. *Integrity* means most nearly _____

   A) wealth   C) honesty
   B) temper   D) understanding

2. *Frugal* means most nearly _____

   A) free   C) pretentious
   B) thrifty   D) profane

3. *Depravity* means most nearly _____

   A) corruption   C) greed
   B) slavery   D) boldness

4. *Awry* means most nearly _____

   A) distant   C) not straight
   B) bitter   D) ironic

5. *Unkempt* means most nearly _____

   A) neat   C) swollen
   B) untidy   D) closed

6. *Unique* means most nearly _____

   A) singular   C) twisted
   B) sexless   D) clownish

7. *Proficient* means most nearly _____

   A) quick   C) skilled
   B) dubious   D) reliable

8. *Judicious* means most nearly _____

   A) trial   C) debatable
   B) wise   D) sweet

9. *Meticulous* means most nearly _____

   A) careful   C) asinine
   B) imitative   D) healthful

10. *Prognosis* means most nearly _____

    A) sickness   C) forecast
    B) difficulty D) forked

11. *Introverted* means most nearly _____

    A) unarguable C) strong
    B) withdrawn   D) upset

12. *Heterogeneous* means most nearly _____

    A) perverted   C) varied
    B) healthy   D) recondite

13. *Feasible* means most nearly _____

    A) practical   C) stealable
    B) expensive   D) ridiculous

14. To *emulate* means most nearly to _____

    A) imitate   C) require
    B) disown   D) disparage

15. *Hirsute* means most nearly _____

    A) historic   C) mounted
    B) hairy   D) armored

16. *Pastoral* means most nearly _____

    A) ancient   C) melodic
    B) rural   D) starving

17. *Homage* means most nearly _____

    A) honor   C) settle
    B) estate   D) vision

18. *Aghast* means most nearly _____

    A) fueled   C) horrified
    B) exhaust   D) left over

19. *Innate* means most nearly _____

    A) human   C) simplistic
    B) overwrought D) in-born

20. *Fetid* means most nearly _____

    A) stinking   C) fallen
    B) productive D) satiated

21. To *embellish* means most nearly to _____

    A) signal   C) ornament
    B) stomach   D) mortify

22. *Paraphernalia* means most nearly _____

    A) spirits   C) fear
    B) equipment   D) illegal

23. To *binder* means most nearly to _____

    A) restrain   C) sharpen
    B) imply   D) pray

24. To *cull* means most nearly to _____

    A) cut   C) select
    B) desert   D) decay

25. *Chaste* means most nearly _____

    A) pursuit   C) satisfaction
    B) pure   D) punishment

Answers for Practice Set 7

1. **(C)** honesty
2. **(B)** thrifty
3. **(A)** corruption
4. **(C)** not straight
5. **(B)** untidy
6. **(A)** singular
7. **(C)** skilled
8. **(B)** wise
9. **(A)** careful
10. **(C)** forecast
11. **(B)** withdrawn
12. **(C)** varied
13. **(A)** practical
14. **(A)** imitate
15. **(B)** hairy
16. **(B)** rural
17. **(A)** honor
18. **(C)** horrified
19. **(D)** in-born
20. **(A)** stinking
21. **(C)** ornament
22. **(B)** equipment
23. **(A)** restrain
24. **(C)** select
25. **(B)** pure

Verbal Abilities Analysis Chart for Word Meaning (Vocabulary)

Use the following chart to carefully analyze your results of the *word meaning (vocabulary)* question type. This will help you evaluate your strengths and weaknesses. This analysis should help you focus your study and review efforts on specific types of problems.

Practice Set	Total Number of Questions	Number Correct	Number Incorrect	Number Unanswered
Set 1	25			
Set 2	25			
Set 3	25			
Set 4	25			
Set 5	25			
Set 6	25			
Set 7	25			

Because there is no penalty for incorrect answers on most of the questions in the Verbal Abilities section, you should have left no question unanswered. Even if you didn't have time to answer a question, you should have at least filled in the answer space with an educated guess.

REVIEWING THE KEY STRATEGIES

Remember to:
1. Look for the best, or closest, meaning.
2. Work as quickly as possible.
3. Use prefixes, suffixes, and roots.
4. Try the word in a clear sentence.
5. Look for positive or negative connotations.

ANALOGIES (WORD RELATIONSHIPS)

This question type tests your vocabulary and your ability to understand relationships. Each question gives you one pair of related words, and one word from a second pair. You are given four choices for completing the second pair, so that it expresses a relationship similar to the first.

For example:

HEN is related to CHICK as HORSE is related to

A) bull   C) colt
B) milk   D) kitten

Notice the first pair, "HEN is related to CHICK." In this pair, the second word is a "young version" of the first word. Now look at the first word of the second pair: HORSE is related to . . . To complete this pair you must express the same relationship as in the first pair, so that the second word is a "young version" of the first word. The answer choice (second word) that best expresses that relationship is COLT. A COLT (second word) is a young version of a HORSE (first word). (C) is the correct answer.

Helpful Techniques and Strategies

1. Always try to determine the relationship expressed in the first pair of words. Is the relationship "cause to effect" or "part to whole," or what? Then look at the first word of the next pair.

2. It may help to read this question type by thinking to yourself, "A is related to B *in the same way* as C is related to (D)." The (D) word is the one you are looking for in your answer choices.

3. Remember that *order* must be the same in both pairs. For example,

STREAM is related to RIVER as LAKE is related to

A) pond   C) fish
B) ocean   D) water

Notice the relationship in the first pair: SMALL is to LARGE. Therefore the second pair should say that LAKE (small) is related to OCEAN (large). If you made the mistake of reversing the order in the second pair, you would have chosen (A) POND, which is incorrect.

4. The parts of speech in each pair should be consistent. Look at the question below:

SKYSCRAPER is related to TALL as FREIGHT TRAIN is related to

A) track   C) quickly
B) engine   D) long

Notice that the first word in each pair is a noun (person, place, or thing) and the second word in the first pair, TALL, is an adjective. Therefore the second word in the second pair must also be an adjective. Notice that answer choice (D), LONG, is an adjective, whereas the other choices are not: SKYSCRAPER (noun) is related to TALL (adjective) as FREIGHT TRAIN (noun) is related to LONG (adjective).

5. Remember that the second pair of words does not have to concern the same "subject" as the first. Look at the following question:

PUPPY is related to DOG as SAPLING is related to

A) house   C) leaf
B) tree   D) syrup

Notice that the "subject" of the first pair is animals and the "subject" of the second pair is plants. However, it is the relationship between words that is important. The *relationship* in the first pair is "younger" to "older." With this relationship in mind, you should conclude that SAPLING (younger) is related to TREE (older).

6. Look at all the choices before deciding on an answer, but don't spend too much time on any one question.

7. Usually you will be able to eliminate one or two choices immediately. Those that remain may all seem like good answers, but remember that you are looking for the *best* answer, one that best expresses the same relationship.

8. Analogies can be classified into specific categories. You will find it helpful to be able to recognize some of these categories and the common relationships immediately. Do not try to memorize these categories or to classify the analogies you are given on the exam. Instead, reason out the relationships shown in the first pair of analogies and then carefully choose a second pair that has a corresponding relationship.

    Following are some BASIC TYPES of analogies:

a. CLASSIFICATIONS—sorts, kinds, general to specific, specific to general, thing to quality or characteristic, opposites, degree, etc.

A broad category is compared to a narrower category:

RODENT	:	SQUIRREL	::	fish	:	flounder
(broad category)		*(narrower category)*		*(broad category)*		*(narrower category)*

A person is compared to a characteristic:

SPRINTER	:	FAST	::	jockey	:	small
(person)		*(characteristic)*		*(person)*		*(characteristic)*

The general is compared to the specific:

SPORT	:	HOCKEY	::	machine	:	typewriter
(general)		*(specific)*		*(general)*		*(specific)*

A word is compared to a synonym of itself:

ENORMOUS	:	HUGE	::	quick	:	speedy
(word)		*(synonym)*		*(word)*		*(synonym)*

A word is compared to an antonym of itself:

SERVANT	:	MASTER	::	sad	:	happy
(word)		*(antonym)*		*(word)*		*(antonym)*

A word is compared to a definition of itself:

REGULATE	:	CONTROL	::	segregate	:	separate
(word)		*(definition)*		*(word)*		*(definition)*

A male is compared to a female:

ROOSTER	:	CHICKEN	::	buck	:	doe
(male)		*(female)*		*(male)*		*(female)*

A family relationship is compared to a similar family relationship:

AUNT	:	NIECE	::	uncle	:	nephew
(family relationship)				*(family relationship)*		

A virtue is compared to a failing:

RESPONSIBILITY	:	CARELESSNESS	::	honesty	:	dishonesty
(virtue)		*(failing)*		*(virtue)*		*(failing)*

An element is compared to an extreme of itself:

DRY SPELL	:	DROUGHT	::	water	:	flood
(element)		*(extreme)*		*(element)*		*(extreme)*

A lesser degree is compared to a greater degree:

HAPPY	:	ECSTATIC	::	hot	:	scorching
(lesser degree)		*(greater degree)*		*(lesser degree)*		*(greater degree)*

The plural is compared to the singular:

CHILDREN	:	CHILD	::	they	:	he
(plural)		*(singular)*		*(plural)*		*(singular)*

b. STRUCTURALS—part to whole, whole to part, part to part, etc.

A part is compared to a whole:

FINGER	:	HAND	::	room	:	house
(part)		*(whole)*		*(part)*		*(whole)*

A whole is compared to a part:

DECK	:	CARD	::	novel	:	chapter
(whole)		*(part)*		*(whole)*		*(part)*

c. COMPONENTS—elements of a compound, ingredients of a recipe, etc.

An ingredient is compared to its finished result:

FLOUR	:	CAKE	::	sulphur	:	gunpowder
(ingredient)		*(finished product)*		*(ingredient)*		*(finished product)*

HYDROGEN	:	WATER	::	sodium	:	salt
(element)		*(compound)*		*(element)*		*(compound)*

d. OPERATIONALS—time sequence, operations, stages, phases, beginning to ending, before to after, etc.

One element of time is compared to another element of time:

DAWN	:	DUSK	::	sunrise	::	sunset
(time element)		*(time element)*		*(time element)*		*(time element)*

A time sequence relationship is expressed:

PROLOGUE	:	EPILOGUE	::	birth	:	death
(beginning)		*(ending)*		*(beginning)*		*(ending)*

A complete operation is compared to a stage:

FOOTBALL GAME	:	QUARTER	::	baseball game	:	inning
(operation)		*(stage)*		*(operation)*		*(stage)*

NOTE: Many analogies (word relationships) will overlap into more than one of the above basic types and will have to be analyzed by their purpose, use, cause-effect relationship, etc.

Practice Set 1

Select the best answer to each question and write the letter of your choice in the space provided.

1. APPOINTMENT is related to CANCEL as BUILDING is related to _____
   A) construct
   B) conference
   C) demolish
   D) design

2. SPORT is related to SPECTATOR as TELEVISION is related to _____
   A) vision
   B) tube
   C) viewer
   D) channel

3. PURITY is related to WHITE as ANGER is related to _____

   A) yellow   C) mad
   B) red   D) mean

4. WALL is related to PAINTING as FLOOR is related to _____

   A) sweeping   C) house
   B) dirty   D) ironing

5. PLUMBER is related to WRENCH as LION-TAMER is related to _____

   A) lion   C) cage
   B) whip   D) fear

6. AUTOMOBILE is related to IGNITION as LAMP is related to _____

   A) bulb   C) switch
   B) wheel   D) steering wheel

7. IMPORTANT is related to INSIGNIFICANT as INTENDED is related to _____

   A) purpose   C) meaningless
   B) required   D) accidental

8. CUISINE is related to KITCHEN as EXPERIMENT is related to _____

   A) living room   C) stadium
   B) airport   D) laboratory

9. ORE is related to MINE as SAP is related to _____

   A) syrup   C) branch
   B) fluid   D) tree

10. WINDOW is related to AWNING as EYES is related to _____

    A) glasses   C) visor
    B) feet   D) hand

11. SALVAGE is related to TREASURE as RESCUE is related to _____

    A) ambulance   C) squad
    B) victim   D) hospital

12. ALLIES is related to ADVERSARIES as FRIENDS is related to _____

    A) foes   C) arbitrators
    B) helpers   D) peacemakers

13. LAGOON is related to BAY as BROOK is related to _____

    A) puddle   C) ocean
    B) river   D) aqueduct

14. TASK is related to FATIGUE as FASTING is related to _____

    A) food   C) weakness
    B) strength   D) slowness

15. DRAPE is related to WINDOW as COSTUME is related to _____

    A) seamstress   C) character
    B) Halloween   D) mask

16. DAWN is related to DAY as PREFACE is related to _____

    A) epilogue   C) book
    B) index   D) chapter

17. TRIAL is related to COURTROOM as BALLGAME is related to _____

    A) clubhouse   C) stadium
    B) league   D) uniform

18. MARRIAGE is related to BACHELOR as EXPERIENCE is related to _____

    A) fun   C) wizard
    B) novice   D) husband

19. HEART is related to HUMAN as ENGINE is related to _____

   A) carburetor   C) automobile
   B) gasoline   D) mechanic

20. BURGLAR is related to ALARM as TRESPASSER is related to _____

   A) bark   C) air raid
   B) steal   D) property

Answer Explanations for Practice Set 1

1. **(C)** The first word is eliminated by the second word.
2. **(C)** The first word is watched by the second word.
3. **(B)** The second word is the color symbolizing the first word.
4. **(A)** The second word is done to the first word.
5. **(B)** The second word is a tool of the first word.
6. **(C)** The second word turns on the first word.
7. **(D)** The first word is the opposite of the second word.
8. **(D)** The first word is produced in the second word.
9. **(D)** The first word is produced in the second word.
10. **(C)** The second word shades the first word.
11. **(B)** The first word saves the second word.
12. **(A)** The first word is the opposite of the second word.
13. **(B)** The first word is similar to but smaller than the second word.
14. **(C)** The first word causes the second word.
15. **(C)** The first word covers the second word.
16. **(C)** The first word begins the second word.
17. **(C)** The first word takes place in the second word.
18. **(B)** The first word ends the second word.
19. **(C)** The first word is the vital center of the second word.
20. **(A)** The first word is frightened away by the second word.

Practice Set 2

Select the best answer to each question and write the letter of your choice in the space provided.

1. SOLO is related to ENSEMBLE as INDIVIDUAL is related to _____

   A) committee   C) instrument
   B) performance   D) partner

2. MELANCHOLY is related to CHEERFUL as TRAGEDY is related to _____

   A) death   C) play
   B) drama   D) comedy

3. BIGOT is related to TOLERANCE as MISER is related to _____

   A) generosity   C) hoard
   B) money   D) spendthrift

4. CLAW is related to LION as TALON is related to _____

   A) snake   C) hand
   B) hawk   D) finger

5. BUSINESS is related to BANKRUPT as TEAM is related to _____

A) fall behind   C) teamwork
B) forfeit   D) play

6. COFFEE is related to BEAN as TEA is related to _____

A) bag   C) instant
B) leaf   D) iced

7. HERD is related to GAME as FLOCK is related to _____

A) lions   C) mice
B) sheep   D) gather

8. ICE is related to GLACIER as SAND is related to _____

A) beach   C) sandstorm
B) heat   D) water

9. CAPTAIN is related to SHIP as PUBLISHER is related to _____

A) newspaper   C) film
B) mint   D) airplane

10. CATASTROPHE is related to EARTHQUAKE as BIRD is related to _____

A) robin   C) accident
B) flight   D) nest

11. EXTINCT is related to DINOSAUR as IMAGINARY is related to _____

A) whale   C) unicorn
B) fantasy   D) real

12. ASTRONOMY is related to STARS as GEOLOGY is related to _____

A) geography   C) rocks
B) maps   D) artifacts

13. REVOLUTION is related to TYRANNY as COURAGE is related to _____

A) fear   C) government
B) anger   D) heroism

14. SACRIFICE is related to MARTYR as RULE is related to _____

A) lawyer   C) despot
B) carpenter   D) measure

15. DAY is related to SOLAR as EVENING is related to _____

A) night   C) dawn
B) dark   D) lunar

16. GARAGE is related to VEHICLES as VAULT is related to _____

A) burglar   C) valuables
B) safe   D) combination

17. LIMP is related to INJURY as LAUGH is related to _____

A) cry   C) joke
B) pain   D) smile

18. WATER is related to EVAPORATE as ICE is related to _____

A) freeze   C) cold
B) melt   D) solid

19. MEAT is related to PROTEIN as POTATOES is related to _____

A) fat   C) calories
B) starch   D) butter

20. DISEMBARK is related to SHIP as DISMOUNT is related to _____

A) train   C) horse
B) rider   D) mountain

Answer Explanations for Practice Set 2

1. **(A)** The second word is the plural of the first word.
2. **(D)** The first word is the opposite of the second word.
3. **(A)** The first word lacks the second word.
4. **(B)** The second word grasps with the first word.
5. **(B)** The second word is the failure of the first word.
6. **(B)** The first word comes originally from the second word.
7. **(B)** The first word is a collection of the second word.
8. **(A)** The second word is composed of the first word.
9. **(A)** The first word is in charge of the second word.
10. **(A)** The second word is a specific example of the first word.
11. **(C)** The first word is a description of the second word.
12. **(C)** The first word is the study of the second word.
13. **(A)** The first word overcomes the second word.
14. **(C)** The first word is an action of the second word.
15. **(D)** The second word is the illumination of the first word.
16. **(C)** The first word stores the second word.
17. **(C)** The second word causes the first word.
18. **(B)** The first word changes by means of the second word.
19. **(B)** The first word provides the second word,
20. **(C)** The first word is the action of getting off the second word.

Practice Set 3

Select the best answer to each question and write the letter of your choice in the space provided.

1. DUNCE is related to SCHOLAR as TRAITOR is related to _____

    A) spy   C) rogue
    B) teaser   D) hero

2. SCARCITY is related to PLENTY as FOOLISHNESS is related to _____

    A) wisdom   C) interests
    B) jokes   D) jesters

3. IMAGE is related to MIRAGE as FACT is related to _____

    A) fantasy   C) thought
    B) oasis   D) reality

4. BOOK is related to INDEX as APARTMENT BUILDING is related to _____

    A) doorbells   C) bedroom
    B) directory   D) driveway

5. IGLOO is related to ESKIMO as NEST is related to _____

    A) Indian   C) family
    B) bird   D) flock

6. NUN is related to HABIT as SOLDIER is related to _____

    A) rifle   C) uniform
    B) battalion   D) infantry

7. VIAL is related to BARREL. as PAMPHLET is related to _____

    A) volume   C) leaflet
    B) box   D) discount

8. WAITER is related to TIP as ACTOR is related to _____

    A) applause C) actress
    B) drama   D) stage

9. BLADE is related to SKATE as WHEEL is related to _____

    A) kick   C) bicycle
    B) foot   D) spoke

10. RAIN is related to DROP as SNOW is related to _____

    A) flake   C) ice
    B) icicle   D) hail

11. BALDNESS is related to HAIR as SILENCE is related to _____

    A) quiet   C) laughter
    B) noise   D) sunshine

12. CIRCLE is related to ARC as LINE is related to _____

    A) parallel C) curve
    B) segment   D) perpendicular

13. DOG is related to WOLF as CAT is related to _____

    A) kitty   C) bear
    B) tiger   D) feline

14. FEATHERS is related to BIRD as SCALES is related to _____

    A) weigh   C) fish
    B) notes   D) animal

15. PACKAGE is related to RIBBON as CAKE is related to _____

    A) chocolate C) icing
    B) wedding   D) sugar

16. FACE is related to EYES as HOUSE is related to _____

    A) windows   C) roof
    B) doors   D) ears

17. PUNCH is related to DUCK as QUESTION is related to _____

    A) answer   C) evade
    B) understand D) teach

18. TREE is related to SAPLING as COW is related to _____

    A) bull   C) calf
    B) milk   D) barn

19. SOCCER is related to BALL as HOCKEY is related to _____

    A) stick   C) goal
    B) ice   D) puck

20. DROWSY is related to NAP as HUNGRY is related to _____

    A) snack   C) siesta
    B) starve   D) drink

Answer Explanations for Practice Set 3

1. **(D)** The first word is the opposite of the second word.
2. **(A)** The first word is the opposite of the second word.
3. **(A)** The second word is an imaginary first word.
4. **(B)** The second word is a contents listing of the first word.
5. **(B)** The second word builds and lives out of the first word.
6. **(C)** The first word wears the second word.

7. **(A)** The second word is a much larger first word.

8. **(A)** The second word is given in appreciation to the first word.

9. **(C)** The first word is a part of the second word.

10. **(A)** The first word falls in the form of the second word.

11. **(B)** The first word lacks the second word.

12. **(B)** The second word is a part of the first word.

13. **(B)** The first word is a domesticated animal in the same family as the second word.

14. **(C)** The first word is the body covering of the second word.

15. **(C)** The second word is what goes around the first word.

16. **(A)** The second word is the "viewing openings" of the first word.

17. **(C)** The second word avoids the first word.

18. **(C)** The second word is an immature first word.

19. **(D)** The second word is the object of control when playing the first word.

20. **(A)** The second word satisfies the biological condition of the first word.

Practice Set 4

Select the best answer to each question and write the letter of your choice in the space provided.

1. LIFEGUARD is related to RESCUE as PROFESSOR is related to _____

    A) instruct   C) school
    B) college   D) student

2. JOKE is related to LAUGHTER as THREAT is related to _____

    A) fear   C) happiness
    B) discovery   D) brawny

3. DEPOSIT is related to WITHDRAWAL as POSITIVE is related to _____

    A) neutral   C) position
    B) negative   D) bankrupt

4. TREMOR is related to EARTHQUAKE as WIND is related to _____

    A) hurricane   C) clock
    B) lightning   D) thunder

5. JAR is related to JAM as SHOES is related to _____

    A) sandals   C) feet
    B) laces   D) soles

6. RADIO is related to TRANSISTOR as SAILBOAT is related to _____

    A) mast   C) engine
    B) rudder   D) wind

7. TOES is related to FOOT as HANDS is related to _____

    A) fingers   C) glove
    B) clock   D) house

8. PREDICTION is related to MYSTIC as PROGNOSIS is related to _____

    A) diagnosis   C) doctor
    B) prescription D) patient

9. MEAT is related to MILK as FORK is related to _____

    A) knife   C) dish
    B) straw   D) cow

10. REHEARSE is related to IMPROVEMENT as PRACTICE is related to _____

    A) perfection   C) failure
    B) study   D) audition

11. HOUSE is related to ROOF as BOX is related to _____

    A) wall   C) side
    B) face   D) lid

12. TEETHING is related to PAIN as TICKLING is related to _____

    A) tenderness   C) friendship
    B) laughter   D) soothing

13. THROTTLE is related to GASOLINE as FAUCET is related to _____

    A) hose   C) water
    B) garden   D) car

14. WRING is related to WASHCLOTH as SQUEEZE is related to _____

    A) mop   C) pail
    B) sponge   D) pillow

15. STAMP is related to POSTAGE as PREMIUM is related to _____

    A) insurance   C) coupon
    B) accident   D) exceptional

16. WEIGHT is related to SCALE as LENGTH is related to _____

    A) speedometer   C) clock
    B) tape measure   D) width

17. SCULPTOR is related to MARBLE as NOVELIST is related to _____

    A) books   C) literature
    B) paper   D) characters

18. MODEST is related to HUMBLE as CAUTIOUS is related to _____

    A) accident   C) reliable
    B) careful   D) braggart

19. SAFARI is related to GAME as POSSE is related to _____

    A) animal   C) fugitive
    B) human   D) western

20. LULLABY is related to BABY as TAPS is related to _____

    A) trumpet   C) bedtime
    B) soldier   D) sleep

Answer Explanations for Practice Set 4

1. **(A)** The second word is the job task of the first word.
2. **(A)** The second word is the result of the first word.
3. **(B)** The first word is the opposite of the second word.
4. **(A)** The second word is larger in size than the first word.
5. **(C)** The first word contains the second word.
6. **(D)** The second word powers the first word.
7. **(B)** The first word is on or a part of the second word.
8. **(C)** The first word is a statement made by the second word.
9. **(B)** The first word relates to solid food; the second word to liquid food.
10. **(A)** The second word is the goal of the first word.
11. **(D)** The second word is atop the first word.
12. **(B)** The second word is a result of the first word.
13. **(C)** The first word regulates the flow of the second word.
14. **(B)** The first word empties the liquid from the second word.
15. **(A)** The first word pays for the second word.
16. **(B)** The second word measures the first word.

17. **(B)** The second word is the raw material used by the first word.
18. **(B)** The first word is a synonym for the second word.
19. **(C)** The second word is the object of capture of the first word.
20. **(B)** The first word precedes the sleeping of the second word.

Practice Set 5

Select the best answer to each question and write the letter of your choice in the space provided.

1. NURSE is related to DOCTOR as SECRETARY is related to _____

    A) man   C) typewriter
    B) office   D) executive

2. ENCOURAGE is related to RIDICULE as SMILE is related to _____

    A) scowl   C) rely
    B) happy   D) wink

3. AMNESIA is related to MEMORIES as SILENCE is related to _____

    A) operation   C) melodies
    B) hearing   D) quiet

4. APPRENTICE is related to MASTER as STUDENT is related to _____

    A) scholar   C) teacher
    B) academic   D) studies

5. SIGNATURE is related to FORGERY as ORIGINAL is related to _____

    A) facsimile   C) reasonable
    B) verbatim   D) criminal

6. ACCIDENT is related to RECKLESSNESS as HUMILIATION is related to _____

    A) resoluteness   C) cleanliness
    B) tactlessness   D) determination

7. NAVIGATOR is related to SEXTANT as WOODSMAN is related to _____

    A) novel   C) axe
    B) work   D) timber

8. BOOK is related to CHAPTER as SYMPHONY is related to _____

    A) musician   C) movement
    B) conductor   D) instrument

9. ONION is related to TEARS as TIREDNESS is related to _____

    A) body   C) yawn
    B) bed   D) exercise

10. GALLOP is related to HORSE as SLITHER is related to _____

    A) snail   C) spider
    B) rat   D) snake

11. IRON is related to RUST as TOOTH is related to _____

    A) incisor   C) decay
    B) toothpaste   D) clean

12. TROPICAL is related to RAIN as ARCTIC is related to _____

    A) ice   C) igloo
    B) snow   D) water

13. ENGINE is related to FUEL as BODY is related to _____

    A) organs   C) food
    B) limb   D) breath

14. SCARCE is related to EXPENSIVE as PLENTIFUL is related to _____

    A) invaluable   C) rotten
    B) cheap   D) valuable

15. ENORMOUS is related to MINUTE as REWARD is related to _____

    A) reprimand   C) restitution
    B) value   D) hour

16. RECKLESS is related to CAREFUL as FACT is related to _____

    A) novel   C) fiction
    B) new   D) antique

17. GINGER is related to ROOT as CHOCOLATE is related to _____

    A) bar   C) bean
    B) candy   D) milk

18. BULLSEYE is related to TARGET as NOSE is related to _____

    A) eyes   C) face
    B) ears   D) body

19. BUTTER is related to MARGARINE as SUGAR is related to _____

    A) sweet   C) saccharin
    B) salt   D) oleomargarine

20. BIRD is related to WORM as CAT is related to _____

    A) dog   C) pet
    B) mouse   D) animal

Answer Explanations for Practice Set 5

1. **(D)** The first word assists the second word.
2. **(A)** The first word is the opposite of the second word.
3. **(C)** The first word is the absence of the second word.
4. **(C)** The first word learns from the second word.
5. **(A)** The second word is a copy of the first word.
6. **(B)** The first word results from the second word.
7. **(C)** The second word is a tool of the first word.
8. **(C)** The second word is a part of the first word.
9. **(C)** The first word causes the second word.
10. **(D)** The first word is how the second word moves.
11. **(C)** The second word is the corrosion of the first word.
12. **(B)** The second word is the precipitation occurring in the region of the first word.
13. **(C)** The second word powers the first word.
14. **(B)** The second word is the cost of the first word.
15. **(A)** The first word is the opposite of the second word.
16. **(C)** The first word is the opposite of the second word.
17. **(C)** The second word is the origin of the first word.
18. **(C)** The first word is the center of the second word.
19. **(C)** The second word is a substitute for the first word.
20. **(B)** The second word is the prey of the first word.

Practice Set 6

Select the best answer to each question and write the letter of your choice in the space provided.

1. COACH is related to TEAM as CONDUCTOR is related to _____

    A) electricity   C) instruments
    B) orchestra   D) music

2. EWE is related to RAM as CHICKEN is related to _____

    A) hen   C) rooster
    B) chick   D) fowl

3. SWORD is related to KNIGHT as RIFLE is related to _____

A) gun C) pistol
B) soldier D) weapon

4. PAPER is related to INK as BLACKBOARD is related to _____

A) writing C) schoolroom
B) lesson D) chalk

5. COOL is related to FRIGID as WARM is related to _____

A) torrid C) crisp
B) lukewarm D) balmy

6. NEWS is related to HEARSAY as FACT is related to _____

A) ideas C) science
B) newspaper D) fiction

7. CROCUS is related to SPRING as THUNDERCLOUD is related to _____

A) sky C) winter
B) storm D) dark

8. OBESE is related to SLENDER as BABBLING is related to _____

A) brook C) talkative
B) quiet D) slim

9. LEMON is related to CITRUS as CHICKEN is related to _____

A) rooster C) fowl
B) hen D) barnyard

10. INFANTS is related to NURSERY as MINNOWS is related to _____

A) hospital C) babies
B) hatchery D) fish

11. WATER is related to JUG as LETTER is related to _____

A) alphabet C) stamp
B) envelope D) literate

12. HICK is related to SOPHISTICATION as BOOR is related to _____

A) tactfulness C) interesting
B) money D) rudeness

13. THUG is related to GUN as BULL is related to _____

A) steer C) matador
B) horns D) sports

14. SCHOLAR is related to ENCYCLOPEDIA as MECHANIC is related to _____

A) dictionary C) manual
B) tools D) transistor

15. OVERALLS is related to TRACTOR as TUXEDO is related to _____

A) farming C) cummerbund
B) limousine D) sportscar

16. FAME is related to DISGRACE as HERO is related to _____

A) criminal C) fortune
B) friendship D) popularity

17. PIANO is related to TUNED as HAIR is related to _____

A) grown C) blonde
B) trimmed D) shaggy

18. PODIUM is related to SPEAKER as STAGE is related to _____

A) coach C) cowboy
B) actor D) soldier

19. ANGLER is related to TROUT as WOLF is related to _____

    A) cub   C) lair
    B) hunter   D) rabbit

20. CRINGE is related to COWARD as DECEIVE is related to _____

    A) spy   C) actor
    B) soldier   D) hero

Answer Explanations for Practice Set 6

1. **(B)** The first word prepares and leads the second word.
2. **(C)** The first word is the female of the species; the second word is the male.
3. **(B)** The first word is the weapon used by the second word.
4. **(D)** The second word is the substance used to write on the first word.
5. **(A)** The second word is a greater degree of the first word.
6. **(D)** The first word is nearer the truth; the second word lacks truth.
7. **(B)** The first word is a sign of the second word.
8. **(B)** The first word is the opposite of the second word.
9. **(C)** The first word is a specific variety of the second word.
10. **(B)** The first word is where the second word lives immediately after birth.
11. **(B)** The second word contains the first word.
12. **(A)** The first word is lacking the second word.
13. **(B)** The second word is the weapon used by the first word.
14. **(C)** The second word is the reference book of the first word.
15. **(B)** The first word is the attire worn by the person using the second word.
16. **(A)** The first word is the opposite of the second word.
17. **(B)** The second word puts the first word "in order."
18. **(B)** The first word is where the second word performs.
19. **(D)** The second word is the prey of the first word.
20. **(A)** The first word is the action of the second word.

Practice Set 7

Select the best answer to each question and write the letter of your choice in the space provided.

1. SCALPEL is related to KNIFE as NURSE is related to _____

    A) doctor   C) hospital
    B) assistant   D) operation

2. BEGGAR is related to POOR as FOX is related to _____

    A) skunk   C) large
    B) slow   D) sly

3. FELONY is related to MISDEMEANOR as KILL is related to _____

    A) maim   C) murder
    B) bury   D) guilty

4. RETRACT is related to STATEMENT as VOID is related to _____

    A) escape   C) contract
    B) avoidance   D) empty

5. STOOPED is related to POSTURE as SLURRED is related to _____

    A) diction   C) music
    B) stance   D) action

6. MOVIES is related to PROJECTOR as RECORDS is related to _____

    A) speakers   C) phonograph
    B) tape recorder D) radio

7. CHEMIST is related to LABORATORY as ARTIST is related to _____

A) canvas   C) easel
B) museum   D) studio

8. AGILE is related to NIMBLE as FAST is related to _____

A) swift   C) perpetual
B) slow   D) racy

9. DELICACY is related to GOURMET as INSECT is related to _____

A) bee   C) frog
B) pollen   D) hive

10. BOOK is related to CHAPTER as SONG is related to _____

A) stanza   C) music
B) sing   D) instrument

11. AMBIGUOUS is related to CLARITY as TEMPORARY is related to _____

A) transient   C) clear
B) permanence   D) fragile

12. SAW is related to CUT as YARDSTICK is related to _____

A) foot   C) measure
B) inch   D) tool

13. PROBLEM is related to SOLUTION as POISON is related to _____

A) hemlock   C) arsenic
B) nitrate   D) antidote

14. SUGGEST is related to REQUIRED as REQUEST is related to _____

A) ask   C) suspect
B) demand   D) allow

15. AUTOMOBILE is related to HIGHWAY as LOCOMOTIVE is related to _____

A) station   C) track
B) train   D) engine

16. DISTANCE is related to MILE as LIQUID is related to _____

A) milk   C) water
B) quart   D) meter

17. TAILOR is related to NEEDLE as MECHANIC is related to _____

A) engineer   C) toolchest
B) screwdriver   D) brush

18. PORCINE is related to PIG as BOVINE is related to _____

A) boy   C) sheep
B) cow   D) iodine

19. BREAD is related to BUTTER as POTATOES is related to _____

A) gravy   C) margarine
B) steak   D) lamb

20. GNASH is related to TEETH as LISTEN is related to _____

A) hear   C) resolve
B) ears   D) dissuade

Answers and Explanations for Practice Set 7

1. **(B)** The first word is the medical term for the second word.
2. **(D)** The second word is a characteristic of the first word.
3. **(A)** The first word is a more serious degree of the second word.
4. **(C)** The first word nullifies the second word.
5. **(A)** The first word is an impairment of the second word.
6. **(C)** The second word plays the first word.

7. **(D)** The second word is where the first word works.
8. **(A)** The first word is a synonym for the second word.
9. **(C)** The first word is eaten by the second word.
10. **(A)** The second word is a part of the first word.
11. **(B)** The first word is the opposite of the second word.
12. **(C)** The first word is the tool to do the second word.
13. **(D)** The second word overcomes the first word.
14. **(B)** The second word is an imperative ("must") of the first word.
15. **(C)** The first word travels on the second word.
16. **(B)** The second word is a measure of the first word.
17. **(B)** The second word is a tool of the first word.
18. **(B)** The first word means "pertaining to" the second word.
19. **(A)** The second is usually put on the first word.
20. **(B)** The first word is the action of the second word.

Practice Set 8

Select the best answer to each question and write the letter of your choice in the space provided.

1. ALUMNUS is related to ALUMNA as ROOSTER is related to _____

   A) hen   C) barnyard
   B) crow   D) chick

2. PRUNE is related to PLUM as RAISIN is related to _____

   A) kumquat   C) peach
   B) grape   D) cereal

3. RUNG is related to LADDER as STEP is related to _____

   A) march   C) stairway
   B) halt   D) prong

4. INTERSECTION is related to RED LIGHT as PROMONTORY is related to _____

   A) lighthouse C) archipelago
   B) peninsula   D) island

5. SUNDIAL is related to CLOCK as ABACUS is related to _____

   A) stopwatch   C) calculator
   B) barometer   D) thermometer

6. TADPOLE is related to FROG as CATERPILLAR is related to _____

   A) worm   C) butterfly
   B) fur   D) forest

7. MAYOR is related to CITY as GOVERNOR is related to _____

   A) country   C) village
   B) nation   D) state

8. MARS is related to RED as SATURN is related to _____

   A) Jupiter   C) planet
   B) rings   D) moons

9. PROFESSOR is related to CAMPUS as LIFEGUARD is related to _____

   A) rescue   C) beach
   B) save   D) summer

10. TELESCOPE is related to CLOSE as MICROSCOPE is related to _____

    A) small   C) far
    B) large   D) near

11. CHILD is related to BIB as ADULT is related to _____

    A) wipe   C) napkin
    B) neck   D) food

12. PEN is related to QUILL as PAPER is related to _____

    A) pencil   C) ink
    B) parchment   D) book

13. APARTMENT is related to RENT as HOME is related to _____

    A) paint   C) live
    B) purchase   D) build

14. JOCKEY is related to SMALL as RACEHORSE is related to _____

    A) big   C) fast
    B) brown   D) old

15. PREFACE is related to BOOK as PREFIX is related to _____

    A) novel   C) suffix
    B) word   D) repair

16. RADIO is related to TELEVISION as AURAL is related to _____

    A) oral   C) film
    B) visual   D) station

17. PERSON is related to SURNAME as BOOK is related to _____

    A) author   C) chapter
    B) subject   D) title

18. ROOM is related to LAMP as SKY related to _____

    A) cloud   C) sun
    B) night   D) day

19. CLOTHING is related to CLOSET as AMMUNITION is related to _____

    A) armory   C) garage
    B) general   D) storeroom

20. INDUSTRY is related to POLLUTION as TRAFFIC is related to _____

    A) cars   C) highway
    B) accidents   D) speed

Answer Explanations for Practice Set 8

1. **(A)** The first word is the male version; the second word is the female version.
2. **(B)** The first word is the second word dried up.
3. **(C)** The first word is one of the parts of the second word.
4. **(A)** The second word is the signal located at the first word.
5. **(C)** The first word is an ancient version of the second word.
6. **(C)** The first word changes into the second word.
7. **(D)** The first word is the elected leader of the second word.
8. **(B)** The second word is a characteristic of the first word.
9. **(C)** The second word is where the first word works.
10. **(B)** The second word is the resulting action of the first word.
11. **(C)** The second word is used while the first word eats.
12. **(B)** The second word is an ancient version of the first word.
13. **(B)** The second word is the common way of obtaining the first word.
14. **(C)** The second word is a characteristic of the first word.
15. **(B)** The first word is the first part of the second word.
16. **(B)** The first word refers to hearing; the second word refers to sight.

17. **(D)** The second word is the identifying name for the first word.

18. **(C)** The second word illuminates the first word.

19. **(A)** The first word is stored in the second word.

20. **(B)** The second word is a harmful result of the first word.

Practice Set 9

Select the best answer to each question and write the letter of your choice in the space provided.

1. TEETH is related to CHEW as NOSE is related to _____

    A) sweet C) center
    B) smell D) nostril

2. BAT is related to BASEBALL as DRUMSTICK is related to _____

    A) instrument C) band leader
    B) triangle D) drum

3. WOOD is related to GLASS as PAPER is related to _____

    A) cellophane C) ripped
    B) page D) book

4. STENOGRAPHER is related to WORDS as ACCOUNTANT is related to _____

    A) typist C) numbers
    B) letters D) terms

5. COTTON is related to SOFT as WOOL is related to _____

    A) sheep C) expensive
    B) warm D) light

6. SMOKE is related to CHIMNEY as LIQUID is related to _____

    A) funnel C) glass
    B) ocean D) water

7. ATHLETE is related to ROOKIE as MOVIE is related to _____

    A) screening C) award
    B) premiere D) cancelation

8. PENDULUM is related to SWING as GYROSCOPE is related to _____

    A) stop C) spin
    B) measure D) boat

9. CHOREOGRAPHER is related to BALLET as INVENTOR is related to _____

    A) laboratory C) electricity
    B) machine D) imagination

10. BASEMENT is related to ATTIC as VALLEY is related to _____

    A) plateau C) mountaintop
    B) crevasse D) pasture

11. BOOK is related to LIBRARY as WHEAT is related to _____

    A) granary C) food
    B) bread D) milk

12. BUST is related to SCULPTOR as PLAY is related to _____

    A) playground C) dramatist
    B) worker D) entertainer

13. FLOWER is related to GARDEN as TREE is related to _____

    A) stump C) weeds
    B) orchard D) branches

14. SHEEP is related to WOOL as GOOSE is related to _____

    A) gander C) down
    B) flock D) beak

15. BLEEDING is related to TOURNIQUET as TRAFFIC is related to _____

    A) green light   C) automobile
    B) red light   D) detour

16. FOOD is related to FASTING as EXERCISE is related to _____

    A) conditioning   C) resting
    B) warming up   D) stretching

17. HAIR is related to HEAD as NAIL is related to _____

    A) hammer   C) arm
    B) finger   D) cut

18. FENCE is related to YARD as BRACELET is related to _____

    A) wrist   C) neck
    B) ring   D) belt

19. SOLDIER is related to BARRACKS as ESKIMO is related to _____

    A) Iceland   C) snow
    B) arctic   D) igloo

20. SOCKET is related to PLUG as HOLE is related to _____

    A) peg   C) shovel
    B) pencil   D) axe

Answer Explanations for Practice Set 9

1. **(B)** The second word is the action of the first word.
2. **(D)** The first word hits the second word.
3. **(A)** The second word has clear, "see-through" qualities, differentiating it from the first word.
4. **(C)** The first word works professionally with the second word.
5. **(B)** The second word is a quality of the first word.
6. **(A)** The first word travels through the second word.
7. **(B)** The second word is the initial introduction of the first word.
8. **(C)** The second word is the movement of the first word.
9. **(B)** The first word creates the second word.
10. **(C)** The first word is at the bottom; the second word is at the top.

11. **(A)** The first word is stored in the second word.
12. **(C)** The second word creates the first word.
13. **(B)** The first word grows in the second word.
14. **(C)** The second word covers the first word.
15. **(B)** The second word stops the flow of the first word.
16. **(C)** The second word is the opposite of the first word.
17. **(B)** The first word grows out of the second word.
18. **(A)** The second word encircles the first word.
19. **(D)** The second word is the structure in which the first word lives.
20. **(A)** The second word fits into the first word.

Verbal Abilities Analysis Chart for Analogies (Word Relationships)

Use the following chart to carefully analyze your results of the *analogies (word relationships)* question type. This will help you evaluate your strengths and weaknesses. This analysis should help you focus your study and review efforts on specific types of problems.

Practice Set	Total Number of Questions	Number Correct	Number Incorrect	Number Unanswered
Set 1	20			
Set 2	20			
Set 3	20			
Set 4	20			
Set 5	20			
Set 6	20			
Set 7	20			
Set 8	20			
Set 9	20			

Because there is no penalty for incorrect answers on most of the questions in the Verbal Abilities section, you should have left no question unanswered. Even if you didn't have time to answer a question, you should have at least filled in the answer space with an educated guess.

> **REVIEWING THE KEY STRATEGIES**
>
> **Remember to:**
> 1. Determine the relationship in the first pair.
> 2. Use "in the same way" to set up relationships.
> 3. Keep the order similar.
> 4. Keep parts of speech consistent.
> 5. Disregard subject matter; only relationship is important.
> 6. Look at all the choices before selecting one.
> 7. Eliminate wrong choices immediately.
> 8. Use categories to recognize relationships.

GRAMMAR (LANGUAGE USAGE)

This question type tests your ability to recognize language that is unsuitable for a formal letter or written report. Knowledge of the rules and conventions of Standard Written English is necessary.

Each question consists of four different sentences. Three of them contain errors; one does not. Consider the following example:

A) Those who can remember well after a period of practice has an advantage over others.
B) Through regular practice, it is possible to develop a good memory, which can be very useful.
C) A good memory is not enjoyed by many people which do not practice at it.
D) Practice is required, being that memory is so difficult of get ahold of.

The correct answer is (B); it demonstrates grammar and usage suitable for a formal letter or report. An explanation of the errors in each of the other choices is included in the following discussion of helpful techniques and strategies.

Helpful Techniques and Strategies

1. Read all four sentences before considering which one is best. Don't jump to conclusions.
2. Sentences that are incorrect will often contain one of the following types of errors:
   a. INCORRECT VERBS—Pay special attention to the verbs in each sentence. One type of verb error occurs in choice (A) of the preceding example: "*Those* who can remember well after a period of practice *has* an advantage over others." In this case, the subject is "those," which is plural, and therefore the verb should also be plural, "have" instead of "has." In this case, the danger lies in presuming that "practice" is the subject of the sentence and concluding that because "practice has" is correct, the sentence is correct. When examining the verb in any sentence, be careful to identify correctly the subject (the "doer" of the action). Here is another sentence in which the subject does no agree with the verb.

   INCORRECT: A *crate* of office supplies have been stored in the closet, until some other space is found.

   CORRECT: A crate of office supplies has been stored in the closet, until some other space is found.

   Besides checking for subject-verb agreement, make sure that the verb tense is correct. Consider the following example:

   By the end of the year, every employee *will had been given* a 10 percent raise.

   In this case, "had" is incorrect; the correct verb is "have."
   b. MISUSE OF PRONOUNS—Pay special attention to pronouns: he, she, him, her, we, us, you, who, whom, which, that. Choice (C) of the example contains a pronoun error: "A good memory is not enjoyed by many people *which* do not practice at it." The pronoun "which" does not refer correctly to "people"; the correct pronoun here is "who." The following sentences also illustrate pronoun errors.

   INCORRECT: When *one* has given dedicated service to the company for so many years, *you* expect a gift upon retirement.

   CORRECT: When *one* has given dedicated service to the company for so many years, *one* expects a gift upon retirement.

It would also be correct, in this case, to write "he expects" or "she expects." "He" and "she" agree with "one."

INCORRECT: The man *whom* delivered the new copier to the office also installed it.

CORRECT: The man *who* delivered the new copier to the office also installed it.

The pronoun "whom" refers to those who receive an action, and the pronoun "who" refers to those who do an action. In this case, the man is doing an action, delivering the copier, so "who" is correct.
Another example of this:

INCORRECT: I will give the bonus to whomever fixes the machine.

In this sentence, *whomever* is incorrect. Although it appears that "whomever" is the object of the preposition "to" and therefore should be correct, it is not the object of "to." The entire phrase, "whomever fixes the machine," is the object of "to," and within that phrase, "whomever" is doing the action: "*whomever* fixes the machine." Therefore, "whomever," as the doer, is incorrect. It should be changed to "whoever."

CORRECT: I will give the bonus to whoever fixes the machine.

c. INCORRECT USAGE—A number of expressions commonly used in conversation are incorrect in Standard Written English. Choice (D) in the original example contains two such expressions: "Practice is required, *being that* memory is so difficult to *get ahold of.*" Here is one way to rewrite this sentence correctly: "Because the improvement of memory, is so difficult, practice is required." The following are some expressions that represent incorrect usage:

all the farther	hissself	ought to of
being as how	in regards	theirselves
being that	that	use to,
had to of	irregardless	suppose to
	no such a	

d. VAGUE OR UNCLEAR MEANING—The meaning of a sentence may be vague or unclear because (1) certain words in the sentence are not used clearly or (2) the structure of the sentence makes the meaning illogical or unclear. Consider the following set of four choices:

A) While proofreading the letter, a mistake was detected in the third line.
B) While proofreading a letter, one should be able to do this perfectly.

C) Through careful proofreading, a number of mistakes can appear in a letter.

D) Those who carefully proofread letters detect errors easily.

The correct choice is (D); the meaning of each of the other choices is unclear. In choice (B), the meaning of "this" is uncertain; "this" may or may not refer to proofreading. In choice (A), the structure of the sentence makes it seem as if "a mistake" is doing the proofreading! Choice (C) makes the inaccurate and illogical statement that mistakes "appear" through proofreading; it is more logical and accurate to say that mistakes are *detected* through proofreading.

e. REPETITION—A sentence is incorrect when it is unnecessarily wordy or repetitious. Consider the following examples:

The memorandum was sent to those who received it, the manager and me.
Everyone was asked to arrive for work early in the morning, at 6 A.M.

Here are less repetitious and wordy versions of the same sentences:

The memorandum was received by the manager and me.
Everyone was asked to arrive for work at 6 A.M.

A few more examples of common errors:

A) The quantity of child care centers have increased during the last decade, along with the increase in working parents.
B) For the work of parents, more child care centers have appeared during the last decade.
C) With more during the last decade, working parents appreciate child care centers.
D) During the last decade, the appearance of more working parents has coincided with the appearance of more child care centers.

Choice (D) is correct. In (A), the verb "have" should be replaced with "has," in order to agree with the subject, "quantity" In (B), "for the work of parents" is an unclear phrase. In (C), the meaning of "more" is unclear.

A) The sales force ought to of achieved much higher sales last week, but were not able to do so.
B) The sales force, who is usually very successful, did a very poor job last week.
C) Selling much less than usual, the weeks ahead might be more productive for the company sales force.
D) Putting a week of poor results behind them, the sales force hoped that the weeks ahead would be more productive.

Choice (D) is correct. In (A), "ought to of" is incorrect usage. In (B), the pronoun "who" is incorrect; "which" is the correct pronoun for referring to "the sales force." The structure of choice (C) makes it seem as if "the weeks ahead," rather than the sales force, are "selling much less than usual."

    A) The lobby of the Brinker Building use to of been much less crowded than it is now.

    B) If the lobby of the Brinker Building would have had been enlarged years ago, it would not be so crowded today.

    C) The lobby of the Brinker Building is much more crowded now than it used to be.

    D) When one enters the lobby of the Brinker Building, you immediately enter a crowd.

Choice (C) is correct. In (A), "use to of been" is incorrect usage. In (B), "would have had been" is an incorrect verb tense; "had been" is correct. In (D), the pronoun "you" is incorrect; "you" should be replaced with "one," "he," or "she," and "enter" should be changed to "enters."

Practice Set 1

Decide which sentence is preferable with respect to grammar and usage suitable for a formal letter or report. Write the letter of your choice in the space provided.

1. A) The prohibition against laying down on the furniture is posted in several places throughout the company lounge.   _____

    B) During lunch and breaks, although laying one down in the company lounge may be inviting, it is prohibited.

    C) Lying down on furniture in the company lounge is not allowed.

    D) With reference to the furnishings in the lounge, lying down or laying on it cannot be permitted.

2. A) Having the drinking of wine frequently in Italy and France contrasts with the regular drinking of water in the United States.   _____

    B) With water the frequent drink in the United States, wine is for Italy and France also a frequent drink.

    C) Drinking wine such as we in the United States drink water are the people of which are in Italy and France.

    D) Many people in Italy and France drink wine as frequently as we in the United States drink water.

3. A) Modern business psychologists, with information on creativity and stress more than long ago, have contributed to improved morale and productivity. _____

B) With valuable information on creativity and stress, modern business psychologists have contributed to improved morale and productivity.

C) Improved morale and productivity has been of modern business psychology, with information on creativity and stress.

D) Creativity and stress have improved morale and productivity, with information from modern business psychologists.

4. A) A longer lunch period will be provided, after it was reported that hastily eating lunch caused an upset stomach. _____

B) Eating lunch too quickly, an upset stomach resulted in lengthening the lunch period.

C) Returning from lunch feeling upset, a longer lunch period was instituted for everyone.

D) Convinced that eating a hasty lunch is not healthy for anyone, we are instituting a longer lunch period.

5. A) People often read a book merely to pass the time, to prove their intelligence, avoiding the real world, and many other ridiculous reasons. _____

B) There are many good reasons for reading, and some ridiculous ones as well.

C) Merely passing the time, to prove their intelligence, and to avoid the real world, many people read a book.

D) Reading for ridiculous reasons are merely to pass the time, to prove their intelligence, and to avoid the real world, among others.

6. A) Manikins, each dressed in an expensive outfit, makes the store window attractive to passersby. _____

B) There are two manikins, dressed in expensive clothes, in the store window.

C) As shoppers pass the store window, expensively dressed manikins pass their view.

D) As for clothes that are attractive and expensive, manikins are on display in the store window.

7. A) Empty since it appeared, a number of you have requested a suggestion box for the office. _____

B) The suggestion box that a number of you requested has remained empty since it appeared.

C) The request for a suggestion box, to which was responded with one, has not as yet resulted with a suggestion.

D) Suggestions for the suggestion box have not appeared as yet, and it is still empty even though a number of you have requested it.

8. A) Having mislain the calendar, _____
   the appointments calendar
   was unable to verify where
   they should be and when.
   B) Scheduling was impossible
   because the appointments secretary had mislain the appointments calendar.
   C) The calendar listing everyone's
   appointments could not be
   found, with the result being
   that no one knew where to be
   and when.
   D) The appointments secretary
   mislaid his calendar, so no one
   knew whether any appointments had been scheduled.

9. A) Associates who we have not _____
   contacted for months should
   be informed of all recent
   decisions.
   B) Inform associates whom we
   have not contacted for months
   of all recent decisions.
   C) Of all associates that we have
   not contacted for months,
   inform them of recent
   decisions.
   D) Not contacting associates for
   months, we are informing
   them of all recent decisions.

10. A) When one has all ready publi- _____
    cized a decision, it is difficult
    to revoke it.
    B) With an already publicized
    decision, revoking it is
    difficult.
    C) With the revoking of a deci-
    sion already publicized, revok-
    ing it is difficult.
    D) It is difficult to revoke a deci-
    sion that has already been
    publicized.

Answer Explanations for Practice Set 1

1. **(C)** The most prominent error in each of
   the other choices is the incorrect use of
   "laying" for "lying."
2. **(D)** "Having" should be omitted in (A).
   (B) is both vague and repetitious (for
   example, "frequent drink"). "Such as we" is
   one incorrect phrase in (C).
3. **(B)** The sentence structure in each of the
   other choices is incoherent, and the meaning
   of several phrases is unclear.
4. **(D)** Choice (B) seems to say that an upset
   stomach is eating lunch, and (C) that the

lunch period returns from lunch. The verb
tenses in (A) are inconsistent.
5. **(B)** (A) and (C) have parallelism errors. (D)
   should begin, "Ridiculous reasons for
   reading . . ."
6. **(B)** in (A), the verb "makes" does not agree
   with the subject "manikins." (C) contains
   the illogical phrase "manikins pass." In (D),
   the connection between the first half of the
   sentence and the second half is unclear.
7. **(B)** The phrase "empty since it appeared"
   in (A) is misplaced. (C) contains awkward

and wordy phrases, for instance, "to which was responded." (D) is wordy and repetitious.

8. **(D)** "Mislain" is incorrect in both (A) and (B). In (C) "with result being that" is wordy and awkward.

9. **(B)** In (A), "who" is incorrect. In (C), the sentence structure is wordy and awkward,

and "that" is used incorrectly. In (D), the verb tense of "not contacting" is incorrect.

10. **(D)** In (A), "all ready" is incorrect; "already" would be correct, Although (B) and (C) do use "already" correctly, both sentences are vague and wordy. The most clear, direct, and correct expression is (D).

Practice Set 2

Decide which sentence is preferable with respect to grammar and usage suitable for a formal letter or report. Write the letter of your choice in the space provided.

1. A) Everyone differs greatly in the   _____ way they listen to and benefit from information.
   B) Listening closely to important information, in order to benefit from it, vary from person to person.
   C) Listening carefully is an important skill, especially when vital information is involved.
   D) Skillful listening is important, while everyone does theirs differently.

2. A) Neither wealth nor power are   _____ the desires of those majoring in business, according to a recent poll.
   B) Business majors polled recently denied that either wealth or power are their desire.
   C) Business majors desire neither wealth nor power as such in a recent poll.
   D) Wealth and power were not the stated goals of business majors polled recently.

3. A) Both the inventor and the   _____ manufacturer received credit for the success of the product.
   B) The inventor was as responsible for the success of the product, with the manufacturer.
   C) High sales figures for the new product delighted not only their inventor, but also the manufacturer.
   D) The inventor and the manufacturer was given publicity for the popularity of their new product.

4. A) Government institutions have   _____ become more powerful, but they have also lost the respect of many citizens.
   B) A rapidly decreasing respect for government institutions and that such institutions are becoming more powerful is a cause of concern.
   C) The status of government institutions, that has changed recently, can result in less respect.
   D) As for the status of government institutions, theirs is not as strong as it was formerly.

5. A) Dealing directly with the question are minor errors in typing to be allowed. _____
   B) Some people question whether minor errors in typing should be allowed.
   C) The allowance of imperfectly typed manuscripts are not to be permitted.
   D) Although typing errors are difficult to avoid, it cannot be permitted.

6. A) Many will agree with the new retirement policy, and many will disagree with it, taking the other side of the issue. _____
   B) Some changes in the retirement policy provokes both positive and negative responses.
   C) Those who drafted the new retirement policy welcome both positive and negative responses from all concerned.
   D) Retirement is an issue to get both pro and con viewpoints.

7. A) The City Council, consisting of twelve members, were scheduled to meet for several hours. _____
   B) With all twelve members of the City Council scheduled to meet, several hours were scheduled.
   C) A City Council meeting may be scheduled soon, if all of the council members are available at a convenient time.
   D) Finding several hours for a meeting of the City Council members were not at all easy.

8. A) To type a letter accurately, spelling must be part of what is watched. _____
   B) Accurate typing and correct spelling are both absolutely necessary.
   C) With accuracy, both for typing and for spelling, a letter will be acceptable.
   D) Typing, spelling, and accuracy are those which any letter must demonstrate.

9. A) Adam is a successful student who never thinks of anything but grades _____
   B) Adam is a successful student whom never thinks of anything but grades.
   C) Adam is a successful student for who grades are all that is important.
   D) Adam, for who grades are most important, is a successful student.

10. A) The people who neglect important tasks until the last minute are usually unable to do a careful job. _____
    B) Those type of people which neglect important tasks usually rush to complete them.
    C) Types of people which neglect important tasks until the last minute do so in a rush.
    D) With the neglect of important tasks by those who prefer to rush, the last minute is popular.

Answer Explanations for Practice Set 2

1. **(C)** In (A), the pronoun "they" and the verbs "listen" and "benefit" should agree with the singular "everyone." One error in (B) is the incorrect use of "vary"; the verb should be "varies." In (D), "theirs" is a plural pronoun, but "everyone" is singular.

2. **(D)** In both (A) and (B), the verb "are" should be changed to "is." In (C), "as such" is awkward.

3. **(A)** In (B), either the "as" or the "with" is incorrect. In (C), "their" should be replaced with "its." In (D), the verb "was given" should be replaced with "were given," in order to agree with the plural subject.

4. **(A)** The sentence structure of (B) is awkward, and "is" is incorrect. (C) is unclear, and (D) is wordy.

5. **(B)** Choice (A) is not a complete sentence. In (C), "are" should be changed to "is" in order to agree with "allowance." In (D), "it" is an incorrect pronoun; "they" would be correct, to agree with "errors."

6. **(C)** Choice (A) is repetitious. In (B), "provokes" should be changed to "provoke," to agree with "changes." in (D), "to get" is an awkward phrase.

7. **(C)** In (A), the verb "were" does not agree with the subject, "City Council." In (B), the repetition of "scheduled" is awkward. In (D), the verb "were" should be changed to "was."

8. **(B)** Choice (A) seems to say that the "spelling" is doing the "typing"! In (C), both instances of "for" may be changed to "in." In (D), "those which" is an incomplete, unclear phrase.

9. **(A)** In the incorrect choices, "whom" and "for who" are used incorrectly.

10. **(A)** In (B), "those type" and "which" are incorrect. In (C), "which" is incorrect ("who" and "whom" are used to refer to people). In (D), "the last minute is popular" has no clear relation to the first part of the sentence.

Practice Set 3

Decide which sentence is preferable with respect to grammar and usage suitable for a formal letter or report. Write the letter of your choice in the space provided.

1. A) The Back & Hammer Corporation has designed a new building that is round in shape and large in size. _____
   B) The new Back & Hammer building will be round and very large, according to the architect's design.
   C) With the new building's design submitted by the architect, Back & Hammer can look forward to a new size and shape.
   D) While conventional buildings are somewhat smaller and more square, the new Back & Hammer building's roundness and size is a reason it is different.

2. A) Whichever of the two companies submits the lowest bid will receive the contract. _____
   B) The contract will be awarded to whoever bids lowest.
   C) Bidding lower than the competitors, the contract will go to whomever does so.
   D) The contract bids are being reviewed by myself, who will select the lowest.

3. A) Those in the company who _____ had worked all the hardest to handle the Christmas rush, were rewarded with large bonuses.
   B) Those who worked hardest to handle the Christmas rush will receive large bonuses.
   C) A well-deserved bonus was paid by the company to the hardest-working employees among them, during the Christmas rush.
   D) Working hardly during the very busy Christmas season brought bonuses to a number of workers.

4. A) Whoever answers the phone _____ must do so courteously.
   B) Courtesy is important, both away from it and on the phone.
   C) Without courtesy on the telephone, any secretary is lacking with a vital skill.
   D) A courteous phone voice, for whomever answers the phone, has great importance.

5. A) Although hundreds of people _____ complained when they changed the taste of their soft drink, sales remained steady.
   B) Sales did not decrease after the company "improved" the taste of its soft drinks, but hundreds of people complained.
   C) The complaints of hundreds of people in the fact of a new taste for the cola had no effect on sales.
   D) Selling cola was no more difficult after changing their taste than before it.

6. A) After establishing its home _____ office in Los Angeles, the small company failed to compete successfully with larger firms in the area.
   B) Although they intended to offer competition to larger firms in the Los Angeles area, the new company was not successful.
   C) Among successful competition among successful firms in the Los Angeles area, a smaller company is unlikely to be successful.
   D) Achieving success in the competitive Los Angeles area, the new company was not able to do so.

7. A) Child safety groups are _____ demanding legislation forbidding the use of glass containers in public places.
   B) Fearing for the safety of children who might be injured by them, child safety groups are forbidding the public use of glass containers.
   C) Because broken glass containers may injure a child, they are demanding legislation prohibiting their public use.
   D) Children, because they may break, should not have access to glass containers.

8. A) One new employee was _____ accused of complaining too much, but denied that he had done so.
   B) One new employee was overheard complaining about his job, but he claimed that he said no such a thing.
   C) Accused of complaining too much, a new employee denied himself.
   D) Complaining excessively, the job was obviously unpleasant for the new employee.

9. A) Everyone on the staff, as well _____ as Jerry and I, supports the new proposal.
   B) Everyone on the staff, as well as Jerry and me, supports the new proposal.
   C) The support of the new proposal by Jerry as well as me goes along with the support of the staff.
   D) Me and Jerry and everyone on the staff support the new proposal.

10. A) Choosing every word care- _____ fully, a writer can communicate even complex ideas with clarity and precision.
    B) Choosing every word carefully, even complex ideas can be written with clarity and precision.
    C) Writing complex ideas with clarity and precision, choosing every word carefully.
    D) As for clarity and precision, it is the task of choosing every word carefully.

Answer Explanations for Practice Set 3

1. **(B)** In (A), "in shape" and "in size" are repetitious. In (C) there is no clear reference to a building, so "a new size and shape" is vague. In (D), the subjects "roundness and size" require a plural verb and "reasons."

2. **(B)** In (A) "lowest" should be "lower" (C) seems to say that the contract itself is doing the bidding, and "whomever" is not the correct form. In (D), "me" should be used, instead of "myself."

3. **(B)** In (A), "all the hardest" is incorrect. In (C), the meaning of "them" is not clear. In (D), "working hardly" is incorrect.

4. **(A)** Choices (B) and (D) both contain pronoun errors: in (B), "it" is vague, and in (D), "whomever" is incorrect. In (C),

"lacking with" should be replaced with "lacking in."

5. **(B)** In (A), the meaning of "they" and "their" is not clear. In (C), "in the fact of" is an incorrect phrase. In (D), the meaning of "it" is not clear, and "their" should be "its."

6. **(A)** In (B), "they" is used incorrectly to refer to "company." In (C), "Among successful competition among" is repetitious. Choice (D) seems to contradict itself.

7. **(A)** In each of the other choices, the use of pronouns "they" and "them" is unclear.

8. **(A)** In (B), "no such a thing" is incorrect. In (C), "denied himself" is not the appropriate phrase. Choice (D), with its unclear

sentence structure, seems to say that the "job" was "complaining excessively."

9. **(A)** In both (B) and (D), "me" is incorrect; "I" is the correct pronoun in both cases. (C) is an unnecessarily wordy expression.

10. **(A)** In (B), the "complex ideas" seem to be doing the "choosing." Choice (C) is not a complete sentence. In (D), "it" is a vague term.

Practice Set 4

Decide which sentence is preferable with respect to grammar and usage suitable for a formal letter or report. Write the letter of your choice in the space provided.

1. A) if the report would have been completed on schedule, everyone would have been able to take the weekend off.   _____
   B) Everyone will be required to work this weekend if the report is not completed on time.
   C) With the possibility of completing the report in order to avoid working all weekend, everyone would have tried staying on schedule.
   D) A report not completed by this weekend, the weekend off will not be available.

2. A) Both men and women, whomever are interested in administrative experience, are invited to apply for a summer internship program.   _____
   B) We are pleased to announce a summer internship program that offers substantial administrative experience.
   C) Those whom are after administrative experience should apply for the summer internship program.
   D) With administrative experience, the summer internship program invites applications from both men and women.

3. A) The special talents of every team member are rarely acknowledged by the coach.   _____
   B) Each member of the team is theirself a unique talent, even though the coach rarely gives anyone credit.
   C) Without any credit of the coach, the unique talent of each team member goes unnoticed.
   D) Talented and unique, the team goes without the acknowledgment of them by the coach.

4. A) In the opinion of the general public, it believes that major corporations are not ethical.   _____
   B) The general public questions the ethics of major corporations, in their opinion.
   C) With a belief regarding major corporations that their ethics are questionable, the general public voices its opinion.
   D) The general public believes that the practices of most major corporations are not ethical.

5. A) Most popular in relation to _____ the flexible interest rate is the fixed rate, even though it is often higher.
   B) With flexible versus fixed rates, the more popular one is the higher of the two.
   C) Flexible interest rates are less popular than fixed rates, even though fixed rates are usually higher.
   D) Less popularity has made flexible interest rates less appealing than the higher fixed rates.

6. A) Because Stupple & Whipple _____ Industries has discontinued the production of microcomputers, they are giving full attention to other possible products.
   B) Having decided to investigate other possibilities, Stupple & Whipple Industries is no longer producing microcomputers.
   C) Microcomputer production is not for Stupple & Whipple Industries any longer, after whose decision to explore other possibilities.
   D) Without microcomputers in production, other possibilities than the computer is the interest of Stupple & Whipple Industries.

7. A) As far as political forces were _____ concerned, industrial growth as well as business grows stronger before 1950.
   B) During the first half of this century, business and industry were becoming dominant political forces in the United States.
   C) As the growth of the United States progressed during the first half of the century, both business and industry was in the forefront,
   D) With the early years of this century came a dominant industry, as a political force, along with business.

8. A) The memorandum was addressed to the office manager, _____ the division supervisor, and me.
   B) Those receiving the communication included myself, along with the division manager, and in addition, the office manager.
   C) A memo—routed to the office manager via the division supervisor and me—was received.
   D) After receiving a memo addressed also to the office manager and me, the division supervisor did also.

9. A) The president of the Rotary _____
   Club won reelection being
   that his past achievements
   were so many.
   B) Being that his past achievements were so many, the president of the Rotary Club won
   reelection.
   C) The president of the
   Rotary Club won reelection
   because of his many past
   achievements.
   D) With his many past achievements in mind, reelection of
   the Rotary Club president was
   because of them.

10. A) In the court's judgment, the _____
    cause of the accident was neg-
    ligence rather than speeding.
    B) The cause of the accident was
    negligence rather than speed-
    ing in the court's judgment.
    C) The cause of the accident was
    negligence instead of speeding
    in the court's judgment.
    D) Negligence rather than speed-
    ing was the cause of the acci-
    dent in the court judgment.

Answer Explanations for Practice Set 4

1. **(B)** in (A), "report would have been" should
   be "report had been." In both (C) and
   (D), the sentence structure is obviously
   confusing.
2. **(B)** "Whomever" and whom" are incorrect
   pronouns in (A) and (C). The sentence
   structure of (D) suggests that the "summer
   program" has "administrative experience."
3. **(A)** In (B), the pronoun "theirself" is incorrect, and in (D), the pronoun "them" is
   incorrect. In (C), "of the coach" should be
   "from the coach."
4. **(D)** In (A), "it believes" is repetitious.
   "Their" is incorrect in (B). In (C) "with
   a belief regarding . . . that" is awkward
   usage.
5. **(C)** In (A), "in relation to" is awkward. In
   (B), the meaning of the sentence is unclear.
   In (D), "less popularity" is an awkward
   phrase.
6. **(B)** In (A) and (C) there are pronoun errors:
   "they" is incorrect in (A), and "whose" contributes to poor sentence structure in (C).
   In (D), "is" should be "are" ("possibilities
   are").
7. **(B)** Both (A) and (C) contain incorrect
   verbs: "grows" in (A), and "was" in (C). The
   relationship between "business" and "industry" is not precisely stated in (D).
8. **(A)** Each of the other is wordy or
   awkward.
9. **(C)** In both (A) and (B), "being that" is an
   incorrect phrase; "because" is correct. Choice
   (D) is awkward and unclear.
10. **(A)** In (B), "speeding in the court's judg-
    ment" seems to say that the speeding took
    place in the court; this same confusing
    phrase occurs in (C). In (D), the comma is
    missing before the final phrase; "court"
    should be "court's."

Practice Set 5

Decide which sentence is preferable with respect to grammar and usage suitable for a formal letter or report. Write the letter of your choice in the space provided.

1. A) A meeting was called for we project supervisors and our assistants. _____
   B) It was important to all concerned that a meeting having been called for both supervisors and assistants be scheduled.
   C) Project supervisors and their assistants were called to a meeting.
   D) Meeting regularly, on the part of both supervisors and assistants, were important to all concerned.

2. A) Not likely to repeat what he had said a moment ago, the teacher was not sure if whether the class understood him or not. _____
   B) Making an important point more than once, the class was not sure of the teacher's meaning until he had repeated it.
   C) Uncertain about whether the class had understood him, the teacher repeated what he had said a moment ago.
   D) After a few moments past, and the class still did not express any understanding, the teacher had repeated himself.

3. A) Several friends have decided to jog on a weekend basis, which can gradually be increased as their heart and lungs grow stronger. _____
   B) Several friends have decided to jog together every Saturday, and perhaps more often as their hearts and lungs grow stronger.
   C) To jog more often as their heart and lungs grow stronger, several friends have decided to jog every Saturday.
   D) With every Saturday, several friends have begun jogging as their hearts and lungs grow stronger.

4. A) Finding the most efficient method for completing a routine task can make it more pleasant. _____
   B) Routine assignments can be very unpleasant without which effort to find a method that is efficient.
   C) The founding of a method, although it does not change the requirement to do a routine task, can be more pleasant.
   D) Routine though they may be, a task can be much better if one is given an efficient method for completing it.

5. A) Friends for years, they sud- _____
denly began arguing frequently
and loudly.
   B) Arguments can upset years of
friendship, as a frequent and
loud one seemed to prove in a
recent case.
   C) With years behind a friendship of frequent and loud
arguments, those involved are
often not capable of continuing the relationship.
   D) How violent an argument
must be before a friendship is
affected, and those involved
in it must change their
relationship.

6. A) As for other appliances, those _____
installed newly have energy
efficiency ratings surpassed the
older ones.
   B) Each of the appliances installed in the new offices is
energy-efficient.
   C) New appliances, even though
more expensive, compare
favorably over those that
required more energy in the
past.
   D) Although new, the energy used
by each new appliance in
each new office could not be
described as efficient.

7. A) All of his sentences are well _____
constructed, and it contributes
to the clarity of his writing.
   B) His well-constructed sentences
contribute to the clarity of his
writing.
   C) Clear sentences, well-
constructed, are contributory
to clarity of writing.
   D) All of his sentences are well
constructed, that being the
contribution to the clarity of
his writing.

8. A) Both days being the same _____
birthday for both Jean and
Joan, we baked only one
cake.
   B) On the same day as Joan,
whose birthday falls along
with Jean's, more than one
cake for both of them was not
necessary.
   C) We baked a cake for Jean,
whose birthday fell on the
same day as Joan's.
   D) With the other's birthday on
the same day as Jean, namely
Joan, we had already baked a
cake for only one.

9. A) Reading the newspaper care- _____
fully, I noticed that an old
English sheepdog was advertised in the column labeled
"Pets for Sale."
   B) Reading the newspaper carefully, an old English sheepdog
that I noticed was advertised
in the column labeled, "Pets
for Sale."
   C) By reading the newspaper
carefully, an old English sheepdog was advertised in the
column labeled "Pets for
Sale."
   D) In the column labeled "Pets
for Sale," reading carefully,
I noticed an old English
sheepdog.

10. A) Everyone should be com- _____
mended for performing admirable well during a recent
evaluation of the department.

B) Everyone should be commended for performing admirably well during a recent
evaluation of the department.

C) With an admirably well
performance, everyone in
the department should be
commended.

D) An admirable good performance deserves commending
everyone in the department.

Answer Explanations for Practice Set 5

1. **(C)** In (A), "for we" is incorrect; "for us" would be correct. In (B) the verb "having been called" is both unnecessary and incorrect. In (D), the verb "were" does not agree with the subject, "meeting"; "Meeting . . . *was* important" would be correct.

2. **(C)** In (A), "if whether" is incorrect; "if" alone would be sufficient. The sentence structure of (B) seems to say that the class, not the teacher, is "making a important point." In (D), both "past" and "had repeated" are incorrect.

3. **(B)** An error in (A) is "heart"; it should be "hearts." An obvious error in (C) is the repetition of "to jog." Choice (D) is unclear.

4. **(A)** in (B), "without which effort" is incorrect. One error in (C) is the incorrect use of "founding." In (D), "they" is used incorrectly to refer to "task."

5. **(A)** (B) is not as clear a statement as (A); the word "one" makes no sense with "frequent." In (C), "with years behind" is awkward. In (D), the sentence structure is not clear.

6. **(B)** in (A), "surpassed," "as for other appliances," and "installed newly" are used incorrectly. In (C), "compare favorably over" should be "compare favorably to." In (D), "new" seems to refer to "energy"; this is an illogical reference.

7. **(B)** "It" is an incorrect pronoun in (A); "they contribute" or just "contribute" would be correct. In (C), "contributory" is incorrect. In (D), "that being" is a vague phrase.

8. **(C)** The sentence structure of each of the other choices is obviously wordy, vague, and confusing.

9. **(A)** Both (B) and (C) seem to say that a sheepdog was reading the paper. In (D), "reading carefully" is placed in an awkward position in the sentence.

10. **(B)** In (A), "admirable" is incorrect. In (C), "admirably well performance" is incorrect. In (D), "admirable good" is incorrect. "Performing admirably well," in (B), is the correct expression.

Practice Set 6

Decide which sentence is preferable with respect to grammar and usage suitable for a formal letter or report. Write the letter of your choice in the space provided.

1. A) A letterhead that is colorful _____ but not having adequate information is useless.
   B) Letterhead design is not nearly as important as the sufficiency of informing them who read it.
   C) If the information on the company letterhead is insufficient, they serve no purpose.
   D) Along with a colorful design, the company letterhead must include sufficient information.

2. A) Visitors are asked to park their _____ cars away from the main building during rush-hour traffic.
   B) Access to the main building during rush-hour traffic is prohibited on visitors.
   C) Parking space is available a long ways from the main building during rush-hour traffic.
   D) Finding a parking space near the main building for visitors is impossible during the rush hour.

3. A) After talking to the accoun- _____ tant, Mr. Wright felt he should audit the report prior to the noon conference.
   B) Mr. Wright asked his accountant whether auditing the report before his conference at noon was possible.
   C) If he could audit the report before the noon conference was what Mr. Wright needed to know of his accountant.
   D) Mr. Wright wondered if his accountant would have time to audit the report prior to the noon conference.

4. A) The final draft of a report _____ should demonstrate not only correct English, with logical organization as well.
   B) Correct English, as well as logical organization, are important in the final draft of a report.
   C) When drafting the final version of a report, writers must pay close attention to both correct English and logical organization.
   D) As for final matters, correctness and effective organization should be the focus of any writer concerned with it.

5. A) Neither welfare benefits nor an improved health plan was discussed by the board members. _____
   B) Neither welfare benefits or an improved health plan was on the agenda at the board meeting.
   C) With more important matters to consider, the board members discussed not welfare benefits or even an improved health plan.
   D) Without discussion of either welfare benefits or an improved health plan at the board meeting.

6. A) Those who require emergency medical attention may do so without loss of pay. _____
   B) When emergency medical attention is necessary to interrupt the workday, no loss of pay results.
   C) Anyone who must leave work for emergency medical attention will not suffer any loss of pay.
   D) Loss of pay is not given to those who need emergency medical attention during the workday.

7. A) "To Whom It May Concern" is one of many popular grammatically correct phrases. _____
   B) Among grammatically popular and correct expressions, "To Whom It May Concern" is one of many.
   C) When beginning correspondence with "To Whom It May Concern," they can be sure of a popular and grammatical phrase.
   D) A number of phrases are both popular and grammatically correct; "To Whom It May Concern" is one of which.

8. A) This year's expenditure for advertising ought to of been much lower. _____
   B) The firm must devote fewer of its budget to advertising.
   C) The advertising budget should be reduced.
   D) Reduction in the budget for advertising would of been a good idea.

9. A) When only one security officer is on duty in the building, there are those of which take special precautions. _____
   B) Those who work after hours should be very cautious, being as how only, one security officer is on duty.
   C) Only one security officer patrols the building after working hours, so everyone staying late should be very cautious.
   D) All should take precautions over any emergency after hours, rather than to depend on only one security officer.

10. A) An unused office, full of obsolete equipment and discarded files, were made ready for the newest member of the firm. _____

    B) To find office space for someone new, an unused area full of old files and useless equipment is available.

    C) New office space is scarce, except of an area that had been used for storage.

    D) A previously unused office will be renovated for the use of the firm's newest member.

Answer Explanations for Practice Set 6

1. **(D)** In (A), to be parallel, "not having" should read "does not have." In (B), "sufficiency of informing them" is incorrect. In (C), "they serve" should be replaced with "it serves."

2. **(A)** In (B), "prohibited on" is incorrect. In (C), "ways" is incorrect. In (D), "for visitors" is awkwardly placed.

3. **(D)** In each of the other choices, the reference of the pronoun "he" or "his" is not clear.

4. **(C)** in (A), the words following the comma are incorrectly phrased; correct phrasing would be "but also logical organization." In (B), "are" should be replaced with "is," in order to agree with the singular subject, "correct English." In (D), "it" is a vague pronoun.

5. **(A)** Both (B) and (C) are incorrect because they do not use "neither/not . . . nor" correctly. (D) is not a complete sentence.

6. **(C)** In (A), "may do so" is an inappropriate phrase. In (B), "to interrupt the workday"

is illogical. Choice (D) is also illogical, because "loss of pay" is not something that is "given."

7. **(A)** In (B), "grammatically popular" is an illogical phrase. In (C), "they" is unclear. In (D), "of which" is unnecessary.

8. **(C)** In (A), "ought to of" is incorrect. In (B), "fewer" should be replaced with "less." In (D), "would of been" is incorrect.

9. **(C)** In (A), "those of which" is an incorrect phrase. In (B), "being as how" is incorrect. In (D), one error is "precautions over," which should be replaced with "precautions for"; another is "rather than to depend"— "to" is incorrect.

10. **(D)** In (A), "were" should be replaced with "was," in order to agree with the subject, "office." (B) illustrates unclear sentence structure and seems to say that the "unused area" is "to find office space. In (C), "except of" should be replaced with "except for."

Practice Set 7

Decide which sentence is preferable with respect to grammar and usage suitable for a formal letter or report.

1. A) Each of the senior staff _____ members regards his work serious enough to excel in every task, according to a recent evaluation.

   B) According to a recent evaluation, each senior staff member regards his work so seriously that he excels in every task.

   C) With a serious regard, according to a recent evaluation, each senior staff member excels in every task.

   D) The excelling in every task by each of the senior staff members is the result of taking work seriously according to a recent evaluation.

2. A) Although the floral arrange- _____ ment smelled sweetly, several people complained about its gaudiness.

   B) Smelling sweetly, the floral arrangement still received complaints from those objecting to its gaudiness.

   C) The sweet-smelling floral arrangement had complaints of gaudiness.

   D) Although gaudy, the floral arrangement smelled sweet.

3. A) The most demanding profes- _____ sor on campus always requires term papers, insists on field studies, and reads all lab reports personally.

   B) The most demanding profes- sor on campus always requires term papers, insists on field studies, and reading all lab reports personally.

   C) Personally reading all lab reports, insisting on field studies, and to require term papers make this professor the most demanding.

   D) With demanding term papers, insisting on field studies, and the reading of all lab reports, this professor is requiring.

4. A) The agency overseas sent _____ several representatives, who present new ideas for market- ing there after they arrived.

   B) The overseas representatives presented new ideas for mar- keting when they arrived here.

   C) The overseas representatives' arrival presented new ideas for marketing.

   D) Having had arrived here, the overseas representatives present new ideas.

5. A) Waste can be eliminated, or at _____ least reduced, if less pencils, pens, and paper clips are left lying around.
   B) Waste can be eliminated, or at least reduced, if fewer pencils, pens, and paper clips are left lying around.
   C) The fewer the pencils, pens, and paper clips, the more of waste is eliminated.
   D) With pencils, pens, and paper clips less wasted, the more it can be eliminated or reduced.

6. A) When only six months old, _____ the committee will review the success of the new manage-ment plan.
   B) After the new management plan has been implemented for six months, the committee will have had it under review.
   C) With six months behind them, the new management plan's success came under the review of the committee.
   D) In six months the committee will review the effects of the new management plan.

7. A) Arriving at the office early, the _____ sun was rising as the manager began work.
   B) The sun rising and arriving at the office early, the manager began work.
   C) The manager arrived at the office before sunrise and began work.
   D) Managing a sunrise arrival at the office to begin work, the manager had been working.

8. A) Juries usually make correct _____ decisions and perform their duties both correctly and effectively.
   B) Juries usually make correct decisions.
   C) Making correct decisions keep juries both correct and effective.
   D) Juries usually make correct decisions and perform their duties both correct and effective.

9. A) Referring to known and _____ proven facts is important in any effective argument.
   B) To know and proving facts for an effective argument is important.
   C) One should include persuasive facts in any argument.
   D) One should put persuasive facts in their argument when-ever possible.

10. A) Thirty-six hours, give or take _____ a few minutes, are the length of time required for the special project.
    B) Required for the special project are thirty-six hours, give or take a few minutes.
    C) The special project will re-quire approximately thirty-six hours.
    D) With a requirement of thirty-six hours, more or less, the special project requires a precise length of time.

Answer Explanations for Practice Set 7

1. **(B)** In (A), "serious" should be "seriously." In (C), "with a serious regard" is unclear. Choice (D) is wordy.

2. **(D)** In both (A) and (B), "sweetly" should be "sweet." In (C), "had complaints of gaudiness" is an unclear phrase.

3. **(A)** Choices (B), (C), and (D) all exhibit faulty parallelism; for instance, in (C), "to require" should be "requiring."

4. **(B)** In both (A) and (D), the verbs are incorrect: "present" in both (A) and (D) should be "presented"; also, "having had" in (D) should be "having." In (C), the "arrival" rather than the "representatives" presented the new ideas.

5. **(B)** In (A), "less" is used incorrectly; when describing items that are *countable*, "fewer" is correct. (C) is an illogical sentence, and "more of waste" is a vague expression. In (D), "less wasted" and "it" are unclear.

6. **(D)** In (A), the sentence seems to say that the committee is "only six months old." (B) contains a verb error: "will have had" is incorrect. (C) is awkward and not clearly "them" should be "it."

7. **(C)** Choices (A) and (B) seem to say that the sun was arriving at the office early. Choice (D) is vague and wordy.

8. **(B)** Choices (A), (C), and (D) are unnecessarily repetitious. In (C), "keep" should be "keeps." In (D), "correct and effective" should be "correctly and effectively."

9. **(C)** In (A), "known and proven facts" is an unnecessarily wordy phrase. In (B), "proving" should be "to prove," and the verb should be plural ("are"). In (D), "their" is incorrect; "one's," "his," or "her" is correct in this case.

10. **(C)** In (A) and (B), the verb "are" should be singular, to agree with the single-unit subject. The sentence structure in (B) is also awkward. Choice (D) is repetitious and also illogical, because "thirty-six hours, more or less" is not a *precise* length of time."

Practice Set 8

Decide which sentence is preferable with respect to grammar and usage suitable for a formal letter or report.

1. A) Whomever reviews last _____ month's financial statements must conclude that the company is in trouble.
   B) With a review of financial statements, one must conclude that it is all the better to see that the company is in trouble.
   C) A review of last month's financial statements suggests that the company is in trouble.
   D) A review of last month's financial statements. Should be referred to whomever will review it thoroughly.

2. A) The hazy ideas and concepts _____ presented in the presentation were vague and indefinite.
   B) The presenter presented hazy ideas and concepts in a vague and indefinite way.
   C) Hazy ideas and concepts were presented only vaguely, and without definitions.
   D) The ideas presented were vague.

3. A) Because she demanded immediate improvement, the manager warned her that dismissal was a possibility. _____

   B) Demanding immediate improvement, the manager threatened her with dismissal.

   C) The manager threatened her with immediate improvement in mind.

   D) Because she demanded immediate improvement, she warned her that dismissal was a possibility.

4. A) Regulations must be enforced all the farther if they are to be effective. _____

   B) The farther enforcement of regulations will guarantee their effectiveness.

   C) Going farther with the enforcement of regulations guarantees farther effectiveness.

   D) Stronger enforcement will make the regulations more effective.

5. A) Merlo's Gift Shop and Nat's Novelty Store sells gifts created by local artists. _____

   B) Gifts created to local artists are sold in both Merlo's Gift Shop and Nat's Novelty Store.

   C) Merlo's and Nat's, selling gifts created by local artists.

   D) Merlo's Gift Shop and Nat's Novelty Store sell gifts created by local artists.

6. A) The office manager hired the most experienced of the two candidates who applied for a clerical position. _____

   B) Deciding experientially on who was better prepared clerically, the office manager decided to choose between two candidates.

   C) Primarily interested in the candidate with more experience, the office manager hired her for the new clerical position.

   D) With a clerical position in mind requiring experience, the decision was for the office manager.

7. A) In order to cut expenses, the supervisor must decide whether to reduce the workload, lay off several employees, or forbid private use of the duplicating machine. _____

   B) Reducing the workload, laying off several employees, or to forbid private use of the duplicating machine were several options open to the supervisor cutting employees.

   C) Reduced workload, or employees, or no private duplication crossed the mind of the supervisor cutting expenses.

   D) The supervisor thought about several ways to cut expenses: workload, employee reduction, or in the area of duplication.

8. A) Having been promoted sud- _____
   denly, the board of directors
   extended their congratulations
   to the new vice-president.
   B) The board of directors congratulated the new vice-
   president on his sudden
   promotion.
   C) To the new vice-president,
   with promotion so sudden,
   the board of directors congratulated him.
   D) The board of directors will
   have had congratulated the
   new vice-president after his
   sudden promotion.

9. A) Promising a bright future, and _____
   to celebrate a wonderful past,
   the Hardy Company awarded
   each of its employees a
   bonus.
   B) To promise a bright future
   and a wonderful past, the
   Hardy Company awarded
   each of its employees a
   bonus.
   C) The future bright and the past
   wonderful, the bonus awarded
   to each of the Hardy Company
   employees.
   D) The Hardy Company awarded
   each of its employees a bonus,
   promising them a bright future
   and thanking them for a wonderful past.

10. A) The lunch he ordered tasted _____
    better than the co-workers.
    B) The lunch he ordered tasted
    better than the others'
    lunches.
    C) The lunch he ordered tasted
    better than the co-workers
    lunching.
    D) Lunching with the co-workers,
    the one he ordered tasted
    best.

Answer Explanations for Practice Set 8

1. **(C)** In (A), "whomever" is incorrect;
   "whoever" would be correct. In (B), "all the
   better" is an incorrect expression. In (D),
   "whomever" should be "whoever."

2. **(D)** Each of the other choices is repetitious;
   for instance, "vague" repeats unnecessarily
   the meaning of "hazy."

3. **(B)** In both (A) and (D), the reference of
   "her" and of "she" is vague. In (C), the
   meaning of "in mind" is not clear.

4. **(D)** "All the farther" and "farther" are
   incorrect in each of the other choices;
   "further" would be a better choice in all
   three cases.

5. **(D)** In (A), the subject of the sentence is plural, so the verb should be plural, "sell" instead of "sells." In (B), "to" should be "by," (C) is not a complete sentence.

6. **(C)** In (A), the correct phrase for comparing two people is "more experienced" rather than "most experienced." In (B), "experientially" improperly refers to the office manager. (D) is vague and illogical, saying that the decision had a mind and that the clerical position was given to the office manager!

7. **(A)** In (B), "to forbid" should be "forbidding" (so that it is parallel with "reducing" and "laying"). Both (C) and (D) are incomplete and unclear.

8. **(B)** In both (A) and (C), the sentence structure is awkward and unclear. Also in (A), the board of directors seems to have been promoted. In (D), "will have had congratulated" is an incorrect verb; "congratulated" alone would be sufficient here.

9. **(D)** In (A), "to celebrate" should be "celebrating," parallel to "promising." Choice (B) is illogical: one cannot *promise* a "wonderful past." (C) is not a complete sentence.

10. **(B)** Choices (A) and (C) compare the taste of lunch with the taste of co-workers. In (D), "one" appears to refer to "co-workers."

Practice Set 9

Decide which sentence is preferable with respect to grammar and usage suitable for a formal letter or report.

1. A) All of them decided it would _____ not be as good for the girls to stay home rather than go to the party.

   B) The girls all decided it would be best to stay at home rather to go to the party.

   C) All the girls decided it would be better to stay home than to go to the party.

   D) To stay home instead of going to the party was decided to be the best according to all the girls.

2. A) When a person reads the _____ instructions, they should remember to follow directions as complete as possible.

   B) When reading the instructions, a person should follow directions as completely as possible.

   C) Following directions as completely as possible, a person reading the instructions.

   D) Remember when reading instructions and following directions as completely as possible.

3. A) Be sure to double check your _____ ticket location to make certain you are in the proper seat.
   B) To make sure you are in the proper seat, double checking your ticket location is to be done.
   C) Making certain you are in the proper seat, your ticket is to be double checked.
   D) To double check your ticket location and to be certain you are in the proper seat.

4. A) Whatever he does or doesn't _____ do, its for sure that he really truly enjoys his work.
   B) Depending on what he does or doesn't do, he sure likes his work.
   C) Not mattering what he does or doesn't do, he enjoys his work.
   D) Whatever he does or doesn't do, he at least enjoys his work.

5. A) Typical of their species, the _____ parrot will thrive where they can find enough fruits and nuts.
   B) Like their species, parrots will thrive wherever it can find enough fruits and nuts.
   C) Finding enough fruits and nuts will enable parrots to thrive like their species.
   D) Typical of their species, parrots will thrive wherever they can find enough fruits and nuts.

6. A) Bernhouse obviously treasured _____ the memory of his father's happiness as much as he did the memory of his own childhood.
   B) The memory of his father's happiness was obviously treasured by Bernhouse as much as he did his father's treasured happiness.
   C) Obviously treasuring his father's happiness as much as the memory of Bernhouse's own childhood.
   D) Bernhouse treasured obviously the memory of his father's happiness as much as his own childhood memory.

7. A) Music and films with a strong _____ Latin theme has helped to unite the community
   B) Music, as well as films with a strong Latin theme, have been mostly helpful for the uniting of the community
   C) Music and films with a strong Latin theme have helped to unite the community.
   D) Uniting the community, music and films with a strong Latin theme have been helpful.

8. A) Sitting in what he called his _____ home away from home, Arnold thought concerning about his future.
   B) Sitting in what he called his home away from home, concerning his future Arnold thought.
   C) Having sat in what he is calling his home away from home, Arnold thinks about his future.
   D) Sitting in what he called his home away from home, Arnold thought about the future.

9. A) Many at the time believed that _____ the alliance with the allies is a trick to confuse their enemy.

   B) Many at the time believes that the alliance with the allies was a trick to confuse their enemies.

   C) Many at the time believed that their alliance with the allies confused the enemy as a trick.

   D) Many at the time believed that their alliance with the allies was a trick to confuse their enemies.

10. A) Going a long way toward _____ improvement of efficiency, they are no doubt useless, computers without humans.

    B) Though they have gone a long way toward improvement of efficiency, computers are no doubt useless, having no humans.

    C) Though they've made major improvements in efficiency, computers are useless without humans.

    D) Being without humans, in spite of their improvements in efficiency, computers have gone a long way.

Answer Explanations for Practice Set 9

1. **(C)** In (A), "not be as good . . . rather than" is incorrect. In (B), "best" is incorrect when comparing two options. It should be "better." In (D), "according to" is awkward, and the sentence is better stated in the active, rather than passive.

2. **(B)** In (A), "they" incorrectly refers to "a person." (C) and (D) are sentence fragments.

3. **(A)** In (B), the sentence would be vastly improved if the phrases were in reverse order. In (C), "Making certain" should be "To make certain." (D) is a sentence fragment.

4. **(D)** In (A), "for sure" and "really truly" are unacceptable idioms, as is "Not mattering" in (C). In (B), "sure" should be "certainly."

5. **(D)** In (A), "the parrot" (singular) does not agree with "their" and "they" Similarly in (B), "parrots" does not agree with "it." In (C), "to thrive like their species" is vague.

6. **(A)** In (B), "as much as he did" is vague. (C) is a sentence fragment. In (D), "treasured obviously" is incorrect sentence structure.

7. **(C)** In (A), "Music and films" (plural) require a plural verb, "have helped" instead of "has helped." In (B), the opposite is required: "Music . . . *has* helped," a singular subject takes a singular verb. Notice in (B) that "films" are not part of the subject. In (D), "have been helpful" is vague.

8. **(D)** In (A), "concerning about" is incorrect usage. (B) uses awkward structure. In (C), verb tenses are inconsistent.

9. **(D)** In (A), "is" should be "was." In (B), "believes" should he "believed." In (C), "confused the enemy as a trick" is awkward structure.

10. **(C)** In (A), "they" is vague, and the structure is awkward. In (B), having no humans" is a vague phrase, as is "being without humans" in (D).

Practice Set 10

Decide which sentence is preferable with respect to grammar and usage suitable for a formal letter or report.

1. A) The salad contains broccoli _____ that has been cooked briefly, crabmeat, and it has two kinds of lettuce.
   B) The salad contains broccoli that is cooked briefly as well as crabmeat and contains two kinds of lettuce.
   C) The salad contains two kinds of lettuce, crabmeat, and also has briefly cooked broccoli.
   D) The salad contains broccoli that has been cooked briefly, crabmeat, and two kinds of lettuce.

2. A) Unlike most modern novel-ists, the novels of the Victo-rian age appeared first in magazines in serial form, sometimes for as long as one year.
   B) Appearing first in magazines in serial form, the novels of the Victorian age were sometimes as long as one year unlike most modern ones.
   C) Appearing first in magazines in serial form, sometimes over the length of a year, most Victorian novels were unlike modern novels.
   D) Unlike most modern novels, those of the Victorian age appeared first in magazines in serial form, sometimes for as long as a year.

3. A) Depressed by urban sprawl _____ and the noise of the traffic, a one-acre garden of produce and flowers has cheered up ten patients at the Westway hospital.
   B) Depressed by urban sprawl and the noise of the traffic, ten patients at the Westway hospi-tal have been cheered Lip by a one-acre garden of produce and flowers.
   C) Ten patients at the Westway hospital who have been cheered up by a one-acre garden of produce and flowers though once depressed by urban sprawl and the noise of the traffic.
   D) Urban sprawl and the noise of traffic depress ten patients at the Westway hospital, cheered up by a one-acre garden of produce and flowers.

4. A) The federal commission had _____ decided to close the Boston Naval Shipyard, and this seemed the end of their jobs to hundreds of workers.
   B) The decision to close the Boston Naval Shipyard was reached by a federal commis-sion, and this decision seems to be the end of their job for hundreds of workers.
   C) The federal commission's deci-sion to close the Boston Naval Shipyard seemed to end the jobs of hundreds of workers.
   D) The federal commission decided to close the Boston Naval Shipyard, which seem-ingly ended the jobs of hun-dreds of workers.

5. A) If you think carefully about your future, one must see the importance of education.
   B) If you think about your future carefully, you must see the importance of education.
   C) If one thinks about your future carefully, one must see the importance of education.
   D) You must see the importance of education, if one thinks about one's future carefully.

6. A) The final results at the end of the game were a total and complete surprise.
   B) The final results of the game were a total and complete surprise.
   C) The results of the game were a complete surprise.
   D) The results at the end were totally and completely surprising.

7. A) After he had mowed the lawn, the gardener put the lawnmower in the garage, and scatters the clippings on the garden.
   B) After he mows the lawn, the gardener put the lawnmower in the garage, and scattered the clippings in the garden.
   C) After he had mowed the lawn, the gardener put the lawnmower in the garage, and scattered the clippings on the garden.
   D) After mowing the lawn, the lawnmower was put into the garage and the clippings were scattered on the garden by the gardener.

8. A) Millions of farm workers who plant, tend, harvest, and package our food without any health insurance.
   B) Millions of farm workers who plant our food, tend it, harvest our food, and package it without any health insurance.
   C) Millions of farm workers, planting, tending, harvesting, and packaging our food without any health insurance.
   D) There are millions of farm workers who plant, tend, harvest, and package our food without any health insurance.

9. A) The senate, because the president, the chief justice, and the mayor were late, were unable to perform any business.
   B) Because the president, the chief justice, and the mayor were late, the senate was unable to perform any business.
   C) Being as the president, chief justice, and mayor were late, the senate was not able to perform any business.
   D) Because the president, chief justice, and mayor were late, the senate were unable to perform any business.

10. A) There is one thing that most kids would rather do with food than eat it: play with it.
    B) Most kids would rather play with food than eat food.
    C) For most kids, they would rather play with it than eat their foods.
    D) Food, most kids believe, is for playing with rather than for eating it.

Answer Explanations for Practice Set 10

1. **(D)** (A), (B), and (C) have second verbs where one is sufficient.

2. **(D)** In (A), the opening phrase dangles. In (B), the verb "were" should be something like "extended" or "lasted." In (C), "novels" is repeated.

3. **(B)** Choice (A) corrects the dangling modifier that begins (A). Choice (C) is a sentence fragment, lacking a main verb, and (D) places the final modifying clause so that it's unclear if it modifies "hospital" or "patients."

4. **(C)** Choice (C) is the most economical version and has no errors. (A) and (D) have a vague pronoun ("this") ("which"); (B) has an awkward repetition ("decision").

5. **(B)** Only (B) uses only one pronoun (you, your) consistently. Each of the other three versions shifts from "one" to "you" or "you" to "one."

6. **(C)** Choice (C) is the most economical version. "Final" and "at the end," as well as "total and complete," are redundant.

7. **(C)** The errors here are in the verb tenses. The correct version uses the past perfect "had mowed" in the clause with "after," and the past tense in the rest of the sentence.

8. **(D)** Only choice (D) is a complete sentence. The three other versions are sentence fragments, missing a main verb.

9. **(B)** Choice (B) has the correct singular verb with "senate" and keeps the subjects and verbs close together. (A) and (D) have agreement errors, and (C) has an idiom error in "Being as."

10. **(A)** The first choice is correct; it avoids the repetition or awkward prepositions and pronouns of the other three.

Verbal Abilities Analysis Chart for Grammar (Language Usage)

Use the following chart to carefully analyze your results of the *grammar (language usage)* question type. This will help you evaluate your strengths and weaknesses. This analysis should help you focus your study and review efforts on specific types of problems.

Practice Set	Total Number of Questions	Number Correct	Number Incorrect	Number Unanswered
Set 1	10			
Set 2	10			
Set 3	10			
Set 4	10			
Set 5	10			
Set 6	10			
Set 7	10			
Set 8	10			
Set 9	10			
Set 10	10			

Because there is no penalty for incorrect answers on most of the questions in the Verbal Abilities section, you should have left no question unanswered. Even if you didn't have time to answer a question, you should have at least filled in the answer space with an educated guess.

REVIEWING THE KEY STRATEGIES

Remember to:
1. Read all four sentences before selecting an answer.
2. Look for common errors first:
   —incorrect verbs
   —misuse of pronouns
   —incorrect usage
   —unclear meaning
   —repetition

SPELLING

This section provides you with examples of two different spelling question types. The strategies presented will help to prepare you for both question types.

SPELLING QUESTION TYPE ONE: FIND THE CORRECT SPELLING.

This question type tests your ability to recognize correct spelling. You are given three different spellings of a certain word and are required to choose the correct spelling, if it appears. If it does not appear, you are to choose answer D.

SPELLING QUESTION TYPE TWO: FIND THE INCORRECT SPELLING.

In question type two, you are given three different spellings of a certain word. You are required to recognize and choose the word that is misspelled, if it appears. If all of the words are spelled correctly, choose answer D.

Helpful Techniques and Strategies

1. SEE the word. Very often, we do not recognize words that are misspelled because of the way they are pronounced. For instance, "accidentally" is pronounced "accidently" and may be misspelled for that reason.

   After looking at the three choices you are given, look away from the test page and attempt to *see* the word in your mind. Write the word mentally, letter by letter. Doing so may help you to avoid a misspelling based on pronunciation alone.

2. Before taking the test, study a list of commonly misspelled words, such as the following. The common trouble spots are underlined.

3. One way to prepare for this part of the test is to create your own sample questions, using the preceding list of commonly misspelled words. Keeping in mind some basic spelling rules and common spelling errors (some examples follow), devise possible misspellings of these words. This way you will

TABLE 3

Some Commonly Misspelled Words

absence	bicycle	correspondence	equipped	independence	necessary	pursuing	sophomore
accept	bulletin	courageous	evidently	influential	neither	quarreling	specimen
accidentally	bureau	course	excitement	ingenious	nickel	really	speech
accommodate	cafeteria	courteous	existence	inoculate	niece	receipt	stomach
accordance	calendar	courtesy	expense	interesting	ninety	received	strength
achievement	campaign	criticism	extension	interfere	ninth	recognize	succeed
acknowledge	captain	crowd	familiar	jealous	noticeable	recommend	success
acquainted	careful	crucial	fascinating	jewelry	occasion	referee	sufficient
acquired	carriage	deceive	fatigue	judgment	occurred	referred	superintendent
across	ceiling	decided	forcibly	justice	often	refugee	surely
advice	cemetery	defendant	forehead	kindergarten	omitted	relieve	surprise
advisable	changeable	dependent	foreign	knowledge	owing	religious	suspense
advise	chaos	descent	foresee	laboratory	pamphlet	remittance	technical
affectionately	chief	desirable	forty	legible	parallel	repetition	terrible
aisle	climbed	despair	forward	lettuce	pastime	reservoir	therefore
allege	cloth	desperate	freight	library	permanent	resistance	thorough
all right	clothes	device	fugitive	lieutenant	personally	restaurant	tobacco
almost	college	disastrous	fundamental	lightning	personnel	rhyme	toward
already	colonel	discipline	further	losing	physically	rhythm	tragedy
altogether	column	disease	generally	lying	planning	ridiculous	transferred
amateur	committee	divided	government	maintenance	possesses	salary	twelfth
annual	common	doubt	grateful	magazine	possibility	sandwich	typical
anxious	comparative	duly	grievance	marriage	possible	scarcely	unusual
apparatus	competition	dying	guarantee	merchandise	preceding	schedule	useful
arctic	confident	effect	guard	miniature	prejudice	secretary	vegetable
article	congratulations	efficiency	handful	mischievous	privilege	seize	village
ascertain	conquer	eighth	harassed	misspelled	probably	sergeant	villain
assistance	conscience	eligible	height	mortgage	procedure	severely	weight
athletic	conscientious	embarrass	heroes	mournful	proceeded	shriek	weird
attacked	conscious	eminent	immediately	movable	prominent	siege	welfare
attendance	consequently	endeavor	incidentally	murmur	proved	sincerely	woman
beggar	convenience	environment	indefinitely	muscle	psychology	skiing	yield
benefited	coolly	equipment					

become familiar not only with the correct spelling, but also with possible types of incorrect spellings that may appear on the test. Examples:

absolutely	absalutely	absolootly
foresee	forsee	foursea
vegetable	vegtable	vegetible

4. Be familiar with basic spelling rules. Study the following:
   a. ADDING ENDINGS—When a word ends with "e," drop the "e" if the ending begins with a vowel (a, e, i, o, u), but do not drop the "e" if the ending begins with a consonant (b, c, d, f, g, h, etc.). Examples:

   age—aging (drop the "e" when adding "ing")
   manage—management (keep the "e" when adding "ment")

   Change "y" to "i" when adding an ending, except when the ending is "ing." Examples:

   study—studies—studying

   Keep the final "I" when you add "ly." Example:

   personal—personally

   b. "I" BEFORE "E" EXCEPT AFTER "C." Examples:

   field   perceive
   relief   ceiling

   When the sound of "ie" is not ē (ee), the usual spelling is "ei." Examples:

   neighbor
   weigh
   height

   Exceptions to these rules: weird, leisure, friend, mischief

5. Be familiar with types of common spelling errors. We have already cautioned you to become familiar with words that are pronounced differently from the way they are spelled. Besides the confusion of pronunciation and spelling, another common error is *confusing words with the same sound but different spellings.* Study the following list:

TABLE 4

Some Commonly Confused Words

air; ere; heir	buy; by
ate; eight	cent; scent; sent
blew; blue	coarse; course
bough; bow	for; four
brake; break	forth; fourth
grate; great	right; write
groan; grown	road; rode
hear; here	sew; so; sow
him; hymn	scene; seen
hole; whole	stationary; stationery
hour; our	steal; steel
its; it's	straight; strait
knew; new	some; sum
know; no	son; sun
lead; led	sweet; suite
mail; male	their; there; they're
meat; meet	threw; through
pail; pale	to; too; two
pair; pare; pear	way; weigh
peace; piece	whose; who's
principal; principle	wood; would
read; red	

6. Keep a personal list of troublesome words. Jot down those words that give you particular spelling problems, and review them regularly.

Sample Questions

Find the correct spelling of the word and write the letter of your choice in the space provided. If no suggested spelling is correct, write choice D.

1. A) accomadate   C) accommodate   _____
   B) accomodate   D) none of these   _____

2. A) calander   C) calendur   _____
   B) calendar   D) none of these   _____

3. A) priviledge   C) priviedge   _____
   B) privilege   D) none of these   _____

4. A) recommend   C) recomend   _____
   B) reccommend   D) none of these   _____

5. A) developement   C) devellopment   _____
   B) development   D) none of these   _____

6. A) nickel   C) nickil   _____
   B) nickle   D) none of these   _____

7. A) catagory   C) cattagory   _____
   B) category   D) none of these   _____

Answers to Sample Questions

1. **(D)**   3. **(B)**   5. **(B)**   7. **(B)**
2. **(B)**   4. **(A)**   6. **(A)**

SPELLING QUESTION TYPE ONE: FIND THE CORRECT SPELLING

Practice Set I

Find the correct spelling of the word and write the letter of your choice in the space provided. If no suggested spelling is correct, write choice D.

1. A) fourty   C) forety   _____
   B) forty   D) none of these

2. A) acheivement   C) acheivment   _____
   B) achievement   D) none of these

3. A) accross   C) acros   _____
   B) across   D) none of these

4. A) advertizement   C) advertisement _____
   B) adverticement   D) none of these

5. A) salary   C) sallary   _____
   B) salery   D) none of these

6. A) permenent   C) purmenent   _____
   B) permanent   D) none of these

7. A) ajourn   C) adjourn   _____
   B) ediourn   D) none of these

8. A) artikle   C) articul   _____
   B) artical   D) none of these

9. A) scarcley   C) scarcly   _____
   B) scarcely   D) none of these

10. A) intresting   C) interesting   _____
    B) intrestting   D) none of these

11. A) magasine   C) magazine   _____
    B) maggazine   D) none of these

12. A) referance   C) reference   _____
    B) refrence   D) none of these

13. A) posible   C) posibel   _____
    B) possible   D) none of these

14. A) gentlemen   C) gentelmen   _____
    B) gentalmen   D) none of these

15. A) consequently   C) consecuentally _____
    B) consequentally   D) none of these

16. A) captian   C) captein   _____
    B) captin   D) none of these

17. A) carrage   C) carriage   _____
    B) cariage   D) none of these

18. A) aquired   C) ackwiered   _____
    B) acuired   D) none of these

19. A) lutenant   C) liutenant   _____
    B) lieutenent   D) none of these

20. A) independance   C) independince   _____
    B) independence   D) none of these

Answers for Practice Set 1

1. **(B)** forty
2. **(B)** achievement
3. **(B)** across
4. **(C)** advertisement
5. **(A)** salary
6. **(B)** permanent
7. **(C)** adjourn
8. **(D)** Correct spelling: article
9. **(B)** scarcely
10. **(C)** interesting

11. **(C)** magazine
12. **(C)** reference
13. **(B)** possible
14. **(A)** gentlemen
15. **(A)** consequently
16. **(D)** Correct spelling: captain
17. **(C)** carriage
18. **(D)** Correct spelling: acquired
19. **(D)** Correct spelling: lieutenant
20. **(B)** independence

Practice Set 2

Find the correct spelling of the word and write the letter of your choice in the space provided. If no suggested spelling is correct, write choice D.

1. A) stomach   C) stommack   _____
   B) stomack   D) none of these

2. A) jewlrey   C) jewelry   _____
   B) jewlry   D) none of these

3. A) superentendent   C) superentendant
   B) superintendant   D) none of these _____

4. A) virticle   C) vertical   _____
   B) verticle   D) none of these

5. A) sofomore   C) sophmore   _____
   B) sophomore   D) none of these

6. A) sarient   C) sargant   _____
   B) sargeant   D) none of these

7. A) vegtable   C) vegetable   _____
   B) vegtabel   D) none of these

8. A) tobaco   C) tabacco   _____
   B) tobacco   D) none of these

9. A) moregage   C) morgage   _____
   B) mortgage   D) none of these

10. A) merchandice C) merchandise   _____
    B) merchandize D) none of these

11. A) omited   C) ommitted   _____
    B) omitted   D) none of these

12. A) memmorandem C) memmorandum
    B) memorandum   D) none of these _____

13. A) minature   C) minatoor   _____
    B) miniature   D) none of these

14. A) greatful   C) graitful   _____
    B) grateful   D) none of these

15. A) fudjitive   C) fugative   _____
    B) fudgitive   D) none of these

16. A) preperations   C) preprarations _____
    B) preparations   D) none of these

17. A) equiptment   C) equipment   _____
    B) eqwuiptment D) none of these

18. A) buereau   C) bureau   _____
    B) beaureau   D) none of these

19. A) accordance   C) acordance   _____
    B) accordence   D) none of these

20. A) assistence   C) assistance   _____
    B) assistince   D) none of these

Answers for Practice Set 2

1. **(A)** stomach
2. **(C)** jewelry
3. **(D)** Correct spelling: superintendent
4. **(C)** vertical
5. **(B)** sophomore
6. **(D)** Correct spelling: sergeant
7. **(C)** vegetable
8. **(B)** tobacco
9. **(B)** mortgage
10. **(C)** merchandise

11. **(B)** omitted
12. **(B)** memorandum
13. **(B)** miniature
14. **(B)** grateful
15. **(D)** Correct spelling: fugitive
16. **(B)** preparations
17. **(C)** equipment
18. **(C)** bureau
19. **(A)** accordance
20. **(C)** assistance

Practice Set 3

Find the correct spelling of the word and write the letter of your choice in the space provided. If no suggested spelling is correct, write choice D.

1. A) artic   C) Artic   _____
    B) arctic   D) none of these

2. A) marrage   C) marriage   _____
    B) marraige   D) none of these

3. A) chiminey   C) chimeny   _____
    B) chimney   D) none of these

4. A) perfession   C) profession   _____
    B) profesion   D) none of these

5. A) excape   C) escape   _____
    B) exkape   D) none of these

6. A) surprize   C) surprise   _____
    B) serprise   D) none of these

7. A) congradalations   C) congratulations
    B) congradulations   D) none of these _____

8. A) reconize   C) recconise   _____
    B) recognize   D) none of these

9. A) tomorow   C) tomorrow   _____
    B) tommorrow   D) none of these

10. A) atheitics   C) athletics   _____
    B) atheletics   D) none of these

11. A) disasterous   C) desasterous   _____
    B) disastrous   D) none of these

12. A) prespire   C) perspire   _____
    B) pirspire   D) none of these

13. A) secratery   C) secratary   _____
    B) secretery   D) none of these

14. A) umberella   C) umberela   _____
    B) umbrella   D) none of these

15. A) lightining   C) litening   _____
    B) lightning   D) none of these

16. A) goverment   C) government   _____
    B) govrenment   D) none of these

17. A) affectionitely   C) affectionately   _____
    B) affectionatly   D) none of these

18. A) requirment   C) requiremint   _____
    B) requirement   D) none of these

19. A) choclate   C) chocolit   _____
    B) chocolet   D) none of these

20. A) asociate   C) assoshiate   _____
    B) associate   D) none of these

Answers for Practice Set 3

1. **(B)** arctic
2. **(C)** marriage
3. **(B)** chimney
4. **(C)** profession
5. **(C)** escape
6. **(C)** surprise
7. **(C)** congratulations
8. **(B)** recognize
9. **(C)** tomorrow
10. **(C)** athletics
11. **(B)** disastrous
12. **(C)** perspire
13. **(D)** Correct spelling: secretary
14. **(B)** umbrella
15. **(B)** lightning
16. **(C)** government
17. **(C)** affectionately
18. **(B)** requirement
19. **(D)** Correct spelling: chocolate
20. **(B)** associate

Practice Set 4

Find the correct spelling of the word and write the letter of your choice in the space provided. If no suggested spelling is correct, write choice D.

1. A) dependent   C) dependint   _____
   B) dependunt   D) none of these

2. A) equasion   C) equazion   _____
   B) equation   D) none of these

3. A) excitment   C) excitement   _____
   B) exsitement   D) none of these

4. A) presense   C) prescence   _____
   B) presence   D) none of these

5. A) environement   C) environment   _____
   B) enviernment   D) none of these

6. A) campaine   C) campaign   _____
   B) campain   D) none of these

7. A) corespondence   C) corraspondence
   B) corispondence   D) none of these   _____

8. A) benefit   C) benafit   _____
   B) benifit   D) none of these

9. A) consequentally   C) consekwentally
   B) consequently   D) none of these   _____

10. A) attendence   C) attendance   _____
    B) atendance   D) none of these

11. A) promanent   C) promenint   _____
    B) promenent   D) none of these

12. A) height   C) heighth   _____
    B) hieght   D) none of these

13. A) dropt   C) dropped   _____
    B) droped   D) none of these

14. A) carefull   C) carful   _____
    B) careful   D) none of these

15. A) busness   C) business   _____
    B) bizness   D) none of these

16. A) suceed   C) succed   _____
    B) succede   D) none of these

17. A) english   C) English   _____
    B) Englesh   D) none of these

18. A) cooperation   C) cooparation   _____
    B) coaparation   D) none of these

19. A) vackume   C) vaccuum   _____
    B) vaccume   D) none of these

20. A) afourmentioned   C) aformentioned
    B) aforementioned   D) none of these   _____

Answers for Practice Set 4

1. **(A)** dependent
2. **(B)** equation
3. **(C)** excitement
4. **(B)** presence
5. **(C)** environment
6. **(C)** campaign
7. **(D)** Correct spelling: correspondence
8. **(A)** benefit
9. **(B)** consequently
10. **(C)** attendance

11. **(D)** Correct spelling: prominent
12. **(A)** height
13. **(C)** dropped
14. **(B)** careful
15. **(C)** business
16. **(D)** Correct spelling: succeed
17. **(C)** English
18. **(A)** cooperation
19. **(D)** Correct spelling: vacuum
20. **(B)** aforementioned

Practice Set 5

Find the correct spelling of the word and write the letter of your choice in the space provided. If no suggested spelling is correct, write choice D.

1. A) relience   C) reliance   _____
   B) relyance   D) none of these

2. A) adition   C) addittion   _____
   B) addition   D) none of these

3. A) innoculate   C) inocculate   _____
   B) inoculate   D) none of these

4. A) probubly   C) probably   _____
   B) probly   D) none of these

5. A) Febuary   C) February   _____
   B) Febrary   D) none of these

6. A) testimonial   C) testemonial   _____
   B) testamonial   D) none of these

7. A) eficient   C) efficcient   _____
   B) effishient   D) none of these

8. A) necesary   C) necessary   _____
   B) nessesary   D) none of these

9. A) temprature   C) temperature   _____
   B) tempereture   D) none of these

10. A) corperation   C) corporation   _____
    B) corparation   D) none of these

11. A) comittment   C) commitment   _____
    B) committment   D) none of these

12. A) facetously   C) fascetiously   _____
    B) facitiously   D) none of these

13. A) barter   C) bartur   _____
    B) bartar   D) none of these

14. A) recquisite   C) recwisite   _____
    B) requisite   D) none of these

15. A) inteligent   C) intelligint   _____
    B) enteligent   D) none of these

16. A) transatory   C) transitory   _____
    B) transitorry   D) none of these

17. A) langauge   C) langwage   _____
    B) language   D) none of these

18. A) liberty   C) library   _____
    B) libary   D) none of these

19. A) resplendent   C) resplendint   _____
    B) resplendant   D) none of these

20. A) propelor   C) propeller   _____
    B) propellor   D) none of these

Answers for Practice Set 5

1. **(C)** reliance
2. **(B)** addition
3. **(B)** inoculate
4. **(C)** probably
5. **(C)** February
6. **(A)** testimonial
7. **(D)** Correct spelling: efficient
8. **(C)** necessary
9. **(C)** temperature
10. **(C)** corporation
11. **(C)** commitment
12. **(D)** Correct spelling: facetiously
13. **(A)** barter
14. **(B)** requisite
15. **(D)** Correct spelling: intelligent
16. **(C)** transitory
17. **(B)** language
18. **(C)** library
19. **(A)** resplendent
20. **(C)** propeller

Practice Set 6

Find the correct spelling of the word and write the letter of your choice in the space provided. If no suggested spelling is correct, write choice D.

1. A) wield   C) weilde   11. A) perogative   C) prerogotive
    B) weild   D) none of these   B) prerogative   D) none of these

2. A) exhilarate   C) exhilerate   12. A) their's   C) theyr's
    B) exilarate   D) none of these   B) theirs   D) none of these

3. A) misspell   C) misspel   13. A) guage   C) gaige
    B) mispell   D) none of these   B) gauge   D) none of these

4. A) grammer   C) grammar   14. A) aggression   C) aggresion
    B) gramar   D) none of these   B) agression   D) none of these

5. A) existance   C) exsistence   15. A) restarant   C) restaurant
    B) existence   D) none of these   B) restrant   D) none of these

6. A) missile   C) misile   16. A) marshul   C) marshalle
    B) missle   D) none of these   B) marshal   D) none of these

7. A) procede   C) proseed   17. A) ristrain   C) restrain
    B) proceed   D) none of these   B) restrane   D) none of these

8. A) repitition   C) repittition   18. A) cemetary   C) cemetery
    B) repetition   D) none of these   B) cemitery   D) none of these

9. A) wierd   C) weerd   19. A) irresistible   C) irrisistable
    B) weird   D) none of these   B) irresistable   D) none of these

10. A) embaras   C) embarrass   20. A) occassion   C) occasion
    B) embarass   D) none of these   B) ocassion   D) none of these

Answers for Practice Set 6

1. **(A)** wield   11. **(B)** prerogative
2. **(A)** exhilarate   12. **(B)** theirs
3. **(A)** misspell   13. **(B)** gauge
4. **(C)** grammar   14. **(A)** aggression
5. **(B)** existence   15. **(C)** restaurant
6. **(A)** missile   16. **(B)** marshal
7. **(B)** proceed   17. **(C)** restrain
8. **(B)** repetition   18. **(C)** cemetery
9. **(B)** weird   19. **(A)** irresistible
10. **(C)** embarrass   20. **(C)** occasion

SPELLING QUESTION TYPE TWO: FIND THE MISSPELLED WORD

Practice Set 1

Find the word that is spelled incorrectly and write the letter of your choice in the space provided. If no word is misspelled, write choice D.

1. A) absorbtion _____
   B) compatible
   C) tolerance
   D) None is misspelled.

2. A) continue _____
   B) logistics
   C) circumfrence
   D) None is misspelled.

3. A) nautical _____
   B) retrospect
   C) condenced
   D) None is misspelled.

4. A) assuage _____
   B) coagulate
   C) crescendo
   D) None is misspelled.

5. A) sincere _____
   B) incinuate
   C) contemptible
   D) None is misspelled.

6. A) abstinent _____
   B) murcurial
   C) limpid
   D) None is misspelled.

7. A) psychosis _____
   B) bureaucratic
   C) autonomie
   D) None is misspelled.

8. A) inclement _____
   B) deciduous
   C) amassed
   D) None is misspelled.

9. A) veluptuous _____
   B) conformist
   C) telekinesis
   D) None is misspelled.

10. A) pronunciation _____
    B) contraversy
    C) intervene
    D) None is misspelled.

11. A) adequate _____
    B) obsequious
    C) vociferous
    D) None is misspelled.

12. A) misterious _____
    B) purview
    C) associate
    D) None is misspelled.

13. A) intractable _____
    B) incorigible
    C) tempestuous
    D) None is misspelled.

14. A) venomous _____
    B) sustenance
    C) cello
    D) None is misspelled.

15. A) sacriledge _____
    B) cantankerous
    C) calligraphy
    D) None is misspelled.

16. A) perseverance _____
    B) existential
    C) constitutional
    D) None is misspelled.

17. A) dynamism   _____
    B) atrophy
    C) syncapation
    D) None is misspelled.

18. A) continuum   _____
    B) vernacular
    C) recieved
    D) None is misspelled.

19. A) acrimony   _____
    B) envellope
    C) nonchalant
    D) None is misspelled.

20. A) bequeath   _____
    B) substantiate
    C) qualatative
    D) None is misspelled.

Answer Explanation for Practice Set 1

1. **(A)** "Absorbtion is a misspelling of the word "absorption."
2. **(C)** "Circumfrence" is a misspelling of the word "circumference."
3. **(C)** "Condenced" is a misspelling of the word "condensed."
4. **(D)** All of the words are spelled correctly.
5. **(B)** "Incinuate" is a misspelling of the word "insinuate"
6. **(B)** "Murcurial" is a misspelling of the word "mercurial."
7. **(C)** "Autonomie" is a misspelling of the word "autonomy."
8. **(D)** All of the words are spelled correctly.
9. **(A)** "Veluptuous" is a misspelling of the world "voluptuous."
10. **(B)** "Contraversy" is a misspelling of the word "controversy."
11. **(D)** All of the words are spelled correctly.
12. **(A)** "Misterious" is a misspelling of the word "mysterious."
13. **(B)** "Incorigible" is a misspelling of the word "incorrigible."
14. **(D)** All of the words are spelled correctly.
15. **(A)** "Sacriledge" is a misspelling of the word "sacrilege."
16. **(D)** All of the words are spelled correctly.
17. **(C)** "Syncapation" is a misspelling of the word "syncopation."
18. **(C)** "Recieved" is a misspelling of the word "received."
19. **(B)** "Envellope" is a misspelling of the word "envelope."
20. **(C)** "Qualatative" is a misspelling of the word "qualitative."

Practice Set 2

Find the word that is spelled incorrectly and write the letter of your choice in the space provided. If no word is misspelled, write choice D.

1. A) fathomable   _____
   B) attest
   C) apetite
   D) None is misspelled.

2. A) judicious   _____
   B) pergatory
   C) succinct
   D) None is misspelled.

3. A) sureal   _____
   B) toupee
   C) oblivious
   D) None is misspelled.

4. A) industrial   _____
   B) nullify
   C) nutrience
   D) None is misspelled.

5. A) ordanance   _____
   B) scrutinize
   C) palatial
   D) None is misspelled.

6. A) boredom   _____
   B) silouette
   C) dexterity
   D) None is misspelled.

7. A) monologue   _____
   B) desirous
   C) enigma
   D) None is misspelled.

8. A) tawdry   _____
   B) recreation
   C) grandios
   D) None is misspelled.

9. A) maledroit   _____
   B) obsequy
   C) prognosis
   D) None is misspelled.

10. A) subtrehend   _____
    B) yataghan
    C) wraith
    D) None is misspelled.

11. A) guerila   _____
    B) indubitable
    C) grotesque
    D) None is misspelled.

12. A) champagne   _____
    B) derelict
    C) iridesence
    D) None is misspelled.

13. A) ecclesiastical   _____
    B) aestheticism
    C) beauteous
    D) None is misspelled.

14. A) frivelous   _____
    B) datum
    C) gracious
    D) None is misspelled.

15. A) cornacopia   _____
    B) schism
    C) decoyed
    D) None is misspelled.

16. A) annual   _____
    B) gorgeous
    C) necessity
    D) None is misspelled.

17. A) emphatic   _____
    B) sacrafice
    C) sarcophagi
    D) None is misspelled.

18. A) requirement   _____
    B) democratic
    C) tendency
    D) None is misspelled.

19. A) sereen   _____
    B) qualm
    C) sundry
    D) None is misspelled.

20. A) temporary   _____
    B) juxtapose
    C) morsal
    D) None is misspelled.

Answer Explanations for Practice Set 2

1. **(C)** "Apetite" is a misspelling of the word "appetite."

2. **(B)** "Pergatory" is a misspelling of the word "purgatory."

3. **(A)** "Sureal" is a misspelling of the word "surreal."

4. **(C)** "Nutrience" is a misspelling of the word "nutrients."

5. **(A)** "Ordanance" is a misspelling of the word "ordinance."
6. **(B)** "Silouette" is a misspelling of the word "silhouette."
7. **(D)** All of the words are spelled correctly.
8. **(C)** "Grandios" is a misspelling of the word "grandiose."
9. **(A)** "Maledroit" is a misspelling of the word "maladroit."
10. **(A)** "Subtrehend" is a misspelling of the word "subtrahend."
11. **(A)** "Guerila" is a misspelling of the word "guerrilla."
12. **(C)** "Iridesence" is a misspelling of the word "iridescence."

13. **(D)** All of the words are spelled correctly.
14. **(A)** "Frivelous" is a misspelling of the word "frivolous."
15. **(A)** "Cornacopia" is a misspelling of the word "cornucopia."
16. **(D)** All of the words are spelled correctly.
17. **(B)** "Sacrafice" is a misspelling of the word "sacrifice."
18. **(D)** All of the words are spelled correctly.
19. **(A)** "Sereen" is a misspelling of the word "serene."
20. **(C)** "Morsal" is a misspelling of the word "morsel."

Practice Set 3

Find the word that is spelled incorrectly and write the letter of your choice in the space provided. If no word is misspelled, write choice D.

1. A) impromptu _____
   B) depoe
   C) requisite
   D) None is misspelled.

2. A) miscellaneous _____
   B) idiosyncrasy
   C) facsimily
   D) None is misspelled.

3. A) adolescence _____
   B) grandiose
   C) maintenence
   D) None is misspelled.

4. A) suseptible _____
   B) improvisation
   C) accompaniment
   D) None is misspelled.

5. A) paraphanelia _____
   B) parsimonious
   C) ameliorate
   D) None is misspelled.

6. A) assumption _____
   B) requirement
   C) derivitive
   D) None is misspelled.

7. A) dubiously _____
   B) intriging
   C) accommodate
   D) None is misspelled.

8. A) pedagogical _____
   B) purturbed
   C) assignment
   D) None is misspelled.

9. A) performance _____
   B) vacume
   C) orphanage
   D) None is misspelled.

10. A) adrenaline _____
    B) delinquent
    C) recency
    D) None is misspelled.

11. A) dutiful   _____
    B) wallowing
    C) presevation
    D) None is misspelled.

12. A) mutuality   _____
    B) colision
    C) decision
    D) None is misspelled.

13. A) ncanderthol   _____
    B) corporate
    C) destitute
    D) None is misspelled.

14. A) simoultaneously   _____
    B) upheaval
    C) betray
    D) None is misspelled.

15. A) genesis   _____
    B) incontrollable
    C) bizzare
    D) None is misspelled.

16. A) combust   _____
    B) consternation
    C) deliberate
    D) None is misspelled.

17. A) interogation   _____
    B) intrusion
    C) corollary
    D) None is misspelled.

18. A) fallicy   _____
    B) adept
    C) exceptional
    D) None is misspelled.

19. A) celibate   _____
    B) cuncussion
    C) accurate
    D) None is misspelled.

20. A) exitement   _____
    B) cascade
    C) embark
    D) None is misspelled.

Answer Explanations for Practice Set 3

1. **(B)** "Depoe" is a misspelling of the word "depot."
2. **(C)** "Facsimily" is a misspelling of the word "facsimile."
3. **(C)** "Maintenence" is a misspelling of the word "maintenance."
4. **(A)** "Suseptible" is a misspelling of the word "susceptible."
5. **(A)** "Paraphanelia" is a misspelling of the word "paraphernalia."
6. **(C)** "Derivitive" is a misspelling of the word "derivative."
7. **(B)** "Intriging" is a misspelling of the word "intriguing."
8. **(B)** "Purturbed" is a misspelling of the word "perturbed."
9. **(B)** "Vacume" is a misspelling of the word "vacuum."
10. **(D)** All of the words are spelled correctly.
11. **(C)** "Presevation" is a misspelling of the word "preservation."
12. **(B)** "Colision" is a misspelling of the word "collision."
13. **(A)** "Neanderthol" is a misspelling of the word "Neanderthal."
14. **(A)** "Simoultaneously" is a misspelling of the word "simultaneously."
15. **(C)** "Bizzare" is a misspelling of the word "bizarre."
16. **(D)** All of the words are spelled correctly.
17. **(A)** "Interogation" is a misspelling of the word "interrogation."
18. **(A)** "Fallicy" is a misspelling of the word "fallacy."
19. **(B)** "Cuncussion" is a misspelling of the word "concussion."
20. **(A)** "Exitement" is a misspelling of the word "excitement."

Practice Set 4

Find the word that is spelled incorrectly and write the letter of your choice in the space provided. If no word is misspelled, write choice D.

1. A) illuminate _____
   B) corps
   C) colegiate
   D) None is misspelled.

2. A) designed _____
   B) insentive
   C) debris
   D) None is misspelled.

3. A) pastell _____
   B) campaigner
   C) dubiously
   D) None is misspelled.

4. A) indignant _____
   B) assasination
   C) cliché
   D) None is misspelled.

5. A) government _____
   B) judgment
   C) intramural
   D) None is misspelled.

6. A) exorbitant _____
   B) gawdy
   C) delinquent
   D) None is misspelled.

7. A) triumph _____
   B) cataclysmic
   C) queue
   D) None is misspelled.

8. A) shyster _____
   B) aesthetic
   C) praized
   D) None is misspelled.

9. A) depravity _____
   B) amature
   C) anguished
   D) None is misspelled.

10. A) ingénue _____
    B) enigmatic
    C) promiscuous
    D) None is misspelled.

11. A) acuity _____
    B) exlamation
    C) sleuth
    D) None is misspelled.

12. A) quandary _____
    B) medieval
    C) designation
    D) None is misspelled.

13. A) awry _____
    B) mollify
    C) typographical
    D) None is misspelled.

14. A) condusive _____
    B) enthralling
    C) dialysis
    D) None is misspelled.

15. A) emblamatic _____
    B) unkempt
    C) antiquated
    D) None is misspelled.

16. A) diplomatic _____
    B) trecherous
    C) confiscate
    D) None is misspelled.

17. A) delineate   _____
    B) centrifuge
    C) corporeal
    D) None is misspelled.

18. A) tariff   _____
    B) breach
    C) choreograph
    D) None is misspelled.

19. A) conceited   _____
    B) amorphous
    C) tribulashuns
    D) None is misspelled.

20. A) convivial   _____
    B) desultury
    C) ecclesiastic
    D) None is misspelled.

Answer Explanations for Practice Set 4

1. **(C)** "Colegiate" is a misspelling of the word "collegiate."
2. **(B)** "Insentive" is a misspelling of the word "incentive."
3. **(A)** "Pastell" is a misspelling of the word "pastel."
4. **(B)** "Assasination" is a misspelling of the word "assassination."
5. **(D)** All of the words are spelled correctly.
6. **(B)** "Gawdy" is a misspelling of the word "gaudy."
7. **(D)** All of the words are spelled correctly.
8. **(C)** "Praized" is a misspelling of the word "praised."
9. **(B)** "Amature" is a misspelling of the word "amateur."
10. **(D)** All of the words are spelled correctly.
11. **(B)** "Exlamation" is a misspelling of the word "exclamation."
12. **(D)** All of the words are spelled correctly.
13. **(D)** All of the words are spelled correctly
14. **(A)** "Condusive" is a misspelling of the word "conducive."
15. **(A)** "Emblamatic" is a misspelling of the word "emblematic."
16. **(B)** "Trecherous" is a misspelling of the word "treacherous."
17. **(D)** All of the words are spelled correctly.
18. **(D)** All of the words are spelled correctly.
19. **(C)** "Tribulashuns" is a misspelling of the word "tribulations."
20. **(B)** "Desultury" is a misspelling of the word "desultory."

Practice Set 5

Find the word that is spelled incorrectly and write the letter of your choice in the space provided. If no word is misspelled, write choice D.

1. A) congragate   _____
    B) contingency
    C) itinerary
    D) None is misspelled.

2. A) integrity   _____
    B) desensitized
    C) comunal
    D) None is misspelled.

3. A) consignment   _____
    B) tertiary
    C) resistence
    D) None is misspelled.

4. A) expedient   _____
    B) dignitary
    C) sentient
    D) None is misspelled.

5. A) endemic _____
   B) philosiphy
   C) burgeoning
   D) None is misspelled.

6. A) liquified _____
   B) aerodynamic
   C) precaution
   D) None is misspelled.

7. A) consternation _____
   B) rebelion
   C) meagerly
   D) None is misspelled.

8. A) confound _____
   B) maximum
   C) indigenous
   D) None is misspelled.

9. A) authentic _____
   B) opportunities
   C) cooperatively
   D) None is misspelled.

10. A) dyeing _____
    B) zealotry
    C) remitance
    D) None is misspelled.

11. A) prophacy _____
    B) receipt
    C) vetoes
    D) None is misspelled.

12. A) potatos _____
    B) tomatoes
    C) parentheses
    D) None is misspelled.

13. A) diphthong _____
    B) canvass
    C) councel
    D) None is misspelled.

14. A) enumeration _____
    B) mannor
    C) courteous
    D) None is misspelled.

15. A) deservedly _____
    B) attention
    C) abhor
    D) None is misspelled.

16. A) cognition _____
    B) implacation
    C) absence
    D) None is misspelled.

17. A) desist _____
    B) capitel
    C) lanyard
    D) None is misspelled.

18. A) adendum _____
    B) sorcerer
    C) requisite
    D) None is misspelled.

19. A) procesor _____
    B) thunderous
    C) nullify
    D) None is misspelled.

20. A) acutely _____
    B) deviant
    C) clientele
    D) None is misspelled.

Answer Explanations for Practice Set 5

1. **(A)** "Congragate" is a misspelling of the word "congregate."

2. **(C)** "Comunal" is a misspelling of the word "communal."

3. **(C)** "Resistence" is a misspelling of the word "resistance."

4. **(D)** All of the words are spelled correctly.

5. **(B)** "Philosiphy" is a misspelling of the word "philosophy"

6. **(A)** "Liquified" is a misspelling of the word "liquefied."

7. **(B)** "Rebelion" is a misspelling of the word "rebellion."

8. **(D)** All of the words are spelled correctly.

9. **(D)** All of the words are spelled correctly.

10. **(C)** "Remitance" is a misspelling of the word "remittance."

11. **(A)** "Prophacy" is a misspelling of the word "prophecy."

12. **(A)** "Potatos" is a misspelling of the word "potatoes."

13. **(C)** "Councel" is a misspelling of the word "counsel" or "council."

14. **(B)** "Mannor" is a misspelling of the word "manner" or "manor."

15. **(D)** All of the words are spelled correctly.

16. **(B)** "Implacation" is a misspelling of the word "implication."

17. **(B)** "Capitel" is a misspelling of the words "capital" or "capitol."

18. **(A)** "Adendum" is a misspelling of the word "addendum."

19. **(A)** "Procesor" is a misspelling of the word "processor."

20. **(D)** All of the words are spelled correctly.

REVIEWING THE KEY STRATEGIES

Remember to:
1. "See" the word.
2. Review your list of commonly misspelled words.
3. Be familiar with basic spelling rules.
4. Be familiar with types of common errors.
5. Keep a personal list of troublesome words.

Verbal Abilities Analysis Chart For Spelling

Use the following chart to carefully analyze your results of the *two different spelling* question types. This will help you evaluate your strengths and weaknesses. This analysis should help you focus your study and review efforts on specific types of problems.

Find the Correct Spelling

Practice Set	Total Number of Questions	Number Correct	Number Incorrect	Number Unanswered
Set 1	20			
Set 2	20			
Set 3	20			
Set 4	20			
Set 5	20			
Set 6	20			

Find the Incorrect Spelling

Practice Set	Total Number of Questions	Number Correct	Number Incorrect	Number Unanswered
Set 1	20			
Set 2	20			
Set 3	20			
Set 4	20			
Set 5	20			

Because there is no penalty for incorrect answers on most of the questions in the Verbal Abilities section, you should have left no question unanswered. Even if you didn't have time to answer a question, you should have at least filled in the answer space with an educated guess.

READING (UNDERSTANDING AND INTERPRETING WRITTEN MATERIAL)

This question type tests your ability to understand the essential meaning of brief paragraphs. No outside information or knowledge is required to answer each question.

Each paragraph is very brief, sometimes no more than one sentence. One question follows each paragraph, with four answer choices.

Helpful Techniques and Strategies for Reading Each Paragraph

1. Each paragraph usually contains only one main idea, often stated in the first sentence. Identify the main idea in the following sample paragraph:

   As the legal profession becomes more specialized and complex, clerical assistance must become more specialized as well. One legal secretary might be an expert in bankruptcy law, another an expert in criminal justice.

   The first sentence, a general statement about increasing specialization in the legal profession states the main idea. It is followed by a more specific statement, which gives additional information. You should practice recognizing this structure: *main idea + additional information.*

2. As you finish reading each paragraph, try to summarize the paragraph mentally, in a few words. For example, after reading the sample paragraph just given, you might summarize it by saying to yourself, "Legal secretaries specialize in different types of law."

3. Note whether the paragraph states a particular attitude toward the subject. Typically, the author will either *approve* or *disapprove* of the main point or remain neutral. In the sample passage just given, the author takes no position pro or con, but delivers the additional information in a matter-of-fact way. Consider the following sample passage:

In the majority of modern families, both husband and wife work full-time. However, many of these couples become more devoted to their jobs than to each other.

Here, the main point receives criticism rather than support. The key to the author's attitude here is the contrast word "however"; when a *contrast word* follows the main point, it may indicate the author's disapproval of the main point.

4. If necessary, read the paragraph twice so that you understand it fully. These paragraphs are so brief that an *occasional* rereading will not seriously shorten your allotted time. However, never reread a paragraph until you have read it completely.

5. Don't dwell on unfamiliar words. Usually the context of a paragraph will help you to understand such words. Consider the following sample passage:

A regular diet of pizza and beer will have deleterious effects. These foods are loaded with fats and carbohydrates, and add more to one's waistline than to physical well-being.

Although "deleterious" may be an unfamiliar word, the remainder of the paragraph makes it clear that the effects of pizza and beer are unhealthy, and suggests that "deleterious" has a meaning similar to "unhealthy."

Helpful Techniques and Strategies for Choosing an Answer

Consider once again a sample paragraph that we examined earlier, this time including a question:

As the legal profession becomes more specialized and complex, clerical assistance must become more specialized as well. One legal secretary might be an expert in bankruptcy law, another an expert in criminal justice.

The paragraph best supports the statement that a legal secretary

A) may understand subjects other than law
B) may have special training in a particular branch of law
C) must be an expert in several types of law
D) is of no use to attorneys

1. When considering the answer choices, try first to eliminate incorrect answers. An incorrect answer often falls into one of three categories:
   a. IRRELEVANT, OR NOT ADDRESSED—Choice (A) is an irrelevant choice. Although particular types of law are mentioned, subjects other than law are not. Note that this statement may certainly be true for some legal secretaries, but receives no support *from the paragraph*.
   b. CONTRADICTORY—Choice (C) contradicts information in the passage. The paragraph discusses legal secretaries who specialize in one type of law, not several.

    c. UNREASONABLE—Choice (D) is an altogether unreasonable statement, according to the paragraph. The passage stresses the special expertise of legal secretaries thus making it unreasonable to conclude that they are useless.

2. In many cases, the correct answer choice will repeat the main point from the paragraph. In this case, the main point is that legal secretaries are becoming more specialized, and the correct answer emphasizes "special training." Notice also that the correct answer here refers as well to the second sentence, which contains additional information about particular branches of law.

    A few more samples:

> A regular diet of pizza and beer may have deleterious effects. These foods are loaded with fats and carbohydrates, and add more to one's waistline than to physical well-being.

The paragraph best supports the statement that pizza and beer

A) should be consumed regularly if they are to have the proper effects
B) should definitely be eaten occasionally
C) can be harmful if they make up the main part of every meal
D) should be consumed separately rather than together

The correct answer is (C); it repeats the main point that pizza and beer, if eaten regularly, can have deleterious (harmful to health) effects. Choice (A) contradicts this point. Choice (B) contradicts the author's negative attitude toward pizza and beer. Choice (D) is irrelevant; the issue whether pizza and beer should be consumed separately or together is not addressed by the passage.

> The belief that positive thinking is the key to success can lead to laziness. It encourages some people to engage in slipshod work, in the hope that an optimistic mental attitude will take the place of hard, careful, dedicated work.

The paragraph best supports the statement that laziness

A) is always the result of positive thinking
B) is practiced by successful people
C) is only permissible after one has completed a hard day's work
D) may result from a reliance on positive thinking

The correct choice is (D), which repeats the main point that "positive thinking . . . can lead to laziness." However, the paragraph does not say that laziness is *always* the result; therefore (A) is not the best answer. Choice (A) *overstates* the main point of the paragraph; the overstatement is evident in the use of the word "always." Choice (B) is unreasonable and is certainly contradicted by the paragraph. Choice (C) is irrelevant; the paragraph does not discuss *when* laziness is permissible.

Practice Set 1

Select the best answer to each question and write the letter of your choice in the space provided.

1. Hundreds of new self-help books _____ have been published over the last decade. These books generally reflect a positive, optimistic approach to modern problems and challenges, informed by current research in psychology.

   The paragraph best supports the statement that the authors of self-help books

   A) are psychologists
   B) may be aware of current research in psychology
   C) are of greatest value to psychologists
   D) have only been published over the last ten years

2. The recent popularity of hot-air _____ ballooning is yet another instance of nostalgia for the past. Certainly these brightly colored floating globes of air are not modern inventions; rather, they recall the spectacle of county fairs and carnivals from the turn of the century.

   The paragraph best supports the statement that hot-air balloons

   A) could be seen at county fairs and carnivals of the past
   B) are more brightly colored today than they were at the turn of the century
   C) are most popular among those who lived at the turn of the century
   D) have been popular in every century

3. It has been said that a weed is a _____ flower whose virtue has not yet been discovered. As if to prove this point, a number of home-owners who are tired of constantly maintaining a pretty lawn and shrubbery have decided to let weeds run wild in their yards. The result, in some cases, has been quite an attractive array of lively shapes and colors.

   The paragraph best supports the statement that

   A) weeds are not flowers
   B) weeds make a pretty lawn even prettier
   C) weeds can be beautiful
   D) most homeowners prefer to let weeds run wild

4. Although every individual is _____ thinking constantly during the course of every day, no one is aware of his thoughts very often. Just walking a few steps entails a number of mental choices and activities that are performed more or less unconsciously. To become conscious of everything going on in the mind would be immobilizing.

   The paragraph best supports the statement that unconscious mental choices

   A) are performed by everyone every day
   B) are most dangerous when one is not thinking
   C) are immobilizing
   D) occur every few steps

5. Science fiction and fantasy have _____ always appealed to the desire to escape from the boredom of conventional life and to experience the adventure and danger of a new environment. Thrilling to the excitement of *Star Wars* is a way of "getting away from it all."

The paragraph best supports the statement that Star Wars

A) is popular only with those who are bored with life
B) provides excitement that conventional life does not
C) is the best example of science fiction and fantasy
D) is more thrilling than any other science fiction movie

6. Hitting a baseball is certainly one _____ of the most difficult feats in sports. Even the greatest hitters of all time have been able only to hit safely once for every three trips to the plate. In other words, even great hitters fail more often than they succeed.

The paragraph best supports the statement that

A) nothing succeeds like success
B) it is unrealistic to expect to get a hit more than once in three tries
C) great hitters must get used to being failures
D) the difficulty of hitting a baseball causes many potential ballplayers to avoid the sport

7. The microwave oven has become _____ a standard appliance in many kitchens, mainly because it offers a fast way of cooking food, and therefore appeals to the growing number of households whose members maintain busy schedules, and have little time for the slow, conventional preparation of a meal.

The paragraph best supports the statement that the microwave oven appeals to

A) everyone living in a busy household
B) those who need time to maintain a busy schedule in the kitchen
C) those who need more standard appliances in the kitchen
D) those who are not able to spend much time cooking

8. Clarity, correctness, and coherence are certainly elements of good _____ writing, but interest is the most important element of all; writing that does not provoke and hold a reader's attention rarely succeeds as effective communication.

The paragraph best supports the statement that

A) clarity, correctness, and coherence are not important elements of good writing
B) good writers are always interesting people
C) it is possible for writing to be correct without being interesting
D) writing is the most effective means of communication

9. Because so many educators have _____ concluded that interacting with students is more effective than dominating and commanding them, student-centered classrooms (typified by open discussion and sharing) have become more numerous than teacher-centered classrooms (typified by passive attention to lectures).

The paragraph best supports the statement that the number of student-centered classrooms

A) is larger than the number of teacher-centered classrooms
B) has been approved by educators
C) means that students are learning more than they ever have before
D) suggests that there are more students dominating teachers than there are teachers dominating students

10. Despite numerous medical studies _____ that publicize health risks associated with caffeine, Americans continue to consume coffee in huge quantities. For most, the benefits of coffee apparently outweigh the dangers.

The paragraph best supports the statement that caffeine

A) is included in all brands of coffee
B) is a popular drink in America
C) receives unwarranted attention from the medical profession
D) is the victim of careless scientific research

Answer Explanations for Practice Set 1

1. **(B)** The paragraph states that self-help books are "generally . . . informed by current research in psychology." However, just because these books may contain research in psychology, they are not necessarily authored by psychologists, so (A) is not the best choice.
2. **(A)** The paragraph associates present-day hot-air balloons with those seen at county fairs and carnivals at the turn of the century.
3. **(C)** The passage states that a collection of weeds can be quite attractive.
4. **(A)** The paragraph states that every day "a number of mental choices" are performed "more or less unconsciously."
5. **(B)** The paragraph states that science fiction and fantasy (of which "Star Wars" is an example) provide "escape from the boredom of conventional life."

6. **(B)** Since even the greatest hitters hit safely only once in three tries, we may logically conclude that it is unrealistic to expect to do better than this.
7. **(D)** The paragraph says that the microwave oven appeals to those who have "little time" for the slow preparation of a meal.
8. **(C)** By emphasizing that interest is more important than correctness, the paragraph strongly implies that it is possible for writing to be correct without being interesting.
9. **(A)** Each of the other choices requires assumptions not supported by the paragraph. The paragraph does explicitly state that student-centered classrooms "have become more numerous" than teacher-centered classrooms.
10. **(B)** The paragraph explicitly states that "Americans . . . consume coffee in huge quantities."

Practice Set 2

Select the best answer to each question and write the letter of your choice in the space provided.

1. Comedy is an art that is constantly _____ changing. What was funny a few years ago seems merely silly now, mainly because the public tastes and public issues that are the substance of comedy have themselves changed. New events result in new blunders, and provide the material for new jokes.

   The paragraph best supports the statement that

   A) today's jokes are different than they were years ago
   B) today's jokes refer only to current events
   C) comedians are finding it difficult to write new material
   D) comedy writers are constantly changing

2. Being new and different does not _____ ensure the success of a product. Advertisers must see to it that buyers who will use the product hear about it; they must place their advertising in the right spot. Little is gained by advertising denture adhesive during a Saturday morning cartoon show.

   The paragraph best supports the statement that

   A) Saturday morning cartoon shows do not contain advertisements
   B) Saturday morning cartoon shows only advertise products that are not new and different
   C) most buyers are shopping rather than watching television on Saturday mornings
   D) those who use denture adhesive are not likely to be the viewers of Saturday morning cartoon shows

3. Some American auto factories are _____ beginning to resemble their Japanese counterparts. In many Japanese factories, the workers enjoy the same status and privileges as their bosses. Everyone works in harmony, and there is much less of the tension and anger that results when one group dominates another.

   The paragraph best supports the statement that

   A) everyone works in harmony in Japan
   B) workers and bosses share the same status in some American factories
   C) there is one main cause of tension and anger
   D) Japanese factories have been influenced by the success of the American auto industry

4. Scientists persist in their efforts _____ to improve on nature. Making advances in genetic engineering, some researchers expect to invent new forms of life soon. One bacterium under development can consume and digest toxic wastes, and thus help clean up the environment.

   The paragraph best supports the statement that

   A) toxic wastes pose the most serious environmental problem, as far as scientists are concerned
   B) it is the responsibility of scientists to improve on nature
   C) a bacterium that can consume and digest toxic wastes would be a new form of life
   D) inventing new forms of life takes persistence

5. The foliage and ground cover _____ growing along the nation's super-highways serve at least two functions. They help make traveling a more pleasant visual experience, and they help absorb the noise of thousands of automobile engines.

The paragraph best supports the statement that

A) foliage and ground cover are planted along superhighways for more than one reason
B) automobile engines become less noisy on superhighways
C) there are only two reasons for planting foliage and ground cover along superhighways
D) pleasant scenery results in safer driving

6. An emphasis on orderly behavior _____ and discipline in junior high school and high school prepares young adults to join the work force upon graduation, where they must adhere to rules and regulations. But a school experience that does not encourage free expression, individuality, and creativity may produce obedient workers who are not able to think for themselves.

The paragraph best supports the statement that junior high school and high school

A) are not educating young adults properly
B) do not employ teachers who can think for themselves
C) should encourage qualities other than orderly behavior and discipline
D) punish those who are creative

7. Comic strips can often provide a _____ commentary on everyday life, along with entertainment. The characters from "Peanuts," for instance, represent types of people that everyone encounters regularly: the bumbling nice guy; the brash, insensitive loudmouth; and the student for whom school is a bore.

The paragraph best supports the statement that the characters in "Peanuts"

A) do not represent particular individuals
B) handle real life better than real people
C) represent the three most common types of people one encounters in everyday life
D) appear in other comic strips as well

8. In the 1930s, the first modern _____ health spas were built, complete with efficient exercise equipment, swimming pools, and full-service locker rooms. But health spas did not become wildly popular until the 1980s; now one cannot travel very far in any big city without seeing one.

The paragraph best supports the statement that the popularity of health spas

A) is the result of improved exercise equipment
B) could not be measured in the 1930s
C) has increased since the 1930s
D) only exists in big cities

9. Poets who wish to compose a Japa- _____
nese haiku must follow a formula:
There are three lines in all, a first
line of five syllables, a second line
of seven syllables, and a third line
of five syllables. The restriction to
precisely seventeen syllables makes
the haiku form quite difficult to
master.

*The paragraph best supports the statement
that* writing a haiku

A) is difficult for someone who is not
Japanese
B) may include more than three lines
C) extends beyond thirty-five syllables in
special cases
D) is not an easy task, even though the
form of the poem is simple

10. The length and structure of the _____
workweek have undergone a good
deal of change in recent years.
Workers who once labored eight
hours each day, forty hours each
week, Monday through Friday,
are now allowed to determine
their own schedules to some
extent. Those who are able to
complete assigned tasks efficiently
and effectively during a shortened
or irregular schedule, or those who
can work better during different
hours from the standard ones, are
allowed an adjusted schedule by
some companies.

*The paragraph best supports the statement
that* some workers

A) are unable to work efficiently and
effectively
B) may work on Saturday or Sunday
C) are employed by old-fashioned companies
D) work much more than forty hours each
week

Answer Explanations for Practice Set 2

1. **(A)** The paragraph repeatedly stresses that
what is funny now is different from what
was funny in the past.

2. **(D)** The paragraph stresses that advertising
must be placed in the "right spots" and concludes by implying that a cartoon show is
not the right spot to appeal to "buyers who
will use the product."

3. **(B)** The passage states that some American
factories are beginning to operate like those
in Japan, relative to the relationship between
workers and bosses.

4. **(C)** The "bacterium under development" is
mentioned as an example of "new forms of
life."

5. **(A)** The passage states that foliage and
ground cover "serve at least two functions."

6. **(C)** The passage calls for the encourage-
ment of "free expression, individuality, and
creativity."

7. **(A)** The passage states that the comic strip's
characters represent "types of people," thus
strongly implying that they do not represent
particular individuals.

8. **(C)** The paragraph states that health spas
became "wildly popular" in the 1980s.

9. **(D)** The paragraph states explicitly that the
haiku form is "quite difficult to master."

10. **(B)** The paragraph stresses that some
workers no longer work during the standard, Monday through Friday, workweek;
this fact strongly implies that some workers
may work on Saturday or Sunday. The
paragraph does not suggest, however, that
the workweek has become longer than forty
hours, so (D) is not the best answer.

Practice Set 3

Select the best answer to each question and write the letter of your choice in the space provided.

1. The relationship between architecture and geometry becomes apparent once one surveys the newest buildings under construction in metropolitan areas. Each structure is a precise combination of triangles, rectangles, and trapezoids, arranged so that angles jut out in unusual places, in an array of lively designs.

   The paragraph best supports the statement that new buildings

   A) are more pleasant to look at than old ones
   B) utilize a number of geometric shapes
   C) were constructed to reflect a love of geometry
   D) are designed to teach geometry to observers

2. Fast food is becoming more nutritious. Salad bars are appearing at places that only served hamburgers once, offering diners the benefits of fresh vegetables. And the menus are expanding in other directions as well, offering chicken sandwiches on whole wheat buns, and low-fat yogurt desserts. With families cooking less often and eating out more often, the diet provided by fast-food chains has a great impact on the health of the nation; it would seem that the budget restaurants are taking seriously their responsibility to nourish us.

   The paragraph best supports the statement that the improved nutrition of fast food is

   A) affecting the health of many people
   B) probably only a temporary trend
   C) mainly based on the availability of more fresh vegetables
   D) a response to widespread malnutrition

3. Few people understand poetry, _____ and few prefer to read it. Although English professors speak in glowing terms about the greatness of Pope's *Rape of the Lock* and Tennyson's *Ulysses*, it seems that only other professors share their enthusiasm. To appreciate the greatness of difficult poetry, readers must exercise great patience and concentration, and must tolerate the unusual, compressed language of rhythm and rhyme; with so many urgent issues demanding our attention at almost every hour of the day, choosing to figure out a poem seems an unlikely possibility.

The paragraph best supports the statement that poetry is popular

A) because so many people love the satisfaction that comes from understanding a great poem
B) because English professors have generated enthusiasm in so many of their students
C) with those who love rhymes
D) with a small, specialized group

4. Those who try to increase their _____ vocabulary by memorizing words and definitions are wasting time. Only by employing language in real situations do we make it familiar. Therefore, the most effective way to learn a new word is to use it, again and again.

The paragraph best supports the statement that people can increase their vocabulary by

A) memorizing more than just word lists and definitions
B) using only the words they need to use
C) creating situations that require unusual language
D) using new words whenever possible

5. Meteorology may qualify as a _____ science, but there is a great deal of guesswork involved as well. Even with tremendous knowledge about wind currents and weather patterns, and the most sophisticated equipment, forecasters' predictions are often wrong. The movement of a phenomenon as prominent as a hurricane cannot even be determined very far in advance. We remain the servants and victims of the weather, not its masters.

The paragraph best supports the statement that the science of weather prediction

A) is accurate only when the weather is fair
B) is useless when it comes to hurricanes
C) is not yet sophisticated enough to achieve accuracy consistently
D) does not qualify as a science

6. More children die each year from _____ automobile accidents than from any other single cause. This fact should be sufficient to force each of the 50 states to enact a mandatory seat belt law, but such laws have not yet swept the country. If we are to preserve our most precious natural resource, however, we must take steps that make buckling up imperative everywhere.

The paragraph best supports the statement that children are

A) our most precious natural resource
B) ignored in most states
C) not willing to wear seat belts
D) dying more frequently than ever

7. A baseball game can be described _____ as a series of solo performances: at any given moment, attention is focused on one player and one play. On the other hand, soccer involves all of the team most of the time: each player interacts with others constantly, so that no single individual seems responsible for success or failure. It is perhaps because spectators enjoy concentrating on individual personalities that baseball remains a much more popular spectator sport than soccer.

The paragraph best supports the statement that the popularity of baseball

A) will always be greater than the popularity of soccer
B) cannot be compared to the popularity of soccer
C) may be related to the preferences of spectators
D) will remain strong as long as individual players maintain their skills

8. Modern word processing equipment makes the preparation of business correspondence easier and more efficient, perhaps. Typing errors disappear from the monitor at the touch of a button, and the final printout takes only seconds to produce. However, some typists have not yet become comfortable with staring at a text displayed on a screen; they are used to black letters on a white background, and cannot perceive textual errors as readily when faced with white letters on a dark background.

The paragraph best supports the statement that the typing errors that appear on a word processor screen

A) are more serious than those that appear on paper
B) are more difficult for some typists to recognize
C) disappear before they can be corrected
D) are more modern than errors produced on a typewriter

9. Student protesters are more polite _____ than they used to be. One need only recall the violent riots of the 1960s, led by ragged, long-haired political activists, to notice the difference that prevails today: while the demonstrators of yesteryear yelled obscenities at the police and openly flouted civic regulations, today's demonstrators cooperate almost meekly with law enforcement officials, maintaining a neat, orderly, peaceful display while they express political dissent.

The paragraph best supports the statement that

A) today's protesters are not as effective as the protesters of the 1960s
B) law enforcement officials encounter less hostility from protesters now than they did in the 1960s
C) today's protesters wear nice clothes and have short hair
D) civic regulations have changed since the 1960s, and are not so offensive to protesters anymore

10. Everyone who collects books is _____ not an avid reader. Some prefer to fill their homes with shelves of novels, travelogues, and self-help guides for the purpose of display and decoration only. They enjoy the accessibility of knowledge and information, but rarely partake of the storehouse.

The paragraph best supports the statement that those who buy books

A) prefer only novels, travelogues, and self-help guides
B) decorate their homes with books alone
C) have added a storehouse onto their home
D) do not necessarily read them

Answer Explanations for Practice Set 3

1. **(B)** The passage states that new buildings display geometric shapes: triangles, rectangles, and trapezoids.
2. **(A)** The paragraph states that the availability of more nutritious fast food "has a great impact on the health of the nation."
3. **(D)** The paragraph states that poetry seems to be popular mainly with professors (2nd sentence); professors are a small, specialized group.
4. **(D)** All the other choices contradict the inforniation in the passage; (D) repeats the point of the third sentence.
5. **(C)** Several times the passage makes the point that predicting the weather involves "a great deal of guesswork" and can be inaccurate.

6. **(A)** The value of children is stressed throughout the passage, and they are called "our most precious natural resource" in the final sentence.
7. **(C)** The final sentence of the paragraph proposes that what the spectators enjoy (individual personalities) mav determine the greater popularity of baseball.
8. **(B)** The passage states that "some typists . . . cannot perceive textual errors as readily" on a word processor screen.
9. **(B)** The major change emphasized in the passage is the increased cooperation with law enforcement officials.
10. **(D)** The paragraph explicitly states that every collector of books "is not an avid reader."

Practice Set 4

Select the best answer to each question and write the letter of your choice in the space provided.

1. The federal government is becoming more vigilant when it comes to toxic waste. Probably as a result of widespread press coverage of the Love Canal disaster a few years ago, politicians and bureaucrats are more sensitive to heightened public attention to mismanaged chemical dumps and the health hazards they pose. Heavy fines are being imposed upon those who have ignored regulations about safe waste disposal.

   _____

   The paragraph best supports the statement that the Love Canal disaster

   A) was the first disaster of its kind
   B) led to a number of other, more serious disasters involving unsafe waste disposal
   C) was the first disaster that attracted the attention of the federal government
   D) involved the issue of toxic waste

2. Sociologists have noted that children today are less "childish" than ever; when they are still very young, perhaps only six or seven years old, children are already mimicking adult fashions and leading relatively independent lives. Dressed in designer jeans, an elementary school child is likely to spend much of every day fending for herself, taking charge of her own life while waiting for her working parents to arrive home. Less dependent on adults for their day-to-day decisions, children "grow up" faster.

   _____

   The paragraph best supports the statement that children today are

   A) likely to wear only fashion jeans
   B) likely to be more intelligent than children of six or seven years ago
   C) not interested in the opinions of their parents
   D) likely to have parents who are employed outside the home during the day

3. The new American revolution is ———— an electronic one. Advances in sophisticated circuitry have yielded more gadgets than anyone could have imagined only a few years ago: calculators as small as a wristwatch and automobile dashboards full of digital readouts are two of the many products that have enhanced the quality of life. There is some fear, however, that we may become so dependent on solid-state circuits to do our thinking that we may forget how to do it ourselves.

The paragraph best supports the statement that although progress in electronic progress has improved the quality of life, it

A) may, affect our ability to think independently
B) has merely provided gadgets
C) has made those who use electronic devices more afraid of them than ever
D) is not nearly as sophisticated as it will become in the next century

4. There are advantages and disad- ———— vantages to clear, simple writing. Sentences that are easy to understand are processed more quickly and efficiently by readers; those who can express themselves in simple terms are rarely misunderstood. However, prose that is crystal clear often lacks both complexity and imagination. Whether one chooses a style that is simple and clear or complex and unusual often depends upon the tolerance of one's readers.

The paragraph best supports the statement that more tolerant readers will

A) be less willing to read simple and clear writing
B) be more willing to read complex and unusual writing
C) be confused easily
D) demand writing that is complex, unusual, and easy to misunderstand

5. Years ago, a nationwide poll con- _____
cluded that there are more televisions than there are bathtubs in
American homes. No doubt that
fact remains today, especially in
light of the growing popularity of
home computers. Now, in addition to owning televisions for
entertainment, more and more
families are purchasing TV moni-
tors for use with a personal computer. We can guess safely that
there are still many more people
staring at a picture tube than
singing in the shower.

*The paragraph best supports the statement
that*

A) cleanliness is less important to
Americans than it used to be
B) most homes do not require more than
one bathtub
C) the general results of the nationwide
poll taken years ago are still true
D) few people have televisions in the
bathroom

6. Some have called Californians the _____
nomads of America. While those
living in the Midwest, the South,
and the East tend to reside in the
same place for a number of years,
Californians change addresses regularly. The constant mobility of
California residents helps to keep
the real estate industry in that
state thriving.

*The paragraph best supports the statement
that* real estate sales

A) are related to how frequently a
population changes addresses
B) have always been better in California
than in any other state
C) are more important to Californians
than to the residents of other states
D) are virtually nonexistent outside
California

7. Recently, cable television firms _____
have faced stiff competition from
the home video industry. Given
the choice of either renting movies
for home viewing or subscribing
to a cable service that offers recent
films, consumers are choosing the
rentals. Many say that local video
stores offer a wider choice of
movies than any cable station, and
that renting movies allows viewers
the freedom to watch them at any
time, so they are not tied to the
cable station schedule.

*The paragraph best supports the statement
that* consumers

A) prefer to rent movies rather than buy
them
B) value freedom of choice
C) would like to upgrade the quality of
cable television firms
D) watch a greater number of movies than
cable television firms have been able to
provide

8. A recent experiment in psychology yielded results that are difficult to interpret. Researchers found that whenever the light bulbs were changed in the workplace, production increased. Although the brightness in the room neither increased nor decreased, the workers worked better each time a custodial crew changed the bulbs. Perhaps just the sight of the light bulbs being changed led the workers to feel that conditions had improved, and to work better.

The paragraph best supports the statement that the results of the psychology experiment

A) will lead to a continual increase in production
B) had no effect on the work of the custodial crew
C) lead to no definite conclusions
D) will be used to improve working conditions in a number of companies

9. Some teachers prefer "creative" writers, and some prefer "correct" writers. Rarely does one encounter a student who writes unconventional and exciting prose while also obeying all the rules and conventions of standard written English. It may be impossible for any writer to be both radical and obedient at the same time.

The paragraph best supports the statement that a writer who is both creative and correct

A) is rarely successful in school
B) is preferred by half of the teachers he encounters
C) tends to confuse being radical with being obedient
D) knows how to deviate from the rules of standard written English

10. Many aviators are also avid sailors, perhaps because the principles of flying are so similar to the principles of sailing, so that participants in both sports enjoy the thrill of riding the wind.

The paragraph best supports the statement that

A) learning to sail qualifies one to fly an airplane
B) flying is most thrilling on windy days
C) many aviators are sailors, but no sailors are aviators
D) many aviators, when not flying, enjoy sailing

Answer Explanations for Practice Set 4

1. **(D)** The paragraph discusses government attention to toxic waste, and the Love Canal disaster is cited as a specific example.

2. **(D)** The individual who represents "children today" in the paragraph waits "for her working parents to arrive home"; the strong implication here is that the parents are employed outside the home.

3. **(A)** The final sentence of the paragraph contrasts the enhanced quality of life with the possibility that electronic devices may "do our thinking" for us.

4. **(B)** The paragraph associates a writer's chosen style with the tolerance of readers and implies that complex and unusual writing requires more tolerant readers because it is not understood as "quickly and efficiently" as simple and clear writing.

5. **(C)** The paragraph states that the "fact remains today" that there are more televisions than bathtubs in American homes.

6. **(A)** The passage associates the "mobility of California residents" with a thriving real estate industry, but does not support any of the other possible choices.

7. **(B)** The paragraph states that consumers prefer the freedom to choose both their movies and their viewing time.

8. **(C)** Although the paragraph reaches a conclusion that is "perhaps" true, it emphasizes that the results of the experiment "are difficult to interpret," and states no definite conclusions.

9. **(D)** The creative and correct writer knows the rules and also knows how to write "unconventional" prose, that is, prose that deviates from the rules.

10. **(D)** The paragraph explicitly states that "many aviators are also avid sailors."

Practice Set 5

Select the best answer to each question and write the letter of your choice in the space provided.

1. Historians accept the fact that _____ writing history requires interpreting the past, not just cataloguing it. As a mere collection of facts, the history of the Civil War means nothing; only when the facts are analyzed and explained does this event become significant.

The paragraph best supports the statement that a list of facts about the Civil War is

A) what most historians are interested in
B) mistaken for history by those who are not historians
C) not so important as the analysis and explanation of those facts
D) usually too dull for any historian

2. The automobile engine is an un- _____ appreciated marvel. Consider its durability alone, as it endures tens of thousands of miles of wear and tear over years and years, and still starts up every morning.

The paragraph best supports the statement that those who drive automobiles

A) abuse their automobile engines
B) do not usually consider the amazing durability of the engine
C) run the engine longer than they should
D) know almost nothing about how an automobile engine works

3. Babe Ruth still holds the official _____ record for the most home runs hit in one season. Roger Maris hit 61 home runs, to top Ruth's record of 60, but Maris batted in 162 games, compared to 154 games for Ruth.

The paragraph best supports the statement that Roger Maris

A) played in a number of unofficial baseball games, but hit home runs in none of them
B) did not hit a home run again after the season in which he hit 61
C) probably had more chances to hit home runs, during the season, than Babe Ruth did
D) was a more powerful hitter than Babe Ruth, despite the existence of Ruth's record

4. Many gamblers seem unwilling to _____ admit that chance and luck largely determine who wins and loses. Many develop elaborate schemes and systems for winning at blackjack and roulette, but only very few leave the casino wealthier than when they entered.

The paragraph best supports the statement that a system for winning at blackjack

A) depends to a great extent upon chance and luck for its success
B) should only be used by gamblers who consider themselves lucky
C) can also be useful for winning at roulette and other casino games
D) has been tried by many gamblers who have relied on chance and luck as well

5. Secretaries must be experts in _____ human relations as well as office procedures. Much of their time every day is spent advising and counseling others about programs and policies, and repeatedly adjusting to the variety of persons and personalities that visits the office each day.

The paragraph best supports the statement that the ability to interact effectively with a variety of different people

A) should not be expected of a secretary, even though it is a valuable skill
B) is only useful during the times that the office is very busy
C) is a very important and necessary secretarial skill
D) should only be demanded of secretaries who have had extensive training in human relations

6. Social observers have noted that _____ "stress," which is such a popular affliction in this decade, was virtually unheard of in the recent past. Our grandparents accorded no special status to everyday tension, and they seem to have experienced less of such tension than we do now. If "stress" did not receive so much publicity these days, perhaps many of us would not feel compelled to suffer from it.

The paragraph best supports the statement that the widespread publicity of stress

A) is something that those of past generations would not have allowed
B) may actually influence the occurrence of stress
C) never compelled our grandparents to pay any attention to everyday tension
D) has gone unnoticed by many of us

7. A neat, orderly workplace encourages calmness and efficiency, just as a messy workplace provokes tension and wastefulness. In other words, the qualities of the workplace draw out related qualities in the workers.

The paragraph best supports the statement that the appearance of a workplace

A) is usually neat and orderly
B) is completely dependent on the abilities of the workers
C) can affect the behavior of the workers
D) must be maintained on a regular basis, just as personal qualities such as wastefulness must be maintained on a regular basis.

8. For inexperienced writers, often the most difficult task is writing an introduction. Therefore, it is sometimes best to delay writing the introductory paragraph until after the body, or "middle" of the essay, is complete.

The paragraph best supports the statement that

A) experienced writers may not need to delay writing the introductory paragraph
B) experienced writers must always write the introductory paragraph before writing the body of the essay
C) without first reading the body of the essay, inexperienced writers cannot tell what they are supposed to write about
D) the introductory paragraph is always a disaster for inexperienced writers

9. As digital clocks replace tradiional, radial timepieces, the connection between time and the rotation of the earth is less evident. As the hands of a radial clock move in a circle, from hour to hour, they mimic the turning of the earth on its axis, during the course of each twenty-four-hour day.

The paragraph best supports the statement that the movement of a radial clock

A) reminds everyone of the rotation of the sun around the earth
B) is less accurate, but more natural, than the movement of a digital clock
C) only pretends to duplicate the rotation of the earth
D) is significantly different from the movement of a digital clock

10. The interior design of a restaurant can invite customers to either dine leisurely, or eat and run. Dark, soft upholstery and soft lighting are conducive to a long, relaxed meal; on the other hand, stiff, thinly padded chairs and brightly illuminated dining areas seem to keep people from remaining for very long.

The paragraph best supports the statement that the length of time that one spends at a restaurant meal

A) is usually spent relaxing in a dark atmosphere
B) can vary with the quality of the food as well as the interior design of the restaurant
C) may be affected by the interior design of the restaurant
D) is never pleasant when the room is brightly lit and the chairs are thinly padded

Answer Explanations for Practice Set 5

1. **(C)** The paragraph stresses that analysis and explanation, rather than facts alone, are important to historians.
2. **(B)** The passage calls the automobile engine an "unappreciated marvel" and follows with a discussion of engine durability, thus implying that drivers do not usually consider the durability of the engine.
3. **(C)** The paragraph states that Maris hit 61 home runs in a season that was longer than the season during which Ruth set his record; therefore, we may conclude that Maris probably had more chances than Ruth to hit home runs.
4. **(A)** The paragraph states explicitly that "chance and luck largely determine who wins and loses."
5. **(C)** The importance of "adjusting to the variety of persons and personalities" is emphasized in the paragraph.
6. **(B)** The final sentence suggests a relationship between the publicity of stress and the occurrence of it.
7. **(C)** The paragraph compares the appearance of the workplace with the "qualities in the workers," pointing out that the workers are affected by the workplace.
8. **(A)** The paragraph suggests that inexperienced writers may need to delay writing the introductory paragraph, and thus implies that experienced writers may not need to delay writing the introductory paragraph.
9. **(D)** The passage contrasts digital clocks with radial timepieces, in the first sentence.
10. **(C)** It is the interior design of the restaurant that invites customers "to either dine leisurely, or eat and run."

Practice Set 6

Select the best answer to each question and write the letter of your choice in the space provided.

1. Any voice heard over the phone is _____ associated with a face and personality, which are sometimes not at all appropriate to the actual person who is speaking. In other words, the telephone can be both an invaluable tool for communication and a source of mistaken impressions.

   The paragraph best supports the statement that the way a person sounds over the phone

   A) will lead a listener to accurately imagine a face and personality
   B) will always fool a listener who is curious about what face and personality match the voice
   C) is often distorted by the mistaken impressions of the telephone
   D) may not always match the face and personality of the person

2. Teachers in several regions are _____ being asked to take competency tests in order to demonstrate their educational preparation and literacy skills. Recently, some officials emphasized the need for a national test for teachers, and some teachers' groups responded angrily.

   The paragraph best supports the statement that

   A) some teachers' groups do not believe that teachers can pass a competency test
   B) the competency tests already in use have received no angry responses
   C) the institution of a national competency test for teachers is a controversial issue
   D) the results of competency tests accurately reflect the educational preparation and literacy skills of teachers

3. Those who find themselves _____ without the time to sit down and read a good book are listening to books instead. A number of literary classics have been recorded on audio cassettes and have become popular with busy professionals as well as with homemakers.

The paragraph best supports the statement that the time required to read books

A) may be used by some people for tasks other than reading
B) is better spent listening to books on audio cassettes
C) is less available today than it was earlier in this century
D) is probably spent on audio and video entertainment

4. The dozens of different languages _____ spoken today may have a common root. A number of linguists and historians believe that the Indo-European language, spoken thousands of years ago, was the basis for many of the languages of more modern times. The precise nature of the Indo-European language is, however, very difficult to determine.

The paragraph best supports the statement that

A) Indo-European is no longer spoken anywhere in the world
B) there were dozens of different ancient languages that were all called Indo-European
C) linguists and historians are no longer interested in the precise nature of Indo-European
D) Indo-European is not the only language that was spoken

5. Although reference books such _____ as a dictionary, thesaurus, and grammar handbook are part of any writer's library, they are not usually consulted with regularity. Too much time looking into reference works leaves little time for the writing itself.

The paragraph best supports the statement that a writer's reference books

A) are best left untouched by any writer who wishes to be productive
B) may be books other than a dictionary, thesaurus, and grammar handbook
C) always require a great deal of time to consult
D) are indispensable for writers, but do not often improve the quality of any writer's work

6. When one is pressed to complete a writing task within a brief time limit, it is often useful to rely on a standard formula for organizing the writing. One very useful formula for writing the first paragraph of an essay is abbreviated TRI, topic-restriction-illustration. Using this formula, one first writes a very general sentence (topic), and then follows with a more focused statement (restriction) and a mention of the examples that will be discussed (illustration).

The paragraph best supports the statement that

A) writing within a brief time limit is very difficult for anyone who does not use a standard formula
B) the time available for writing may determine whether using a formula is necessary
C) those who rely on TRI for writing paragraphs will complete writing tasks more quickly than those who do not
D) there are no standard formulas for writing the paragraphs that follow the first one

7. A skillful typist is much more than a transcriber of words. Given a rough draft filled with scribbles and awkward phrases, the typist must not only type the copy, but also decipher and make clear ideas that the original writer left vague.

The paragraph best supports the statement that

A) typists do not always receive rough drafts that are neat and clear
B) typists prefer to revise and correct the writer's rough draft
C) all typists have worked for writers who were imaginative but not able to produce a clear rough draft
D) most typists expect that a rough draft will be difficult to read

8. At most major universities, the availability of parking spaces is a substantial problem. There are always far fewer spaces than there are students, faculty, and staff who drive to school, and unless one arrives very early in the morning, the likelihood of securing a space is slim indeed.

The paragraph best supports the statement that many people who attend major universities

A) arrive early in the morning
B) do not park on campus
C) are not bothered by parking problems
D) prefer to walk to school

9. When individual personalities _____ conflict, the best solution is honesty and compromise. Only by airing the problem and discussing mutually agreeable terms for solving it, can a group put conflict behind them and get on with useful work.

The paragraph best supports the statement that when a conflict arises between individuals

A) honesty on the part of either individual is unusual
B) solving the problem is much more difficult than continuing to work together
C) one of the individuals is not willing to be honest and compromise
D) an individual who refuses to compromise is an obstacle to solving the problem

10. With advances in medical tech- _____ nology, and increased public interest in exercise and nutrition, the average life expectancy in America continues to increase, and consequently, the average age of the population continues to rise. America is getting older.

The paragraph best supports the statement that exercise and nutrition

A) have offset the decay of American culture
B) are less advanced than medical technology, but more interesting to the public
C) have contributed to longer lives, and affected the average age of the population
D) are most valuable before one passes the average age of the population

Answer Explanations for Practice Set 6

1. **(D)** The paragraph implies that listeners will not always *accurately* imagine the face and personality associated with a voice on the telephone, so (A) is not the best choice. (D) sums up the overall point of the paragraph.

2. **(C)** The paragraph states that "some officials" and "some teachers' groups" disagree about the need for a national competency test; such disagreement makes the issue controversial, rather than agreeable to all.

3. **(A)** The paragraph stresses the popularity of books on cassettes and suggests that some people are listening to books rather than reading them, thus spending the time during which they might be reading in other ways.

4. **(A)** While (D) may be true, in general, it is not supported by information in the passage. Because the passage states that Indo-European is an ancient language that remains more or less unknown today, we may

conclude that it is no longer spoken; otherwise, its nature would not be "difficult to determine."

5. **(B)** Each of the other choices is an extreme conclusion that extends beyond the information in the paragraph. In the paragraph, the particular books mentioned are offered as examples of reference books in general and are not referred to as the *only* reference books useful or available to a writer.

6. **(B)** The paragraph mentions "time limit" as a factor related to using a formula for writing. Each of the other choices may be true in general, but none is supported by the paragraph.

7. **(A)** The paragraph describes a rough draft that is neither neat nor clear as something that a typist may receive.

8. **(B)** The availability of "far fewer spaces" than drivers allows us to conclude that many people do not park on campus.

9. **(D)** The paragraph connects compromise with the "best solution" and allows us to conclude that a solution is blocked by one who is unwilling to compromise.

10. **(C)** The passage explicitly states that exercise and nutrition have caused Americans to live longer.

Practice Set 7

Select the best answer to each question and write the letter of your choice in the space provided.

1. Most college graduates do not _____ pursue a career relevant to their college major. Part of the reason for this is fast-changing job market, which creates new jobs and job categories, and eliminates old jobs and job categories at such a rapid pace that college training in a particular area may become obsolete very quickly.

The paragraph best supports the statement that a student entering college today

A) will encounter a much-changed job market when she graduates
B) will be unable to find a job when she graduates
C) will need to create a new job for herself, taking account of the old jobs that have been eliminated
D) should not pursue a major that is not relevant to the future job market

2. The past is the mirror of the _____ present. By studying history we encounter the same general problems that cultures and societies face today, and we learn possible solutions to those problems. We may also learn that some problems can never be absolutely solved.

The paragraph best supports the statement that history

A) always provides the necessary solutions to modern social problems
B) makes the solution of modern problems even more difficult
C) is a source of solutions that may be used to address problems in modern times
D) does not necessarily repeat itself

3. Perhaps it is true, as the old saying ———— goes, that knowledge is power. But sometimes knowledge brings pain rather than power: the more we learn and the more we read, the more we realize that the world is filled with violence and corruption. This knowledge may leave us feeling more powerless than powerful.

The paragraph best supports the statement that knowledge

A) may be possible only after violence and corruption are eliminated forever
B) is mainly the result of reading about violence and corruption
C) may not lead to power
D) really exists only in old sayings, and is rarely available from any other source

4. Office procedures are not inflexi- ———— ble. Although each employee has been assigned specific tasks to be performed at specific times, all must be sensitive to the needs and problems of others and help out whenever necessary. In order to be ready to help, everyone is advised to become familiar with the jobs and responsibilities of others, to become as skilled as possible in as many different tasks as possible.

The paragraph best supports the statement that

A) assisting co-workers is important and desirable
B) most employees are not willing to help one another
C) some employees are more skilled than others
D) learning many different tasks is difficult

5. With expert clerical assistance, a ———— business executive is free to concentrate on important issues and decisions, and can rely on the staff to give expert attention to correspondence, bookkeeping, and appointments. Without expert clerical assistance, an executive must compromise her talents and her time. Clearly, it is the clerical staff that allows any executive to be an executive, a talented staff guarantees that business will thrive.

The paragraph best supports the statement that expert attention to correspondence, bookkeeping, and appointments

A) utilizes the talents and time of some business executives
B) leaves the staff free to concentrate on other issues
C) are tasks that all executives should master
D) are best accomplished by a talented staff

6. In most cases, prefer active verbs _____ to passive verbs. A sentence such as "The salaries were raised by the board of directors," should be revised to read, "The board of directors raised the salaries." In this case, and in so many others, the active construction results in a more economical statement, one that is understood more quickly and clearly. Of course, passive constructions cannot and should not be discarded altogether.

The paragraph best supports the statement that passive constructions

A) will be thought incorrect by most readers
B) are useful at times
C) can be understood more clearly than active constructions
D) must always be revised

7. County clerks, who issue marriage _____ licenses and retain records of confidential marriages, have reported numerous abuses of the confidential marriage law. In San Diego, for instance, the Immigration and Naturalization Service has found that illegal aliens take advantage of the law's privacy to wed citizens they may never have met, in order to gain legal residency status.

The paragraph best supports the statement that the confidential marriage law

A) can be abused by illegal aliens who want to become legal residents
B) is often abused by the county clerks who issue marriage licenses
C) is used by illegal aliens to marry citizens outside the United States
D) privately issues licenses and records of marriage

8. By investing $10 million in the _____ shuttle salvage operation, underwriters for the Palapa and Westar now have a chance to recover some of the $100 million they paid to the Indonesian government and to Western Union after the satellite launch fizzled last February.

The paragraph best supports the statement that the salvage operation

A) was a failure last February
B) will earn $100 million from the Indonesian government
C) may help reduce the losses incurred by the underwriters
D) will recover $100 million paid by Western Union

9. With the growing popularity of _____ radio talk shows, it becomes possible to spend most of the day listening to interesting conversations on a variety of significant topics, even while working at a solitary job. Listening to music all day may not be nearly as rewarding or informative.

The paragraph best supports the statement that listening to music

A) has become a popular alternative to listening to talk shows
B) is never as interesting as participating in a conversation
C) may be less preferable than listing to radio talk shows
D) makes it impossible to listen to radio talk shows

10. Those who have difficulty reading ———
    are usually those who have not
    read much. The habit of reading
    is probably instilled during child-
    hood; those children with parents
    who like to read also tend to
    acquire a fondness for books.
    Adults who have never learned to
    like reading are likely to avoid it.

    *The paragraph best supports the statement
    that* those who have avoided reading
    during childhood

    A) will probably not find reading easier as
       they get older
    B) will transmit a hateful attitude toward
       books and reading to their children
    C) were probably kept from reading by
       their parents
    D) did so only because interesting reading
       material was not made available by
       their parents

Answer Explanations for Practice Set 7

1. **(A)** The passage stresses the "fast-changing job market."

2. **(C)** The passage stresses the similarity between the "general problems" of the past and those of the present, but does not suggest that the study of history will answer all questions or solve all problems.

3. **(C)** The passage states that having knowledge may leave the holder of such knowledge feeling "more powerless than powerful."

4. **(A)** None of the other choices is supported by information in the paragraph. (A) repeats the overall point of the paragraph.

5. **(D)** This choice restates the overall point of the paragraph.

6. **(B)** The final sentence states that "passive constructions . . . should not be discarded altogether" and thus implies that passive constructions are useful at times.

7. **(A)** The passage states that illegal aliens take advantage of the law "in order to gain legal residency status."

8. **(C)** The paragraph states that the under-writers "now have a chance to recover" some of the money they lost because of the failed launch.

9. **(C)** The paragraph states that listening to music "may not be nearly as rewarding or informative" as listening to radio talk shows.

10. **(A)** The paragraph reveals that children who have not read much will probably become adults who avoid reading and have difficulty reading. Each of the other choices makes assumptions about parents that are not expressed or implied in the paragraph.

Practice Set 8

Select the best answer to each question and write the letter of your choice in the space provided.

1. Noting that drug abuse has _____ increased markedly since the 1960s, we must ask why. Put simply, people use drugs because the complexity and difficulty of modern life is simply overwhelming, and the temptation to escape from it all with cocaine is often impossible to resist.

   The paragraph best supports the statement that cocaine

   A) was not used previous to the 1960s
   B) is part of the complexity and difficulty of modern life
   C) is a temptation that can be resisted when life is more simple and easy
   D) is one of the drugs whose abuse has increased since the 1960s

2. The ability to recognize grammar _____ and usage errors in the writing of others is not the same as the ability to see such errors in one's own writing. Often a writer is not aware of his own errors until they are pointed out by a good editor.

   The paragraph best supports the statement that errors in grammar and usage

   A) are difficult to recognize in one's own writing
   B) are only apparent to professional editors who are not writers
   C) are not usually a problem for an editor reading her own writing
   D) must be pointed out before they are recognized

3. Since 1890, the federal govern- _____ ment and the states have passed a number of laws against corrupt political practices. But today many feel that political corruption is a regular occurrence, and deeply mistrust their public leaders.

   The paragraph best supports the statement that many citizens

   A) are not in favor of laws against corrupt political practices
   B) changed their attitude toward political corruption after 1890
   C) think that their political leaders are probably corrupt
   D) are even more corrupt than their political leaders

4. People who easily adapt them- _____ selves to different social situations, who mingle easily with many different personalities, might be compared to the chameleon, that lizard who changes color to match the environment.

   The paragraph best supports the statement that

   A) it is possible to compare people with animals
   B) adaptable people tend to resemble reptiles
   C) the chameleon is a very social animal
   D) the ability to change color is not limited to the chameleon

5. Some scientists have proposed _____ that, over two hundred million years ago, one giant land mass—rather than various continents and islands—covered one-third of the earth.

The paragraph best supports the statement that the different continents that exist now

A) were all larger in the past
B) may not have always existed as such
C) have been challenged by scientists
D) now occupy two-thirds of the earth

6. Antifreeze lowers the melting _____ point of any liquid to which it is added, so that the liquid will not freeze in cold weather. It is commonly used to maintain the cooling system in automobile radiators. Of course, the weather may become so cold that even antifreeze is not effective, but such a severe climatic condition rarely occurs in well-traveled places.

The paragraph best supports the statement that antifreeze is

A) usually effective only in automobile radiators
B) usually effective wherever automobile travel is common
C) usually effective even in the coldest climates on earth
D) not nearly as effective as it could be

7. In the twelfth century, people _____ used the abacus (a simple device made of beads strung on wire) to perform complex calculations. Today we use electronic calculators, and the abacus has become obsolete. One thousand years from now, who knows?

The paragraph best supports the statement that

A) the abacus is useless for performing calculations today
B) in the distant future, the electronic calculator of today may seem obsolete
C) devices used for calculating undergo a vast improvement every 1,000 years
D) modern calculations are more complex than ancient calculations

8. It has been estimated that only _____ one out of 500 drunken drivers on the highway is flagged down by the police. The odds against being arrested make it tempting for drinkers to give themselves the benefit of the doubt when they are considering whether they should get behind the wheel.

The paragraph best supports the statement that drinkers are

A) usually not driving when they are detained by the police
B) likely to drive even though they are drunk
C) quite frequently stopped by the police while on the highway
D) never stopped by the police while driving on the highway

9. One of the most important works _____ of the Middle Ages was *The Principles of Letter Writing*, authored by an anonymous Italian educator. It became the basis for formal communication, and many of the principles it advocates have become part of clerical education today.

The paragraph best supports the statement that clerical workers today

A) should be more familiar with relevant books from the Middle Ages
B) study some principles of communication that were available in the Middle Ages
C) are not familiar with *The Principles of Letter Writing*
D) study some principles that contradict those proposed in the Middle Ages

10. Although the acceptable format _____ for writing reports varies from profession to profession, certain rules are invariable. For example, all writers must avoid faulty parallelism and misplaced modifiers; such grammatical errors are incorrect in any context.

The paragraph best supports the statement that different professions

A) tend to disapprove of grammatical errors in written reports
B) are only concerned with errors involving parallelism and modifiers
C) consult grammatical rules before the preparation of any written report
D) follow the same basic format for written reports, although there are variations

Answer Explanations for Practice Set 8

1. **(D)** Cocaine is mentioned as a specific example of the general increase in drug abuse.
2. **(A)** The paragraph's second sentence strongly supports this choice.
3. **(C)** The passage states that "many . . . deeply mistrust their public leaders."
4. **(A)** The paragraph is itself a comparison between people and animals, thus supporting the statement that people and animals can be compared.
5. **(B)** The paragraph discusses the possibility that the various continents of today were once contained in "one giant land mass."
6. **(B)** The final sentence implies that antifreeze is effective in "well-traveled places," that is, places where automobile travel is common.

7. **(B)** The paragraph concludes by questioning what sort of calculation device will exist in 1,000 years, strongly implying that the electronic calculator, like the abacus, will become obsolete.
8. **(B)** The paragraph states that drunken drivers are tempted to "give themselves the benefit of the doubt" when deciding whether to drive; in other words, drunken drivers are tempted to drive in spite of their condition.
9. **(B)** The paragraph states that principles from the Middle Ages "have become part of clerical education today."
10. **(A)** The paragraph stresses the incorrectness of grammatical errors in all professions, saying that certain rules are "invariable."

Practice Set 9

Select the best answer to each question and write the letter of your choice in the space provided.

1. Being the financial center of the _____ United States has advantages and disadvantages. New York is also the fraud capital of the country with more than a thousand criminal fraud convictions this year. Gullible investors lost more than five billion dollars.

   The paragraph best supports the statement that

   A) gains and losses on financial investments in New York are equal
   B) New York is the financial center of the United States
   C) convictions for criminal fraud are lowest where financial activity is lowest
   D) losses in financial fraud are seldom the fault of gullible investors

2. The tobacco industry has filed a _____ law suit charging that the EPA report on second-hand smoke should be declared null and void because it overlooked evidence showing second-hand smoke is not dangerous. The report, the tobacco industry claims, has caused a sharp rise in the number of no smoking ordinances and a sharp decline in cigarette sales.

   The paragraph best supports the statement that

   A) the tobacco industry is genuinely concerned with scientific truth
   B) governments should pass no smoking ordinances to protect the health of the public
   C) the tobacco industry is concerned about the effect of the EPA report on tobacco sales
   D) the tobacco industry is likely to win its lawsuit

3. Just under 300,000 people have _____ been murdered in the United States by guns in the last 25 years. Each year, an increasing percentage of these deaths involve children. Laws that punish adults who leave weapons where children can reach them cannot bring back a dead child. And these laws certainly do not prevent adults from buying the guns that kill the children.

   The paragraph best supports the statement that

   A) guns don't kill people, people do
   B) any laws controlling the sales or handling of a gun will fail to reduce the number of gun-related deaths
   C) more children are killed by guns in the United States every year
   D) we have not yet found a way to prevent the deaths by gunshot of a large number of American children

4. Throughout the nation, utility companies are looking for ways to reduce the consumption of energy instead of building new power plants. Since 20 percent of an average household's electricity is used to run refrigerators, any improvement in their energy efficiency would reduce the demand for electric power. A new, more efficient refrigerator developed by Whirlpool Corporation is expected to use just half as much electricity as older refrigerators, but should not cost buyers more than similar models cost now.

The paragraph best supports the statement that

A) consumers who use the new refrigerator can expect a drop of about 50 percent in their electric bills
B) consumers who use the new refrigerator can expect a drop of about 10 percent in their electric bills
C) the reduction of energy consumption is counterbalanced by an increase in the use of environmentally unsafe materials such as freon
D) other companies will market energy efficient refrigerators at a lower price if the Whirlpool model is successful

5. Federal law now requires all television sets to be equipped with built-in capacity to display captions. Captions enable the nation's 24 million hearing-impaired people to read subtitles on the screen. It will now be possible to watch television in a silent room, in case someone is sleeping. It will be easier for the illiterate to learn to read or for non-English speakers to learn English. The rise in the cost of television sets is expected to be no more than ten dollars, while separate decoders to access captions now cost much more.

The paragraph best supports the statement that

A) television sets with caption-display capabilities will be useful for both the hearing and the hearing-impaired public
B) technological advances usually are accompanied by a rise in cost for consumers
C) in the past, deaf people would not hear what was being said on television programs
D) captioned television programs will make the use of earphones obsolete

6. If the United States presses too _____ hard on an issue, we are accused of forcing our views upon our allies. But if we consult with them and refuse to act without their agreement, we are accused of lack of leadership. It is difficult to find a way to be neither too hard nor too soft.

The paragraph best supports the statement that

A) the United States should give up trying to win the favor of its allies
B) the opinion of its allies plays a part in the policies of the United States
C) the United States should pay more attention to the concerns of its allies
D) the United States lacks leadership in world affairs

7. In Indianapolis, sewer billing, _____ microfilming, public golf courses, and building inspections are all handled by private firms. Public services, in competition with private operations, have become more efficient. But other communities that have turned public services over to private companies report higher costs while workers receive lower wages or fewer benefits. Privatization is not always the best choice a city can make.

The paragraph best supports the statement that

A) by privatizing such services as building inspections and microfilming, large cities can save money
B) in cities where privatization has been used, workers receive fewer benefits than in cities that retain control over the public services
C) a city should study the possible effects carefully before handing public services over to private industry
D) cities with both privatized and public services are more efficient than those having only one or the other.

8. As long as something is based on _____ a true story, Americans are eager to buy it. Fiction is no longer necessary when so many facts are available. Television no longer shows mystery stories. It shows true stories of husbands who kill their wives or children who murder their parents. Is it any wonder that fiction sales fall lower every year?

The paragraph best supports the statement that novelists

A) are no longer interested in writing mystery stories
B) face a declining number of readers
C) can earn more money by writing for television than by writing novels
D) are more likely to write crime stories based upon real life than on imagined crimes

9. Everyone agrees that military bases _____ that have been closed should be put to other uses; but as long as they are not cleaned up, no one can go near them safely. Half of the closed bases are dangerously polluted, either with hazardous chemicals or explosives. The federal government's willingness to sell these lands at somewhat reduced prices to the states is of no use unless the toxic wastes are cleaned up prior to the sale.

The paragraph best supports the statement that those states that purchase army bases from the federal government

A) will be unable to use them for nonmilitary purposes
B) should ascertain that the lands are pollution free before completing any transaction
C) should use the land for the construction of prisons unwanted in other areas of the state
D) can expect, in the long run, a modest improvement in the rate of unemployment

10. In South Africa, both the ruling _____ government party and the African National Congress have been consistently willing to consider new ideas, to change positions, and to compromise. They are opponents, but both see the need to change South Africa. It is the extreme left and the extreme right that are incapable of seeing any point of view other than their own. Both are racist, violent, and determined that the flexible parties of the center will not succeed.

The paragraph best supports the statement that

A) the ruling government party and the African National Congress are no longer the most important forces in South Africa

B) the African National Congress is more willing to compromise than the ruling government party

C) the extremists of both political persuasions present a real threat to the possible solution of political differences

D) the most plausible solution to problems of South Africa is the separation of country into two independent nations

Answer Explanations for Practice Set 9

1. **(B)** The first sentence speaks of the "financial center" and the second of New York as *also* the fraud capital. None of the other answers is supported by the text of the paragraph.

2. **(C)** Though (A), (B), and (D) may be true, there is nothing to support them in the paragraph. That the tobacco industry has filed suit is a good indication of its concern with the effect of the report on sales.

3. **(D)** The passage is concerned with the failure to prevent the death by gunshot of so many American children. The problem with (C) is that the passage speaks of an increasing percentage of children killed but not a larger number each year. It is possible the total would decline, while the percentage increased.

4. **(B)** Since the refrigerator consumes 20 percent of the average household electricity and the new refrigerators use only half as much energy, the electric bill should decrease by about 10 percent.

5. **(A)** The paragraph points out the benefits of captions to both the hearing and the hearing-impaired audience. The other choices may be true but they are not nearly so well supported by this paragraph.

6. **(B)** Of the four answers, only choice (B) can be supported by the information in this paragraph. The paragraph implies that the United States wishes to find an answer because its allies do influence policy.

7. **(C)** Since the paragraph presents both the possible advantages and disadvantages of privatization, it supports only choice (C). Choice (B) overstates and distorts a detail from the paragraph.

8. **(B)** Choices (A), (C), and (D) are not supported by the paragraph, but if fiction sales are falling, the novelist probably faces a declining number of readers.

9. **(B)** The passage warns against pollution on army bases. Choice (A) overstates, while choices (C) and (D) may or may not be true but then, are not relevant to this passage.

10. **(C)** The passage does prefer the African National Congress to the extremes, but not above the ruling party (B). Neither (A) nor (D) can be supported by this paragraph. The point of the paragraph is summed up by choice (C).

Verbal Abilities Analysis Chart for Reading (Understanding and Intepreting Written Material)

Use the following chart to carefully analyze your results of the *reading (understanding and interpreting written material)* question type. This will help you evaluate your strengths and weaknesses. This analysis should help you focus your study and review efforts on specific types of problems.

Practice Set	Total Number of Questions	Number Correct	Number Incorrect	Number Unanswered
Set 1	10			
Set 2	10			
Set 3	10			
Set 4	10			
Set 5	10			
Set 6	10			
Set 7	10			
Set 8	10			
Set 9	10			

Because there is no penalty for incorrect answers on most of the questions in the Verbal Abilities section, you should have left no question unanswered. Even if you didn't have time to answer a question, you should have at least filled in the answer space with an educated guess.

REVIEWING THE KEY STRATEGIES

Remember to:

1. Eliminate incorrect answers first. They may be:
   —irrelevant
   —contradicton
   —unreasonable
2. Look for correct answer choices that repeat or reemphasize main points of the passage.

PUNCTUATION

This question type tests your ability to recognize punctuation errors and when punctuation is being used correctly. For each question, you will be given four sentences, all of which have the same words but only one of which is punctuated correctly. Your task will be to select the correctly punctuated sentence.

Helpful Techniques and Strategies

The best way to prepare for this question type is to review basic punctuation rules and then practice applying those rules doing questions similar to those on the verbal part of your required Civil Service Clerical Examination. This list of punctuation rules listed below is not complete. It does, however, provide fundamentals for answering many of the punctuation questions that will appear in this section of the exam. Answering the practice questions and checking why your answers are correct—or not—will help you to fine-tune your punctuation skills.

Punctuation Basic Rules

Use a Comma . . .

To separate each item in a listing of three or more: *Kyle enjoys playing basketball, soccer, and rugby.*

If a pause is needed to make the sentence easier to read, and its meaning would be misconstrued without the pause: *After all, the arguments were over nothing important.* versus *After all the arguments were over nothing important.*

Between two or more terms that modify a noun: *The large, brown, mysterious package remained on the desk.*

After an introductory phrase: *Being his sister's caretaker, Tom drove Sally to and from school every day.*

To set off a quotation from an author or speaker: *Lincoln wrote, "You cannot fool all of the people all of the time."*

To set off an expression that interrupts the flow of a sentence: *We did not, however, have enough money to pay the bill.*

Before a conjunction (and, but, however, etc.) that joins two complete clauses, each with its own subject: *Yoshio likes to play board games, but Susan decided to teach him poker instead.*

To separate an "appositional word or phrase" (extra information not essential to the intent of the sentence) from the rest of the sentence: *My neighbor, Carol, leaves for work every morning at 6 a.m.* If it were necessary to distinguish Carol as the neighbor, then the sentence would be written: *My neighbor Carol leaves for work every morning at 6 a.m.*

To set off an appositional word or phrase that is descriptive: *Jim, a large man of great proportions, enjoyed playing football.*

To separate a noun of address: *So I'm begging you, Susan, to stop smoking cigarettes.*

Use a Period . . .

To end a sentence: *The quick fox jumped over the lazy dog.*

As part of, or at the end of, an abbreviation (except for American states in postal codes): *She purchased a U.S. government bond for her grandchild.*

After the initial(s) in a person's name: *J. P. Morgan was an American financier.*

As part of a person's title: *Jerry Bobrow, Ph.D. or Ms. Mondragon*

To indicate whether day or night: *At exactly 3:30 a.m. the dogs began to bark.*

Use an Exclamation Point . . .

To indicate a command: *Stop that horrible noise right now!*

To express a strong emotion: *Wonderful! I can't believe you remembered my birthday!*

Use an Apostrophe . . .

To show ownership or belonging: Judith's *bicycle rested against the tree.* Note that the apostrophe serves as a little "arrow" pointing to whoever possesses the item. So, for example, "women's rights" are rights that belong to women.

To replace one or more letters or numbers in a contraction: *He didn't remember anything from the decade of the '70s.*

To create the plural of letters or numbers used as words: *The presenter left time at the end of the meeting for Q's and A's.*

Use a Colon . . .

To introduce a list: *John purchased six paint colors: red, blue, orange, yellow, white, and black.*

In showing time: *The curtain went up at exactly 8:30 p.m.*

To introduce an example: *Here's an example of a palindrome: Madam, I'm Adam.*

Use a Semicolon . . .

To link two independent sentences with related meaning: *The birds were nowhere in view; they had flown south for the winter.*

To separate phrases within a list, where using only commas may cause confusion: *The starting roster includes four players from our town: Tom Banks, freshman, first baseman, and best fielder; Regina Morris, sophomore, pitcher, and team captain; Fredrick Fuller, junior, second baseman, and star hitter; and Cameron Smart, sophomore, catcher, and most valuable player.*

Use the Em-Dash . . .

To set off an explanatory phrase: *We witnessed the revolution—a remarkable set of events—and the birth of a new populist government.*

To interject a new idea or thought different from the flow of the sentence: *The party took place in Amsterdam—I remember it well—at the end of last year.*

Use the Hyphen . . .

To express numbers between *twenty-one* and *ninety-nine*.

When adding certain prefixes and suffixes: *all-county, ex-major, self-serving, pre-conditioned, post-partum,* and others.

When creating a compound adjective that modifies a noun: *twenty-nine-year-old mother of two, six-month text, sure-thing principle, interest-rate disclosures,* and so on.

To avoid uncertainty in meaning: *re-create* is different in meaning from *recreate*; *re-present* differs from *represent*.

Use Quotation Marks . . .

To indicate words that are spoken or written: *"It's getting late,"* he remarked. *"Let's leave town!"*

To indicate the titles of certain creative works (poems, essays, songs, stories, articles in magazines and journals, but not books, plays, or films which are usually italicized: *"Yesterday" is one of the Beatles' most famous ballads.*

Note that in the United States, commas and periods go inside the end-quotation marks (whereas in the United Kingdom they go outside): *"I love roses,"* she said.

Colons and semicolons go outside the end-quotation marks.

Exclamation points and question marks depend upon whether or not they are part of the quotation. If so, they go inside the end-quotation marks. *"Let's run!"* he shouted. *"Why not?"* she replied.

Use Single Quotation Marks . . .

When indicating a quote inside another spoken sentence: *"I thought I heard you say, 'Everyone should leave now,' and so therefore I left without you,"* Susan replied.

Practice Set 1

This question type tests your ability to recognize the correct usage of punctuation rules. Each question shows four sentences, but only one sentence contains correct punctuation. Find the correctly punctuated sentence and choose the corresponding letter to match your answer choice.

1. A) A customer needs assistance in the womens department.
   B) A customer needs assistance in the women's department.
   C) A customer needs assistance in the womens' department.
   D) A customer needs assistance in the womens's department.

2. A) There were many available players to substitute into the game. Billy, Tyler, Steven, Kelly, or even Ryan.
   B) There were many available players to substitute into the game, Billy, Tyler, Steven, Kelly, or even Ryan.
   C) There were many available players to substitute into the game: Billy, Tyler, Steven, Kelly, or even Ryan.
   D) There were many available players to substitute into the game; Billy, Tyler, Steven, Kelly, or even Ryan.

3. A) The man, while quite friendly, was seemingly unaware of the attention that he was drawing. .

B) The man, while quite friendly was seemingly unaware of the attention that he was drawing.

C) The man while quite friendly was seemingly unaware of the attention that he was drawing.

D) The man, while quite friendly; was seemingly unaware of the attention that he was drawing.

4. A) While strenuous, the customer service job was quite well paid.

B) While strenuous, the customer service job was quite well-paid.

C) While strenuous, the customer-service job was quite well paid.

D) While strenuous, the customer-service job was quite well-paid.

5. A) Jenny called Joey, Amy, Carl, and Jane, none of them answered.

B) Jenny called Joey, Amy, Carl, and Jane: none of them answered.

C) Jenny called Joey, Amy, Carl, and Jane; none of them answered.

D) Jenny called Joey, Amy, Carl, and Jane; no answer.

6. A) She always paid the bills, the mortgage, etc.. Still, she never complained.

B) She always paid the bills, the mortgage, etc., still, she never complained.

C) She always paid the bills, the mortgage, etc, still, she never complained.

D) She always paid the bills, the mortgage, etc. Still, she never complained.

7. A) It was a beautiful pristine beach. The young married couple was happy.

B) It was a beautiful pristine beach. The young, married couple was happy

C) It was a beautiful, pristine beach. The young married couple was happy.

D) It was a beautiful, pristine beach. The young, married couple was happy.

8. A) The three candidates were Blake, an accountant, Kate, a salesperson, and Shawn, an account executive.

B) The three candidates were Blake, an accountant; Kate, a salesperson; and Shawn, an account executive.

C) The three candidates were Blake an accountant, Kate a salesperson, and Shawn an account executive.

D) The three candidates were Blake, an accountant; Kate, a salesperson, and Shawn, an account executive.

9. A) Alan had never really liked riding in the Jones' car.

B) Alan had never really liked riding in the Joneses car.

C) Alan had never really liked riding in the Jones's car.

D) Alan had never really liked riding in the Joneses' car.

10. A) Anne's three friends; Mary, Rich, and Cody; were all quite tall.

B) Anne's three friends Mary, Rich, and Cody were all quite tall.

C) Anne's three friends, Mary, Rich, and Cody, were all quite tall.

D) Anne's three friends—Mary, Rich, and Cody—were all quite tall.

11. A) Mark's in—laws will be visiting from April 12th to April 15th this year.

B) Mark's in-laws will be visiting from April 12th to April 15th this year.

C) Mark's inlaws will be visiting from April 12th to April 15th this year.

D) Mark's—in—laws will be visiting from April 12th to April 15th this year.

12. A) No, Craig, I will not be able to pick you up from the airport.

B) No Craig, I will not be able to pick you up from the airport.

C) No, Craig I will not be able to pick you up from the airport.

D) No, Craig: I will not be able to pick you up from the airport.

13. A) Tina has a book club meeting on Tuesday, Alan goes running on Thursdays.
    B) Tina has a book club meeting on Tuesday; Alan goes running on Thursdays.
    C) Tina has a book club meeting on Tuesday. Alan goes running on Thursdays.
    D) Tina has a book club meeting on Tuesday—Alan goes running on Thursdays.

14. A) He's going to pick up his car at the shop and leave her's there.
    B) He's going to pick up his car at the shop and leave hers there.
    C) Hes going to pick up his car at the shop and leave hers there.
    D) Hes going to pick up his car at the shop and leave her's there.

15. A) Their old car ran, and it ran well; but it was not pretty.
    B) Their old car ran, and it ran well, but it was not pretty.
    C) Their old car ran, and it ran well. But it was not pretty.
    D) Their old car ran, and it ran well but it was not pretty.

16. A) The game will most likely be canceled, if it rains.
    B) The game will most likely be canceled; if it rains.
    C) The game will most likely be canceled if it rains.
    D) The game will most likely be canceled: if it rains.

17. A) Unfortunately, its not the first time that shes done this.
    B) Unfortunately, its not the first time that she's done this.
    C) Unfortunately, it's not the first time that shes done this.
    D) Unfortunately, it's not the first time that she's done this.

18. A) The first meeting was on March 14, 2007 in Paris.
    B) The first meeting was on March 14, 2007, in Paris.
    C) Their first meeting was on March 14 2007, in Paris.
    D) Their first meeting was on March 14 2007 in Paris.

19. A) If Tom takes the expressway, he will be late.
    B) If Tom takes the expressway he will be late.
    C) If Tom takes the expressway; he will be late.
    D) If Tom takes the expressway. He will be late.

20. A) Jon and Kathy's laptops are both broken.
    B) Jon and Kathy's laptop's are both broken.
    C) Jon's and Kathy's laptops are both broken.
    D) Jons and Kathys laptops are both broken.

Answer Explanations for Practice Set 1

1. **(B)** The plural form of woman is "women," and because this plural form does not end in an "s," the plural possessive form requires an apostrophe followed by an "s."

2. **(C)** If a list is preceded by a clause that can stand by itself, a colon should be used after the preceding clause. Because the list following the colon is not a stand-alone clause, a period or semicolon would not be appropriate.

3. **(A)** Because "while quite friendly" is a non-essential phrase that adds extra information to the sentence, it should be set off by commas.

4. **(C)** "Customer-service" is a compound adjective comprised of two separate words and modifying a noun that follows it, and so should be hyphenated. Notice that "well paid," however, does **not** precede any noun and so does not require a hyphen.

5. **(C)** A semicolon is used to separate two complete sentences that are related in meaning.

6. **(D)** If the last word in a sentence ends in a period, it should not be followed with another period. Answers B and C are incorrect because two sentences cannot be combined with only a comma.

7. **(C)** If two adjectives can be separated by the word "and," a comma should go between them.

8. **(B)** In a list where at least one of the items contains a comma, semicolons should be used to separate the items.

9. **(D)** The plural of "Jones" is "Joneses," so the plural possessive would be "Joneses'."

10. **(D)** A midsentence list that adds extra information to the sentence should be set off by em-dashes.

11. **(B)** A hyphen, not an em-dash, should be used for the word "in-laws."

12. **(A)** If a person is being addressed directly, the name or title of the person being addressed should be set off by commas.

13. **(C)** The two clauses are complete sentences with no relation or connector word between them, so they should be separated with a period.

14. **(B)** An apostrophe should be used to separate two contracted words (he's, she's), but not in possessive pronouns (his, hers, theirs, ours).

15. **(A)** When two independent clauses are connected by a coordinating conjunction and the first contains a comma, they should be separated by a semicolon.

16. **(C)** A comma should not be used before a dependent phrase when it comes at the end of a sentence.

17. **(D)** Both "it's" and "she's" are contractions in this sentence: it's for it is; she's for she has. Therefore, apostrophes should be used in both cases.

18. **(B)** In a date that includes the day, month, and year, there should be commas before and after the year.

19. **(A)** When a sentence begins with a dependent clause, the clause should be followed by a comma.

20. **(C)** The apostrophe should be used on both names because they are not referring to the same item. The laptops belong to both Jon and Kathy.

Practice Set 2

This question type tests your ability to recognize the correct usage of punctuation rules. Each question shows four sentences, but only one sentence contains correct punctuation. Find the correctly punctuated sentence and choose the corresponding letter to match your answer choice.

1. A) Tim's expression turned to horror when he saw his new teacher: Ms. Knight.
   B) Tim's expression turned to horror when he saw his new teacher; Ms. Knight.
   C) Tim's expression turned to horror when he saw his new teacher. Ms. Knight.
   D) Tim's expression turned to horror when he saw his new teacher! Ms. Knight.

2. A) The student's all turned to look at the children's work.
   B) The students all turned to look at the childrens work.
   C) The student's all turned to look at the childrens work.
   D) The students all turned to look at the children's work.

3. A) Marie said something implying that Mark "shouldn't even come."
   B) Marie said something implying that Mark, "shouldn't even come."
   C) Marie said something implying "that Mark shouldn't even come."
   D) Marie said something implying that Mark shouldn't even come.

4. A) The old house had creaky floors, dusty walls and termites.
   B) The old house had creaky floors; dusty walls, and termites.
   C) The old house had creaky floors, dusty walls, and termites.
   D) The old house had creaky floors—dusty walls—and termites.

5. A) She went to pick up the car and he went to the grocery store.
   B) She went to pick up the car. And he went to the grocery store.
   C) She went to pick up the car; and he went to the grocery store.
   D) She went to pick up the car, and he went to the grocery store.

6. A) Cindy moved quickly but did not show any signs of panic.
   B) Cindy moved quickly; but did not show any signs of panic.
   C) Cindy moved quickly, but did not show any signs of panic.
   D) Cindy moved quickly. But did not show any signs of panic.

7. A) It was a very quickly-assembled team, but it was also an effective team.
   B) It was a very quickly assembled team, but it was also an effective team.
   C) It was a very-quickly-assembled team, but it was also an effective team.
   D) It was a very quickly assembled team; but it was also an effective team.

8. A) Terry could transfer to Waco, Texas, Buffalo, New York, or Reno, Nevada.
   B) Terry could transfer to Waco Texas, Buffalo New York, or Reno Nevada.
   C) Terry could transfer to Waco, Texas; Buffalo, New York; or Reno, Nevada.
   D) Terry could transfer to Waco, Texas— Buffalo, New York—or Reno, Nevada.

9. A) "But" she wondered aloud, "what would give him that idea?"
   B) "But," she wondered aloud, "what would give him that idea?"
   C) "But," she wondered aloud "what would give him that idea?"
   D) "But" she wondered aloud "what would give him that idea?"

10. A) The Smiths were delighted to receive Jess's wedding invitation.
    B) The Smith's were delighted to receive Jess's wedding invitation.
    C) The Smiths were delighted to receive Jesses wedding invitation.
    D) The Smiths' were delighted to receive Jess's wedding invitation.

11. A) He wondered where she had gone and wished she had stayed.
    B) He wondered where she had gone, and wished she had stayed.
    C) He wondered where she had gone; and wished she had stayed.
    D) He wondered where she had gone. And wished she had stayed.

12. A) My dog, which happens to be a Dalmatian, is twelve years old.
    B) My dog which happens to be a Dalmatian, is twelve years old.
    C) My dog which happens to be a Dalmatian is twelve years old.
    D) My dog, which happens to be a Dalmatian is twelve years old.

13. A) Marilyn always took the blue route; Joe the green route.
    B) Marilyn always took the blue route; Joe, the green route.
    C) Marilyn always took the blue route; Joe—the green route.
    D) Marilyn always took the blue route; Joe: the green route.

14. A) "Where is the nearest subway station?," asked the man.
    B) "Where is the nearest subway station," asked the man.
    C) "Where is the nearest subway station?" asked the man.
    D) "Where is the nearest subway station"? asked the man.

15. A) The building; large and glass; stood out from the rest of the skyline.
    B) The building, large and glass; stood out from the rest of the skyline.
    C) The building, large, and glass, stood out from the rest of the skyline.
    D) The building, large and glass, stood out from the rest of the skyline.

16. A) We always used to let his little brother, and sister, tag along.
    B) We always used to let his little brother and sister, tag along.
    C) We always used to let his little brother and sister tag along.
    D) We always used to let his little brother, and sister tag along.

17. A) He told me he would give me the card, when I gave him the money.
    B) He told me he would give me the card; when I gave him the money.
    C) He told me he would give me the card: when I gave him the money.
    D) He told me he would give me the card when I gave him the money.

18. A) She smiled and said "You can run but you can't hide."
    B) She smiled and said, "You can run but you can't hide."
    C) She smiled and said "You can run, but you can't hide."
    D) She smiled and said, "You can run, but you can't hide."

19. A) Karen asked, if she could see the ring?
    B) Karen asked if she could see the ring?
    C) Karen asked if she could see the ring.
    D) Karen asked, if she could see the ring.

20. A) I hate hearing it; nevertheless, I know that it is true.
    B) I hate hearing it, nevertheless, I know that it is true.
    C) I hate hearing it—nevertheless, I know that it is true.
    D) I hate hearing it, nevertheless; I know that it is true.

Answer Explanations for Practice Set 2

1. **(A)** A colon should be used to introduce an appositive at the end of the sentence (an appositive is a clause that describes or renames a preceding noun or pronoun).

2. **(D)** "Students" is not used in the possessive form, so there should be no apostrophe. "Children's" is the possessive form of "children," so there should be an apostrophe.

3. **(D)** Because the quote is an indirect quote rather than a direct quote, quotation marks should not be used.

4. **(C)** While omitting the comma before the conjunction in a list is sometimes optional, it would cause confusion in this sentence in that it would make "dusty" seem to apply to both "walls" and "termites."

5. **(D)** When two strong clauses are connected by a coordinating conjunction, they should be separated by a comma.

6. **(A)** If two verbs refer to the same subject and the subject does not appear in front of the second verb, do not use a comma.

7. **(B)** Because "quickly" ends in "ly," it should not be hyphenated with "assembled" even though the compound modifier precedes the noun it is modifying.

8. **(C)** Because a comma must go between the city and state name, semicolons should be used to separate the list items to avoid confusion.

9. **(B)** Commas should be used to interrupt and introduce direct quotations.

10. **(A)** "Smiths" is simply a plural form of the noun, so there is no need for an apostrophe. "Jess's" is meant to show possession, and although the word "Jess" ends in an "s," the extra apostrophe-s should be added because it would be pronounced.

11. **(A)** Because there is only one subject in the sentence to which both verbs refer, no comma is required.

12. **(A)** Because the added information about the Dalmation breed of the dog is unessential to the central meaning of the sentence, its phrase should be set off by commas.

13. **(B)** When a word is clearly and intentionally omitted from a clause, a comma should be inserted in place of the word. In this case, the missing word is "took."

14. **(C)** The quote is a question, so it must end in a question mark and the question mark should come before the end-quotation mark. Also, when a quote ends in a question mark, a comma should not be used.

15. **(D)** When adjectives follow the noun they modify, they should be connected by the word "and" and should be set off by commas even if they provide essential information.

16. **(C)** Because "brother" and "sister" are compound subjects that are referred to by the same verb, they should not be separated by a comma.

17. **(D)** Because the sentence ends in a dependent clause, it should not be set off by a comma or other punctuation.

18. **(D)** A quote in a sentence should be set off by a comma. Also, the sentence in quotations is made up of two independent clauses connected by a coordinating conjunction, so it should be separated with a comma.

19. **(C)** Because the quotation is not a direct quotation, it should not be set off by a

comma. Also, because the sentence is describing a question rather than asking or quoting a question, a question mark should not be used.

20. **(A)** When two independent clauses are connected by a conjunctive adverb like "nevertheless," they should be separated by a semicolon before the conjunctive adverb.

Practice Set 3

This question type tests your ability to recognize the correct usage of punctuation rules. Each question shows four sentences, but only one sentence contains correct punctuation. Find the correctly punctuated sentence and choose the corresponding letter to match your answer choice.

1. A) The CEO could not decide which department's funding to cut; Research, Marketing, or Sales.
   B) The CEO could not decide which department's funding to cut. Research, Marketing, or Sales.
   C) The CEO could not decide which department's funding to cut: Research, Marketing, or Sales.
   D) The CEO could not decide which department's funding to cut, Research, Marketing, or Sales.

2. A) All of the high salary jobs were filled; the only positions left were poorly paid.
   B) All of the high-salary jobs were filled; the only positions left were poorly-paid.
   C) All of the high salary jobs were filled; the only positions left were poorly-paid.
   D) All of the high-salary jobs were filled; the only positions left were poorly paid.

3. A) That is true. He did, however, leave a great tip.
   B) That is true. He did, however leave a great tip.
   C) That is true. He did however leave a great tip.
   D) That is true. He did however leave a great tip.

4. A) The bill was passed in August, 1922, but it did not take effect until 1923.
   B) The bill was passed in August 1922 but it did not take effect until 1923.
   C) The bill was passed in August 1922, but it did not take effect until 1923.
   D) The bill was passed in August 1922, but, it did not take effect until 1923.

5. A) She ran towards the truck and he followed her.
   B) She ran towards the truck, and he followed her.
   C) She ran towards the truck; and he followed her.
   D) She ran towards the truck. And, he followed her.

6. A) There were four employees in the meeting: Dan, from accounting; Sarah, from legal; Trish, from Marketing; and Charles, from legal.
   B) There were four employees in the meeting, Dan, from accounting; Sarah, from legal; Trish, from Marketing; and Charles, from legal.
   C) There are four employees in the meeting: Dan, from accounting, Sarah, from legal, Trish, from Marketing, and Charles, from legal.
   D) There are four employees in the meeting, Dan, from accounting, Sarah, from legal, Trish, from Marketing, and Charles, from legal.

7. A) He looked over the spreadsheet once more, and then he forwarded it along to his boss.
   B) He looked over the spreadsheet once more and then he forwarded it along to his boss.
   C) He looked over the spreadsheet once more, and then he forwarded it along, to his boss.
   D) He looked over the spreadsheet once more. And then he forwarded it along to his boss.

8. A) Obviously she would not want to do that!
   B) Obviously; she would not want to do that!
   C) Obviously: she would not want to do that!
   D) Obviously, she would not want to do that!

9. A) Don't touch that fence Robert. It looks rusty.
   B) Don't touch that fence Robert, it looks rusty.
   C) Don't touch that fence Robert it looks rusty.
   D) Don't touch that fence, Robert; it looks rusty.

10. A) Tyler, who's hair is red, is the only boy who's coming.
    B) Tyler, who's hair is red, is the only boy who's coming.
    C) Tyler, whose hair is red, is the only boy whose coming.
    D) Tyler, whose hair is red, is the only boy who's coming.

11. A) Any kind of candy, jelly beans, for instance, did the trick.
    B) Any kind of candy—jelly beans, for instance—did the trick.
    C) Any kind of candy; jelly beans, for instance; did the trick.
    D) Any kind of candy: jelly beans, for instance, did the trick.

12. A) There were four-hundred-twenty-six attendees at the concert.
    B) There were four hundred twenty six attendees at the concert.
    C) There were four hundred twenty-six attendees at the concert.
    D) There were four-hundred twenty-six attendees at the concert.

13. A) Marcia gave him one last stern look, and then walked out the door.
    B) Marcia gave him one last stern look and then walked out the door.
    C) Marcia gave him one last stern look; and then walked out the door.
    D) Marcia gave him one last stern look, and then, walked out the door.

14. A) Ken wants to know where you put the television remote?
    B) Ken wants to know, where you put the television remote?
    C) Ken wants to know where you put the television remote.
    D) Ken wants to know, where you put the television remote.

15. A) It was Kaylee, not Ashley, who borrowed my car.
    B) It was Kaylee not Ashley, who borrowed my car.
    C) It was Kaylee; not Ashley, who borrowed my car.
    D) It was Kaylee not Ashley who borrowed my car.

16. A) Without a doubt; Jason was the one who took it.
    B) Without a doubt Jason was the one who took it.
    C) Without a doubt, Jason was the one who took it.
    D) Without a doubt. Jason was the one who took it.

17. A) Surely, confused was the flustered man.
    B) Surely confused was the flustered man.
    C) Surely; confused was the flustered man.
    D) Surely confused, was the flustered man.

18. A) The CFO said that he would review the numbers but he made no promises.
    B) The CFO said that he would review the numbers; but he made no promises.
    C) The CFO said that he would review the numbers. But, he made no promises.
    D) The CFO said that he would review the numbers, but he made no promises.

19. A) Five sizes are currently in stock. S, M, L, XL, and XXL.
    B) Five sizes are currently in stock, S, M, L, XL, and XXL.
    C) Five sizes are currently in stock: S, M, L, XL, and XXL.
    D) Five sizes are currently in stock; S, M, L, XL, and XXL.

20. A) The north Georgia plains seemed to stretch on forever in the rearview mirror.
    B) The north-Georgia plains seemed to stretch on forever in the rearview mirror.
    C) The north-Georgia plains seemed to stretch on forever in the rear-view mirror.
    D) The north, Georgia plains seemed to stretch on forever in the rearview mirror.

Answer Explanations for Practice Set 3

1. **(C)** The list should be set off by a colon because it is preceded by a complete, independent sentence.
2. **(D)** Compound adjectives should only be hyphenated when they directly precede the noun they modify. Also, compound adjectives containing parts that end in "ly" should not be hyphenated.
3. **(A)** When words such as "however" are used mid-sentence as a transitional adverb or interjection that produces a distinct break in thought, they should be set off by commas.
4. **(C)** If any part of the date is missing, there should not be a comma.
5. **(B)** Because the two clauses that "and" connects are independent and because both contain subjects, they should be separated by a comma.
6. **(A)** Semicolons should be used to separate the list items because the list items contain commas. Also, the list should be set off by a colon because it is preceded by a complete, independent clause.
7. **(A)** A comma should be used to separate two independent clauses that are combined with a conjunction. "To his boss" is a subordinate clause and should not be set off by a comma.
8. **(D)** An introductory adverb should be followed by a comma unless it directly precedes the word that it modifies.
9. **(D)** When directly addressing someone, their name should be set off by commas no matter where it falls in the sentence. A semicolon should be used to combine two independent complete clauses when there is no conjunction and their meanings are related.
10. **(D)** "Whose" is the possessive form of "who," and should be used in the first instance. "Who's" is the contraction of "who

is," and should be used in the second instance.

11. **(B)** A mid-sentence modifying phrase that contains a comma should be set off by em-dashes.

12. **(C)** A hyphen should be used between the tens digit and the ones digit when spelling out the numbers twenty-one through ninety-nine.

13. **(B)** Because "Marcia" is referred to by both verbs, this is a single clause and should not be separated by any punctuation.

14. **(C)** Because the quotation is indirect rather than direct, it should not be set off by a comma or end in a question mark.

15. **(A)** A contrasting expression beginning with "not" should always be set off by commas.

16. **(C)** A common phrase that has no grammatical connection to the sentence should be set off by a comma.

17. **(B)** Because "surely" modifies "mistaken," it should not be set off by a comma. Although the sentence reads awkwardly, it is grammatically correct.

18. **(D)** Two independent and complete clauses connected by a conjunction should be separated by a comma.

19. **(C)** A colon should be used to separate the list from the preceding complete, independent clause. A semicolon or period would be appropriate only if the second clause were also a complete, independent clause.

20. **(A)** Compound adjectives should not be hyphenated if they contain a part that is a proper noun or an adjective.

Practice Set 4

This question type tests your ability to recognize the correct usage of punctuation rules. Each question shows four sentences, but only one sentence contains correct punctuation. Find the correctly punctuated sentence and choose the corresponding letter to match your answer choice.

1. A) Whenever I get too sleepy I always pull over and take a nap.
   B) Whenever I get too sleepy; I always pull over and take a nap.
   C) Whenever I get too sleepy, I always pull over and take a nap.
   D) Whenever I get too sleepy. I always pull over and take a nap.

2. A) Susie lived at 17 Maplewood Court, Springfield, OH.
   B) Susie lived at 17, Maplewood Court, Springfield, OH.
   C) Susie lived at 17 Maplewood Court Springfield, OH.
   D) Susie lived at 17 Maplewood Court Springfield OH.

3. A) Its not the size of the racehorse that matters most, it's the size of its heart.
   B) It's not the size of the racehorse that matters most, it's the size of it's heart.
   C) It's not the size of the racehorse that matters most, it's the size of its heart.
   D) Its not the size of the racehorse that matters most, its the size of it's heart.

4. A) The company had issued additional shares of stock on: April 4, 2007; September 18, 2007; and August 21, 2008.
   B) The company had issued additional shares of stock on April 4, 2007; September 18, 2007; and August 21, 2008.
   C) The company had issued additional shares of stock on April 4 2007, September 18 2007, and August 21 2008.
   D) The company had issued additional shares of stock on April 4, 2007, September 18, 2007, and August 21, 2008.

5. A) I went to the gym, did some laundry, went shopping, and cooked dinner.
   B) I went to the gym; did some laundry; went shopping; and cooked dinner.
   C) I went to the gym. Did some laundry. Went shopping. And cooked dinner.
   D) I went to the gym did some laundry went shopping and cooked dinner.

6. A) She ran the numbers one last time, but still could not find the error.
   B) She ran the numbers one last time; but still could not find the error.
   C) She ran the numbers one last time but still could not find the error.
   D) She ran the numbers one last time, but still, could not find the error.

7. A) I would be happy to accompany you, of course.
   B) I would be happy to accompany you of course.
   C) I would be happy to accompany you. Of course.
   D) I would be happy to accompany you; of course.

8. A) "Wow!" she exclaimed "What was he thinking?"
   B) "Wow," she exclaimed, "What was he thinking?"
   C) "Wow" she exclaimed "What was he thinking?"
   D) "Wow!" she exclaimed, "What was he thinking?"

9. A) By coincidence, Ellen moved from Jackson, Georgia, to Jackson, Louisiana.
   B) By coincidence, Ellen moved from Jackson Georgia to Jackson Louisiana.
   C) By coincidence, Ellen moved from Jackson, Georgia to Jackson, Louisiana.
   D) By coincidence, Ellen moved from Jackson, Georgia; to Jackson, Louisiana.

10. A) The fully functional machine looked quite sleek and was clearly well built.
    B) The fully-functional machine looked quite sleek and was clearly well built.
    C) The fully functional machine looked quite sleek and was clearly well-built.
    D) The fully-functional machine looked quite sleek and was clearly well-built.

11. A) Her hometown—Dallas, Texas—never had winters like this.
    B) Her hometown: Dallas, Texas, never had winters like this.
    C) Her hometown, Dallas, Texas, never had winters like this.
    D) Her hometown Dallas Texas never had winters like this.

12. A) Make sure you turn the lights out when you go to bed, unless I'm still up.
    B) Make sure you turn the lights out when you go to bed; unless I'm still up.
    C) Make sure you turn the lights out when you go to bed unless I'm still up.
    D) Make sure you turn the lights out when you go to bed. Unless I'm still up.

13. A) He was not present at the time;
      therefore, it could not have been him.
   B) He was not present at the time;
      therefore it could not have been him.
   C) He was not present at the time,
      therefore, it could not have been him.
   D) He was not present at the time,
      therefore it could not have been him.

14. A) Jack promised it would be okay but
      she still wasn't quite sure.
   B) Jack promised it would be okay, but
      she still wasn't quite sure.
   C) Jack promised it would be okay. But,
      she still wasn't quite sure.
   D) Jack promised it would be okay; but
      she still wasn't quite sure.

15. A) Strangely he did not even raise an
      eyebrow; he just stared straight ahead.
   B) Strangely, he did not even raise an
      eyebrow, he just stared straight ahead.
   C) Strangely he did not even raise an
      eyebrow, he just stared straight ahead.
   D) Strangely, he did not even raise an
      eyebrow; he just stared straight ahead.

16. A) I thought I told you, Alan, that we're
      not leaving until 7 o'clock.
   B) I thought I told you Alan, that we're
      not leaving until 7 o'clock.
   C) I thought I told you, Alan. That we're
      not leaving until 7 o'clock.
   D) I thought I told you, Alan, that we're
      not leaving, until 7 o'clock.

17. A) Kelly thought she had left her keys by
      the door but now could not find them.
   B) Kelly thought she had left her keys by
      the door; but now could not find them.
   C) Kelly thought she had left her keys by
      the door. But now could not find them.
   D) Kelly thought she had left her keys by
      the door, but now could not find them.

18. A) There were four different color schemes
      available, green, red, blue, and black.
   B) There were four different color schemes
      available; green, red, blue, and black.
   C) There were four different color schemes
      available. Green, red, blue, and black.
   D) There were four different color schemes
      available: green, red, blue, and black.

19. A) At least three fourths of the cake was
      gone by the time we arrived.
   B) At least three-fourths of the cake was
      gone by the time we arrived.
   C) At least, three fourths of the cake was
      gone by the time we arrived.
   D) At least, three-fourths of the cake was
      gone by the time we arrived.

20. A) Your not the guy with the racing
      stripe on your car, are you?
   B) You're not the guy with the racing
      stripe on you're car, are you?
   C) Your not the guy with the racing
      stripe on you're car, are you?
   D) You're not the guy with the racing
      stripe on your car, are you?

Answer Explanations for Practice Set 4

1. **(C)** An introductory adverb clause should be set off by a comma.
2. **(A)** In an address, commas should separate the street address from the city and the city from the state.
3. **(C)** "It's" is the contraction of "it is," and should be used in the first two instances.

"Its" is the possessive form of "it," and should be used in the third instance.

4. **(B)** Because a comma must separate the year of a date from the day and month, a semicolon must be used to separate the list of dates. The list should not be set off by a colon because the preceding clause ends in

a preposition and is not complete and independent.

5. **(A)** List items should be separated by commas. Semicolons are unnecessary because none of the list items contain commas.

6. **(C)** Because "she" is the subject referred to by both verbs, this is a single clause and should not be separated by any punctuation.

7. **(A)** A common expression such as "of course" should be set off by a comma, no matter where it falls in the sentence.

8. **(D)** "Wow" should be followed by an exclamation point, as it is clearly an exclamation. Also, the quotation should be set off by a comma.

9. **(A)** In place names, a comma should separate the city from the state, and should also come after the state. A semicolon is unnecessary because there are only two items, rather than a list.

10. **(A)** Compound adjectives should not be hyphenated if they do not precede the noun they modify nor if they contain a part that ends in "ly."

11. **(A)** A mid-sentence modifying phrase should be set of by em-dashes when it contains a comma (a comma must be used to separate "Dallas" from "Texas").

12. **(C)** Because "unless I'm still up" is a subordinate clause at the end of a sentence, it should not be set off by a comma.

13. **(A)** Two complete, independent clauses connected by a conjunctive adverb ("therefore") should be separated by a semicolon. Also, conjunctive adverbs should always be set off by commas.

14. **(B)** Two complete, independent clauses connected by a conjunction should be separated by a comma.

15. **(D)** "Strangely" should be set off by a comma because it is an introductory adverb that is not directly followed by the word it modifies. The two clauses should be separated with a semicolon because they are two complete, independent clauses with no connecting conjunction and related meanings.

16. **(B)** When addressing someone directly, their name should be set off by commas.

17. **(A)** Because both "thought" and "find" refer to the subject "Kelly," this is a single clause and should not be separated by any punctuation.

18. **(D)** The list should be set off by a colon because the list is preceded by an independent complete clause.

19. **(A)** Spelled-out fractions should not be hyphenated unless the fraction is used as an adjective.

20. **(D)** "You're" is the contraction of "you are" and should be used in the first instance. "Your" is the possessive form of "you" and should be used in the second instance.

Practice Set 5

This question type tests your ability to recognize the correct usage of punctuation rules. Each question shows four sentences, but only one sentence contains correct punctuation. Find the correctly punctuated sentence and choose the corresponding letter to match your answer choice.

1. A) She left her laundry all over the floor so I picked it up for her.
   B) She left her laundry all over the floor, so I picked it up for her.
   C) She left her laundry all over the floor. So I picked it up for her.
   D) She left her laundry all over the floor; so I picked it up for her.

2. A) Martin, more or less, understood what Katelyn was trying to say.
   B) Martin more or less understood what Katelyn was trying to say.
   C) Martin, more or less understood what Katelyn was trying to say.
   D) Martin; more or less; understood what Katelyn was trying to say.

3. A) I have always wanted to go to: France, Italy, China, and Brazil.
   B) I have always wanted to go to, France, Italy, China, and Brazil.
   C) I have always wanted to go to France, Italy, China, and Brazil.
   D) I have always wanted to go to; France, Italy, China, and Brazil.

4. A) The only players left were John Davis, a guard, Al Horner, a center, and Ray Skinner, a forward.
   B) The only players left were John Davis, a guard; Al Horner, a center; and Ray Skinner, a forward.
   C) The only players left were John Davis a guard, Al Horner a center, and Ray Skinner a forward.
   D) The only players left were: John Davis, a guard; Al Horner, a center; and Ray Skinner, a forward.

5. A) Obviously, we never actually tried it, but it was always a tempting idea.
   B) Obviously we never actually tried it; but it was always a tempting idea.
   C) Obviously, we never actually tried it; but it was always a tempting idea.
   D) Obviously we never actually tried it, but it was always an tempting idea.

6. A) The dog eared clipping described how Grandpa had been the last one out.
   B) The dog-eared clipping described how Grandpa had been the last one out.
   C) The dog-eared clipping described how Grandpa had been the last-one out.
   D) The dog eared clipping described how Grandpa had been the last-one out.

7. A) Twentyseven students enrolled in the class.
   B) Twenty seven students enrolled in the class.
   C) Twenty-seven students enrolled in the class.
   D) 27 students enrolled in the class.

8. A) "I'm not sure what I'll do now." He said.
   B) "I'm not sure what I'll do now" he said.
   C) "I'm not sure what I'll do now," he said.
   D) "I'm not sure what I'll do now;" he said.

9. A) Henry closed out all of his windows before leaving, and then logged out.
   B) Henry closed out all of his windows, before leaving, and then logged out.
   C) Henry closed out all of his windows before leaving; and then logged out.
   D) Henry closed out all of his windows before leaving and then logged out.

10. A) Sir I thought I had made myself clear; we are not interested thank you.
    B) Sir, I thought I had made myself clear; we are not interested thank you.
    C) Sir, I thought I had made myself clear; we are not interested, thank you.
    D) Sir I thought I had made myself clear; we are not interested, thank you.

11. A) Clark has been trying to figure out, who we left out?
    B) Clark has been trying to figure out who we left out.
    C) Clark has been trying to figure out, who we left out.
    D) Clark has been trying to figure out who we left out?

12. A) He wanted to go to the water park, not the beach, for his birthday.
    B) He wanted to go to the water park, not the beach for his birthday.
    C) He wanted to go to the water park not the beach for his birthday.
    D) He wanted to go to the water park not the beach, for his birthday.

13. A) After I eat dinner I always like to relax for a little while.
    B) After I eat dinner, I always like to relax for a little while.
    C) After I eat dinner; I always like to relax for a little while.
    D) After I eat dinner, I always like to relax, for a little while.

14. A) We drove through Tennessee; we did not have time to stop, however.
    B) We drove through Tennessee, we did not have time to stop, however.
    C) We drove through Tennessee; we did not have time to stop however.
    D) We drove through Tennessee, we did not have time to stop however.

15. A) He had been there the whole time; and I hadn't even noticed him.
    B) He had been there the whole time. And I hadn't even noticed him.
    C) He had been there the whole time and I hadn't even noticed him.
    D) He had been there the whole time, and I hadn't even noticed him.

16. A) The class's star student wont even turn in a paper without proofreading it.
    B) The class' star student won't even turn in a paper without proofreading it.
    C) The classes star student won't even turn in a paper without proofreading it.
    D) The class's star student won't even turn in a paper without proofreading it.

17. A) The only things he had with him—a pen, business card, and some loose change—were useless here.
    B) The only things he had with him: a pen, business card, and some loose change, were useless here.
    C) The only things he had with him, a pen, business card, and some loose change, were useless here.
    D) The only things he had with him: a pen, business card, and some loose change. Were useless here.

18. A) The high-paid executives were generally not well-liked in the mailroom.
    B) The high-paid executives were generally not well liked in the mailroom.
    C) The high paid executives were generally not well liked in the mailroom.
    D) The high paid executives were generally not well-liked in the mailroom.

19. A) There were several pieces of furniture inside. A couch, a table, a desk, and several chairs.
    B) There were several pieces of furniture inside; a couch, a table, a desk, and several chairs.
    C) There were several pieces of furniture inside: a couch, a table, a desk, and several chairs.
    D) There were several pieces of furniture inside, a couch, a table, a desk, and several chairs.

20. A) Their not gone, are they? They're car was right there a minute ago.
    B) They're not gone, are they? They're car was right there a minute ago.
    C) Their not gone, are they? Their car was right there a minute ago.
    D) They're not gone, are they? Their car was right there a minute ago.

Answer Explanations for Practice Set 5

1. **(B)** Two independent and complete clauses connected by a conjunction should be separated by a comma.

2. **(A)** A common expression such as "more or less" that is not grammatically connected to the sentence should be set off by commas.

3. **(C)** Neither the list nor the preceding clause is a complete, independent clause. The entire phrase is one clause, and so the list should not be set off by any punctuation.

4. **(B)** The list items should be separated by semicolons because the list items contain commas. The list itself should not be set off by any punctuation because the preceding clause is not a complete, independent clause.

5. **(C)** "Obviously" should be set off by a comma because it is an introductory word. The two independent clauses should be separated by a semicolon because the first clause contains a comma.

6. **(B)** "Dog-eared" should be hyphenated because it is a compound adjective preceding the noun it modifies. "Last one" should not be hyphenated because "one" is the noun being modified.

7. **(C)** A hyphen should be used between the tens digit and the ones digit when spelling out the numbers twenty-one through ninety-nine. If a number begins a sentence, it must be spelled out.

8. **(C)** Direct quotations should be set off by commas.

9. **(D)** Both "closed" and "logged" refer to the subject "Henry," which means that this is a single clause and so should not be separated by any punctuation.

10. **(C)** "Sir" should be set off by a comma because it is a direct address. "Thank you"

should also be set off by a comma because it is a common expression that is not grammatically connected to the sentence.

11. **(B)** The quotation is indirect, so it should not be set off by a comma or end in a question mark.

12. **(A)** A contrasting expression beginning with "not" should be set off by commas.

13. **(B)** "After I eat dinner" is an introductory adverb phrase, and so should be set off by a comma.

14. **(A)** The two clauses are complete and independent, and so should be separated by a semicolon. "However" is a conjunctive adverb, which should always be set off by commas.

15. **(D)** Two independent and complete clauses connected by a conjunction should be separated by a comma.

16. **(D)** "Class's" should have an apostrophe-s because it shows possession and would be pronounced as such. "Won't" is a contraction and so should also have an apostrophe.

17. **(A)** Em-dashes should be used to set off mid-sentence modifying phrases that contain commas.

18. **(B)** Compound adjectives should be hyphenated only when they directly precede the word they modify.

19. **(C)** When a complete, independent clause precedes a list, it should be set off by a colon.

20. **(D)** "They're" is the contraction of "they are," and should be used in the first instance. "Their" is the possessive form of "they," and should be used in the second instance.

Verbal Abilities Analysis Chart for Punctuation

Use the following chart to carefully analyze your results of the *punctuation* question type. This will help you evaluate your strengths and weaknesses. This analysis should help you focus your study and review efforts on specific types of problems.

Practice Set	Total Number of Questions	Number Correct	Number Incorrect	Number Unanswered
Set 1	20			
Set 2	20			
Set 3	20			
Set 4	20			
Set 5	20			

Because there is no penalty for incorrect answers on most of the questions in the Verbal Abilities section, you should have left no question unanswered. Even if you didn't have time to answer a question, you should have at least filled in the answer space with an educated guess.

REVIEWING THE KEY STRATEGIES

1. Review the fundamental punctuation rules published in this chapter.
2. Practice applying these rules when taking the Practice Set questions. Reviewing the answer explanations will add to your understanding of punctuation rules.

PART II

THE CLERICAL EXAM: CLERICAL ABILITIES PART

Clerical Abilities
General Strategies:
A Diagnostic Test

with Answers and Explanations/ Analysis of Strengths and Weaknesses

THE CLERICAL ABILITIES PART

The Clerical Abilities Part tests speed and accuracy on typical clerical tasks. Possible question types include:

- Alike or different (name and number checking)
- Alphabetizing
- Arithmetic computation (arithmetic operations)
- Number and letter scramble (name and number comparison)
- Clerical operations with letters and numbers (number sequencing/ordering)
- Record keeping (chart reading)
- Using a directory
- Filing
- Customer service (office practices, interpersonal skills, and decision making)

These question types are frequently "cycled" throughout the test; that is, there are about 5 questions of each type, repeated until the exam is complete. Each question has equal value toward your final score. Your score on the Clerical Abilities Part, unlike that on the Verbal Abilities Part, may be penalized for incorrect answers. (See the section on "Guessing" that follows.)

Procedure

You will have about 10 minutes to study the directions and sample questions on the front of your test booklet and to mark the answers to these sample questions in the space provided. (However, since time is at a premium on this test, it is important that you become familiar with the test question types *long before you take the actual exam.*) You will be told when to begin the actual test.

General Strategies

Since there is a limited amount of time for answering the questions, some essential considerations come into play. We recommend that you reread the general strategies explained in the Verbal Abilities Part section of this book (pages 3–6). There may be one very important difference in the strategies for the Clerical Abilities Part, however, in regard to guessing.

Guessing

It is important for you to find out if choosing a wrong answer will penalize your score. If so, don't guess blindly. The score for this test, unlike the Verbal Abilities Part, may be determined by the number of right answers *minus one-fourth* the number of wrong answers. Blank answers are given neither plus nor minus credit. Therefore every filled-in but incorrect answer lowers your test score very slightly. For example, if on this test you answer

90 questions correctly,
20 questions incorrectly, and leave
10 questions unanswered,

you will get 90 credits for your correct answers, minus 5 points for your incorrect answers (¼ × 20), for a total of 85 points. Notice that your final score is 5 points lower because of the 20 wrong answers.

Because of this possible adjustment, it is not wise to guess blindly on the Clerical Abilities Part, as a wrong choice can decrease your total score. (A "blind" guess is answering a question where you have no insight into the problem and no way of eliminating any choices.)

But if you are able to eliminate even one of the answer choices as incorrect, then you will have increased the odds of guessing correctly and, in the long run, you should get more points in your favor than taken away.

Of course, if you can eliminate *two* choices as incorrect, your chances of guessing correctly are even greater.

So, to summarize, don't guess blindly on this test, but do guess when you can eliminate one or more answer choices as incorrect.

Remember, if you skip a question, be careful to place your next answer mark in the proper space on your answer sheet, not in the space you just skipped!

SPEED

The Clerical Abilities Part is primarily a test of *speed* in carrying out relatively simple clerical tasks. While accuracy on these tasks is important and will be taken into account in the scoring, experience has shown that many persons are so concerned about accuracy that they do the test more slowly than they should. Speed as well as accuracy is important to achieve a good score. Therefore, do not spend undue time on any particular question.

How to Determine the Total Test Score

The score on the Verbal Abilities Part is the number of right answers. The score on the Clerical Abilities Part may be the number of right answers minus ¼ the number of wrong answers (R − ¼W).

The scores on both tests will be added to determine total score. The passing point on the total test will vary according to the grade and kind of position to be filled. In general, a score of approximately 60 percent of the 85 questions on the Verbal Abilities Test is considered good performance. Therefore, a score of 50 or better on the Verbal Abilities Part and a score of 100 on the Verbal and Clerical Abilities Parts combined are considered good scores. These scores will probably qualify a prospective applicant, providing all other test and experience requirements for a particular position are met. Similarly, a score of less than 50 percent of the questions on the Verbal Abilities Part is considered poor. Less than 40 on the Verbal Abilities Part and less than 80 on the Verbal and Clerical Abilities Parts combined indicate relatively poor performance.

A review of how you answered the test questions in the Model Tests will provide useful information to see whether more work is needed in spelling, grammar, etc., whether greater speed or accuracy is needed in the Clerical Abilities Test, and whether the nature of the tasks in the two tests has been clearly understood.

A DIAGNOSTIC TEST WITH ANSWER EXPLANATIONS

The purpose of this diagnostic test is to familiarize you with the Clerical Abilities Part. It is designed to introduce you to the testing areas and assist you in evaluating your strengths and weaknesses. This will help you focus your review. Chapter 4 will give you a more complete range of problem types and specific strategies for each section. After correcting the diagnostic exam and assessing your strengths and weaknesses, you should start your area reviews and practice in the next chapter.

The diagnostic test should be taken under strict test conditions.

NOTE: Sample questions are usually distributed with the announcement and if so may not be given in the official examination.

First take 10 minutes to review the sample questions given here before starting this exam. Now tear out your answer sheet from this book, turn to the next page, and begin the exam.

Answer Sheet

CLERICAL ABILITIES GENERAL STRATEGIES

1 Ⓐ Ⓑ Ⓒ Ⓓ	31 Ⓐ Ⓑ Ⓒ Ⓓ	61 Ⓐ Ⓑ Ⓒ Ⓓ	91 Ⓐ Ⓑ Ⓒ Ⓓ
2 Ⓐ Ⓑ Ⓒ Ⓓ	32 Ⓐ Ⓑ Ⓒ Ⓓ	62 Ⓐ Ⓑ Ⓒ Ⓓ	92 Ⓐ Ⓑ Ⓒ Ⓓ
3 Ⓐ Ⓑ Ⓒ Ⓓ	33 Ⓐ Ⓑ Ⓒ Ⓓ	63 Ⓐ Ⓑ Ⓒ Ⓓ	93 Ⓐ Ⓑ Ⓒ Ⓓ
4 Ⓐ Ⓑ Ⓒ Ⓓ	34 Ⓐ Ⓑ Ⓒ Ⓓ	64 Ⓐ Ⓑ Ⓒ Ⓓ	94 Ⓐ Ⓑ Ⓒ Ⓓ
5 Ⓐ Ⓑ Ⓒ Ⓓ	35 Ⓐ Ⓑ Ⓒ Ⓓ	65 Ⓐ Ⓑ Ⓒ Ⓓ	95 Ⓐ Ⓑ Ⓒ Ⓓ
6 Ⓐ Ⓑ Ⓒ Ⓓ	36 Ⓐ Ⓑ Ⓒ Ⓓ	66 Ⓐ Ⓑ Ⓒ Ⓓ	96 Ⓐ Ⓑ Ⓒ Ⓓ
7 Ⓐ Ⓑ Ⓒ Ⓓ	37 Ⓐ Ⓑ Ⓒ Ⓓ	67 Ⓐ Ⓑ Ⓒ Ⓓ	97 Ⓐ Ⓑ Ⓒ Ⓓ
8 Ⓐ Ⓑ Ⓒ Ⓓ	38 Ⓐ Ⓑ Ⓒ Ⓓ	68 Ⓐ Ⓑ Ⓒ Ⓓ	98 Ⓐ Ⓑ Ⓒ Ⓓ
9 Ⓐ Ⓑ Ⓒ Ⓓ	39 Ⓐ Ⓑ Ⓒ Ⓓ	69 Ⓐ Ⓑ Ⓒ Ⓓ	99 Ⓐ Ⓑ Ⓒ Ⓓ
10 Ⓐ Ⓑ Ⓒ Ⓓ	40 Ⓐ Ⓑ Ⓒ Ⓓ	70 Ⓐ Ⓑ Ⓒ Ⓓ	100 Ⓐ Ⓑ Ⓒ Ⓓ
11 Ⓐ Ⓑ Ⓒ Ⓓ	41 Ⓐ Ⓑ Ⓒ Ⓓ	71 Ⓐ Ⓑ Ⓒ Ⓓ	101 Ⓐ Ⓑ Ⓒ Ⓓ
12 Ⓐ Ⓑ Ⓒ Ⓓ	42 Ⓐ Ⓑ Ⓒ Ⓓ	72 Ⓐ Ⓑ Ⓒ Ⓓ	102 Ⓐ Ⓑ Ⓒ Ⓓ
13 Ⓐ Ⓑ Ⓒ Ⓓ	43 Ⓐ Ⓑ Ⓒ Ⓓ	73 Ⓐ Ⓑ Ⓒ Ⓓ	103 Ⓐ Ⓑ Ⓒ Ⓓ
14 Ⓐ Ⓑ Ⓒ Ⓓ	44 Ⓐ Ⓑ Ⓒ Ⓓ	74 Ⓐ Ⓑ Ⓒ Ⓓ	104 Ⓐ Ⓑ Ⓒ Ⓓ
15 Ⓐ Ⓑ Ⓒ Ⓓ	45 Ⓐ Ⓑ Ⓒ Ⓓ	75 Ⓐ Ⓑ Ⓒ Ⓓ	105 Ⓐ Ⓑ Ⓒ Ⓓ
16 Ⓐ Ⓑ Ⓒ Ⓓ	46 Ⓐ Ⓑ Ⓒ Ⓓ	76 Ⓐ Ⓑ Ⓒ Ⓓ	106 Ⓐ Ⓑ Ⓒ Ⓓ
17 Ⓐ Ⓑ Ⓒ Ⓓ	47 Ⓐ Ⓑ Ⓒ Ⓓ	77 Ⓐ Ⓑ Ⓒ Ⓓ	107 Ⓐ Ⓑ Ⓒ Ⓓ
18 Ⓐ Ⓑ Ⓒ Ⓓ	48 Ⓐ Ⓑ Ⓒ Ⓓ	78 Ⓐ Ⓑ Ⓒ Ⓓ	108 Ⓐ Ⓑ Ⓒ Ⓓ
19 Ⓐ Ⓑ Ⓒ Ⓓ	49 Ⓐ Ⓑ Ⓒ Ⓓ	79 Ⓐ Ⓑ Ⓒ Ⓓ	109 Ⓐ Ⓑ Ⓒ Ⓓ
20 Ⓐ Ⓑ Ⓒ Ⓓ	50 Ⓐ Ⓑ Ⓒ Ⓓ	80 Ⓐ Ⓑ Ⓒ Ⓓ	110 Ⓐ Ⓑ Ⓒ Ⓓ
21 Ⓐ Ⓑ Ⓒ Ⓓ	51 Ⓐ Ⓑ Ⓒ Ⓓ	81 Ⓐ Ⓑ Ⓒ Ⓓ	111 Ⓐ Ⓑ Ⓒ Ⓓ
22 Ⓐ Ⓑ Ⓒ Ⓓ	52 Ⓐ Ⓑ Ⓒ Ⓓ	82 Ⓐ Ⓑ Ⓒ Ⓓ	112 Ⓐ Ⓑ Ⓒ Ⓓ
23 Ⓐ Ⓑ Ⓒ Ⓓ	53 Ⓐ Ⓑ Ⓒ Ⓓ	83 Ⓐ Ⓑ Ⓒ Ⓓ	113 Ⓐ Ⓑ Ⓒ Ⓓ
24 Ⓐ Ⓑ Ⓒ Ⓓ	54 Ⓐ Ⓑ Ⓒ Ⓓ	84 Ⓐ Ⓑ Ⓒ Ⓓ	114 Ⓐ Ⓑ Ⓒ Ⓓ
25 Ⓐ Ⓑ Ⓒ Ⓓ	55 Ⓐ Ⓑ Ⓒ Ⓓ	85 Ⓐ Ⓑ Ⓒ Ⓓ	115 Ⓐ Ⓑ Ⓒ Ⓓ
26 Ⓐ Ⓑ Ⓒ Ⓓ	56 Ⓐ Ⓑ Ⓒ Ⓓ	86 Ⓐ Ⓑ Ⓒ Ⓓ	116 Ⓐ Ⓑ Ⓒ Ⓓ
27 Ⓐ Ⓑ Ⓒ Ⓓ	57 Ⓐ Ⓑ Ⓒ Ⓓ	87 Ⓐ Ⓑ Ⓒ Ⓓ	117 Ⓐ Ⓑ Ⓒ Ⓓ
28 Ⓐ Ⓑ Ⓒ Ⓓ	58 Ⓐ Ⓑ Ⓒ Ⓓ	88 Ⓐ Ⓑ Ⓒ Ⓓ	118 Ⓐ Ⓑ Ⓒ Ⓓ
29 Ⓐ Ⓑ Ⓒ Ⓓ	59 Ⓐ Ⓑ Ⓒ Ⓓ	89 Ⓐ Ⓑ Ⓒ Ⓓ	119 Ⓐ Ⓑ Ⓒ Ⓓ
30 Ⓐ Ⓑ Ⓒ Ⓓ	60 Ⓐ Ⓑ Ⓒ Ⓓ	90 Ⓐ Ⓑ Ⓒ Ⓓ	120 Ⓐ Ⓑ Ⓒ Ⓓ

Clerical Abilities Diagnostic Test

Time allotted—15 minutes

Directions

This test contains some of the kinds of questions that may appear on your test. The time limit for the test will be announced by the examiner.

Study the sample questions carefully. Each question has five suggested answers. Decide which one is the best answer. Find the question number on the Sample Answer Sheet. Show your answer to the question by darkening completely the space corresponding to the letter that is the same as the letter of your answer. Keep your mark within the space. If you have to erase a mark, be sure to erase it completely. Mark only one answer for each question.

Selected Sample Questions

In each line across the page there are three names or numbers that are much alike. Compare the three names or numbers and decide which ones are exactly alike. On the Sample Answer Sheet at the right, mark the answer—

A if ALL THREE names or numbers are exactly ALIKE
B if only the FIRST and SECOND names or numbers are exactly ALIKE
C if only the FIRST and THIRD names or numbers are exactly ALIKE
D if only the SECOND and THIRD names or numbers are exactly ALIKE
E if ALL THREE names or numbers are DIFFERENT

I. Davis Hazen	David Hozen	David Hazen
II. Lois Appel	Lois Appel	Lois Apfel
III. June Allan	Jane Allan	Jane Allan
IV. 10235	10235	10235
V. 32614	32164	32614

SAMPLE ANSWER SHEET

1 Ⓐ Ⓑ Ⓒ Ⓓ Ⓔ
2 Ⓐ Ⓑ Ⓒ Ⓓ Ⓔ
3 Ⓐ Ⓑ Ⓒ Ⓓ Ⓔ
4 Ⓐ Ⓑ Ⓒ Ⓓ Ⓔ
5 Ⓐ Ⓑ Ⓒ Ⓓ Ⓔ
6 Ⓐ Ⓑ Ⓒ Ⓓ Ⓔ
7 Ⓐ Ⓑ Ⓒ Ⓓ Ⓔ

It will be to your advantage to learn what A, B, C, D, and E stand for. If you finish the sample questions before you are told to turn to the test, study them.

In the next group of sample questions, there is a name in a box at the left, and four other names in alphabetical order at the right. Find the correct space for the boxed name so that it will be in alphabetical order with the others, and mark the letter of that space as your answer.

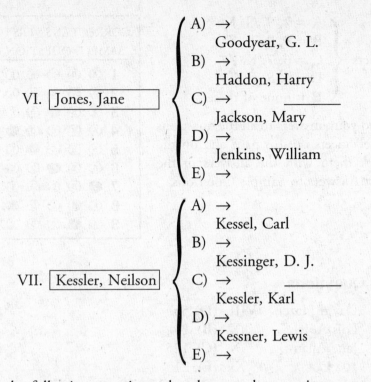

VI. Jones, Jane

A) →
Goodyear, G. L.
B) →
Haddon, Harry
C) → _____
Jackson, Mary
D) →
Jenkins, William
E) →

VII. Kessler, Neilson

A) →
Kessel, Carl
B) →
Kessinger, D. J.
C) → _____
Kessler, Karl
D) →
Kessner, Lewis
E) →

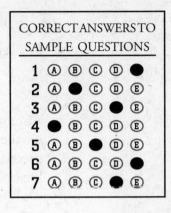

CORRECT ANSWERS TO
SAMPLE QUESTIONS

1 Ⓐ Ⓑ Ⓒ Ⓓ ●
2 Ⓐ ● Ⓒ Ⓓ Ⓔ
3 Ⓐ Ⓑ Ⓒ ● Ⓔ
4 ● Ⓑ Ⓒ Ⓓ Ⓔ
5 Ⓐ Ⓑ ● Ⓓ Ⓔ
6 Ⓐ Ⓑ Ⓒ Ⓓ ●
7 Ⓐ Ⓑ Ⓒ ● Ⓔ

In the following questions, do whatever the question says, and find your answer among the list of suggested answers for that question. Mark the Sample Answer Sheet A, B, C, or D, for the answer you obtained; or if your answer is not among these, mark E for that question.

	Answers			*Answers*	
VIII. Add:	A) 44	B) 45	X. Multiply:	A) 100	B) 115
22	C) 54	D) 55	25	C) 125	D) 135
+ 33	E) none of these		× 5	E) none of these	
IX. Subtract:	A) 20	B) 21	XI. Divide:	A) 20	B) 22
24	C) 27	D) 29	6)126	C) 24	D) 26
− 3	E) none of these			E) none of these	

There is one set of suggested answers for the next group of sample questions. Do not try to memorize these answers, because there will be a different set on each page in the test.

To find the answer to a question, find which suggested answer contains numbers and letters all of which appear in the question. If no suggested answer fits, mark E for that question.

XII. 8 N K 9 G T 4 6

XIII. T 9 7 Z 6 L 3 K

XIV. Z 7 G K 3 9 8 N

XV. 3 K 9 4 6 G Z L

XVI. Z N 7 3 8 K T 9

SAMPLE ANSWER
SHEET

1 Ⓐ Ⓑ Ⓒ Ⓓ Ⓔ
2 Ⓐ Ⓑ Ⓒ Ⓓ Ⓔ
3 Ⓐ Ⓑ Ⓒ Ⓓ Ⓔ
4 Ⓐ Ⓑ Ⓒ Ⓓ Ⓔ
5 Ⓐ Ⓑ Ⓒ Ⓓ Ⓔ
6 Ⓐ Ⓑ Ⓒ Ⓓ Ⓔ
7 Ⓐ Ⓑ Ⓒ Ⓓ Ⓔ
8 Ⓐ Ⓑ Ⓒ Ⓓ Ⓔ
9 Ⓐ Ⓑ Ⓒ Ⓓ Ⓔ

Suggested Answers $\begin{cases} A = 7, 9, G, K \\ B = 8, 9, T, Z \\ C = 6, 7, K, Z \\ D = 6, 8, G, T \\ E = \text{none of these} \end{cases}$

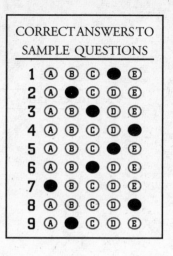

CORRECT ANSWERS TO
SAMPLE QUESTIONS

After you have marked your answers to all the questions on the Sample Answer Sheets on this page and on the preceding page, check them with the answers in the boxes marked Correct Answers to Sample Questions.

Answer Explanations for Sample Questions

I. **(E)** Davis Hazen   David Hozen   David Hazen   VIII. **(D)** 55

II. **(B)** Lois Appel   Lois Appel   Lois Apfel   IX. **(B)** 21

III. **(D)** June Allan   Jane Allan   Jane Allan   X. **(C)** 125

IV. **(A)** 10235   10235   10235   XI. **(E)** 21

V. **(C)** 32614   32164   32614   XII. **(D)** 8 N K 9 G T 4 6

VI. **(E)** Jenkins, William   XIII. **(C)** T 9 Z Z 6 L 3 K

      Jones, Jane   XIV. **(A)** Z Z G K 3 9 8 N

VII. **(D)** Kessier, Karl   XV. **(E)** 3 K 9 Z 6 G Z L

      Kessler, Neilson   XVI. **(B)** Z N 7 3 8 K T 9

      Kessner, Lewis

The Test

In questions 1 through 5, compare the three names or numbers, and mark the answer—

A if ALL THREE names or numbers are exactly ALIKE
B if only the FIRST and SECOND names or numbers are exactly ALIKE
C if only the FIRST and THIRD names or numbers are exactly ALIKE
D if only the SECOND and THIRD names or numbers are exactly ALIKE
E if ALL THREE names or numbers are DIFFERENT

1.	5261383	5261383	5261338
2.	8125690	8126690	8125609
3.	W. E. Johnston	W. E. Johnson	W. E. Johnson
4.	Vergil L. Muller	Vergil L. Muller	Vergil L. Muller
5.	Atherton R. Warde	Asheton R. Warde	Atherton P. Warde

In questions 6 through 10, find the correct place for the name in the box.

6. Hackett, Gerald

A) →
   Habert, James
B) →
   Hachett, J. J.
C) →
   Hachetts, K. Larson
D) →
   Hachettson, Leroy
E) →

7. Margenroth, Alvin

A) →
   Margeroth, Albert
B) →
   Margestein, Dan
C) →
   Margestein, David
D) →
   Margue, Edgar
E) →

8. Bobbitt, Olivier E.

A) →
   Bobbitt, D. Olivier
B) →
   Bobbitt, Olive B.
C) →
   Bobbitt, Olivia H.
D) →
   Bobbitt, R. Olivia
E) →

9. Mosely, Werner

A) →
   Mosely, Albert J.
B) →
   Mosley, Alvin
C) →
   Mosley, S. M.
D) →
   Mozley, Vinson N.
E) →

10. Youmuns, Frank I.

A) →
   Youmons, Frank G.
B) →
   Youmons, Frank H.
C) →
   Youmons, Frank K.
D) →
   Youmons, Frank M.
E) →

GO ON TO THE NEXT COLUMN.

Answers

11. Add:
   43
   + 32

   A) 55 B) 65
   C) 66 D) 75
   E) none of these

12. Subtract:
   83
   − 4

   A) 73 B) 79
   C) 80 D) 89
   E) none of these

13. Multiply:
   41
   × 7

   A) 281 B) 287
   C) 291 D) 297
   E) none of these

14. Divide:

   6)306

   A) 44 B) 51
   C) 52 D) 60
   E) none of these

15. Add:
   37
   + 15

   A) 42 B) 52
   C) 53 D) 62
   E) none of these

For each question below, find which one of the suggested answers appears in that question.

16. 6 2 5 K 4 P T G

17. L 4 7 2 T 6 V K

18. 3 5 4 L 9 V T G

19. G 4 K 7 L 3 5 Z

20. 4 K 2 9 N 5 T G

Suggested Answers
A = 4, 5, K, T
B = 4, 7, G, K
C = 2, 5, G, L
D = 2, 7, L, T
E = none of these

GO ON TO THE NEXT PAGE.

In questions 21 through 25, compare the three names or numbers, and mark the answer—

A if ALL THREE names or numbers are exactly ALIKE
B if only the FIRST and SECOND names or numbers are exactly ALIKE
C if only the FIRST and THIRD names or numbers are exactly ALIKE
D if only the SECOND and THIRD names or numbers are exactly ALIKE
E if ALL THREE names or numbers are DIFFERENT

21.	2395890	2395890	2395890
22.	1926341	1926347	1926314
23.	E. Owens McVey	E. Owen McVey	E. Owen McVay
24.	Emily Neal Rouse	Emily Neal Rowse	Emily Neal Rowse
25.	H. Merritt Audubon	H. Merriott Audubon	H. Merritt Audubon

In questions 26 through 30, find the correct place for the name in the box.

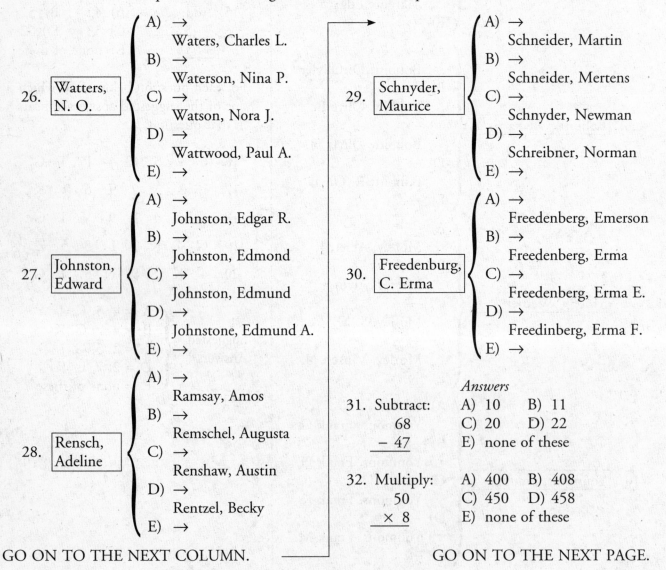

26. Watters, N. O.

A) →
Waters, Charles L.
B) →
Waterson, Nina P.
C) →
Watson, Nora J.
D) →
Wattwood, Paul A.
E) →

27. Johnston, Edward

A) →
Johnston, Edgar R.
B) →
Johnston, Edmond
C) →
Johnston, Edmund
D) →
Johnstone, Edmund A.
E) →

28. Rensch, Adeline

A) →
Ramsay, Amos
B) →
Remschel, Augusta
C) →
Renshaw, Austin
D) →
Rentzel, Becky
E) →

29. Schnyder, Maurice

A) →
Schneider, Martin
B) →
Schneider, Mertens
C) →
Schnyder, Newman
D) →
Schreibner, Norman
E) →

30. Freedenburg, C. Erma

A) →
Freedenberg, Emerson
B) →
Freedenberg, Erma
C) →
Freedenberg, Erma E.
D) →
Freedinberg, Erma F.
E) →

Answers

31. Subtract:
   68
   − 47

A) 10   B) 11
C) 20   D) 22
E) none of these

32. Multiply:
   50
   × 8

A) 400   B) 408
C) 450   D) 458
E) none of these

GO ON TO THE NEXT COLUMN.

GO ON TO THE NEXT PAGE.

Answers

33. Divide: A) 20   B) 29
                C) 30   D) 39

$9\overline{)180}$ E) none of these

34. Add: A) 131   B) 140
    78   C) 141   D) 151
 + 63   E) none of these

35. Subtract: A) 9   B) 18
   89   C) 19   D) 29
 − 70   E) none of these

For each question below, find which one of the suggested answers appears in that question.

GO ON TO THE NEXT COLUMN.

36. 9 G Z 3 L 4 6 N

37. L 5 N K 4 3 9 V

38. 8 2 V P 9 L Z 5

39. V P 9 Z 5 L 8 7

40. 5 T 8 N 2 9 V L

Suggested Answers
$$\begin{cases} A = 4, 9, L, V \\ B = 4, 5, N, Z \\ C = 5, 8, L, Z \\ D = 8, 9, N, V \\ E = \text{none of these} \end{cases}$$

In questions 41 through 45, compare the three names or numbers, and mark the answer—

A if ALL THREE names or numbers are exactly ALIKE
B if only the FIRST and SECOND names or numbers are exactly ALIKE
C if only the FIRST and THIRD names or numbers are exactly ALIKE
D if only the SECOND and THIRD names or numbers are exactly ALIKE
E if ALL THREE names or numbers are DIFFERENT

41.	6219354	6219354	6219354
42.	2312793	2312793	2312793
43.	1065407	1065407	1065047
44.	Francis Ransdell	Frances Ramsdell	Francis Ramsdell
45.	Cornelius Detwiler	Cornelius Detwiler	Cornelius Detwiler

In questions 46 through 50, find the correct place for the name in the box.

46. DeMattia, Jessica
- A) →
  DeLong, Jesse
- B) →
  DeMatteo, Jessie
- C) →
  Derby, Jessie S.
- D) →
  DeShazo, L. M.
- E) →

47. Theriault, Louis
- A) →
  Therien, Annette
- B) →
  Therien, Elaine
- C) →
  Thibeault, Gerald
- D) →
  Thiebeault, Pierre
- E) →

48. Gaston M. Hubert
- A) →
  Gaston, Dorothy M.
- B) →
  Gaston, Henry N.
- C) →
  Gaston, Isabel
- D) →
  Gaston, M. Melvin
- E) →

49. SanMiguel, Carlos
- A) →
  SanLuis, Juana
- B) →
  Santilli, Laura
- C) →
  Stinnett, Nellie
- D) →
  Stoddard, Victor
- E) →

50. DeLaTour, Hall F.
- A) →
  Delargy, Harold
- B) →
  DeLathouder, Hilda
- C) →
  Lathrop, Hillary
- D) →
  LaTour, Hullbert E.
- E) →

GO ON TO THE NEXT COLUMN.

Answers

51. Multiply:
62
× 5
A) 300 B) 310
C) 315 D) 360
E) none of these

52. Divide:
3)153
A) 41 B) 43
C) 51 D) 53
E) none of these

53. Add:
47
+ 21
A) 58 B) 59
C) 67 D) 68
E) none of these

54. Subtract:
87
− 42
A) 34 B) 35
C) 44 D) 45
E) none of these

55. Multiply:
37
× 3
A) 91 B) 101
C) 104 D) 114
E) none of these

For each question below, find which one of the suggested answers appears in that question.

56. N 5 4 7 T K 3 Z

57. 8 5 3 V L 2 Z N

58. 7 2 5 N 9 K L V

59. 9 8 L 2 5 Z K V

60. Z 6 5 V 9 3 9 N

Suggested Answers
- A = 3, 8, K, N
- B = 5, 8, N, V
- C = 3, 9, V, Z
- D = 5, 9, K, Z
- E = none of these

GO ON TO THE NEXT PAGE.

In questions 61 through 65, compare the three names or numbers, and mark the answer—

A if ALL THREE names or numbers are exactly ALIKE
B if only the FIRST and SECOND names or numbers are exactly ALIKE
C if only the FIRST and THIRD names or numbers are exactly ALIKE
D if only the SECOND and THIRD names or numbers are exactly ALIKE
E if ALL THREE names or numbers are DIFFERENT

61.	6452054	6452654	6452054
62.	8501268	8501268	8501286
63.	Ella Burk Newham	Ella Burk Newnham	Elena Burk Newnham
64.	Jno. K. Ravencroft	Jno. H. Ravencroft	Jno. H. Ravnecoft
65.	Martin Wills Pullen	Martin Wills Pulen	Martin Wills Pullen

In questions 66 through 70, find the correct place for the name in the box.

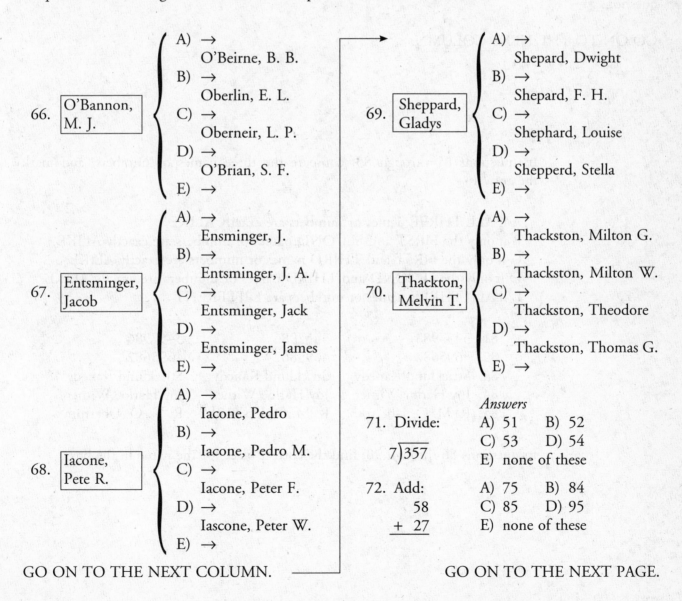

66. O'Bannon, M. J.
A) →
O'Beirne, B. B.
B) →
Oberlin, E. L.
C) →
Oberneir, L. P.
D) →
O'Brian, S. F.
E) →

67. Entsminger, Jacob
A) →
Ensminger, J.
B) →
Entsminger, J. A.
C) →
Entsminger, Jack
D) →
Entsminger, James
E) →

68. Iacone, Pete R.
A) →
Iacone, Pedro
B) →
Iacone, Pedro M.
C) →
Iacone, Peter F.
D) →
Iascone, Peter W.
E) →

69. Sheppard, Gladys
A) →
Shepard, Dwight
B) →
Shepard, F. H.
C) →
Shephard, Louise
D) →
Shepperd, Stella
E) →

70. Thackton, Melvin T.
A) →
Thackston, Milton G.
B) →
Thackston, Milton W.
C) →
Thackston, Theodore
D) →
Thackston, Thomas G.
E) →

Answers

71. Divide:

$7\overline{)357}$

A) 51 B) 52
C) 53 D) 54
E) none of these

72. Add:
    58
  + 27

A) 75 B) 84
C) 85 D) 95
E) none of these

GO ON TO THE NEXT COLUMN.   GO ON TO THE NEXT PAGE.

Answers

73. Subtract:
    86
    − 57

A) 18   B) 29
C) 38   D) 39
E) none of these

74. Multiply:
    68
    × 4

A) 242   B) 264
C) 272   D) 274
E) none of these

75. Divide:
    9)639

A) 71   B) 73
C) 81   D) 83
E) none of these

For each question below, find which one of the suggested answers appears in that question.

GO ON TO THE NEXT COLUMN.

76. 6 Z T N 8 7 4 V

77. V 7 8 6 N 5 P L

78. N 7 P V 8 4 2 L

79. 7 8 G 4 3 V L T

80. 4 8 G 2 T N 6 L

Suggested Answers
{
A = 2, 7, L, N
B = 2, 8, T, V
C = 6, 8, L, T
D = 6, 7, N, V
E = none of these
}

In questions 81 through 85, compare the three names or numbers, and mark the answer—

A if ALL THREE names or numbers are exactly ALIKE
B if only the FIRST and SECOND names or numbers are exactly ALIKE
C if only the FIRST and THIRD names or numbers are exactly ALIKE
D if only the SECOND and THIRD names or numbers are exactly ALIKE
E if ALL THREE names or numbers are DIFFERENT

81. 3457988	3457986	3457986
82. 4695682	4695862	4695682
83. Stricklund Kanedy	Stricklund Kanedy	Stricklund Kanedy
84. Joy Harlor Witner	Joy Harloe Witner	Joy Harloe Witner
85. R. M. O. Uberroth	R. M. O. Uberroth	R. N. O. Uberroth

In questions 86 through 90, find the correct place for the name in the box.

86. | Dunlavery, M. Hilary |

A) →
Dunleavy, Hilary G.
B) →
Dunleavy, Hilary K.
C) →
Dunleavy, Hilary S.
D) →
Dunleavy, Hilery W.
E) →

87. | Yarbrough, Maria |

A) →
Yabroudy, Margy
B) →
Yarboro, Marie
C) →
Yarborough, Marina
D) →
Yarborough, Mary
E) →

88. | Prouty, Martha |

A) →
Proutey, Margaret
B) →
Proutey, Maude
C) →
Prouty, Myra
D) →
Prouty, Naomi
E) →

89. | Pawlowicz, Ruth M. |

A) →
Pawalek, Edward
B) →
Pawelek, Flora G.
C) →
Pawlowski, Joan M.
D) →
Pawtowski, Wanda
E) →

90. | Vanstory, George |

A) →
Vanover, Eva
B) →
VanSwinderen, Floyd
C) →
VanSyckle, Harry
D) →
Vanture, Laurence
E) →

GO ON TO THE NEXT COLUMN.

Answers

91. Add:
28
+ 35
A) 53 B) 62 C) 64 D) 73 E) none of these

92. Subtract:
78
− 69
A) 7 B) 8 C) 18 D) 19 E) none of these

93. Multiply:
86
× 6
A) 492 B) 506 C) 516 D) 526 E) none of these

94. Divide:
8)648
A) 71 B) 76 C) 81 D) 89 E) none of these

95. Add:
97
+ 34
A) 131 B) 132 C) 140 D) 141 E) none of these

For each question below, find which one of the suggested answers appears in that question.

96. V 5 7 Z N 9 4 T

97. 4 6 P T 2 N K 9

98. 6 4 N 2 P 8 Z K

99. 7 P 5 2 4 N K T

100. K T 8 5 4 N 2 P

Suggested Answers
A = 2, 5, N, Z
B = 4, 5, N, P
C = 2, 9, P, T
D = 4, 9, T, Z
E = none of these

GO ON TO THE NEXT PAGE.

In questions 101 through 105, compare the three names or numbers, and mark the answer—

A if ALL THREE names or numbers are exactly ALIKE
B if only the FIRST and SECOND names or numbers are exactly ALIKE
C if only the FIRST and THIRD names or numbers are exactly ALIKE
D if only the SECOND and THIRD names or numbers are exactly ALIKE
E if ALL THREE names or numbers are DIFFERENT

101.	1592514	1592574	1592574
102.	2010202	2010202	2010220
103.	6177396	6177936	6177396
104.	Drusilla S. Ridgeley	Drusilla S. Ridgeley	Drusilla S. Ridgeley
105.	Andrei I. Toumantzev	Andrei I. Tourmantzev	Aňdrei I. Toumantzov

In questions 106 through 110, find the correct place for the name in the box.

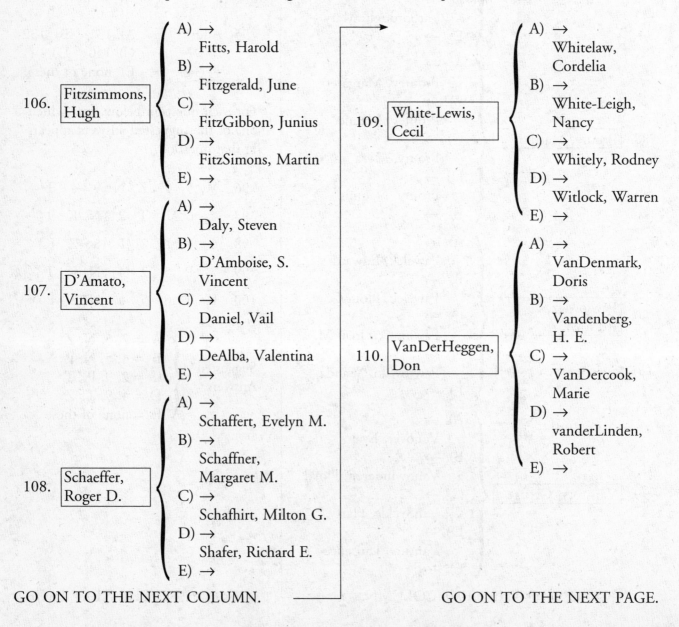

106. **Fitzsimmons, Hugh**
A) →
Fitts, Harold
B) →
Fitzgerald, June
C) →
FitzGibbon, Junius
D) →
FitzSimons, Martin
E) →

107. **D'Amato, Vincent**
A) →
Daly, Steven
B) →
D'Amboise, S. Vincent
C) →
Daniel, Vail
D) →
DeAlba, Valentina
E) →

108. **Schaeffer, Roger D.**
A) →
Schaffert, Evelyn M.
B) →
Schaffner, Margaret M.
C) →
Schafhirt, Milton G.
D) →
Shafer, Richard E.
E) →

109. **White-Lewis, Cecil**
A) →
Whitelaw, Cordelia
B) →
White-Leigh, Nancy
C) →
Whitely, Rodney
D) →
Witlock, Warren
E) →

110. **VanDerHeggen, Don**
A) →
VanDenmark, Doris
B) →
Vandenberg, H. E.
C) →
VanDercook, Marie
D) →
vanderLinden, Robert
E) →

GO ON TO THE NEXT COLUMN.   GO ON TO THE NEXT PAGE.

Answers

111. Add: A) 124   B) 125

       75   C) 134   D) 225

    + 49   E) none of these

112. Subtract: A) 14   B) 23

       69   C) 24   D) 26

    − 45   E) none of these

113. Multiply: A) 246   B) 262

       36   C) 288   D) 368

    × 8   E) none of these

114. Divide: A) 31   B) 41

             C) 42   D) 48

   8)328   E) none of these

115. Multiply: A) 472   B) 513

       58   C) 521   D) 522

    × 9   E) none of these

For each question below, find which one of the suggested answers appears in that question.

GO ON TO THE NEXT COLUMN.

116. Z 3 N P G 5 4 2

117. 6 N 2 8 G 4 P T

118. 6 N 4 T V G 8 2

119. T 3 P 4 N 8 G 2

120. 6 7 K G N 2 L 5

Suggested Answers
$$\begin{cases} A = 2, 3, G, N \\ B = 2, 6, N, T \\ C = 3, 4, G, K \\ D = 4, 6, K, T \\ E = \text{none of these} \end{cases}$$

IF YOU FINISH BEFORE THE TIME IS UP, YOU MAY GO BACK AND CHECK YOUR ANSWERS.

Answer Key for Diagnostic Test

Alike or Different

1. **B**	21. **A**	41. **A**	61. **C**	81. **D**	101. **D**
2. **E**	22. **E**	42. **A**	62. **B**	82. **C**	102. **B**
3. **D**	23. **E**	43. **B**	63. **E**	83. **A**	103. **C**
4. **A**	24. **D**	44. **E**	64. **E**	84. **D**	104. **A**
5. **E**	25. **C**	45. **A**	65. **C**	85. **B**	105. **E**

Alphabetizing

6. **E**	26. **D**	46. **C**	66. **A**	86. **A**	106. **D**
7. **A**	27. **D**	47. **A**	67. **D**	87. **E**	107. **B**
8. **D**	28. **C**	48. **D**	68. **C**	88. **C**	108. **A**
9. **B**	29. **C**	49. **B**	69. **D**	89. **C**	109. **C**
10. **E**	30. **D**	50. **C**	70. **E**	90. **B**	110. **D**

Arithmetic

11. **D**	31. **E**	51. **B**	71. **A**	91. **E**	111. **A**
12. **B**	32. **A**	52. **C**	72. **C**	92. **E**	112. **C**
13. **B**	33. **A**	53. **D**	73. **B**	93. **C**	113. **C**
14. **B**	34. **C**	54. **D**	74. **C**	94. **C**	114. **B**
15. **B**	35. **C**	55. **E**	75. **A**	95. **A**	115. **D**

Letters and Numbers

16.	**A**	36.	**E**	56.	**E**	76.	**D**	96.	**D**	116.	**A**
17.	**D**	37.	**A**	57.	**B**	77.	**D**	97.	**C**	117.	**B**
18.	**E**	38.	**C**	58.	**E**	78.	**A**	98.	**E**	118.	**B**
18.	**B**	39.	**C**	59.	**D**	79.	**E**	99.	**B**	119.	**A**
20.	**A**	40.	**D**	60.	**C**	80.	**C**	100.	**B**	120.	**E**

Analysis Chart for Diagnostic Test

Now that you've corrected your exam, use the following chart to carefully analyze your results and spot your strengths and weaknesses. This analysis should help you focus your study and review efforts.

Section	Total Number of Questions	Number Correct	Number Incorrect	Number Unanswered*
Alike or Different	30			
Alphabetizing	30			
Arithmetic	30			
Letters and Numbers	30			
TOTAL	120			

Since there is no penalty for incorrect answers on the Clerical Aptitude Part, you should not guess "blindly." Try to eliminate one or more of the choices before you take your educated guess.

Answer Explanations for Diagnostic Test

1. **(B)** 5261383   5261383   5261338
2. **(E)** 8125690   8126690   8125609
3. **(D)** W. E. Johnston   W. E. Johnson   W. E. Johnson
4. **(A)** Vergil L. Muller   Vergil L. Muller   Vergil L. Muller
5. **(E)** Atherton R. Warde   Asheton R. Warde   Atherton P. Warde
6. **(E)** Hachettson, Leroy
   Hackett, Gerald
7. **(A)** *Margenroth, Alvin*
   Margeroth, Albert
8. **(D)** Bobbitt, Olivia H.
   Bobbitt, Olivier E.
   Bobbitt, R. Olivia
9. **(B)** Mosely, Albert J.
   Mosely Werner
   Mosley, Alvin
10. **(E)** Youmotis, Frank M.
    Youmuns, Frank L.
11. **(D)** 75
12. **(B)** 79
13. **(B)** 287

14. **(B)** 51
15. **(B)** 52
16. **(A)** 6 2 <u>5</u> <u>K</u> <u>4</u> P T G
17. **(D)** L 4 <u>7</u> 2 <u>T</u> 6 V K
18. **(E)** 3 5 T L 9 V T G
19. **(B)** <u>G</u> <u>4</u> <u>K</u> <u>7</u> L 3 5 Z
20. **(A)** <u>4</u> <u>K</u> 2 9 N <u>5</u> <u>T</u> G
21. **(A)** 2395890   2395890   2395890
22. **(E)** 192634<u>1</u>   192634<u>7</u>   19263<u>14</u>
23. **(E)** E. Owen<u>s</u> McVey   E. Owen McVey   E. Owen McV<u>a</u>y
24. **(D)** Emily Neal Ro<u>u</u>se   Emily Neal Rowse   Emily Neal Rowse
25. **(C)** H. Merritt Audubon   H. Merri<u>ott</u> Audubon   H. Merritt Audubon
26. **(D)** Watson, Noraj.
         Wat<u>ters</u>, N. O.
         Wattwood, Paul A.
27. **(D)** Johnston, Edmund
         Johns<u>ton</u>, Edward
         Johnstone, Edmund A.
28. **(C)** Remschel, Augusta
         Ren<u>sch</u>, Adeline
         Renshaw, Austin
29. **(C)** Schneider, Mertens
         Sch<u>nyder</u>, Maurice
         Schnyder, Newman
30. **(D)** Freedenberg, Erma E.
         Freeden<u>burg</u>, C. Erma
         Freedinberg, Erma F.
31. **(E)** 21
32. **(A)** 400
33. **(A)** 20
34. **(C)** 141
35. **(C)** 19
36. **(E)** 9 G Z 3 L 4 6 N
37. **(A)** <u>L</u> 5 N K <u>4</u> 3 <u>9</u> <u>V</u>
38. **(C)** <u>8</u> 2 V P 9 <u>L</u> <u>Z</u> <u>5</u>
39. **(C)** V P 9 <u>Z</u> <u>5</u> <u>L</u> <u>8</u> 7
40. **(D)** 5 T <u>8</u> <u>N</u> 2 <u>9</u> <u>V</u> L
41. **(A)** 6219354   6219354   6219354
42. **(A)** 2312793   2312793   2312793
43. **(B)** 1065407   1065407   1065<u>04</u>7
44. **(E)** Francis Ra<u>n</u>sdell   Franc<u>es</u> Ramsdell   Francis Ramsdell
45. **(A)** Cornelius Detwiler   Corn<u>i</u>lius Detwiler   Cornelius Detwiler
46. **(C)** DeMatteo, Jessie
         DeMat<u>tia</u>, Jessica
         Derby, Jessie S.
47. **(A)** *Theri<u>a</u>ult, Louis*
         Therien, Annette

48. **(D)** Gaston, Isabel
Gaston, M. Hubert
Gaston, M. Melvin

49. **(B)** SanLuis, Juana
San Miguel, Carlos
Santilli, Laura

50. **(C)** DeLathouder, Hilda
DeLaTour, Hall F.
Lathrop, Hillary

51. **(B)** 310
52. **(C)** 51
53. **(D)** 68
54. **(D)** 45
55 **(E)** 111
56. **(E)** N 5 4 7 T K 3 Z
57. **(B)** 8 5 3 V L 2 Z N
58. **(E)** 7 2 5 N 9 K L V
59. **(D)** 9 8 L 2 5 Z K V
60. **(C)** Z 6 5 V 9 3 P N

61. **(C)** 6452054   6452654   6452054
62 **(B)** 8501268   8501268   8501286
63. **(E)** Ella Burk Newham   Ella Burk Newnham   Elena Burk Newnham
64. **(E)** Jno. K. Ravencroft   Jno. H. Ravencroft   Jno. H. Ravencoft
65. **(C)** Martin Wills Pullen   Martin Wills Pulen   Martin Wills Pullen

66. **(A)** *O'Bannon, M. J.*
O'Beirne, B. B.

67. **(D)** Entsminger, Jack
Entsminger, Jacob
Entsminger, James

68. **(C)** Iacone, Pedro M.
Iacone, Pete R.
Iacone, Peter F.

69. **(D)** Shephard, Louise
Sheppard, Gladys
Shepperd, Stella

70. **(E)** Thackston, Thomas G.
Thackton, Melvin T.

71. **(A)** 51
72. **(C)** 85
73. **(B)** 29
74. **(C)** 272
75. **(A)** 71
76. **(D)** 6 Z T N 8 7 4 V
77. **(D)** V 7 8 6 N 5 P L
78. **(A)** N 7 P V 8 4 2 L
79. **(E)** 7 8 G 4 3 V L T
80. **(C)** 4 8 G 2 T N 6 L

81.	**(D)**	3457988	3457986	3457986
82.	**(C)**	4695682	4695862	4695682
83.	**(A)**	Stricklund, Kanedy	Stricklund, Kanedy	Stricklund, Kanedy
84.	**(D)**	Joy Harlor Witner	Joy Harloe Witner	Joy Harloe Witner
85.	**(B)**	R. M. O. Uberroth	R. M. O. Uberroth	R. N. O. Uberroth

86. **(A)** *Dunlavey, M. Hilary*
Dunleavy, Hilary G.

87. **(E)** Yarborough, Mary
Yarbrough, Maria

88. **(C)** Proutey, Maude
Prouty, Martha
Prouty, Myra

89. **(C)** Pawelek, Flora G.
Pawlowicz, Ruth M.
Pawlowski, Joan M.

90. **(B)** Vanover, Eva
Vanstory, George
VanSwinderen, Floyd

91. **(E)** 63

92. **(E)** 9

93. **(C)** 516

94. **(C)** 81

95. **(A)** 131

96. **(D)** V 5 7 Z N 9 4 T

97. **(C)** 4 6 P T 2 N K 9

98. **(E)** 6 4 N 2 P 8 Z K

99. **(B)** 7 P 5 2 4 N K T

100. **(B)** K T 8 5 4 N 2 P

101.	**(D)**	1592514	1592574	1592574
102.	**(B)**	2010202	2010202	2010220
103.	**(C)**	6177396	6177936	6177396
104.	**(A)**	Drusilla S. Ridgeley	Drusilia S. Ridgeley	Drusilia S. Ridgeley
105.	**(E)**	Andrei I. Toumantzev	Andrei I. Tourmantzev	Andrei I. Toumantzov

106. **(D)** FitzGibbon, Junius
Fitzsimmons, Hugh
FitzSimons, Martin

107. **(B)** Daly, Steven
D'Amato, Vincent
D'Amboise, S. Vincent

108. **(A)** *Schaeffer, Roger D.*
Schaffert, Evelyn M.

109. **(C)** White-Leigh, Nancy
White-Lewis, Cecil
Whitely, Podney

110. **(D)** VanDercook, Marie
VanDerHeggen, Don
vanderLinden, Robert

111. **(A)** 124
112. **(C)** 24
113. **(C)** 288
114. **(B)** 41
115. **(D)** 522
116. **(A)** Z 3 N P G 5 4 2
117. **(B)** 6 N 2 8 G 4 P T
118. **(B)** 6 N 4 T V G 8 2
119. **(A)** T 3 P 4 N 8 G 2
120. **(E)** 6 7 K G N 2 L 5

Understanding the Clerical Abilities Sections: Key Strategies

CHAPTER 4

Practice, Practice, Practice

ALIKE OR DIFFERENT (NAME AND NUMBER CHECKING)

This question type tests your observation skills. You are given three names or three sets of numbers and are asked to determine if

ALL THREE are alike (answer A)
only the FIRST and SECOND are alike (answer B)
only the FIRST and THIRD are alike (answer C)
only the SECOND and THIRD are alike (answer D)
NONE of them are alike (answer E)

For example:

Harmon A. Killebrew
Harmon A. Killebrew
Harmonn A. Killebrew

Notice that the third name has a double "n," making it different from the first two names. Therefore since only the FIRST and SECOND are alike, the answer is B.
Or another example:

3546798
3547698
3546798

Notice here that the first and third are alike, but the second set of numbers is different—the 6 and 7 are reversed. Therefore the answer is C.

Helpful Techniques and Strategies

1. Before you take your actual test, be sure to understand and memorize what each answer choice indicates. You should not have to keep looking back and forth from the problems to the directions for every question.

2. Practice the many questions in this book, finding a particular technique that works best for you. Here are some suggestions:

FOR THE NUMBERS

a. Because there are seven numbers in each set, you may read the set as if it's a telephone number. If you are used to working with phone numbers, saying to yourself ("subvocalizing") a telephone "exchange" (the first three numbers) followed by four digits may be a helpful method.
For example:

2698621
2698612
2698612

Thus, you might subvocalize "269-8621" for the first set. Then, since the beginning of the next set, "269-," sounds the same, you continue with the last four digits "8612." These sound different from the four digits in the first set. Therefore, you know sets 1 and 2 are different, because of the last four digits. Now try the third set: "269-" (the "exchange" sounds the same) "8612." Which last four digits does the third set duplicate? Quickly checking, you find the last four digits of set 2 are also "8612." The answer is (D).

b. This telephone technique has variations. You may wish to compare the first three digits (the "exchange") in each set separately; then compare the last four digits in each set—a divide and conquer strategy.

c. Or you may wish to try "Odd Man Out" checking the first two sets to determine if they're similar. If they are, you then go to the third to see whether you have an (A) answer (all ALIKE) or a (B) answer (only the first two ALIKE). If the first two are different, then proceed to the third to see if the third matches the first set (answer C), or the second set (answer D), or neither set (answer E).

d. Whichever technique you develop, watch out for "reversals."
For example:

4695862
4695682
4695862

Notice that sets 1 and 3 are alike, but that 8 and 6 are reversed in set 2. Such reversals are often easily missed.

FOR THE NAMES

a. Saying the names *carefully* in your mind may be helpful, but sometimes names spelled differently can sound alike.

b. You may wish to "divide and conquer": first comparing first names, then initials, then last names.

c. Watch for the following:

Double letters. Often a letter will be single in one name but doubled in another.

> Bob Ubcrroth
> Bob Uberroth
> Bob Uberoth

The third name has a single "r."

Silent letters

> Emiley Smyth
> Emiley Smyth
> Emily Smith

Notice how all three first names will sound the same despite the last name not having the second "e."

Reversals. Especially look for reversals of vowels, easy to miss. For example:

> Annette Tharien
> Annette Tharien
> Annette Tharein

Notice the "i" and "e" reversed in the third name.

Different common spellings. Be aware of names (like Francis/Frances) that have more than one correct spelling. For example:

> Francis Ramsdell
> Frances Ramsdell
> Frances Ramsdell

Only the second and the third names are alike, because "Francis" is spelled with an "i" in the first name.

Reverse letters. Some letters arc the mirror image of other letters, and these can sometimes be confusing, especially if you are working at top speed. For example, "p" is the mirror image of "q." The letter "b" is the reverse of the letter "d." Some people have special difficulties with these kinds of letters. Try these:

> Larry P. Dobkin
> Larry P. Dobkin
> Larry P. Dodkin

Notice the "d" in the last name; the others contain a "b."

Look-alike letters. And finally keep on your toes when you see certain letters that can be easily misread as other letters. For instance, an "m" may often be misread as an "n," and vice versa. An "s" may be misread as a "z," and a "q" as a "g." As you practice, you'll begin to spot these, and you should try to remember them. For example:

Ernest Ramsdell
Ernest Ransdell
Ernest Ramsdell

Notice that "Ramsdell" is spelled with an "n," rather than an "m," in the second case. Or:

Alfredo C. Lopes
Alfredo C. Lopez
Alfredo C. Lopez

Notice the "s" in the first name, the others end in "z."

Practice Set 1

Compare the three names or numbers, and mark the answer—

A if ALL THREE names or numbers are exactly ALIKE
B if only the FIRST and SECOND names or numbers are exactly ALIKE
C if only the FIRST and THIRD names or numbers are exactly ALIKE
D if only the SECOND and THIRD names or numbers are exactly ALIKE
E if ALL THREE names or numbers are DIFFERENT

1. 9854688	9854688	9854668	_____
2. 1003873	1003873	1003873	_____
3. 4837261	4837621	4837621	_____
4. Oswald Dunleavey	Oswald Dunleavey	Oswals Dunleavy	_____
5. Joseph Willierdite	Joseph Willierdite	Joseph Willierdite	_____
6. 6978459	6974859	6974589	_____
7. 3823145	3832145	3823145	_____
8. Stacey Baum Pleskoff	Stacy Baum Plesckoff	Stacey Baum Pleskof	_____
9. C. J. Farleighbacker	C. J. Farleighbacker	C. J. Farleighbacher	_____
10. Arnold M. Goulian	Arnold M. Goulain	Arnold M. Goulian	_____

11. 8093472   8093472   8093472   _____

12. 4768523   4765823   4765833   _____

13. 9487297   9482797   9482797   _____

14. Dona Leszyzski   Dona Leszyczski Donna Leszyzski _____

15. Joy Mondragon   Joy Mondragon   Joy Mondragan   _____

16. 7465938   7465398   7465938   _____

17. 1489235   1489325   1489325   _____

18. William E. Jerzsinski   William E. Jerszinski   William E. Jerzsinski   _____

19. Ernest VanSwickerton   Ernest VanSwikirten   Ernest VanSwickerten   _____

20. Fredda Wilmarettez   Fredda Wilmarettez   Freda Wilmarettez   _____

21. 5839287   5832987   5832987   _____

22. 9372638   9732368   9732368   _____

23. Lazaro F. Cosgrove   Lasaro F. Cosgrove   Lazaro F. Casgrove   _____

24. Lucila Fontanez   Lucila Fonanes   Lunita Fontanez   _____

25. Armand Cisalissi   Armand Cisilissi   Armand Cisalissi   _____

26. 4873983   4873983   4783983   _____

27. 9578246   9578246   9578246   _____

28. 5797358   5797358   5797538   _____

29. Robin I. Gastongauy   Robin I. Gastonguay   Robin I. Gastanquay   _____

30. Alfred Geisthardt   Alfred Geisthartd   Alfred Geisthardt   _____

Answer Explanations for Practice Set 1

1. **(B)** 9854688   9854688   9854668
2. **(A)** 1003873   1003873   1003873
3. **(D)** 4837261   4837621   4837621
4. **(B)** Oswald Dunleavey   Oswald Dunleavey   Oswals Dunleavy
5. **(A)** Joseph Willierdite   Joseph Willierdite   Joseph Willierdite

6. **(E)** 6978459   6974859   6974589
7. **(C)** 3823145   3832145   3823145
8. **(E)** Stacey Baum Pleskoff   Stacy Baum Plesckoff   Stacey Baum Pleskof
9. **(B)** C. J. Farleighbacker   C. J. Farleighbacker   C.J. Farteighbacher
10. **(C)** Arnold M. Goulian   Arnold M. Goulain   Arnold M. Goulian
11. **(A)** 8093472   8093472   8093472
12. **(E)** 4768523   4765823   4765833
13. **(D)** 9487297   9482797   9482797
14. **(E)** Dora Leszyzski   Dona Leszyczski   Donna Leszyzski
15. **(B)** Joy Mondragon   Joy Mondragon   Joy Mondragan
16. **(C)** 7465938   7465398   7465938
17. **(D)** 1489235   1489325   1489325
18. **(C)** William E. Jerzsinski   William E. Jerszinski   William E. Jerzsinski
19. **(E)** Ernest VanSwickerton   Ernest VanSwikirten   Ernest VanSwickerten
20. **(B)** Fredda Wilniarettez   FreddaWilmarettez   Freda Wilmarettez
21. **(D)** 5839287   5832987   5832987
22. **(D)** 9372638   9732368   9732368
23. **(E)** Lazaro F. Cosgrove   Lasaro F. Cosgrove   Lazaro F. Casgrove
24. **(E)** Lucila Fontanez   Lucila Fonanes   Lunita Fontanez
25. **(C)** Armand Cisalissi   Armand Cisilissi   Armand Cisalissi
26. **(B)** 4873983   4873983   4783983
27. **(A)** 9578246   9578246   9578246
28. **(B)** 5797358   5797358   5797538
29. **(E)** Robin I. Gastongauy   Robin I. Gastonguay   Robin I. Gastanguay
30. **(C)** Alfred Geisthardt   Alfred Geisthartd   Alfred Geisthardt

Practice Set 2

Compare the three names or numbers, and mark the answer—

A if ALL THREE names or numbers are exactly ALIKE
B if only the FIRST and SECOND names or numbers are exactly ALIKE
C if only the FIRST and THIRD names or numbers are exactly ALIKE
D if only the SECOND and THIRD names or numbers are exactly ALIKE
E if ALL THREE names or numbers are DIFFERENT

1. 9358745   9358745   9357845   _____

2. 8574690   8547690   8547690   _____

3. Raymond H.   Raymond H.   Raymond H.   _____
   Didsbury   Diddsbury   Didsburry

4. Stephen M. Tranz   Stephen M. Tranz   Stephen M. Tramz   _____

5. Kevin C. Kretchmer   Kevin C. Kretchmer   Kevin C. Kretchmer   _____

6. 7534689   7354689   7534689   _____

7. 4736258	4736258	4736258	_____
8. 9273415	9274315	9274315	_____
9. Douglas S. Borghi	Douglass S. Borghi	Douglass S. Borghi	_____
10. Vartan Bergquist	Vartan Berquist	Vartan Berquist	_____
11. 7493876	4793876	4739876	_____
12. 9073484	9073484	9074384	_____
13. Shehani D. Housel	Shahani D. Housel	Shehani D. Housel	_____
14. Mansoor Hornblithe	Mansoor Hornblithe	Mansoor Hornblithe	_____
15. George Komashko	George Komashko	George Kamashko	_____
16. 7287394	7287934	7827934	_____
17. 4736297	4736297	4736297	_____
18. 5398247	5389247	5389247	_____
19. Steven P. Fuschia	Stephen P. Fuschia	Stephen P. Fuschia	_____
20. Farrah Berstmilier	Farrah Berstmilier	Farrah Berstmileir	_____
21. 3827394	3827394	3827934	_____
22. 4839271	4289271	4839271	_____
23. Powers S. Boothe	Powers S. Booth	Power S. Boothe	_____
24. Evyln Schaeffert	Evyln Shaeffert	Evyln Schaeffert	_____
25. Armantine Rogioso	Armatine Rogioso	Armatine Rogioso	_____
26. 9864837	9864387	9864837	_____
27. 8725137	8725137	8725137	_____
28. 6468931	6469831	6468931	_____
29. Rogers Hornsbrath	Rogers Hornsbrath	Rogers Hornsbrathe	_____
30. Mikael Maggliocco	Mikeal Maggliocco	Mikael Magglioco	_____

Answer Explanations for Practice Set 2

1.	**(B)** 9358745	9358745	935<u>7</u>845
2.	**(D)** 85<u>74</u>690	8547690	8547690
3.	**(E)** Raymond H. Didsbury	Raymond H. Did<u>d</u>sbury	Raymond H. Didsbur<u>r</u>y
4.	**(B)** Stephen M. Tranz	Stephen M. Tranz	Stephen M. Tra<u>mz</u>
5.	**(A)** Kevin C. Kretchmer	Kevin C. Kretchmer	Kevin C. Kretchmer
6.	**(C)** 7534689	7<u>35</u>4689	7534689
7.	**(A)** 4736258	4736258	4736258
8.	**(D)** 927<u>34</u>15	9274315	9274315
9.	**(D)** Dougla<u>s</u> S. Borghi	Douglass S. Borghi	Douglass S. Borghi
10.	**(D)** Vartan Ber<u>g</u>quist	Vartan Berquist	Vartan Berquist
11.	**(E)** <u>7</u>493876	4793876	47<u>39</u>876
12.	**(B)** 9073484	9073484	907<u>4</u>384
13.	**(C)** Sh<u>e</u>hani D. Housel	Sh<u>a</u>hani D. Housel	Sh<u>a</u>hani D. Housel
14.	**(A)** Mansoor Hornblithe	Mansoor Hornblithe	Mansoor Hornblithe
15.	**(B)** George Komashko	George Komashko	George K<u>a</u>mashko
16.	**(E)** 7287<u>39</u>4	7287934	7<u>82</u>7934
17.	**(A)** 4736297	4736297	4736297
18.	**(D)** 53<u>98</u>247	5389247	5389247
19.	**(D)** Ste<u>v</u>en P. Fuschia	Stephen P. Fuschia	Stephen P. Fuschia
20.	**(B)** Farrah Berstmilier	Farrah Berstmilier	Farrah Berstmil<u>ei</u>r
21.	**(B)** 3827394	3827394	3827<u>93</u>4
22.	**(C)** 4839271	<u>42</u>89271	4839271
23.	**(E)** Power<u>s</u> S. Booth<u>e</u>	Power<u>s</u> S. Booth	Power S. Booth<u>e</u>
24.	**(C)** Evyln Schaeffert	Evyln <u>Sh</u>aeffert	Evyln Schaeffert
25.	**(D)** Arma<u>n</u>tine Rogioso	Armatine Rogioso	Armatine Rogioso
26.	**(C)** 9864837	9864<u>38</u>7	9864837
27.	**(A)** 8725137	8725137	8725137
28.	**(C)** 6468931	646<u>98</u>31	6468931
29.	**(B)** Rogers Hornsbrath	Rogers Hornsbrath	Rogers Hornsbrath<u>e</u>
30.	**(E)** Mikael Maggliocco	Mik<u>ea</u>l Maggliocco	Mikael Magglio<u>co</u>

Practice Set 3

Compare the three names or numbers, and mark the answer—

A if ALL THREE names or numbers are exactly ALIKE
B if only the FIRST and SECOND names or numbers are exactly ALIKE
C if only the FIRST and THIRD names or numbers are exactly ALIKE
D if only the SECOND and THIRD names or numbers are exactly ALIKE
E if ALL THREE names or numbers are DIFFERENT

1.	5839478	5839478	5839478	_____
2.	9382739	9382789	9382789	_____

3. Alxis Kordumdrong   Alxis Kordumdrong   Alxis Kordomdrung   _____

4. Blossom Koneczka   Blossom Koneszka   Blossom Konezska   _____

5. Bethina Ploesser   Bethina Pleosser   Bettina Ploesser   _____

6. 3746893   3746983   3746983   _____

7. 4278345   4278345   4278345   _____

8. 2875291   2785291   2785291   _____

9. Krokor Pechakjian   Krokor Pechakjian   Krokor Pecharjian   _____

10. Lynette Preistley   Lynnette Preistley   Lynnette Priestley   _____

11. 3826387   3862837   3826837   _____

12. 4739826   4739836   4739826   _____

13. 3982635   3983625   3982635   _____

14. Rafael Morrison   Rafael Morrison   Rafael Morrisson   _____

15. Randise Rappoport   Randice Rappoport   Randice Rapopport   _____

16. 3675214   3675214   3675214   _____

17. 8672391   8673291   8672391   _____

18. Quenten C. Fischbeim   Quentin C. Fischbeim   Quentin C. Fischbiem   _____

19. Jenifer Robesgiase   Jenifer Robesgiase   Jennifer Robesgiase   _____

20. Florel Petersen   Florel Peterson   Florel Peterson   _____

21. 4872364   4873264   4873264   _____

22. 7483092   7480392   7480932   _____

23. 7348234   7348234   7348234   _____

24. G. Raymund Pafalcko   G. Ramund Pafalcko   G. Raymund Pafalcko   _____

25. M. L. K. Carrutthers   M. L. K. Carruthers   M. L. K. Carruthers   _____

26. 3678362   3687362   3687362   _____

27. 9376982	9736982	9736982	_____
28. 3892761	3892761	3892761	_____
29. Rogeiio Gonzalez	Rogeiio Gonzales	Rogeiio Gonzales	_____
30. Ferdinan Bulliekeir	Ferdinan Bulleikeir	Ferdinan Bulliekier	_____

Answer Explanations for Practice Set 3

1. **(A)** 5839478	5839478	5839478
2. **(D)** 9382739	9382789	9382789
3. **(B)** Alxis Kordumdrong	Aixis Kordumdrong	Alxis Kordomdrung
4. **(E)** Blossom Koneczka	Blossom Koneszka	Blossom Konezska
5. **(E)** Bethina Ploesser	Bethina Pleosser	Bettina Ploesser
6. **(D)** 3746893	3746983	3746983
7. **(A)** 4278345	4278345	4278345
8. **(D)** 2875291	2785291	2785291
9. **(B)** Krokor Pechakjian	Krokor Pechakjian	Krokor Pecharjian
10. **(E)** Lynette Preistley	Lynnette Preistley	Lynnette Priestley
11. **(E)** 3826387	3862837	3826837
12. **(C)** 4739826	4739836	4739826
13. **(C)** 3982635	3983625	3982635
14. **(B)** Rafael Morrison	Rafael Morrison	Rafael Morrisson
15. **(E)** Randise Rappoport	Randice Rappoport	Randice Rapopport
16. **(A)** 3675214	3675214	3675214
17. **(C)** 8672391	8673291	8672391
18. **(E)** Quenten C. Fischbeim	Quentin C. Fischbeim	Quentin C. Fischbiem
19. **(B)** Jenifer Robesgiase	Jenifer Robesgiase	Jennifer Robesgiase
20. **(D)** Florel Petersen	Florel Peterson	Florel Peterson
21. **(D)** 4872364	4873264	4873264
22. **(E)** 7483092	7480392	7480932
23. **(A)** 7348234	7348234	7348234
24. **(C)** G. Raymund Pafalcko	G. Ramund Pafalcko	G. Raymund Pafalcko
25. **(D)** M. L. K. Carrutthers	M. L. K. Carruthers	M. L. K. Carruthers
26. **(D)** 3678362	3687362	3687362
27. **(D)** 9376982	9736982	9736982
28. **(A)** 3892761	3892761	3892761
29. **(D)** Rogeiio Gonzalez	Rogeiio Gonzales	Rogeiio Gonzales
30. **(E)** Ferdinan Bulliekeir	Ferdinan Bulleikeir	Ferdinan Bulliekier

Practice Set 4

Compare the three names or numbers, and mark the answer—

A if ALL THREE names or numbers are exactly ALIKE
B if only the FIRST and SECOND names or numbers are exactly ALIKE

C if only the FIRST and THIRD names or numbers are exactly ALIKE
D if only the SECOND and THIRD names or numbers are exactly ALIKE
E if ALL THREE names or numbers are DIFFERENT

1. 5732837   5372837   5372837   _____

2. 4802736   4802736   4802376   _____

3. Michel St. Johns   Michel St. John   Mishel St. Johns   _____

4. Terrence Vanespreaux   Terrence Vanesprauex   Terrence Vanespreaux   _____

5. U. Yoshima Chaingo   U. Yoshina Chaingo   U. Yoshina Chiango   _____

6. 4869482   4869482   4869482   _____

7. 8394276   8392476   8392746   _____

8. 4829487   4829487   4892487   _____

9. Dana Cammer Lynd   Dana Cammer Lynde   Dana Cammer Lynde   _____

10. Epimena Sainzt   Epimena Saintz   Epimena Sainzt   _____

11. Louis Sagakuchi   Louis Sagsgughi   Louis Sagakuchi   _____

12. Festron Armandoff   Festron Armadoff   Festron Armadoff   _____

13. Hermine Pakhanians   Hermine Pakanians   Hermine Pakhanian   _____

14. 3846398   3846389   3846398   _____

15. 7493183   7493183   7493183   _____

16. 4839273   4832973   4839273   _____

17. 4698264   4698264   4698624   _____

18. Nicholas Palladino   Nickolas Palladino   Nicholas Palladino   _____

19. Jaime Prestridge   Jaime Pestridge   Jaime Pestredge   _____

20. Alonzo Forsythe   Alonzo Forsythe   Alonzo Forthythe   _____

21. 4832472   4832472   4832472   _____

22. 3659624   2695624   2695624   _____

23. 3825983   8325938   9325983   _____

24. Marietta Rogolizzo   Marieta Rogolizzo   Marieta Rogolizzo   _____

25. Jacob Rietdokog   Jacob Rietdokog   Jakob Rietdokog   _____

26. 5784963   5784693   5784963   _____

27. 3124785   3124785   3124875   _____

28. Edwardo Pimpernott   Edwardo Pimpernott   Eduardo Pimpernott   _____

29. Frencesca Moisely   Francesca Moisely   Francesca Moisely   _____

30. Olivier R. Dudlees   Oliver R. Dudlees   Oliver R. Dudless   _____

Answer Explanations for Practice Set 4

1. **(D)** 5732837   5372837   5372837
2. **(B)** 4802736   4802736   4802376
3. **(E)** Michel St. Johns   Michel St. John   Mishel St. Johns
4. **(C)** Terrence Vanespreaux   Terrence Vanesprauex   Terrence Vanespreaux
5. **(E)** U. Yoshima Chaingo   U. Yoshina Chaingo   U. Yoshina Chiango
6. **(A)** 4869482   4869482   4869482
7. **(E)** 8394276   8392476   8392746
8. **(B)** 4829487   4829487   4892487
9. **(D)** Dana Cammer Lynd   Dana Cammer Lynde   Dana Cammer Lynde
10. **(C)** Epimena Sainzt   Epimena Saintz   Epimena Sainzt
11. **(C)** Louis Sagakuchi   Louis Sagsgughi   Louis Sagakuchi
12. **(D)** Festron Armandoff   Festron Armadoff   Festron Armadoff
13. **(E)** Hermine Pakhanians   Hermine Pakanians   Hermine Pakhanian
14. **(C)** 3846398   3846389   3846398
15. **(A)** 7493183   7493183   7493183
16. **(C)** 4839273   4832973   4839273
17. **(B)** 4698264   4698264   4698624
18. **(C)** Nicholas Palladino   Nickolas Palladino   Nicholas Palladino
19. **(E)** Jaime Prestridge   Jaime Pestridge   Jaime Pestredge
20. **(B)** Alonzo Forsythe   Alonzo Forsythe   Alonzo Forthythe
21. **(A)** 4832472   4832472   4832472
22. **(D)** 3659624   2695624   2695624
23. **(E)** 3825983   8325938   9325983
24. **(D)** Marietta Rogolizzo   Marieta Rogolizzo   Marieta Rogolizzo
25. **(B)** Jacob Rietdokog   Jacob Rietdokog   Jakob Rietdokog
26. **(C)** 5784963   5784693   5784963
27. **(B)** 3124785   3124785   3124875
28. **(B)** Edwardo Pimpernott   Edwardo Pimpernott   Eduardo Pimpernott

29. **(D)** Frencesca Moisely   Francesca Moisely   Francesca Moisely
30. **(E)** Olivier R. Dudlees   Oliver R. Dudlees   Oliver R. Dudless

Practice Set 5

Compare the three names or numbers, and mark the answer—

A if ALL THREE names or numbers are exactly ALIKE
B if only the FIRST and SECOND names or numbers are exactly ALIKE
C if only the FIRST and THIRD names or numbers are exactly ALIKE
D if only the SECOND and THIRD names or numbers are exactly ALIKE
E if ALL THREE names or numbers are DIFFERENT

1. 9374653   9374653   9374653   _____

2. 4763981   4769381   4769831   _____

3. 5847291   5847291   5842791   _____

4. Atherton Jacquesman   Atherton Jaquesman   Atherton Jacqueman   _____

5. Willis Undertopper   Willis Undertopper   Willes Undertopper   _____

6. 6493759   6439759   6439759   _____

7. 3928404   3298404   3928404   _____

8. Langer F. Feltmann   Langer F. Feltman   Langar F. Feltman   _____

9. Oskar Fischman   Oskar Fischman   Oskar Ficshman   _____

10. Norris Feuchtwangar   Norris Feuchtwanger   Norris Fuechtwanger   _____

11. 4736948   4376948   4376948   _____

12. 4257389   4257389   4257389   _____

13. 8294735   2894735   8294735   _____

14. Arthur Fidelibus   Arthur Fidelibus   Arther Fidelibus   _____

15. Gerald M. Dudkins   Gerald M. Dudkins   Gerard M. Dudkins   _____

16. 4879326   4873926   4879326   _____

17. 6948732   6948732   6948732   _____

18. Haruko Kamakura   Hurako Kamakura   Hurako Kamakura   _____

19. Simmons Werthingten   Simmons Werthington   Simmins Werthington   _____

20. DeRonda Nocerino   DeRonda Nocerino   DaRonda Nocerino   _____

21. Marc Nochiela   Marc Nocheila   Marc Nochiela   _____

22. Cleveland Noburski   Cleveland Nobruski   Cleveland Nobruski   _____

23. 2839747   2839747   2839747   _____

24. 9372875   9732875   9732875   _____

25. 3729854   3729584   3798254   _____

26. 4839734   4839734   4837934   _____

27. 3526791   3526971   3526891   _____

28. 3749825   3749825   2949825   _____

29. Mallery J. Pearre   Mallory J. Peare   Mallory J. Pearre   _____

30. Stacey Rudashmann   Stacy Rudashmann   Stacey Rudashmann   _____

Answer Explanations for Practice Set 5

1. **(A)** 9374653   9374653   9374653
2. **(E)** 4763981   4769381   4769831
3. **(B)** 5847291   5847291   5842791
4. **(E)** Atherton Jacquesman   Atherton Jaquesman   Atherton Jacqueman
5. **(B)** Willis Undertopper   Willis Undertopper   Willes Undertopper
6. **(D)** 6493759   6439759   6439759
7. **(C)** 3928404   3298404   3928404
8. **(E)** Langer F. Feltmann   Langer F. Feltman   Langar F. Feltman
9. **(B)** Oskar Fischman   Oskar Fischman   Oskar Ficshman
10. **(E)** Norris Feuchtwangar   Norris Feuchtwanger   Norris Fuechtwanger
11. **(D)** 4736948   4376948   4376948
12. **(A)** 4257389   4257389   4257389
13. **(C)** 8294735   2894735   8294735
14. **(B)** Arthur Fidelibus   Arthur Fidelibus   Arther Fidelibus
15. **(B)** Gerald M. Dudkins   Gerald M. Dudkins   Gerard M. Dudkins
16. **(C)** 4879326   4873926   4879326
17. **(A)** 6948732   6948732   6948732
18. **(D)** Haruko Kamakura   Hurako Kamakura   Hurako Kamakura

19. **(E)** Simmons Werthing<u>ten</u>   Simmons Werthington   Sim<u>min</u>s Werthington
20. **(B)** DeRonda Nocerino   DeRonda Nocerino   D<u>a</u>Ronda Nocerino
21. **(C)** Marc Nochiela   Marc Noch<u>ei</u>la   Marc Nochiela
22. **(D)** Cleveland Nob<u>ur</u>ski   Cleveland N<u>o</u>bruski   Cleveland Nobruski
23. **(A)** 2839747   2839747   2839747
24. **(D)** 9<u>3</u>72875   9732875   9732875
25. **(E)** 3729<u>8</u>54   3729<u>58</u>4   37<u>98</u>254
26. **(B)** 4839734   4839734   483<u>79</u>34
27. **(E)** 3526<u>7</u>91   3526<u>97</u>1   3526<u>8</u>91
28. **(B)** 3749825   3749825   <u>2</u>949825
29. **(E)** Mal<u>ler</u>y J. Pearre   Mall<u>or</u>y J. Pe<u>are</u>   Mall<u>or</u>y J. Pearre
30. **(C)** Stacey Rudashmann   Stac<u>y</u> Rudashmann   Stacey Rudashmann

Practice Set 6

Compare the three names or numbers, and mark the answer—

A if ALL THREE names or numbers are exactly ALIKE
B if only the FIRST and SECOND names or numbers are exactly ALIKE
C if only the FIRST and THIRD names or numbers are exactly ALIKE
D if only the SECOND and THIRD names or numbers are exactly ALIKE
E if ALL THREE names or numbers are DIFFERENT

1. Abebaye Tearleney   Abebaya Tearleney   Abebaya Tearleney   _____

2. Mimi P. Teisan   Mimi P. Tiesman   Mimi P. Tiesman   _____

3. Forest Peuterman   Forrest Peuterman   Forrest Peuterman   _____

4. 6483947   6483947   6438947   _____

5. 3926598   3925698   3925968   _____

6. 4378947   4378947   4378947   _____

7. 4628479   4624879   4628479   _____

8. Claude Versailes   Claude Versailles   Claude Versailles   _____

9. Phillip Waddillove   Phillip Waddillove   Philip Waddillove   _____

10. Pinkerten Chesneiy   Pinkerton Chesneiy   Pinkerton Chesniey   _____

11. 4893263   4893262   4893623   _____

12. 4832764   4832764   4832746   _____

13. 6382749   6832749   6832749   _____

14. Hugh L. Wyannicki   Huge L. Wyannicki   Hugh L. Wyannicki   _____

15. Otto C. Wichert   Otto C. Wichert   Otto C. Wichirt   _____

16. Maurice E. Tyson   Maurice E. Tyson   Maurice E. Tyson   _____

17. Tzivskos Tittlemen   Tzivzkos Tittlemen   Tzvizkos Tittlemen   _____

18. Peter E. Villasenor   Peter E. Villiasenor   Peter E. Villiasenor   _____

19. 7362456   7364256   7342456   _____

20. 3829756   3829576   3829756   _____

21. 4839876   4839876   4839876   _____

22. 7328631   7328361   7328631   _____

23. 3907356   3907356   3907365   _____

24. Illay Vischmid   Illay Vischmed   Illay Vischmed   _____

25. Benjamin Weinenger   Benjamen Weinenger   Benjamin Weininger   _____

26. 4983675   4983675   4983675   _____

27. 8109354   8109534   8109354   _____

28. Marion Wyanicki   Marian Wyanicki   Marian Wyanicki   _____

29. Whitney Williston   Whitney Willisten   Whitney Wiliston   _____

30. Garry Wohmgemuth   Garry Wohmgemuth   Garry Wohmgemuth   _____

Answer Explanations for Practice Set 6

1. **(D)** Abeba<u>ye</u> Tearleney   Abebaya Tearleney   Abebaya Tearleney
2. **(D)** Mimi P. T<u>ei</u>san   Mimi P. Tiesman   Mimi P. Tiesman
3. **(D)** F<u>or</u>est Peuterman   Forrest Peuterman   Forrest Peuterman
4. **(B)** 6483947   6483947   6<u>43</u>8947
5. **(E)** 3926<u>5</u>98   3925698   3925<u>96</u>8
6. **(A)** 4378947   4378947   4378947
7. **(C)** 4628479   4624<u>87</u>9   4628479
8. **(D)** Claude Versai<u>le</u>s   Claude Versailles   Claude Versailles

9.	**(B)** Phillip Waddillove	Phillip Waddillove	Philip Waddillove
10.	**(E)** Pinkerten Chesneiy	Pinkerton Chesneiy	Pinkerton Chesniey
11.	**(E)** 4893263	4893262	4893623
12.	**(B)** 4832764	4832764	4832746
13.	**(D)** 6382749	6832749	6832749
14.	**(C)** Hugh L. Wyannicki	Huge L. Wyannicki	Hugh L. Wyannicki
15.	**(B)** Otto C. Wichert	Otto C. Wichert	Otto C. Wichirt
16.	**(A)** Maurice E. Tyson	Maurice E. Tyson	Maurice E. Tyson
17.	**(E)** Tzivskos Tittlemen	Tzivzkos Tittlemen	Tzvizkos Tittlemen
18.	**(D)** Peter E. Villasenor	Peter E. Villiasenor	Peter E. Villiasenor
19.	**(E)** 7362456	7364256	7342456
20.	**(C)** 3829756	3829576	3829756
21.	**(A)** 4839876	4839876	4839876
22.	**(C)** 7328631	7328361	7328631
23.	**(B)** 3907356	3907356	3907365
24.	**(D)** Illay Vischmid	Illay Vischmed	Illay Vischmed
25.	**(E)** Benjamin Weinenger	Benjamen Weinenger	Benjamin Weininger
26.	**(A)** 4983675	4983675	4983675
27.	**(C)** 8109354	8109534	8109354
28.	**(D)** Marion Wyanicki	Marian Wyanicki	Marian Wyanicki
29.	**(E)** Whitney Williston	Whitney Willisten	Whitney Wiliston
30.	**(A)** Garry Wohmgemuth	Garry Wohmgemuth	Garry Wohmgemuth

Practice Set 7

Compare the three names or numbers, and mark the answer—

A if ALL THREE names or numbers are exactly ALIKE
B if only the FIRST and SECOND names or numbers are exactly ALIKE
C if only the FIRST and THIRD names or numbers are exactly ALIKE
D if only the SECOND and THIRD names or numbers are exactly ALIKE
E if ALL THREE names or numbers are DIFFERENT

1.	4826489	4824689	4826489	_____
2.	3825431	3825431	3825431	_____
3.	4763901	4769301	4769301	_____
4.	Worthington Pistle	Worthington Pistel	Worthington Pistle	_____
5.	Merriam Riwonla	Merriam Riwonia	Merriam Riwonia	_____
6.	3926528	3926528	3925628	_____
7.	1930283	1930823	1930283	_____

8. Sima Serrafzadeh	Sima Serrafzadah	Sima Serrafzadeh	_____
9. Victor I. Sarquez	Victor T. Sarquez	Victor I. Sarquez	_____
10. Shizuyi Uchiyama	Shizuyi Uchiyama	Shizuyi Uchiyama	_____
11. 9038717	9037217	9037218	_____
12. 2983014	2983014	2938014	_____
13. 3826798	3826978	3826978	_____
14. Leonard Wibbelsman	Leonard Wibblesman	Leonard Wibbelsmann	_____
15. Heidi Claire Whotlock	Heidi Claire Whotlock	Hiedi Claire Whotlock	_____
16. 8372918	8372981	8372981	_____
17. 2837192	2837912	2837192	_____
18. Sigemin Ziegler	Sigemin Zeigler	Sigemin Ziegler	_____
19. Fern Frederics	Fern Fredricks	Fern Fredericks	_____
20. J. Michael Zigovras	J. Michael Zigovras	J. Michael Zigorvas	_____
21. 4819287	4819287	3891287	_____
22. 3782619	3782619	3782619	_____
23. 2736510	2735610	2736510	_____
24. Judith A. Streigel	Judith A. Streigel	Judith A. Striegel	_____
25. Nicholas Strimling	Nicholas Strimler	Nichlas Strimling	_____
26. 3921038	3912038	3923038	_____
27. 2710935	2701935	2701935	_____
28. Neilson Saemaidahr	Neilson Saemaidhar	Neilson Saemaidahr	_____
29. Stephanie R. Sharron	Stephanie R. Sharon	Stephanie R. Sharon	_____
30. Jefferey Paige Sacks	Jefferey Paige Sachs	Jeffrey Paige Sachs	_____

Answer Explanations for Practice Set 7

1.	**(C)** 4826489	4824689	4826489
2.	**(A)** 3825431	3825431	3825431
3.	**(D)** 4763901	4769301	4769301
4.	**(C)** Worthington Pistle	Worthington Pistel	Worthington Pistle
5.	**(D)** Merriam Riwonla	Merriam Riwonia	Merriam Riwonia
6.	**(B)** 3926528	3926528	3925628
7.	**(C)** 1930283	1930823	1930283
8.	**(C)** Sima Serrafzadeh	Sima Serrafzadah	Sima Serrafzadeh
9.	**(C)** Victor I. Sarquez	Victor T. Sarquez	Victor I. Sarquez
10.	**(A)** Shizuyi Uchiyama	Shizuyi Uchiyama	Shizuyi Uchiyama
11.	**(E)** 9038717	9037217	9037218
12.	**(B)** 2983014	2983014	2938014
13.	**(D)** 3826798	3826978	3826978
14.	**(E)** Leonard Wibbelsman	Leonard Wibblesman	Leonard Wibbeismann
15.	**(B)** Heidi Claire Whotlock	Heidi Claire Whotlock	Hiedi Claire Whotlock
16.	**(D)** 8372918	8372981	8372981
17.	**(C)** 2837192	2837912	2837192
18.	**(C)** Sigemin Ziegler	Sigeniin Zeigler	Sigemin Ziegler
19.	**(E)** Fern Frederics	Fern Fredricks	Fern Fredericks
20.	**(B)** J. Michael Zigovras	J. Michael Zigovras	J. Michael Zigorvas
21.	**(B)** 4819287	4819287	4891287
22.	**(A)** 3782619	3782619	3182619
23.	**(C)** 2736510	2735610	2736510
24.	**(B)** Judith A. Streiget	Judith A. Streigel	Judith A. Striegel
25.	**(E)** Nicholas Strimling	Nicholas Strimler	Nichlas Strimling
26.	**(E)** 3921038	3912038	3923038
27.	**(D)** 2710935	2701935	2701935
28.	**(C)** Neilson Saemaidahr	Neilson Saemaidhar	Neilson Saemaidahr
29.	**(D)** Stephanie R. Sharron	Stephanie R. Sharon	Stephanie R. Sharon
30.	**(E)** Jefferey Paige Sacks	Jefferey Paige Sachs	Jeffrey Paige Sachs

Practice Set 8

Compare the three names or numbers, and mark the answer—

A if ALL THREE names or numbers are exactly ALIKE
B if only the FIRST and SECOND names or numbers are exactly ALIKE
C if only the FIRST and THIRD names or numbers are exactly ALIKE
D if only the SECOND and THIRD names or numbers are exactly ALIKE
E if ALL THREE names or numbers are DIFFERENT

1. 3870936	3879036	3870963	_____
2. 3827092	3827902	3827902	_____

3. 3701234	3702324	3701234	_____
4. Arno Wojecieski	Arno Wojeceiski	Arno Wojecieski	_____
5. Laurence Zwisen	Latirence Zwiseti	Lawrence Zwisen	_____
6. 2873012	2870312	2873012	_____
7. 2870283	2870283	2870283	_____
8. 2983121	2981231	2981231	_____
9. Magdalena Koltunik	Madalena Koltunik	Magdalina Koltunik	_____
10. Gavrilo Romendicth	Gavrilo Romendicth	Gavrilo Romenditch	_____
11. Ronald T. Kullaway	Ronald T. Kullaway	Ronald F. Kullaway	_____
12. Ernest Teversen	Ernest Iversen	Ernest Ieversen	_____
13. 4836194	4836914	4836194	_____
14. 3129378	3123978	3129738	_____
15. 2356421	2354621	2354621	_____
16. Lorraine Timbershun	Lorraine Timbershun	Loraine Timbershun	_____
17. Michele R. Spencer	Michelle R. Spencer	Michele R. Spenser	_____
18. Jake Lazarwitz	Jake Lazarwits	Jake Lazarwitz	_____
19. 3826129	3826129	3826127	_____
20. 4837910	4837910	4837910	_____
21. 9810236	9810236	9870236	_____
22. 3784615	3786415	3786415	_____
23. 3892767	3892767	3892767	_____
24. Kelley Millie Laykin	Kelley Millie Layken	Kelley Millie Layken	_____
25. Alexander Mueller	Alexandra Mueller	Alexandra Meuller	_____
26. 3829742	3829742	3829742	_____

27. 3783465   3738465   3783465   _____

28. L. M. Pisarkiewicz   L. M. Pisarkiewicz   M. L. Pisarkiewicz   _____

29. Francis Pivrnec   Frances Pivrnec   Francis Pivnrec   _____

30. Lloyd J. Pfitzer   Lloyd J. Pfitzer   Lloyd J. Pfitzer   _____

Answer Explanations for Practice Set 8

1. **(E)** 3870936   3879036   3870963
2. **(D)** 3827092   3827902   3827902
3. **(C)** 3701234   3702324   3701234
4. **(C)** Arno Wojecieski   Arno Wojeceiski   Arno Wojecieski
5. **(B)** Laurence Zwisen   Laurence Zwisen   Lawrence Zwisen
6. **(C)** 2873012   2870312   2873012
7. **(A)** 2870283   2870283   2870283
8. **(D)** 2983121   2981231   2981231
9. **(E)** Magdalena Koltunik   Madalena Koltunik   Magdalina Koltunik
10. **(B)** Gavrilo Romendicth   Gavrilo Romendicth   Gavrilo Romenditch
11. **(B)** Ronald T. Kullaway   Ronald T. Kullaway   Ronald F. Kullaway
12. **(E)** Ernest Teversen   Ernest Iversen   Ernest Ieversen
13. **(C)** 4836194   4836914   4836194
14. **(E)** 3129378   3123978   3129738
15. **(D)** 2356421   2354621   2354621
16. **(B)** Lorraine Timbershun   Lorraine Timbershun   Loraine Timbershun
17. **(E)** Michele R. Spencer   Michelle R. Spencer   Michele R. Spenser
18. **(C)** Jake Lazarwitz   Jake Lazarwits   Jake Lazarwitz
19. **(B)** 3826129   3826129   3826127
20. **(A)** 4837910   4837910   4837910
21. **(B)** 9810236   9810236   9870236
22. **(D)** 3784615   3786415   3786415
23. **(A)** 3892767   3892767   3892767
24. **(D)** Kelley Millie Laykin   Kelley Millie Layken   Kelley Millie Layken
25. **(E)** Alexander Mueller   Alexandra Mueller   Alexandra Meuller
26. **(A)** 3829742   3829742   3829742
27. **(C)** 3783465   3738465   3783465
28. **(B)** L. M. Pisarkiewicz   L. M. Pisarkiewicz   M. L. Pisarkiewicz
29. **(E)** Francis Pivrnec   Frances Pivrnec   Francis Pivnrec
30. **(A)** Lloyd J. Pfitzer   Lloyd J. Pfitzer   Lloyd J. Pfitzer

Clerical Abilities Analysis Chart for Alike or Different (Name and Number Checking)

Use the following chart to carefully analyze your results of the *alike or different (name and number checking)* question type. This will help you evaluate your strengths and weaknesses. This analysis should help you focus your study and review efforts on specific types of problems.

Practice Set	Total Number of Questions	Number Correct	Number Incorrect	Number Unanswered
Set 1	30			
Set 2	30			
Set 3	30			
Set 4	30			
Set 5	30			
Set 6	30			
Set 7	30			
Set 8	30			

Because there is no penalty for incorrect answers on most of the questions in the Clerical Abilities section, you should have left no question unanswered. Even if you didn't have time to answer a question, you should have at least filled in the answer space with an educated guess.

REVIEWING THE KEY STRATEGIES

Remember to:
1. Understand and memorize the directions before your test.
2. Find the technique that works best for you, and practice it.
3. Watch out for those "troublesome" numbers and letters.

ALPHABETIZING

The rules for placing names in proper alphabetical order are simple and straightforward. They require you to follow several steps:

DIFFERENT LAST NAMES

1. First, alphabetize by the first letter of the last name:
   Brown, James
   Harris, Arthur
   Thomas, Peter

2. If two or more last names begin with the same letter, then look to the second letter in the last name:
   Brown, James
   Sanders, Fred
   Smith, Gloria
   Notice that both "S" names come after *Brown* and that *Sanders* comes before *Smith* because of their second letters ("a" and "m").

3. If the first and second letters of the last name are alike, then look to the third letter:
   Peterson, Roberta
   Pezzari, Thomas
   Ulmer, Janice

4. If the first three letters of the last name are similar, look to the fourth letter, and so on:

> Bronson, Eloise
> Brown, Ferdinand
> Browvort, Michael

Notice in the last example that Bron comes before *Brow*, but *Brown* comes before *Browv*.

5. If the letters are identical in two names, but one name is longer, the shorter name, which runs out of letters, goes first. For example,

> Prout, Marie
> Proute, Harry

Notice that *Prout* comes before *Proute*.

6. Don't let lowercase letters, apostrophes, or hyphens in last names confuse you. Continue to follow rules 1 to 5. For example:

> Daly, Ernest
> D'Ambrose, Evelyn

Above, *Dal* comes before *DAm*. Or:

> VanDercook, Stephen
> vanLitton, Morris
> Vans-Harrold, Martha

Notice the order: VanD, vanl, Vans.

IDENTICAL LAST NAMES

What happens if the last names are exactly the same? Then look at the first name or first initial and follow these rules:

7. Alphabetize, using the first letter of the first name:

> Smith, Albert
> Smith, George
> Smith, Harold

8. If the first name begins with the same letter, look to the second letter:

> Jones, Richard
> Jones, Roberta
> Jones, Ruben

9. If a first name is merely an initial, that initial will precede any first name beginning with that same letter. For example:

> White, N.
> White, Norbert

10. Even if there is a middle name after the first initial, or two initials, a first initial will always precede a full first name:

> Chan, G. Ling
> Chan, George

Another example:

> Forrest, R. Peter
> Forrest, Rae

11. Of course, if the first initial comes after the first letter of the full first name, it must follow the usual alphabetical rules. For example:

    Johnson, Albert
    Johnson, C. David
    Johnson, Charles
    Johnson, F. K.
    Johnson, Louise

12. And, of course, given only first initials, follow the usual rules:

    Abbott, C.
    Abbott, C. A.
    Abbott, E.
    Abbott, F.
    Abbott, H.

    Note that Abbott, C. A. comes after Abbott, C.

13. Finally, if the first names are exactly the same, or the first initials are the same, then look to the middle initial or the middle name, and follow the standard rules. For example:

    Brown, John
    Brown, John A.
    Brown, John Albert
    Brown, John H.
    Brown, John Herbert
    Brown, John Thomas
    Brown, John Z.

    Notice that here the alphabetizing begins with the middle name or initial: *Brown, John* is first because there is no middle name or initial; then A., then *Albert*, then *H.*, then *Herbert*, then *Thomas*, then Z.

Practice Set 1

Find the correct place for the name in the box, and mark the letter of that space as your answer.

1. **Waverley, S. Q.**

A) →
    Watkins, Roger
B) →
    Watson, Gabriele
C) →
    Watsonian, Franklin
D) →
    Wetson, McDougle
E) →

2. **Burmingbam, Emma A.**

A) →
    Birmingham, Hal
B) →
    Birminghoff, Brinker
C) →
    Birminghuller, Daisy
D) →
    Burningham, Morris
E) →

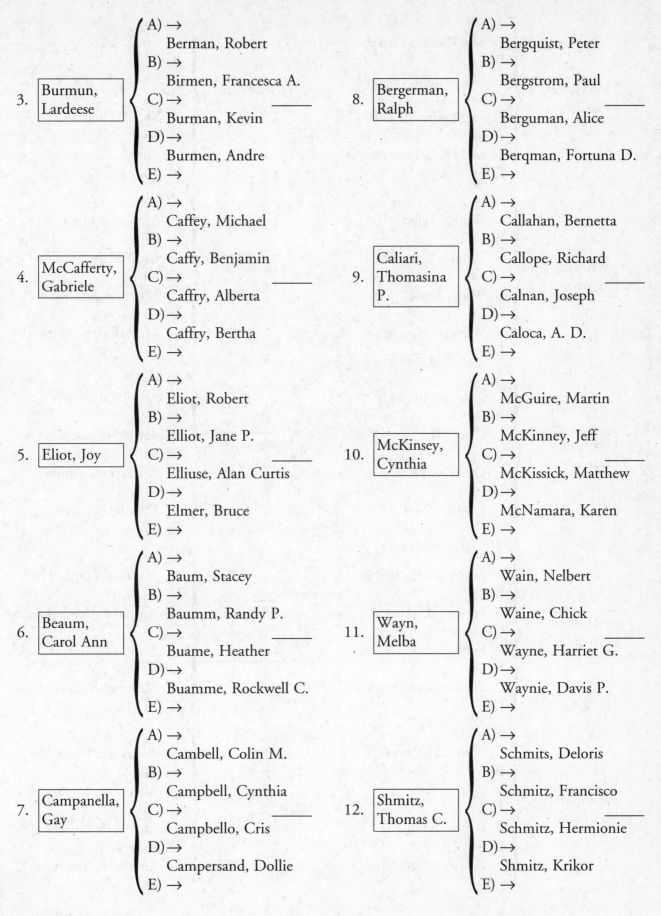

3. Burmun, Lardeese

A) →
Berman, Robert
B) →
Birmen, Francesca A.
C) → _____
Burman, Kevin
D) →
Burmen, Andre
E) →

4. McCafferty, Gabriele

A) →
Caffey, Michael
B) →
Caffy, Benjamin
C) → _____
Caffry, Alberta
D) →
Caffry, Bertha
E) →

5. Eliot, Joy

A) →
Eliot, Robert
B) →
Elliot, Jane P.
C) → _____
Elliuse, Alan Curtis
D) →
Elmer, Bruce
E) →

6. Beaum, Carol Ann

A) →
Baum, Stacey
B) →
Baumm, Randy P.
C) → _____
Buame, Heather
D) →
Buamme, Rockwell C.
E) →

7. Campanella, Gay

A) →
Cambell, Colin M.
B) →
Campbell, Cynthia
C) → _____
Campbello, Cris
D) →
Campersand, Dollie
E) →

8. Bergerman, Ralph

A) →
Bergquist, Peter
B) →
Bergstrom, Paul
C) → _____
Berguman, Alice
D) →
Berqman, Fortuna D.
E) →

9. Caliari, Thomasina P.

A) →
Callahan, Bernetta
B) →
Callope, Richard
C) → _____
Calnan, Joseph
D) →
Caloca, A. D.
E) →

10. McKinsey, Cynthia

A) →
McGuire, Martin
B) →
McKinney, Jeff
C) → _____
McKissick, Matthew
D) →
McNamara, Karen
E) →

11. Wayn, Melba

A) →
Wain, Nelbert
B) →
Waine, Chick
C) → _____
Wayne, Harriet G.
D) →
Waynie, Davis P.
E) →

12. Shmitz, Thomas C.

A) →
Schmits, Deloris
B) →
Schmitz, Francisco
C) → _____
Schmitz, Hermionie
D) →
Shmitz, Krikor
E) →

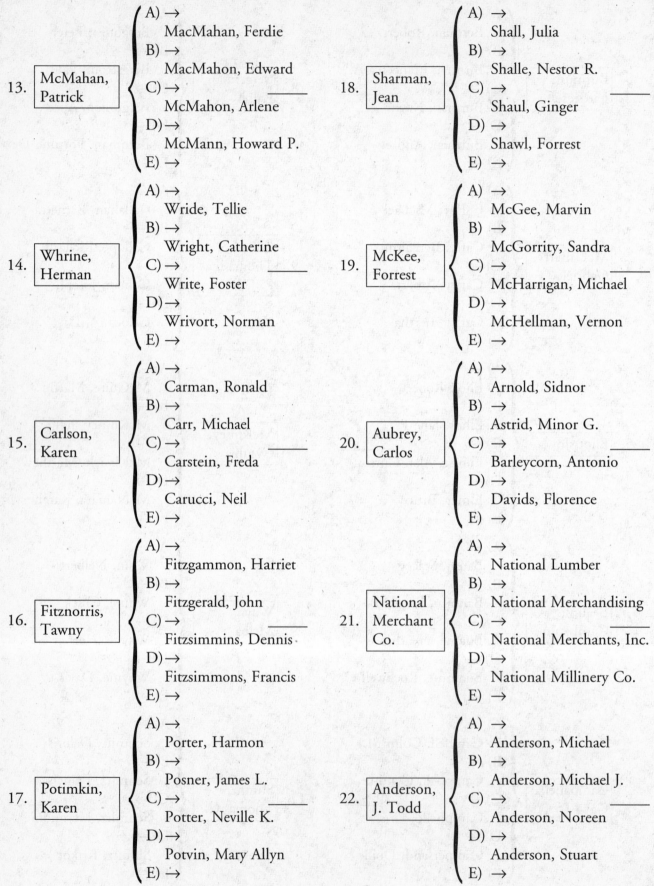

13. McMahan, Patrick

A) →
MacMahan, Ferdie
B) →
MacMahon, Edward
C) → _____
McMahon, Arlene
D) →
McMann, Howard P.
E) →

14. Whrine, Herman

A) →
Wride, Tellie
B) →
Wright, Catherine
C) → _____
Write, Foster
D) →
Wrivort, Norman
E) →

15. Carlson, Karen

A) →
Carman, Ronald
B) →
Carr, Michael
C) → _____
Carstein, Freda
D) →
Carucci, Neil
E) →

16. Fitznorris, Tawny

A) →
Fitzgammon, Harriet
B) →
Fitzgerald, John
C) → _____
Fitzsimmins, Dennis
D) →
Fitzsimmons, Francis
E) →

17. Potimkin, Karen

A) →
Porter, Harmon
B) →
Posner, James L.
C) → _____
Potter, Neville K.
D) →
Potvin, Mary Allyn
E) →

18. Sharman, Jean

A) →
Shall, Julia
B) →
Shalle, Nestor R.
C) → _____
Shaul, Ginger
D) →
Shawl, Forrest
E) →

19. McKee, Forrest

A) →
McGee, Marvin
B) →
McGorrity, Sandra
C) → _____
McHarrigan, Michael
D) →
McHellman, Vernon
E) →

20. Aubrey, Carlos

A) →
Arnold, Sidnor
B) →
Astrid, Minor G.
C) → _____
Barleycorn, Antonio
D) →
Davids, Florence
E) →

21. National Merchant Co.

A) →
National Lumber
B) →
National Merchandising
C) → _____
National Merchants, Inc.
D) →
National Millinery Co.
E) →

22. Anderson, J. Todd

A) →
Anderson, Michael
B) →
Anderson, Michael J.
C) → _____
Anderson, Noreen
D) →
Anderson, Stuart
E) →

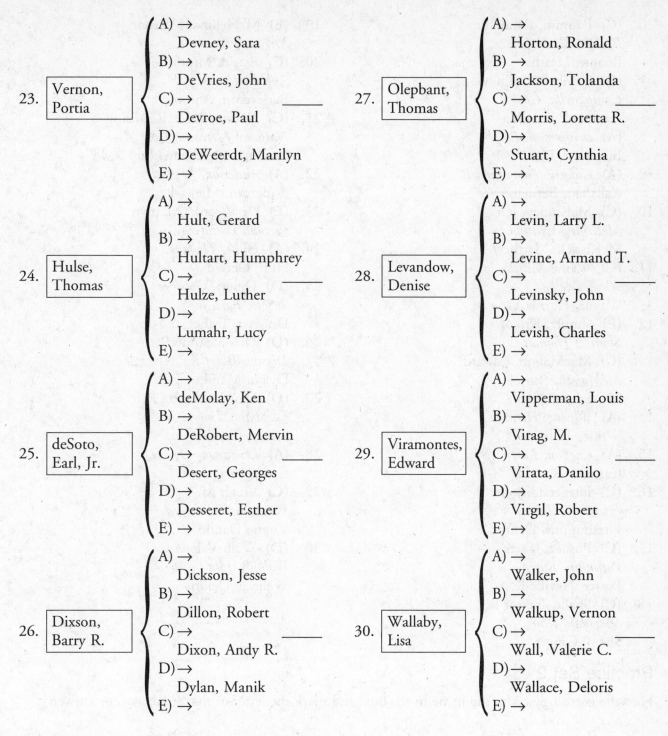

23. Vernon, Portia
   - A) →
   - Devney, Sara
   - B) →
   - DeVries, John
   - C) → _____
   - Devroe, Paul
   - D) →
   - DeWeerdt, Marilyn
   - E) →

24. Hulse, Thomas
   - A) →
   - Hult, Gerard
   - B) →
   - Hultart, Humphrey
   - C) → _____
   - Hulze, Luther
   - D) →
   - Lumahr, Lucy
   - E) →

25. deSoto, Earl, Jr.
   - A) →
   - deMolay, Ken
   - B) →
   - DeRobert, Mervin
   - C) → _____
   - Desert, Georges
   - D) →
   - Desseret, Esther
   - E) →

26. Dixson, Barry R.
   - A) →
   - Dickson, Jesse
   - B) →
   - Dillon, Robert
   - C) → _____
   - Dixon, Andy R.
   - D) →
   - Dylan, Manik
   - E) →

27. Olepbant, Thomas
   - A) →
   - Horton, Ronald
   - B) →
   - Jackson, Tolanda
   - C) → _____
   - Morris, Loretta R.
   - D) →
   - Stuart, Cynthia
   - E) →

28. Levandow, Denise
   - A) →
   - Levin, Larry L.
   - B) →
   - Levine, Armand T.
   - C) → _____
   - Levinsky, John
   - D) →
   - Levish, Charles
   - E) →

29. Viramontes, Edward
   - A) →
   - Vipperman, Louis
   - B) →
   - Virag, M.
   - C) → _____
   - Virata, Danilo
   - D) →
   - Virgil, Robert
   - E) →

30. Wallaby, Lisa
   - A) →
   - Walker, John
   - B) →
   - Walkup, Vernon
   - C) → _____
   - Wall, Valerie C.
   - D) →
   - Wallace, Deloris
   - E) →

Answer Explanations for Practice Set 1

1. **(D)** Watsonian, Franklin
   Wa_verley, S. Q.
   Wetson, McDougle

2. **(D)** Birminghuller, Daisy
   Burmingbam, Emma A.
   Burningham, Morris

3. **(E)** Burmen, Andre
   Burm_un, Lardeese

4. **(E)** Caffry, Bertha
   McCafferty, Gabriele

5. **(A)** *Eliot, Joy*
   Eliot, Robert

6. **(C)** Baumm, Randy P.
Beaum, Carol Ann
Buame, Heather

7. **(B)** Cambell, Colin M.
Campanella, Gay
Campbell, Cynthia

8. **(A)** *Bergerman, Ralph*
Bergquist, Peter

9. **(A)** *Caliari, Thomasina P.*
Callahan, Bernetta

10. **(C)** McKinney, Jeff
McKinsey, Cynthia
McKissick, Matthew

11. **(C)** Waine, Chick
Wayn, Melba
Wayne, Harriet G.

12. **(E)** Shmitz, Krikor
Shmitz, Thomas C.

13. **(C)** MacMahon, Edward
McMahan, Patrick
McMahon, Arlene

14. **(A)** *Whrine, Herman*
Wride, Tellie

15. **(A)** *Carlson, Karen*
Carman, Ronald

16. **(C)** Fitzgerald, John
Fitznorris, Tawny
Fitzsimmins, Dennis

17. **(C)** Posner, James L.
Potimkin, Karen
Potter, Neville K.

18. **(C)** Shalle, Nestor R.
Sharman, Jean
Shaul, Ginger

19. **(E)** McHellman, Vernon
McKee, Forrest

20. **(C)** Astrid, Minor G.
Aubrey, Carlos
Barleycorn, Antonio

21. **(C)** National Merchandising
National Merchant Co.
National Merchants, Inc.

22. **(A)** *Anderson, J. Todd*
Anderson, Michael

23. **(E)** De Weerdt, Marilyn
Vernon, Portia

24. **(A)** *Hulse, Thomas*
Hult, Gerard

25. **(D)** Desert, Georges
deSoto, Earl, Jr.
Desseret, Esther

26. **(D)** Dixon, Andy R.
Dixson, Barry R.
Dylan, Manik

27. **(D)** Morris, Loretta R.
Olepbant, Thomas
Stuart, Cynthia

28. **(A)** *Levandow, Denise*
Levin, Larry L.

29. **(C)** Virag, M.
Viramontes, Edward
Virata, Danilo

30. **(D)** Wall, Valerie C.
Wallaby, Lisa
Wallace, Deloris

Practice Set 2

Find the correct place for the name in the box, and mark the letter of that space as your answer.

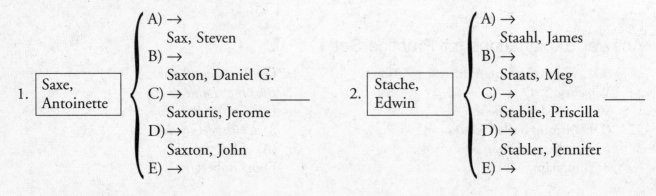

1. Saxe, Antoinette
  A) →
    Sax, Steven
  B) →
    Saxon, Daniel G.
  C) → _____
    Saxouris, Jerome
  D) →
    Saxton, John
  E) →

2. Stache, Edwin
  A) →
    Staahl, James
  B) →
    Staats, Meg
  C) → _____
    Stabile, Priscilla
  D) →
    Stabler, Jennifer
  E) →

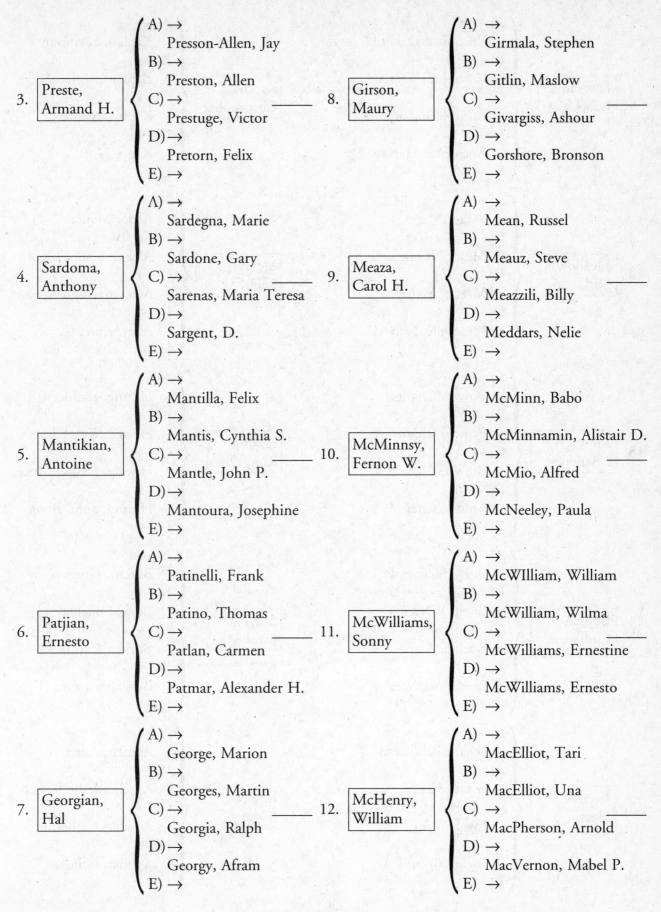

3. Preste, Armand H.
- A) →
  Presson-Allen, Jay
- B) →
  Preston, Allen
- C) → _____
  Prestuge, Victor
- D) →
  Pretorn, Felix
- E) →

8. Girson, Maury
- A) →
  Girmala, Stephen
- B) →
  Gitlin, Maslow
- C) → _____
  Givargiss, Ashour
- D) →
  Gorshore, Bronson
- E) →

4. Sardoma, Anthony
- A) →
  Sardegna, Marie
- B) →
  Sardone, Gary
- C) → _____
  Sarenas, Maria Teresa
- D) →
  Sargent, D.
- E) →

9. Meaza, Carol H.
- A) →
  Mean, Russel
- B) →
  Meauz, Steve
- C) → _____
  Meazzili, Billy
- D) →
  Meddars, Nelie
- E) →

5. Mantikian, Antoine
- A) →
  Mantilla, Felix
- B) →
  Mantis, Cynthia S.
- C) → _____
  Mantle, John P.
- D) →
  Mantoura, Josephine
- E) →

10. McMinnsy, Fernon W.
- A) →
  McMinn, Babo
- B) →
  McMinnamin, Alistair D.
- C) → _____
  McMio, Alfred
- D) →
  McNeeley, Paula
- E) →

6. Patjian, Ernesto
- A) →
  Patinelli, Frank
- B) →
  Patino, Thomas
- C) → _____
  Patlan, Carmen
- D) →
  Patmar, Alexander H.
- E) →

11. McWilliams, Sonny
- A) →
  McWIlliam, William
- B) →
  McWilliam, Wilma
- C) → _____
  McWilliams, Ernestine
- D) →
  McWilliams, Ernesto
- E) →

7. Georgian, Hal
- A) →
  George, Marion
- B) →
  Georges, Martin
- C) → _____
  Georgia, Ralph
- D) →
  Georgy, Afram
- E) →

12. McHenry, William
- A) →
  MacElliot, Tari
- B) →
  MacElliot, Una
- C) → _____
  MacPherson, Arnold
- D) →
  MacVernon, Mabel P.
- E) →

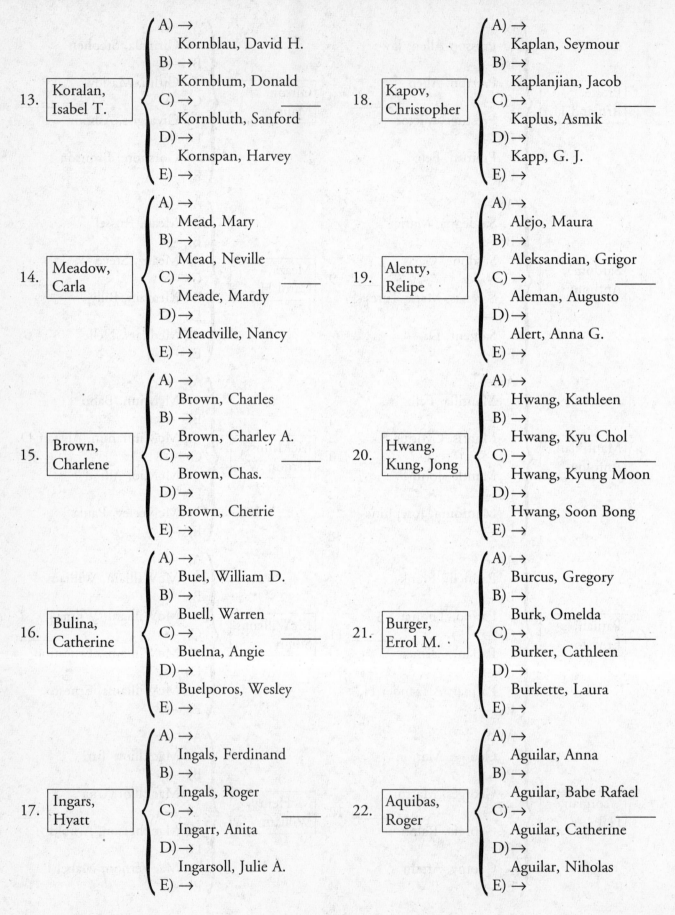

13. Koralan, Isabel T.
A) →
Kornblau, David H.
B) →
Kornblum, Donald
C) → _____
Kornbluth, Sanford
D) →
Kornspan, Harvey
E) →

14. Meadow, Carla
A) →
Mead, Mary
B) →
Mead, Neville
C) → _____
Meade, Mardy
D) →
Meadville, Nancy
E) →

15. Brown, Charlene
A) →
Brown, Charles
B) →
Brown, Charley A.
C) → _____
Brown, Chas.
D) →
Brown, Cherrie
E) →

16. Bulina, Catherine
A) →
Buel, William D.
B) →
Buell, Warren
C) → _____
Buelna, Angie
D) →
Buelporos, Wesley
E) →

17. Ingars, Hyatt
A) →
Ingals, Ferdinand
B) →
Ingals, Roger
C) → _____
Ingarr, Anita
D) →
Ingarsoll, Julie A.
E) →

18. Kapov, Christopher
A) →
Kaplan, Seymour
B) →
Kaplanjian, Jacob
C) → _____
Kaplus, Asmik
D) →
Kapp, G. J.
E) →

19. Alenty, Relipe
A) →
Alejo, Maura
B) →
Aleksandian, Grigor
C) → _____
Aleman, Augusto
D) →
Alert, Anna G.
E) →

20. Hwang, Kung, Jong
A) →
Hwang, Kathleen
B) →
Hwang, Kyu Chol
C) → _____
Hwang, Kyung Moon
D) →
Hwang, Soon Bong
E) →

21. Burger, Errol M.
A) →
Burcus, Gregory
B) →
Burk, Omelda
C) → _____
Burker, Cathleen
D) →
Burkette, Laura
E) →

22. Aquibas, Roger
A) →
Aguilar, Anna
B) →
Aguilar, Babe Rafael
C) → _____
Aguilar, Catherine
D) →
Aguilar, Niholas
E) →

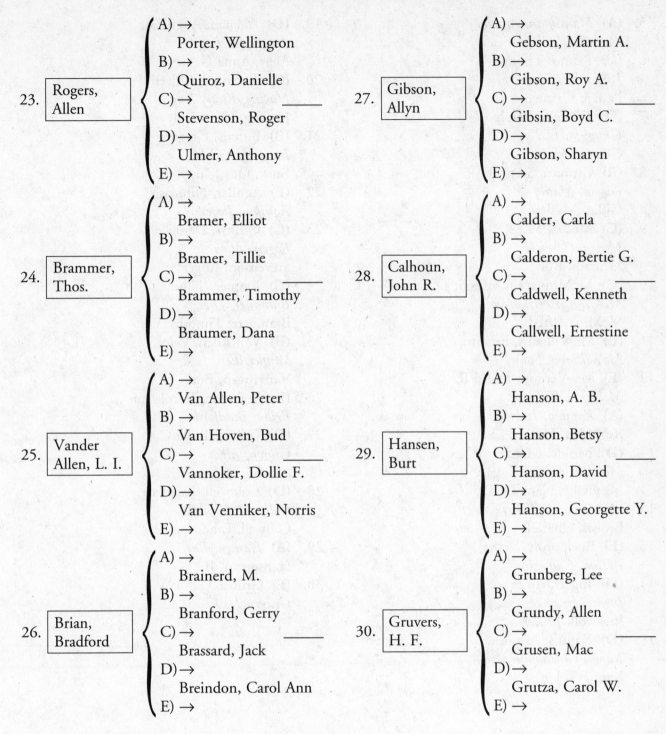

23. Rogers, Allen
- A) →
  Porter, Wellington
- B) →
  Quiroz, Danielle
- C) → _____
  Stevenson, Roger
- D) →
  Ulmer, Anthony
- E) →

24. Brammer, Thos.
- A) →
  Bramer, Elliot
- B) →
  Bramer, Tillie
- C) → _____
  Brammer, Timothy
- D) →
  Braumer, Dana
- E) →

25. Vander Allen, L. I.
- A) →
  Van Allen, Peter
- B) →
  Van Hoven, Bud
- C) → _____
  Vannoker, Dollie F.
- D) →
  Van Venniker, Norris
- E) →

26. Brian, Bradford
- A) →
  Brainerd, M.
- B) →
  Branford, Gerry
- C) → _____
  Brassard, Jack
- D) →
  Breindon, Carol Ann
- E) →

27. Gibson, Allyn
- A) →
  Gebson, Martin A.
- B) →
  Gibson, Roy A.
- C) → _____
  Gibsin, Boyd C.
- D) →
  Gibson, Sharyn
- E) →

28. Calhoun, John R.
- A) →
  Calder, Carla
- B) →
  Calderon, Bertie G.
- C) → _____
  Caldwell, Kenneth
- D) →
  Callwell, Ernestine
- E) →

29. Hansen, Burt
- A) →
  Hanson, A. B.
- B) →
  Hanson, Betsy
- C) → _____
  Hanson, David
- D) →
  Hanson, Georgette Y.
- E) →

30. Gruvers, H. F.
- A) →
  Grunberg, Lee
- B) →
  Grundy, Allen
- C) → _____
  Grusen, Mac
- D) →
  Grutza, Carol W.
- E) →

Answer Explanations for Practice Set 2

1. **(B)** Sax, Steven
   Saxe, Antoinette
   Saxon, Daniel G.
2. **(E)** Stabler, Jennifer
   Stache, Edwin

3. **(B)** Presson Allen, Jay
   Preste, Armand H.
   Preston, Allen
4. **(B)** Sardegna, Marie
   Sardoma, Anthony
   Sardone, Gary

5. **(A)** *Mantikian, Antoine*
   Mantifla, Felix
6. **(C)** Patino, Thomas
   Patjian, Ernesto
   Patfan, Carmen
7. **(D)** Georgia, Ralph
   Georgian, Hal
   Georgy, Afram
8. **(B)** Girmala, Stephen
   Girson, Maury
   Gitlin, Maslow
9. **(C)** Meauz, Steve
   Meaza, Carol II
   Meazzili, Billy
10. **(C)** McMinnamin, Alistair D.
    McMinnsy, Fernon W.
    McMio, Alfred
11. **(E)** McWilliams, Ernesto
    McWilliams, Sonny
12. **(E)** MacVernon, Mabel R.
    McHenry, William
13. **(A)** *Koralan, Isabel T.*
    Kornblau, David H.
14. **(D)** Meade, Mardy
    Meadow, Carla
    Meadville, Nancy
15. **(A)** *Brown, Charlene*
    Brown, Charles
16. **(E)** Buelporos, Wesley
    Bulina, Catherine
17. **(D)** Ingarr, Anita
    Ingars, Hyatt
    Ingarsoll, Julie A.
18. **(D)** Kaptus, Asmik
    Kapov, Christopher
    Kapp, G. J.

19. **(D)** Aleman, Augusto
    Alenty, Relipe
    Alert, Anna G.
20. **(B)** Hwang, Kathleen
    Hwang, Kung, Jong
    Hwang, Kyu Chol
21. **(B)** Burcus, Gregory
    Burger, Errol M.
    Burk, Omelda
22. **(E)** Aguilar, Niholas
    Aquibas, Roger
23. **(C)** Quiroz, Danielle
    Rogers, Allen
    Stevenson, Roger
24. **(C)** Bramer, Tillie
    Brammer, Thos.
    Brammer, Timothy
25. **(B)** Van Allen, Peter
    VanderAllen, L. I.
    VanHoven, Bud
26. **(E)** Breindon, Carol Ann
    Brian, Bradford
27. **(D)** Gibsin, Boyd C.
    Gibson, Allyn
    Gibson, Sharyn
28. **(D)** Caldwell, Kenneth
    Calhoun, John R.
    Callwell, Ernestine
29. **(A)** *Hansen, Burt*
    Hanson, A. B.
30. **(E)** Grutza, Carol W.
    Gruver, H. F.

Practice Set 3

Find the correct place for the name in the box, and mark the letter of that space as your answer.

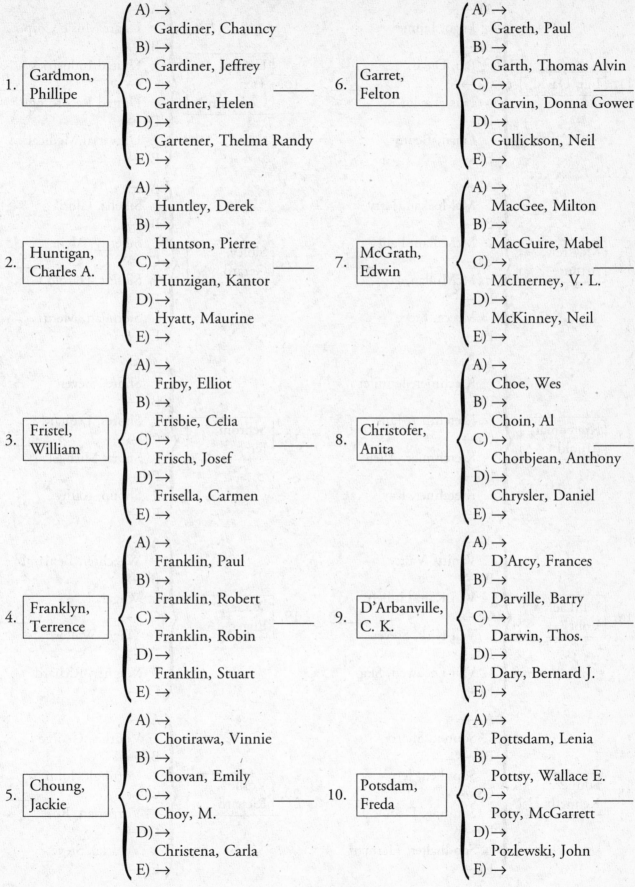

1. Gardmon, Phillipe
- A) →
  Gardiner, Chauncy
- B) →
  Gardiner, Jeffrey
- C) → _____
  Gardner, Helen
- D) →
  Gartener, Thelma Randy
- E) →

2. Huntigan, Charles A.
- A) →
  Huntley, Derek
- B) →
  Huntson, Pierre
- C) → _____
  Hunzigan, Kantor
- D) →
  Hyatt, Maurine
- E) →

3. Fristel, William
- A) →
  Friby, Elliot
- B) →
  Frisbie, Celia
- C) → _____
  Frisch, Josef
- D) →
  Frisella, Carmen
- E) →

4. Franklyn, Terrence
- A) →
  Franklin, Paul
- B) →
  Franklin, Robert
- C) → _____
  Franklin, Robin
- D) →
  Franklin, Stuart
- E) →

5. Choung, Jackie
- A) →
  Chotirawa, Vinnie
- B) →
  Chovan, Emily
- C) → _____
  Choy, M.
- D) →
  Christena, Carla
- E) →

6. Garret, Felton
- A) →
  Gareth, Paul
- B) →
  Garth, Thomas Alvin
- C) → _____
  Garvin, Donna Gower
- D) →
  Gullickson, Neil
- E) →

7. McGrath, Edwin
- A) →
  MacGee, Milton
- B) →
  MacGuire, Mabel
- C) → _____
  McInerney, V. L.
- D) →
  McKinney, Neil
- E) →

8. Christofer, Anita
- A) →
  Choe, Wes
- B) →
  Choin, Al
- C) → _____
  Chorbjean, Anthony
- D) →
  Chrysler, Daniel
- E) →

9. D'Arbanville, C. K.
- A) →
  D'Arcy, Frances
- B) →
  Darville, Barry
- C) → _____
  Darwin, Thos.
- D) →
  Dary, Bernard J.
- E) →

10. Potsdam, Freda
- A) →
  Pottsdam, Lenia
- B) →
  Pottsy, Wallace E.
- C) → _____
  Poty, McGarrett
- D) →
  Pozlewski, John
- E) →

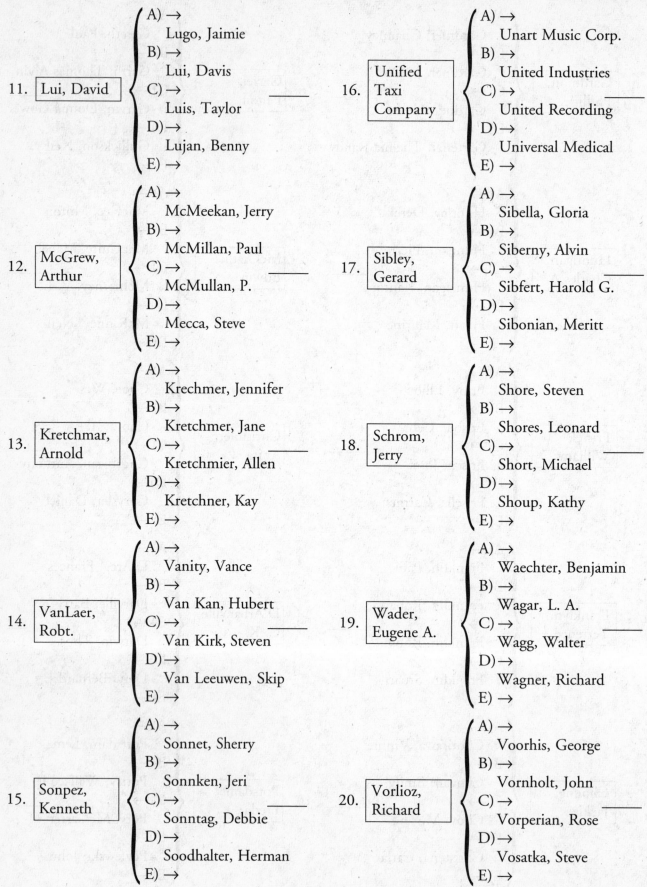

11. Lui, David
A) →
Lugo, Jaimie
B) →
Lui, Davis
C) → _____
Luis, Taylor
D) →
Lujan, Benny
E) →

12. McGrew, Arthur
A) →
McMeekan, Jerry
B) →
McMillan, Paul
C) → _____
McMullan, P.
D) →
Mecca, Steve
E) →

13. Kretchmar, Arnold
A) →
Krechmer, Jennifer
B) →
Kretchmer, Jane
C) → _____
Kretchmier, Allen
D) →
Kretchner, Kay
E) →

14. VanLaer, Robt.
A) →
Vanity, Vance
B) →
Van Kan, Hubert
C) → _____
Van Kirk, Steven
D) →
Van Leeuwen, Skip
E) →

15. Sonpez, Kenneth
A) →
Sonnet, Sherry
B) →
Sonnken, Jeri
C) → _____
Sonntag, Debbie
D) →
Soodhalter, Herman
E) →

16. Unified Taxi Company
A) →
Unart Music Corp.
B) →
United Industries
C) → _____
United Recording
D) →
Universal Medical
E) →

17. Sibley, Gerard
A) →
Sibella, Gloria
B) →
Siberny, Alvin
C) → _____
Sibfert, Harold G.
D) →
Sibonian, Meritt
E) →

18. Schrom, Jerry
A) →
Shore, Steven
B) →
Shores, Leonard
C) → _____
Short, Michael
D) →
Shoup, Kathy
E) →

19. Wader, Eugene A.
A) →
Waechter, Benjamin
B) →
Wagar, L. A.
C) → _____
Wagg, Walter
D) →
Wagner, Richard
E) →

20. Vorlioz, Richard
A) →
Voorhis, George
B) →
Vornholt, John
C) → _____
Vorperian, Rose
D) →
Vosatka, Steve
E) →

21. Darin, Louise
A) →
Darran, Robert
B) →
Darren, Jean Louise
C) → _____
Darrin, Sarah
D) →
Darryn, Josiane
E) →

22. Cassity, Michael
A) →
Casady, Henry
B) →
Casidy, Nestor
C) → _____
Cassady, Roland
D) →
Cassidy, Darryl R.
E) →

23. Carson, Adam
A) →
Carsen, Roger
B) →
Carsen, Teresa R.
C) → _____
Carsin, Foster
D) →
Carsini, Elaine
E) →

24. Dolph, Ralph
A) →
Dogherty, Frederick
B) →
Dougherty, Cinthia
C) → _____
Doughrty, Benta
D) →
Douph, Patricia
E) →

25. Collins, Denise
A) →
Collins, Collie
B) →
Collins, Dolley
C) → _____
Collins, Dorothy
D) →
Collins, Dova
E) →

26. Homer, Nelson
A) →
Hooker, Dennis
B) →
Hooper, Margie
C) → _____
Hooper, Peter D.
D) →
Hoover, Phyllis
E) →

27. Matthau, Warren
A) →
Mathews, Ginger
B) →
Matthews, Aaron
C) → _____
Matthews, Neville
D) →
McMathow, Lynne
E) →

28. Dipman, Maria
A) →
Desmond, Ronald C.
B) →
Diamond, Leslie Ann
C) → _____
Dimond, Laura
D) →
Dizmond, Jennie
E) →

29. Cummings, James
A) →
Cummings, Eric
B) →
Cummings, James T.
C) → _____
Cummings, Phyllis
D) →
Cummings, Stuart
E) →

30. Abrahms, Corinna
A) →
Abrahams, Tara
B) →
Abrams, Marcus J.
C) → _____
Abramson, Arthur
D) →
Abrasnov, Clarence
E) →

Answer Explanations for Practice Set 3

1. **(C)** Gardiner, Jeffrey
Gard<u>m</u>on, Phillipe
Gardner, Helen

2. **(A)** *Hunti<u>g</u>an, Charles A.*
Huntley, Derek

3. **(E)** Friselia, Carmen
Fris<u>t</u>el, William

4. **(E)** Franklin, Stuart
Frank<u>l</u>yn, Terrence

5. **(B)** Chotirawa, Vinnie
Cho<u>u</u>ng, Jackie
Chovan, Emily

6. **(B)** Gareth, Paul
Gar<u>r</u>et, Felton
Garth, Thomas Alvin

7. **(C)** MacGuire, Mabel
M<u>c</u>Grath, Edwin
McInerney, V. L.

8. **(D)** Chorbjean, Anthony
Ch<u>r</u>istofer, Anita
Chrysler, Daniel

9. **(A)** *D'Ar<u>b</u>anville, C. K.*
D'Arcy, Frances

10. **(A)** *Pot<u>s</u>dam, Freda*
Pottsdam, Lenia

11. **(B)** Lugo, Jaimie
Lu<u>i, David</u>
Lui, Davis

12. **(A)** *Mc<u>G</u>rew, Arthur*
McKeekan, Jerry

13. **(B)** Krechmer, Jennifer
Kre<u>tch</u>mar, Arnold
Kretchmer, Jane

14. **(D)** Van Kirk, Steven
Van<u>L</u>aer, Robt.
Van Leeuwen, Skip

15. **(D)** Sonntag, Debbie
Son<u>p</u>ez, Kenneth
Soodhalter, Herman

16. **(B)** Unart Music Corp.
Uni<u>f</u>ied Taxi Company
United Industries

17. **(D)** Sibfert, Harold G.
Sibl<u>e</u>y, Gerard
Sibonian, Meritt

18. **(A)** *S<u>c</u>hrom, Jerry*
Shore, Steven

19. **(A)** *Wa<u>d</u>er, Eugene A.*
Waechter, Benjamin

20. **(B)** Voorhis, George
Vo<u>r</u>lioz, Richard
Vornholt, John

21. **(A)** *Da<u>r</u>in, Louise*
Darran, Robert

22. **(E)** Cassidy, Darryl R.
Cass<u>i</u>ty, Michael

23. **(E)** Carsini, Elaine
Cars<u>on</u>, Adam

24. **(B)** Dogherty, Frederick
Dol<u>p</u>h, Ralph
Dougherty, Cinthia

25. **(B)** Collins, Collie
Collins, <u>D</u>enise
Collins, Dolley

26. **(A)** *Ho<u>m</u>er, Nelson*
Hooker, Dennis

27. **(B)** Mathews, Ginger
Mat<u>th</u>au, Warren
Matthews, Aaron

28. **(D)** Dimond, Laura
Di<u>p</u>man, Maria
Dizmond, Jennie

29. **(B)** Cummings, Eric
Cummings, <u>J</u>ames
Cummings, James T.

30. **(B)** Abrahams, Tara
Abra<u>hm</u>s, Corinna
Abrams, Marcus J.

Practice Set 4

Find the correct place for the name in the box, and mark the letter of that space as your answer.

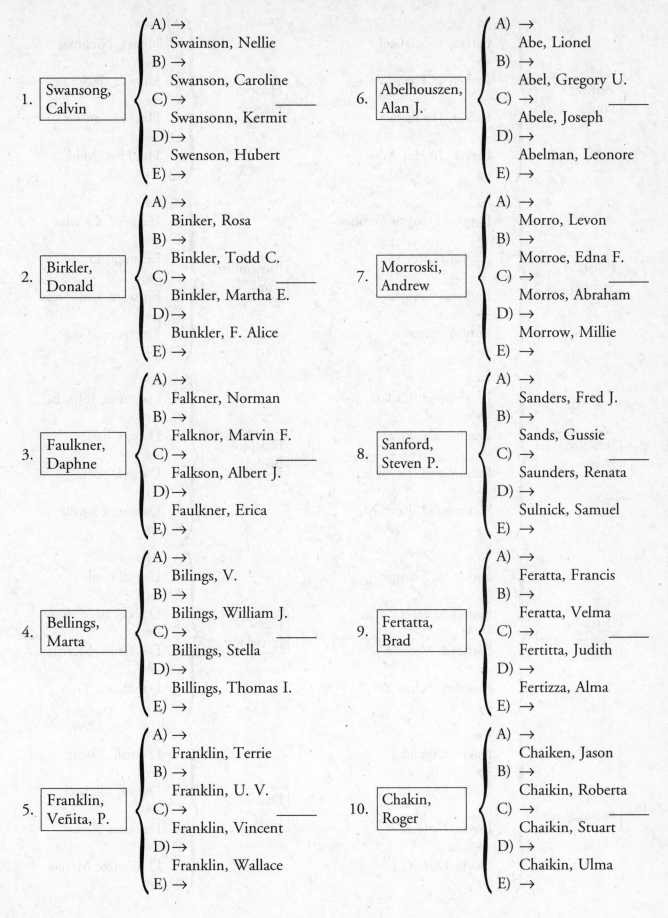

1. Swansong, Calvin
   - A) →
     Swainson, Nellie
   - B) →
     Swanson, Caroline
   - C) → _____
     Swansonn, Kermit
   - D) →
     Swenson, Hubert
   - E) →

2. Birkler, Donald
   - A) →
     Binker, Rosa
   - B) →
     Binkler, Todd C.
   - C) → _____
     Binkler, Martha E.
   - D) →
     Bunkler, F. Alice
   - E) →

3. Faulkner, Daphne
   - A) →
     Falkner, Norman
   - B) →
     Falknor, Marvin F.
   - C) → _____
     Falkson, Albert J.
   - D) →
     Faulkner, Erica
   - E) →

4. Bellings, Marta
   - A) →
     Bilings, V.
   - B) →
     Bilings, William J.
   - C) → _____
     Billings, Stella
   - D) →
     Billings, Thomas I.
   - E) →

5. Franklin, Veñita, P.
   - A) →
     Franklin, Terrie
   - B) →
     Franklin, U. V.
   - C) → _____
     Franklin, Vincent
   - D) →
     Franklin, Wallace
   - E) →

6. Abelhouszen, Alan J.
   - A) →
     Abe, Lionel
   - B) →
     Abel, Gregory U.
   - C) → _____
     Abele, Joseph
   - D) →
     Abelman, Leonore
   - E) →

7. Morroski, Andrew
   - A) →
     Morro, Levon
   - B) →
     Morroe, Edna F.
   - C) → _____
     Morros, Abraham
   - D) →
     Morrow, Millie
   - E) →

8. Sanford, Steven P.
   - A) →
     Sanders, Fred J.
   - B) →
     Sands, Gussie
   - C) → _____
     Saunders, Renata
   - D) →
     Sulnick, Samuel
   - E) →

9. Fertatta, Brad
   - A) →
     Feratta, Francis
   - B) →
     Feratta, Velma
   - C) → _____
     Fertitta, Judith
   - D) →
     Fertizza, Alma
   - E) →

10. Chakin, Roger
   - A) →
     Chaiken, Jason
   - B) →
     Chaikin, Roberta
   - C) → _____
     Chaikin, Stuart
   - D) →
     Chaikin, Ulma
   - E) →

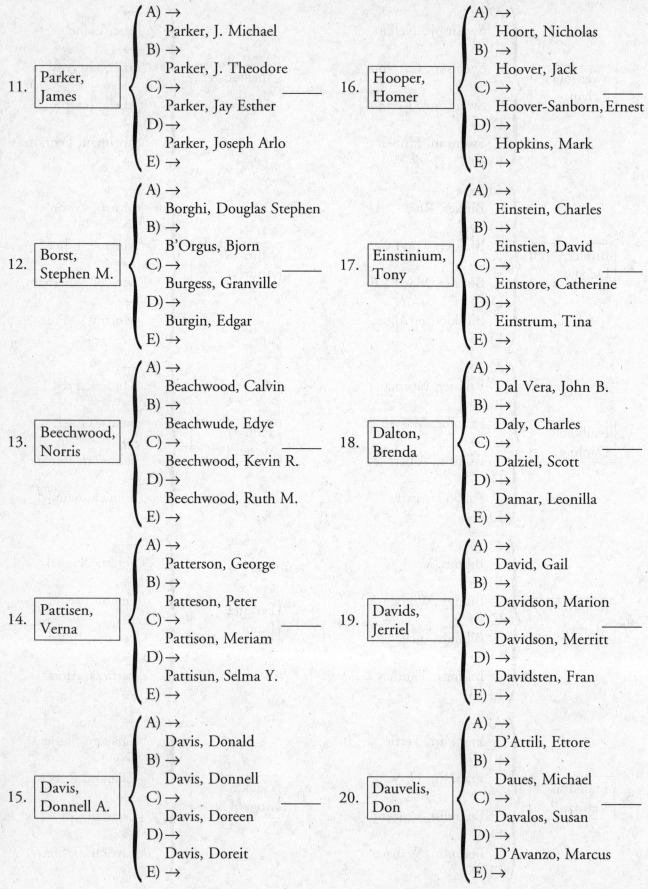

11. Parker, James
A) →
Parker, J. Michael
B) →
Parker, J. Theodore
C) → _____
Parker, Jay Esther
D) →
Parker, Joseph Arlo
E) →

12. Borst, Stephen M.
A) →
Borghi, Douglas Stephen
B) →
B'Orgus, Bjorn
C) → _____
Burgess, Granville
D) →
Burgin, Edgar
E) →

13. Beechwood, Norris
A) →
Beachwood, Calvin
B) →
Beachwude, Edye
C) → _____
Beechwood, Kevin R.
D) →
Beechwood, Ruth M.
E) →

14. Pattisen, Verna
A) →
Patterson, George
B) →
Patteson, Peter
C) → _____
Pattison, Meriam
D) →
Pattisun, Selma Y.
E) →

15. Davis, Donnell A.
A) →
Davis, Donald
B) →
Davis, Donnell
C) → _____
Davis, Doreen
D) →
Davis, Doreit
E) →

16. Hooper, Homer
A) →
Hoort, Nicholas
B) →
Hoover, Jack
C) → _____
Hoover-Sanborn, Ernest
D) →
Hopkins, Mark
E) →

17. Einstinium, Tony
A) →
Einstein, Charles
B) →
Einstien, David
C) → _____
Einstore, Catherine
D) →
Einstrum, Tina
E) →

18. Dalton, Brenda
A) →
Dal Vera, John B.
B) →
Daly, Charles
C) → _____
Dalziel, Scott
D) →
Damar, Leonilla
E) →

19. Davids, Jerriel
A) →
David, Gail
B) →
Davidson, Marion
C) → _____
Davidson, Merritt
D) →
Davidsten, Fran
E) →

20. Dauvelis, Don
A) →
D'Attili, Ettore
B) →
Daues, Michael
C) → _____
Davalos, Susan
D) →
D'Avanzo, Marcus
E) →

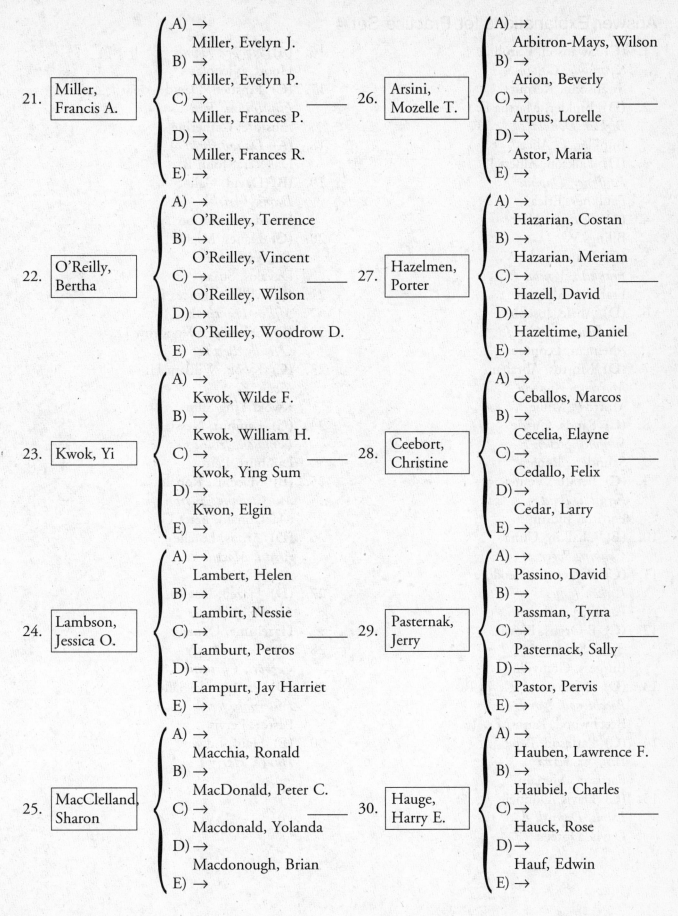

21. Miller, Francis A.
- A) →
  Miller, Evelyn J.
- B) →
  Miller, Evelyn P.
- C) → _____
  Miller, Frances P.
- D) →
  Miller, Frances R.
- E) →

22. O'Reilly, Bertha
- A) →
  O'Reilley, Terrence
- B) →
  O'Reilley, Vincent
- C) → _____
  O'Reilley, Wilson
- D) →
  O'Reilley, Woodrow D.
- E) →

23. Kwok, Yi
- A) →
  Kwok, Wilde F.
- B) →
  Kwok, William H.
- C) → _____
  Kwok, Ying Sum
- D) →
  Kwon, Elgin
- E) →

24. Lambson, Jessica O.
- A) →
  Lambert, Helen
- B) →
  Lambirt, Nessie
- C) → _____
  Lamburt, Petros
- D) →
  Lampurt, Jay Harriet
- E) →

25. MacClelland, Sharon
- A) →
  Macchia, Ronald
- B) →
  MacDonald, Peter C.
- C) → _____
  Macdonald, Yolanda
- D) →
  Macdonough, Brian
- E) →

26. Arsini, Mozelle T.
- A) →
  Arbitron-Mays, Wilson
- B) →
  Arion, Beverly
- C) → _____
  Arpus, Lorelle
- D) →
  Astor, Maria
- E) →

27. Hazelmen, Porter
- A) →
  Hazarian, Costan
- B) →
  Hazarian, Meriam
- C) → _____
  Hazell, David
- D) →
  Hazeltime, Daniel
- E) →

28. Ceebort, Christine
- A) →
  Ceballos, Marcos
- B) →
  Cecelia, Elayne
- C) → _____
  Cedallo, Felix
- D) →
  Cedar, Larry
- E) →

29. Pasternak, Jerry
- A) →
  Passino, David
- B) →
  Passman, Tyrra
- C) → _____
  Pasternack, Sally
- D) →
  Pastor, Pervis
- E) →

30. Hauge, Harry E.
- A) →
  Hauben, Lawrence F.
- B) →
  Haubiel, Charles
- C) → _____
  Hauck, Rose
- D) →
  Hauf, Edwin
- E) →

Answer Explanations for Practice Set 4

1. **(C)** Swanson, Caroline
   Swansong, Calvin
   Swansonn, Kermit
2. **(D)** Binkler, Martha E.
   Birkler, Donald
   Bunkler, F. Alice
3. **(D)** Falkson, Albert J.
   Faulkner, Daphne
   Faulkner, Erica
4. **(A)** *Bellings, Marta*
   Bilings, V.
5. **(C)** Franklin, U. V.
   Franklin, Venita, P.
   Franklin, Vincent
6. **(D)** Abele, Joseph
   Abelhouszen, Alan J.
   Abelman, Leonore
7. **(D)** Morros, Abraham
   Morroski, Andrew
   Morrow, Millie
8. **(C)** Sands, Gussie
   Sanford, Steven P.
   Saunders, Renata
9. **(C)** Feratta, Velma
   Fertatta, Brad
   Fertitta, Judith
10. **(E)** Chaikin, Ulma
    Chakin, Roger
11. **(C)** Parker, J. Theodore
    Parker, James
    Parker, Jay Esther
12. **(C)** B'Orgus, Bjorn
    Borst, Stephen M.
    Burgess, Granville
13. **(D)** Beechwood, Kevin R.
    Beechwood, Norris
    Beechwood, Ruth M.
14. **(C)** Patteson, Peter
    Pattisen, Verna
    Pattison, Meriam
15. **(C)** Davis, Donnell
    Davis, Donnell A.
    Davis, Doreen
16. **(A)** *Hooper, Homer*
    Hoort, Nicholas
17. **(C)** Einstien, David
    Einstinium, Tony
    Einstore, Catherine
18. **(A)** *Dalton, Brenda*
    Dal Vera, John B.
19. **(B)** David, Gail
    Davis, Jerriel
    Davidson, Marion
20. **(C)** Daues, Michael
    Dauvelis, Don
    Davalos, Susan
21. **(E)** Miller, Frances R.
    Miller, Francis A.
22. **(E)** O'Reilley, Woodrow D.
    O'Reilly, Bertha
23. **(C)** Kwok, William H.
    Kwok, Yi
    Kwok, Ying Sum
24. **(C)** Lambirt, Nessie
    Lambson, Jessica O.
    Lamburt, Petros
25. **(B)** Macchia, Ronald
    MacClelland, Sharon
    MacDonald, Peter C.
26. **(D)** Arpus, Lorelle
    Arsini, Mozelle T.
    Astor, Maria
27. **(D)** Hazell, David
    Hazelmen, Porter
    Hazeltime, Daniel
28. **(E)** Cedar, Larry
    Ceebort, Christine
29. **(D)** Pasternack, Sally
    Pasternak, Jerry
    Pastor, Pervis
30. **(E)** Hauf, Edwin
    Hauge, Harry E.

Practice Set 5

Find the correct place for the name in the box, and mark the letter of that space as your answer.

1. SanMarco, Antonio
   - A) →
     SanLuis, Phillip
   - B) →
     Sanlummis, Douglas
   - C) → _____
     Sanlutent, Wilfred
   - D) →
     SanMiguel, Maria
   - E) →

5. Merlino, Flavio
   - A) →
     Merino, Joseph
   - B) →
     Merinoff, Anton
   - C) → _____
     Merkley, Allen L.
   - D) →
     Merluzzo, Paul Michael
   - E) →

2. Arunges, Artin
   - A) →
     Arto, Raoul
   - B) →
     Artz, M. G.
   - C) → _____
     Arutyun, Adam
   - D) →
     Arvin, Stefanie
   - E) →

6. Soleman, Brooke G.
   - A) →
     Solmon, Sylvia
   - B) →
     Solomon, Rose
   - C) → _____
     Solomon, William
   - D) →
     Soltman, Neil
   - E) →

3. Felard, Stephanie
   - A) →
     Falana, Ariel
   - B) →
     Falardeau, George
   - C) → _____
     Falcasantos, Lea
   - D) →
     Falck, Raymond
   - E) →

7. Smith, Robert Z.
   - A) →
     Smith, R. Ruth
   - B) →
     Smith, Richard
   - C) → _____
     Smith, Rodney
   - D) →
     Smith, Sara
   - E) →

4. Aryzinault, Paul
   - A) →
     Arye, Israel
   - B) →
     Aryee, Enoch
   - C) → _____
     Arzola, Luz
   - D) →
     Arzouman, Merry
   - E) →

8. Kuhn, Frank P.
   - A) →
     Kuh, Grace
   - B) →
     Kuhl, Gregory
   - C) → _____
     Kuhner, Maryann
   - D) →
     Kulh, Eugene R.
   - E) →

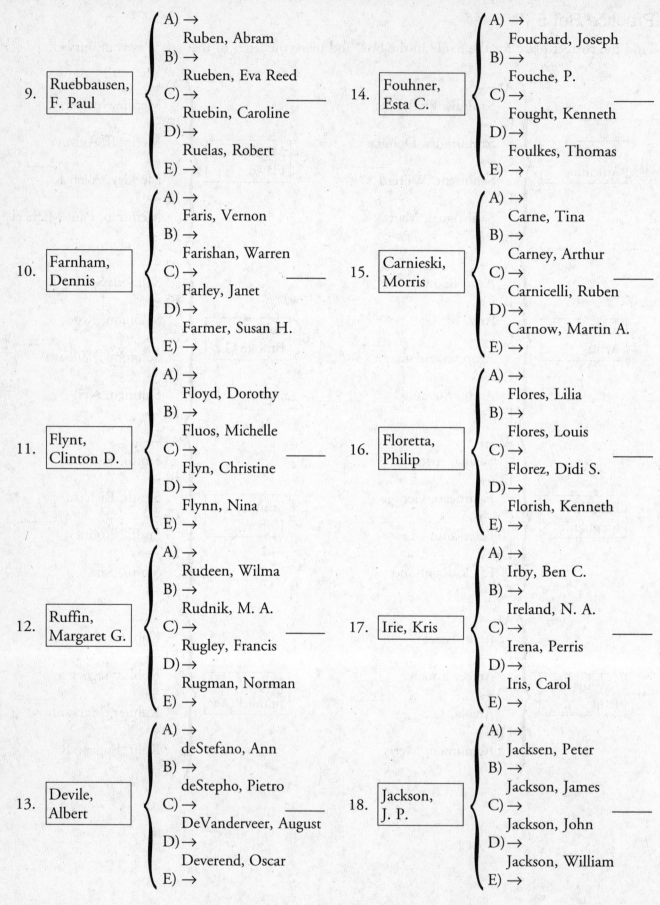

9. Ruebbausen, F. Paul
- A) →
  Ruben, Abram
- B) →
  Rueben, Eva Reed
- C) → _____
  Ruebin, Caroline
- D) →
  Ruelas, Robert
- E) →

10. Farnham, Dennis
- A) →
  Faris, Vernon
- B) →
  Farishan, Warren
- C) → _____
  Farley, Janet
- D) →
  Farmer, Susan H.
- E) →

11. Flynt, Clinton D.
- A) →
  Floyd, Dorothy
- B) →
  Fluos, Michelle
- C) → _____
  Flyn, Christine
- D) →
  Flynn, Nina
- E) →

12. Ruffin, Margaret G.
- A) →
  Rudeen, Wilma
- B) →
  Rudnik, M. A.
- C) → _____
  Rugley, Francis
- D) →
  Rugman, Norman
- E) →

13. Devile, Albert
- A) →
  deStefano, Ann
- B) →
  deStepho, Pietro
- C) → _____
  DeVanderveer, August
- D) →
  Deverend, Oscar
- E) →

14. Fouhner, Esta C.
- A) →
  Fouchard, Joseph
- B) →
  Fouche, P.
- C) → _____
  Fought, Kenneth
- D) →
  Foulkes, Thomas
- E) →

15. Carnieski, Morris
- A) →
  Carne, Tina
- B) →
  Carney, Arthur
- C) → _____
  Carnicelli, Ruben
- D) →
  Carnow, Martin A.
- E) →

16. Floretta, Philip
- A) →
  Flores, Lilia
- B) →
  Flores, Louis
- C) → _____
  Florez, Didi S.
- D) →
  Florish, Kenneth
- E) →

17. Irie, Kris
- A) →
  Irby, Ben C.
- B) →
  Ireland, N. A.
- C) → _____
  Irena, Perris
- D) →
  Iris, Carol
- E) →

18. Jackson, J. P.
- A) →
  Jacksen, Peter
- B) →
  Jackson, James
- C) → _____
  Jackson, John
- D) →
  Jackson, William
- E) →

19. Berland, Helen Ann
A) →
Berk, Lillian O.
B) →
Berker, S. R.
C) → _____
Berkey, Maurice
D) →
Berkey, Maurice
E) →

20. Berry, Charles
A) ›
Berry, Bill
B) →
Berry, Brian
C) → _____
Berry, C. Douglas
D) →
Berry, Jonathan
E) →

21. McAllister, Virginia
A) →
MacMenamin, Peter
B) →
MacMullory, Nigel
C) → _____
McNoughton, Foster
D) →
McOleny, Santa
E) →

22. Kramer, Edward
A) →
Kramer, A.
B) →
Kramer, Allen
C) → _____
Kramer, E. J.
D) →
Kramer, Rubin
E) →

23. Jurimasat, Patricia
A) →
Juodeika, G. Rowena
B) →
Jura, John
C) → _____
Jurow, Stasia
D) →
Justice, Edgar J.
E) →

24. Harding, Gary
A) →
Hardin, Timothy
B) →
Harding, Gary D.
C) → _____
Harding, Gary T.
D) →
Harding, George
E) →

25. O'Reilley, Sarah
A) →
O'Donnell, William
B) →
Orofino, Roger
C) → _____
Oshorn, Margaret
D) →
Oviello, Jennifer
E) →

26. Caban, Thomas O.
A) →
Cahn, Cathy
B) →
Canen, Franklin R.
C) → _____
Cohan, Martha
D) →
Cohen, Phillip
E) →

27. Murshente, Betsy
A) →
Muray, Michael
B) →
Murtaugh, Danny
C) → _____
Muscente, Kathlene
D) →
Musgrove, Stanley A.
E) →

28. Myers, Arthur G.
A) →
Meyers, Alma
B) →
Meyers, Arno
C) → _____
Meyers, Eleanor G.
D) →
Meyers, Terrence
E) →

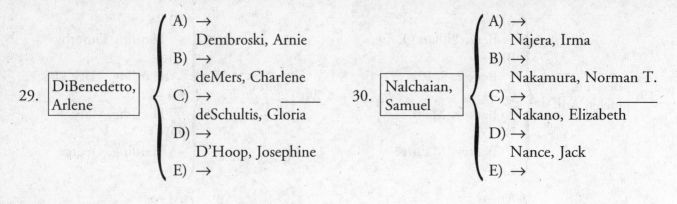

29. DiBenedetto, Arlene
A) →
   Dembroski, Arnie
B) →
   deMers, Charlene
C) → _____
   deSchultis, Gloria
D) →
   D'Hoop, Josephine
E) →

30. Nalchaian, Samuel
A) →
   Najera, Irma
B) →
   Nakamura, Norman T.
C) → _____
   Nakano, Elizabeth
D) →
   Nance, Jack
E) →

Answer Explanations for Practice Set 5

1. **(D)** Sanlutent, Wilfred
   San<u>M</u>arco, Antonio
   SanMiguel, Maria

2. **(C)** Artz, M. G.
   Ar<u>u</u>nges, Artin
   Arutyun, Adam

3. **(E)** Faick, Raymond
   Fe<u>l</u>ard, Stephanie

4. **(C)** Aryee, Enoch
   Ary<u>z</u>inault, Paul
   Arzola, Luz

5. **(D)** Merkley, Allen L.
   Merl<u>i</u>no, Flavio
   Merluzzo, Paul Michael

6. **(A)** *Sol<u>e</u>man, Brooke G.*
   Solmon, Sylvia

7. **(C)** Smith, Richard
   Smith, <u>R</u>obert Z.
   Smith, Rodney

8. **(C)** Kuhl, Gregory
   Kuh<u>n</u>, Frank P.
   Kuhner, Maryann

9. **(C)** Rueben, Eva Reed
   Rueb<u>h</u>ausen, F. Paul
   Ruebin, Caroline

10. **(E)** Farmer, Susan H.
    Far<u>n</u>ham, Dennis

11. **(E)** Flynn, Nina
    Flyn<u>t</u>, Clinton D.

12. **(C)** Rudnik, M. A.
    Ru<u>ff</u>in, Margaret G.
    Rugley, Francis

13. **(E)** Deverend, Oscar
    Dev<u>i</u>le, Albert

14. **(D)** Fought, Kenneth
    Fou<u>h</u>ner, Esta C.
    Fou<u>l</u>kes, Thomas

15. **(D)** Carnicelli, Ruben
    Carni<u>e</u>ski, Morris
    Carnow, Martin A.

16. **(C)** Flores, Louis
    Flor<u>e</u>tta, Philip
    Florez, Didi S.

17. **(D)** Irena, Perris
    Iri<u>e</u>, Kris
    Iris, Carol

18. **(B)** Jacksen, Peter
    <u>Jackson, J. P.</u>
    Jackson, James

19. **(E)** Berkquist, Peter
    Ber<u>l</u>and, Helen Ann

20. **(D)** Berry, C. Douglas
    Berry, <u>C</u>harles
    Berry, Jonathan

21. **(C)** MacMullory, Nigel
    M<u>c</u>Allister, Virginia
    McNoughton, Foster

22. **(D)** Kramer, E. J.
    Kramer, <u>E</u>dward
    Kramer, Rubin

23. **(C)** Jura, John
    Ju<u>r</u>imasat, Patricia
    Jurow, Stasia

24. **(B)** Hardin, Timothy
    Hard<u>in</u>g, Gary
    Harding, Gary D.

25. **(B)** O'Donnell, William
    O'<u>R</u>eilley, Sarah
    Orofino, Roger

26. **(A)** *Caban, Thomas O.*
    Cahn, Cathy
27. **(B)** Murray, Michael
    Murshente, Betsy
    Murtaugh, Danny
28. **(E)** Meyers, Terrence
    Myers, Arthur G.

29. **(E)** D'Hoop, Josephine
    DiBenedetto, Arlene
30. **(D)** Nakano, Elizabeth
    Nalchaian, Samuel
    Nance, Jack

Practice Set 6

Find the correct place for the name in the box, and mark the letter of that space as your answer.

1. **Mercadante, Alicia**
   - A) →
     Mensor, Arthur C.
   - B) →
     Meono, Michael
   - C) → _____
     Mercado, Mary
   - D) →
     Mercer, Elmer
   - E) →

2. **Hawkins, Mary**
   - A) →
     Hawkins, M. C.
   - B) →
     Hawkins, Nick
   - C) → _____
     Hawkins, Odie
   - D) →
     Hawkins, Phillipa
   - E) →

3. **Bujol, Leslie**
   - A) →
     Buitrago, Belma
   - B) →
     Buiza, Carmen
   - C) → _____
     Buizzie, Ralph
   - D) →
     Sukowski, Richard
   - E) →

4. **Gomez, Anna**
   - A) →
     Gomes, Peter
   - B) →
     Gomes, Ricardo
   - C) → _____
     Gomes, Rosalina
   - D) →
     Gomes, Steven
   - E) →

5. **Rubenstein, Blanche**
   - A) →
     Rubey, Michelle
   - B) →
     Rubins, Brady
   - C) → _____
     Rubrick, Michael
   - D) →
     Ruffert, Maggy
   - E) →

6. **Sobel, Allyn D.**
   - A) →
     Snow, Wade
   - B) →
     Snyder, Libbie
   - C) → _____
     Sonsini, P.
   - D) →
     Soria, Erica
   - E) →

7. **San Benito, Adele**
   - A) →
     Sabo, George
   - B) →
     Sabocur, Dwight
   - C) → _____
     Sabosian, Dorothy
   - D) →
     Saobine, Judith
   - E) →

8. **McEnninger, Vivian**
   - A) →
     McElleny, Thomas
   - B) →
     McElroy, Anna
   - C) → _____
     McEnney, Hazel
   - D) →
     McEntosh, Belle
   - E) →

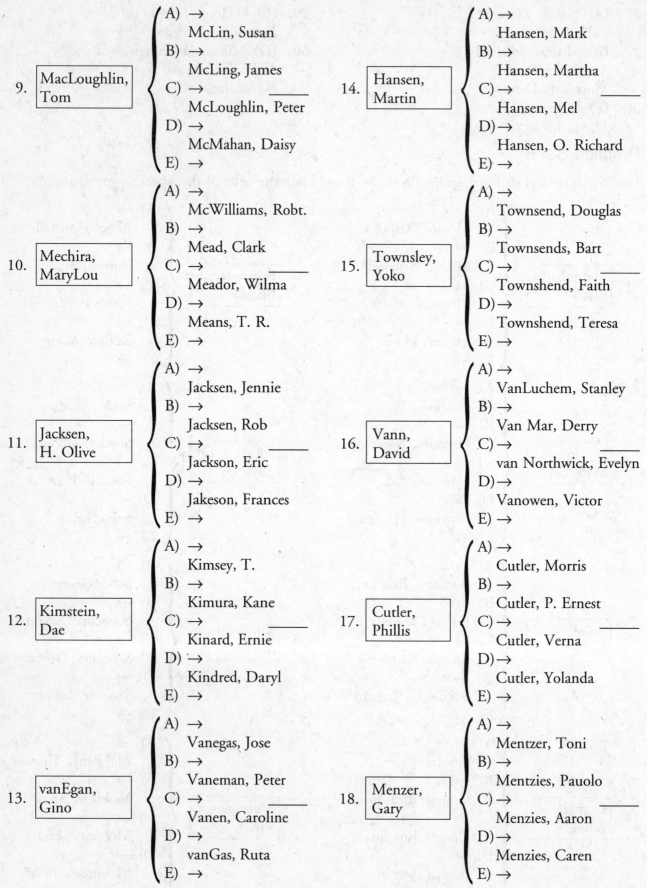

9. MacLoughlin, Tom
A) →
   McLin, Susan
B) →
   McLing, James
C) → _____
   McLoughlin, Peter
D) →
   McMahan, Daisy
E) →

10. Mechira, MaryLou
A) →
   McWilliams, Robt.
B) →
   Mead, Clark
C) → _____
   Meador, Wilma
D) →
   Means, T. R.
E) →

11. Jacksen, H. Olive
A) →
   Jacksen, Jennie
B) →
   Jacksen, Rob
C) → _____
   Jackson, Eric
D) →
   Jakeson, Frances
E) →

12. Kimstein, Dae
A) →
   Kimsey, T.
B) →
   Kimura, Kane
C) → _____
   Kinard, Ernie
D) →
   Kindred, Daryl
E) →

13. vanEgan, Gino
A) →
   Vanegas, Jose
B) →
   Vaneman, Peter
C) → _____
   Vanen, Caroline
D) →
   vanGas, Ruta
E) →

14. Hansen, Martin
A) →
   Hansen, Mark
B) →
   Hansen, Martha
C) → _____
   Hansen, Mel
D) →
   Hansen, O. Richard
E) →

15. Townsley, Yoko
A) →
   Townsend, Douglas
B) →
   Townsends, Bart
C) → _____
   Townshend, Faith
D) →
   Townshend, Teresa
E) →

16. Vann, David
A) →
   VanLuchem, Stanley
B) →
   Van Mar, Derry
C) → _____
   van Northwick, Evelyn
D) →
   Vanowen, Victor
E) →

17. Cutler, Phillis
A) →
   Cutler, Morris
B) →
   Cutler, P. Ernest
C) → _____
   Cutler, Verna
D) →
   Cutler, Yolanda
E) →

18. Menzer, Gary
A) →
   Mentzer, Toni
B) →
   Mentzies, Pauolo
C) → _____
   Menzies, Aaron
D) →
   Menzies, Caren
E) →

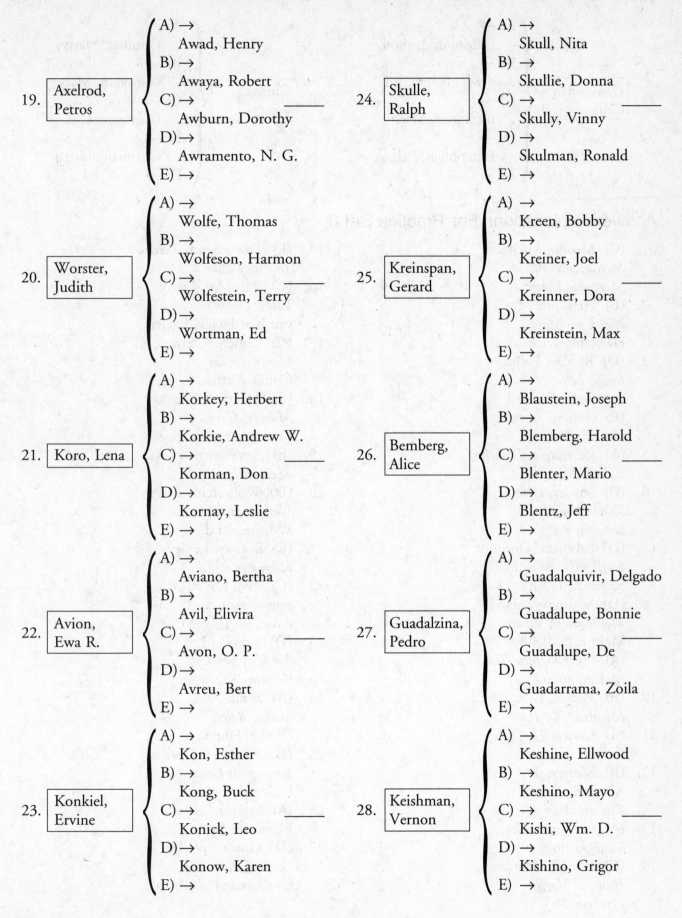

19. Axelrod, Petros
A) →
Awad, Henry
B) →
Awaya, Robert
C) → _____
Awburn, Dorothy
D) →
Awramento, N. G.
E) →

20. Worster, Judith
A) →
Wolfe, Thomas
B) →
Wolfeson, Harmon
C) → _____
Wolfestein, Terry
D) →
Wortman, Ed
E) →

21. Koro, Lena
A) →
Korkey, Herbert
B) →
Korkie, Andrew W.
C) → _____
Korman, Don
D) →
Kornay, Leslie
E) →

22. Avion, Ewa R.
A) →
Aviano, Bertha
B) →
Avil, Elivira
C) → _____
Avon, O. P.
D) →
Avreu, Bert
E) →

23. Konkiel, Ervine
A) →
Kon, Esther
B) →
Kong, Buck
C) → _____
Konick, Leo
D) →
Konow, Karen
E) →

24. Skulle, Ralph
A) →
Skull, Nita
B) →
Skullie, Donna
C) → _____
Skully, Vinny
D) →
Skulman, Ronald
E) →

25. Kreinspan, Gerard
A) →
Kreen, Bobby
B) →
Kreiner, Joel
C) → _____
Kreinner, Dora
D) →
Kreinstein, Max
E) →

26. Bemberg, Alice
A) →
Blaustein, Joseph
B) →
Blemberg, Harold
C) → _____
Blenter, Mario
D) →
Blentz, Jeff
E) →

27. Guadalzina, Pedro
A) →
Guadalquivir, Delgado
B) →
Guadalupe, Bonnie
C) → _____
Guadalupe, De
D) →
Guadarrama, Zoila
E) →

28. Keishman, Vernon
A) →
Keshine, Ellwood
B) →
Keshino, Mayo
C) → _____
Kishi, Wm. D.
D) →
Kishino, Grigor
E) →

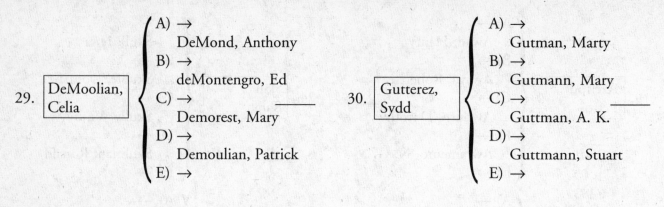

29. DeMoolian, Celia
- A) →
- DeMond, Anthony
- B) →
- deMontengro, Ed
- C) → _____
- Demorest, Mary
- D) →
- Demoulian, Patrick
- E) →

30. Gutterez, Sydd
- A) →
- Gutman, Marty
- B) →
- Gutmann, Mary
- C) → _____
- Guttman, A. K.
- D) →
- Guttmann, Stuart
- E) →

Answer Explanations For Practice Set 6

1. **(C)** Meono, Michael
   Mercadante, Alicia
   Mercado, Mary
2. **(B)** Hawkins, M. C.
   Hawkins, Mary
   Hawkins, Wick
3. **(D)** Buizzie, Ralph
   Bujol, Leslie
   Bukowski, Richard
4. **(E)** Gomes, Steven
   Gomez, Anna
5. **(A)** *Rubenstein, Blanche*
   Rubey, Michelle
6. **(C)** Snyder, Libbie
   Sobel, Allyn D.
   Sonsini, P.
7. **(D)** Sabosian, Dorothy
   SanBenito, Adele
   Saobine, Judith
8. **(D)** McEnney, Hazel
   McEnninger, Vivian
   McEntosh, Belle
9. **(A)** *MacLoughlin, Tom*
   McLin, Susan
10. **(E)** Means, T. R.
    Mechira, MaryLou
11. **(A)** *Jacksen, H. Olive*
    Jacksen, Jennie
12. **(B)** Kimsey, T.
    Kimstein, Dae
    Kimura, Kane
13. **(A)** *vanEgan, Gino*
    Vanegas, Jose
14. **(C)** Hansen, Martha
    Hansen, Martin
    Hansen, Mel

15. **(E)** Townshend, Teresa
    Townsley, Yoko
16. **(C)** Van Mar, Derry
    Vann, David
    van Northwick, Evelyn
17. **(C)** Cutler, P. Ernest
    Cutler, Phillis
    Cutler, Verna
18. **(C)** Mentzies, Pauolo
    Menzer, Gary
    Menzies, Aaron
19. **(E)** Awramento, N. G.
    Axelrod, Petros
20. **(D)** Wolfestein, Terry
    Worster, Judith
    Wortman, Ed
21. **(E)** Kornay, Leslie
    Koro, Lena
22. **(C)** Avil, Elivira
    Avion, Ewa R.
    Avon, O. P.
23. **(D)** Konick, Leo
    Konkiel, Ervine
    Konow, Karen
24. **(B)** Skull, Nita
    Skulle, Ralph
    Skullie, Donna
25. **(D)** Kreinner, Dora
    Kreinspan, Gerard
    Kreinstein, Max
26. **(A)** *Bemberg, Alice*
    Blaustein, Joseph
27. **(D)** Guadalupe, De
    Guadalzina, Pedro
    Guadarrama, Zoila

28. **(A)** *Keishman, Vernon*
    Keshine, Ellwood
29. **(C)** deMontengro, Ed
    DeMoolian, Celia
    Demorest, Mary

30. **(C)** Gutmann, Mary
    Gutterez, Sydd
    Guttman, A. K.

Practice Set 7

Find the correct place for the name in the box, and mark the letter of that space as your answer.

1. | Dembart, Lee |
   - A) →
     Demaree, Ona
   - B) →
     Demars, James
   - C) →
     Demas, Maxine
   - D) →
     de Melo, Paul
   - E) →

5. | Labosian, Angeline |
   - A) →
     Labossiere, Phillipe
   - B) →
     Labossiereaux, Jean
   - C) →
     Labowitz, Edward
   - D) →
     Labowitz, Ian
   - E) →

2. | Dennison, Larry |
   - A) →
     Denko, Bee
   - B) →
     Dennis, Harold A.
   - C) →
     Denny, Larry
   - D) →
     DePiero, Carlos
   - E) →

6. | Dennis, Harold |
   - A) →
     Dennen, A. J.
   - B) →
     Denner, Paul
   - C) →
     Denney, Al
   - D) →
     Denning, Darryl
   - E) →

3. | Laughlin, Thomas |
   - A) →
     LaFleur, Guy
   - B) →
     Lathoulder, Hilda
   - C) →
     McLatchaw, Paul
   - D) →
     McLaugher, Jerry
   - E) →

7. | Covino, Wendy A. |
   - A) →
     Covino, Bill
   - B) →
     Covino, William
   - C) →
     Covino, William A.
   - D) →
     Covino, Zelda
   - E) →

4. | Cilley, Allan |
   - A) →
     Caity, Katy
   - B) →
     Cilly, Vernon
   - C) →
     Ciyley, T. F.
   - D) →
     Cyley, Dennis
   - E) →

8. | DeVore, Cinthia |
   - A) →
     Deveren, Billy
   - B) →
     Devereu, Ernest
   - C) →
     Devoreaux, Robert
   - D) →
     Devoreu, Carol
   - E) →

9. **Afitson, Roger**
A) →
Afif, Sharon
B) →
Afifi, Gevorik
C) →
Afilador, Phillip
D) →
Afiniyev, Rudolf
E) →

10. **Adams, L. L.**
A) →
Adams, Larry
B) →
Adams, Leroy
C) →
Adams, Lindy
D) →
Adams, Louis R.
E) →

11. **Hatchikan, Cindy**
A) →
Hatch, Mark S.
B) →
Hatcher, George
C) →
Hatem, Carl
D) →
Hathaway, Carol
E) →

12. **Ain, Juan**
A) →
Aiki, Terri
B) →
Aikido, Thomas
C) →
Aimone, Charles
D) →
Aintabulos, Phyllis
E) →

13. **Rawkins, Bert**
A) →
Rawkens, Robert
B) →
Rawkens, Stuart
C) →
Rawkins, Annabel
D) →
Rawkins, B. A.
E) →

14. **Hayad, Orville**
A) →
Hay, Harry
B) →
Hayak, Salem
C) →
Hayakama, N.
D) →
Hayashi, Shinro
E) →

15. **Odom, Rick**
A) →
O'Davorin, Kenneth
B) →
O'Day, Dennis
C) →
O'Dell, David
D) →
O'Donnell, Gene
E) →

16. **Hawkins, Norbert**
A) →
Hawkins, Lee
B) →
Hawkins, Lewis
C) →
Hawkins, N. M.
D) →
Hawkins, Wm. S.
E) →

17. **Gutierrez, Beth**
A) →
Gutana, Edmund
B) →
Gutenberg, Bessie
C) →
Gutentag, Chas.
D) →
Guthrie, Bob
E) →

18. **Ole, Bente**
A) →
O'Lares, Enid
B) →
O'Leary, Tim
C) →
Oleas, Patrick
D) →
Olender, Missy
E) →

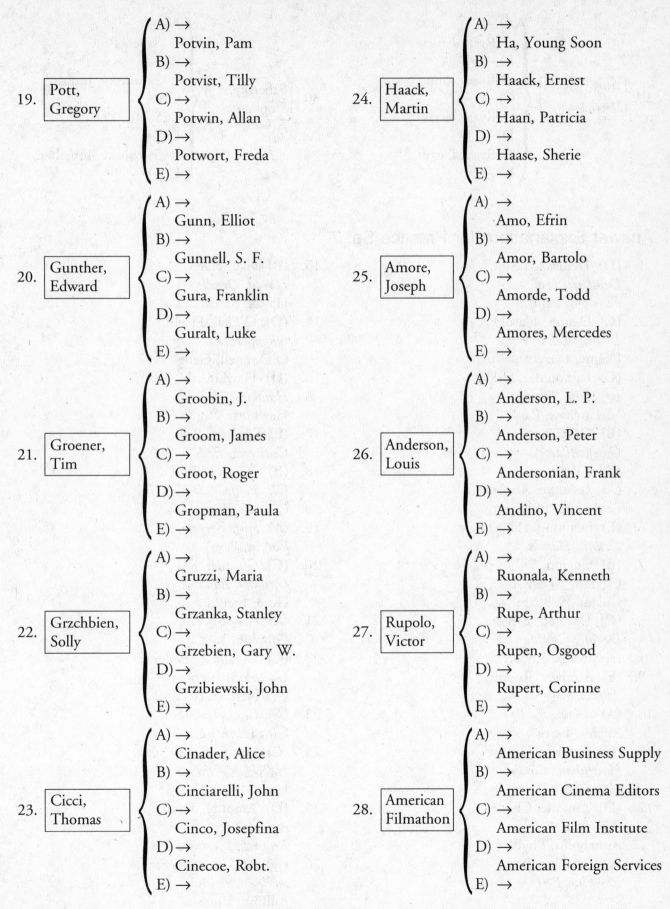

19. Pott, Gregory
A) →
   Potvin, Pam
B) →
   Potvist, Tilly
C) →
   Potwin, Allan
D) →
   Potwort, Freda
E) →

20. Gunther, Edward
A) →
   Gunn, Elliot
B) →
   Gunnell, S. F.
C) →
   Gura, Franklin
D) →
   Guralt, Luke
E) →

21. Groener, Tim
A) →
   Groobin, J.
B) →
   Groom, James
C) →
   Groot, Roger
D) →
   Gropman, Paula
E) →

22. Grzchbien, Solly
A) →
   Gruzzi, Maria
B) →
   Grzanka, Stanley
C) →
   Grzebien, Gary W.
D) →
   Grzibiewski, John
E) →

23. Cicci, Thomas
A) →
   Cinader, Alice
B) →
   Cinciarelli, John
C) →
   Cinco, Josepfina
D) →
   Cinecoe, Robt.
E) →

24. Haack, Martin
A) →
   Ha, Young Soon
B) →
   Haack, Ernest
C) →
   Haan, Patricia
D) →
   Haase, Sherie
E) →

25. Amore, Joseph
A) →
   Amo, Efrin
B) →
   Amor, Bartolo
C) →
   Amorde, Todd
D) →
   Amores, Mercedes
E) →

26. Anderson, Louis
A) →
   Anderson, L. P.
B) →
   Anderson, Peter
C) →
   Andersonian, Frank
D) →
   Andino, Vincent
E) →

27. Rupolo, Victor
A) →
   Ruonala, Kenneth
B) →
   Rupe, Arthur
C) →
   Rupen, Osgood
D) →
   Rupert, Corinne
E) →

28. American Filmathon
A) →
   American Business Supply
B) →
   American Cinema Editors
C) →
   American Film Institute
D) →
   American Foreign Services
E) →

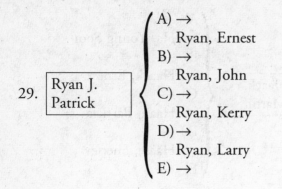

29. Ryan J. Patrick
A) →
Ryan, Ernest
B) →
Ryan, John
C) →
Ryan, Kerry
D) →
Ryan, Larry
E) →

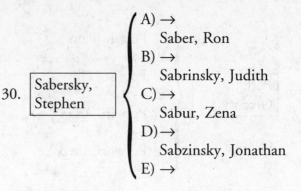

30. Sabersky, Stephen
A) →
Saber, Ron
B) →
Sabrinsky, Judith
C) →
Sabur, Zena
D) →
Sabzinsky, Jonathan
E) →

Answer Explanations for Practice Set 7

1. **(D)** Demas, Maxine
   Dembart, Lee
   de Melo, Paul

2. **(C)** Dennis, Harold A.
   Dennison, Larry
   Denny, Larry

3. **(C)** Lathoulder, Hilda
   Laughlin, Thomas
   McLatchaw, Paul

4. **(B)** Caity, Katy
   Cilley, Allan
   Cilly, Vernon

5. **(A)** *Labosian, Angeline*
   Labossiere, Phillipe

6. **(E)** Denning, Darryl
   Dennis, Harold

7. **(B)** Covino, Bill
   Covino, *Wendy A.*
   Covino, William

8. **(C)** Devereu, Ernest
   DeVore, Cinthia
   Devoreaux, Robert

9. **(E)** Afiniyev, Rudolf
   Afitson, Roger

10. **(A)** *Adams, L. L.*
    Adams, Larry

11. **(C)** Hatcher, George
    Hatchikan, Cindy
    Hatem, Carl

12. **(D)** Aimone, Charles
    Ain, Juan
    Aintabulos, Phyllis

13. **(E)** Rawkins, B. A.
    Rawkins, Bert

14. **(B)** Hay, Harry
    Hayad, Orville
    Hayak, Salem

15. **(D)** O'Dell, David
    Odom, Rick
    O'Donnell, Gene

16. **(D)** Hawkins, N. M.
    Hawkins, Norbert
    Hawkins, Wm. S.

17. **(E)** Guthrie, Bob
    Gutierrez, Beth

18. **(B)** O'Lares, Enid
    Ole, Bente
    O'Leary, Tm

19. **(A)** *Pott, Gregory*
    Potvin, Pam

20. **(C)** Gunnell, S. F.
    Gunther, Eduard
    Gura, Franklin

21. **(A)** *Groener, Tim*
    Groobin, J.

22. **(C)** Grzanka, Stanley
    Grzchbien, Solly
    Grzebien, Gary, W.

23. **(A)** *Cicci, Thomas*
    Cinader, Alice

24. **(C)** Haack, Ernest
    Haack, Martin
    Haan, Patricia

25. **(D)** Amorde, Todd
    Amore, Joseph
    Amores, Mercedes

26. **(D)** Andersonian, Frank
    Andeson, Louis
    Andino, Vincent

27. **(E)** Rupert, Corinne
    Ru<u>po</u>lo, Victor
28. **(D)** American Film Institute
    American <u>Fil</u>mathon
    American Foreign Services

29. **(B)** Ryan, Ernest
    Ryan, <u>J</u>. Patrick
    Ryan, John
30. **(B)** Saber, Ron
    Sab<u>er</u>sky, Stephen
    Sabrinsky, Judith

Practice Set 8

Find the correct place for the name in the box, and mark the letter of that space as your answer.

1. Melody, Rogers
   - A) →
     Melodee, Wilson
   - B) →
     Melodie, Merry
   - C) →
     Meloeny, Vincent
   - D) →
     Melore, Joseph P.
   - E) →

2. Sachs, George
   - A) →
     Sack, Uthbert
   - B) →
     Sacker, Peter Z.
   - C) →
     Sackett, Bennett
   - D) →
     Sackley, Daniel
   - E) →

3. Laidler, Clovis
   - A) →
     Lai, Christine
   - B) →
     Laib, Robin
   - C) →
     Laine, Bob
   - D) →
     Laird, P. J.
   - E) →

4. Mentzel, Donald
   - A) →
     Mensor, Albert
   - B) →
     Menzies, Peter
   - C) →
     Menzilla, Arnold
   - D) →
     Meono, Miguel
   - E) →

5. Deluccio, D. M.
   - A) →
     De Luna, Ronald
   - B) →
     Delva, Rex
   - C) →
     Del Valle, Antonio
   - D) →
     Delvecchio, Alex
   - E) →

6. King, Anthony P.
   - A) →
     King, Alma M.
   - B) →
     King, Anna Kris
   - C) →
     King, Arden
   - D) →
     King, Arthur
   - E) →

7. Abovid, Maria
   - A) →
     Abosch, Albert
   - B) →
     Abowd, Harriet
   - C) →
     Abraham, Joseph
   - D) →
     Abrahams, Roasamid
   - E) →

8. Addison, Tracey
   - A) →
     Addams, Dick
   - B) →
     Adderly, D. J.
   - C) →
     Addotta, Cosimo
   - D) →
     Adduman, Nikolas
   - E) →

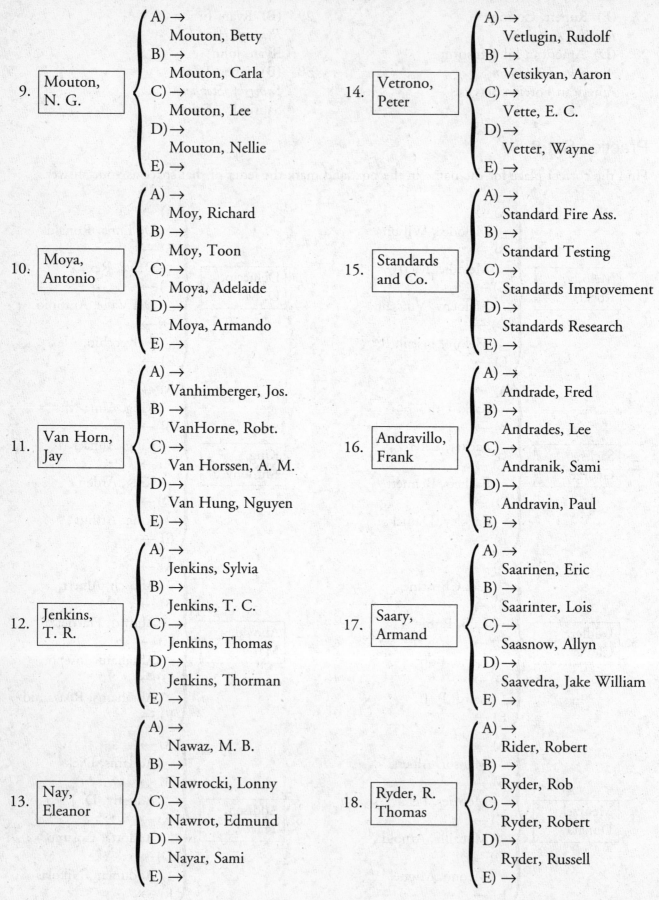

9. Mouton, N. G.
A) →
Mouton, Betty
B) →
Mouton, Carla
C) →
Mouton, Lee
D) →
Mouton, Nellie
E) →

10. Moya, Antonio
A) →
Moy, Richard
B) →
Moy, Toon
C) →
Moya, Adelaide
D) →
Moya, Armando
E) →

11. Van Horn, Jay
A) →
Vanhimberger, Jos.
B) →
VanHorne, Robt.
C) →
Van Horssen, A. M.
D) →
Van Hung, Nguyen
E) →

12. Jenkins, T. R.
A) →
Jenkins, Sylvia
B) →
Jenkins, T. C.
C) →
Jenkins, Thomas
D) →
Jenkins, Thorman
E) →

13. Nay, Eleanor
A) →
Nawaz, M. B.
B) →
Nawrocki, Lonny
C) →
Nawrot, Edmund
D) →
Nayar, Sami
E) →

14. Vetrono, Peter
A) →
Vetlugin, Rudolf
B) →
Vetsikyan, Aaron
C) →
Vette, E. C.
D) →
Vetter, Wayne
E) →

15. Standards and Co.
A) →
Standard Fire Ass.
B) →
Standard Testing
C) →
Standards Improvement
D) →
Standards Research
E) →

16. Andravillo, Frank
A) →
Andrade, Fred
B) →
Andrades, Lee
C) →
Andranik, Sami
D) →
Andravin, Paul
E) →

17. Saary, Armand
A) →
Saarinen, Eric
B) →
Saarinter, Lois
C) →
Saasnow, Allyn
D) →
Saavedra, Jake William
E) →

18. Ryder, R. Thomas
A) →
Rider, Robert
B) →
Ryder, Rob
C) →
Ryder, Robert
D) →
Ryder, Russell
E) →

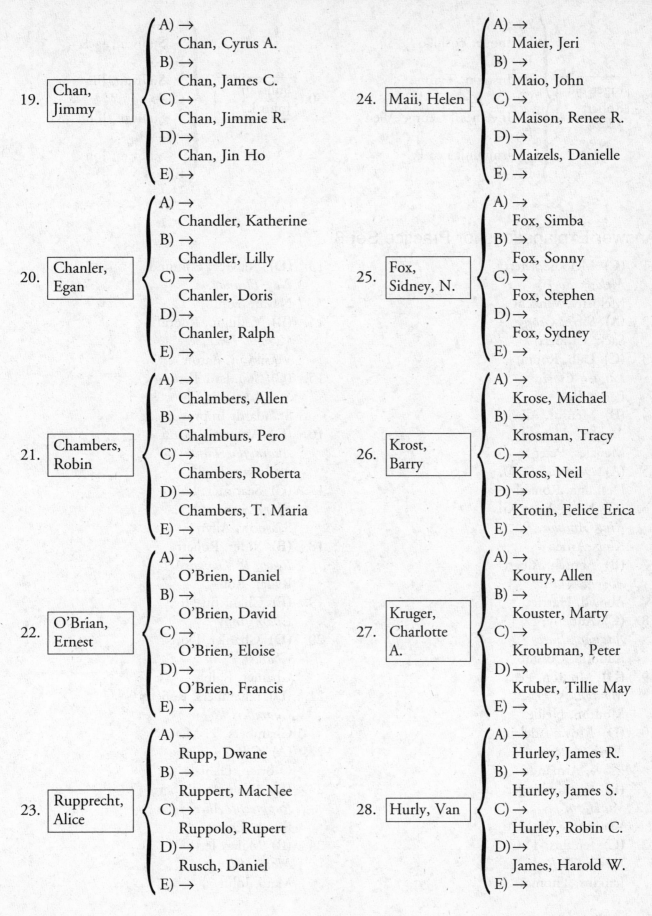

19. Chan, Jimmy
- A) →
  Chan, Cyrus A.
- B) →
  Chan, James C.
- C) →
  Chan, Jimmie R.
- D) →
  Chan, Jin Ho
- E) →

20. Chanler, Egan
- A) →
  Chandler, Katherine
- B) →
  Chandler, Lilly
- C) →
  Chanler, Doris
- D) →
  Chanler, Ralph
- E) →

21. Chambers, Robin
- A) →
  Chalmbers, Allen
- B) →
  Chalmburs, Pero
- C) →
  Chambers, Roberta
- D) →
  Chambers, T. Maria
- E) →

22. O'Brian, Ernest
- A) →
  O'Brien, Daniel
- B) →
  O'Brien, David
- C) →
  O'Brien, Eloise
- D) →
  O'Brien, Francis
- E) →

23. Rupprecht, Alice
- A) →
  Rupp, Dwane
- B) →
  Ruppert, MacNee
- C) →
  Ruppolo, Rupert
- D) →
  Rusch, Daniel
- E) →

24. Maii, Helen
- A) →
  Maier, Jeri
- B) →
  Maio, John
- C) →
  Maison, Renee R.
- D) →
  Maizels, Danielle
- E) →

25. Fox, Sidney, N.
- A) →
  Fox, Simba
- B) →
  Fox, Sonny
- C) →
  Fox, Stephen
- D) →
  Fox, Sydney
- E) →

26. Krost, Barry
- A) →
  Krose, Michael
- B) →
  Krosman, Tracy
- C) →
  Kross, Neil
- D) →
  Krotin, Felice Erica
- E) →

27. Kruger, Charlotte A.
- A) →
  Koury, Allen
- B) →
  Kouster, Marty
- C) →
  Kroubman, Peter
- D) →
  Kruber, Tillie May
- E) →

28. Hurly, Van
- A) →
  Hurley, James R.
- B) →
  Hurley, James S.
- C) →
  Hurley, Robin C.
- D) →
  James, Harold W.
- E) →

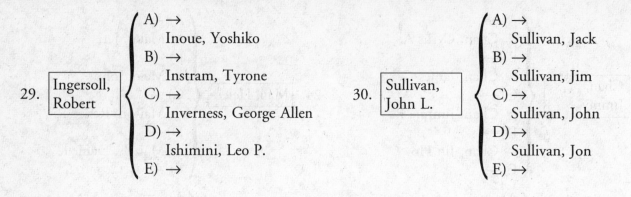

29. Ingersoll, Robert
- A) →
  - Inoue, Yoshiko
- B) →
  - Instram, Tyrone
- C) →
  - Inverness, George Allen
- D) →
  - Ishimini, Leo P.
- E) →

30. Sullivan, John L.
- A) →
  - Sullivan, Jack
- B) →
  - Sullivan, Jim
- C) →
  - Sullivan, John
- D) →
  - Sullivan, Jon
- E) →

Answer Explanations for Practice Set 8

1. **(C)** Melodie, Merry
   Melody, Rogers
   Meloeny, Vincent
2. **(A)** *Sachs, George*
   Sack, Uthbert
3. **(C)** Laib, Robin
   Laidler, Clovis
   Laine, Bob
4. **(B)** Mensor, Albert
   Mentzel, Donald
   Menzies, Peter
5. **(A)** *Deluccio, D. M.*
   De Luna, Ronald
6. **(C)** King, Anna Kris
   King, Anthony P.
   King, Arden
7. **(B)** Abosch, Albert
   Abovid, Maria
   Abowd, Harriet
8. **(C)** Adderly, D. J.
   Addison, Tracey
   Addotta, Cosimo
9. **(D)** Mouton, Lee
   Mouton, N. G.
   Mouton, Nellie
10. **(D)** Moya, Adelaide
    Moya, Antonio
    Moya, Armando
11. **(B)** Vanhimberger, Jos.
    VanHorn, Jay
    VanHorne, Robt.
12. **(C)** Jenkins, T. C.
    Jenkins, T. R.
    Jenkins, Thomas

13. **(D)** Nawrot, Edmund
    Nay, Eleanor
    Nayar, Sami
14. **(B)** Vetlugin, Rudolf
    Vetrono, Peter
    Vetsikyan, Aaron
15. **(C)** Standard Testing
    Standards and Co.
    Standards Improvement
16. **(D)** Andranik, Sami
    Andravillo, Frank
    Andravin, Paul
17. **(C)** Saarinter, Lois
    Saary, Armand
    Saasnow, Allyn
18. **(B)** Rider, Robert
    Ryder, R. Thomas
    Ryder, Rob
19. **(E)** Chan, Jin Ho
    Chan, Jinny
20. **(D)** Chanler, Doris
    Chanler, Egan
    Chanier, Ralph
21. **(D)** Chambers, Roberta
    Chambers, Robin
    Chambers, T. Maria
22. **(A)** *O'Brian, Ernest*
    O'Brien, Daniel
23. **(D)** Ruppolo, Rupert
    Rupprecht, Alice
    Rusch, Daniel
24. **(B)** Maier, Jeri
    Maii, Helen
    Maio, John

25. **(A)** *Fox, Si<u>d</u>ney N.*
    Fox, Simba
26. **(D)** Kross, Neil
    Kro<u>st</u>, Barry
    Krotin, Felice Erica
27. **(E)** Kruber, Tillie May
    Kruger, Charlotte A.
28. **(D)** Hurley, Robin C.
    <u>Hurly</u>, Van
    James, Harold W.

29. **(A)** *Ingersoll, Robert*
    Inoue, Yoshiko
30. **(D)** Sullivan, John
    Sullivan, <u>John L</u>.
    Sullivan, Jon

Clerical Abilities Analysis Chart for Alphabetizing

Use the following chart to carefully analyze your results of the *alphabetizing* question type. This will help you evaluate your strengths and weaknesses. This analysis should help you focus your study and review efforts on specific types of problems.

Practice Set	Total Number of Questions	Number Correct	Number Incorrect	Number Unanswered
Set 1	30			
Set 2	30			
Set 3	30			
Set 4	30			
Set 5	30			
Set 6	30			
Set 7	30			
Set 8	30			

Because there is no penalty for incorrect answers on most of the questions in the Clerical Abilities section, you should have left no question unanswered. Even if you didn't have time to answer a question, you should have at least filled in the answer space with an educated guess.

REVIEWING THE KEY STRATEGIES
Remember to:
1. Learn the definite rules for alphabetizing.
2. Practice them.

ARITHMETIC COMPUTATION (ARITHMETIC OPERATIONS)

These question types measure your ability to do simple computations, without the use of an adding machine or calculator. There are four types of questions: addition, subtraction, multiplication, and division.

Addition

Add:

$$
\begin{array}{r}
19 \\
+\ 23 \\
\end{array}
$$

To answer this question type you must be familiar with basic addition facts (for example, $9 + 3 = 12$). You should also know how to "carry." In the example just given, for the ones column $9 + 3$ equals 12. The 2 is written in the total ones column, but the 1 (from the 12) is carried to the tens column, which now equals $1 + 1 + 2 = 4$. The answer is 42.

$$
\begin{array}{r}
^{1}19 \\
+\ \ 23 \\
\hline
42 \\
\end{array}
$$

Subtraction

Subtract:

$$
\begin{array}{r}
92 \\
-\ 37 \\
\end{array}
$$

To answer this question type, you must be familiar with basic subtraction facts (for example, $12 - 7 = 5$). You should also know how to "borrow." Notice in the example just given, in the one's column, you cannot compute $2 - 7$. Therefore, you must borrow a 1 (which means 10) from the 9 (ninety), and add it to the 2, which now becomes 12:

$$
\begin{array}{r}
8_{1} \\
\not{9}2 \\
-\ 37 \\
\end{array}
$$

When you borrow 1 (ten) from the 9 (tens), the 9 (ninety) now becomes 8 (eighty), and the 2 becomes 12. Now you can subtract in the onescolumn, $12 - 7 = 5$, and in the tens column, $8 - 3 = 5$. The answer is 55.

A TIP: You may check your subtraction, by adding up from the total. in this example:

$$
\begin{array}{r}
92 \\
-\ 37 \\
\hline
55 \\
\end{array}
$$

Does $55 + 37 = 92$? It should, if 55 is the correct answer. If it does not, then you have made a calculation error.

Multiplication

Multiply:

$$
\begin{array}{r}
46 \\
\times\ 3 \\
\end{array}
$$

To answer this question type, you must be familiar with basic multiplication skills (times tables). You should also know how to "carry." In the example just given, the 3 is first multiplied with the 6:

$$
\begin{array}{r}
{}^{1}46 \\
\times\ \ 3 \\
\hline
8 \\
\end{array}
$$

$3 \times 6 = 18$. Notice that the 8 is placed in the ones column, but the 1 (ten) is carried to the tens column. Now the 4 is multiplied by the 3: $3 \times 4 = 12$. And the "1" (ten) carried over is added on to the 12: $12 + 1 = 13$.

$$
\begin{array}{r}
{}^{1}46 \\
\times\ \ 3 \\
\hline
138 \\
\end{array}
$$

Division

Divide:

$$6\overline{)258}$$

To answer this question type, you must be familiar with basic division skills (for example, 15 divided by 3 = 5). You should also know how to do simple "long division." In the example just given, 6 does not go into 2, but it will go into 25 a total of 4 times. Write the 4 above the 5 in 25:

$$
\begin{array}{r}
4\ \ \\
6\overline{)258}
\end{array}
$$

Now multiply 4×6, and write the answer, 24, below the 25:

$$
\begin{array}{r}
4\ \ \\
6\overline{)258} \\
24\ \ \\
\end{array}
$$

Now subtract:

$$
\begin{array}{r}
4\ \ \\
6\overline{)258} \\
24\ \ \\
\hline
1\ \ \\
\end{array}
$$

Now "bring down" the next digit, 8:

$$
\begin{array}{r}
4\\
6\overline{)258}\\
24\\
\hline
18
\end{array}
$$

Does 6 go into 18? Yes, 3 times. Therefore, write 3 on the line above the 8: 43

$$
\begin{array}{r}
43\\
6\overline{)258}\\
24\\
\hline
18
\end{array}
$$

Now multiply, as before: $3 \times 6 = 18$. Write that below the 18 and subtract:

$$
\begin{array}{r}
43\\
6\overline{)258}\\
24\\
\hline
18\\
18\\
\hline
0
\end{array}
$$

Because the difference is 0, there is no remainder. (The questions on your test will not have any remainder answer.) The final answer is 43.

A TIP: One quick way to check your answer is to multiply it by the divisor: in this case, 43×6. The result should be 258.

Helpful Techniques and Strategies

1. Review the basic addition and subtraction facts, as well as the multiplication (times tables) and division facts, long before taking your exam. If you are weak in any area, try to strengthen your skills in that area so that it will not slow you down when you are taking the test.
2. Practice the many arithmetic question types in this book to increase your speed, skill, and confidence.
3. Although the words "add," "subtract," "divide," or "multiply" are printed above each arithmetic question on the actual test, it is wise also to look at the "sign" in the question. For example:

   Subtract:

   $$
   \begin{array}{r}
   85\\
   -\ 32\\
   \hline
   \end{array}
   $$

   The minus sign reinforces this as a subtraction problem. Under time and test pressure it can be easy to make a careless mistake and add when you should be *subtracting*. Looking at the sign will help reinforce the operation required.
4. All the problems have answer (E), "none of these." if the answer you arrive at is not listed in choices (A), (B), (C), or (D), then you are to choose answer (E).

5. As with the other question types on the test, if any particular question gives you trouble, then skip it; if you can eliminate one choice take a guess, or come back to it later if time permits.

Practice Set 1

Make the following computations, and indicate which of the answer choices is the correct one.

Answers

1. Add:
   82
   + 41
   A) 121   B) 123   _____
   C) 133   D) 141
   E) none of these

2. Subtract:
   90
   − 31
   A) 59   B) 61   _____
   C) 63   D) 69
   E) none of these

3. Multiply:
   57
   × 2
   A) 104   B) 114   _____
   C) 124   D) 134
   E) none of these

4. Divide:
   7)602
   A) 68   B) 76   _____
   C) 86   D) 88
   E) none of these

5. Add:
   24
   + 16
   A) 30   B) 40   _____
   C) 50   D) 60
   E) none of these

6. Subtract:
   86
   − 21
   A) 57   B) 65   _____
   C) 67   D) 78
   E) none of these

7. Multiply:
   85
   × 5
   A) 406   B) 415   _____
   C) 425   D) 435
   E) none of these

8. Divide:
   2)682
   A) 324   B) 340   _____
   C) 341   D) 342
   E) none of these

9. Add:
   123
   + 348
   A) 461   B) 463   _____
   C) 471   D) 473
   E) none of these

Answers

10. Subtract:
    88
    − 31
    A) 57   B) 59   _____
    C) 67   D) 119
    E) none of these

11. Multiply:
    72
    × 3
    A) 213   B) 246   _____
    C) 261   D) 266
    E) none of these

12. Divide:
    6)630
    A) 102   B) 105   _____
    C) 150   D) 160
    E) none of these

13. Add:
    91
    + 45
    A) 126   B) 136   _____
    C) 146   D) 156
    E) none of these

14. Subtract:
    72
    − 14
    A) 52   B) 58   _____
    C) 62   D) 68
    E) none of these

15. Multiply:
    52
    × 8
    A) 406   B) 412   _____
    C) 416   D) 418
    E) none of these

16. Divide:
    9)981
    A) 19   B) 101   _____
    C) 109   D) 190
    E) none of these

17. Add:
    82
    + 14
    A) 76   B) 84   _____
    C) 86   D) 92
    E) none of these

18. Subtract:
    89
    − 14
    A) 73   B) 75   _____
    C) 85   D) 94
    E) none of these

Answers

19. Multiply: A) 141 B) 151 ____
    23 C) 171 D) 181
    × 7 E) none of these

20. Divide: A) 34 B) 36 ____
    6)204 C) 44 D) 48
    E) none of these

21. Add: A) 81 B) 83 ____
    36 C) 91 D) 93
    + 57 E) none of these

22. Subtract: A) 65 B) 75 ____
    162 C) 77 D) 85
    − 87 E) none of these

23. Multiply: A) 140 B) 144 ____
    28 C) 160 D) 164
    × 5 E) none of these

24. Divide: A) 70 B) 71 ____
    5)350 C) 75 D) 80
    E) none of these

Answers

25. Add: A) 84 B) 86 ____
    36 C) 88 D) 98
    + 52 E) none of these

26. Subtract: A) 63 B) 65 ____
    82 C) 73 D) 75
    − 17 E) none of these

27. Multiply: A) 282 B) 284 ____
    72 C) 288 D) 298
    × 4 E) none of these

28. Divide: A) 205 B) 215 ____
    4)860 C) 225 D) 235
    E) none of these

29. Add: A) 64 B) 66 ____
    29 C) 68 D) 74
    + 35 E) none of these

30. Subtract: A) 113 B) 118 ____
    134 C) 123 D) 128
    − 21 E) none of these

Answers for Practice Set 1

1. **(B)** 123
2. **(A)** 59
3. **(B)** 114
4. **(C)** 86
5. **(B)** 40
6. **(B)** 65
7. **(C)** 425
8. **(C)** 341
9. **(C)** 471
10. **(A)** 57
11. **(E)** Correct answer: 216.
12. **(B)** 105
13. **(B)** 136
14. **(B)** 58
15. **(C)** 416

16. **(C)** 109
17. **(E)** Correct answer: 96.
18. **(B)** 75
19. **(E)** Correct answer: 161.
20. **(A)** 34
21. **(D)** 93
22. **(B)** 75
23. **(A)** 140
24. **(A)** 70
25. **(C)** 88
26. **(B)** 65
27. **(C)** 288
28. **(B)** 215
29. **(A)** 64
30. **(A)** 113

Practice Set 2

Make the following computations, and indicate which of the answer choices is the correct one.

Answers

1. Multiply: A) 12   B) 102   _____
   30   C) 120   D) 140
   × 4   E) none of these

2. Divide: A) 19   B) 91   _____
                C) 99   D) 100
   9)810   E) none of these

3. Add: A) 106   B) 108   _____
   32   C) 110   D) 118
   + 84   E) none of these

4. Subtract: A) 77   B) 78   _____
   93   C) 88   D) 93
   − 15   E) none of these

5. Multiply: A) 401   B) 410   _____
   82   C) 411   D) 420
   × 5   E) none of these

6. Divide: A) 17   B) 70   _____
                C) 71   D) 77
   7)497   E) none of these

7. Add: A) 83   B) 87   _____
   15   C) 93   D) 98
   + 82   E) none of these

8. Subtract: A) 54   B) 55   _____
   89   C) 65   D) 66
   − 34   E) none of these

9. Multiply: A) 216   B) 226   _____
   54   C) 236   D) 264
   × 4   E) none of these

10. Divide: A) 71   B) 72   _____
                C) 73   D) 75
    3)219   E) none of these

11. Add: A) 82   B) 94   _____
    74   C) 92   D) 94
    + 18   E) none of these

Answers

12. Subtract: A) 58   B) 62   _____
    71   C) 63   D) 68
    − 13   E) none of these

13. Multiply: A) 150   B) 154   _____
    38   C) 180   D) 190
    × 5   E) none of these

14. Divide: A) 8   B) 18   _____
                C) 80   D) 81
    9)720   E) none of these

15. Add: A) 81   B) 87   _____
    39   C) 91   D) 97
    + 52   E) none of these

16. Subtract: A) 46   B) 48   _____
    92   C) 56   D) 58
    − 36   E) none of these

17. Multiply: A) 128   B) 135   _____
    23   C) 136   D) 148
    × 6   E) none of these

18. Divide: A) 50   B) 51   _____
                C) 53   D) 57
    7)357   E) none of these

19. Add: A) 73   B) 78   _____
    38   C) 80   D) 83
    + 45   E) none of these

20. Subtract: A) 60   B) 62   _____
    95   C) 67   D) 73
    − 32   E) none of these

21. Multiply: A) 85   B) 95   _____
    15   C) 105   D) 115
    × 7   E) none of these

22. Divide: A) 60   B) 61   _____
                C) 66   D) 71
    6)366   E) none of these

Answers

23. Add: A) 76   B) 79   _____
    19   C) 84   D) 86
    + 57   E) none of these

24. Subtract: A) 35   B) 45   _____
    93   C) 55   D) 58
    − 48   E) none of these

25. Multiply: A) 103   B) 113   _____
    19   C) 133   D) 153
    × 7   E) none of these

26. Divide: A) 80   B) 81   _____
               C) 88   D) 91
    8)648   E) none of these

Answers

27. Add: A) 64   B) 65   _____
    26   C) 67   D) 75
    + 39   E) none of these

28. Subtract: A) 38   B) 42   _____
    93   C) 48   D) 52
    − 51   E) none of these

29. Multiply: A) 222   B) 322   _____
    84   C) 332   D) 342
    × 3   E) none of these

30. Divide: A) 55   B) 61   _____
               C) 65   D) 68
    5)325   E) none of these

Answers for Practice Set 2

1. **(C)** 120
2. **(E)** Correct answer: 90.
3. **(E)** Correct answer: 116.
4. **(B)** 78
5. **(B)** 410
6. **(C)** 71
7. **(E)** Correct answer: 97.
8. **(B)** 55
9. **(A)** 216
10. **(C)** 73
11. **(C)** 92
12. **(A)** 58
13. **(D)** 190
14. **(C)** 80
15. **(C)** 91
16. **(C)** 56
17. **(E)** Correct answer: 138.
18. **(B)** 51
19. **(D)** 83
20. **(E)** Correct answer: 63.
21. **(C)** 105
22. **(B)** 61
23. **(A)** 76
24. **(B)** 45
25. **(C)** 133
26. **(B)** 81
27. **(B)** 65
28. **(B)** 42
29. **(E)** Correct answer: 252.
30. **(C)** 65

Practice Set 3

Make the following computations, and indicate which of the answer choices is the correct one.

Answers

1. Add: A) 51   B) 61   _____
    25   C) 63   D) 71
    + 36   E) none of these

2. Subtract: A) 34   B) 36   _____
    71   C) 46   D) 56
    − 35   E) none of these

Answers

3. Multiply: A) 28   B) 48   _____
    17   C) 58   D) 68
    × 4   E) none of these

4. Divide: A) 41   B) 47   _____
              C) 51   D) 57
    7)287   E) none of these

Answers

5. Add:
   44
   + 71

   A) 105   B) 113
   C) 115   D) 125
   E) none of these   _____

6. Multiply:
   23
   × 9

   A) 181   B) 191
   C) 201   D) 207
   E) none of these   _____

7. Subtract:
   53
   − 21

   A) 21   B) 23
   C) 32   D) 33
   E) none of these   _____

8. Divide:

   8)168

   A) 12   B) 20
   C) 21   D) 22
   E) none of these   _____

9. Add:
   19
   + 56

   A) 65   B) 77
   C) 78   D) 85
   E) none of these   _____

10. Multiply:
    22
    × 3

    A) 60   B) 62
    C) 66   D) 69
    E) none of these   _____

9. Subtract:
   92
   − 13

   A) 71   B) 75
   C) 79   D) 81
   E) none of these   _____

12. Divide:

    8)248

    A) 13   B) 23
    C) 30   D) 31
    E) none of these   _____

13. Add:
    49
    + 34

    A) 73   B) 81
    C) 75   D) 93
    E) none of these   _____

15. Multiply:
    13
    × 6

    A) 48   B) 68
    C) 78   D) 88
    E) none of these   _____

14. Subtract:
    89
    − 64

    A) 23   B) 27
    C) 35   D) 37
    E) none of these   _____

16. Divide:

    7)357

    A) 41   B) 50
    C) 55   D) 61
    E) none of these   _____

Answers

17. Add:
    53
    + 25

    A) 77   B) 78
    C) 87   D) 88
    E) none of these   _____

18. Subtract:
    84
    − 17

    A) 67   B) 69
    C) 75   D) 77
    E) none of these   _____

19. Multiply:
    23
    × 3

    A) 66   B) 68
    C) 69   D) 96
    E) none of these   _____

20. Divide:

    4)256

    A) 61   B) 62
    C) 64   D) 66
    E) none of these   _____

21. Add:
    17
    + 81

    A) 76   B) 88
    C) 97   D) 98
    E) none of these   _____

22. Subtract:
    84
    − 13

    A) 61   B) 69
    C) 71   D) 73
    E) none of these   _____

23. Multiply:
    24
    × 7

    A) 148   B) 158
    C) 168   D) 188
    E) none of these   _____

24. Divide:

    8)648

    A) 81   B) 82
    C) 83   D) 84
    E) none of these   _____

25. Add:
    28
    + 54

    A) 72   B) 74
    C) 82   D) 84
    E) none of these   _____

26. Subtract:
    93
    − 31

    A) 60   B) 61
    C) 62   D) 63
    E) none of these   _____

27. Multiply:
    93
    × 4

    A) 362   B) 366
    C) 372   D) 376
    E) none of these   _____

28. Divide:

    7)805

    A) 113   B) 120
    C) 125   D) 127
    E) none of these   _____

Answers

29. Add:
    83
    + 59

    A) 132   B) 138   _____
    C) 142   D) 144
    E) none of these

Answers

30. Subtract:
    169
    − 23

    A) 144   B) 146   _____
    C) 156   D) 158
    E) none of these

Answers for Practice Set 3

1. **(B)** 61
2. **(B)** 36
3. **(D)** 68
4. **(A)** 41
5. **(C)** 115
6. **(D)** 207
7. **(C)** 32
8. **(C)** 21
9. **(E)** Correct answer: 75.
10. **(C)** 66
11. **(C)** 79
12. **(D)** 31
13. **(E)** Correct answer: 83.
14. **(C)** 78
15. **(E)** Correct answer: 25.

16. **(E)** Correct answer: 51.
17. **(B)** 78
18. **(A)** 67
19. **(C)** 69
20. **(C)** 64
21. **(D)** 98
22. **(C)** 71
23. **(C)** 168
24. **(A)** 81
25. **(C)** 82
26. **(C)** 62
27. **(C)** 372
28. **(E)** Correct answer: 115.
29. **(C)** 142
30. **(B)** 146

Practice Set 4

Make the following computations, and indicate which of the answer choices is the correct one.

Answers

1. Multiply:
   82
   × 7

   A) 546   B) 564   _____
   C) 568   D) 574
   E) none of these

2. Divide:
   5)850

   A) 107   B) 130   _____
   C) 170   D) 190
   E) none of these

3. Add:
   23
   + 81

   A) 104   B) 106   _____
   C) 108   D) 114
   E) none of these

4. Subtract:
   812
   − 408

   A) 402   B) 404   _____
   C) 408   D) 410
   E) none of these

5. Multiply:
   92
   × 3

   A) 216   B) 236   _____
   C) 256   D) 276
   E) none of these

Answers

6. Divide:
   8)648

   A) 18   B) 80   _____
   C) 88   D) 89
   E) none of these

7. Add:
   81
   + 18

   A) 98   B) 99   _____
   C) 100   D) 109
   E) none of these

8. Subtract:
   98
   − 31

   A) 37   B) 39   _____
   C) 67   D) 69
   E) none of these

9. Multiply:
   72
   × 4

   A) 238   B) 288   _____
   C) 328   D) 368
   E) none of these

10. Divide:
    7)497

    A) 17   B) 70   _____
    C) 71   D) 701
    E) none of these

Answers

11. Add:
    35
    + 81
    A) 106 B) 111
    C) 116 D) 119
    E) none of these _____

12. Subtract:
    52
    − 19
    A) 31 B) 33
    C) 41 D) 43
    E) none of these _____

13. Multiply:
    106
    × 5
    A) 53 B) 503
    C) 530 D) 630
    E) none of these _____

14. Divide:
    6)612
    A) 21 B) 102
    C) 111 D) 112
    E) none of these _____

15. Add:
    123
    + 304
    A) 227 B) 337
    C) 427 D) 437
    E) none of these _____

16. Subtract:
    82
    − 31
    A) 31 B) 41
    C) 51 D) 61
    E) none of these _____

17. Multiply:
    72
    × 8
    A) 562 B) 566
    C) 568 D) 574
    E) none of these _____

18. Divide:
    4)256
    A) 44 B) 46
    C) 64 D) 66
    E) none of these _____

19. Add:
    19
    + 82
    A) 81 B) 83
    C) 91 D) 101
    E) none of these _____

20. Subtract:
    101
    − 48
    A) 43 B) 45
    C) 55 D) 58
    E) none of these _____

Answers

21. Multiply:
    21
    × 8
    A) 160 B) 168
    C) 169 D) 186
    E) none of these _____

22. Divide:
    6)906
    A) 115 B) 150
    C) 151 D) 155
    E) none of these _____

23. Add:
    56
    + 81
    A) 135 B) 137
    C) 139 D) 147
    E) none of these _____

24. Subtract:
    92
    − 31
    A) 61 B) 63
    C) 67 D) 71
    E) none of these _____

25. Multiply:
    23
    × 5
    A) 105 B) 115
    C) 135 D) 155
    E) none of these _____

26. Divide:
    7)784
    A) 112 B) 114
    C) 118 D) 121
    E) none of these _____

27. Add:
    62
    + 35
    A) 93 B) 97
    C) 107 D) 111
    E) none of these _____

28. Subtract:
    148
    − 74
    A) 64 B) 68
    C) 72 D) 74
    E) none of these _____

29. Multiply:
    74
    × 3
    A) 144 B) 212
    C) 222 D) 224
    E) none of these _____

30. Divide:
    3)936
    A) 302 B) 311
    C) 313 D) 318
    E) none of these _____

Answers for Practice Set 4

1. **(D)** 574
2. **(C)** 170
3. **(A)** 104
4. **(B)** 404

5. **(D)** 276
6. **(E)** Correct answer: 81.
7. **(B)** 99
8. **(C)** 67

9. **(B)** 288
10. **(C)** 71
11. **(C)** 116
12. **(B)** 33
13. **(C)** 530
14. **(B)** 102
15. **(C)** 427
16. **(C)** 51
17. **(E)** Correct answer: 576.
18. **(C)** 64
19. **(D)** 101

20. **(E)** Correct answer: 53.
21. **(B)** 168
22. **(C)** 151
23. **(B)** 137
24. **(A)** 61
25. **(B)** 115
26. **(A)** 112
27. **(B)** 97
28. **(D)** 74
29. **(C)** 222
30. **(E)** Correct answer: 312.

Practice Set 5

Make the following computations, and indicate which of the answer choices is the correct one.

Answers

1. Add:
   82
   + 21
   A) 102 B) 113
   C) 137 D) 143
   E) none of these _____

2. Subtract:
   96
   − 41
   A) 45 B) 47
   C) 55 D) 57
   E) none of these _____

3. Multiply:
   81
   × 3
   A) 241 B) 243
   C) 253 D) 283
   E) none of these _____

4. Divide:
   8)840
   A) 15 B) 51
   C) 105 D) 150
   E) none of these _____

5. Add:
   87
   + 83
   A) 160 B) 170
   C) 180 D) 190
   E) none of these _____

6. Subtract:
   182
   − 31
   A) 111 B) 141
   C) 143 D) 151
   E) none of these _____

7. Multiply:
   71
   × 5
   A) 350 B) 355
   C) 365 D) 375
   E) none of these _____

8. Divide:
   7)910
   A) 13 B) 103
   C) 130 D) 133
   E) none of these _____

Answers

9. Add:
   283
   + 46
   A) 229 B) 289
   C) 329 D) 349
   E) none of these _____

10. Subtract:
    261
    − 130
    A) 130 B) 131
    C) 138 D) 141
    E) none of these _____

11. Multiply:
    23
    × 8
    A) 164 B) 174
    C) 184 D) 194
    E) none of these _____

12. Divide:
    4)484
    A) 112 B) 120
    C) 121 D) 122
    E) none of these _____

13. Add:
    92
    + 18
    A) 100 B) 106
    C) 108 D) 110
    E) none of these _____

14. Subtract:
    82
    − 15
    A) 57 B) 59
    C) 67 D) 77
    E) none of these _____

15. Multiply:
    18
    × 3
    A) 34 B) 44
    C) 54 D) 64
    E) none of these _____

16. Divide:
    8)168
    A) 12 B) 22
    C) 24 D) 31
    E) none of these _____

Answers   *Answers*

17. Add: A) 92   B) 95   _____   24. Divide: A) 18   B) 38   _____
        42   C) 99   D) 109   C) 80   D) 81
      + 57   E) none of these   3)243   E) none of these

18. Subtract: A) 68   B) 78   _____   25. Add: A) 84   B) 86   _____
       130   C) 88   D) 98   56   C) 94   D) 98
      − 42   E) none of these   + 32   E) none of these

19. Multiply: A) 123   B) 132 _____   26. Subtract: A) 47   B) 53   _____
        19   C) 143   D) 153   84   C) 55   D) 57
      × 7   E) none of these   − 31   E) none of these

20. Divide: A) 61   B) 66   _____   27. Multiply: A) 342   B) 344 _____
                C) 71   D) 76   96   C) 364   D) 384
      6)366   E) none of these   × 4   E) none of these

21. Add: A) 131   B) 133 _____   28. Divide: A) 52   B) 53   _____
        32   C) 137   D) 141   C) 54   D) 55
      + 81   E) none of these   7)392   E) none of these

22. Subtract: A) 76   B) 84   _____   29. Add: A) 781   B) 783 _____
       122   C) 86   D) 94   472   C) 791   D) 797
      − 38   E) none of these   + 319   E) none of these

23. Multiply: A) 82   B) 88   _____   30. Subtract: A) 69   B) 71   _____
        23   C) 92   D) 104   94   C) 77   D) 79
      × 4   E) none of these   − 25   E) none of these

Answers for Practice Set 5

1. **(E)** Correct answer: 103.   16. **(E)** Correct answer: 21.
2. **(C)** 55   17. **(C)** 99
3. **(B)** 243   18. **(C)** 88
4. **(C)** 105   19. **(E)** Correct answer: 133.
5. **(B)** 170   20. **(A)** 61
6. **(D)** 151   21. **(E)** Correct answer: 113.
7. **(B)** 355   22. **(B)** 84
8. **(C)** 130   23. **(C)** 92
9. **(C)** 329   24. **(D)** 81
10. **(B)** 131   25. **(E)** Correct answer: 88.
11. **(C)** 184   26. **(B)** 53
12. **(C)** 121   27. **(D)** 384
13. **(D)** 110   28. **(E)** Correct answer: 56.
14. **(C)** 67   29. **(C)** 791
15. **(C)** 54   30. **(A)** 69

Practice Set 6

Make the following computations, and indicate which of the answer choices is the correct one.

Answers

1. Multiply:
   32
   × 5
   A) 150   B) 155
   C) 160   D) 170
   E) none of these
   _____

2. Divide:
   8)248
   A) 13   B) 30
   C) 31   D) 41
   E) none of these
   _____

3. Add:
   52
   + 49
   A) 91   B) 97
   C) 101   D) 103
   E) none of these
   _____

4. Subtract:
   44
   − 13
   A) 19   B) 21
   C) 31   D) 39
   E) none of these
   _____

5. Multiply:
   28
   × 6
   A) 148   B) 168
   C) 188   D) 208
   E) none of these
   _____

6. Divide:
   6)384
   A) 34   B) 44
   C) 64   D) 74
   E) none of these
   _____

7. Add:
   123
   + 38
   A) 141   B) 151
   C) 161   D) 171
   E) none of these
   _____

8. Subtract:
   47
   − 19
   A) 18   B) 26
   C) 28   D) 36
   E) none of these
   _____

9. Multiply:
   31
   × 3
   A) 39   B) 36
   C) 91   D) 93
   E) none of these
   _____

10. Divide:
    2)572
    A) 266   B) 271
    C) 281   D) 286
    E) none of these
    _____

11. Add:
    84
    + 32
    A) 114   B) 118
    C) 126   D) 132
    E) none of these
    _____

Answers

12. Subtract:
    92
    − 35
    A) 57   B) 59
    C) 63   D) 67
    E) none of these
    _____

13. Multiply:
    81
    × 4
    A) 314   B) 324
    C) 342   D) 432
    E) none of these
    _____

14. Divide:
    3)372
    A) 122   B) 126
    C) 128   D) 132
    E) none of these
    _____

15. Add:
    95
    + 28
    A) 121   B) 123
    C) 131   D) 133
    E) none of these
    _____

16. Subtract:
    142
    − 71
    A) 61   B) 71
    C) 73   D) 79
    E) none of these
    _____

17. Multiply:
    56
    × 7
    A) 352   B) 372
    C) 392   D) 402
    E) none of these
    _____

18. Divide:
    4)108
    A) 23   B) 27
    C) 29   D) 32
    E) none of these
    _____

19. Add:
    28
    + 91
    A) 111   B) 119
    C) 121   D) 127
    E) none of these
    _____

20. Subtract:
    88
    − 32
    A) 54   B) 55
    C) 56   D) 57
    E) none of these
    _____

21. Multiply:
    17
    × 7
    A) 109   B) 119
    C) 129   D) 131
    E) none of these
    _____

22. Divide:
    9)918
    A) 92   B) 98
    C) 102   D) 120
    E) none of these
    _____

Answers

23. Add: A) 141   B) 144   _____
    57   C) 153   D) 157
 + 93   E) none of these

24. Subtract: A) 77   B) 78   _____
   108   C) 87   D) 97
 – 21   E) none of these

25. Multiply: A) 164   B) 194   _____
   28   C) 204   D) 224
 × 8   E) none of these

26. Divide: A) 73   B) 78   _____
            C) 79   D) 83
 8)624   E) none of these

Answers

27. Add: A) 127   B) 132   _____
    78   C) 133   D) 143
 + 45   E) none of these

28. Subtract: A) 46   B) 48   _____
   92   C) 52   D) 56
 – 44   E) none of these

29. Multiply: A) 42   B) 52   _____
   18   C) 62   D) 72
 × 4   E) none of these

30. Divide: A) 73   B) 77   _____
            C) 79   D) 83
 7)539   E) none of these

Answers for Practice Set 6

1. **(C)** 160
2. **(C)** 31
3. **(C)** 101
4. **(C)** 31
5. **(B)** 168
6. **(C)** 64
7. **(C)** 161
8. **(C)** 28
9. **(D)** 93
10. **(D)** 286
11. **(E)** Correct answer: 116.
12. **(A)** 57
13. **(B)** 324
14. **(E)** Correct answer: 124.
15. **(B)** 123
16. **(B)** 71
17. **(C)** 392
18. **(B)** 27
19. **(B)** 119
20. **(C)** 56
21. **(B)** 119
22. **(C)** 102
23. **(E)** Correct answer: 150.
24. **(C)** 87
25. **(D)** 224
26. **(B)** 78
27. **(E)** Correct answer: 123.
28. **(B)** 48
29. **(D)** 72
30. **(B)** 77

Practice Set 7

Make the following computations, and indicate which of the answer choices is the correct one.

Answers

1. Add: A) 66   B) 67   _____
   29   C) 76   D) 78
 + 47   E) none of these

2. Subtract: A) 66   B) 76   _____
   108   C) 78   D) 88
 – 32   E) none of these

Answers

3. Multiply: A) 132   B) 138   _____
   19   C) 152   D) 158
 × 8   E) none of these

4. Divide: A) 57   B) 58   _____
            C) 59   D) 61
 8)472   E) none of these

Answers   *Answers*

5. Add: A) 321   B) 331   _____   17. Add: A) 511   B) 515   _____
    147   C) 341   D) 441   203   C) 521   D) 535
    + 204   E) none of these   + 318   E) none of these

6. Subtract: A) 33   B) 37   _____   18. Subtract: A) 54   B) 56   _____
    75   C) 39   D) 43   106   C) 58   D) 62
    − 38   E) none of these   − 48   E) none of these

7. Multiply: A) 480   B) 640   _____   19. Multiply: A) 169   B) 183   _____
    210   C) 840   D) 1040   27   C) 191   D) 199
    × 4   E) none of these   × 7   E) none of these

8. Divide: A) 38   B) 39   _____   20. Divide: A) 31   B) 301   _____
                C) 41   D) 49   C) 311   D) 313
    9)369   E) none of these   3)903   E) none of these

9. Add: A) 123   B) 125   _____   21. Add: A) 93   B) 95   _____
    27   C) 127   D) 129   39   C) 103   D) 105
    + 98   E) none of these   + 64   E) none of these

10. Subtract: A) 76   B) 78   _____   22. Subtract: A) 64   B) 66   _____
    92   C) 74   D) 86   98   C) 68   D) 74
    − 18   E) none of these   − 32   E) none of these

11. Multiply: A) 275   B) 295   _____   23. Multiply: A) 124   B) 128   _____
    35   C) 305   D) 315   32   C) 132   D) 136
    × 9   E) none of these   × 4   E) none of these

12. Divide: A) 801   B) 810   _____   24. Divide: A) 80   B) 81   _____
                C) 811   D) 880   C) 82   D) 83
    4)3240   E) none of these   8)656   E) none of these

13. Add: A) 618   B) 638   _____   25. Add: A) 124   B) 126   _____
    483   C) 718   D) 738   94   C) 136   D) 144
    + 235   E) none of these   + 32   E) none of these

14. Subtract: A) 59   B) 61   _____   26. Subtract: A) 5   B) 13   _____
    92   C) 69   D) 71   29   C) 18   D) 19
    − 31   E) none of these   − 14   E) none of these

15. Multiply: A) 94   B) 96   _____   27. Multiply: A) 84   B) 94   _____
    19   C) 104   D) 114   13   C) 104   D) 114
    × 6   E) none of these   × 8   E) none of these

16. Divide: A) 64   B) 82   _____   28. Divide: A) 51   B) 53   _____
                C) 108   D) 112   C) 55   D) 61
    4)488   E) none of these   7)385   E) none of these

	Answers				*Answers*	
29. Add:	A) 141	B) 143	_____	30. Subtract:	A) 53	B) 55	_____

29. Add:
85
+ 66
A) 141   B) 143
C) 151   D) 153
E) none of these

30. Subtract:
92
− 37
A) 53   B) 55
C) 65   D) 67
E) none of these

Answers for Practice Set 7

1. **(C)** 76
2. **(B)** 76
3. **(C)** 152
4. **(C)** 59
5. **(E)** Correct answer: 351.
6. **(B)** 37
7. **(C)** 840
8. **(C)** 41
9. **(B)** 125
10. **(E)** Correct answer: 74.
11. **(D)** 315
12. **(B)** 810
13. **(C)** 718
14. **(B)** 61
15. **(D)** 114
16. **(E)** Correct answer: 122.
17. **(C)** 521
18. **(C)** 58
19. **(E)** Correct answer: 189.
20. **(B)** 301
21. **(C)** 103
22. **(B)** 66
23. **(B)** 128
24. **(C)** 82
25. **(B)** 126
26. **(E)** Correct answer: 15.
27. **(C)** 104
28. **(C)** 55
29. **(C)** 151
30. **(B)** 55

Practice Set 8

Make the following computations, and indicate which of the answer choices is the correct one.

Answers

1. Multiply:
23
× 6
A) 122   B) 128
C) 138   D) 198
E) none of these

2. Divide:
4)168
A) 41   B) 42
C) 43   D) 48
E) none of these

3. Add:
46
+ 31
A) 74   B) 75
C) 87   D) 89
E) none of these

4. Subtract:
98
− 31
A) 55   B) 57
C) 67   D) 73
E) none of these

5. Multiply:
72
× 8
A) 562   B) 566
C) 568   D) 576
E) none of these

Answers

6. Divide:
7)637
A) 90   B) 91
C) 92   D) 97
E) none of these

7. Add:
23
+ 84
A) 107   B) 109
C) 117   D) 119
E) none of these

8. Subtract:
96
− 31
A) 64   B) 65
C) 75   D) 86
E) none of these

9. Multiply:
19
× 6
A) 54   B) 64
C) 104   D) 114
E) none of these

10. Divide:
6)660
A) 11   B) 101
C) 112   D) 118
E) none of these

Answers   *Answers*

11. Add: A) 55   B) 65   _____   21. Multiply: A) 72   B) 92   _____
    28   C) 75   D) 85   19   C) 132   D) 152
    + 57   E) none of these   × 8   E) none of these

12. Subtract: A) 2   B) 4   _____   22. Divide: A) 111   B) 121   _____
    92   C) 6   D) 16   C) 122   D) 128
    − 86   E) none of these   7)784   E) none of these

13. Multiply: A) 84   B) 88   _____   23. Add: A) 172   B) 174   _____
    26   C) 94   D) 114   93   C) 176   D) 178
    × 4   E) none of these   + 81   E) none of these

14. Divide: A) 92   B) 94   _____   24. Subtract: A) 62   B) 66   _____
                  C) 96   D) 98   82   C) 68   D) 72
    3)288   E) none of these   − 14   E) none of these

15. Add: A) 123   B) 134   _____   25. Multiply: A) 82   B) 102   _____
    93   C) 143   D) 144   23   C) 112   D) 122
    + 41   E) none of these   × 4   E) none of these

16. Subtract: A) 53   B) 57   _____   26. Divide: A) 42   B) 46   _____
    75   C) 63   D) 67   C) 64   D) 68
    − 18   E) none of these   3)138   E) none of these

17. Multiply: A) 154   B) 164   _____   27. Add: A) 172   B) 175   _____
    58   C) 174   D) 182   83   C) 178   D) 183
    × 3   E) none of these   + 95   E) none of these

18. Divide: A) 13   B) 18   _____   28. Subtract: A) 70   B) 72   _____
                  C) 103   D) 108   134   C) 78   D) 82
    8)824   E) none of these   − 62   E) none of these

19. Add: A) 64   B) 66   _____   29. Multiply: A) 140   B) 150   _____
    28   C) 68   D) 76   28   C) 170   D) 190
    + 38   E) none of these   × 5   E) none of these

20. Subtract: A) 64   B) 68   _____   30. Divide: A) 12   B) 21   _____
    81   C) 74   D) 78   C) 28   D) 81
    − 17   E) none of these   9)108   E) none of these

Answers for Practice Set 8

1. **(C)** 138   5. **(D)** 576
2. **(B)** 42   6. **(B)** 91
3. **(E)** Correct answer: 77.   7. **(A)** 107
4. **(B)** 57   8. **(B)** 65

9. **(D)** 114
10. **(E)** Correct answer: 110.
11. **(D)** 85
12. **(C)** 6
13. **(E)** Correct answer: 104.
14. **(C)** 96
15. **(B)** 134
16. **(B)** 57
17. **(C)** 174
18. **(C)** 103
19. **(B)** 66

20. **(A)** 64
21. **(D)** 152
22. **(E)** Correct answer: 112.
23. **(B)** 174
24. **(C)** 68
25. **(E)** Correct answer: 92.
26. **(B)** 46
27. **(C)** 178
28. **(B)** 72
29. **(A)** 140
30. **(A)** 12

Clerical Abilities Analysis Chart for Arithmetic Computation (Arithmetic Operations)

Use the following chart to carefully analyze your results of the *arithmetic computation (arithmetic operations)* question type. This will help you evaluate your strengths and weaknesses. This analysis should help you focus your study and review efforts on specific types of problems.

Practice Set	Total Number of Questions	Number Correct	Number Incorrect	Number Unanswered
Set 1	30			
Set 2	30			
Set 3	30			
Set 4	30			
Set 5	30			
Set 6	30			
Set 7	30			
Set 8	30			

Because there is no penalty for incorrect answers on most of the questions in the Clerical Abilities section, you should have left no question unanswered. Even if you didn't have time to answer a question, you should have at least filled in the answer space with an educated guess.

REVIEWING THE KEY STRATEGIES

Remember to:
1. Review the basic addition, subtraction, multiplication, and division facts.
2. Practice arithmetic questions to increase speed.
3. Look at the "sign" in each problem.
4. Note all problems also contain a choice (E), "none of the these."
5. Leave the difficult questions for last.

NUMBER AND LETTER SCRAMBLE
(NAME AND NUMBER COMPARISON)

This question type tests your observation skills. You are given five sets of eight letters and numbers (four of each), followed by five suggested answers, (A), (B), (C), (D), and (E). Answer (E) is always "none of these." For example:

1. V 5 7 Z N 9 4 T

2. 4 6 P T 2 N K 9

3. 6 4 N 2 P 8 Z K

4. 7 P 5 2 4 N K T

5. K T 8 5 4 N 2 P

$$
\text{Suggested Answers} \begin{cases} A &= 2, 5, N, Z \\ B &= 4, 5, N, P \\ C &= 2, 9, P, T \\ D &= 4, 9, T, Z \\ E &= \text{none of these} \end{cases}
$$

For each numbered question, you must find which of the suggested answers contains letters and numbers *all*, of which appear in that question. For example, the answer to question 1 is (D), because all of the numbers and letters in answer (D) (4, 9, T, Z) appear in question 1.

Suggested Strategy

Because the first problem is solved, let's go on to question 2. Place your finger so that it points to the numbers in question 2, and now look at the two numbers in (A): 2 and 5. Are they contained in question 2? The 2 is, but 5 is not, so go on to answer (B). The two numbers there are 4 and 5. The 4 is in question 2, but the 5 is not, so go on to answer (C). The two numbers there are 2 and 9, *both* of which are contained in question 2. So keep going in answer (C) to the letters: P and T. Are they contained in question 2? They are, so you can stop—the answer to question 2 is (C).

If either P or T were *not* contained in the question, you would then have gone on to answer (D). If the numbers and letters in (D) were not contained in question 2, you would then choose answer (E).

Now try practicing this technique to increase your skill and speed.

Reminders:

1. Only one suggested answer will be correct for each question.
2. A suggested answer, (A), (B), (C), (D), or (E), may be used more than once for different questions in each five-question set. For example, the answers to 1, 2, 3, 4, and 5 are (D), (C), (E), (B), and (B). Notice that the (B) answer appears twice in this set of five questions.

Practice Set 1

For each of the following questions, find which one of the suggested answers appears in that question.

1. F 2 Q S W 4 3 9 _____
2. 5 Q 9 7 W 3 S Z _____
3. 5 Q 3 Z X W 7 9 _____
4. Z 2 S 3 Q 7 W 9 _____
5. 5 7 H W Q 9 J 4 _____

Suggested Answers $\begin{cases} A = 9, 2, W, Q \\ B = 9, 5, Q, Z \\ C = 2, 3, W, H \\ D = 3, 5, H, Z \\ E = \text{none of these} \end{cases}$

6. Q 4 3 6 Z H 2 F _____
7. 7 4 2 X J 9 F Q _____
8. 6 9 4 Q 8 H J X _____
9. 8 7 J 9 4 F H X _____
10. F 5 4 X 8 2 S Q _____

Suggested Answers $\begin{cases} A = 2, 7, H, Q \\ B = 4, 7, Q, X \\ C = 2, 8, X, F \\ D = 4, 8, H, F \\ E = \text{none of these} \end{cases}$

11. 5 9 4 H 3 S Z W _____
12. J 3 6 9 Z 5 X H _____
13. 2 4 3 J 8 X Z W _____
14. W 3 H 6 J 2 4 F _____
15. 3 H 9 8 Q 4 Z W _____

Suggested Answers $\begin{cases} A = 3, 4, H, Z \\ B = 3, 6, W, H \\ C = 9, 4, W, J \\ D = 9, 6, J, Z \\ E = \text{none of these} \end{cases}$

16. 8 W F 2 J 3 5 Q _____
17. J 4 Q H 3 2 8 X _____
18. 7 9 X S 8 J F 4 _____
19. X S 8 F 4 J 7 6 _____
20. 4 Z 7 Q 9 8 X J _____

Suggested Answers $\begin{cases} A = 3, 8, J, X \\ B = 3, 4, Q, F \\ C = 4, 7, J, F \\ D = 7, 8, Q, X \\ E = \text{none of these} \end{cases}$

21. 5 F Z Q 7 6 3 X _____
22. X 6 7 5 Q 4 S J _____
23. Q 6 S X 7 3 9 J _____
24. 6 7 W 3 2 X J Z _____
25. 3 7 W 9 Z Q 5 J _____

Suggested Answers $\begin{cases} A = 9, 6, J, Q \\ B = 9, 7, Z, X \\ C = 5, 7, J, Z \\ D = 5, 6, Q, X \\ E = \text{none of these} \end{cases}$

26. X 4 6 F Q 8 3 Z _____
27. 3 5 S Z 9 Q H 8 _____
28. 5 3 Q 9 S 7 F H _____
29. 6 S 4 9 3 Q H Z _____
30. H Z 7 4 3 Q 9 S _____

Suggested Answers $\begin{cases} A = 9, 4, Q, F \\ B = 3, 4, Q, S \\ C = 9, 8, S, Z \\ D = 3, 8, Z, F \\ E = \text{none of these} \end{cases}$

Answer Explanations for Practice Set 1

1. **(A)** F 2 Q S W 4 3 9
2. **(B)** 5 Q 9 7 W 3 S Z
3. **(B)** 5 Q 3 Z X W 7 9
4. **(A)** Z 2 S 3 Q 7 W 9
5. **(E)** 5 7 H W Q 9 J 4
6. **(E)** Q 4 3 6 Z H 2 F
7. **(B)** 7 4 2 X J 9 F Q
8. **(E)** 6 9 4 Q 8 H J X
9. **(D)** 8 7 J 9 4 F H X
10. **(C)** F 5 4 X 8 2 S Q
11. **(A)** 5 9 4 H 3 S Z W
12. **(D)** J 3 6 9 Z 5 X H
13. **(E)** 2 4 3 J 8 X Z W
14. **(B)** W 3 H 6 J 2 4 F
15. **(A)** 3 H 9 8 Q 4 Z W

16. **(E)** 8 W F 2 J 3 5 Q
17. **(A)** J 4 Q H 3 2 8 X
18. **(C)** Z 9 X S 8 J F 4
19. **(C)** X S 8 F 4 J 7 6
20. **(D)** 4 Z Z Q 9 8 X J
21. **(D)** 5 F Z Q 7 6 3 X
22. **(D)** X 6 7 5 Q 4 S J
23. **(A)** Q 6 S X 7 3 9 J
24. **(E)** 6 7 W 3 2 X J Z
25. **(C)** 3 Z W 9 Z Q 5 J
26. **(D)** X 4 6 F Q 8 3 Z
27. **(C)** 3 5 S Z 9 Q H 8
28. **(E)** 5 3 Q 9 S 7 F H
29. **(B)** 6 S 4 9 3 Q H Z
30. **(B)** H Z 7 4 3 Q 9 S

Practice Set 2

For each of the following questions, find which one of the suggested answers appears in that question.

1. Y 5 R U H 7 6 4 _____
2. 8 R 4 2 H 6 U Z _____
3. 8 R 6 Z I H 2 4 _____
4. Z 5 U 6 R 2 H 4 _____
5. 8 9 X H R 4 M 7 _____

11. 3 H Y 5 M 6 8 R _____
12. M 7 R X 6 5 3 1 _____
13. 2 4 I U 3 M Y 7 _____
14. I U 3 Y 7 M 2 9 _____
15. 7 Z 2 R 4 3 I M _____

Suggested Answers
{
A = 4, 5, H, R
B = 4, 8, R, Z
C = 5, 6, H, X
D = 6, 8, X, Z
E = none of these
}

Suggested Answers
{
A = 6, 3, M, I
B = 6, 7, R, Y
C = 7, 2, M, Y
D = 2, 3, R, I
E = none of these
}

6. 8 4 7 X 6 U Z H _____
7. M 6 9 4 Z 8 I X _____
8. 5 7 6 M 3 I Z H _____
9. H 6 X 9 M 5 7 Y _____
10. 6 X 4 3 R 7 Z H _____

16. 8 Y Z R 2 9 6 I _____
17. I 9 2 8 R 7 U M _____
18. R 9 U I 2 6 4 M _____
19. 9 2 H 6 5 I M Z _____
20. 6 2 H 4 Z R 8 M _____

Suggested Answers
{
A = 6, 7, X, Z
B = 6, 9, H, X
C = 4, 7, H, M
D = 4, 9, M, Z
E = none of these
}

Suggested Answers
{
A = 4, 9, M, R
B = 4, 2, Z, I
C = 8, 2, M, Z
D = 8, 9, R, I
E = none of these
}

21. I   7   9   Y   R   3   6   Z   _____
22. 6   8   U   Z   4   R   X   3   _____
23. 8   6   R   4   U   2   Y   X   _____
24. 9   U   7   4   R   X   Z   _____
25. X   Z   2   7   6   R   4   U   _____

26. R   7   6   9   Z   X   5   Y   _____
27. 2   7   5   I   M   4   Y   R   _____
28. 9   4   7   R   3   X   M   I   _____
29. 3   2   M   4   7   Y   X   I   _____
30. Y   8   7   I   3   5   U   R   _____

Suggested Answers
$$\begin{cases} A = 4, 7, R, Y \\ B = 6, 7, R, U \\ C = 4, 3, U, Z \\ D = 6, 3, Z, Y \\ E = \text{none of these} \end{cases}$$

Suggested Answers
$$\begin{cases} A = 5, 2, X, R \\ B = 7, 2, R, I \\ C = 5, 3, I, Y \\ D = 7, 3, X, Y \\ E = \text{none of these} \end{cases}$$

Answer Explanations for Practice Set 2

1. **(A)** Y 5 R U H 7 6 4
2. **(B)** 8 R 4 2 H 6 U Z
3. **(B)** 8 R 6 Z I H 2 4
4. **(A)** Z 5 U 6 R 2 H 4
5. **(E)** 8 9 X H R 4 M 7
6. **(A)** 8 4 7 X 6 U Z H
7. **(D)** M 6 9 4 Z 8 I X
8. **(E)** 5 7 6 M 3 I Z H
9. **(B)** H 6 X 9 M 5 7 Y
10. **(A)** 6 X 4 3 R Z Z H
11. **(E)** 3 H Y 5 M 6 8 R
12. **(A)** M 7 R X 6 5 3 I
13. **(C)** 2 4 I U 3 M Y 7
14. **(C)** I U 3 Y 7 M 2 9
15. **(D)** 7 Z 2 R 4 3 I M

16. **(D)** 8 Y Z R 2 9 6 I
17. **(D)** I 9 2 8 R 7 U M
18. **(A)** R 9 U 1 2 6 4 M
19. **(E)** 9 2 H 6 5 I M Z
20. **(C)** 6 2 H 4 Z R 8 M
21. **(D)** I 7 9 Y R 3 6 Z
22. **(C)** 6 8 U Z 4 R X 3
23. **(E)** 8 6 R 4 U 2 Y X
24. **(E)** 9 U 7 4 R X Z
25. **(B)** X Z 2 7 6 R 4 U
26. **(E)** R 7 6 9 Z X 5 Y
27. **(B)** 2 7 5 I M 4 Y R
28. **(E)** 9 4 7 R 3 X M I
29. **(D)** 3 2 M 4 7 Y X I
30. **(C)** Y 8 7 I 3 5 U R

Practice Set 3

For each of the following questions, find which one of the suggested answers appears in that question.

1. Q   9   8   3   X   Z   7   M   _____
2. 4   9   7   U   W   6   M   Q   _____
3. 3   6   9   Q   5   Z   W   U   _____
4. 5   4   W   6   9   M   Z   U   _____
5. M   2   9   U   5   7   R   Q   _____

Suggested Answers
$$\begin{cases} A = 7, 4, Z, Q \\ B = 9, 4, Q, U \\ C = 7, 5, U, M \\ D = 9, 5, Z, M \\ E = \text{none of these} \end{cases}$$

6. U 9 3 M Q 5 8 X _____

7. 8 2 R X 6 Q Z 5 _____

8. 2 8 Q 6 R 4 M Z _____

9. 3 R 9 6 8 Q Z X _____

10. Z X 4 9 8 Q 6 R _____

Suggested Answers
{
A = 6, 9, Q, M
B = 8, 9, Q, R
C = 6, 5, R, X
D = 8, 5, X, M
E = none of these
}

11. 2 M X Q 4 3 8 U _____

12. U 3 4 2 Q 9 R W _____

13. Q 3 R U 4 8 6 W _____

14. 3 4 F 8 7 U W X _____

15. 8 4 F 6 X Q 2 W _____

Suggested Answers
{
A = 6, 3, W, Q
B = 6, 4, X, U
C = 2, 4, W, X
D = 2, 3, Q, U
E = none of these
}

16. 5 F M 7 W 8 2 Q _____

17. W 9 Q Z 8 7 5 U _____

18. 4 6 U R 5 W M 9 _____

19. U R 5 M 9 W 4 3 _____

20. 9 X 4 Q 6 5 U W _____

Suggested Answers
{
A = 8, 5, W, U
B = 8, 9, Q, M
C = 9, 4, W, M
D = 4, 5, Q, U
E = none of these
}

21. 2 6 9 Z 8 R X F _____

22. W 8 3 6 X 2 U Z _____

23. 7 9 8 W 5 U X F _____

24. F 8 Z 3 W 7 9 M _____

25. 8 Z 6 5 Q 9 X F _____

Suggested Answers
{
A = 8, 9, Z, X
B = 8, 3, F, Z
C = 6, 9, F, W
D = 6, 3, W, X
E = none of these
}

26. M 7 Q R F 9 8 6 _____

27. 2 Q 6 4 F 8 R X _____

28. 2 Q 8 X U F 4 6 _____

29. X 7 R 8 Q 4 F 6 _____

30. 2 3 Z F Q 6 W 9 _____

Suggested Answers
{
A = 6, 7, F, Q
B = 6, 2, Q, X
C = 7, 8, F, Z
D = 8, 2, Z, X
E = none of these
}

Answer Explanations for Practice Set 3

1. **(E)** Q 9 8 3 X Z 7 M
2. **(B)** 4 9 7 U W 6 M Q
3. **(E)** 3 6 9 Q 5 Z W U
4. **(D)** 5 4 W 6 9 M Z U
5. **(C)** M 2 9 U 5 7 R Q
6. **(D)** U 9 3 M Q 5 8 X
7. **(C)** 8 2 R X 6 Q Z 5
8. **(E)** 2 8 Q 6 R 4 M Z

9. **(B)** 3 R 9 6 8 Q Z X
10. **(B)** Z X 4 9 8 Q 6 R
11. **(D)** 2 M X Q 4 3 8 U
12. **(D)** U 3 4 2 Q 9 R W
13. **(A)** Q 3 R U 4 8 6 W
14. **(E)** 3 4 F 8 7 U W R
15. **(C)** 8 4 F 6 X Q 2 W
16. **(E)** 5 F M 7 W 8 2 Q

17. **(A)** <u>W</u> 9 Q Z <u>8</u> <u>7</u> <u>5</u> <u>U</u>
18. **(C)** <u>4</u> 6 U R 5 <u>W</u> <u>M</u> 9
19. **(C)** U R 5 <u>M</u> <u>9</u> <u>W</u> <u>4</u> 3
20. **(D)** 9 X <u>4</u> Q 6 <u>5</u> <u>U</u> W
21. **(A)** 2 6 <u>9</u> Z <u>8</u> R <u>X</u> F
22. **(D)** <u>W</u> 8 <u>3</u> <u>6</u> <u>X</u> 2 U Z
23. **(E)** 7 9 8 W 5 U X F

24. **(B)** <u>F</u> <u>8</u> <u>Z</u> <u>3</u> W 7 9 M
25. **(A)** <u>8</u> <u>Z</u> 6 5 Q <u>9</u> <u>X</u> F
26. **(A)** M <u>7</u> Q R <u>F</u> 9 8 <u>6</u>
27. **(B)** <u>2</u> Q <u>6</u> 4 F 8 R <u>X</u>
28. **(B)** <u>2</u> Q 8 <u>X</u> U F 4 <u>6</u>
29. **(A)** X <u>7</u> R 8 Q 4 <u>F</u> <u>6</u>
30. **(E)** 2 3 Z F Q 6 W 9

Practice Set 4

For each of the following questions, find which one of the suggested answers appears in that question.

1. 4   5   J   Q   M   8   H   3   _____
2. Y   9   R   2   M   6   Q   8   _____
3. 4   M   2   Y   W   Q   6   8   _____
4. 4   M   8   6   Q   2   R   Y   _____
5. S   9   M   R   Q   3   2   8   _____

Suggested Answers
$\begin{cases} A = 2, & 7, & H, & W \\ B = 2, & 3, & M, & S \\ C = 3, & 6, & H, & S \\ D = 6, & 7, & M, & W \\ E = \text{none of these} \end{cases}$

Suggested Answers
$\begin{cases} A = 8, & 9, & Q, & M \\ B = 8, & 4, & M, & Y \\ C = 9, & 2, & Q, & J \\ D = 2, & 4, & J, & Y \\ E = \text{none of these} \end{cases}$

6. 2   J   8   7   M   3   Y   Q   _____
7. Q   2   J   5   H   9   3   S   _____
8. 9   3   2   H   7   W   Y   Q   _____
9. H   2   5   8   Y   4   W   J   _____
10. 4   8   3   J   2   R   Y   Q   _____

Suggested Answers
$\begin{cases} A = 2, & 3, & J, & Y \\ B = 2, & 5, & Q, & J \\ C = 8, & 3, & Q, & H \\ D = 8, & 5, & H, & Y \\ E = \text{none of these} \end{cases}$

11. 3   Y   6   M   8   7   W   H   _____
12. W   R   7   S   3   H   6   5   _____
13. 6   8   W   R   7   H   S   3   _____
14. H   3   M   J   2   9   7   W   _____
15. 7   Q   S   9   H   2   4   M   _____

16. 2   6   Q   8   Y   M   4   H   _____
17. 5   6   Q   2   9   W   H   Y   _____
18. M   5   R   W   6   2   8   H   _____
19. W   5   6   4   M   3   R   H   _____
20. 4   S   Y   M   6   5   2   W   _____

Suggested Answers
$\begin{cases} A = 8, & 5, & H, & M \\ B = 8, & 6, & Y, & W \\ C = 4, & 6, & H, & Y \\ D = 4, & 5, & M, & W \\ E = \text{none of these} \end{cases}$

21. J   Y   6   3   2   M   8   R   _____
22. 5   R   3   8   2   M   J   Y   _____
23. 4   2   M   8   R   6   S   J   _____
24. 2   4   R   Y   8   M   J   7   _____
25. W   3   5   S   M   7   2   Y   _____

Suggested Answers
$\begin{cases} A = 8, & 3, & M, & S \\ B = 2, & 3, & M, & R \\ C = 8, & 7, & R, & Y \\ D = 2, & 7, & Y, & S \\ E = \text{none of these} \end{cases}$

26. S 4 3 W 7 9 R M _____

27. 7 6 H 8 3 S J W _____

28. 5 8 3 M 7 J H W _____

29. 6 3 9 W H 8 S M _____

30. M 3 2 5 Y J 9 S _____

Suggested Answers
$\begin{cases} A = 9, & 6, & J, & M \\ B = 3, & 6, & M, & W \\ C = 9, & 7, & W, & S \\ D = 3, & 7, & J, & S \\ E = & \text{none of these} \end{cases}$

Answer Explanations for Practice Set 4

1. **(E)** 4 5 J Q M 8 H 3
2. **(A)** Y 9 R 2 M 6 Q 8
3. **(B)** 4 M 2 Y W Q 6 8
4. **(B)** 4 M 8 6 Q 2 R Y
5. **(A)** S 9 M R Q 3 2 8
6. **(A)** 2 J 8 7 M 3 Y Q
7. **(B)** Q 2 J 5 H 9 3 S
8. **(E)** 9 3 2 H 7 W Y Q
9. **(D)** H 2 5 8 Y 4 W J
10. **(A)** 4 8 3 J 2 R Y Q
11. **(D)** 3 Y 6 M 8 7 W H
12. **(C)** W R 7 S 3 H 6 5
13. **(C)** 6 8 W R 7 H S 3
14. **(A)** H 3 M J 2 9 7 W
15. **(E)** 7 Q S 9 H 2 4 M

16. **(C)** 2 6 Q 8 Y M 4 H
17. **(E)** 5 6 Q 2 9 W H Y
18. **(A)** M 5 R W 6 2 8 H
19. **(D)** W 5 6 4 M 3 R H
20. **(D)** 4 S Y M 6 5 2 W
21. **(B)** J Y 6 3 2 M 8 R
22. **(B)** 5 R 3 8 2 M J Y
23. **(E)** 4 2 M 8 R 6 S J
24. **(C)** 2 4 R Y 8 M J Z
25. **(D)** W 3 5 S M Z 2 Y
26. **(C)** S 4 3 W Z 9 R M
27. **(D)** Z 6 H 8 3 S J W
28. **(E)** 5 8 3 M 7 J H W
29. **(B)** 6 3 9 W H 8 S M
30. **(E)** M 3 2 5 Y J 9 S

Practice Set 5

For each of the following questions, find which one of the suggested answers appears in that question.

1. T 3 2 G 6 8 L K _____

2. 6 5 P 7 2 T N G _____

3. 4 7 2 K 6 N P G _____

4. 5 2 8 G P 7 T K _____

5. K 2 9 4 Z N 8 T _____

6. N Z 5 2 9 K 7 L _____

7. 4 L 2 7 9 K N Z _____

8. 3 9 K 7 L 5 T N _____

9. 9 3 L Z 7 K N 6 _____

10. G 2 4 T K 6 9 Z _____

Suggested Answers
$\begin{cases} A = 8, & 5, & N, & K \\ B = 2, & 5, & K, & G \\ C = 8, & 6, & G, & T \\ D = 2, & 6, & N, & T \\ E = & \text{none of these} \end{cases}$

Suggested Answers
$\begin{cases} A = 7, & 6, & Z, & T \\ B = 9, & 3, & K, & L \\ C = 7, & 6, & L, & Z \\ D = 9, & 6, & Z, & T \\ E = & \text{none of these} \end{cases}$

11. 9 5 V 7 Z K 3 P _____ 21. 9 N 7 6 K 2 Z V _____

12. 4 5 V 9 8 G P Z _____ 22. V 9 N 4 P 8 2 T _____

13. K 4 L G 5 9 7 P _____ 23. 8 2 9 P 6 G Z V _____

14. G 4 5 3 K 2 L P _____ 24. P 9 3 7 Z 3 G N _____

15. 3 T Z K 5 4 9 G _____ 25. 3 7 2 N 9 L Z V _____

Suggested Answers
{
A = 7, 4, P, K
B = 7, 5, Z, G
C = 3, 5, P, Z
D = 3, 4, K, G
E = none of these
}

Suggested Answers
{
A = 9, 2, N, Z
B = 9, 3, V, N
C = 7, 2, V, P
D = 7, 3, P, Z
E = none of these
}

16. 2 Z 5 K 7 6 G P _____ 26. 3 4 N V K 7 P 2 _____

17. G L 6 T 2 P 5 4 _____ 27. Z 8 L 9 K 5 V 7 _____

18. 5 7 G L 6 P T 2 _____ 28. 3 K 9 Z G V 5 7 _____

19. P 2 K N 9 8 6 G _____ 29. 3 K 7 5 V 9 L Z _____

20. 6 V T 8 P 9 3 K _____ 30. T 8 K L V 2 9 7 _____

Suggested Answers
{
A = 9, 6, P, G
B = 9, 2, K, T
C = 2, 5, P, T
D = 5, 6, K, G
E = none of these
}

Suggested Answers
{
A = 7, 8, V, K
B = 7, 3, K, Z
C = 8, 9, V, N
D = 9, 3, N, Z
E = none of these
}

Answer Explanations for Practice Set 5

1. **(C)** T 3 2 G 6 8 L K 16. **(D)** 2 Z 5 K 7 6 G P
2. **(D)** 6 5 P 7 2 T N G 17. **(C)** G L 6 T 2 P 5 4
3. **(E)** 4 7 2 K 6 N P G 18. **(C)** 5 7 G L 6 P T 2
4. **(B)** 5 2 8 G P 7 T K 19. **(A)** P 2 K N 9 8 6 G
5. **(E)** K 2 9 7 Z N 8 T 20. **(E)** 6 V T 8 P 9 3 K
6. **(B)** N Z 5 2 9 K 7 L 21. **(A)** 9 N 7 6 K 2 Z V
7. **(B)** 4 L 2 7 9 K N Z 22. **(E)** V 9 N 4 P 8 2 T
8. **(E)** 3 9 K 7 L 5 T N 23. **(E)** 8 2 9 P 6 G Z V
9. **(C)** 9 3 L Z 7 K N 6 24. **(D)** P 9 3 7 Z 3 G N
10. **(D)** G 2 4 T K 6 9 Z 25. **(A)** 3 7 2 N 9 L Z V
11. **(C)** 9 5 V 7 Z K 3 P 26. **(E)** 3 4 N V K 7 P 2
12. **(E)** 4 5 V 9 8 G P Z 27. **(A)** Z 8 L 9 K 5 V 7
13. **(A)** K 4 L G 5 9 7 P 28. **(B)** 3 K 9 Z G V 5 7
14. **(D)** G 4 5 3 K 2 L P 29. **(B)** 3 K 7 5 V 9 L Z
15. **(D)** 3 T Z K 5 4 9 G 30. **(A)** T 8 K L V 2 9 7

Practice Set 6

For each of the following questions, find which one of the suggested answers appears in that question.

1. 3   P   U   4   M   T   7   9
2. T   4   2   R   9   Y   6   U
3. R   2   M   U   6   4   3   P
4. 6   U   4   7   9   M   R   Y
5. R   P   2   6   3   U   T   4

Suggested Answers
$\begin{cases} A = 2, 4, M, U \\ B = 3, 4, T, R \\ C = 9, 2, U, R \\ D = 9, 3, M, T \\ E = \text{none of these} \end{cases}$

16. M   Q   3   7   4   Z   X   5
17. 7   Z   5   8   2   F   M   W
18. M   3   F   Z   7   5   4   Q
19. X   5   3   M   2   W   7   Z
20. 4   Q   Z   5   F   X   8   2

Suggested Answers
$\begin{cases} A = 3, 5, F, Z \\ B = 4, 5, X, M \\ C = 2, 3, Z, M \\ D = 2, 4, F, Z \\ E = \text{none of these} \end{cases}$

6. T   K   4   8   5   N   Z   6
7. 8   N   6   9   3   V   T   P
8. T   4   V   N   8   6   5   K
9. Z   6   4   T   3   P   8   N
10. 5   K   N   6   V   Z   9   3

Suggested Answers
$\begin{cases} A = 4, 6, V, N \\ B = 5, 6, Z, T \\ C = 3, 4, N, T \\ D = 3, 5, V, Z \\ E = \text{none of these} \end{cases}$

21. 7   Q   H   8   W   Z   3   5
22. Z   8   6   F   5   J   2   H
23. F   6   W   H   2   8   7   Q
24. 2   H   8   3   5   W   F   J
25. F   Q   6   2   7   H   Z   8

Suggested Answers
$\begin{cases} A = 6, 8, W, H \\ B = 7, 8, Z, F \\ C = 5, 6, H, F \\ D = 5, 7, W, Z \\ E = \text{none of these} \end{cases}$

11. 6   M   1   7   Q   Y   2   4
12. Y   7   5   S   4   H   9   J
13. S   5   Q   J   9   7   6   M
14. 9   J   7   2   4   Q   S   H
15. S   M   5   9   6   J   Y   7

Suggested Answers
$\begin{cases} A = 5, 7, Q, J \\ B = 6, 7, Y, S \\ C = 4, 5, J, S \\ D = 4, 6, Q, Y \\ E = \text{none of these} \end{cases}$

26. Y   R   9   5   2   X   Z   3
27. 5   X   3   6   8   H   Y   M
28. Y   9   H   X   5   3   2   R
29. Z   3   9   Y   8   M   5   X
30. 2   R   X   3   H   Z   6   8

Suggested Answers
$\begin{cases} A = 9, 3, H, X \\ B = 2, 3, Z, Y \\ C = 8, 9, X, Y \\ D = 8, 2, H, Z \\ E = \text{none of these} \end{cases}$

Answer Explanations for Practice Set 6

1. **(D)** 3 P U 4 M T 7 9
2. **(C)** T 4 2 R 9 Y 6 U
3. **(A)** R 2 M U 6 4 3 P
4. **(E)** 6 U T 7 9 M R Y
5. **(B)** R P 2 6 3 U T 4
6. **(B)** T K 4 8 5 N Z 6
7. **(E)** 8 N 6 9 3 V T P
8. **(A)** T 4 V N 8 6 5 K
9. **(C)** Z 6 4 T 3 P 8 N
10. **(D)** 5 K N 6 V Z 9 3
11. **(D)** 6 M J 7 Q Y 2 4
12. **(C)** Y 7 5 S 4 H 9 J
13. **(A)** S 5 Q J 9 7 6 M
14. **(E)** 9 J 7 2 4 Q S H
15. **(B)** S M 5 9 6 J Y Z

16. **(B)** M Q 3 7 4 Z X 5
17. **(E)** 7 Z 5 8 2 F M W
18. **(A)** M 3 F Z 7 5 4 Q
19. **(C)** X 5 3 M 2 W 7 Z
20. **(D)** 4 Q Z 5 F X 8 2
21. **(D)** Z Q H 8 W Z 3 5
22. **(C)** Z 8 6 F 5 J 2 H
23. **(A)** F 6 W H 2 8 7 Q
24. **(E)** 2 H 8 3 5 W F J
25. **(B)** F Q 6 2 7 H Z 8
26. **(B)** Y R 9 5 2 X Z 3
27. **(E)** 5 X 3 6 8 H Y M
28. **(A)** Y 9 H X 5 3 2 R
29. **(C)** Z 3 9 Y 8 M 5 X
30. **(D)** 2 R X 3 H Z 6 8

Practice Set 7

For each of the following questions, find which one of the suggested answers appears in that question.

1. R 6 7 4 F M 8 Q
2. 3 6 8 X V 9 Q R
3. 4 9 6 R 2 M V X
4. 2 3 V 9 6 Q M X
5. Q 5 6 X 2 8 Z R

Suggested Answers
A = 8, 3, M, R
B = 6, 3, R, X
C = 8, 2, X, Q
D = 6, 2, M, Q
E = none of these

6. 5 9 6 M 7 Z F Y
7. V 7 1 9 F 5 X M
8. 8 6 7 V 2 X F Y
9. Y 7 M 4 V 8 6 Q
10. 7 M 9 2 R 6 F Y

Suggested Answers
A = 7, 6, M, F
B = 7, 4, Y, M
C = 9, 6, Y, V
D = 9, 4, V, F
E = none of these

11. X 6 4 Q R 2 7 F
12. 7 5 Z F 9 R M 2
13. 5 7 R 9 Z 3 Q M
14. 4 Z 6 9 7 R M F
15. M F 3 6 7 R 9 Z

Suggested Answers
A = 9, 6, R, Q
B = 7, 6, R, Z
C = 9, 2, Z, F
D = 7, 2, F, Q
E = none of these

16. 5 Q F R 3 4 7 X
17. X 4 3 5 R 6 Z V
18. R 4 Z X 3 7 9 V
19. 4 3 Y 7 8 X V F
20. 7 3 Y 9 F R 5 V

Suggested Answers
A = 9, 4, V, R
B = 9, 3, F, X
C = 5, 3, V, F
D = 5, 4, R, X
E = none of these

21. Q 8 R Z Y 6 7 9
22. 5 R 9 3 Y 7 Z F
23. 5 R 7 F X Y 3 9
24. F 8 Z 7 R 3 Y 9
25. 5 4 M Y R 9 V 6

26. 2 Y Q 8 V 7 5 R
27. V 6 R M 7 8 2 X
28. 3 9 X Z 2 V Q 6
29. X Z 2 Q 6 V 3 4
30. 6 F 3 R 9 2 X V

Suggested Answers
$$\begin{cases} A = 9, 8, Y, R \\ B = 9, 5, R, F \\ C = 8, 7, Y, M \\ D = 7, 5, M, F \\ E = \text{none of these} \end{cases}$$

Suggested Answers
$$\begin{cases} A = 7, 2, V, X \\ B = 7, 6, R, Q \\ C = 6, 3, V, Q \\ D = 3, 2, R, X \\ E = \text{none of these} \end{cases}$$

Answer Explanations for Practice Set 7

1. **(E)** R 6 7 4 F M 8 Q
2. **(B)** 3 6 8 X V 9 Q R
3. **(E)** 4 9 6 R 2 M V X
4. **(D)** 2 3 V 9 6 Q M X
5. **(C)** Q 5 6 X 2 8 Z R
6. **(A)** 5 9 6 M 7 Z F Y
7. **(D)** V 7 4 9 F 5 X M
8. **(E)** 8 6 7 V 2 X F Y
9. **(B)** Y 7 M 4 V 8 6 Q
10. **(A)** 7 M 9 2 R 6 F Y
11. **(D)** X 6 4 Q R 2 7 F
12. **(C)** 7 5 Z F 9 R M 2
13. **(E)** 5 7 R 9 Z 3 Q M
14. **(B)** 4 Z 6 9 7 R M F
15. **(B)** M F 3 6 7 R 9 Z

16. **(D)** 5 Q F R 3 4 7 X
17. **(D)** X 4 3 5 R 6 Z V
18. **(A)** R 4 X 3 7 9 V
19. **(E)** 4 3 Y 7 8 X V F
20. **(C)** 7 3 Y 9 F R 5 V
21. **(A)** Q 8 R Z Y 6 7 9
22. **(B)** 5 R 9 3 Y 7 Z F
23. **(B)** 5 R 7 F X Y 3 9
24. **(A)** F 8 Z 7 R 3 Y 9
25. **(E)** 5 4 M Y R 9 V 6
26. **(E)** 2 Y Q 8 V 7 5 R
27. **(A)** V 6 R M 7 8 2 X
28. **(C)** 3 9 X Z 2 V Q 6
29. **(C)** X Z 2 Q 6 V 3 4
30. **(D)** 6 F 3 R 9 2 X V

Practice Set 8

For each of the following questions, find which one of the suggested answers appears in that question.

1. 7 U 5 4 P 8 T M
2. M 7 U 2 Y 6 8 R
3. 6 8 7 Y 4 X T M
4. Y 7 2 5 T 9 X U
5. 9 5 8 U 7 Q T M

6. 8 T 3 P 5 4 X Y
7. X Q 4 R 8 Y 3 2
8. 3 5 X Q 4 Y R 8
9. Y 8 P U 7 6 4 X
10. 4 M R 6 Y 7 9 P

Suggested Answers
$$\begin{cases} A = 7, 8, U, T \\ B = 7, 2, M, U \\ C = 5, 8, M, Y \\ D = 5, 2, Y, T \\ E = \text{none of these} \end{cases}$$

Suggested Answers
$$\begin{cases} A = 7, 4, Y, X \\ B = 7, 8, P, R \\ C = 8, 3, Y, R \\ D = 3, 4, P, X \\ E = \text{none of these} \end{cases}$$

11. R   9   8   X   4   6   Q   P
12. 4   3   Y   5   8   R   U   X
13. 2   5   8   P   4   U   Y   X
14. 3   8   6   X   Y   5   R   P
15. P   8   7   2   T   U   6   R

21. U   T   3   8   7   P   5   Q
22. 2   Q   8   5   7   P   U   T
23. 9   7   P   5   Q   3   R   U
24. 7   9   Q   T   5   P   U   4
25. X   8   2   R   P   4   7   T

Suggested Answers
{
A = 6, 3, U, P
B = 8, 3, P, X
C = 6, 4, X, R
D = 8, 4, U, R
E = none of these
}

Suggested Answers
{
A = 5, 8, P, R
B = 7, 8, P, Q
C = 5, 4, Q, T
D = 7, 4, T, R
E = none of these
}

16. 7   3   M   5   T   P   9   Y
17. 2   3   M   7   6   X   Y   T
18. P   2   Q   X   3   7   5   Y
19. X   2   3   9   P   8   Q   Y
20. 9   R   T   P   3   2   7   X

26. 9   2   U   M   P   5   Y   8
27. T   6   Q   7   P   3   M   5
28. 9   P   7   T   X   M   3   5
29. 9   P   5   3   M   7   Q   T
30. R   6   P   Q   M   8   7   5

Suggested Answers
{
A = 5, 2, Y, P
B = 5, 3, T, X
C = 9, 3, Y, T
D = 9, 2, P, X
E = none of these
}

Suggested Answers
{
A = 5, 6, M, P
B = 5, 9, P, T
C = 6, 7, M, U
D = 7, 9, U, T
E = none of these
}

Answer Explanations for Practice Set 8

1. **(A)** 7 U 5 4 P 8 T M
2. **(B)** M 7 U 2 Y 6 8 R
3. **(E)** 6 8 7 Y 4 X T M
4. **(D)** Y 7 2 5 T 9 X U
5. **(A)** 9 5 8 U 7 Q T M
6. **(D)** 8 T 3 P 5 4 X Y
7. **(C)** X Q 4 R 8 Y 3 2
8. **(C)** 3 5 X Q 4 Y R 8
9. **(A)** Y 8 P U 7 6 4 X
10. **(E)** 4 M R 6 Y 7 9 P
11. **(C)** R 9 8 X 4 6 Q P
12. **(D)** 4 3 Y 5 8 R U X
13. **(E)** 2 5 8 P 4 U Y X
14. **(B)** 3 8 6 X Y 5 R P
15. **(E)** P 8 7 2 T U 6 R

16. **(C)** 7 3 M 5 T P 9 Y
17. **(E)** 2 3 M 7 6 X Y T
18. **(A)** P 2 Q X 3 7 5 Y
19. **(D)** X 2 3 9 P 8 Q Y
20. **(D)** 9 R T P 3 2 7 X
21. **(B)** U T 3 8 7 P 5 Q
22. **(B)** 2 Q 8 5 7 P U T
23. **(E)** 9 7 P 5 Q 3 R U
24. **(C)** 7 9 Q T 5 P U 4
25. **(D)** X 8 2 R P 4 7 T
26. **(E)** 9 2 U M P 5 Y 8
27. **(A)** T 6 Q 7 P 3 M 5
28. **(B)** 9 P 7 T X M 3 5
29. **(B)** 9 P 5 3 M 7 Q T
30. **(A)** R 6 P Q M 8 7 5

Clerical Abilities Analysis Chart for Number And Letter Scramble (Name and Number Comparison)

Use the following chart to carefully analyze your results of the *number and letter scramble (name and number comparison)* question type. This will help you evaluate your strengths and weaknesses. This analysis should help you focus your study and review efforts on specific types of problems.

Practice Set	Total Number of Questions	Number Correct	Number Incorrect	Number Unanswered
Set 1	30			
Set 2	30			
Set 3	30			
Set 4	30			
Set 5	30			
Set 6	30			
Set 7	30			
Set 8	30			

Because there is no penalty for incorrect answers on most of the questions in the Clerical Abilities section, you should have left no question unanswered. Even if you didn't have time to answer a question, you should have at least filled in the answer space with an educated guess.

REVIEWING THE KEY STRATEGIES

Remember to:
1. Practice a technique and become comfortable with it.
2. Only one suggested answer will be correct for each question.
3. A choice may be used more than once within a five-question set.

CLERICAL OPERATIONS WITH LETTERS AND NUMBERS (NUMBER SEQUENCING/ORDERING)

This question type tests your ability to be detail oriented in a number of different operations: alphabetizing, comparing sets of numbers and/or letters, counting items in a group or within lists, and more. The question types are varied, but each type relies on your ability to discern differences and similarities among groups of elements, typically names, numbers, and letters.

Helpful Techniques and Strategies

1. If required to count within a long line of numbers or letters, use your answer sheet as a straightedge to keep your place as you reveal each letter or number one at a time.

2. Know the difference between odd and even numbers.
3. Practice in order to be able to alphabetize quickly.
4. Double-check your answer by working from left to right first, and then work from right to left to verify your response.
5. Use the same approach with a stacked list: work from bottom-up the second time to check.
6. If permitted to write in the test booklet, mark or circle lightly in the lists if such notations will be helpful.
7. Getting used to these unusual question types and becoming comfortable with your own approach is probably the best advice. So practice, practice, practice.

Practice Set 1

This question type tests your ability to compare the similarities and differences among selected groups. Use your knowledge of ordering and sequencing to answer the questions following each data group.

The following four questions are based on this list of employees:

Robinson, Angela
Brown, Gary
Johnson, Tracy
Staley, George
Garrett, Sheila
Jackson, Shawn

1. Which employee's name would come third in an alphabetized list?

   A) Robinson, Angela
   B) Johnson, Tracy
   C) Garrett, Sheila
   D) Jackson, Shawn

2. Which employee's first name starts with the letter in the alphabet that is five letters after the first letter of their last name?

   A) Johnson, Tracy
   B) Brown, Gary
   C) Jackson, Shawn
   D) Garrett, Sheila

3. How many of the employees have either a first or a last name that starts with the letter "G"?

   A) 1
   B) 2
   C) 3
   D) 4

4. How many employees have last names that are exactly 7 letters long?

   A) 1
   B) 2
   C) 3
   D) 4

The following four questions are based on these sets of letters and numbers:

ETRSF7F3W
MWE3V86RS
ZXSC1Y752
UEF4WEB9L

5. Which set of letters and numbers contains the most numerical digits?

   A) ETRSF7F3W
   B) MWN3V86RS
   C) ZXSC1Y752
   D) UEF4WEB9L

6. What is the sum of all of the numerical digits in the set "MWN3V86RS"?

A) 11
B) 14
C) 16
D) 17

7. How many times does the letter "E" occur in the four sets?

A) 1
B) 2
C) 3
D) 4

8. If the four sets were alphabetized by the first letter in the set, which set would come third?

A) ETRSF7F3W
B) MWN3V86RS
C) ZXSC1Y752
D) UEF4WEB9L

The following four questions are based on this sentence:

"The executive decided to resign rather than face the prospect of a no-confidence vote from the Board of Directors."

9. How many words in the sentence are greater than six letters long?

A) 4
B) 5
C) 6
D) 7

10. How many times is "e" the second letter of a word in the sentence?

A) 1
B) 2
C) 3
D) 4

11. Which letter is NOT present in the sentence?

A) y
B) v
C) x
D) f

12. How many words in the sentence begin with a vowel (a, e, i, o, u)?

A) 2
B) 3
C) 4
D) 5

The following four questions are based on this series of numbers:

134,088; 478,234; 280,838; 251,021; 23,874; 89,216; 929,183

13. Which number contains the most repeated numbers?

A) 478,234
B) 929,183
C) 251,021
D) 280,838

14. How many of the numbers have an odd digit at either end?

A) 1
B) 2
C) 3
D) 4

15. How many times does the digit 4 occur in the series of numbers?

A) 2
B) 3
C) 4
D) 5

16. Which number has the largest fourth digit, counting from the left?

A) 280,838
B) 134,088
C) 929,183
D) 23,874

Answer Explanations for Practice Set 1

1. **(D)** Alphabetize the list of names by last name. The first name would be Gary Brown, the second name would be Sheila Garrett, and the third name would be Shawn Jackson.

2. **(B)** For each employee, take the first letter of their last name and count five letters forward in the alphabet. Then compare this letter to the first letter of their first name. The employee whose first name starts with the letter that is five letters after the first letter of their last name in the alphabet is Gary Brown.

3. **(C)** Three employees have either a first or a last name that starts with the letter "G": Gary Brown, George Staley, and Sheila Garrett.

4. **(C)** Three employees have last names that are exactly 7 letters long: Tracy Johnson, Sheila Garrett, and Shawn Jackson.

5. **(C)** The set "ZXSC1Y752" contains the four numerical digits: 1 (digit five), 7 (digit seven), 5 (digit eight), and 2 (digit nine).

6. **(D)** First, identify all of the numerical digits in the set. They are 3 (digit four), 8 (digit six), and 6 (digit seven). Then add them together: $3 + 8 + 6 = 17$.

7. **(D)** The letter "E" occurs four times in the sets. It is digit one of the first set, digit three of the second set, and digits two and six of the fourth set.

8. **(D)** Alphabetize the four sets by the first letter in the set. The first set is ETRSF7F3W, the second set is MYN3V86RS, and the third set is UEF4WHB9L.

9. **(B)** Count the number of letters in each word in the sentence. Five words in the sentence are more than six letters long: "executive," "decided," "prospect," "no-confidence," and "Directors."

10. **(B)** Scan the sentence and count the number of words where "E" is the second letter. The letter "E" is the second letter of two words in the sentence: "decided" and "resign."

11. **(A)** Scan the sentence for each letter listed. The letter "V" is present in the words "executive" and "vote," the letter "X" is present in the word "executive," and the letter "F" is present in the words "face" and "no-confidence." The only letter listed that is not present in the sentence is the letter "Y."

12. **(C)** Scan the sentence and count the number of words beginning with a vowel. There are four words in the sentence that begin with a vowel: "executive," "of," "a," and another "of."

13. **(D)** Compare all numbers in the series. The number 280,838 has three 8s. None of the other numbers have more than two of the same number.

14. **(C)** Scan the end digits of every number. Three numbers have an odd digit at either end: 134,088; 251,021; and 929,183.

15. **(C)** Scan the series of numbers and count every time the digit 4 occurs. The digit 4 occurs four times: once in 134,088, twice in 478,234, and once in 23,874.

16. **(A)** Compare the fourth digit from the left in each number. The number with the largest fourth digit is 280,838, with a fourth digit of 8.

Practice Set 2

This question type tests your ability to compare the similarities and differences among selected groups. Use your knowledge of ordering and sequencing to answer the questions following each data group.

The following questions are based on these four sentences:

1) Mr. Brown sits at the second cubicle from the wall.
2) Ms. Black sits at the front corner cubicle.
3) Mr. Smith's cubicle is fifth from the back wall.
4) Cubicle 11-B belongs to Ms. Jones.

1. Which sentence would come third in an alphabetized list?

   A) Sentence 1
   B) Sentence 2
   C) Sentence 3
   D) Sentence 4

2. Which vowel does not appear in sentence 4?

   A) a
   B) u
   C) i
   D) o

3. How many sentences include two consecutive words that begin with the same letter?

   A) 1
   B) 2
   C) 3
   D) 4

4. Which sentence contains the most capital letters?

   A) Sentence 1
   B) Sentence 2
   C) Sentence 3
   D) Sentence 4

The following questions are based on these columns of numbers, each having three digits:

Column 1	Column 2
239	942
596	670
124	189
841	723
670	124
239	345

5. How many numbers appear in both columns?

   A) 1
   B) 2
   C) 3
   D) 4

6. Which number appears more than once in Column 1?

   A) 596
   B) 670
   C) 124
   D) 239

7. How many numbers in both columns are lower in numeric value than 300?

   A) 2
   B) 3
   C) 4
   D) 5

8. Which digit appears the most times in Column 2?

   A) 1
   B) 4
   C) 7
   D) 9

The following questions are based on this series of last names:

   Adams, Jacobs, Williams, Rastanaan, Martinez, Abrams, Horton, Vickers, Tinsley, Fairchild, Lawrence

9. Which name would be third in an alphabetized list of all of the names?

   A) Adams
   B) Horton
   C) Fairchild
   D) Jacobs

10. Which name in the list would be last if the names were alphabetized?

   A) Lawrence
   B) Horton
   C) Williams
   D) Yarrow

11. Which name contains the most letters that are vowels?

    A) Williams
    B) Rastanaan
    C) Fairchild
    D) Martinez

12. How many names in the series contain at least two of the same letter?

    A) 4
    B) 5
    C) 6
    D) 7

The following questions are based on these four sets of letters:

    Set 1: DKDNEBGJRCA
    Set 2: SLSNFNESNEN
    Set 3: AKFNSBSLJOJE
    Set 4: PIOFUOSJNCAQR

13. Which set would be last if the sets were alphabetized by the second letter in each set?

    A) Set 1
    B) Set 2
    C) Set 3
    D) Set 4

14. In which set does the letter "S" occur most frequently?

    A) Set 1
    B) Set 2
    C) Set 3
    D) Set 4

15. Which set would be first if the sets were alphabetized by the first vowel in each set?

    A) Set 1
    B) Set 2
    C) Set 3
    D) Set 4

16. Which set contains two consecutive letters that immediately follow each other in the alphabet? (For example, "M" and "N" immediately follow each other in the alphabet.)

    A) Set 1
    B) Set 2
    C) Set 3
    D) Set 4

Answer Explanations for Practice Set 2

1. **(C)** The first sentence in an alphabetized list would be sentence 4, because it starts with the letter "C" and the others start with "M." The second sentence would be sentence 1, because it starts with "Mr." The third sentence would be sentence 3, because it starts with "Mr. Smith." The fourth, and last sentence, in an alphabetized list would be sentence 2, because it starts with the word "Ms."

2. **(A)** Check the sentence for the vowel in each answer choice. The vowels "u" and "i" appear in the word "cubicle," and "o" appears in "belongs," "to," and "Jones." The vowel "a" does not appear in sentence 4.

3. **(B)** Check each sentence for two consecutive words that begin with the same letter. Two sentences include two consecutive words that begin with the same letter: Sentence 2 ("corner cubicle") and Sentence 3 ("fifth from").

4. **(D)** Count the number of capital letters in each sentence. Each sentence contains two capital letters except sentence 4. Sentence 4 has four capital letters (Cubicle, 11-B, Ms., and Jones).

5. **(B)** Compare the numbers in the two columns. There are two numbers that appear in both columns: 124 (line 3 of Column 1 and line 5 of column 2) and

670 (line 5 of Column 1 and line 2 of Column 2).

6. **(D)** Check Column 1 for numbers that appear multiple times. The number 239 appears more than once in Column 1: in line 1 and in line 6.

7. **(D)** Five numbers are lower than 300: 239, 124, and 239 again in Column 1, and 189 and 124 in Column 2.

8. **(B)** Count the number of times each digit occurs in Column 2. The digit 4 appears three times in Column 2, more than any other digit.

9. **(C)** In an alphabetized list, Abrams would be first, Adams would come second, and Fairchild would come third.

10. **(C)** If the names were alphabetized, Williams would be last. Note that (D) Yarrow is not a name included in the list.

11. **(B)** The name Rastanaan contains the most letters that are vowels (4). The other three choices contain only three letters each that are vowels.

12. **(D)** Seven names contain at least two of the same letter: Adams (two a's), Williams (two i's and l's), Rastanaan (two n's and four a's), Abrams (two a's), Horton (two o's), Fairchild (two i's), and Lawrence (two e's).

13. **(B)** Set 2 would come last if the sets were alphabetized by the second letter in each set, because its second letter is "L." The second letters of Set 1, Set 3, and Set 4 are "K," "K," and "I," respectively.

14. **(B)** The letter "S" appears most frequently—three times—in Set 2. Set 3 has two "S's," Set 4 has one "S," and Set 1 has no "S."

15. **(C)** Set 3 would come first if the sets were alphabetized by the first vowel in each set, because the first vowel in Set 3 is "A." The first vowels in Set 1, Set 2, and Set 4 are "E," "E," and "I," respectively.

16. **(D)** Set 4 contains two consecutive letters that are next to each other in the alphabet, as its last two letters are "Q" and "R."

Practice Set 3

This question type tests your ability to compare similarities and differences among selected groups. Use your knowledge of ordering and sequencing to answer the questions following each data group.

Questions 1–4 are based on the following list of employee user names. The user names are constructed of the first initial of the employee's first name with the employee's entire last name.

hdonovan
kmartin
abarrinson
wbrown
rtennison
sadams
fmiller
erodriguez

1. Which user name would be second in the list if the user names were alphabetized by the first letter of each user name?

A) fmiller
B) abarrinson
C) hdonovan
D) erodriguez

2. Which user name would be first in the list if the user names were alphabetized by the employees' last names?

A) abarrinson
B) wbrown
C) sadams
D) hdonovan

3. Which user name contains the least amount of vowels (a, e, i, o, u)?

   A) sadams
   B) wbrown
   C) fmiller
   D) kmartin

4. How many of the user names contain at least ten letters?

   A) 1
   B) 2
   C) 3
   D) 4

Questions 5–8 are based on the following series of letters and numbers:

S7T89L1M7N-JFE24H82BW-QB54VYU52-33NBVDA

5. How many numbers are to the left of the first dash?

   A) 4
   B) 5
   C) 9
   D) 10

6. How many characters are to the right of the third dash?

   A) 6
   B) 7
   C) 8
   D) 9

7. Which section between hyphens contains the most letters? (The first section is section #1; the second section is section #2; and so on.)

   A) Section #4
   B) Section #3
   C) Section #2
   D) Section #1

8. Which section between hyphens contains the highest single numerical digit? (The first section is section #1; the second section is section #2; and so on.)

   A) Section #4
   B) Section #3
   C) Section #2
   D) Section #1

Questions 9–12 are based on the following four groups of names:

Group 1: Lewis, Johnson, Stevens, Carrington
Group 2: Brooks, Charles, Logston, Manor
Group 3: Kilbourne, Vanderlay, Gregory, Allen
Group 4: Burris, Flaherty, Horton, Ziebinsky

9. Which group contains the name with the most letters?

   A) Group 1
   B) Group 2
   C) Group 3
   D) Group 4

10. Which group would be second in a list if the groups were alphabetized by the second name in each group?

    A) Group 1
    B) Group 2
    C) Group 3
    D) Group 4

11. How many of the groups contain at least one name that contains the letter "y"?

    A) 1
    B) 2
    C) 3
    D) 4

12. Which name in Group 2 contains the most consecutive consonants (not a, e, i, or u)?

   A) Brooks
   B) Charles
   C) Logston
   D) Manor

Questions 13–16 are based on the following list of company departments:

   Information Technology
   Accounting
   Digital Media
   Public Relations
   Marketing
   Administrative
   Human Resources
   Security
   Sales
   Customer Service

13. Which department would be second to last in an alphabetized list?

   A) Public Relations
   B) Security
   C) Sales
   D) Information Technology

14. How many of the departments have names consisting of multiple words?

   A) 3
   B) 4
   C) 5
   D) 6

15. How many letters does the longest single word in the list contain?

   A) 11
   B) 12
   C) 13
   D) 14

16. For how many departments does the second letter of the department name come alphabetically before the first letter of that department name?

   A) 3
   B) 4
   C) 5
   D) 6

Answer Explanations for Practice Set 3

1. **(D)** If the user names were alphabetized by the first letter of each user name, "abarrinson" would be first and "erodriguez" would be second.

2. **(C)** If the user names were alphabetized by the employees' last names (which begin with the second letter of each username), "sadams" would be first because it is the user name for an employee with the last name "Adams."

3. **(B)** Compare the four answer choices. Only "wbrown" contains one vowel. All the other choices contain two vowels.

4. **(B)** The user names "abarrinson" and "erodriguez" each contain ten letters. The next longest user name is "rtennison," which contains only nine letters.

5. **(B)** Five numbers are before the first dash: 7, 8, 9, 1, and 7 again.

6. **(B)** Seven characters are after the third dash: 3, 3, N, B, V, D, and A.

7. **(C)** The section "JFE24H82BW" contains the most letters, with six (J, F, E, H, B, and W). The other three sections contain only five letters each.

8. **(D)** The section "S7T89L1M7N" contains the largest numerical digit, as the fifth character in the section is a "9."

9. **(A)** Group 1 contains the name with the most letters: Carrington, which is ten letters long. The next longest names are Kilbourne, Vanderlay, and Ziebinsky, which each contain nine letters.

10. **(D)** If the groups were alphabetized by the second name in each group, Group 2 would be first ("Charles") and Group 4 would be second ("Flaherty").

11. **(B)** Two of the groups contain at least one name that contains the letter "y": Group 3 ("Vanderlay") and Group 4 ("Flaherty" and "Ziebinsky").

12. **(C)** Of the names in Group 2, the name "Logston" contains the most consecutive consonants, with three (g-s-t). None of the other three names contain more than two consecutive consonants.

13. **(C)** "Security" would be last in an alphabetized list, as it begins with "Se." "Sales" would be second to last, as it begins with "Sa."

14. **(C)** Five of the departments have names that consist of multiple words: "Information Technology," "Digital Media," "Public Relations," "Human Resources," and "Customer Service."

15. **(D)** The longest word in the list in "administrative," which contains 14 letters.

16. **(A)** The second letter of the department name comes alphabetically before the first letter of that department name for three departments: "Marketing," "Security," and "Sales."

Practice Set 4

This question type tests your ability to compare the similarities and differences among selected groups. Use your knowledge of ordering and sequencing to answer the questions following each data group.

Questions 1–4 are based on the following two sentences:

> Make checks payable to "Nelson, Sanders, & French" in the amount stated on the invoice. If you have further questions on this matter, please contact Customer Service at 1-800-555-0293.

1. If all the words in the first sentence were alphabetized, which word would come last?

   A) stated
   B) you
   C) to
   D) questions

2. How many capital letters are in the two sentences?

   A) 4
   B) 5
   C) 6
   D) 7

3. How many commas are in the two sentences?

   A) 1
   B) 2
   C) 3
   D) 4

4. How many digits in the phone number in the second sentence are odd numbers?

   A) 4
   B) 5
   C) 6
   D) 7

Questions 5–8 are based on the following list of cities:

Decatur, Alabama
Savannah, Georgia
Buffalo, New York
Johnson City, Tennessee
Buxton, North Carolina
Biloxi, Mississippi
Riverside, California
Newark, New Jersey

5. If the list of cities were alphabetized by city name, which state would come first?

   A) New York
   B) North Carolina
   C) Mississippi
   D) Alabama

6. If the list of cities were alphabetized by state name, which city would come first?

   A) Decatur
   B) Savannah
   C) Biloxi
   D) Riverside

7. Every state name in the list—except one state—has a letter repeated in its name. For example, New Jersey has three e's. One listed state has no repeated letters. Which city in the list represents that state?

   A) Savannah
   B) Buffalo
   C) Riverside
   D) Buxton

8. Only one state name in the list contains four different vowels. (Vowels are a, e, i, o, u, and y.) Which city represents that state?

   A) Buxton
   B) Newark
   C) Savannah
   D) Johnson City

Questions 9–12 are based on the following list of radio station call letters and frequencies:

   WQBX 107.1
   WTVP 101.3
   WRVJ 98.7
   WBZX 104.9
   WDNJ 93.1
   WPDP 96.5

9. Which letter does NOT appear in any of the radio stations' call letters?

   A) N
   B) T
   C) J
   D) M

10. Which of the following radio stations contains only odd-numbered digits in its frequency?

    A) WBZX
    B) WRVJ
    C) WDNJ
    D) WPDP

11. If the list were to be alphabetized, which station's frequency would come second?

    A) 98.7
    B) 104.9
    C) 93.1
    D) 96.5

12. What numbered digit does NOT appear in any of the listed frequencies?

    A) 2
    B) 3
    C) 4
    D) 5

Questions 13–16 are based on the following list of employees and their extensions:

   Mr. Kendrick, ext. 5181
   Ms. Manning, ext. 8209
   Mr. Harrison, ext. 2809
   Ms. Benson, ext. 3547
   Mr. Lane, ext. 0987
   Ms. Armstrong, ext. 1276
   Mr. Garrett, ext. 2395
   Ms. Arnette, ext. 7012

13. If the employees were alphabetized by last name, which employee would come last?

    A) Ms. Manning
    B) Mr. Lane
    C) Ms. Armstrong
    D) Mr. Kendrick

14. Which male employee does not have an "8" in his extension?

    A) Mr. Kendrick
    B) Mr. Harrison
    C) Mr. Lane
    D) Mr. Garrett

15. How many of the female employees have extensions that contain at least two digits that are odd numbers?

    A) 1
    B) 2
    C) 3
    D) 4

16. How many times does the digit "1" appear in the entire list?

    A) 3
    B) 4
    C) 5
    D) 6

Answer Explanations for Practice Set 4

1. **(C)** If all of the words in the first sentence were alphabetized, the word "to" would come last. The word "the" (which is not included in the answer choices) would come second to last. The word "you" occurs in the second sentence, not the first.

2. **(D)** Seven capital letters are in the two sentences, in the words "Make," "Nelson," "Sanders," "French," "If," "Customer," and "Service."

3. **(C)** Three commas are in the two sentences: two commas are in the first sentence, after the words "Nelson" and "Sanders," and one comma is in the second sentence after the word "matter."

4. **(C)** Six digits in the phone number's second sentence are odd numbers: 1, 5, 5, 5, 9, and 3.

5. **(C)** If the list were alphabetized by city name, Biloxi would come first because it starts with "Bi." Biloxi is in Mississippi.

6. **(D)** If the list were alphabetized by state name, Decatur would come first because it is in the state of Alabama.

7. **(B)** New York is the only state that does not contain at least two of the same letter. Georgia contains two of the letter "G," California contains two of the letters "A" and "I," and North Carolina contains two of the letters "O" and "A."

8. **(C)** The state name Georgia contains four different vowels: e, o, i, and a. The city of Savannah represents Georgia.

9. **(D)** The letter "M" does not appear in any of the radio stations' call letters. The letter "N" appears in "WDNJ," the letter "T" appears in "WTVP," and the letter "J" appears in "WRVJ" and "WDNJ."

10. **(C)** "WDNJ 93.1" contains only odd-numbered digits in its frequency. "WBZX 104.9" contains a "4," "WRVJ 98.7" contains an "8," and "WPDP 96.5" contains a "6."

11. **(C)** In an alphabetized list, "WBZX 104.9" would come first because it starts with "WB." "WDNJ 93.1" would come second because it starts with "WD."

12. **(A)** The digit 2 does not appear in any of the listed frequencies.

13. **(A)** If the employees were alphabetized by last name, Ms. Manning would come last because her last name starts with "M."

14. **(D)** Mr. Garrett does not have an "8" in his extension number, which is "2395." The other three male employees have extensions of "5181," "2809," and "0987."

15. **(C)** Ms. Benson (ext. 3547), Ms. Armstrong (ext. 1276), and Ms. Arnette (ext. 7012) all have extension numbers that contain at least two digits that are odd numbers. Ms. Manning (ext. 8209) has only one odd-numbered digit in her extension number.

16. **(B)** The number "1" appears four times in the list: twice in Mr. Kendrick's extension, once in Ms. Armstrong's extension, and once in Ms. Arnette's extension.

Clerical Abilities Analysis Chart for Clerical Operations with Letters and Numbers (Number Sequencing/Ordering)

Use the following chart to carefully analyze your results of the *clerical operations with letters and numbers (number sequencing/ordering)* question type. This will help you evaluate your strengths and weaknesses. This analysis should help you focus your study and review efforts on specific types of problems.

Practice Set	Total Number of Questions	Number Correct	Number Incorrect	Number Unanswered
Set 1	16			
Set 2	16			
Set 3	16			
Set 4	16			

Because there is no penalty for incorrect answers on most of the questions in the Clerical Abilities section, you should have left no question unanswered. Even if you didn't have time to answer a question, you should have at least filled in the answer space with an educated guess.

REVIEWING THE KEY STRATEGIES
Remember to:
1. If helpful, use your answer sheet to cover up a list, revealing numbers or letters one by one as you count.
2. If permitted to write in the test booklet, mark or circle lightly elements in the list if such notations will be helpful.
3. Double-check your answers by working from right to left the second time after first working left to right.
4. Use the same approach with a stacked list: work from bottom-up the second time to check.
5. Become familiar with the test question types. Practice, practice, practice.

RECORD KEEPING (CHART READING)

This question type tests your ability to perform common record-keeping tasks. It requires you to read a chart, to understand the meanings and relationships among numbers within the chart, and to work with selected numbers within the chart as indicated by each question. Typical problems involve identifying amounts, and creating totals, subtotals, averages, and percentages. You will need to use simple arithmetic (adding, subtracting, averaging, finding percentages, etc.) to derive the answers.

Each set includes a chart followed by one or more questions based on the chart. The questions will vary in difficulty: some easy, some moderate, and some difficult. As you may not be allowed to use a calculator for this section of the text, it's recommended that you practice these questions without using one.

Sample question set:

Price per Gallon of Gasoline in the Cities of Oxford and Hillsboro, by Grade and Month

Month	Oxford			Hillsboro		
	Regular	Premium	Super	Regular	Premium	Super
July	$3.50	$3.75	$3.85	$3.35	$3.50	$3.55
August	$3.40	$3.60	$3.70	$3.15	$3.40	$3.45
September	$2.70	$2.85	$2.95	$2.50	$2.60	$2.70
October	$2.80	$2.95	$3.00	$2.45	$2.65	$2.70

Helpful Techniques and Strategies

Before you look at the questions, it is important for you to get a quick understanding of the chart and what the numbers in the rows and columns mean. The best way to do that is to first read the chart title—the title of the chart—and any subheadings. Doing so should inform you of what the numbers represent and how the columns and rows mean different things. Don't look for numerical relationships at this point although some may be obvious. This first task is to get a quick sense of what the columns and rows signify.

In the example above, you would start by understanding that the chart shows the prices of three different blends of gasoline in two cities during four different months.

Now try the first question:

1. What was the largest single-month decrease in the price of Premium gasoline in either city?

   A) $0.65
   B) $0.70
   C) $0.75
   D) $0.80

First you must realize that this question concerns the price of *only* Premium gasoline in both cities. So your focus should be limited to just two columns of information:

Price per Gallon of Gasoline in the Cities of Oxford and Hillsboro by Grade and Month

Month	Oxford Premium	Hillsboro Premium
July	$3.75	$3.50
August	$3.60	$3.40
September	$2.85	$2.60
October	$2.95	$2.65

This is typical of this problem type. Your first action will be to identify just the part(s) of the chart that are relevant to that question, and ignore the rest of the information in the chart.

Your next step in this question is to look for the largest single-month decrease in the price of Premium. A "single-month decrease" means the price goes down from one month to the next. This occurs two times in Oxford (from July to August and from August to September) and two times in Hillsboro (from July to August and from August to September). The price in both cities goes up in October, so you no longer concern yourself with the October numbers:

Price per Gallon of Gasoline in the Cities of Oxford and Hillsboro, by Grade and Month

Month	Oxford Premium	Hillsboro Premium
July	$3.75	$3.50
August	$3.60	$3.40
September	$2.85	$2.60

Limiting your focus to only these amounts, you move to your final action: to identify which of these decreases is the largest. From July to August, the decrease in Oxford is $0.15 and the decrease in Hillsboro is $0.10. Perhaps you can even compute these differences in your head without using pencil and paper. The remaining two decreases may require you to use pencil and paper to do the subtraction. In Oxford, the price dropped from $3.60 in August to $2.85 in September; in Hillsboro the price dropped from $3.40 in August to $2.60 in September. The larger of the two decreases was the $0.80 in Hillsboro. The correct answer is (D) $0.80.

Let's look at another question:

2. For the city of Oxford, which month had the greatest difference in price between Super and Regular?

    A) July
    B) August
    C) September
    D) October

This question is about only the city of Oxford and only the prices of Super and Regular. So your focus should be:

Price per Gallon of Gasoline in the Cities of Oxford and Hillsboro, by Grade and Month

| Month | Oxford | | |
	Regular		Super
July	$3.50		$3.85
August	$3.40		$3.70
September	$2.70		$2.95
October	$2.80		$3.00

To find the greatest difference in price, your actions now will be to subtract across, either from left to right or from right to left, whichever is necessary, to identify the greatest difference in any month. The largest difference is in July: $3.85 − $3.50 = $0.35. None of the other differences is as large.

These two questions relied on subtraction to derive the correct answers. Other questions may require addition, averaging (adding and then dividing), finding percentages, or ordering numbers to find the highest, lowest, second highest, and so forth. Now practice with several more questions using the chart. The correct answers and explanations follow.

Price per Gallon of Gasoline in the Cities of Oxford and Hillsboro, by Grade and Month

| Month | Oxford | | | Hillsboro | | |
	Regular	Premium	Super	Regular	Premium	Super
July	$3.50	$3.75	$3.85	$3.35	$3.50	$3.55
August	$3.40	$3.60	$3.70	$3.15	$3.40	$3.45
September	$2.70	$2.85	$2.95	$2.50	$2.60	$2.70
October	$2.80	$2.95	$3.00	$2.45	$2.65	$2.70

3. In which month was the price of Regular gasoline in the two cities the closest?

   A) July
   B) August
   C) September
   D) October

4. During how many months did the price of Premium gasoline in Hillsboro cost less than $3.00?

   A) 1
   B) 2
   C) 3
   D) 4

5. What was the average price per month for Regular gasoline in Oxford during the entire four-month period?

   A) $2.80
   B) $3.00
   C) $3.10
   D) $3.20

6. What was the highest price for any grade of gasoline in either city during the entire four-month period?

   A) $3.55
   B) $3.75
   C) $3.85
   D) $3.95

Answers and Explanations

3. **(A)** For each month, subtract the price of Regular in Hillsboro from the price of Regular in Oxford. The month with the smallest absolute difference (either positive or negative) was July, with a difference of $3.50 − $3.35 = $0.15.

4. **(B)** The price of Premium cost less than $3.00 in Hillsboro during two months in September ($2.60) and in August ($2.65).

5. **(C)** To find the average price first, add the four prices in the Oxford Regular column together. Then divide this sum by 4 to get the average price per month. The average price per month for Regular in Oxford was $12.40 / 4 = $3.10.

6. **(C)** The highest price for any grade in either city during the entire four-month period was $3.85 in July in Oxford.

Practice Set 1

Use the chart below to answer questions 1–6.

Dollars Spent in Company Budget, by Year and Department, in Thousands

Department	2007		2008	
	Dollars	Percent	Dollars	Percent
Research and Development	30	40	20	16
Overhead	5	7	10	8
Payroll	25	33	50	40
Marketing	15	20	45	36
Totals	75	100	125	100

1. Which department had the second-largest increase in dollars spent from 2007 to 2008?

   A) Research and Development
   B) Overhead
   C) Payroll
   D) Marketing

2. Which department had the highest per-year average of percentage of company budget?

   A) Research and Development
   B) Overhead
   C) Payroll
   D) Marketing

3. For the two years combined, how many more dollars were spent on Research and Development than on Overhead?

   A) $10,000
   B) $15,000
   C) $25,000
   D) $35,000

4. Which department experienced the largest change in percentage of company budget from 2007 to 2008?

   A) Research and Development
   B) Overhead
   C) Payroll
   D) Marketing

5. Which department(s) experienced double-digit increases in percentage of company budget from 2007 to 2008?

   A) Research and Development and Overhead
   B) Overhead, Marketing, and Payroll
   C) Marketing and Payroll
   D) Marketing

6. Which departments used less than one quarter of the company's budget during either 2007 or 2008?

   A) Overhead and Marketing
   B) Overhead, Marketing, and Payroll
   C) Research and Development and Overhead
   D) Research and Development, Overhead, and Marketing

Use the chart below to answer questions 7–12.

Share Price in Dollars of Company Stock by Quarter, 2005–2008

Year	Q1	Q2	Q3	Q4
2008	24	26	37	25
2007	19	31	32	26
2006	14	12	21	17
2005	11	11	14	12

7. Which quarter averaged the highest share price for the four-year period?

   A) Q1
   B) Q2
   C) Q3
   D) Q4

8. How many times did the share price change more than $8 from one quarter to the next?

   A) 2
   B) 3
   C) 4
   D) 5

9. For which year was the Q2 share price less than the Q1 share price?

   A) 2008
   B) 2007
   C) 2006
   D) 2005

10. Which year had the second-largest increase in share price from Q1 to Q4?

   A) 2005
   B) 2006
   C) 2007
   D) 2008

11. How many times did the share price decrease from one quarter to the next?

   A) 3
   B) 4
   C) 5
   D) 6

12. What was the third-highest share price during the entire time period?

   A) $24
   B) $26
   C) $31
   D) $32

Answer Explanations for Practice Set 1

1. **(C)** For each department, subtract the number of dollars spent in 2007 from the number of dollars spent in 2008. Then rank the departments from largest to smallest based on these results. The department with the largest increase in dollars spent was Marketing with an increase of $30,000. The second-largest increase in dollars spent was Payroll, with an increase of $25,000.

2. **(C)** Add each department's 2007 percentage to its 2008 percentage, and then divide each sum by 2 to get each department's average percentage. The highest average percentage was Payroll, with an average percentage of 36.5%.

3. **(D)** Add the total dollars spent on each of Overhead in 2007 and 2008, and then on Research and Development in those two years. The difference is $50,000 − $15,000 = $35,000.

4. **(A)** For each department, subtract the number in the 2007 Percent column from the number in the 2008 Percent column. Then identify the difference with the largest absolute value (since the change could be either positive or negative). The largest change in percent was in Research and

Development, which spent 24 percent less of the company's budget in 2008 than in 2007.

5. **(D)** For each department, subtract the number in the 2007 Percent column from the number in the 2008 Percent column. The only double-digit increase was in Marketing, from 20 percent to 36 percent, an increase of 16 percent.

6. **(D)** Research & Development, Overhead, and Marketing all used less than 25 percent of the company's budget in either 2007 or 2008. Research and Development used only 16 percent in 2008, Overhead used only 7 percent in 2007 and 8 percent in 2008, and Marketing used only 20 percent in 2007.

7. **(C)** For each quarter, add the share prices in each column. No need to divide each total by 4 because the greatest total will have the greatest average. The quarter with the highest total share price was Q3, with a total of $104. So Q3 had the greatest per-year average.

8. **(C)** For each year, subtract the share price of the previous quarter from its next quarter share price. Count the number of instances in which the difference is plus or minus 8.

There are four such instances: Q2 to Q3 in 2006, Q1 to Q2 in 2007, Q2 to Q3 in 2008, and Q3 to Q4 in 2008.

9. **(C)** For each year, compare the share prices from Q1 to Q2. Only in 2006 did the share price drop, from $14 to $12. In the other years, the share price either increased or remained the same from Q1 to Q2.

10. **(B)** For each year, subtract the Q1 share price from the Q4 share price. Then rank the years from largest to smallest based on these differences. The largest increase from Q1 to Q4 was in 2007, with an increase of $7. The second-largest increase was in 2006, with an increase of $3.

11. **(D)** The share price decreased from one quarter to the next six times: Q3 to Q4 in 2005, Q1 to Q2 in 2006, Q3 to Q4 in 2006, Q3 to Q4 in 2007, Q4 in 2007 to Q1 in 2008, and Q3 to Q4 in 2008.

12. **(C)** Scanning for the highest number, and then the next highest is a quick way to rank the listed share prices from all quarters and years from highest to lowest. The highest share price was $37 in Q3 of 2008, the second highest was $32 in Q3 of 2007, and the third highest was $31 in Q2 of 2007.

Practice Set 2

Use the chart below to answer questions 1 through 6.

Points per Game Scored by Players A, B, C, and D During 8-Game Season

Games:	1	2	3	4	Midseason Total	5	6	7	8	Season Total
Player A	12	17	15	22	66	15	19	14	18	132
Player B	20	21	13	18	72	25	12	10	17	136
Player C	14	13	16	21	64	20	18	24	15	141
Player D	18	16	28	19	81	21	23	15	16	156

1. Which player scored the most points during the second half of the season?

   A) Player A
   B) Player B
   C) Player C
   D) Player D

2. Which player had the highest-scoring game of the season?

   A) Player A
   B) Player B
   C) Player C
   D) Player D

3. What was the average number of points scored per player in game 1?

   A) 13
   B) 14
   C) 15
   D) 16

4. How many times did a player score 20 or more points in two consecutive games?

   A) 1
   B) 2
   C) 3
   D) 4

5. Who was the only player to lead the other players in scoring in three games?

   A) Player A
   B) Player B
   C) Player C
   D) Player D

6. How many times did Player C score fewer points than in the previous game?

   A) 2
   B) 3
   C) 4
   D) 5

Use the chart below to answer questions 7–12.

GDP by Country for the Years 1995, 2000, and 2005 in Trillions of Dollars

Country	1995	2000	2005
United States	10	14	15
Japan	4.5	4.5	3.5
China	1	3	5.5
Germany	3.5	4	4
France	3	3.5	3.5
United Kingdom	2.5	3	2.5
Italy	2.5	3	4
Russia	2	3	2.5
Spain	1.5	2	3
Brazil	1	2	2

7. How many countries experienced no change in GDP from 2000 to 2005?

   A) 1
   B) 2
   C) 3
   D) 4

8. What was the average GDP for the United States for the three years listed (in trillions)?

   A) 12
   B) 12.5
   C) 13
   D) 14

9. What was the only country to experience a net decrease in GDP from 1995 to 2005?

   A) United Kingdom
   B) Russia
   C) France
   D) Japan

10. Which country had the fourth highest GDP in 2000?

    A) France
    B) China
    C) Germany
    D) Japan

11. Which country experienced the second largest increase in GDP from 1995 to 2000?

    A) United States
    B) China
    C) Italy
    D) Spain

12. What was the average increase in GDP in the United States *per year* from 1995 to 2005 (in trillions)?

    A) 0.1
    B) 0.5
    C) 1
    D) 2.5

Answer Explanations for Practice Set 2

1. **(C)** Subtract each player's midseason point total from that player's full-season point total. This gives each player's point total for the second half of the season. The player with the highest second-half point total was Player C, with 77 points.

2. **(D)** Scan each player's point totals and note the highest score among them. The player with the highest-scoring game is Player D, who scored 28 points in game 3.

3. **(D)** Add the four numbers in the game 1 column together, and then divide the sum by 4 to get the average points scored per player in game 1. The average points scored per player for game 1 was 64/4 = 16.

4. **(C)** A player scoring 20 or more points in consecutive games occurred three times: Player B in games 1 and 2, Player C in games 4 and 5, and Player D in games 5 and 6.

5. **(B)** For each game, make a note of which player scored the highest number of points, and then tally the results. Only Player B scored the highest number of points in three games: game 1, game 2, and game 5.

6. **(C)** For each of Player C's games, calculate the change in points from the previous game. Player C's point production was less than that of the previous game in four games: game 2 (from 14 to 13 points), game 5 (from 21 to 20 points), game 6 (from 20 to 18 points), and game 8 (from 24 to 15 points).

7. **(C)** For each country, compare the 2000 GDP and the 2005 GDP. Count each comparison in which there was no change. Three countries experienced no change in GDP from 2000 to 2005: Germany, France, and Brazil.

8. **(C)** Add together the U.S. GDP numbers for each year, and then divide the sum by 3 to find the average GDP. The average GDP is $39 trillion/3 = $13 trillion.

9. **(D)** For each country, subtract the 1995 GDP from the 2005 GDP. Any country for which this difference is a negative number experienced a decrease in GDP over this period. The only country to experience a decrease in GDP from 1995 to 2005 was Japan, with a decrease of $1 trillion.

10. **(A)** Rank the countries from highest to lowest based on their 2000 GDP. The countries with the three highest GDPs were the United States, Japan, and Germany, with respective GDPs of $12 trillion, $4.5 trillion, and $4 trillion. The country with the fourth largest GDP in 2000 was France, with a GDP of $3.5 trillion.

11. **(B)** For each country, subtract the 1995 GDP from the 2000 GDP. Then rank the countries from largest to smallest based on these differences. The country with the largest increase in GDP from 1995 to 2000 was the United States, with an increase of $4 trillion. The country with the second largest increase was China, with an increase of $2 trillion.

12. **(B)** Subtract the U.S. 1995 GDP from its 2005 GDP to get its total increase during the period, which was $5 trillion. Then divide this difference by 10 (years) to get the average yearly increase over the 10-year period. The 10-year average was $0.5 trillion.

Practice Set 3

Use the chart below to answer questions 1–6.

County Population by Town and Age Range

Age Range	Springfield	%	Franklin	%	Riverside	%	Jackson	%
0–17	11,000	35	12,000	37	7,500	38	16,500	20
18–34	4,000	13	8,000	25	4,500	23	30,000	36
35–64	9,500	30	7,000	22	1,500	8	18,000	22
65+	7,000	22	5,500	17	6,500	33	19,000	23
Total	**31,500**	**100**	**32,500**	**100**	**20,000**	**100**	**83,500**	**100**

1. Which town has the second-highest percentage of 18- to 34-year-olds?

   A) Springfield
   B) Franklin
   C) Riverside
   D) Jackson

2. How many county residents are age 65 or older?

   A) 19,000
   B) 38,000
   C) 39,000
   D) 83,500

3. How many Jackson residents are under age 35?

   A) 16,500
   B) 30,000
   C) 46,500
   D) 64,500

4. What is the average number of 35- to 64-year-olds living in each town?

   A) 7,500
   B) 8,000
   C) 8,500
   D) 9,000

5. For how many towns is the 35- to 64-year-old age range the smallest population segment?

   A) 1
   B) 2
   C) 3
   D) 4

6. How many more residents in Springfield are 18 years old or older than are residents in Springfield under 18 years old?

   A) 9,000
   B) 9,500
   C) 10,500
   D) 11,000

Use the chart below to answer questions 7–12.

Sales of Books by Week, in Thousands of Copies				
Week	**Book #1**	**Book #2**	**Book #3**	**Book #4**
Week 1	100	50	135	120
Week 2	85	55	90	95
Week 3	60	70	60	70
Week 4	45	80	40	60
Month 1 Sales	**290**	**255**	**325**	**345**
Week 5	40	75	35	50
Week 6	35	65	35	40
Week 7	45	60	30	25
Week 8	40	55	30	20
Month 2 Sales	**160**	**255**	**130**	**135**

7. Which book had the largest decrease in sales from Week 1 to Week 8?

   A) Book #1
   B) Book #2
   C) Book #3
   D) Book #4

8. What was the average number of copies sold per book in Month 2?

   A) 140,000
   B) 150,000
   C) 160,000
   D) 170,000

9. During which week did Book #2 sell the most copies?

   A) Week 1
   B) Week 2
   C) Week 3
   D) Week 4

10. How many times did a book sell more copies in a given week than it did the previous week?

    A) 1
    B) 2
    C) 3
    D) 4

11. Which book sold the third most copies during Week 2?

    A) Book #1
    B) Book #2
    C) Book #3
    D) Book #4

12. Which book sold the most copies during the entire two-month period?

    A) Book #1
    B) Book #2
    C) Book #3
    D) Book #4

Answer Explanations for Practice Set 3

1. **(B)** Rank the towns from largest to smallest based on the percentage of their population that is aged 18–34. The town with the highest percentage of 18- to 34-year-olds is Jackson, with 36 percent. The town with the second-highest percentage of 18- to 34-year olds is Franklin, with 25 percent.

2. **(B)** Add together the 65+ populations of all four towns. There are 38,000 total residents aged 65 or older in the county.

3. **(C)** Add together the 0- to 17-year-old and 18- to 34-year-old populations for the town of Jackson. This produces a total of 46,500 Jackson residents under the age of 35.

4. **(D)** First, add together the 35- to 64-year-old populations of all four towns. That total is 36,000. Then divide this sum by 4 to get the average number of 35- to 64-year olds living in each town. The average number of 35- to 64-year-olds per town is 9,000.

5. **(A)** For each town, make a note of which age range represents the smallest percentage of that town's population. The only town for which the 35- to 64-year-old age group represents the smallest population segment is Riverside, with only 1,500 residents between the ages of 35 and 64.

6. **(B)** First, add together the populations aged 18–34, 35–64, and 65+ for Springfield to get the total number of Springfield residents who are 18 years old or older. Then subtract the 0–17 population of Springfield from this sum to get the difference between the two populations. There are 20,500 − 11,000 = 9,500 more residents who are 18 years old or older residents than there are residents under 18 years of age in Springfield.

7. **(C)** For each book, subtract its Week 1 sales from its Week 8 sales. The book with the largest difference is the book with the largest decrease. Book #3 experienced the largest decrease in sales from Week 1 to Week 8, with a decrease of 105,000 copies.

8. **(D)** First, add together the Month 2 sales of each book. Then divide this sum by 4 to obtain the average sales per book. The average number of copies sold per book in Month 2 was 170,000.

9. **(D)** Rank the weeks from largest to smallest, based on the number of copies of Book #2 sold. Book #2 sold the most copies in Week 4, during which it sold 80,000 copies.

10. **(D)** A book sold more copies than in it did in the previous week four times. Book #1 experienced an increase in sales from Week 6 to Week 7, and Book #2 experienced increases in sales from Week 1 to Week 2, from Week 2 to Week 3, and from Week 3 to Week 4.

11. **(A)** Rank the book sales from most to least based on Week 2 sales. Book #4 sold the most copies (95,000), Book #3 sold the second most copies (90,000), and Book #1 sold the third most copies (85,000) during Week 2.

12. **(B)** Add each book's Month 1 sales to its Month 2 sales. Then rank the books from most to least based on these sums. The book that sold the most copies during the entire two-month period was Book #2, with 510,000 copies sold.

Practice Set 4

Use the chart below to answer questions 1–6.

Students Enrolled in a College Business Program, by Major and by Year

Major	2006	%	2007	%	2008	%	2009	%
Finance	77	32	68	27	69	27	59	23
Marketing	65	27	71	28	64	25	71	27
Management	58	24	63	25	62	25	65	25
Info Tech (IT)	41	17	52	20	58	23	67	26
Total	241	100	254	100	253	100	262	100

1. In which year did the fewest number of students major in Marketing?

   A) 2006
   B) 2007
   C) 2008
   D) 2009

2. In how many years did more than 30 percent of business students major in a subject?

   A) 0
   B) 1
   C) 2
   D) 3

3. How many different times during the years indicated in the chart did exactly one fourth of the total number of business students major in any subject?

   A) 1
   B) 2
   C) 3
   D) 4

4. Which major subject experienced the greatest increase in number of students from 2006 to 2009?

   A) Finance
   B) Marketing
   C) Management
   D) Info Tech (IT)

5. What was the greatest change in percentage in consecutive years for any major subject?

   A) 3 percent
   B) 4 percent
   C) 5 percent
   D) 6 percent

6. Which major subjects had more than 70 students enrolled at any time during the four-year span?

   A) Finance and Marketing
   B) Marketing and Management
   C) Finance and Management
   D) Management and Info Tech (IT)

Use the chart below to answer questions 7–12.

Sales and Sales Leads Generated per Month by Salespeople A, B, C, and D

Month	Salesperson A Sales	Leads	Salesperson B Sales	Leads	Salesperson C Sales	Leads	Salesperson D Sales	Leads
April	50	35	25	40	70	15	40	45
May	60	20	50	55	75	20	50	50
June	45	25	35	40	65	15	55	65
July	40	45	30	45	80	20	60	55
Total	**195**	**125**	**140**	**180**	**290**	**70**	**205**	**215**

7. Which salesperson had the most combined sales and leads during the four-month period?

   A) Salesperson A
   B) Salesperson B
   C) Salesperson C
   D) Salesperson D

8. Which salesperson made the least number of sales during the four-month period?

   A) Salesperson A
   B) Salesperson B
   C) Salesperson C
   D) Salesperson D

9. What were the most leads any salesperson generated during a single month?

   A) 60
   B) 65
   C) 80
   D) 215

10. Which salesperson had more leads than sales during every month?

    A) Salesperson A
    B) Salesperson B
    C) Salesperson C
    D) Salesperson D

11. What were the average sales per salesperson in June?

    A) 50
    B) 55
    C) 60
    D) 65

12. Which salesperson had the greatest difference between number of May sales and number of May leads?

    A) Salesperson A
    B) Salesperson B
    C) Salesperson C
    D) Salesperson D

Answer Explanations for Practice Set 4

1. **(C)** Rank the years from fewest to greatest based on the number of students majoring in Marketing. The year with the fewest number of students majoring in Marketing was 2008, with only 64 students majored in Marketing.

2. **(B)** More than 30 percent of business students majored in a subject in only one year: 32 percent of business students majored in Finance in 2006.

3. **(D)** According to the percentages in the chart, exactly one fourth (25 percent) of the total number of business students majored in a subject four times: Management in 2007, 2008, and 2009, and Marketing in 2008.

4. **(D)** For each major, subtract its 2006 number of students from its 2009 number of students. Then rank the majors from largest to smallest based on these differences. The major with the largest increase in number of students from 2006 to 2009 was Info Tech (IT), with an increase of 26 students.

5. **(C)** For each major, calculate the change in percentage between consecutive years. The largest percentage change was in Finance: its percentage of total business students decreased by 5 percent between 2006 and 2007.

6. **(A)** Both Finance and Marketing had more than 70 students enrolled at any time during the four-year span: Finance in 2006, and Marketing in 2007 and 2009.

7. **(D)** For each salesperson, combine their sales and leads numbers from the Total row. The salesperson with the most combined sales and leads was Salesperson D, with 420 combined sales and leads.

8. **(B)** Compare each salesperson's sales number from the Total row. The salesperson who made the least sales during the four-month period was Salesperson B, with 140 sales.

9. **(B)** For each salesperson, compare the numbers from each month in the Leads column and make a note of the largest number. The most leads any salesperson generated during any month was 65, by Salesperson D in June.

10. **(B)** For each salesperson, compare the sales number and the leads number from each month. The only salesperson to have more leads than sales in every month was Salesperson B.

11. **(A)** Add together sales numbers of each salesperson in the month of June. Divide this sum by 4 to get the average sales. The average sales per salesperson in June were 200/4 = 50 sales.

12. **(C)** For each salesperson, subtract the number of May leads from the number of May sales. Then identify the salesperson with the greatest difference. The salesperson with the greatest difference between number of May sales and number of May leads was Salesperson C, with a difference of 55.

Practice Set 5

Use the chart below to answer questions 1–6.

Television Viewers (in Millions) and Ratings Share per Week

Week	Program A Viewers	Program A Nielson	Program B Viewers	Program B Nielson	Program C Viewers	Program C Nielson	Program D Viewers	Program D Nielson
Week 1	20	2.60	11	1.43	15	1.95	18	2.34
Week 2	18	2.34	12	1.56	19	2.47	15	1.95
Week 3	17	2.21	13	1.69	18	2.34	14	1.82
Week 4	17	2.21	18	2.34	17	2.21	24	3.12
Total	72	9.36	54	7.02	69	8.97	71	9.23

1. What was the largest single-week increase in number of viewers for any of the four programs?

   A) 1,300,000
   B) 4,000,000
   C) 10,000,000
   D) 24,000,000

2. What was the only program to increase its Nielson Ratings Share every week?

   A) Program A
   B) Program B
   C) Program C
   D) Program D

3. How many people watched any of the four programs during Week 3?

   A) 60,000,000
   B) 62,000,000
   C) 64,000,000
   D) 64,500,000

4. How many times did any of the four programs have a Nielson Ratings Share lower than 2.00?

   A) 4
   B) 5
   C) 6
   D) 7

5. Which program experienced the largest change in number of viewers from Week 1 to Week 4?

   A) Program A
   B) Program B
   C) Program C
   D) Program D

6. How many viewers did Program A average per week?

   A) 16,500,000
   B) 17,000,000
   C) 17,500,000
   D) 18,000,000

Use the chart below to answer questions 7–12.

Nutritional Content of Menu Items at a Fast Food Chain

Nutritional Content	Bacon Cheeseburger	Chicken Sandwich	Large French Fries	Chicken Caesar Salad
Calories	1,100	700	450	620
Fat (g)	48	20	17	15
%DV	74%	31%	26%	23%
Saturated Fat (g)	20	6	7	1
%DV	133%	40%	47%	7%
Carbohydrates (g)	65	45	50	40
%DV	41%	28%	31%	25%
Sodium (mg)	1,600	790	950	510
%DV	107%	53%	63%	34%
Sugar (g)	6	11	0	14
%DV	n/a	n/a	n/a	n/a
Protein (g)	46	25	6	28
%DV	54%	29%	7%	33%

7. Which menu item has more than 100 percent of the %DV of any nutritional item?

A) Bacon Cheeseburger
B) Chicken Sandwich
C) Large French Fries
D) Chicken Caesar Salad

8. Which menu item has the largest difference between the amount of protein and the amount of saturated fat?

A) Bacon Cheeseburger
B) Chicken Sandwich
C) Large French Fries
D) Chicken Caesar Salad

9. What is the average amount of carbohydrates per menu item?

A) 40
B) 45
C) 50
D) 60

10. Which menu item has more grams of saturated fat than grams of protein?

A) Bacon Cheeseburger
B) Chicken Sandwich
C) Large French Fries
D) Chicken Caesar Salad

11. Which menu items contain more sugar than saturated fat?

A) Bacon Cheeseburger and Chicken Caesar Salad
B) Chicken Sandwich and Chicken Caesar Salad
C) Chicken Sandwich and Large French Fries
D) Large French Fries and Chicken Caesar Salad

12. Which nutritional item has the third-highest %DV in the Chicken Sandwich?

A) Fat
B) Saturated Fat
C) Carbohydrates
D) Protein

Answer Explanations for Practice Set 5

1. **(C)** For each week and each program, subtract the previous week's number of viewers from that week's number of viewers. The largest difference will be the largest increase. The largest single-week increase in number of viewers was 10,000,000, from Week 3 to Week 4 for Program D.

2. **(B)** Program B was the only program to increase its Nielson Ratings Share during every week (1.43 in Week 1, 1.56 in Week 2, 1.69 in Week 3, and 2.34 in Week 4).

3. **(B)** Add together the number of Week 3 viewers for all four programs. The total was 17M + 13M + 18M + 14M = 62,000,000 viewers for the four programs combined in Week 3.

4. **(C)** A program had a Nielson Ratings Share of less than 2.00 on six occasions: Program B in Weeks 1, 2, and 3, Program C in Week 1, and Program D in Weeks 2 and 3.

5. **(B)** For each program, subtract the number of viewers in Week 1 from the number of viewers in Week 4. The largest absolute difference will be the largest change (ignore signs because the question did not specify positive or negative change). The program that experienced the largest change in number of viewers from Week 1 to Week 4 was Program C, with an increase of 18M − 11M = 7,000,000 viewers.

6. **(D)** Divide the total number of Program A viewers during the period by 4 (the four-week totals are already calculated in the Total row). The average number of Program A viewers per week was 72M/4 = 18,000,000.

7. **(A)** Look through the %DV rows, and make a note of which menu items have more than 100 percent of the %DV of any nutritional item. The only menu item with more than 100 percent of the %DV of any nutritional item is the Bacon Cheeseburger, with 133 percent of the %DV of saturated fat and 107 percent of the %DV of sodium.

8. **(D)** For each menu item, subtract the number of grams of saturated fat from the number of grams of protein. The largest difference is in the Chicken Caesar Salad, with a difference of 28 − 1 = 27 grams.

9. **(C)** First, add together the number of grams of carbohydrates of every menu item. Then divide this sum by 4 to get the average. The average number of carbohydrates per menu item is 200/4 = 50 grams.

10. **(C)** Compare the number of grams of saturated fat for each menu item with the number of grams of protein. Only the Large French Fries menu item has more grams of saturated fat (7 g) than grams of protein (6 g).

11. **(B)** For each menu item, subtract the number of grams of saturated fat from the number of grams of sugar. Each menu item with a positive difference contains more sugar than saturated fat. The menu items that contain more sugar than saturated fat are the Chicken Sandwich and the Chicken Caesar Salad.

12. **(A)** Rank each nutritional item for the Chicken Sandwich from highest to lowest based on its %DV. The nutritional item with the highest %DV in the Chicken Sandwich is sodium (53%), then saturated fat (40%), and then fat (31%).

Clerical Abilities Analysis Chart for Record Keeping (Chart Reading)

Use the following chart to carefully analyze your results of the *record keeping (chart reading)* question type. This will help you evaluate your strengths and weaknesses. This analysis should help you focus your study and review efforts on specific types of problems.

Practice Set	Total Number of Questions	Number Correct	Number Incorrect	Number Unanswered
Set 1	12			
Set 2	12			
Set 3	12			
Set 4	12			
Set 5	12			

Because there is no penalty for incorrect answers on most of the questions in the Clerical Abilities section, you should have left no question unanswered. Even if you didn't have time to answer a question, you should have at least filled in the answer space with an educated guess.

REVIEWING THE KEY STRATEGIES

Remember to:

1. Understand the meaning of the chart by reading its title and subheadings before answering the questions.
2. Isolate and focus only on the parts of the chart that are relevant to the question you are answering.
3. If it helps to keep your place, use your answer sheet as a straightedge to read across columns.
4. If a chart set contains several questions, answer the easy questions first and leave the difficult question(s) for after you've become more familiar with the chart.
5. Use pencil and paper (or a calculator, if permitted) to do difficult computations. Do easy ones in your head.

USING A DIRECTORY

This question type tests your ability to refer back continually to a listing of names and numbers plus a list of revisions and to assess how the original information changes based upon the revisions.

Sample Practice Set

Questions 1–3 are based on the following directory and list of changes:

Directory

Name	Emp. Type	Position
Robert, Bell,	Warehouse	Packer
Ventre, Judith	Offlce	Secretary
Proctor, June	Warehouse	Packer
Underwood, Vicky	Office	Salesperson
Lackey, Joseph	Office	Salesperson
Walker, Carlos	Office	Manager
Duvall, Harrison	Warehouse	Packer
Kaiser, Hilary	Warehouse	Supervisor
Graham, Albert	Office	Salesperson
Schaffer, Tom	Office	Salesperson
Ingram, Jeannie	Office	Accountant
Sims, Harvey	Warehouse	Packer
White, Gail	Office	Salesperson
Brugman, Steve	Warehouse	Packer
Wheeler, Kyle	Office	Accountant

List of Changes:

- Employee email addresses follow the format *firstname.lastname@companyabcd. com* (ex: Kyle Wheeler is *kyle.wheeler@companyabcd.com*). However, all warehouse employees share the common email address *inventory@companyabcd.com*.
- The "Secretary" position is now called "Administrative Assistant."
- Harvey Sims has been promoted to a Supervisor position in the warehouse and is no longer a Packer. All warehouse employees work under the two Supervisors, and all office employees work under the Manager.

1. How many Packers currently work in the warehouse?

   A) 4
   B) 5
   C) 6
   D) 7

Notice that in the Directory, five Packers are listed. However, Harvey Sims was promoted to Supervisor and, according to the List of Changes Sims "is no longer a Packer." Therefore the correct answer is (A) 4, and not (B) 5. This is a typical *using a directory* question, in that the information in the Directory is slightly altered by the information in the List of Changes.

2. What position does Judith Ventre currently hold?

A) Secretary
B) Administrative Assistant
C) Salesperson
D) Packer

Here again the Directory information is slightly altered by the List of Changes. Judith Ventre is listed in the Directory as a "Secretary," but as per the changes, her position is now officially called "Administrative Assistant." So the correct answer is (B), not (A).

3. To which email address should an email for the office manager be sent?

A) *manager@companyabcd.com*
B) *carloswalker@companyabcd.com*
C) *carlos.walker@companyabcd.com*
D) *cwalker@companyabcd.com*

The office manager is Carlos Walker. As per the list of changes, an email for Carlos Walker should be sent to the address *carlos.walker@companyabcd.com*, which is answer choice (C).

Helpful Techniques and Strategies

1. Nearly all the questions in each set will require an alteration in the Directory information. So your focus should be primarily on the information in the List of Changes, which you will use as you refer back to the Directory listing as you alter the information.
2. When starting a problem set, first quickly scan the Directory to understand how it is laid out, but don't worry about learning or memorizing its contents. Rather, your main focus should be on the List of Changes. Carefully read the List of Changes to be aware of which items in the Directory will be affected by the revisions. You don't have to memorize this information, but you should stay aware of which names and items are affected as you answer the questions.
3. If permitted to write on your test booklet, circle or mark directly in the List of Changes the names of the elements that change in the Directory listing. Then make needed changes (strike outs, alterations, notations, etc.) directly in the Listing based upon the List of Changes to call your attention to items that are affected by the changes.

Practice Set 1

Use the directory and list of changes below to answer questions 1–5.

Directory

Name	RM. No.	Ext.
Anderson, Terry	105	2809
Chapman, Karen	127	3913
Edwards, Michelle	229	3652
Kent, Edward	251	7163
Markham, Eric	237	5245
Ray, Tammy	207	1823
Reese, Benjamin	346	4092
Sutton, Dave	313	6364
Thompson, Ruth	322	5238
Williams, Janice	348	8271

List of Changes:

- Dave Sutton and Michelle Edwards have switched offices and extension numbers since the directory was published.
- Tammy Ray has moved to room 330, but her extension has not changed.
- All calls for employees with room numbers higher than 300 should be directed to Janice Williams.

1. Which of the following room numbers does not currently belong to anyone listed in the directory?

   A) 207
   B) 330
   C) 346
   D) 348

2. Which of the following employees takes calls directly at the extension listed in the directory?

   A) Michelle Edwards
   B) Eric Markham
   C) Tammy Ray
   D) Ruth Thompson

3. What is Michelle Edwards's room number?

   A) 229
   B) 207
   C) 313
   D) 348

4. To which extension should a call for Tammy Ray be directed?

   A) 207
   B) 330
   C) 1823
   D) 8271

5. To which extension should a call for Dave Sutton be directed?

   A) 6364
   B) 8271
   C) 3652
   D) 7163

Use the directory and list of changes below to answer questions 6–10.

Directory

Name	Floor	Dept.	Ext.
Marshall, Kirk	1	Administrative	113
Vance, Joel	1	Administrative	121
Cole, Pamela	2	Accounting	212
Gibson, Mary	2	Accounting	243
Powers, Leslie	2	Marketing	251
Utley, Damien	3	Legal	339
Allen, Jackie	3	Legal	307
Rucker, April	4	Legal	414
Vaughn, Jerry	4	Legal	402
Nixon, Kevin	4	Sales	425
Witherspoon, Randy	4	Sales	434
Majors, Rachel	4	Sales	471

List of Changes:

- All calls for the legal department should be directed to Joel Vance.
- All calls for employees on the fourth floor should be directed to Kirk Marshall, unless the employee is in the legal department.
- Leslie Powers has moved to the third floor and is now at extension 352. Mary Gibson moved into Leslie's old office and can now be reached at Leslie's old extension.

6. To which extension should a call for Rachel Majors be directed?

   A) 113
   B) 121
   C) 352
   D) 471

7. Which of the following employees takes their calls directly?

   A) Jackie Allen
   B) Kirk Marshall
   C) April Rucker
   D) Kevin Nixon

8. If a caller dials extension 251, which employee will the caller reach?

   A) Mary Gibson
   B) Leslie Powers
   C) Kirk Marshall
   D) Joel Vance

9. Which floor currently houses the second-most number of employees?

   A) floor 1
   B) floor 2
   C) floor 3
   D) floor 4

10. To which extension should a call for Jerry Vaughn be directed?

   A) 113
   B) 121
   C) 412
   D) 414

Answer Explanations for Practice Set 1

1. **(A)** Becase Tammy Ray moved out of room 207 into room 330, room 207 does not currently belong to anyone in the directory.

2. **(B)** Of the answer choices, Eric Markham is the only employee who takes his calls directly at his listed extension. Michelle Edwards has switched extensions with Dave Sutton, and Tammy Ray's and Ruth Thompson's calls are directed to Janice Williams because they both have room numbers larger than 300.

3. **(C)** Michelle Edwards switched rooms with Dave Sutton, so she is now in room 313.

4. **(D)** Tammy Ray moved to room 330, so her calls should be directed to Janice Williams (because her room number is higher than 330). Janice' Williams's extension is 8271.

5. **(C)** Because Dave Sutton switched offices and extension numbers with Michelle Edwards, he is now in room 229 and at extension 3652.

6. **(A)** Because all calls for employees on the fourth floor should be directed to Kirk Marshall, the call should be directed to extension 113.

7. **(B)** Kirk Marshall takes his calls directly. Calls for Jackie Allen and April Rucker go to Joel Vance as they are in the legal department, and calls for Kevin Nixon go to Kirk Marshall as he is on the fourth floor.

8. **(A)** A caller who dials extension 251 will reach Mary Gibson. Extension 251 was formerly Leslie Powers's extension, but it now belongs to Mary Gibson.

9. **(C)** Because Leslie Powers moved to floor 3, floor 3 currently houses the second-most number of employees, with three. The floor with the most employees is floor 4, with five employees.

10. **(B)** Because Jerry Vaughn is in the legal department, his calls should be directed to Joel Vance at extension 121.

Practice Set 2

Use the directory and list of changes below to answer questions 1–5.

Directory

Name	Floor	Office#	Ext.
Kaitlin Wall	1	101	0
Craig Mendez	1	102	1
Sean Wagner	1	103	2
Emmett Dodson	1	104	3
Erin Ashmore	1	105	4
Anna Zeigler	2	201	5
Ashley Nichols	2	202	6
Kenneth Green	2	203	7
James Esposito	2	204	8
Melody Freeman	2	205	9
General Voicemail	n/a	n/a	1111

List of Changes:

- Kenneth Green and Melody Freeman are currently in a meeting in Erin Ashmore's office. All other listed employees are in their offices.
- Three zeroes have been added to the beginning of every extension number except for Kaitlin Wall's and General Voicemail.
- Anna Ziegler is meeting with a client, and has requested her calls be forwarded to General Voicemail. All calls for unlisted employees should also be forwarded to General Voicemail.

1. How many listed employees are currently on floor 2?

   A) 3
   B) 4
   C) 5
   D) 6

2. To which extension should a call for Jason Tucker be directed?

   A) 0
   B) 4
   C) 0004
   D) 1111

3. If a caller wants to leave a message on Melody Freeman's voicemail, which extension should be dialed?

   A) 0
   B) 9
   C) 1111
   D) 0009

4. Which office number is Kenneth Green currently in?

   A) 105
   B) 202
   C) 203
   D) 205

5. To which extension should a call to Anna Ziegler be directed?

   A) 0
   B) 4
   C) 0004
   D) 1111

Use the directory and list of changes below to answer questions 6–10.

Directory

Name	Ext.	Mail Code	Name	Ext.	Mail Code
Angle, Brian	871	A-17	Powell, Eleanor	234	C-12
Corsi, John	305	B-14	Philips, Marie	601	B-28
Davis, Rita	624	A-04	Stinson, Nelson	725	B-01
Erickson, Joann	012	C-28	Walsh, Linda	944	B-18
Fisher, Randall	333	B-22	Webb, Lauren	109	A-11
Lawrence, Mark	296	A-36	Wilson, Keith	352	C-33
Meyers, Todd	142	C-16	York, Jennifer	515	A-09

List of Changes:

- All mail addressed to employees with mail codes beginning with "B" should be delivered to Nelson Stinson.
- Jennifer York is an administrative assistant for Brian Angle, Joann Erickson, and Keith Wilson, and takes all of their calls and mail.
- Eleanor Powell and Marie Phillips have switched offices and mail codes, but not extensions.

6. To which mail code should a letter addressed to Randall Fisher be delivered?

   A) 333
   B) B-22
   C) B-01
   D) A-09

7. To which extension should a call for Keith Wilson be directed?

   A) 352
   B) C-33
   C) A-09
   D) 515

8. To which extension should a call for Marie Phillips be directed?

   A) 234
   B) 601
   C) C-22
   D) C-12

9. To which mail code should a letter addressed to Eleanor Powell be delivered?

   A) 601
   B) C-12
   C) B-28
   D) B-01

10. Which of the following employees receives calls and mail directly at the extension and mail code listed in the directory?

    A) John Corsi
    B) Todd Meyers
    C) Brian Angle
    D) Linda Walsh

Answer Explanations for Practice Set 2

1. **(A)** Normally five employees are on floor 2, but because Kenneth Green and Melody Freeman are currently in a meeting in Erin Ashmore's office on floor 1, there are now only three employees on floor 2.
2. **(D)** Because Jason Tucker is not listed in the directory, the call should be directed to General Voicemail at extension 1111.
3. **(D)** Although Melody Freeman is in a meeting, her extension is still 0009 (as three zeroes were added to the beginning of her extension number). This is the extension that should be dialed to reach her voicemail.

4. **(A)** Kenneth Green is currently in a meeting in Erin Ashmore's office, which is office number 105.
5. **(D)** Anna has requested her calls be forwarded to General Voicemail, so the call should be directed to extension 1111.
6. **(C)** Randall Fisher has a mail code beginning with "B," so the letter should be delivered to Nelson Stinson at mail code B-01.
7. **(D)** Calls for Keith Wilson should be directed to Jennifer York at extension 515.
8. **(B)** A call for Marie Phillips should be directed to extension 601. Though she

switched offices and mail codes with Eleanor Powell, they did not switch extensions.

9. **(D)** Eleanor Powell switched mail codes with Marie Phillips, so her new mail code is B-28. This mail code begins with a "B," so her mail should be delivered to Nelson Stinson at mail code B-01.

10. **(B)** Todd Meyers receives his calls and mail directly at the extension and mail code listed in the directory. John Corsi and Linda Walsh have their mail forwarded to Nelson Stinson, and Brian Angle has his calls and mail forwarded to Jennifer York.

Practice Set 3

Use the directory and list of changes below to answer questions 1–5.

Directory

Name	Floor	Dept.	Divison
Porter, Mark	5	Accounting	Auditing
Monroe, Melissa	1	Marketing	Sales
Boatman, Anne	4	Information Tech.	Help Desk
Donaldson, Cheryl	3	Accounting	Budgeting
Osborne, John	1	Information Tech.	Systems
Talley, Trent	1	Marketing	Advertising
Quinn, Anthony	1	Marketing	Research
Ceraluso, Stephanie	1	Marketing	Sales
Blair, Herbert	3	Accounting	Auditing
Yates, Annie	5	Information Tech.	Help Desk
Ward, Brett	2	Marketing	Research
Jefferson, Leigh	5	Accounting	Auditing

List of Changes:

- All employees in the Help Desk division have been moved to the first floor.
- All employees with offices on floor 3 have been temporarily moved to floor 4 while renovations are completed.

1. Which of the following is NOT a division of the Marketing department?

   A) Budgeting
   B) Sales
   C) Advertising
   D) Research

2. On what floor does the only listed employee in the Budgeting division work?

   A) 1
   B) 2
   C) 3
   D) 4

3. Which of the following groups of employees all work on the same floor?

   A) Mark Porter, Annie Yates, Leigh Jefferson
   B) Melissa Monroe, Anthony Quinn, Brett Ward
   C) Cheryl Donaldson, Herbert Blair, Leigh Jefferson
   D) Anne Boatman, Anthony Quinn, Annie Yates

4. Which of the following departments has no listed employees on floors 2, 3, 4, or 5?

   A) Marketing
   B) Information Tech.
   C) Sales
   D) Accounting

5. Which of the following divisions currently has/have employees on floor 4?

   A) Help Desk
   B) Information Tech.
   C) Help Desk, Budgeting, and Auditing
   D) Budgeting and Auditing

Use the directory and list of changes below to answer questions 6–10.

Directory

Name	Dept.	Phone #	Email ID
Dixon, Helena	Accounting	617-555-0129	hdixon
Durham, Harold	Client Relations	617-555-3582	hdurham
Edgehill, Daniel	Administrative	617-555-1111	info
Frederick, Connie	Client Relations	617-555-2360	cfrederick
Goodwin, Martha	Legal	617-555-0437	mgoodwin
Hampton, Frank	Engineering	617-555-3249	fhampton
Montrose, Betty	Engineering	617-555-1672	bmontrose
Norris, Anna	Legal	617-555-2010	anorris
Puckett, Cindy	Landstar	818-555-4401	cpuckett
Rice, Richard	Engineering	617-555-8390	rrice
Summers, Wade	Landstar	818-555-0124	wsummers
Young, Landon	Landstar	818-555-7268	lyoung

List of Changes:

- Employee email addresses are the employee's email ID followed by "@companyabcd.com." However, email addresses of employees in the Landstar department are the employee's email ID followed by "@landstarinc.net."
- Email IDs for all unlisted employees are comprised of the first letter of the first name followed by the entire last name.
- Connie Frederick has moved to the Landstar department, but kept her phone # and email ID.
- Anna Norris and Helena Dixon have switched offices and telephone numbers.

6. What is Landstar employee Wesley Stevens's email address?

   A) *wesley.stevens@landstarinc.net*
   B) *wstevens@landstarinc.net*
   C) *wstevens@companyabcd.com*
   D) wstevens

7. What is the telephone number for the only listed Accounting employee?

   A) 617-555-1029
   B) 617-555-3582
   C) 617-555-1111
   D) 617-555-2010

8. What is Daniel Edgehill's email address?

   A) *dedgehill@companyabcd.com*
   B) *daniel.edgehill@companyabcd.com*
   C) *dedgehill@landstarinc.net*
   D) *info@companyabcd.com*

9. What is the telephone number for the employee with the email ID "anorris"?

   A) Anna Norris
   B) 617-555-0129
   C) 617-555-2010
   D) 818-555-4401

10. What is Connie Frederick's email address?

   A) cfrederick
   B) *cfrederick@companyabcd.com*
   C) *cfrederick@landstarinc.net*
   D) *connie.frederick@companyabcd.com*

Answer Explanations for Practice Set 3

1. **(A)** Budgeting is not a division of the Marketing department. It is a division of the Accounting department.

2. **(D)** Cheryl Donaldson is the only listed Budgeting employee, and because all employees with offices on floor 3 have been moved to floor 4, she currently works on floor 4.

3. **(D)** Because all Help Desk employees were moved to the first floor, Anne Boatman, Anthony Quinn, and Annie Yates all work on the first floor.

4. **(B)** Information Tech. has no listed employees on floors 2, 3, 4 or 5, since all Help Desk employees were moved to the first floor. There are also no Sales employees on these floors, but Sales is a division and not a department.

5. **(D)** Since all Help Desk employees were moved to the first floor and all third floor employees were moved to the fourth floor, Budgeting and Auditing are now currently the only divisions with employees on floor 4.

6. **(B)** Because Wesley Stevens is an unlisted employee, his email handle is "wstevens." He is a Landstar employee, so his email address is *wstevens@landstarinc.net*.

7. **(D)** Helena Dixon is the only listed Accounting employee, and she has switched offices and telephone numbers with Anna Norris. Therefore, her phone number is 617-555-2010.

8. **(D)** As per the directory, Daniel Edgehill's email address is *info@companyabcd.com*.

9. **(B)** The employee with the email ID "anorris" is Anna Norris. Because Anna Norris switched offices and telephone numbers with Helena Dixon, her telephone number is 617-555-0129.

10. **(C)** Connie Frederick has moved to the "Landstar" department, so her email address is *cfrederick@landstarinc.net*.

Practice Set 4

Use the directory and list of changes below to answer questions 1–5.

Directory

Name	Ext.	Supervisor
Applegate, Roger	2356	Jenny Gillen
Britton, Ellen	6910	Carl Vickers
Eubanks, Victoria	9513	Carl Vickers
Morrison, Stephen	2865	Shawn Carlson
Moore, Denise	1074	Jenny Gillen
Owens, Laura	3562	Shawn Carlson
Parker, Jack	1039	Shawn Carlson
Vanhooser, Wesley	8515	Carl Vickers
Weaver, Lance	9874	Jenny Gillen
Wyatt, Marlene	3798	Jenny Gillen

List of Changes:

- Calls for employees under Carl Vickers should go to his extension, 2321.
- Shawn Carlson is no longer with the company. All employees listed under Shawn are now under Taylor Greene, except for Jack Parker, who now works under Jenny Gillen.

1. Who is the supervisor for the employee at extension 2865?

   A) Jenny Gillen
   B) Shawn Carlson
   C) Carl Vickers
   D) Taylor Greene

2. How many employees currently work under Jenny Gillen?

   A) 3
   B) 4
   C) 5
   D) 6

3. Which of the following employees is NOT currently a supervisor at the company?

   A) Jenny Gillen
   B) Shawn Carlson
   C) Carl Vickers
   D) Taylor Greene

4. To which extension should a call for Wesley Vanhooser be directed?

   A) 1039
   B) 8515
   C) 9874
   D) 2321

5. What are the extensions of the two employees who are alphabetized incorrectly in the company directory?

   A) 2865 and 1074
   B) 9513 and 2865
   C) 9874 and 3798
   D) 8515 and 9874

Use the directory and list of changes below to answer questions 6–10.

Directory

Name	Ext.	Mailbox#	Name	Ext.	Mailbox#
Avery, Barbara	237	2B	Prosser, Josh	248	2B
Caveny, Dennis	256	2C	Reid, Shirley	255	2D
Easley, Hubert	274	2C	Tedder, Amelia	273	2D
Fleming, Amy	242	2B	Valdez, Dawn	227	2C
Irwin, Louise	203	2A	Vier, Wendy	214	2A
Moore, Cheryl	201	2D	Wright, Edgar	262	2A
O'Brien, Floyd	283	2A	Zimmerman, Tim	202	2D

List of Changes:

- All calls for employees with mailbox number 2A should be forwarded to Cheryl Moore.
- All employees with extensions beginning with "20" are administrative staff, and mail addressed to them should be delivered to the general mailbox (mailbox number 1A).
- Hubert Easley and Shirley Reid were temporary staff and have since left the company. Stan Pressley is now at Hubert's old extension and mailbox number, and Charlotte Wall is now at Shirley's old extension and mailbox number.

6. To which mailbox should a letter to Tim Zimmerman be delivered?

   A) 2A
   B) 2D
   C) 202
   D) 1A

7. Which employee receives calls at extension 255?

   A) Shirley Reid
   B) Charlotte Wall
   C) Cheryl Moore
   D) Stan Pressley

8. Which of the following employees currently receives calls at his or her listed extension?

   A) Floyd O'Brien
   B) Shirley Reid
   C) Cheryl Moore
   D) Hubert Easley

9. To which extension should a call for Edgar Wright be directed?

   A) 2A
   B) 2D
   C) 262
   D) 201

10. To which mailbox should a package for Wendy Vier be delivered?

    A) 2A
    B) 2B
    C) 2C
    D) 2D

Answer Explanations for Practice Set 4

1. **(D)** Stephen Morrison is the employee at extension 2865, and he now works under Taylor Greene, as per the list of changes.

2. **(C)** Four employees are listed under Jenny Gillen in the directory, and Jack Parker is now also under Jenny Gillen as per the list of changes. Therefore, five employees are currently working under Jenny Gillen.

3. **(B)** Shawn Carlson is no longer with the company, as per the list of change. Shawn's employees are now under Taylor Greene.

4. **(D)** Because Wesley Vanhooser works under Carl Vickers, his calls should go to extension 2321.

5. **(A)** In a correctly alphabetized directory, Denise Moore should be listed before Stephen Morrison, because "Moo" comes before "Mor." Their extensions are 2865 and 1074.

6. **(D)** Tim Zimmerman is administrative staff, so his mail should be delivered to mailbox number 1A, as per the list of changes.

7. **(B)** Charlotte Wall now receives calls at extension 255, as she is now at Shirley Reid's old extension.

8. **(C)** Cheryl Moore currently receives her calls at her listed extension, though her mail is forwarded to the general mailbox. Floyd O'Brien has his calls forwarded to Cheryl Moore. Shirley Reid and Hubert Easley are no longer with the company.

9. **(C)** Edgar Wright has the mailbox number 2A, so his calls should be forwarded to Cheryl Moore at extension 201.

10. **(A)** A package for Wendy Vier should be delivered to her listed mailbox, 2A. Although employees with mailbox number 2A have their calls forwarded to Cheryl Moore, they receive their mail directly.

Practice Set 5

Use the directory and list of changes below to answer questions 1–5.

Directory

Name	Sales Team	Email ID	Ext.
Patrick Flintson	Blue	pflana	283
Susan Hutton	Blue	shutto	529
Bob Irvine	Green	birvin	686
Karl Jansen	Purple	kjanse	821
Henry Kelley	Green	hkelle	125
Julia Lamb	Purple	jlamb	583
Deborah Lee	Blue	dlee	704
Jim Mangum	Green	jmangu	236
Beverly Oakley	Purple	boakle	581
Gloria Tucker	Blue	gtucke	909

List of Changes:

- Calls for all employees should be directed to the leader of their respective sales teams. Henry Kelley, Beverly Oakley, and Gloria Tucker are the leaders of their respective teams.

- Due to a request by their team leader, the email IDs of the employees on the purple team have been expanded to include their entire last names.
- Patrick Flintson has moved to the green team, and is now at extension 214.

1. Which of the following employees takes their emails at their listed email ID and takes their calls directly at their listed extension?

A) Deborah Lee
B) Beverly Oakley
C) Henry Kelley
D) Jim Mangum

2. To which extension should a call for Susan Hutton be directed?

A) 529
B) 125
C) 581
D) 909

3. To which extension should a call for Patrick Flintson be directed?

A) 283
B) 125
C) 214
D) 909

4. What is the email ID of the team leader of the purple team?

A) boakle
B) boakley
C) gtucke
D) hkelle

5. Which of the following email IDs contains the employee's entire last name?

A) birvin
B) jlamb
C) gtucke
D) pflint

Use the directory and list of changes below to answer questions 6–10.

Directory			
Name	**RM No.**	**Ext**	**Dept**
Healy, Bernice	121	1409	Human Resources
Hines, Skip	254	3621	Engineering
Jenning, Carolyn	174	4986	Marketing
Jones, Jeff	316	7057	Engineering
Kessler, Bruce	305	2308	Human Resources
Malone, Emily	209	8473	Accounting
Oliver, Amy	189	2280	Marketing
Quarles, Marvin	163	0894	Human Resources
Ramos, Isaac	230	2847	Marketing
Short, Elizabeth	351	1091	Engineering
Tyler, Suzanne	227	8652	Accounting
Wade, Thomas	114	2485	Engineering

List of Changes:

- The Engineering department has been renamed "Research and Development." The new room number for all employees in this department is "LAB."
- Bernice Healy has been promoted to CFO and head of the Financial department. Isaac Ramos has taken her position in Human Resources and now has her old room number and extension.
- Jon Henley has recently been hired to work in the Research and Development department, and can be reached at extension 3306.

6. Based on the information above, which department currently has the most employees?

   A) Human Resources
   B) Research & Development
   C) Engineering
   D) Finance

7. What is Jon Henley's room number?

   A) 3306
   B) 121
   C) 254
   D) LAB

8. To which extension should a call for Isaac Ramos be directed?

   A) 1409
   B) 230
   C) 2847
   D) 121

9. In what department does the employee at extension 7057 work?

   A) Engineering
   B) Research and Development
   C) Human Resources
   D) Engineering

10. In what department does Bernice Healy work?

   A) Marketing
   B) Human Resources
   C) Financial
   D) Engineering

Answer Explanations for Practice Set 5

1. **(C)** Henry Kelley takes his emails at his listed email ID and takes his calls directly at his listed extension because he is a team leader. Beverly Oakley is also a team leader, but her email ID has changed since the directory was published.

2. **(D)** Susan Hutton is now part of the blue team, so her calls should be directed to Gloria Tucker at extension 909.

3. **(B)** Patrick Flintson is now part of the green team, so his calls should be directed to Henry Kelley at extension 125.

4. **(B)** The team leader of the purple team is Beverly Oakley. Because the email IDs of the employees on the purple team have been expanded to include their entire last names, her email ID is boakley.

5. **(B)** The email ID "jlamb" contains Julia Lamb's entire last name.

6. **(B)** Based on the information in the directory and list of changes, the Research and Development department has the most employees with five. This includes the four employees listed in the Engineering department, plus Jon Henley.

7. **(D)** Because Jon Henley works in the Research and Development department, his room number is "LAB."

8. **(A)** Isaac Ramos now has Bernice Healy's old extension, so the call should be directed to extension 1409.

9. **(B)** The employee at extension 7057 is Jeff Jones, who works in Research and Development (which was formerly Engineering).

10. **(C)** As per the list of changes, Bernice Healy has been promoted to the CFO and head of the Financial department.

Practice Set 6

Use the directory and list of changes below to answer questions 1–5.

Directory

Name	Office	Phone#	Dept
Cortner, Blake	New York	212-555-8240	A & R
Fullerton, Gary	Los Angeles	213-555-1532	Marketing
Harper, Angie	Miami	305-555-8509	Marketing
Jamison, Leonard	Los Angeles	213-555-4201	Finance
Landry, Hector	Chicago	312-555-6237	A & R
Maddox, Christina	New York	212-555-2479	Production
Radford, Janie	New York	212-555-3310	Marketing
Smith, Valerie	Miami	305-555-4291	A & R
Wallace, Joyce	New York	213-555-9175	Production
Woodard, Lewis	Chicago	312-555-4458	Marketing

List of Changes:

- The Chicago office has been closed, and its employees have been transferred to the Los Angeles office. They can now be reached at Gary Fullerton's phone number.
- All finance employees have been transferred to the New York office.
- The Miami office has moved to a new location across town and is now in area code 786. The last seven digits of its employees phone numbers did not change.

1. How many different departments are represented in the New York office?

   A) 2
   B) 3
   C) 4
   D) 5

2. At what phone number can Hector Landry be reached?

   A) 312-555-6237
   B) 213-555-4201
   C) 312-555-4458
   D) 213-555-1532

3. Which city does NOT have an office with an A & R employee?

   A) New York
   B) Los Angeles
   C) Miami
   D) Chicago

4. In which office does Leonard Jamison work?

   A) New York
   B) Los Angeles
   C) Miami
   D) Chicago

5. At what phone number can the A & R employee in Miami be reached?

   A) 305-555-4291
   B) 305-555-8509
   C) 786-555-4291
   D) 786-555-8509

Use the directory and list of changes below to answer questions 6–10.

Directory

Name	Daily Hrs.	Dept
Gardner, Arthur	9:00AM–5:00PM	Sales
Hudson, Charles	8:30AM–5:30PM	Sales
Jordan, Bill	7:30AM–3:00PM	Research
Keane, Jane	9:00AM–4:00PM	Sales
Kemp, Donna	9:00AM–4:30PM	Research
Lilly, Helen	9:30AM–6:00PM	Information Tech.
Roberts, Katie	8:30AM–5:00PM	Accounting
Scales, Darrell	10:30AM–6:30PM	Research
Taylor, Terri	8:00AM–6:00PM	Sales
Weston, Michael	9:00AM–5:00PM	Accounting

List of Changes:

- All employees take lunch breaks 3.5 hours into their work days. Bill Jordan, Charles Hudson, and Jane Keane take half-hour lunch breaks, and all other employees take 1-hour lunch breaks.
- Michael Weston now works in the Sales department.
- Helen Lilly leaves an hour early on Mondays and stays an hour late on Tuesdays.

6. How many employees work in the Sales department?

   A) 2
   B) 3
   C) 4
   D) 5

7. At which of the following times will both employees in the Research department be in their offices?

   A) 10:23AM
   B) 12:26PM
   C) 2:46PM
   D) 4:49PM

8. What is the latest time any employee is ever scheduled to leave work?

   A) 5:30PM
   B) 6:00PM
   C) 6:30PM
   D) 7:00PM

9. Which of the following employees will be in their office at 12:45PM?

   A) Charles Hudson
   B) Jane Keane
   C) Donna Kemp
   D) Katie Roberts

10. Which employee works the most hours per day?

    A) Charles Hudson
    B) Bill Jordan
    C) Terri Taylor
    D) Darrell Scales

Answer Explanations for Practice Set 6

1. **(C)** Three different departments are listed in New York in the directory: A & R, Production, and Marketing. Because all Finance employees were also transferred to New York, there are now a total of four departments represented at the New York office.

2. **(D)** As per the list of changes, all listed Chicago employees can now be reached at Gary Fullerton's phone number: 213-555-1532.

3. **(D)** Because the Chicago office closed and its employees were transferred to the Los Angeles office, Chicago does not have an office with an A & R employee.

4. **(A)** Because all Finance employees have been transferred to the New York office, Leonard Jamison works in the New York office.

5. **(C)** Valerie Smith is the A & R employee in Miami. The Miami office is now in area code 786, so her phone number is 786-555-4291.

6. **(D)** Four employees are listed as working in the Sales department, and Michael Weston also now works in the Sales department. Therefore, five total employees work in the Sales department.

7. **(B)** At 12:26PM, both Research employees should be in their offices. Darrell Scales will not have arrived yet at 10:23AM and will be at lunch at 2:46PM, and Donna Kemp will have left by 4:49PM.

8. **(D)** As per the list of changes, Helen Lilly stays until 7PM on Tuesdays.

9. **(A)** Charles Hudson's lunch break lasts from 12:00PM–12:30PM, so he should be in his office at 12:45PM.

10. **(C)** Terri Taylor works 9 hours per day, more than any other employee. Charles Hudson works the second-most hours per day: 8.5 hours.

Clerical Abilities Analysis Chart for Using a Directory

Use the following chart to carefully analyze your results of the *using a directory* question type. This will help you evaluate your strengths and weaknesses. This analysis should help you focus your study and review efforts on specific types of problems.

Practice Set	Total Number of Questions	Number Correct	Number Incorrect	Number Unanswered
Set 1	10			
Set 2	10			
Set 3	10			
Set 4	10			
Set 5	10			
Set 6	10			

Because there is no penalty for incorrect answers on most of the questions in the Clerical Abilities section, you should have left no question unanswered. Even if you didn't have time to answer a question, you should have at least filled in the answer space with an educated guess.

REVIEWING THE KEY STRATEGIES

Remember to:

1. Quickly assess how the Directory is constructed, but don't memorize its contents.
2. Focus on the List of Changes, reading its information carefully.
3. Be aware that most questions will require altering the information in the Directory based upon revisions in the List of Changes.
4. If permitted to write in your test booklet, mark key elements in the List of Changes and note such alterations in the Directory.

FILING

This question type tests your ability to recognize commonalities appearing down columns or across rows and to recognize their distinctions. You will be asked to find the correct placement for a piece of information based upon the specific labels of each cell in a matrix diagram.

Helpful Techniques and Strategies

First identify if commonalities run down the columns or across the rows, and if so, what they are. For example, you may see running down the left-hand column labels each of which include the word "Sports":

File Cabinet A	File Cabinet B	File Cabinet C	File Cabinet D
1. Girls' Sports Applications	5. Equipment Company Files A–G	9. Non Profit Files A–M	13. Coaching Applications A–N
2. Boys' Sports Applications	6. Equipment Company Files H–M	10. Non Profit Files N–Z	14. Coaching Applications O–Z
3. Women's Sports Applications	7. Equipment Company Files N–R	11. Rejected Applications A–M	15. Sports Licensing—State & Federal
4. Men's Sports Applications	8. Equipment Company Files S–Z	12. Rejected Applications N–Z	16. Sports Licensing—City & County

You are now aware that "Sports" files run down the left-hand column. Briefly do the same with the other columns in order to be familiar with their organization. Note that another sports category—"Sports Licensing"—sits at the bottom right-hand column.

Once you get a sense of the general layout of the matrix, proceed to the questions. You will need to address not only a general topic but also its more specific label within that generality.

Sometimes the matrix may have a common relationship across the rows instead of down the columns. Sometimes the matrix may have no commonality down a column or across a row.

Be aware that some questions may require a multiple-cell answer. In other words, some questions may have more than one cell (say, a drawer) as an appropriate place to find or file information. In this example, a Rejected Men's Sports Application by Orangecrunch will be double-filed in Drawer 4 and Drawer 12.

Practice Set 1

A local insurance company has four file cabinets, each with four drawers. The drawers are numbered 1 through 16 and are labeled according to their contents.

Use the chart below to answer questions 1–8.

File Cabinet A	File Cabinet B	File Cabinet C	File Cabinet D
1. Client Files A–G	5. Insurance Company Files A–G	9. Sample Policies A–M	13. Advertising Materials—Print Media
2. Client Files H–M	6. Insurance Company Files H–M	10. Sample Policies N–Z	14. Advertising Materials—Broadcast Media
3. Client Files N–R	7. Insurance Company Files N–R	11. Blank Applications A–M	15. Agency Licensing—State & Federal
4. Client Files S–Z	8. Insurance Company Files S–Z	12. Blank Applications N–Z	16. Agency Licensing—City & County

1. A client named James Thomas completes an application and subsequently purchases a new insurance policy. Which file drawer is the best place for this client's file?

   A) Drawer 1, because it is labeled "Client Files"
   B) Drawer 2, because it should be filed under "J"
   C) Drawer 4, because it should be filed under "T"
   D) Drawer 12, because he used an application

2. The ABC Insurance Company issues a new policy form that will be used for all new life insurance policies sold through this Agency. Which drawer is best for this document?

   A) Drawer 5, because the document came from ABC Insurance Company and drawer 5 contains files for Insurance Companies from A through G
   B) Drawer 6, because it came from an insurance company, but it should go under "L" for Life Insurance
   C) Drawer 9, because it should go in the file for "ABC Insurance"
   D) Drawer 13, because the new Life Insurance policy might be used in print advertising

3. A new client, Mary Smith, requests a blank application for a Life Insurance policy through the ABC Insurance Company. Where would you find this form for her?

   A) Drawer 2, because her name starts with an "M" for Mary
   B) Drawer 4, because her last name begins with "S" for Smith
   C) Drawer 5, because she wants coverage through the ABC Insurance Company
   D) Drawer 11, because she needs a blank application for ABC Insurance Company

4. The XYZ Insurance Company issues a revised policy form that will replace the old-style Life Insurance policy held by some XYZ policyholders. This revised policy from XYZ Insurance would need to go into all of the following drawers EXCEPT:

   A) Drawer 8, because it contains files for Insurance Companies from S to Z, the location of the XYZ Insurance Company files
   B) Drawer 10, because it contains all sample policies from N to Z
   C) Drawers 1–4, because it must go into all of the client files for current XYZ policyholders
   D) Drawer 15, because the new revision relates to the Agency's Insurance License

5. A License Renewal form is received from the State Department of Insurance. Where is the best location to file this document?

   A) Drawers 5–8, because the form might relate to different insurance companies
   B) Drawers 9 and 10, because the form might relate to different policy forms
   C) Drawers 11 and 12, because the form might relate to different applications
   D) Drawer 15, because the form might relate to state licensing requirements

6. You receive a new marketing brochure layout from an out-of-state advertising agency. Where would be the most logical place to file it?

   A) Drawer 9
   B) Drawer 13
   C) Drawer 14
   D) Drawer 10

7. A client named Maryam Bashmati requests a copy of her current *Homeowner's Insurance* Policy. Where would you be likely to find this file?

A) Drawer 1
B) Drawer 3
C) Drawer 9
D) Drawer 10

8. A client named Maryam Basmati requests a copy of her current *Life Insurance* Policy. Where would you be likely to find this file?

A) Drawer 1
B) Drawer 3
C) Drawer 9
D) Drawer 10

Answers Explanations to Practice Set 1

1. **(C)** Drawer 4 is the correct location to place a file for a client named James Thomas. His file must go into one of the four "Client Files" drawers, and Drawer 4 contains all of the files for clients with last names beginning with "T."

2. **(A)** All new policies for future use must go into the specific file for the issuing insurance company. By reviewing the four drawers for insurance companies, Drawers 5–8, you see that Drawer 5 is the appropriate drawer to find the ABC Insurance Company file.

3. **(D)** Drawer 11 is the correct place to look. The key element is that she is requesting a blank application (so it must be in either Drawer 11 or 12), and an application from a company beginning with "A" must be in Drawer 11.

4. **(D)** Drawer 15 is the correct exception to this question. Because this is a *revised* policy form, which affects both past and future cus-

tomers, the new document must be filed in all the other locations: the company file, the policy file, and the client files.

5. **(D)** All the agency's license-related documents are filed in Drawers 15 and 16. This new paperwork is a State License Renewal Form, so it should be filed in Drawer 15.

6. **(B)** This new brochure layout needs to go into the correct drawer for print advertising materials, Drawer 13.

7. **(A)** Because this is a request for a file of a *current* client, the file must be in one of the Drawers 1–4. The client's last name begins with a "B," so her file would be found in the first drawer.

8. **(A)** Similar to question 7, this is a request for a file of a *current* client, so the file must be in one of the first four drawers. The client's last name begins with a "B," so her file would be found in the first drawer. Note that the *type* of policy is irrelevant.

Practice Set 2

The City's Parks and Recreation Department has four file cabinets, each with four drawers. The drawers are numbered 1 through 16 and are labeled according to their contents.

Use the chart below to answer questions 1–8.

File Cabinet A	File Cabinet B	File Cabinet C	File Cabinet D
1. City Parks A–H	5. Youth Soccer Leagues A–M	9. Administrative Files A–M	13. Public Correspondence, Current A–M
2. City Parks I–P	6. Youth Soccer Leagues N–Z	10. Administrative Files N–Z	14. Public Correspondence, Current N–Z
3. City Parks Q–Z	7. Boys' Baseball Leagues A–Z	11. Personnel Files A–M	15. Internal Correspondence, Current A–Z
4. County Parks A–Z	8. Girls' Softball Leagues A–Z	12. Personnel Files N–Z	16. Archived Correspondence (12 Months+) A–Z

1. If the Parks Department receives a newly updated version of the rules and regulations affecting the *Town Square City Park*, which is the best drawer to file this document?

   A) Drawer 1
   B) Drawer 3
   C) Drawer 4
   D) Drawer 15

2. If the Parks Department receives a newly updated version of the rules and regulations affecting only *Riverside County Park*, which is the best drawer to file this document?

   A) Drawer 1
   B) Drawer 3
   C) Drawer 4
   D) Drawer 8

3. If Park Supervisor Smith requests a copy of a recent memo from Park Supervisor Jones, where is the logical location to look for this memo?

   A) Drawer 9, *Administrative Files*, filed under "J" for Jones
   B) Drawer 13, *Correspondence*, filed under "S" for Smith
   C) Drawer 14, *Correspondence*, filed under "J" for Jones
   D) Drawer 15, *Internal Correspondence*, filed under "J" for Jones

4. If Supervisor Smith requests a copy of a two-year-old memo from Supervisor Jones, where is the logical location to look for this memo?

   A) Drawer 13, *Correspondence*, filed under "S" for Smith
   B) Drawer 14, *Correspondence*, filed under "J" for Jones
   C) Drawer 15, *Internal Correspondence*, filed under "J" for Jones
   D) Drawer 16, *Archived Correspondence*, filed under "J" for Jones

5. The coach of a girls' youth soccer team, *The Amazing Pink Unicorns*, requests a copy of her team's upcoming season schedule. Where would it be located?

   A) Drawer 5, filed under "A" for Amazing
   B) Drawer 6, filed under "P" for Pink
   C) Drawer 6, filed under "U" for Unicorns
   D) Drawer 8, because it is a Girls team

6. If a department supervisor wants to see all files for this year's team sports, which of the following is a complete and accurate list of the drawers you would need to access?

   A) Drawers 1, 2, 3, and 4
   B) Drawers 5 and 6
   C) Drawers 7 and 8
   D) Drawers 5, 6, 7, and 8

7. If Chief Park Administrator Jimenez requests the individual file for a Mr. Ramirez, an employee of the Parks and Recreation Department, it would be most logical to look for the file first in which of the following drawers?

   A) Drawer 9, *Administrative Files*, because Jimenez is an Administrator
   B) Drawer 10, *Administrative Files*, filed under "R" for Ramirez
   C) Drawer 11, *Personnel Files*, because this is a personnel matter
   D) Drawer 12, *Personnel Files*, filed under "R" for Ramirez

8. Where would you look for a file for the *Ragin' Renegades*, a Boys' Baseball Team?

   A) Drawer 5
   B) Drawer 6
   C) Drawer 7
   D) Drawer 8

Answer Explanations for Practice Set 2

1. **(B)** *Town Square City Park* information should be placed with other city parks and alphabetized by the letter "T" in Drawer 3.
2. **(C)** This question deals with a *county* park, and all county park files belong in Drawer 4.
3. **(D)** Park Supervisor Smith is requesting a memo from another Park Supervisor, which makes it an internal correspondence. Look in Drawer 15.
4. **(D)** The memo that Park Supervisor Smith wants is older than one year. Therefore, look in Drawer 16.
5. **(A)** Drawer 5 holds all information for youth soccer teams beginning with letters A–M. *The Amazing Pink Unicorns'* schedule can be found there.
6. **(D)** Drawers 5–8 house all sports information. No other drawers have any sports information.
7. **(D)** Information about personnel is located alphabetically. Look for Mr. Ramirez's file in Drawer 12.
8. **(C)** Boys' baseball files are housed in Drawer 7. The *Ragin' Renegades* information will be located here.

Practice Set 3

The City Maintenance Department has four file cabinets, each with four drawers. The drawers are numbered 1 through 16 and are labeled according to their contents.

Use the chart below to answer questions 1–8.

File Cabinet A	File Cabinet B	File Cabinet C	File Cabinet D
1. Facility Maintenance (south)	5. Park Maintenance (south)	9. Solid Waste Management	13. Landscape Maintenance
2. Facility Maintenance (north)	6. Park Maintenance (north)	10. Street Maintenance (A–K)	14. Tree Maintenance
3. Facility Maintenance (east)	7. Park Maintenance (east)	11. Street Maintenance (L–Z)	15. Fleet Maintenance (south)
4. Facility Maintenance (west)	8. Park Maintenance (west)	12. Street Maintenance (numbered streets)	16. Fleet Maintenance (north)

1. Where should you file a folder of customer feedback on tree height in center medians?

   A) Drawer 13
   B) Drawer 14
   C) Drawer 7
   D) Drawer 9

2. In which drawer will you find files of maintenance records for the Southern Regional Park?

   A) Drawer 3
   B) Drawer 1
   C) Drawer 5
   D) Drawer 13

3. Which drawer holds information about maintenance for city buildings in the western portion of the city?

   A) Drawer 4
   B) Drawer 1
   C) Drawer 15
   D) Drawer 16

4. Where would you file a report that documents a paving problem on Demeter Lane?

   A) Drawer 11
   B) Drawer 16
   C) Drawer 12
   D) Drawer 10

5. If you received a complaint about an oil-leaking garbage truck in the northern section of the city, where would you file it?

   A) Drawer 16
   B) Drawer 15
   C) Drawer 2
   D) Drawer 1

6. A supervisor wants you to find all the files on sprinkler repair. In which drawer will you find the information?

   A) Drawer 5
   B) Drawer 13
   C) Drawer 8
   D) Drawer 14

7. Where would you file the quarterly report for maintenance on oak trees?

   A) Drawer 5
   B) Drawer 7
   C) Drawer 14
   D) Drawer 13

8. Where would you file a citizen's complaint about a traffic signal on South 29th Avenue?

   A) Drawer 7
   B) Drawer 10
   C) Drawer 11
   D) Drawer 12

Answer Explanations for Practice Set 3

1. **(B)** Drawer 14 holds all tree maintenance documentation, which will include trees in the medians.
2. **(C)** Drawer 5 contains maintenance records for all parks in the south sector of the city.
3. **(A)** City buildings fall under the "facilities" category, and buildings in the west sector are in Drawer 4.
4. **(D)** Street maintenance drawers are arranged alphabetically. Therefore, Drawer 10, containing street names from A–L, would be the drawer for a file regarding Demeter Lane.

5. **(A)** The maintenance records for vehicles ("Fleet") in the northern section are in Drawer 16.
6. **(B)** Sprinkler maintenance information would be located under "Landscape Maintenance," in Drawer 13.
7. **(C)** All records of tree maintenance can be found in Drawer 14.
8. **(D)** Information about numbered streets is filed in Drawer 12.

Practice Set 4

The County Department of Permits and Licensing has four file cabinets, each with four drawers. The drawers are numbered 1 through 16 and are labeled according to their contents.

Use the chart below to answer questions 1–8.

File Cabinet A	File Cabinet B	File Cabinet C	File Cabinet D
1. Zoning Permits	5. Business Property Statements	9. Business Names	13. Dog Licenses
2. Building Permits	6. Encroachment Permits	10. Nursery Licensing	14. Marriage Licenses
3. Online Building Permit Processing	7. Hazardous Material Forms	11. Body Art Health Permits	15. Concealed Weapons License Applications
4. Business Licenses	8. Air Quality	12. Special Event Permits	16. Temporary Food Facility Permits

1. Where should a worker file an application to carry a gun?

   A) Drawer 11
   B) Drawer 13
   C) Drawer 7
   D) Drawer 15

2. In which drawer will you find information about smog reports?

   A) Drawer 1
   B) Drawer 8
   C) Drawer 6
   D) Drawer 5

3. In which drawer would you file a list of permits for new companies?

   A) Drawer 4
   B) Drawer 9
   C) Drawer 5
   D) Drawer 2

4. A complaint has been received about a neighbor's barking Rottweiler. In which drawer would you investigate whether or not the canine has a license?

   A) Drawer 1
   B) Drawer 16
   C) Drawer 13
   D) Drawer 10

5. In which drawer would you file a permit for a new tattoo parlor?

   A) Drawer 16
   B) Drawer 11
   C) Drawer 12
   D) Drawer 5

6. A local high school Academic Team holds its annual picnic in the park. In which drawer will you find the permit they need to file?

   A) Drawer 16
   B) Drawer 6
   C) Drawer 5
   D) Drawer 12

7. A customer wants to file a permit to add a new deck to his home. Which drawer will you place it in?

A) Drawer 1
B) Drawer 6
C) Drawer 2
D) Drawer 12

8. A local citizen wants to start a new business, the *Speedy Auto Detailing Service*. In which drawer will you search for any other business that already has this name?

A) Drawer 9
B) Drawer 5
C) Drawer 1
D) Drawer 4

Answer Explanations for Practice Set 4

1. **(D)** Guns are weapons, so one should look in Drawer 15, which contains applications for concealed weapons licenses.
2. **(B)** Drawer 8 has air-quality licensing and permit information. This is the place to look for smog reports.
3. **(A)** Permits for new companies (business licenses) are in Drawer 4.
4. **(C)** All dog license information is located in Drawer 13.
5. **(B)** Tattoo parlors would fall under the category of "Body Art Health Permits." Drawer 11 contains these files information.

6. **(D)** A high school Academic Team's annual picnic would fall under the category of special events, so you should look in Drawer 12 for the correct permit.
7. **(C)** The homeowner wants to build an addition onto his home. Building permits can be found in Drawer 2.
8. **(A)** The citizen needs to know if another business has already been licensed under the name he wants to use. Look in Drawer 9 for business names.

Practice Set 5

The State Department of Motor Vehicles (DMV) has four file cabinets, each with four drawers. The drawers are numbered 1 through 16 and are labeled according to their contents.

Use the chart below to answer questions 1–7.

File Cabinet A	File Cabinet B	File Cabinet C	File Cabinet D
1. Driver Handbook	5. Driver License Applications (A–K)	9. Automobile Bill of Sale Forms	13. Car Buyer's Bill of Rights
2. Commercial Driver Handbook	6. Driver License Applications (L–Z)	10. Lost or Stolen Driver License	14. Driver Safety Information
3. Motorcycle Driver Handbook	7. Driver License Renewals (A–K)	11. Request for Driving Record	15. Personalized License Plate Applications
4. Vehicle Registration	8. Driver License Renewals (L–Z)	12. Automobile Title Information	16. Accident Involvement Forms

1. A customer, Mr. Salisbury, wants to report that he cannot find his driver's license. From which drawer will you get the form for this report?

   A) Drawer 10
   B) Drawer 8
   C) Drawer 6
   D) Drawer 1

2. The *Riverfront Cab Company* wants to hire a new taxicab driver. To which drawer will you go to get information for the new employee?

   A) Drawer 1
   B) Drawer 2
   C) Drawer 11
   D) Drawer 16

3. A concerned parent of a teenaged driver comes to your DMV window asking for information about making her son a better driver. Which drawer will you go to for the information?

   A) Drawer 11
   B) Drawer 16
   C) Drawer 1
   D) Drawer 14

4. A driver has just received another speeding ticket, and he wants to know how many points he has accumulated against his license. From which drawer will you get him the form he needs to obtain this information?

   A) Drawer 12
   B) Drawer 16
   C) Drawer 1
   D) Drawer 11

5. A resident, Ms. Nagai, who has just moved from another state, comes to your window to file for her new driver's license. In which drawer will you place her application?

   A) Drawer 5
   B) Drawer 8
   C) Drawer 6
   D) Drawer 7

6. A private citizen wants to purchase a car from another private citizen. Which drawer will you need to go to in order to find the proper forms for the sale?

   A) Drawer 9
   B) Drawer 13
   C) Drawer 15
   D) Drawer 12

7. A citizen has bought a car from a shady dealer. Upon completion of the sale, on the drive home the car's engine blows a gasket. Which drawer will contain information about the buyer's rights?

   A) Drawer 1
   B) Drawer 12
   C) Drawer 13
   D) Drawer 9

Answer Explanations for Practice Set 5

1. **(A)** Mr. Salisbury has apparently lost his driver's license. Look in Drawer 10 for the forms to report a lost and stolen license.

2. **(B)** Drawer 2 contains the handbook for commercial drivers. The taxicab company's new driver needs to be familiar with the information in this handbook.

3. **(D)** The concerned parent and the teenaged driver will be best served by reading about driver safety, which can be found in Drawer 14.

4. **(D)** The Request for Drivers Records Forms are located in Drawer 11. This concerned driver will need you to get a form from this location.

5. **(C)** The application Ms. Nagai submits is for a new driver's license. Alphabetically, her new application belongs in Drawer 6, which contains applications for drivers with last names between "L" and "Z."

6. **(A)** To sell a car, the participants need an Automobile Bill of Sale Form that is located in Drawer 9.

7. **(C)** The buyer needs to understand his rights. Look in Drawer 13 to find the proper information.

Practice Set 6

The City and County Offices have three file cabinets, each with five drawers. The drawers are numbered 1 through 15 and are labeled according to their contents.

Use the chart below to answer questions 1–7.

File Cabinet A	File Cabinet B	File Cabinet C
1. Bills, Laws and Ordinances	6. Financial Disclosure Records	11. Police Records
2. Birth and Death Records	7. Foreclosure and Real Estate Auctions	12. Property Taxes and Real Estate Records
3. Building Inspection Records	8. Land Survey Records	13. Restaurant Inspection Records
4. County Court Records	9. Marriage Records	14. Traffic Records
5. Election Records	10. Neighborhood Census Records	15. Utility Records

1. A Public Defender wants to find the arrest record of a client. Which drawer will have the file she needs?

   A) Drawer 10
   B) Drawer 6
   C) Drawer 11
   D) Drawer 14

2. Where would you file a report you have received about the number of electrical blackouts during a one-year period?

   A) Drawer 3
   B) Drawer 15
   C) Drawer 13
   D) Drawer 14

3. You need a copy of your birth certificate in order to get a marriage license. Which drawer will have the birth certificate?

   A) Drawer 9
   B) Drawer 4
   C) Drawer 6
   D) Drawer 2

4. Which drawer would contain the most recent report regarding the ethnic makeup of the various sections of the city?

   A) Drawer 13
   B) Drawer 2
   C) Drawer 1
   D) Drawer 10

5. Where would you file a complaint about the cleanliness of a hamburger stand?

A) Drawer 4
B) Drawer 3
C) Drawer 10
D) Drawer 13

6. For an investigative report, a customer asks you to find the salary of the top elected officials in the city. Which drawer will contain this information?

A) Drawer 5
B) Drawer 1
C) Drawer 6
D) Drawer 10

7. A City Council Member has asked you to find the number of city intersections where traffic exceeds 20,000 cars per day. Which drawer will you look in for the information?

A) Drawer 11
B) Drawer 14
C) Drawer 4
D) Drawer 10

Answer Explanations for Practice Set 6

1. **(C)** The Public Defender needs a file from the Police Records because they contain the arrest records.

2. **(B)** Electrical outages would fall under the category of Utilities. Drawer 15 is the best place to look.

3. **(D)** Birth certificates would be found in Drawer 2, which contains all birth and death records.

4. **(D)** Drawer 10 with the Neighborhood Census Records would have information about population ethnicity.

5. **(D)** Health issues for public restaurants should be filed in Drawer 13.

6. **(C)** Drawer 6, with Financial Disclosure Records, will have the information about elected officials' salaries.

7. **(B)** All traffic information, including the number of cars passing through various intersections, should be filed in Drawer 14.

Practice Set 7

The City's Volunteer Services Department has four file cabinets, each with four drawers. The drawers are numbered 1 through 16 and are labeled according to their contents.

Use the following chart to answer questions 1–7.

File Cabinet A	File Cabinet B	File Cabinet C	File Cabinet D
1. Adult Education and Literacy	5. Community Events	9. Health and Wellness: Cancer and AIDS Assistance	13. Justice and Legal Support
2. Animal Support Services	6. Disaster Relief	10. Health and Wellness: Donations Sorting	14. Special Events Support
3. Arts and Culture	7. Environment: Cleanups	11. Health and Wellness: Women's Services	15. Renovation and Repairs: Community Centers
4. Children and Youth	8. Environment: Planting Shrubs and Trees	12. Hospital and Hospice Services	16. Senior Citizen Services

1. In which drawer would you place a list of volunteers who participated in beach cleanups?

    A) Drawer 7
    B) Drawer 8
    C) Drawer 15
    D) Drawer 5

2. In which of the four file cabinets would you find information about volunteering for Women's Domestic Abuse Services?

    A) File Cabinet A
    B) File Cabinet B
    C) File Cabinet C
    D) File Cabinet D

3. You want to volunteer at the local animal shelter. Which drawer has information to assist you?

    A) Drawer 14
    B) Drawer 4
    C) Drawer 5
    D) Drawer 2

4. You need to file a report on the number of volunteer hours spent at the County Courthouse in the last month. In which drawer will you place the report?

    A) Drawer 5
    B) Drawer 13
    C) Drawer 1
    D) Drawer 16

5. You want to volunteer to help with the city's weekly Jazz Concerts in the Park that occur during the summer. The file clerk needs to look in which drawer for information to help you?

    A) Drawer 14
    B) Drawer 15
    C) Drawer 7
    D) Drawer 3

6. Your supervisor has asked you to file a list of all the volunteers who read books to school children in elementary schools. In which drawer will you place the file?

    A) Drawer 1
    B) Drawer 4
    C) Drawer 14
    D) Drawer 3

7. In which drawer will you place a file of the museum's volunteer docents?

    A) Drawer 5
    B) Drawer 14
    C) Drawer 1
    D) Drawer 3

Answer Explanations for Practice Set 7

1. **(A)** Beach cleanup activities, including a list of volunteers who participated, would fall into the category of "Environment: Clean-ups," filed in Drawer 7.

2. **(C)** All Health Services documents are in File Cabinet C. Therefore, all information about volunteering for Women's Domestic Abuse will be located in that cabinet.

3. **(D)** All information related to Animal Services is located in Drawer 2.

4. **(B)** Information about volunteer hours at the County Courthouse will be located in Drawer 13, which contains all of the Legal Services data.

5. **(A)** Summer music programs would fall under the category of special events. The clerk needs to look in Drawer 14 for that information.

6. **(B)** A list of volunteers for any children's activity should be filed in Drawer 4.

7. **(D)** Information about museum volunteers should be filed with "Arts and Culture," so place this file in Drawer 3.

Practice Set 8

A mid-sized city has four file cabinets devoted to local businesses; each cabinet has four drawers. The drawers are numbered 1 through 16 and they are labeled according to their contents.

Use the chart below to answer questions 1–8.

File Cabinet A	File Cabinet B	File Cabinet C	File Cabinet D
1. Floodplain Management	5. Water and Wastewater Issues	9. Oversize Vehicle Restrictions	13. Adopt-a-Street Program
2. City Ordinances	6. Building Specifications	10. Construction and Service Vehicle Permits	14. Small-Business Tax Responsibilities
3. Zoning Rules	7. Load Restrictions	11. Landlord Training	15. Downtown Storefront Requirements
4. City Growth Plan	8. Truck Routes	12. Alcohol-Server Training	16. Garbage Disposal Regulations

1. A city resident wants preliminary information about how to open a new bagel shop in a downtown storefront location. The information she needs is likely to be in which of the following groups of drawers?

   A) Drawers 4, 13, and 16
   B) Drawers 14, 15, and 12
   C) Drawers 10, 8, and 3
   D) Drawers 2, 3, and 15

2. In which drawer will you file a report about volunteer groups who pick up litter on city streets?

   A) Drawer 1
   B) Drawer 13
   C) Drawer 16
   D) Drawer 14

3. A city resident requests information about opening a home-based business in her residential neighborhood. Which drawer will contain the necessary regulations?

   A) Drawer 4
   B) Drawer 14
   C) Drawer 3
   D) Drawer 11

4. Your supervisor has asked you to file a new set of regulations regarding solid-waste refuse collection. In which drawer should you file it?

   A) Drawer 10
   B) Drawer 13
   C) Drawer 8
   D) Drawer 16

5. A downtown restaurant is remodeling its kitchen facilities. The owners need to know when large construction trucks can be legally parked on Main Street. Which drawer will contain this information?

   A) Drawer 9
   B) Drawer 10
   C) Drawer 6
   D) Drawer 15

6. Which drawer would be the best place to file documents from a recent City Council meeting which discussed future expansion plans for the downtown area?

   A) Drawer 2
   B) Drawer 15
   C) Drawer 4
   D) Drawer 1

7. A brand-new commercial management firm has taken over a large downtown building that houses several small businesses. Which of the following drawers contains information pertinent to the management company's new role?

   A) Drawer 11
   B) Drawer 12
   C) Drawer 14
   D) Drawer 13

8. Which drawer is the best place to file a new study on the amount of water used annually by each business in the downtown area?

   A) Drawer 1
   B) Drawer 5
   C) Drawer 3
   D) Drawer 4

Answer Explanations for Practice Set 8

1. **(D)** For a new business in the downtown area, the customer needs information from several drawers. She will need to know about City Ordinances (Drawer 2), Zoning Rules (Drawer 3), and Downtown Storefront Requirements (Drawer 15).
2. **(B)** All records of the volunteer teams who pick up street litter will be filed under the Adopt-a-Street Programs, in Drawer 13.
3. **(C)** To ascertain if the customer can legally operate a business out of her home, you will need to check the city's zoning regulations, which are in Drawer 3.
4. **(D)** All relevant regulations regarding solid-waste refuse (i.e., city garbage collection)

should be filed in Drawer 16, Garbage Disposal Regulations.
5. **(A)** The city rules and regulations governing large construction trucks would be found in Drawer 9, Oversize Vehicle Restrictions.
6. **(C)** Documentation of the discussion regarding possible future expansion of the downtown area should be filed in Drawer 4, City Growth Plans.
7. **(A)** The new management company will be well-served if they learn about the city requirements for landlord training. Look in Drawer 11.
8. **(B)** All water usage reports, for commercial and residential users alike, should be filed in Drawer 5, Water and Wastewater Issues.

Clerical Abilities Analysis Chart for Filing

Use the following chart to carefully analyze your results of the *filing* question type. This will help you evaluate your strengths and weaknesses. This analysis should help you focus your study and review efforts on specific types of problems.

Practice Set	Total Number of Questions	Number Correct	Number Incorrect	Number Unanswered
Set 1	8			
Set 2	8			
Set 3	8			
Set 4	8			
Set 5	7			
Set 6	7			
Set 7	7			
Set 8	8			

Because there is no penalty for incorrect answers on most of the questions in the Clerical Abilities section, you should have left no question unanswered. Even if you didn't have time to answer a question, you should have at least filled in the answer space with an educated guess.

REVIEWING THE KEY STRATEGIES

Before answering the questions, first briefly get a sense of the "lay of the land" by looking down columns and across rows to identify how the commonalities live within the matrix.

Be aware that some questions may require two or more locations (drawers, files, folders, etc.) for the correct answer.

If seeing too much information (the entire matrix) all at once distracts you, you can use your answer sheet to cover up columns or rows, revealing only one row or column at a time.

CUSTOMER SERVICE (OFFICE PRACTICES, INTERPERSONAL SKILLS, AND DECISION MAKING)

This question type tests your knowledge of how best to provide customer service and how to perform professionally in a business office. You will be given common situations between a clerk and a client, or between a clerk and a supervisor, or between employees, and asked to indicate the best response to that situation.

Helpful Techniques and Strategies

For example:

A customer steps up to your desk, smoking a cigarette. You politely inform him that smoking is not permitted in government buildings and ask that he extinguish his cigarette, but he ignores you. Which of the following would NOT be an acceptable course of action?

A) Ask again politely, restating government policy about smoking in buildings.
B) Ensure that the client speaks your language and can understand what you are requesting.
C) Gently take the client by his arm and, in a friendly manner, escort him out of the building.
D) Advise the customer that there are smoking areas outside the building, and ask if he needs directions to them.

Many of the questions in this section do not require a deep understanding of business procedures and policies. Rather, you can usually arrive at a correct answer by considering how *you*, as the customer or client, would prefer to be treated in each situation.

In this situation, the correct answer is (C). Except for emergency situations, it is rarely appropriate to physically touch a customer, even gently or in a friendly manner. All of the other choices treat the customer with respect but still endeavor to enforce the no-smoking rule.

Even though many of these questions have answers that are intuitive, a few rules of thumb will be good to keep in mind:

Whenever possible, try to answer a question or resolve a problem yourself without escalating to a supervisor or colleague.

If you do not immediately know the answer, it is appropriate to let the customer know, and offer to call back with the answer later.

Speed, accuracy, and personal attention are paramount in working with customers.

Even if the mistake was not yours, apologizing to the customer on behalf of your organization will often diffuse his or her anger. Then solve the problem.

Reminders

1. Watch out for words such as NOT and EXCEPT in the questions. They require you to select the answer choice that is inappropriate within business conduct guidelines and customer service.
2. You can usually eliminate one or more of the answer choices as obviously incorrect. If so, take your best guess of the remaining choices.
3. A few of the questions may be overly wordy or time consuming. If so, skip them, do the quick questions first, and then, if time permits, come back and answer those you skipped. Be sure to mark your answers in the appropriate bubbles of your answer sheet.

Practice Set 1

Read the questions that follow and select the answer that *best* represents an excellent customer service response.

1. A customer begins a phone conversation by complaining about having to wait too long to get connected. Which of the following should you do?

    A) Apologize and ask how you may address the customer's needs.
    B) Explain that all customers' calls are taken in order and you cannot control how long it takes for any call to be answered.
    C) Tell the caller that you can serve all customers faster when they do not take time to complain.
    D) Immediately connect the caller to your supervisor.

2. Which of the following is most likely to produce successful customer service employees?

    A) Supervisors hold a competition to see who can help the most customers in a month.
    B) Employees know that they will be promoted to a higher-paying position after one year of service.
    C) The department offers frequent training seminars providing effective customer service practices.
    D) Supervisors spend more time observing their customer service staff as they help customers.

3. A customer says he cannot complete one part of a form required for a building permit. Which of the following demonstrates your best response?

    A) "We are not supposed to take time to do this, but I'll see if I can help."
    B) "I cannot take time to help you personally right now, but if you make an appointment, I'll try to give you as much time as you need at that time."
    C) "Our department does not provide that service. You'll need to go to some other department."
    D) "You need assistance with your form? I'll get you a copy of our step-by-step directions that explain each of the items you have to complete."

4. Your department has recently developed a web page that provides email contact information. What is the most essential procedure to follow when processing incoming email questions?

    A) Train employees to prioritize email inquiries and decide which ones need to be answered first in a given day.
    B) Take the time to draft responses carefully. When customer service representatives are comfortable in replying to emails, they will get faster.
    C) Reply succinctly to all emails within 48 hours.
    D) Reply immediately with a standard letter explaining that a longer, more detailed reply will follow within three days.

5. Which of the following questions about customer service is most likely to elicit the largest number of constructive responses?

   A) Which of our customer service representatives was most helpful to you during your visit to our office?
   B) On a scale from 1 to 5 (5 = best), how would you rate the service you received?
   C) If you worked for our department, what changes would you want to see?
   D) How many times did you have to call before you received a correct answer to your question?

6. Which of the following would be the LEAST effective policy for a customer service department?

   A) Providing customer service training only to employees who deal directly with customers
   B) Providing recognition for employees who provide good service, such as an "employee of the month" award
   C) Knowing which time of day is the busiest and staffing customer-service positions accordingly
   D) Providing an easy way for customers to offer suggestions for improvement

7. Which of the following is NOT a skill learned in effective email training?

   A) Mastering proper email etiquette
   B) Managing an inbox effectively
   C) Understanding legal issues of email
   D) Knowing when not to reply to a customer inquiry

8. If a supervisor is facing a serious morale problem in his/her department, which of the following is most likely to be an effective way to approach the issue?

   A) Have private meetings with each individual involved in the problem.
   B) Use training sessions to discuss the problem and brainstorm possible solutions.
   C) Call your supervisor and urge that he/she fix the problem.
   D) Ask to have the difficult employee(s) transferred to other departments.

9. If an irate customer berates you for incorrect information received from a different customer service representative, which of the following would be the best immediate reply?

   A) "I am not responsible for the previous clerk's mistake, but I am sorry you had to return to customer service."
   B) "I'll call my supervisor who can handle your complaint."
   C) "Everyone makes mistakes; I'm sure that the clerk didn't mean to give you inaccurate information."
   D) "I apologize for your having been inconvenienced. Let me get the accurate answer for you right now."

10. Which of the following is essential information to include on a web site for your department?

   A) The phone number to contact the department
   B) The hierarchy of the department so the customer knows who is at the top position
   C) Pictures of all the current employees
   D) The department's mission statement

Answer Explanations for Practice Set 1

1. **(A)** Customers appreciate a quick apology and then attention to their needs. They are not interested in a lengthy rationale for the long wait, and they certainly do not want to be corrected.

2. **(C)** Customer service representatives become more effective when they are regularly trained in successful customer service strategies.

3. **(D)** Customer service representatives are most effective when they know how to constructively address the customer's specific question.

4. **(C)** As a general rule for business, employees should provide a concise reply to all emails within 48 hours.

5. **(B)** Questionnaires with specific questions tend to generate the most useful replies. Many customer service questionnaires are structured like answer choice (B), using a numeric scale on which the customer can simply place a checkmark.

6. **(A)** A customer service department works best when effective training is provided for all department employees, not just employees with direct customer contact. A department best serves the public when all its members are familiar with the policies for dealing with customers.

7. **(D)** As a general rule, a customer service department should reply to every customer inquiry. Ignoring any customer question should not be part of email training.

8. **(B)** Morale will be stronger when employees know they have a voice. Providing an outlet, perhaps via staff meeting, a suggestion box, or a similar method, will help give employees a venue to express their concerns.

9. **(D)** If a customer is angry, you must always try to diffuse that anger. Remember that you are there to help. Although customers may initially be frustrated, they will leave satisfied if you address their needs quickly, and with a smile.

10. **(A)** Customers want to be able to call any department for quick answers to their questions. Although it may be helpful to know other information, a contact phone number is essential.

Practice Set 2

Read the questions that follow and select the answer that *best* represents an excellent customer service response.

1. If other people are within hearing distance while you are taking a confidential phone message, what is the best way to verify that you have correctly noted the message?

   A) Repeat the caller's message so the customer can verify the facts.
   B) Tell the customer to call back at a later time when you can discuss the message confidentially.
   C) Offer to call the customer back at a time when others are not present to overhear.
   D) Ask the caller to repeat the information in the message as you check your written notes.

2. A customer comes into your office to submit an application. When you give her several additional forms to complete, she complains about all the "bureaucratic red tape" involved in the application. Which of the following would be the best response to this customer?

   A) Be patient and hope that she will calm down.
   B) Clarify the reasons that the office needs the information.
   C) Gently suggest that she can contact the state legislature if she wants the procedures changed.
   D) Indicate that you understand her frustration, but you cannot process her application until she has completed the required forms.

3. You are taking a telephone message for a co-worker who is not in the office at the time. Of the following, which is the LEAST important item to write on the message?

   A) The caller's name
   B) The length of the call
   C) The caller's phone number
   D) The time and day of the call

4. All of the following are core principles of customer service EXCEPT . . .

   A) staffing the phone system so that calls are answered quickly.
   B) greeting each customer cordially and professionally.
   C) promoting exemplary employees from within the department.
   D) providing clear and concise answers to customer questions.

5. Which of the following behaviors may most likely annoy customers?

   A) Telling customers you'll be able to address their needs within a certain time period even if you doubt you can
   B) Referring customers to a different department, one that can better help meet their needs
   C) Accepting and processing customers' forms as efficiently as possible
   D) Apologizing for the time customers may have had to spend "on hold" on the phone

6. Which of the following is NOT a high-priority skill for a trainee in customer service?

   A) Knowing how to diffuse a customer's anger from customers
   B) Knowing how to listen to customer requests
   C) Knowing department budget requirements
   D) Knowing proper telephone etiquette

7. Which of the following is the LEAST important aspect of training customer service employees?

   A) Developing strategies for asking questions that get to the heart of the customer's needs
   B) Providing reminders to begin and end each customer contact with a positive attitude and smile
   C) Confirming that the employee can answer every potential customer question
   D) Giving the employee a variety of techniques to deal with frustrated customers

8. In order to complete a certain task, you need to ask a favor of a worker you know well. Which of the following is the best way to accomplish this?

   A) Ask for your co-worker's help, quickly explaining your reasoning.
   B) Explain how your superior will think well of the worker's effort.
   C) Discuss the benefits the co-worker's career will have after helping.
   D) Offer that you will help the co-worker in the future.

9. A customer comes to your window to submit an application for a permit for a special event in the local park. What is the best way to make the customer feel appreciated?

   A) Refer the customer to the Parks and Recreation department.
   B) Notice the customer's name on the permit and call the customer by name throughout the conversation.
   C) Take the form as quickly as possible and move on to the next customer.
   D) Ask the customer clarifying questions about the event.

10. Customer service employees need to be well-trained in good listening skills. Which of the following would NOT be a component of strong listening skills?

    A) Noticing the customer's body language
    B) Asking clarifying questions when needed
    C) Maintaining eye contact with the customer
    D) Immediately suggesting a solution to the customer

Answer Explanations for Practice Set 2

1. **(D)** Having the telephone caller repeat the main points is the best way to ensure customer confidentiality and privacy while maintaining professionalism and efficiency.

2. **(D)** Always be professional. Let the customer know you understand how difficult it can be to fill out many forms, but that you cannot help meet her needs until she fills out the forms.

3. **(B)** When taking phone messages for others, it is most important to record the caller's name, phone number, the time the call was made, and a concise message.

4. **(C)** Good customer service involves using common sense and treating customers respectfully. Promoting employees only internally does not necessarily make for good customer service.

5. **(A)** Being unreliable as to time deadlines is a major area of complaint in customers' eyes. When you tell customers you can do something, be sure you can fulfill that promise on time.

6. **(C)** Customer service training should focus on "people skills" to serve the public effectively. Understanding the department budget is not nearly as high a priority as knowing how to handle people well.

7. **(C)** Customer service employees cannot be expected to know the specific answer to every potential question, but they can be expected to know where to find the answer to such questions.

8. **(A)** The best practice is to be businesslike, professional, and efficient. There is no need to flatter a fellow employee by suggesting future rewards.

9. **(B)** Customers feel appreciated when service representatives take a personal interest in them. By using the customer's name, you demonstrate that you are personally invested in the individual's satisfaction.

10. **(D)** Immediately suggesting solutions typically interferes with listening carefully and completely to everything the customer has to relate. Instead, give the customer your undivided attention, make direct eye contact, and demonstrate a desire to help.

Practice Set 3

Read the questions that follow and select the answer that *best* represents an excellent customer service response.

1. A customer approaches you with an obscure question about a form you have never seen. What is your best plan of action?

   A) Send the customer to a different clerk for assistance.
   B) Explain that you are unfamiliar with the form but will get an answer immediately from a clerk who is.
   C) Ask the clerk next to you for assistance.
   D) Advise the customer to contact a supervisor for this specialized information.

2. Which of the following is NOT a viable way to reinforce good customer service in employees?

A) Using a system of demerits and charting mistakes to correct employee errors.

B) Displaying a "Customer Service Tip of the Week" poster in the employee workroom.

C) Having employees experience role playing as a way to understand customer needs.

D) Continue training through monthly employee-development sessions.

3. You supervise a public service workers department. What is the best way to maintain an effective department?

A) Ensure all employees understand the department hierarchy and follow it when communicating.

B) Require employees to check with you before making decisions.

C) Explain that you have to report to your supervisors and what it feels like to be under pressure.

D) Provide means for employees to voice their concerns and comments.

4. You answer a call from a customer who has a strong foreign accent and you are unsure that you understand all her needs. Which of the following is the best plan of action?

A) Tell the customer that you have trouble understanding her accent and that you will have someone else return the call.

B) Explain to the customer that you speak only English and cannot follow what she needs.

C) Ask the customer if you can repeat her request in your own words to clarify her needs.

D) Put the customer on hold while you get someone who can understand the caller's accent.

5. Which of the following is the best approach to answer a phone call from a customer?

A) "Hello. It is a beautiful day here in our city."

B) "Good afternoon. We are busy here at the XYZ city offices, but if you can hold we will return your call as soon as possible."

C) "Hello. You have reached the customer service department of the XYZ city offices. Our goal is to provide you the best service possible. We are sincerely interested in achieving an effective solution to your issue. How can I help you?"

D) "Hello. This is Bob Jonsson at the XYZ city offices. How may I direct your call?"

6. When responding to a telephone inquiry about the city's process for getting a building permit approved, which of the following is an appropriate course of action?

    A) Offer the customer a brief verbal overview of the process.
    B) Offer the customer a written brochure explaining the City Building Permit Process.
    C) Offer the customer the address of the city's web site and indentify the page with building permit information.
    D) All of the above are effective strategies.

7. When a customer service representative is faced with many customers in the waiting room all requiring attention, which is usually the best strategy to follow?

    A) Organize the customer list by their time of arrival, and then take them in order on a "first come, first served" basis.
    B) Organize the customer list according to their importance, and serve the most important customers first.
    C) Organize the customer list according to the type of service they require, and then do the type of task you deem most pressing first.
    D) All of the above are effective strategies.

8. If a customer service representative feels vaguely threatened by a verbally abusive customer who then stalks out, which of the following would be the best course of action?

    A) Make a note in the customer's file clearly describing the confrontation so that if it happens again, you have documentation of the pattern.
    B) Alert your supervisor, describe the confrontation, and then proceed according to his instructions.
    C) Immediately contact your security office, describe the confrontation, and then proceed according to their instructions.
    D) All of the above are appropriate strategies, depending on the severity of the confrontation and the degree of perceived threat.

9. When a telephone customer service representative is faced with a very long-winded customer, which of the following is probably NOT an appropriate response?

    A) Get the customer back on track by reminding him of his main point.
    B) Get the customer to avoid repeating himself by getting as quickly as possible to the main point.
    C) Get the customer to realize that his verbosity is the problem preventing him from getting service.
    D) Get the customer to state specifically how you can help him.

10. When a City Hall customer service representative receives a telephone call from a local city resident complaining about potholes in the streets in his local neighborhood, which of the following is probably the best place to refer the resident?

    A) To the City Streets department
    B) To the County Roads department
    C) To the State Highways department
    D) To the Federal Interstate Highways department

Answer Explanations for Practice Set 3

1. **(B)** Customers want to know that they will get service. If you cannot answer a customer's questions, quickly find someone who can.

2. **(A)** Most employees do not react well to only negative messages. Charting demerits and complaints is not likely to maintain effective employees.

3. **(D)** Employees need a sense of empowerment. Providing forums for their comments and concerns will keep communication open.

4. **(C)** Whenever you're not sure of a customer's needs, try repeating the customer's phrasing. This will ensure that you have heard the customer correctly.

5. **(D)** Customers appreciate knowing the name of the employee who answers the phone, but they want quick, efficient service. They do not want to hear clichéd platitudes, long-winded introductions, and they do not want to be initially placed on hold.

6. **(D)** By offering the customer a range of various options, you can most effectively provide the services that are best for each individual customer.

7. **(A)** Customers are accustomed to a "first come, first served" organization for a waiting room. When they see that everyone is waiting their turn, the process is both reassuring and calming to everyone.

8. **(D)** Each of the actions listed may be appropriate, depending upon the situation. Above all, it is essential to respond to a confrontational customer in a measured, effective, nonemotional manner. This will help to defuse the situation and will ensure that adequate follow-up is undertaken.

9. **(C)** A customer service representative should always try to avoid aggravating the customer by in any way "blaming the victim."

10. **(A)** The citizen is a "local city resident" who is complaining about potholes in his "local neighborhood" streets, so the local authority—the City Streets department—is the best place to refer this call.

Practice Set 4

Read the questions that follow and select the answer that *best* represents an excellent customer service response.

1. You are working on routine duties, and a co-worker asks you to help with a high-priority, "rush" assignment. What is your best course of action?

   A) Explain that you can help after you have finished your current task.
   B) Suggest that the co-worker ask someone else not as busy as you are.
   C) Help the co-worker with the high-priority task and then return to your own work.
   D) Inform your supervisor that the co-worker cannot work effectively without other's help.

2. You are in charge of training new customer service employees. Which of the following should be the LEAST important element for you to emphasize?

   A) Establishing appropriate eye contact with the customer
   B) Ensuring the customer understands you have many people to serve
   C) Using the customer's name whenever possible
   D) Showing you value the customer's time and attention

3. You are employed by a city office answering calls about a wide variety of services. A caller asks about holding a church function in a local park. To which department should you direct the call?

   A) Local Ordinances
   B) City Planning
   C) Crowd Control Services
   D) Special Event Permits

4. Which of the following responses would be most appropriate to respond to a customer irritated because another clerk had misinformed him about a required form?

   A) "I'm terribly sorry you received incorrect information. Let me help you fill out the correct form now."
   B) "Some people in our department may not have correct information. It's a shame you had to return, but I can help you."
   C) "I'll tell my supervisor about your situation. The form you need is on the table by the door."
   D) "You know how some government workers can be. It's a good thing you were able to get to me this time."

5. To provide the best community service, it is sometimes essential for members of one department to notify other departments about issues that need correcting. Of the following problems encountered in the course of your city job, which is the most important one to report? You see . . .

   A) a chain-link fence bordering a city park is leaning toward a homeowner's trees outside of the park.
   B) a high-voltage electrical wire is hanging down over a busy street intersection.
   C) several apparently wild dogs are roaming in a vacant city-owned lot.
   D) a small group of people are convening at a park but without the required city permit.

6. A customer complains about the attitude of another clerk whom you know has been dealing with the recent death of a loved one. Which of the following is the most sensitive way to handle the customer?

   A) Tell the customer about the clerk's difficulty, so the customer can understand and be more sensitive to others.
   B) Acknowledge briefly that the clerk is dealing with personal trauma but quickly move to serve the customer's needs.
   C) Remind the customer that everyone has an occasional bad day.
   D) Agree with the customer that the clerk should not be dealing with the public at this time.

7. During your lunch break, a person from another department relates an embarrassing story about a co-worker's behavior at a weekend party. What should you do?

   A) Move to another table and ignore the story and storyteller.
   B) Admit you'll have to report this improper behavior to your supervisor.
   C) Tell the speaker you are uncomfortable listening to such information and you wish not to hear more.
   D) Tell the co-worker what was said about him during lunch and give him the opportunity to deny it.

8. You are a volunteer worker who greets visitors to City Hall. Someone asks you where to file a Business Name form. To which floor of the building will you send the customer?

   A) Second floor: Zoning and Encroachment Permits
   B) Third Floor: Marriage and Dog Licenses
   C) Fourth Floor: Special Event Permits
   D) First Floor: Business Licensing and Permits

9. Which of the following jobs is likely to have the least interaction with the public?

   A) A clerk filing arrest warrants for the police department
   B) An organizer for the Parks and Recreation Department's volunteer trail-maintenance program
   C) A bailiff working at the County Courthouse
   D) A state employee who gives exams to driver's license applicants at the Department of Motor Vehicles

10. You notice a customer letting an elderly, frail-looking gentleman go ahead of her in line. When that customer comes to your window, which of the following do you do?

    A) Do not mention her act, but provide her with the best service you can to reward her kindness.
    B) Announce her kind deed to everyone still waiting in line.
    C) Assume she knows the gentleman and helps him often.
    D) Thank her for her kindness and then help her with her needs.

Answer Explanations for Practice Set 4

1. **(C)** A department is most efficient overall when the workers help each other with urgent, high-priority tasks on an as-needed basis.
2. **(B)** Customers are well aware of the waiting line and do not need to be reminded that you have more people to serve. But when a customer finally makes it to your window, he or she wants and deserves your undivided attention.
3. **(D)** When any organization wants to have a group event in a public facility such as a city park, a special permit is in order.
4. **(A)** To present the most professional appearance, apologize briefly and quickly move on to helping the customer with his needs. You want the customer to forget the earlier incident and leave with a smile after receiving good service.
5. **(B)** For all city workers, public safety is of paramount importance. Thus, you must immediately notify the proper authorities about the high-voltage wire that may pose an imminent threat to human safety.
6. **(B)** Dealing with trauma is never easy for anyone. You want to remain sensitive to your fellow worker, but remember that the customer simply wants to be served efficiently.
7. **(C)** It is important to maintain professionalism in the workplace. Thus it is a good policy neither to spread gossip about others, nor to listen it.
8. **(D)** In this case, all business needs, including the filing of a Business Name, will be tended to in the first-floor offices.
9. **(A)** All government employees need to have the requisite skills for potential interactions with the public. However, a filing clerk working for the police department is the least likely to have regular face-to-face interaction with the public.
10. **(D)** It is never improper to acknowledge another person's act of kindness. You do not wish to dwell or gush over the customer's kind deed. Simply thank her and move on to her business.

Practice Set 5

Read the questions that follow and select the answer that *best* represents an excellent customer service response.

1. You are conducting a monthly staff meeting. Which of the following behaviors is an example of poor meeting skills?

   A) Asking department members for responses to a given idea being discussed
   B) Maintaining eye contact with the department member who is speaking
   C) Paraphrasing what someone has said to make sure it is well understood
   D) Glancing at your watch often to ensure the meeting stays on schedule

2. A customer asks you a question about data obtained from the most recent catalog, but you do not know the specific answer. How should you proceed?

   A) Explain that because you know only general information about the catalog, you'll research the specific information and provide the answer later.
   B) Give the customer a general answer about the catalog figures that you know to be accurate.
   C) Put the customer on hold and attempt to find someone knowledgeable who may be able to answer the question.
   D) Refer the customer to another contact number where the customer service representative may know the answer.

3. A Spanish-speaking customer is obviously frustrated trying to complete a form printed only in English. You speak limited Spanish and cannot provide complete assistance. What is the best course of action for you to take?

   A) Try your best to interpret the customer's words and help him to complete the form.
   B) Ask if there are any Spanish-speaking customers in the room who would be willing to help.
   C) Using your limited Spanish, excuse yourself and indicate you'll return quickly with a company interpreter to help the customer.
   D) Apologize to the customer that you don't speak Spanish well and share his frustration about the form.

4. You answer a call from an irate customer who says that he has been referred to the wrong office several times. Which of the following responses will best serve to defuse his anger?

   A) "I know our phone system can be confusing. Those operators refer people to the wrong departments much of the time."
   B) "I'm so sorry you reached the wrong department several times. I'll be happy to help you right now."
   C) "Everyone knows how it feels to get the re-directed to the wrong department. It's so frustrating."
   D) "We have so many departments that it's understandable you got sent to the wrong place more than once."

5. Which of the following is NOT a successful way of establishing rapport with a customer?

   A) Using body language that shows interest
   B) Establishing and maintaining eye contact
   C) Hurrying so you can meet the next customer's needs
   D) Using the customer's name often

6. Your customer service department wants to provide the best customer service in the county. Which of the following is probably NOT one of the best methods for your department to adopt?

   A) Have an enthusiastic employee greet customers at the entrance to the building to ask questions about what they like most about the city's services.
   B) Place suggestion boxes with pencils and cards in strategic locations to allow customers to provide input about how to improve service.
   C) At every window distribute an easy-to-use customer survey that has room to write comments and provide a postage-paid envelope for mailing.
   D) Encourage the customer service representatives to always ask, "Is there anything else that I can help you with?"

7. Which of the following tactics may be most useful in calming an initially hostile phone caller?

   A) Try to pinpoint the most important aspect of the caller's anger and address it.
   B) Say nothing. Your silence will eventually allow the customer to stop ranting. You can then proceed with helping the customer.
   C) Frequently let the speaker know you are listening with interjections such as "Yes" and "I understand."
   D) Repeat each of the customer's complaints to show that you heard them.

8. You told a customer it would take you "only a few minutes" to get an answer to her question, but you were gone ten minutes and still have not found the answer. Which of the following should you NOT do upon your return?

   A) Apologize for the extra time you took and explain that the answer has been harder to find than you anticipated.
   B) Explain to the customer that you understand how frustrating it is to wait so long and thank her for her patience.
   C) Offer alternative solutions to the customer, such as continuing to wait while you seek extra help or allowing you to call her later with the answer.
   D) Explain all the steps you have taken so far and say that it would have been easier to get an answer faster if the question was not so difficult.

9. Which of the following tends to inhibit a customer service representative's effectiveness in serving the public?

   A) Attending training sessions for efficient practices
   B) Beginning and ending every customer interaction with a smile
   C) Assuming that you know what the customer needs and providing it quickly
   D) Politely using the customer's name

10. You are the new supervisor for the clerical department at the Parks and Recreation Bureau and you want to improve the efficiency of customer service. Which of the following is the most important skill you want your clerks to have?

    A) Understanding when—and when not—to come to you for help
    B) Asking each other for help before coming to you for an answer
    C) Taking the time to always figure things out for themselves
    D) Telling the customer to return after you have managed to find an answer

Answer Explanations for Practice Set 5

1. **(D)** Good listening skills are demonstrated by your body language, by paying attention, and by maintaining eye contact. If you glance repeatedly at your watch, you are sending a message that the speaker's words are not important to you.

2. **(A)** Generally speaking, try to answer every customer question yourself. If research is necessary, give the customer a reasonable, approximate time it will take for you to get back to her. And then be sure to follow up in a timely way. The customer will appreciate your honesty and efficiency.

3. **(C)** Getting the assistance of an interpreter is probably the best plan of action. The customer's overall needs will be met most effectively by someone who can speak the customer's language.

4. **(B)** All that the irate customer wants is to have the problem fixed quickly, so it's usually best to immediately issue a brief apology and efficiently proceed to the customer's needs.

5. **(C)** Customers want to see you providing efficient service, but they also want a sense of being welcomed and valued. Thus, it is as important to smile and to use the customer's name as it is to move professionally and efficiently to meet his or her needs.

6. **(A)** Meeting an enthusiastic employee at the door may be a pleasant experience for some customers, but most people will not appreciate having to answer a series of questions before they even get past the front door.

7. **(B)** The judicious use of silence can be a good technique for telephone operators to use in disarming initially hostile callers. By simply waiting a few seconds after the caller stops ranting, and then quietly asking exactly how you can help, the customer service representative allows the customer a chance to calm down and accept your assistance.

8. **(D)** In general, customers who pose specific questions tend to understand that it may take longer to get an answer. It is never helpful to imply that the problem

is the customer's own fault for asking such a hard-to-answer question. Remember, your job is to provide answers, not excuses.

9. **(C)** Customers can immediately sense an inappropriate attitude. Avoid being seen as a know-it-all. Always be positive, and act as if this customer is the most important job you will face all day.

10. **(A)** Make sure your clerks know when and how to ask for help and which types of questions you can answer more quickly and efficiently than they can. Remind them not to waste each other's time or the customer's time.

Clerical Abilities Analysis Chart for Customer Service (Office Practices, Interpersonal Skills, and Decision Making)

Use the following chart to carefully analyze your results of the *customer service (office practices, interpersonal skills, and decision making)* question type. This will help you evaluate your strengths and weaknesses. This analysis should help you focus your study and review efforts on specific types of problems.

Practice Set	Total Number of Questions	Number Correct	Number Incorrect	Number Unanswered
Set 1	10			
Set 2	10			
Set 3	10			
Set 4	10			
Set 5	10			

Because there is no penalty for incorrect answers on most of the questions in the Clerical Abilities section, you should have left no question unanswered. Even if you didn't have time to answer a question, you should have at least filled in the answer space with an educated guess.

REVIEWING THE KEY STRATEGIES

Remember to:

1. Look at all the choices before marking your answer.
2. Watch out for negative words, such as NOT or EXCEPT, in the question stem.
3. Eliminate obvious wrong choices and then guess, if necessary.
4. If necessary, think of how *you* would like to be treated as a customer.

PART III

THE TYPING (WORD PROCESSING) TEST

Introduction:
A Diagnostic Test

Analysis

THE TYPING (WORD PROCESSING) TEST—COPYING FROM PLAIN COPY

In this test, which is part of the Stenographer-Typist Examination, the applicant meets a single task, that of copying material exactly, as it is presented. The candidate must demonstrate how rapidly he or she can do so and with what accuracy.

The typing test is used by agencies at the agencies' discretion. Agencies may use the tests developed by the Office of Personnel Management or a different test.

Agencies have included an automated version of the Typing Performance Test. This enables agencies to administer the Typing Performance Test using a computer keyboard instead of a typewriter. This version only tests typing skills, not word processing skills.

How the Test Is Given

In the usual typewriter examination procedure, each competitor is given a copy of the test and two sheets of typewriter paper. About 15 minutes is needed for the complete typing test.

Three minutes are allowed for reading the instructions on the face of the test and 3 minutes for the practice typing. The practice exercise consists of typing instructions as to spacing, capitalization, etc., and contains a warning that any erasures will be penalized. The practice typing helps make sure that the typewriter is functioning properly.

After the 3 minutes' practice typing, the competitors put fresh paper in their machines, and turn the test page over and read the test for 2 minutes. After the 2 minutes, they are instructed to start typing the test. Five minutes are allowed for the test proper.

How the Test Is Rated

The exercise must have been typed about once to meet the speed requirement of 40 words a minute. If this speed is not attained, the test is not scored for accuracy.

As shown in Example A, which follows the Diagnostic Test, a test paper that contains 17 lines meets the minimum speed requirement. Applicants have been instructed to begin and end each line precisely as in the printed test copy. From Example A it can be quickly determined whether a typing test is to be rated for accuracy and, if so, the greatest number of errors permitted for the lines typed.

The next step is to compare the test paper with the printed test exercise and to mark charge errors. The basic principles in charging typing errors are as follows:

Charge 1 for each–
WORD or PUNCTUATION MARK incorrectly typed or in which there is an erasure. (An error in spacing which follows an incorrect word or punctuation mark is not further charged.)
SERIES of consecutive words omitted, repeated, inserted, transposed, or erased. Charge for errors within such series, but the total charge cannot exceed the number of words.
LINE or part of line typed over other material, typed with all capitals, or apparently typed with the fingers on the wrong keys.
Change from the MARGIN where most lines begin by the applicant or from the PARAGRAPH INDENTION most frequently used by the applicant.

The typing score used in the official examination reflects both speed and accuracy, with accuracy weighted twice as heavily as speed. Other methods of rating typing often used in schools are based on gross words per minute or net words per minute (usually with not more than a fixed number of errors). Using Example B, teachers and applicants can calculate typing proficiency in terms of gross words per minute and errors, and can determine whether that proficiency meets the minimum standards of eligibility required in the regular Civil Service examination.

Example B, following the Diagnostic Test, gives the maximum number of errors permitted at various typing speeds. For example, at the minimum acceptable speed of 17 lines, or 40 gross words per minute, 3 errors are permitted for eligibility.

DIAGNOSTIC TEST

The purpose of this diagnostic test and analysis is to familiarize you with the Typing Test and to help you assess your typing skills.

Chapter 6 will give you eight full-length practice sets.

TYPING TEST—COPYING FROM PLAIN COPY

Directions

A practice exercise appears at the bottom of this page and the text exercise itself is on the next page. First study these directions. Then, when the signal is given, begin to practice by typing the practice exercise below on the paper that has been given you. The examiner will tell you when to stop typing the practice exercise.

In both the practice and the test exercises, *space, paragraph, spell, punctuate, capitalize, and begin and end each line* precisely as shown in the exercise.

The examiner will tell you the exact time you will have to make repeated copies of the test exercise. Each time you complete the exercise, simply double space and begin again. If you fill up one side of the paper, turn it over and continue typing on the other side. Keep on typing until told to stop.

Keep in mind that you must meet minimum standards in both speed and accuracy and that, above these standards, accuracy is twice as important as speed. Make no erasures, insertions, or other corrections in this plain-copy test. Since errors are penalized whether or not they are erased or otherwise "corrected," it is best to keep on typing even though you detect an error.

PRACTICE EXERCISE

This practice exercise is similar in form and in difficulty to the one that you will be required to typewrite for the plain-copy test. You are to space, capitalize, punctuate, spell, and begin and end each line precisely as in the copy. Make no erasures, insertions, or other changes in this test because errors will be penalized even if they are erased or otherwise corrected. Practice typewriting this material on scratch paper until the examiner tells you to stop, remembering that for this examination it is more important for you to typewrite accurately than to typewrite rapidly.

DO NOT TURN TO THE TEST UNTIL TOLD TO DO SO BY THE EXAMINER.

TEST EXERCISE

Because they have often learned to know types of architecture by decoration, casual observers sometimes fail to realize that the significant part of a structure is not the ornamentation but the body itself. Architecture, because of its close contact with human lives, is peculiarly and intimately governed by climate. For instance, a home built for comfort in the cold and snow of the northern areas of this country would be unbearably warm in a country with weather such as that of Cuba. A Cuban house, with its open court, would prove impossible to heat in a northern winter.

Since the purpose of architecture is the construction of shelters in which human beings may carry on their numerous activities, the designer must consider not only climatic conditions but also the function of a building. Thus, although the climate of a certain locality requires that an auditorium and a hospital have several features in common, the purposes for which they will be used demand some difference in structure. For centuries builders have first complied with these two requirements and later added whatever ornamentation they wished. Logically, we should see as mere additions, not as basic parts, the details by which we identify architecture.

EACH TIME YOU REACH THIS POINT, DOUBLE SPACE AND BEGIN AGAIN.

Example A—Line Key for Typing Test

(LINE KEY FOR 5 MINUTE TYPING TEST SHOWING MAXIMUM NUMBER OF ERRORS PERMISSIBLE FOR VARIOUS TYPING SPEEDS, AT GRADES GS-2 TYPIST AND GS-3 STENOGRAPHER)

SPEED.—In the following example, more than 16 lines must have been typed for any speed rating. This sample key is constructed on the premise that if the competitor made the first stroke in the final line (even if it was an error), he or she is given credit for that line in determining the gross words per minute.

ACCURACY.—The gross words per minute typed, at any line, is the number *outside* the parentheses opposite that line. The numbers *in* the parentheses show the maximum number of errors permitted for that number of gross words per minute typed. The number of errors permitted increases with the speed. If the number of strokes per line were different, this table would have to be altered accordingly.

	Maximum Number of Errors Per Gross Words Per Minute Typed	
	1st typing of exercise	2d typing of exercise
Because they have often learned to know types of archi-	_____	52 (7)
tecture by decoration, casual observers sometimes fail to	_____	54 (7)
realize that the significant part of a structure is not the	_____	56 (8)
ornamentation but the body itself. Architecture, because	_____	59 (8)
of its close contact with human lives, is peculiarly and	_____	61 (9)
intimately governed by climate. For instance, a home built	_____	64 (9)
for comfort in the cold and snow of the northern areas of	_____	66 (10)
this country would be unbearably warm in a country with	_____	68 (10)
weather such as that of Cuba. A Cuban house, with its open	_____	71 (11)
court, would prove impossible to heat in a northern winter.	_____	73 (11)
Since the purpose of architecture is the construction of	_____	76 (12)
shelters in which human beings may carry on their numerous	_____	78 (12)
activities, the designer must consider not only climatic con-	_____	80 (12)[2]
ditions, but also the function of a building. Thus, although	_____	_____
the climate of a certain locality requires that an auditorium	_____	_____
and a hospital have several features in common, the purposes	_____	_____
for which they will be used demand some difference in struc-	40 (3)[1]	_____
ture. For centuries builders have first complied with these	42 (4)	_____
two requirements and later added whatever ornamentation they	44 (5)	_____
wished. Logically, we should see as mere additions, not as	47 (6)	_____
basic parts, the details by which we identify architecture.	49 (6)	_____

[1]The minimum rated speed is 40 gross words per minute for typing from printed copy.
[2]Any material typed after 80 gross words per minute (which is considered 100 in speed) is *not* rated for accuracy.
Note: The number of errors shown above must be proportionately increased for tests that are longer than 5 minutes.

TABLE 5

Example B—Errors Permitted at Various Typing Speeds (MAXIMUM NUMBER OF ERRORS PERMITTED ON 5-MINUTE TESTS AT VARIOUS SPEEDS FOR TYPING SCORES REQUIRED FOR TYPIST AND STENOGRAPHER POSITIONS)

Speed	Maximum Number of Errors Permitted
Gross Words Per Minute	*GS-2, GS-3, GS-4 Clerk-Typist* *GS-3, GS-4, GS-5 Clerk-Stenographer*
Under 40	Ineligible
40	3
41–42	4
43–44	5
45–47	6
48–49	6
50–52	7
53–54	7
55–56	8
57–59	8
60–61	9
62–64	9
65–66	10
67–68	10
69–71	11
72–73	11
74–76	12
77–78	12
79–80	12

NOTE: THE NUMBER OF ERRORS SHOWN ABOVE MUST BE PROPORTIONATELY INCREASED FOR TESTS THAT ARE LONGER THAN 5 MINUTES.

Some Common Errors to Watch For

Practice, Practice, Practice

(NOTE: Each practice set should be taken as a 5-minute timed writing. Gross words a minute are listed next to each line.)

Common Typing Errors to Watch For

As you practice, beware of the following most common typing errors:

1. *Striking one letter for another.* The most common examples of this are hitting "r" for "t," or "t" for "r"; hitting "i" for "o," or "o" for "i"; hitting "a" for "s," or "s" for "a"; hitting "i" for "e," or "e" for "i"; and hitting "m" for "n," or "n" for "m." As you look over your practice typing watch for these errors.

2. *Transposing letters.* Some common examples of typing letters in reverse order are: "re" instead of "er"; "op" instead of "po"; "ew" instead of "we"; "oi" instead of "io"; and "to" instead of "ot." If you find these in your work, practice hitting those letters in the correct order.

3. *Omitted letter errors.* Incorrect hand alignment, weakness in the smaller fingers, and reading too far ahead may cause omitted-letter errors. If you find letters missing in your words, you may wish to practice improving in this area.

Practice Set 1

Type the following exercise, being careful to space, paragraph, spell, punctuate, capitalize, and begin and end each line precisely as shown. Each time you complete the exercise, double space and begin again. If you fill up one side of the paper, turn it over and continue typing on the other side. Keep typing until the time is up. Make no erasures, insertions, or other corrections.

	wpm: 5
Most people want to make sure their own welfare is being taken	3
care of properly. This need will embrace such items as job security,	6
fringe benefits, and final retirement. There are dozens of other items	8
that could be grouped under personal welfare; but, people can cope with	11
these other items if the basic three are covered. For most people, per-	14

sonal welfare means more than acquiring the mere basics of life—food,	17
clothing, and shelter; they want to be able to afford a few luxuries.	20
Job security, to some, is recognized as the single most critical	22
category, of these items. If you do not possess good job security, you	25
may not have adequate fringe benefits and a good retirement program. If	28
you are like most people, you expect a job that is pleasant and finan-	31
cially rewarding as well; however, a good environment is ofttimes of more	34
importance than wages to some people. Your whole outlook on life can be	37
more positive when there is no significant concern about your job security.	40
The next category that is of big concern to most workers is fringe	42
benefits. Some of the most common fringe benefits that we now tend to	45
expect are health and major medical insurance, sick leave, retirement	48
paid for by the employer, and adequate vacation and holidays. Even	51
though wages are often the center of concern for most people, the single	54
largest item of controversy between workers and employers is the size of	57
the fringe benefits package that will be paid for by the firm.	59
Retirement should be a major item of concern to all individuals.	62
Today, more than ever, the need for well-planned and well-financed	64
retirement programs is essential. Most of us can expect to spend many	67
years in retirement; hence, we should begin planning for retirement the	70
day we begin our very first job. After we have arranged the financial	73
part of our retirement, we must be just as eager to organize the kinds	76
of activities in which we can participate when we finally quit working.	79

Practice Set 2

Type the following exercise, being careful to space, paragraph, spell, punctuate, capitalize, and begin and end each line precisely as shown. Each time you complete the exercise, double space and begin again. If you fill up one side of the paper, turn it over and continue typing on the other side. Keep typing until the time is up. Make no erasures, insertions, or other corrections.

	wpm: 5
On display at several of the offices in our city is a small sign	3
showing what is surely a very important message. The sign says quite	5
simply "Think." Busy workers and customers hastily look at the sign,	8
and it is interesting to conjecture that maybe the message says some-	11
thing a little bit different to every one who reads it. To some, for	14
example, it might portend that they should exercise greater caution in	17
their work; to others, it could offer encouragement to attack a pressing	19
problem that needs solving; while a third group might interpret it to be	22
a note of stimulation toward expanded creativity. That a five-letter	25
word printed on a sign should, like a tiny, mystical beacon, flash an	28
individualized message to those who read it, is itself thought provoking.	31

Every person can think. In the kingdom of animals, anthropologists	34
tell us, the power to reason is a distinctive characteristic of humans.	37
Although there appears to be little unanimity about why people can think,	40
it seems evident that we do our best job of it when faced with the pos-	42
sibility of making a mistake. At such times, we feel quite forced to	45
"act wisely," to "make a basic decision," to "use good judgment"—in	48
other words, to "think." The ability to think, therefore, is a valuable	51
prize to us; and, we will, ideally speaking, take advantage of any chance	54
to improve our capacity for it if in so doing we can develop our abil-	57
ity to avoid dangerous and expensive errors that could affect our family,	59
our friends, our city, our employer—and us.	61

Practice Set 3

Type the following exercise, being careful to space, paragraph, spell, punctuate, capitalize, and begin and end each line precisely as shown. Each time you complete the exercise, double space and begin again. If you fill up one side of the paper, turn it over and continue typing on the other side. Keep typing until the time is up. Make no erasures, insertions, or other corrections.

	wpm: 5
You can safely consider that poor stroking habits are generally the	3
cause of failure to achieve high typing speeds and are the major reasons	5
for plateaus; but you can find material especially designed to help develop	8
quick, easy stroking. Use a part of the drill period each day to	11
work on these special drill exercises. You may not notice an immediate	14
change, but it will come if you work for it and if you analyze your	18
stroking habits very carefully. Among other specific ideas to keep before	21
you is the advice that all drills must be practiced with a definite goal in	24
mind. Unless you know what you are trying to attain, you can't hope to	26
achieve any particular degree of success. It is useless to pound away at	30
the keyboard day after day, hoping that practice will make your typing per-	32
fect. Your drills should be done with very specific objectives in mind. Ask	35
yourself about your objectives to determine if your exercises are right for	38
you.	38
A good course has long-term goals, or at least desired outcomes,	41
for all of its students. In order to reach these goals, each student	43
must decide upon the daily practice objectives that are appropriate to his	46
or her immediate requirements. There should be a specific objective for	49
a specific need. At times, a student will need to increase speed;	52
at other times, a student will require a reduction in speed in order to elim-	55
inate error. At still other times, the goal may be to improve a	58
vital technique: keystroking, spacing, shifting, and the like.	60

Practice Set 4

Type the following exercise, being careful to space, paragraph, spell, punctuate, capitalize, and begin and end each line precisely as shown. Each time you complete the exercise, double space and begin again. If you fill up one side of the paper, turn it over and continue typing on the other side. Keep typing until the time is up. Make no erasures, insertions, or other corrections.

	wpm: 5
A business firm may use one of many letter formats that are in	3
use today; but, most companies are using of the following styles:	6
block, modified block, and modified block with paragraphs indented.	8
Some companies have now decided to use a letter style that helps them	11
to avoid sex bias in their letter writing. That style is a simplified	14
letter style, which does not include a salutation, and therefore,	17
does not show the bias against women that was found in the usual salu-	19
tations of the past. The block style and the simplified style are quite easy	23
to type because all parts of both styles begin at the left margin. The major	26
difference between the block style and the simplified style is that the	28
salutation and the complimentary close are included in the block style but	31
are excluded from the simplified format. In addition, the simplified letter	34
style always has a subject line; the block style may or may not include one.	37
According to one study, the block style is used in about a fourth of business	40
firms. The simplified style, however, enjoys only limited use.	43
The modified block style differs from the block and the simplified	46
styles in that the date and the closing lines in the former begin at	49
the horizontal center of the paper rather than at the left margin.	51
The modified block style—which may use paragraph indention, but more	54
often does not—is the most generally used letter style. It results in	57
a well-balanced, attractive letter with only a limited amount of time	60
spent in operating the tab control to indent the date and closing lines.	63

Practice Set 5

Type the following exercise, being careful to space, paragraph, spell, punctuate, capitalize, and begin and end each line precisely as shown. Each time you complete the exercise, double space and begin again. If you fill up one side of the paper, turn it over and continue typing on the other side. Keep typing until the time is up. Make no erasures, insertions, or other corrections.

	wpm: 5
A typist for an accounting firm is expected to be one who can type	3
a great quantity of numbers and symbols quickly and accurately. Some-	6
times the job is almost entirely quantitative, which means that the	8
typist must be alert to see that no errors are allowed to remain uncor-	11
rected. A wrong number or symbol can't be recognized like a misspelled	14

word, so a typist must make sure that the number or symbol has been	17
typed correctly. Accuracy is very important. The preparation of charts and	19
tables will just naturally become a considerable part of the work-load	21
arrangement when you become a typist in an accounting office. Since so	24
much accounting work is quantitative, it stands to reason that some parts	27
of longer reports can be presented best in graphic or tabulated form, such	30
as charts or tables. It is not unusual for a longer report to have, perhaps, as	33
many as a dozen displays in its appendix.	36

A typist in an accounting office may not journalize but will type many	39
letters and memorandums. When a change in procedure is to be	42
effected, a memo is typed and sent to all concerned. A typist will need	45
to know the exact number of copies to make before starting to type. This	48
ensures that all people affected will be sure to receive the notice of	51
change. Most internal communication queries between the accounting	53
office and other locations within the business are done by memo.	56

Practice Set 6

Type the following exercise, being careful to space, paragraph, spell, punctuate, capitalize, and begin and end each line precisely as shown. Each time you complete the exercise, double space and begin again. If you fill up one side of the paper, turn it over and continue typing on the other side. Keep typing until the time is up. Make no erasures, insertions, or other corrections.

	wpm: 5
Telephone etiquette demands that a person should follow specific	3
rules when answering a telephone call. First, answer quickly; no one	5
likes a delay. If at all possible, the telephone should be picked up	8
on the first ring. Second, identify yourself properly; give your com-	11
pany's name, then your own name. Third, screen an incoming call; tell	14
why your boss cannot talk now, and then mention some other way in which	17
you may aid the caller. Fourth, give only essential information; you	20
must be very careful not to give any information that your employer may	22
not want you to provide. Fifth, get the necessary information from the	25
person; be polite, but try to determine who is calling and why he or	28
she is calling. And sixth, take messages accurately; have a pencil and	31
pad by your phone on which to jot down messages. If you will abide by	34
these simple rules, you will avoid many problems.	36
When placing a telephone call, be sure to follow the advice given	38
by the experts. First, be sure you have the correct number; a wrong	41
area code may cause a delay and embarrassment. Second, know the name of	44
the person you are calling; even a short hesitation may cause difficul-	47
ties with the person to whom you are speaking. Third, plan your con-	50
versation prior to making the call; respect the other person and don't	53
waste time. Fourth, give the person you are calling time to answer the	55

telephone; a rule of thumb is to allow the phone to ring a minimum of 58
ten times. Fifth, identify yourself properly and give the reason for 61
the call; avoid embarrassment and delays—the person you are calling 64
may not recognize your voice. And sixth, terminate your call promptly 67
and thank the individual you called for helping you. 69

Practice Set 7

Type the following exercise, being careful to space, paragraph, spell, punctuate, capitalize, and begin and end each line precisely as shown. Each time you complete the exercise, double space and begin again. If you fill up one side of the paper, turn it over and continue typing on the other side. Keep typing until the time is up. Make no erasures, insertions, or other corrections.

wpm: 5

What factors determine if an employee will be a success? The three 3
basic factors of success on the job are: good technical skills, good 6
human relations skills, and a good work attitude. A person must be able 8
to exhibit the required technical skills in order to perform in an ade- 11
quate manner. Also, the need to get along with other people is equal 14
in importance to technical skills. And, even if a person builds good 17
technical skills and good human relations skills, a positive feeling 20
about the job is still essential in order to be a success. Cognizance 22
of these factors plays an important part in attaining success; if any 25
one of them is not realized, an employee may feel unsuccessful. 28

A person needs to prepare adequately in order to succeed on a job. 31
Preparation for a job must start long before the first day at work. A 33
part of this preparation is building a job entry-level skill. Also, an 36
employee must learn to develop a good, positive interpersonal relation- 39
ship with others. This ability to get along well with others is not an 42
instinct—much time and effort must be devoted to achieving good human 45
relations skills. Finally, an employee should took forward to work with 48
pleasure; therefore, a positive attitude toward work must be developed 51
if the job is to be rewarding. Remember, anyone can learn to succeed as 54
an employee; all it takes is a real desire and work. 56

Practice Set 8

Type the following exercise, being careful to space, paragraph, spell, punctuate, capitalize, and begin and end each line precisely as shown. Each time you complete the exercise, double space and begin again. If you fill up one side of the paper, turn it over and continue typing on the other side. Keep typing until the time is up. Make no erasures, insertions, or other corrections.

wpm: 5

The development and expanded use of the computer has not caused 3
the large number of jobs to be lost that so many people expected about 6
twenty-five years ago. In fact, the total number of people in the work force 8

has increased during the past twenty-five years, and the computer has   11
had the effect of creating many of the new jobs. While it is indeed   14
true that the development of the computer has made many of the routine,   17
less-skilled jobs unnecessary, it has also created many other highly   20
skilled jobs that call for employees who are trained for such fields   22
as data entry and computer operations, programming, and systems analy-   25
sis. In short, the occupations that call for specialized training, judgment,   28
and knowledge have increased in number; and thus, the computer has, in   31
fact, helped to create even more jobs and, in turn, to increase wages.   34

There are many people who insist that the computer has not had a   37
positive effect on the worker. They assert that many firms are more   39
concerned with net profit than they are with satisfied workers. In   42
many firms, the telephone calls, the invoices, the letters, and the   45
reports can all be done with the aid of a computer. Some firms are now   48
to the point where they can see how negative the impact of technology   51
is on their employees, and these firms are beginning job enrichment pro-   53
grams that will help their employees gain greater personal satisfaction   56
from their jobs. Perhaps the development of the computer may, in the end,   59
force firms to do what should have been done earlier—create pleas-   62
ant and satisfying jobs for all workers.   64

REVIEWING THE KEY STRATEGIES

Watch out for common errors:
—striking one letter for another
—transposing letters
—omitted letter errors

PART IV

THE DICTATION TEST

Introduction: A Diagnostic Test

With Answers

CHAPTER 7

THE DICTATION TEST

The dictation test, which is a part of the Stenographer-Typist Examination, includes a practice dictation and a test exercise, each consisting of 240 words. The rate of dictation is 80 words a minute.

The dictation passages are nontechnical subject matter that might be given a stenographer in a government office. Sentence structure is not complicated and sentences are not extremely long or short. The words average 1.5 syllables in length.

As shown in Example C, Practice Dictation, each dictation passage is printed with spacing to show the point that the dictator should reach at the end of each 10 seconds in order to maintain an even dictation rate of 80 words a minute. This indication of timing is one device for assisting all examiners to conform to the intended dictation rate. All examiners are also sent instructions for dictating and a sample passage to be used in practicing dictating before the day of the test. By using these devices for securing uniform dictating and by providing alternate dictation passages that are as nearly equal as possible, government agencies can give each applicant a test that is neither harder nor easier than those given others competing for the same jobs.

The test differs from the conventional dictation test in the method of transcribing the notes. The applicant is not required to type a transcript of the notes, but follows a procedure that permits machine scoring of the test. When typewritten transcripts were still required, examiners rated the test by comparing every word of a competitor's paper with the material dictated and by charging errors. Fairness to those competing for employment required that comparable errors be penalized equally. Because of the variety of errors and combinations of errors that can be made in transcripts, the scoring of typewritten transcripts required considerable training and consumed much time—many months for large nationwide examinations. After years of experimentation, a transcript booklet procedure was devised that simplified and speeded the scoring procedure.

How the Transcript Booklet Works

The transcript booklet (see Example D, Diagnostic Test) gives the stenographer parts of the dictated passage, but leaves blank spaces where many of the words belong. With adequate shorthand notes, the stenographer can readily fit the correct words into the blank spaces, which are numbered 1 through 125. At the left of the printed partial transcript is a list of words, each word with a capital letter A, B, C, or D beside it. Knowing from the notes what word belongs in a blank space, the competitor looks for it among the words in the list. The letter beside the word or phrase in the list is the answer to be marked in the space on the transcript. In the list there are other words that a competitor with inadequate notes might guess belong in that space, but the capital letter beside these words would be an incorrect answer. *(Some persons find it helpful to write the word or the shorthand symbol in the blank space before looking for it in the word list. There is no objection to doing this.)*

Look, for example, at the Practice Dictation Transcript Sheet, Example D, question 10. The word dictated is "physical"; it is in the word list with a capital "D." In the transcript, blank number 10 should be answered "D."

None of the words in the list is marked "E," because the answer "E" is reserved for any question when the word dictated for that spot does not appear in the list. Every transcript booklet has spots for which the list does not include the correct words. This provision reduces the possibility that competitors may guess correct answers.

After the stenographer has written the letter of the missing word or phrase in each numbered blank of the transcript, he or she transfers the answers to the proper spaces on the answer sheet. Directions for marking the separate answer sheet are given on page 387 of Example E, Diagnostic Test.

How the Test Is Administered

Each competitor is given a copy of the Practice Dictation Transcript Sheet (Example D), a copy of the Transcript Booklet (Example C), and an answer sheet. These are distributed at the times indicated below.

First, the Practice Dictation (see Example C) is dictated at the rate indicated by the 10-second divisions in which it is printed. This will be at the rate of 80 words a minute, for a total of 3 minutes. Then each competitor is given a copy of the Practice Dictation Transcript Sheet and allowed 7 minutes to study the instructions and to transcribe part of the practice dictation.

The test exercise (reverse side—here, page 383—of Example C) is also dictated at the rate of 80 words a minute, for 3 minutes. Then each competitor is given a Transcript Booklet and an answer sheet, and is told that he or she will have 3 minutes to read the directions on the face page, followed by 30 minutes to write the answers in the blank spaces, and then 10 minutes to transfer the answers to the answer sheet. These time limits have been found ample.

How the Answer Sheet Is Scored

In some rare instances where the typewritten transcript is still used, the passing standard on the total transcript is 24 or fewer errors for Clerk-Stenographer.

Comparable standards on the parts of the dictation measured by the machine-scored method of transcription are 14 or fewer errors for higher-level positions.

A stenographer who can take dictation at 80 words a minute with this degree of accuracy is considered fully qualified. Positions such as Reporting Stenographer and Shorthand Reporter require ability to take dictation at much higher speeds. The test for Reporting Stenographer is dictated at 120 words a minute. Two rates of dictation, 160 and 175 words a minute, are used for the Shorthand Reporter tests for different grade levels.

A DIAGNOSTIC TEST WITH ANSWERS

The purpose of this diagnostic exam is to familiarize you with the Dictation Test and to help you focus your practice.

Chapter 8 will give you five practice sets to help build strengths and reduce weaknesses.

Answer Sheet

DICTATION

1 Ⓐ Ⓑ Ⓒ Ⓓ	33 Ⓐ Ⓑ Ⓒ Ⓓ	65 Ⓐ Ⓑ Ⓒ Ⓓ	97 Ⓐ Ⓑ Ⓒ Ⓓ
2 Ⓐ Ⓑ Ⓒ Ⓓ	34 Ⓐ Ⓑ Ⓒ Ⓓ	66 Ⓐ Ⓑ Ⓒ Ⓓ	98 Ⓐ Ⓑ Ⓒ Ⓓ
3 Ⓐ Ⓑ Ⓒ Ⓓ	35 Ⓐ Ⓑ Ⓒ Ⓓ	67 Ⓐ Ⓑ Ⓒ Ⓓ	99 Ⓐ Ⓑ Ⓒ Ⓓ
4 Ⓐ Ⓑ Ⓒ Ⓓ	36 Ⓐ Ⓑ Ⓒ Ⓓ	68 Ⓐ Ⓑ Ⓒ Ⓓ	100 Ⓐ Ⓑ Ⓒ Ⓓ
5 Ⓐ Ⓑ Ⓒ Ⓓ	37 Ⓐ Ⓑ Ⓒ Ⓓ	69 Ⓐ Ⓑ Ⓒ Ⓓ	101 Ⓐ Ⓑ Ⓒ Ⓓ
6 Ⓐ Ⓑ Ⓒ Ⓓ	38 Ⓐ Ⓑ Ⓒ Ⓓ	70 Ⓐ Ⓑ Ⓒ Ⓓ	102 Ⓐ Ⓑ Ⓒ Ⓓ
7 Ⓐ Ⓑ Ⓒ Ⓓ	39 Ⓐ Ⓑ Ⓒ Ⓓ	71 Ⓐ Ⓑ Ⓒ Ⓓ	103 Ⓐ Ⓑ Ⓒ Ⓓ
8 Ⓐ Ⓑ Ⓒ Ⓓ	40 Ⓐ Ⓑ Ⓒ Ⓓ	72 Ⓐ Ⓑ Ⓒ Ⓓ	104 Ⓐ Ⓑ Ⓒ Ⓓ
9 Ⓐ Ⓑ Ⓒ Ⓓ	41 Ⓐ Ⓑ Ⓒ Ⓓ	73 Ⓐ Ⓑ Ⓒ Ⓓ	105 Ⓐ Ⓑ Ⓒ Ⓓ
10 Ⓐ Ⓑ Ⓒ Ⓓ	42 Ⓐ Ⓑ Ⓒ Ⓓ	74 Ⓐ Ⓑ Ⓒ Ⓓ	106 Ⓐ Ⓑ Ⓒ Ⓓ
11 Ⓐ Ⓑ Ⓒ Ⓓ	43 Ⓐ Ⓑ Ⓒ Ⓓ	75 Ⓐ Ⓑ Ⓒ Ⓓ	107 Ⓐ Ⓑ Ⓒ Ⓓ
12 Ⓐ Ⓑ Ⓒ Ⓓ	44 Ⓐ Ⓑ Ⓒ Ⓓ	76 Ⓐ Ⓑ Ⓒ Ⓓ	108 Ⓐ Ⓑ Ⓒ Ⓓ
13 Ⓐ Ⓑ Ⓒ Ⓓ	45 Ⓐ Ⓑ Ⓒ Ⓓ	77 Ⓐ Ⓑ Ⓒ Ⓓ	109 Ⓐ Ⓑ Ⓒ Ⓓ
14 Ⓐ Ⓑ Ⓒ Ⓓ	46 Ⓐ Ⓑ Ⓒ Ⓓ	78 Ⓐ Ⓑ Ⓒ Ⓓ	110 Ⓐ Ⓑ Ⓒ Ⓓ
15 Ⓐ Ⓑ Ⓒ Ⓓ	47 Ⓐ Ⓑ Ⓒ Ⓓ	79 Ⓐ Ⓑ Ⓒ Ⓓ	111 Ⓐ Ⓑ Ⓒ Ⓓ
16 Ⓐ Ⓑ Ⓒ Ⓓ	48 Ⓐ Ⓑ Ⓒ Ⓓ	80 Ⓐ Ⓑ Ⓒ Ⓓ	112 Ⓐ Ⓑ Ⓒ Ⓓ
17 Ⓐ Ⓑ Ⓒ Ⓓ	49 Ⓐ Ⓑ Ⓒ Ⓓ	81 Ⓐ Ⓑ Ⓒ Ⓓ	113 Ⓐ Ⓑ Ⓒ Ⓓ
18 Ⓐ Ⓑ Ⓒ Ⓓ	50 Ⓐ Ⓑ Ⓒ Ⓓ	82 Ⓐ Ⓑ Ⓒ Ⓓ	114 Ⓐ Ⓑ Ⓒ Ⓓ
19 Ⓐ Ⓑ Ⓒ Ⓓ	51 Ⓐ Ⓑ Ⓒ Ⓓ	83 Ⓐ Ⓑ Ⓒ Ⓓ	115 Ⓐ Ⓑ Ⓒ Ⓓ
20 Ⓐ Ⓑ Ⓒ Ⓓ	52 Ⓐ Ⓑ Ⓒ Ⓓ	84 Ⓐ Ⓑ Ⓒ Ⓓ	116 Ⓐ Ⓑ Ⓒ Ⓓ
21 Ⓐ Ⓑ Ⓒ Ⓓ	53 Ⓐ Ⓑ Ⓒ Ⓓ	85 Ⓐ Ⓑ Ⓒ Ⓓ	117 Ⓐ Ⓑ Ⓒ Ⓓ
22 Ⓐ Ⓑ Ⓒ Ⓓ	54 Ⓐ Ⓑ Ⓒ Ⓓ	86 Ⓐ Ⓑ Ⓒ Ⓓ	118 Ⓐ Ⓑ Ⓒ Ⓓ
23 Ⓐ Ⓑ Ⓒ Ⓓ	55 Ⓐ Ⓑ Ⓒ Ⓓ	87 Ⓐ Ⓑ Ⓒ Ⓓ	119 Ⓐ Ⓑ Ⓒ Ⓓ
24 Ⓐ Ⓑ Ⓒ Ⓓ	56 Ⓐ Ⓑ Ⓒ Ⓓ	88 Ⓐ Ⓑ Ⓒ Ⓓ	120 Ⓐ Ⓑ Ⓒ Ⓓ
25 Ⓐ Ⓑ Ⓒ Ⓓ	57 Ⓐ Ⓑ Ⓒ Ⓓ	89 Ⓐ Ⓑ Ⓒ Ⓓ	121 Ⓐ Ⓑ Ⓒ Ⓓ
26 Ⓐ Ⓑ Ⓒ Ⓓ	58 Ⓐ Ⓑ Ⓒ Ⓓ	90 Ⓐ Ⓑ Ⓒ Ⓓ	122 Ⓐ Ⓑ Ⓒ Ⓓ
27 Ⓐ Ⓑ Ⓒ Ⓓ	59 Ⓐ Ⓑ Ⓒ Ⓓ	91 Ⓐ Ⓑ Ⓒ Ⓓ	123 Ⓐ Ⓑ Ⓒ Ⓓ
28 Ⓐ Ⓑ Ⓒ Ⓓ	60 Ⓐ Ⓑ Ⓒ Ⓓ	92 Ⓐ Ⓑ Ⓒ Ⓓ	124 Ⓐ Ⓑ Ⓒ Ⓓ
29 Ⓐ Ⓑ Ⓒ Ⓓ	61 Ⓐ Ⓑ Ⓒ Ⓓ	93 Ⓐ Ⓑ Ⓒ Ⓓ	125 Ⓐ Ⓑ Ⓒ Ⓓ
30 Ⓐ Ⓑ Ⓒ Ⓓ	62 Ⓐ Ⓑ Ⓒ Ⓓ	94 Ⓐ Ⓑ Ⓒ Ⓓ	
31 Ⓐ Ⓑ Ⓒ Ⓓ	63 Ⓐ Ⓑ Ⓒ Ⓓ	95 Ⓐ Ⓑ Ⓒ Ⓓ	
32 Ⓐ Ⓑ Ⓒ Ⓓ	64 Ⓐ Ⓑ Ⓒ Ⓓ	96 Ⓐ Ⓑ Ⓒ Ⓓ	

Example C—Practice Dictation

INSTRUCTIONS TO THE EXAMINER: This Practice Dictation and one exercise will be dictated at the rate of 80 words a minute. Do not dictate the punctuation except for periods, but dictate with the expression that the punctuation indicates. Use a watch with a second hand to enable you to read the exercises at the proper speed.

Exactly on a minute, start dictating.	Finish reading each two lines at the number of seconds indicated below
I realize that this practice dictation is not a part of the examination	10
proper and is not to be scored. (Period) The work of preventing and correcting	20
physical defects in children is becoming more effective as a result of a change	30
in the attitude of many parents. (Period) In order to bring about this change,	40
mothers have been invited to visit the schools when their children are being examined	50
and to discuss the treatment necessary for the correction of defects. (Period)	1 min.
There is a distinct value in having a mother see that her child is not the	10
only one who needs attention. (Period) Otherwise a few parents might feel that they	20
were being criticized by having the defects of their children singled out for medical	30
treatment. (Period) The special classes that have been set up have shown the value of	40
the scientific knowledge that has been applied in the treatment of children. (Period)	50
In these classes the children have been taught to exercise by a trained teacher	2 min.
under medical supervision. (Period) The hours of the school days have been divided	10
between school work and physical activity that helps not only to correct their defects	20
but also to improve their general physical condition. (Period) This method of treatment	30

has been found to be very effective except for those who have severe medical	40
defects. (Period) Most parents now see how desirable it is to have these classes	50
that have been set up in the regular school system to meet special needs. (Period)	3 min.

After dictating the practice, pause for 15 seconds to permit competitors to complete their notes. Then continue in accordance with the directions for conducting the examination.

After the Practice Dictation Transcript has been completed, dictate the test below.

The Test

Exactly on a minute, start dictating.	Finish reading each two lines at the number of seconds indicated below
The number enrolled in shorthand classes in the high schools has shown a marked increase. (Period)	10
Today this subject is one of the most popular offered in the field of	20
business education. (Period) When shorthand was first taught, educators claimed that it was of	30
value mainly in sharpening the powers of observation and discrimination. (Period)	40
However, with the growth of business and the increased demand for office workers,	50
educators have come to realize the importance of stenography as a vocational	1 min.
tool. (Period) With the differences in the aims of instruction came changes in	10
the grade placement of the subject. (Period) The prevailing thought has always been that it	20
should be offered in high school. (Period) When the junior high school first came into	30
being, shorthand was moved down to that level with little change in the manner in which	40
the subject was taught. (Period) It was soon realized that shorthand had no place there	50
because the training had lost its vocational utility by the time the student could	2 min.

graduate. (Period) Moreover, surveys of those with education only through junior	10
high school seldom found them at work as stenographers. (Period) For this reason, shorthand	20
was returned to the high school level and is offered as near as possible to the time	30
of graduation so that the skill will be retained when the student takes a job. (Period)	40
Because the age at which students enter office jobs has advanced, there is now	50
a tendency to upgrade business education into the junior college. (Period)	3 min.

After completing the dictation, pause for 15 seconds. Give a Transcript to each competitor.

Example D—Practice Dictation Transcript Sheet

The TRANSCRIPT below is part of the material that was dictated to you for practice, except that many of the words have been left out. From your notes, you are to tell what the missing words are. Proceed as follows:

Compare your notes with the TRANSCRIPT and, when you come to a blank in the TRANSCRIPT, decide what word or words belong there. For example, you will find that the word "practice" belongs in blank number 1. Look at the WORD LIST to see whether you can find the same word there. Notice what letter (A, B, C, or D) is printed beside it, and write that letter in the blank. For example, the word "practice" is listed, followed by the letter "B." We have already written "B" in blank number I to show you how you are to record your choice. Now decide what belongs in each of the other blanks. (You may also write the word or words, or the shorthand for them, if you wish.) The same word may belong in more than one blank. If the exact answer is not listed, write "E" in the blank.

Example D—continued.

Alphabetic Word List

about—B
against—C
attitude—A

being—D

childhood—B
children—A
correcting—C

doctors—B

effective—D
efficient—A
examination—A
examining—C

for—B

health—B

mothers—C

never—C
not—D

paper—B
parents—B
part—C
physical—D
portion—D
practical—A
practice—B
preliminary—D
preventing—B
procedure—A
proper—C

reason for—A
result—B
result of—C

schools—C

to be—C
to prevent—A

Transcript

I realize that this __B__ dictation is _____
.......................1...........................2

a _____ of the _____ _____ and is _____
.....3................4...........5.................6

_____ scored.
..7

The work of _____ and _____ _____
.................................8.............9.........10

defects in _____ is becoming more _____ as
................11...............................12

a _____ a change in the _____ of many
.....13.............................14

_____. . . .
..15

SAMPLE ANSWER SHEET	
1 Ⓐ ● Ⓒ Ⓓ Ⓔ	
2 Ⓐ Ⓑ Ⓒ Ⓓ Ⓔ	
3 Ⓐ Ⓑ Ⓒ Ⓓ Ⓔ	
4 Ⓐ Ⓑ Ⓒ Ⓓ Ⓔ	
5 Ⓐ Ⓑ Ⓒ Ⓓ Ⓔ	
6 Ⓐ Ⓑ Ⓒ Ⓓ Ⓔ	
7 Ⓐ Ⓑ Ⓒ Ⓓ Ⓔ	
8 Ⓐ Ⓑ Ⓒ Ⓓ Ⓔ	

Each numbered blank in the TRANSCRIPT is a question. You will be given a separate answer sheet like the sample here, to which you will transfer your answers. The answer sheet has a numbered row of circles for each question. The answer for blank number 1 is "B." We have already transferred this to number 1 in the Sample Answer Sheet, by darkening the circle marked "B."

Now transfer your answer for each of questions 2 through 15 to the answer sheet. That is, beside each number on the answer sheet find the letter that is the same as the letter you wrote in the blank with the same number in the TRANSCRIPT, and darken the circle marked with that letter.

After you have marked 15, continue with blank number 16 on the next page WITHOUT WAITING FOR A SIGNAL.

SAMPLE ANSWER SHEET (CONTINUED)	
9 Ⓐ Ⓑ Ⓒ Ⓓ Ⓔ	
10 Ⓐ Ⓑ Ⓒ Ⓓ Ⓔ	
11 Ⓐ Ⓑ Ⓒ Ⓓ Ⓔ	
12 Ⓐ Ⓑ Ⓒ Ⓓ Ⓔ	
13 Ⓐ Ⓑ Ⓒ Ⓓ Ⓔ	
14 Ⓐ Ⓑ Ⓒ Ⓓ Ⓔ	
15 Ⓐ Ⓑ Ⓒ Ⓓ Ⓔ	

Example D—continued.

Alphabetic Word List

all—A	know—A	to discover—A
at—C	knows—D	to discuss—D
		to endorse—C
bring—A	needed—B	to visit—B
collection—B	promote—B	treatments—A
correction—C		
	recognizing—D	understand—D
discuss—C		undertake—B
during—D	reducing—A	
		virtue—D
friend—A	satisfied—D	visit—A
	say—C	volume—B
indicated—C	see—B	
insisted—D	soon—C	young—C
is—B		
is not—A	their—D	

Transcript (continued)

In order to _____ _____ this change,
16   17

mothers have been invited _____ the schools
18

when _____ children are being examined and
19

_____ the _____ necessary for the _____ of
20   21   22

defects. There is a distinct _____ in having a
23

mother _____ that her child _____ the only
24   25

one who needs attention. . . .

(The rest of the practice dictation is not transcribed here.)

Your notes should show that the word "bring" goes in blank 16, and "about" in blank 17. But "about" is *not in the list*; so "E" should be your answer for question 17.

The two words, "to visit—B," are needed for 18, and the one word "visit—A," would be an incorrect answer.

Compare your answers with the correct answers. If one of your answers does not agree with the correct answer, again compare your notes with the samples and make certain you understand the instructions. The correct answers for 16 through 25 are as follows: 16 A; 17 E; 18 B; 19 D; 20 D; 21 E; 22 C; 23 E; 24 B; and 25 A.

For the actual test you will use a separate answer sheet. As scoring will be done by an electronic scoring machine, it is important that you follow directions carefully. Use a medium No. 2 pencil. You must keep your mark for a question within the box. If you have to erase a mark, be sure to erase it completely. Mark only one answer for each question.

For any stenographer who missed the practice dictation, part of it is given below:

"I realize that this practice dictation is not a part of the examination proper and is not to be scored.

SAMPLE ANSWER SHEET

16 Ⓐ Ⓑ ● Ⓓ Ⓔ
17 Ⓐ Ⓑ Ⓒ Ⓓ ●
18 Ⓐ ● Ⓒ Ⓓ Ⓔ
19 Ⓐ Ⓑ Ⓒ ● Ⓔ
20 Ⓐ Ⓑ Ⓒ ● Ⓔ
21 Ⓐ Ⓑ Ⓒ Ⓓ ●
22 Ⓐ Ⓑ ● Ⓓ Ⓔ
23 Ⓐ Ⓑ Ⓒ Ⓓ ●
24 Ⓐ ● Ⓒ Ⓓ Ⓔ
25 ● Ⓑ Ⓒ Ⓓ Ⓔ

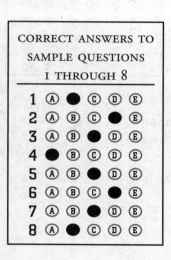

CORRECT ANSWERS TO SAMPLE QUESTIONS I THROUGH 8

1 Ⓐ ● Ⓒ Ⓓ Ⓔ
2 Ⓐ Ⓑ Ⓒ ● Ⓔ
3 Ⓐ Ⓑ ● Ⓓ Ⓔ
4 ● Ⓑ Ⓒ Ⓓ Ⓔ
5 Ⓐ Ⓑ ● Ⓓ Ⓔ
6 Ⓐ Ⓑ Ⓒ ● Ⓔ
7 Ⓐ Ⓑ ● Ⓓ Ⓔ
8 Ⓐ ● Ⓒ Ⓓ Ⓔ

CORRECT ANSWERS TO SAMPLE QUESTIONS 9 THROUGH 15

9 Ⓐ Ⓑ ● Ⓓ Ⓔ
10 Ⓐ Ⓑ Ⓒ ● Ⓔ
11 ● Ⓑ Ⓒ Ⓓ Ⓔ
12 Ⓐ Ⓑ Ⓒ ● Ⓔ
13 Ⓐ Ⓑ ● Ⓓ Ⓔ
14 ● Ⓑ Ⓒ Ⓓ Ⓔ
15 Ⓐ ● Ⓒ Ⓓ Ⓔ

"The work of preventing and correcting physical defects in children is becoming more effective as a result of a change in the attitude of many parents. In order to bring about this change, mothers have been invited to visit the schools when their children are being examined and to discuss the treatment necessary for the correction of defects. There is a distinct value in having a mother see that her child is not the only one who needs attention......"

Example E—Dictation Test Transcript Booklet

Directions for Completing the Transcript

A TRANSCRIPT of the dictation you have just taken is given on the following pages. As in the TRANSCRIPT for the practice dictation, there are numbered blank spaces for many of the words that were dictated. You are to compare your notes with the TRANSCRIPT and, when you come to a blank, decide what word or words belong there. For most of the blanks the words are included in the list beside the TRANSCRIPT; each is followed by a letter, A, B, C, or D. To show that you know which word or words belong in each blank space, you are to write the letter in the blank. You are to write E if the answer is NOT listed. (In addition you may write the word or words, or the shorthand for them, if you wish.) The same choice may belong in more than one blank.

After you have compared your notes with the TRANSCRIPT and have chosen the answer for each blank space, you will be given additional time to transfer your answers to a separate answer sheet.

Directions for Marking the Separate Answer Sheet

On the answer sheet, each question number stands for the blank with the same number in the TRANSCRIPT. For each number, you are to darken the circle with the letter that is the same as the letter you wrote in the TRANSCRIPT. (The answers in this booklet will not be rated.) Be sure to use your pencil and record your answers on the separate answer sheet. You must keep your mark within the circle. If you have to erase a mark, be sure to erase it completely. Make only one mark for each question.

Work quickly so that you will be able to finish in the time allowed. First you should darken the circles on the answer sheet for the blanks you have lettered. You may continue to use your notes if you have not finished writing letters in the blanks in the TRANSCRIPT, or if you wish to make sure you have lettered them correctly.

DO NOT OPEN THIS BOOKLET UNTIL TOLD TO DO SO.

Word List

Write *E* if the answer is NOT listed.

administration—C increase—A   shorthand—D
along the—B   in the—D   shown—C
area—A   stenography—B
at first—A   known—D   study—C
                               subject—A

claimed—C   line—C
classes—B   taught—D
concluded—D   mainly—B   that—C
could be—D   marked—B   the—D
courses—C   mostly—D   these—B
                               this—A
decrease—D   observation—B thought—B
discriminating—C observing—A to be—A
discrimination—D offered—C   training—D
                  of value—C
education—B   open—A   valuable—A
enrolled—D   vast—A
entering—A   popular—B
                  power—B
field—D   powers—D
first—D   practical—A

given—B   shaping—A
great—C   sharpen—B

Transcript

The number _____ in shorthand _____
          1   2

_____ high schools has _____ a _____
3   4   5

_____. Today _____ _____ is one of the
6   7   8

most _____ _____ _____ _____ of busi-
     9   10   11   12

ness _____. When _____ _____ _____
    13   14   15   16

_____ educators _____ that it _____
17   18   19

_____ _____ in _____ _____ _____ of
20   21   22   23   24

_____ and _____. . . .
25   26

CONTINUE ON THE NEXT PAGE WITHOUT WAITING FOR A SIGNAL.

Word List

Write *E* if the answer is NOT listed.

a change—D	has—C	schools—D
administration—C	had—B	shorthand—D
aims—A	have come—A	should be—A
always been—A	high school—B	significance—C
		stenography—B
begun—D	increased—D	study—C
businesses—A	increasing—C	subject—A
	institutions—D	
came—D	instruction—C	thinking—C
changes—B	it—B	this—A
come—C		thought—B
	offered—C	tool—B
defects—B	office—A	to realize—B
demand—B	official—C	to recognize—B
differences—D	often been—B	
	ought to be—B	valuable—A
education—B		vocational—C
educators—D	place—B	
	placement—D	when the—D
for—D	prevailing—B	with—A
		without—C
given—B	rule—D	workers—C
grade—C		
grading—B		

Transcript (continued)

... However, _____, the growth of _____
      27   28
and the _____ _____ for _____ _____,
      29   30   31   32
_____ have _____ _____ the _____ of
33   34   35   36
_____ _____ a _____ _____. With the
37   38   39   40
_____ in the _____ of _____ _____
41   42   43   44
_____ in the _____ _____ of the _____.
45   46   47   48
The _____ _____ _____ _____ that
     49   50   51   52
_____ _____ _____ in _____. ....
53   54   55   56

CONTINUE ON THE NEXT PAGE WITHOUT WAITING FOR A SIGNAL.

Word List

Write *E* if the answer is NOT listed.

became—B   junior high—D   study—C
because—B   subject—A
                    less—B
came—D   lessened—C   taught—D
change—A   level—C   that—C
changed—C   little—A   the—D
could—C   lost—D   their—B
could be—D   there—B
                    manner—B   this—A
date—D   method—C   time—B
                    moved—C   training—D
                    moved down—B
first—D   usefulness—B
graduate—D   occupational—B   utility—C
graduated—B
                    recognized—A   vocational—C
had little—C
had no—A   shorthand—D   which—A
here—D   since—C
high—C   soon—C
                    stenography—B
into being—A   student—A
into business—C   students—C

Transcript (continued)

... When the _____ school _____ _____
              57   58   59

_____, _____ was _____ to _____ _____
60   61   62   63   64

with _____ _____ in _____ _____ _____
     65   66   67   68   69

the _____ was _____. It was _____ _____
    70   71   72   73

that _____ _____ place _____ _____ the
     74   75   76   77

_____ had _____ _____ _____ _____ by
78   79   80   81   82

the _____ the _____ _____ ....
    83   84   85   86

CONTINUE ON THE NEXT PAGE WITHOUT WAITING FOR A SIGNAL.

Word List

Write *E* if the answer is NOT listed.

advanced—A   job—B   showed—A
age—A   junior high—D   so—A
as far as—C   stenographers—C
at which—D   level—C   studies—B
at work—A   surveys—A

may be—C

be—B   takes—A
near as—A   taught—D
date—D   nearly as—C   tendency—B
that—C
education—B   offered—C   there—B
enter—D   often—B   this—A
only—B   through—D
found—D   time—B
possible—D   training—D
graduating—A
graduation—C   rarely—D   undertake—A
reason—B   until—A
has—C   reasons—D   upgrade—D
high school—B   retained—B

when—C
in—A   school—A   which—A
in order—D   secretaries—D   will—B
increased—D   secures—D   would—D
into—B   seldom—C   working—B

Transcript (continued)

. . . Moreover, _____ of _____ with _____
           87   88   89

_____ _____ _____ school _____ _____
90   91   92   93   94

them _____ as _____. For _____ _____,
      95   96   97   98

shorthand was _____ to the _____ _____
           99   100   101

and is _____ as _____ _____ to the _____
     102   103   104   105

of _____ _____ _____ the skill _____
   106   107   108   109

_____ _____ _____ the student _____ a
110   111   112   113

_____. Because the _____ _____ students
114   115   116

_____ office _____ _____ _____, there is
117   118   119   120

_____ a _____ to _____ _____ education
121   122   123   124

_____ the junior college.
125

DICTATION TEST

Answer Key

1. D	33. D	65. A	97. A
2. B	34. C	66. A	98. B
3. D	35. B	67. D	99. E
4. C	36. E	68. B	100. B
5. B	37. E	69. E	101. C
6. A	38. E	70. A	102. C
7. A	39. C	71. D	103. A
8. A	40. B	72. C	104. D
9. B	41. D	73. E	105. B
10. C	42. A	74. D	106. C
11. D	43. C	75. A	107. A
12. D	44. D	76. B	108. C
13. B	45. B	77. B	109. B
14. D	46. C	78. D	110. B
15. E	47. D	79. D	111. B
16. D	48. A	80. E	112. C
17. D	49. B	81. C	113. A
18. C	50. B	82. C	114. B
19. E	51. C	83. B	115. A
20. C	52. A	84. A	116. D
21. B	53. B	85. C	117. D
22. E	54. A	86. D	118. E
23. D	55. C	87. A	119. C
24. D	56. B	88. E	120. A
25. B	57. D	89. B	121. E
26. D	58. D	90. B	122. B
27. A	59. D	91. D	123. D
28. E	60. A	92. D	124. E
29. D	61. D	93. C	125. B
30. B	62. B	94. D	
31. A	63. C	95. A	
32. C	64. C	96. C	

Dictation

Practice, Practice, Practice

(NOTE: You will need another person to dictate each practice exercise. Allow 30 minutes to finish the transcript and mark your answers.)

Practice Set 1

The Dictation

	Finish reading each two lines at the number of seconds indicated below
To be able to express your ideas simply and clearly, it is necessary	10
that you have a good command of the language. (Period) The greater your vocabulary,	20
the more interesting and effective your conversation. (Period) Dr. Eliot, former	30
president of Harvard, said, "I recognize but one mental acquisition that	40
is an essential part of the education of a lady or a gentleman; namely,	50
an accurate and refined use of the mother tongue." (Period) Fortunately, this	1 min.
is an acquisition within the reach of everyone. (Period) Only two things	10
are necessary: a good dictionary and a desire to speak well. (Period)	20
Add to these the association with educated, intelligent people	30
and ready access to a public library, and there is no reason	40
in the world why you cannot acquire a rich and colorful	50
vocabulary. (Period) When you hear a new word or read it in	2 min.
a book, learn its meaning and pronunciation. (Period) Until you are	10
wholly familiar with the word and are able to use it in	20

your conversation, it is not		
a part of your vocabulary. (Period) It		30
is not enough to know how to		
pronounce a word and to have a general		40
idea of its meaning; you		
must know how to use it correctly in		50
your speech. (Period) Remember that there		
is always a right word for every purpose. (Period)		3 min.

Reprinted with permission from Gregg Shorthand Simplified for Colleges, *Leslie, Zoubeck, and Hosler. 1958, Gregg Publishing Division, McGraw-Hill Book Co., Inc.*

The Transcript

Compare your notes with the transcript. Then select the correct word for each blank space and write the letter of your choice in the space.

Word List

Write *E* if the answer is NOT listed.

ability—B	goal—B	one—D
able—C	great—C	only—B
accurate—D	greater—B	our—D
acquire—D	greatest—D	
acquisition—B		part—A
acquisitive—C	Harvard—C	partial—C
actual—C		present—D
	ideal—B	president—A
capable—D	ideas—A	
clear—C	interest—B	realize—D
clearly—B	interesting—A	refined—D
command—C		remind—C
conservation—B	ladies—A	
conversation—B	lady—B	sensual—B
converse—C	language—A	simple—D
	length—B	
educate—C		to exist—C
effect—C	many—B	to express—B
effecting—B	mature—D	tongue—C
effective—D	medical—C	
essence—D	mental—A	use—A
essential—C	more—C	used—B
	mortal—D	
formal—C	most—A	woman—C
former—A		won—C
	natural—C	
gentleman—A	necessary—D	your—C
gentlemen—C	needed—C	

Transcript

To be _____ _____ _____ _____
        1   2   3   4

_____ and _____, it is _____ that you have
  5   6   7

a _____ _____ of the _____. The _____
   8   9   10   11

your _____, the _____ _____ and _____
     12   13   14   15

your _____.
     16

Dr. Eliot, _____ _____ of _____, said,
          17   18   19

"I _____ but _____ _____ _____ that is
  20   21   22   23

an _____ _____ of the _____ of a _____
   24   25   26   27

or a _____; namely, an _____ and _____
   28   29   30

_____ of the _____ _____." . . .
 31   32   33

Word List

Write *E* if the answer is NOT listed.

acquaint—D	intellect—B	their—A
acquire—C	intelligent—A	there—D
acquired—B		these—A
acquisition—A	liberty—D	they're—B
association—B		this—B
assumption—D	necessary—D	those—B
	needed—A	to—B
can—B	no—A	to say—B
cannot—A	now—C	to speak—C
colored—D		too—D
colorful—B	people—C	two—A
	persons—B	
desire—A	public—B	vocality—C
dream—D		
	rare—B	well—B
educated—D	rationale—B	when—C
education—C	reach—C	where—A
everybody—C	reading—A	why—D
everyone—B	realm—B	will—D
	reason—C	within—D
grand—B	republic—C	without—C
great—D	rich—C	

Transcript (continued)

. . . Fortunately, _____ is an _____ _____
34   35   36

the _____ of _____. Only _____ _____ are
37   38   39   40

_____: a _____ _____ and a _____ _____
41   42   43   44   45

_____. Add to _____ the _____ with
46   47   48

_____, _____ _____ and _____ _____ to
49   50   51   52   53

a _____ _____, and _____ is _____
54   55   56   57

_____ in the _____ _____ you _____
58   59   60   61

_____ a _____ and _____ _____. . . .
62   63   64   65

Word List

Write *E* if the answer is NOT listed.

a—C   is—B   the—A
able—A   it—A   these—B
air—D   its—C   this—C
also—D   to abuse—D
an—B   know—C   to lose—B
and—B   to use—C
as—A   lean—A
             learn—D   vocabulary—B
book—B   learned—C   vocality—D
buck—D
             meaning—B   which—B
conservation—C means—C   whole—D
conversation—A mental—D   wholly—B
converse—B   moaning—A   within—A
                           word—B
familiar—D   new—D   world—D
family—C   now—B
                           you—B
hear—C   our—B   your—D
heard—D
here—B   part—D
holy—C   partial—B
             pronounced—C
in—C
into—D   red—C

Transcript (continued)

. . . When _____ _____ a _____ _____
            66   67   68   69

or _____ _____ _____ a _____ , _____
   70   71   72   73   74

_____ _____ and _____. Until you _____
75   76   77   78

_____ _____ _____ _____ word _____
79   80   81   82   83

are _____ _____ it in _____ _____, it
    84   85   86   87

_____ _____ _____ _____ _____ your
88   89   90   91   92

_____ . . . .
93

Word List

Write *E* if the answer is NOT listed.

all—C	into—B	there—A
alright—B	is—D	to abuse—A
an—A	it—C	to have—C
as—A	its—B	to hold—B
		to know—A
correct—B	meaning—C	to pronounce—B
correction—C	morning—B	to propose—D
correctly—D	most—D	to say—C
	must—B	to use—B
every—D		to utilize—C
everyone—B	not—B	tonight—B
	now—C	
for—C	us—C	
four—A	our—C	
		warn—C
general—A	propose—A	who—C
gentle—C		word—A
	speak—D	work—B
how—D	speech—A	write—C
idea—D	than—C	your—B
ideal—B	that—D	
in—A	their—B	
inside—C		

Transcript (continued)

... It _____ _____ _____ _____
     94   95   96   97

_____ _____ a _____ _____ _____ a
 98   99   100   101   102

_____ _____ of _____ _____ ; you _____
 103 104   105 106   107

know _____ _____ it _____ _____ _____
    108 109   110 111 112

_____.
 113

Remember _____ _____ is _____ a
       114 115   116

_____ word _____ _____ _____.
 117   118 119 120

Answers for Practice Set 1

1. **C**	19. **C**	37. **C**	55. **E**
2. **B**	20. **E**	38. **B**	56. **D**
3. **C**	21. **D**	39. **A**	57. **A**
4. **A**	22. **A**	40. **E**	58. **C**
5. **E**	23. **B**	41. **D**	59. **B**
6. **B**	24. **C**	42. **E**	60. **D**
7. **D**	25. **A**	43. **E**	61. **A**
8. **E**	26. **E**	44. **A**	62. **C**
9. **C**	27. **B**	45. **C**	63. **C**
10. **A**	28. **A**	46. **B**	64. **B**
11. **B**	29. **D**	47. **A**	65. **E**
12. **E**	30. **D**	48. **B**	66. **B**
13. **C**	31. **A**	49. **D**	67. **C**
14. **A**	32. **E**	50. **A**	68. **D**
15. **D**	33. **C**	51. **C**	69. **B**
16. **B**	34. **B**	52. **E**	70. **E**
17. **A**	35. **A**	53. **E**	71. **A**
18. **A**	36. **D**	54. **B**	72. **C**

73. **B**	85. **C**	97. **A**	109. **B**
74. **D**	86. **D**	98. **C**	110. **D**
75. **C**	87. **A**	99. **B**	111. **A**
76. **B**	88. **B**	100. **A**	112. **B**
77. **E**	89. **E**	101. **E**	113. **A**
78. **C**	90. **C**	102. **C**	114. **D**
79. **B**	91. **D**	103. **A**	115. **A**
80. **D**	92. **E**	104. **D**	116. **E**
81. **E**	93. **B**	105. **B**	117. **E**
82. **A**	94. **D**	106. **C**	118. **C**
83. **B**	95. **B**	107. **B**	119. **D**
84. **A**	96. **E**	108. **D**	120. **E**

Practice Set 2

The Dictation

Finish reading each two lines
at the number of seconds
indicated below

Each year you, with millions of other Americans, spend an agonizing	10
period of indecision considering the pros and cons of the various trips presented	20
in the travel folders you have accumulated. (Period) The fact that your	30
budget may be definitely limited does not detract from the enjoyment you	40
derive from reading of the far-off places so attractively described and	50
pictured in the literature of the various bus, railroad, steamship, and	1 min.
airlines. (Period) The annual search for something different to do during the	10
vacation period adds to the zest of the vacation itself. (Period) The extensive	20
airline services now available make it possible for one to consider trips that	30
previously were impossible because of time limitations. (Period) High among	40
the trips that might appeal to you is travel in Europe. (Period) You can relax	50
in the scenic splendor of the Old World and revel in its art masterpieces,	2 min.
its colorful native pageants, and its quaint customs and costumes. (Period)	10

Flying the Atlantic to Europe will
save you precious days of that   20

all-too-short vacation period. (Period)
You will have more time to spend   30

in visiting each country. (Period) It will
be possible for you to become better   40

acquainted with the people and their
everyday pursuits. (Period) You can   50

see some of the byways that the
average tourist so frequently misses. (Period)   3 min.

Reprinted with permission from Gregg Shorthand Simplified for Colleges, *Leslie, Zoubeck, and Hosler. 1958,
Gregg Publishing Division, McGraw-Hill Book Co., Inc.*

The Transcript

Compare your notes with the transcript. Then select the correct word for each blank
space and write the letter of your choice in the space.

Word List

Write *E* if the answer is NOT listed.

accumulated—A	enjoyable—D	present—C
accustomed—C	enjoyment—B	presented—D
airlines—C		pros—D
airplanes—D	faced—D	prose—A
airways—B	fact—C	
Americas—D	fat—B	railroad—B
Americans—A	folders—B	railway—C
another—B	folds—D	reading—A
attraction—D		reads—B
attractively—C	indecision—A	
	indigestion—B	spend—D
budding—A		spent—B
budget—B	limitation—B	steamer—A
bus—A	literate—D	steamship—D
bussed—B	literature—B	
		trail—C
cans—C	million—C	travel—A
cons—B	millions—D	traveled—B
considerate—C		tricks—A
	organizing—A	
defined—C	other—C	varied—D
definitely—D		various—C
derailed—D	period—C	very—B
derived—C	picture—A	
describe—C	pictured—D	year—B
detract—A	pitcher—C	your—C
distract—C	placed—B	
disturbed—B	places—A	

Transcript

Each _____ you, with _____ of _____
      1   2   3

_____, _____ an _____ _____ of _____
4   5   6   7   8

_____ the _____ and _____ of the _____
9   10   11   12

_____ _____ in the _____ _____ you have
13   14   15   16

_____. The _____ that your _____ may
17   18   19

be _____ _____ does not _____ from the
20   21   22

_____ you _____ from _____ of the far-off
23   24   25

_____ so _____ _____ and _____ in the
26   27   28   29

_____ of the _____ _____, _____,
30   31   32   33

_____, and _____. . . .
34   35

Word List

Write *E* if the answer is NOT listed.

aids—C   limitations—D   siege—B
airplane—B   limitless—A   someone—A
annual—B   limits—C
annul—C   time—B
are—B   made—A   to conclude—C
available—B   make—D   to conduct—A
availed—D   mate—C   to dew—D
                                       to do—B
because—A   new—D   to due—A
become—C   now—C   tricks—D
                                       trips—A
different—C   one—B
diverse—D   vacation—A
during—C   period—D   vocation—B
                       possible—A
expensive—A   predated—D   wear—A
extensive—D   previously—B   were—C
                       probable—C   won—D
improbable—B
its—C   search—A   zeal—B
itself—B   seek—D   zest—C
                       servants—D
just—D   services—A

Transcript (continued)

. . . The _____ _____ for _____ _____
       36   37   38   39

_____ _____ the _____ _____ _____ to
  40   41   42   43   44

the _____ of the vacation _____.
   45   46

The _____ _____ _____ _____ _____
     47   48   49   50   51

_____ it _____ for _____ _____ _____
  52   53   54   55   56

that _____ _____ _____ _____ of _____
    57   58   59   60   61

_____ . . . .
  62

Word List

Write *E* if the answer is NOT listed.

able—A	masterworks—B	scene—C
aged—D	may—A	scenery—A
amid—D	might—D	scenic—B
among—B		splendid—C
appear—C	native—A	
arch—C	natural—B	than—B
art—A	nature—D	that—C
	night—B	travail—D
can—D		travel—C
can't—C	old—C	tricks—C
colored—A		trips—A
colorful—C	pageants—A	
costumes—B	pages—B	world—A
customs—D		
	quaint—C	you—B
England—B	queer—D	your—A
Europe—A	quick—A	
globe—B	rebel—C	
	relapse—B	
it's—A	relax—D	
its—D	revel—B	

Transcript (continued)

. . . High _____ the _____ _____ _____
63   64   65   66

_____ to _____ is _____ in _____. You
67 68   69   70

_____ _____ in the _____ _____ of the
71 72   73 74

_____ _____ and _____ in _____ _____
75 76   77   78   79

_____, its _____ _____ _____, and its
80   81   82   83

_____ _____ and _____. . . .
84 85   86

Word List

Write *E* if the answer is NOT listed.

acquainted—A	misses—A	than—B
acquitted—D	misuse—C	their—C
Atlanta—B	more—C	there—B
Atlantic—B	most—D	to become—A
avarice—D	Mrs.—B	to begin—B
average—C	much—A	to share—B
		to spend—A
be—B	often—D	tourism—D
best—B	overage—B	tourist—A
better—C		twist—C
bylaws—A	passable—C	
byways—B	people—D	Utopia—A
	period—C	
can—B	person—C	vacation—A
could—D	possible—D	visited—B
country—A	possibility—A	visiting—C
county—B	precious—B	visitor—A
	precocious—D	vocation—C
day—B	pursues—B	
days—C	pursuits—C	will—D
daze—A		would—C
	safe—C	
every—C	save—A	
everyday—A	sea—A	
everyone—D	see—D	
	shall—A	
had—A	some—A	
have—B	sum—C	

Transcript (continued)

. . . Flying the _____ to _____ will _____

         87   88   89

you _____ _____ of _____ all-to-short

     90   91   92

_____ . You _____ _____ _____

 93   94   95   96   97

_____ _____ in _____ _____ _____ . It

 98   99   100   101   102

_____ _____ _____ for you _____ _____

 103   104   105   106   107

_____ with the _____ and _____ _____

 108   109   110   111

_____ . You _____ _____ _____ of the

 112   113   114   115

_____ that the _____ _____ so _____

 116   117   118   119

_____ .

 120

Answers for Practice Set 2

1. **B**	15. **A**	29. **D**	43. **D**
2. **D**	16. **B**	30. **B**	44. **E**
3. **C**	17. **A**	31. **C**	45. **C**
4. **A**	18. **C**	32. **A**	46. **B**
5. **D**	19. **B**	33. **B**	47. **D**
6. **E**	20. **D**	34. **D**	48. **E**
7. **C**	21. **E**	35. **C**	49. **A**
8. **A**	22. **A**	36. **B**	50. **C**
9. **E**	23. **B**	37. **A**	51. **B**
10. **D**	24. **C**	38. **E**	52. **D**
11. **B**	25. **A**	39. **C**	53. **A**
12. **C**	26. **A**	40. **B**	54. **B**
13. **E**	27. **C**	41. **C**	55. **D**
14. **D**	28. **E**	42. **A**	56. **A**

57.	B	73.	B	89.	A	105.	D
58.	C	74.	E	90.	B	106.	A
59.	E	75.	C	91.	C	107.	C
60.	A	76.	A	92.	E	108.	A
61.	B	77.	B	93.	A	109.	D
62.	D	78.	D	94.	C	110.	C
63.	B	79.	A	95.	D	111.	A
64.	A	80.	E	96.	B	112.	C
65.	C	81.	C	97.	C	113.	B
66.	D	82.	A	98.	E	114.	D
67.	E	83.	A	99.	A	115.	A
68.	B	84.	C	100.	C	116.	B
69.	C	85.	D	101.	E	117.	C
70.	A	86.	B	102.	A	118.	A
71.	D	87.	C	103.	D	119.	E
72.	D	88.	E	104.	B	120.	A

Practice Set 3

The Dictation

	Finish reading each two lines at the number of seconds indicated below

The boy was ten years old, and
he had a passion for machinery. (Period) He — 10

tinkered with all the clocks in the old
white farmhouse until they kept time — 20

properly. (Period) One Sunday morning after
church a neighbor took out his big gold — 30

huntingcase watch. (Period) He said, "Henry,
can you fix my old turnip?" (Question mark) The — 40

boy found that a jewel was loose in the
works. (Period) He put it back into place and — 50

the watch ran. (Period) The neighbors around
Dearborn began to bring their ailing old — 1 min.

timepieces. (Period) So young Henry Ford set up
shop on a shelf in his bedroom, working — 10

nights after chores. (Period) In the winter
he kept warm with an oil lantern — 20

between his feet. (Period) He ground a shingle
nail down into a tiny screwdriver and made — 30

files from knitting needles. (Period) All
his life he tinkered with watches and — 40

never had to use a jeweler's eyeglass. (Period)
He could almost see with his long, thin, — 50

steel-spring fingers: the fingers of
the hands that put the nation on wheels. (Period) — 2 min.

His passion for machinery became an idea, and the power of that idea has	10
rolled on through the years. (Period) He learned how to run, repair, and make every	20
kind of machine there was. (Period) Then he began on the machine that wasn't	30
a horseless carriage. (Period) In 1896, seven years before the founding of the	40
Ford Motor Company, he trundled his first little two-passenger machine out	50
into one of the alleys of Detroit and ran it around the block. (Period)	3 min.

Reprinted with permission from Gregg Shorthand Simplified for Colleges, *Leslie, Zoubeck, and Hosler. 1958, Gregg Publishing Division, McGraw-Hill Book Co., Inc.*

The Transcript

Compare your notes with the transcript. Then select the correct word for each blank space and write the letter of your choice in the space.

Word List

Write *E* if the answer is NOT listed.

all—C	large—B	till—B
		time—A
big—B	machine—C	timed—B
bigger—D	machinery—B	tinker—A
boat—D	meaning—C	tinkered—D
boy—A	morning—A	took—D
		turned—A
can—D	neighbor—B	turnip—B
can't—C	neighbors—C	
charge—B		until—D
church—C	oil—D	
clock—A	our—D	watch—B
		water—A
farm—A	passion—A	while—B
farmhouse—C	position—C	white—A
fix—A	proper—D	
fixed—C	properly—C	years—C
fox—B	property—A	yours—A
gold—C	take—A	
good—D	taken—B	
	ten—D	
keep—C	then—C	
kept—B	tied—C	

Transcript

The _____ was _____ _____ _____, and
     1   2   3   4

he had a _____ for _____. He _____ with
     5   6   7

_____ the _____ in the _____ _____
 8   9   10   11

_____ _____ they _____ _____ _____.
 12   13   14   15   16

One _____ _____ _____ _____ a
    17   18   19   20

_____ _____ _____ his _____ _____
 21   22   23   24   25

huntingcase _____. He said, "Henry, _____
      26   27

you _____ my _____ _____?" . . .
  28   29   30

Word List

Write *E* if the answer is NOT listed.

abound—C	in—A	sat—A
ailed—B	into—B	self—D
ailing—C		sharp—A
around—A	jewel—B	shelf—C
	jeweler—D	ship—B
back—C		shop—D
backed—B	keep—D	sit—D
bedroom—B		
begin—A	lecture—B	their—D
between—C	loose—C	there—C
bog—C	lose—D	timepieces—A
book—D		timers—D
bottom—D	neighborhood—D	to bring—B
brought—C	neighborhoods—A	
	night—D	under—C
chores—B	nights—C	
		warm—B
feel—C	oil—A	warn—C
feet—D	old—D	water—A
find—B		winner—C
foot—B	pat—C	winter—D
found—D	please—C	work—B
	put—D	worked—D
him—B		works—A
his—A	ran—D	
	run—C	

Transcript (continued)

. . . The _____ _____ that a _____ was
     31   32   33

_____ in the _____. He _____ it _____
  34   35   36   37

_____ _____ and the _____ _____.
  38   39   40   41

The _____ _____ Dearborn _____ ____
      42   43   44   45

__ _____ _____ _____ _____. So _____
  46   47   48   49   50

Henry Ford _____ _____ _____ on a
             51   52   53

_____ in his _____, _____ _____ after
  54   55   56   57

_____. In the _____ he _____ _____ with
  58   59   60   61

an _____ _____ _____ his _____. . . .
     62   63   64   65

Word List

Write *E* if the answer is NOT listed.

almost—B	knitted—C	puts—D
always—C	knitting—B	
	knotting—A	saw—C
can—D		see—D
could—C	life—C	seen—A
	live—B	single—C
down—B	long—B	
	lung—A	than—C
eyeball—B		then—D
eyeglass—A	made—A	thin—A
	maid—B	tinny—C
file—D	make—A	tiny—D
filed—A		
files—C	nail—D	us—B
fingered—A	nailed—B	used—A
fingers—B	nation—C	
	national—A	watched—D
grind—B	needled—A	watches—A
ground—A	needles—D	wheeled—B
	noodles—C	wheels—D
had—D	null—A	
hard—C		
	pat—B	
jewels—C	put—A	

Transcript (continued)

. . . He _____ a _____ _____ _____
     66   67   68   69

into a _____ _____ and _____ _____ from
   70   71   72   73

_____ _____. All his _____ he tinkered
74   75   76

with _____ and _____ _____ to _____ a
    77   78 79   80

_____ _____.
81   82

He _____ _____ _____ with his _____,
   83   84   85   86

_____, steel spring _____: the fingers of
87   88

the _____ that _____ the _____ on
   89   90   91

_____. . . .
92

Word List

Write *E* if the answer is NOT listed.

all—A foremost—C power—A
alleys—B founded—D powerful—D
allied—D founding—C
allies—C ran—A
horse sense—A repaint—C
became—D repair—A
bccome—A ideal—C roll—C
began—C rolled—B
begin—D kin—B run—B
black—A kind—A
blacked—C seven—B
blocked—D learn—A small—B
learned—C
carriage—A little—D threw—A
carried—C through—D
machine—D to rule—B
earned—D made—D to run—D
every—C make—B trampled—A
everything—D trundled—D
passion—C
finding—B pasture—A year—A
first—A patient—D yours—B

Transcript (continued)

. . . His _____ for _____ _____ an
     93   94   95

_____, and the _____ of that idea has _____
96   97   98

on _____ the _____.
    99   100

IIe _____ _____ _____, _____, and
    101   102   103   104

_____ _____ _____ of _____ there was.
105   106   107   108

Then he _____ on the machine that wasn't—a
      109

_____ _____.
110   111

In 1896, _____ _____ before the _____
      112   113   114

of the Ford Motor Company, he _____ his
                       115

_____ _____ two-passenger machine out
116   117

into one of the _____ of Detroit and _____
          118   119

it around the _____.
    120

Answers for Practice Set 3

1. **A**	16. **C**	31. **E**	46. **D**
2. **D**	17. **E**	32. **D**	47. **C**
3. **C**	18. **A**	33. **B**	48. **D**
4. **E**	19. **E**	34. **C**	49. **A**
5. **A**	20. **C**	35. **A**	50. **B**
6. **B**	21. **B**	36. **D**	51. **E**
7. **D**	22. **D**	37. **C**	52. **E**
8. **C**	23. **E**	38. **B**	53. **D**
9. **E**	24. **A**	39. **E**	54. **C**
10. **E**	25. **C**	40. **E**	55. **B**
11. **A**	26. **B**	41. **D**	56. **E**
12. **C**	27. **D**	42. **E**	57. **C**
13. **D**	28. **A**	43. **A**	58. **B**
14. **B**	29. **E**	44. **E**	59. **D**
15. **A**	30. **B**	45. **B**	60. **E**

61. **B**	76. **C**	91. **C**	106. **C**
62. **A**	77. **A**	92. **D**	107. **A**
63. **E**	78. **B**	93. **C**	108. **D**
64. **C**	79. **D**	94. **B**	109. **C**
65. **D**	80. **E**	95. **D**	110. **E**
66. **A**	81. **E**	96. **E**	111. **A**
67. **E**	82. **A**	97. **A**	112. **B**
68. **D**	83. **C**	98. **B**	113. **A**
69. **B**	84. **B**	99. **D**	114. **C**
70. **C**	85. **D**	100. **A**	115. **D**
71. **E**	86. **B**	101. **C**	116. **A**
72. **A**	87. **A**	102. **E**	117. **D**
73. **C**	88. **B**	103. **D**	118. **B**
74. **B**	89. **E**	104. **A**	119. **A**
75. **D**	90. **A**	105. **B**	120. **C**

Practice Set 4

The Dictation

Finish reading each two lines
at the number of seconds
indicated below

The retail salesperson who plays such
a vital part in the process of distribution — 10

may well be considered one of the most
important spark plugs of our economy. (Period) — 20

He makes our free-enterprise system
work. (Period) He persuades us to exchange — 30

our money for the things that make for
better and more enjoyable living. (Period) — 40

By keeping the cash registers of America
ringing, he also keeps our factories — 50

humming. (Period) The high-pressure
salesperson of yesterday, who misrepresented — 1 min.

merchandise, is as obsolete today as the
Model T and the patent-medicine man. (Period) — 10

in the buyer's market of today, the good
salesperson is the one who induces the — 20

customer to purchase by showing him how he
will benefit. (Period) The retail salesperson — 30

should not only make people want what he has
to sell, but he should also make them want to — 40

but it from him. (Period) What a challenge! (Exclamation
Point) What he does in the place of business in which — 50

he serves reflects upon the firm, and
the firm's reputation reflects upon — 2 min.

him. (Period) The successful salesperson is
more interested in keeping the customer's   10
good will than in turning a quick
sale. (Period) Good will is an intangible   20
asset that is not visible except as
it is reflected in the faces of satisfied   30
customers. (Period) However, it is the most
valuable asset that any business can possess. (Period)   40
It is indeed more valuable than the building, the
merchandise, or the equipment. (Period) Every   50
salesperson holds the goodwill of the
establishment in his hands. (Period)   3 min.

Reprinted with permission from Gregg Shorthand Simplified for Colleges, *Leslie, Zoubeck, and Hosler. 1958,
Gregg Publishing Division, McGraw-Hill Book Co., Inc.*

The Transcript

Compare your notes with the transcript. Then select the correct word for each blank
space and write the letter of your choice in the space.

Word List

Write *E* if the answer is NOT listed.

allow—A   improved—C   retail—C
American—A   items—B   role—A

business—B   key—D   salesman—B
                                salesperson—A
can—C   life—C   seller—C
cash—D   living—D   such—C
considered—C   system—A
considering—A   make—B   systems—C
convinces—D   may—D
                   money—C   takes—C
demonstrates—A   most—D   the—C
distribution—A   much—A   things—D
                                thought of—D
economy—B   our—D   to exchange—A
enjoyable—A   to trade—C
enjoyed—B   part—B
essential—D   perhaps—A   very—C
                   persuades—B
goods—A   plays—D   way—B
                   plug—D   well—B
happen—C   plugs—C   wholesale—A
                   procedure—C work—D
important—B   process—A   worthwhile—D

Transcript

The _____ _____ who _____ _____ a
    1   2   3   4

_____ _____ in the _____ of _____
   5   6   7   8

_____ _____ be _____ one of the _____
   9   10   11   12

_____ _____ _____ of our _____. He
  13   14   15   16

makes _____ _____ _____ _____. He
        17   18   19   20

_____ us _____ our _____ for the _____
  21   22   23   24

that _____ for _____ and more _____
     25   26   27

_____ . . . .
  28

Word List

Write *E* if the answer is NOT listed.

allowing—B	industries—C	past—B
America—A	introduces—C	pressure—A
benefitting—B	keeping—C	registers—B
buyer—C	keeps—A	represented—B
buyer's—A		
	machines—C	show—B
cash—D	making—A	showing—C
coin—C	man—B	
consumer—C	market—D	to buy—D
continues—C	marketing—C	to peruse—B
customer—B	medical—D	to purchase—A
	medicinal—B	today—C
factories—D	medicine—C	
	mercantile—B	when—D
going—A	merchandise—A	where—C
good—B	merchant—B	who—C
goods—A	mistaken—C	whom—A
	Model T—B	why—D
high—C		working—B
how—A	now—B	
humming—B		yesterday—D
	obsolete—D	yesteryear—C
induces—A	opposite—C	

Transcript (continued)

. . . By _____ the _____ _____ of _____
        29   30   31   32

_____, he also _____ our _____ _____.
33   34   35   36

The _____-_____ salesperson of _____,
       37   38   39

_____ _____ _____, is as _____ _____ as
40   41   42   43   44

the _____ and the patent-_____ _____.
    45   46   47

In the _____ _____ of today, the _____
       48   49   50

salesperson is the _____ who _____ the
                   51   52

_____ _____ by _____ him _____ he
53   54   55   56

will _____. . . .
     57

Word List

Write *E* if the answer is NOT listed.

business—D   make—D   sold—C
buying—A   may—C   success—C
   might—A   successful—A

challenge—A
could—C   office—B   than—B
customer—D   one—C   them—A
customer's—A   only—A   then—D
   over—D   they—C
do—D   to bring—D

   people—D   to buy—B
faith—B   persons—A   to say—B
firm—D   place—A   to sell—A
from—C   placed—C   turning—C

goes—B   quiet—B   up—C
good—C   upon—B
   reflected—A
he—B   reflects—B   want—D
her—A   reputation—A   wanted—C
   reputed—C   which—A
interest—B   retail—B   will—A
interested—D   with—B
   sale—A
keep—C   serve—D
keeping—B   serves—C

Transcript (continued)

. . . The ___58___ salesperson ___59___ not ___60___ make ___61___ ___62___ what he has ___63___, but ___64___ ___65___ also ___66___ ___67___ want ___68___ it ___69___ him. What a ___70___! What he ___71___ in the ___72___ of ___73___ in ___74___ he ___75___ ___76___ ___77___ the ___78___, and the firm's ___79___ reflects ___80___ ___81___. The ___82___ salesperson is more ___83___ in ___84___ the ___85___ ___86___ ___87___ ___88___ in ___89___ a ___90___ ___91___. . . .

Word List

Write *E* if the answer is NOT listed.

accept—D
am—B
any—A
are—D
assist—D

built—A
business—C
busy—B

can—A
can't—B
could—D

established—B
establishment—A
except—A
exception—B

faced—D
faces—B

hands—A
has—C

helps—A
his—D
holds—B
honor—C
hour—A

indeed—A
indication—C
intangible—D
invisible—C
is—A
it—C
its—B

many—A
merchandise—A
merchant—B
more—B
most—D
much—C

or—C
our—B

possess—B
possessed—C
possession—D

reflect—B
reflected—A
reflects—C

satisfaction—C
satisfying—B

than—D
the—B
then—C

valuable—A
value—D
valued—B
viable—A
visible—B

was—D
will—C
won't—B

Transcript (continued)

. . . Good _____ _____ an _____ _____
       92   93   94   95

that is not _____ _____ as _____ is _____
       96   97   98   99

in the _____ of _____ customers.
     100   101

However, it is the _____ _____ _____
             102   103   104

that _____ _____ _____ _____. It is
    105   106   107   108

_____ _____ valuable _____ the _____,
109   110   111   112

the _____, _____ the _____. Every _____
   113   114   115   116

_____ the good will of the _____ in _____
117   118   119

_____.
120

Answers for Practice Set 4

1. C	17. D	33. E	49. D
2. A	18. E	34. A	50. B
3. D	19. A	35. D	51. E
4. C	20. D	36. B	52. A
5. E	21. B	37. C	53. B
6. B	22. A	38. A	54. A
7. A	23. C	39. D	55. C
8. A	24. D	40. C	56. A
9. D	25. B	41. E	57. E
10. B	26. E	42. A	58. B
11. C	27. A	43. D	59. E
12. D	28. D	44. C	60. A
13. B	29. C	45. B	61. D
14. E	30. D	46. C	62. D
15. C	31. B	47. B	63. A
16. B	32. A	48. A	64. B

65.	E	79.	A	93.	A	107.	A
66.	D	80.	B	94.	D	108.	B
67.	A	81.	E	95.	E	109.	A
68.	B	82.	A	96.	B	110.	B
69.	C	83.	D	97.	A	111.	D
70.	A	84.	B	98.	C	112.	E
71.	E	85.	A	99.	A	113.	A
72.	A	86.	C	100.	B	114.	C
73.	D	87.	A	101.	E	115.	E
74.	A	88.	B	102.	D	116.	E
75.	C	89.	C	103.	A	117.	B
76.	B	90.	E	104.	E	118.	A
77.	B	91.	A	105.	A	119.	D
78.	D	92.	C	106.	C	120.	A

Practice Set 5

The Dictation

Finish reading each two lines
at the number of seconds
indicated below

We say that Father keeps the house running. (Period) Father says that the house	10
keeps him running. (Period) Probably both statements are true. (Period) Let us look	20
at it in the most favorable light— the light of a lovely summer evening. (Period)	30
Father has come home from the office, has had his dinner, and has arbitrated	40
all the children's quarrels. (Period) He has settled down in his favorite chair	50
on the porch to relax and enjoy the summer evening. (Period) Right away we know	1 min.
that Father is either new to country living or that he is an incurable	10
optimist. (Period) Every beautiful summer evening he sits in that same chair to	20
relax, and every beautiful summer evening something drags him out of the chair. (Period)	30
This evening perhaps the telephone bell rings. (Period) Almost immediately Father hears	40
Mother say, "Of course, he will be delighted." (Period) Then Mother	50
comes out and breaks the news to Father that Mrs. Jones, their neighbor,	2 min.
has offered to give her some plants if Father will get them	10

now. (Period) So, Father climbs into		
the car and drives over to get the		20
plants and drives back, only to find,		
naturally, that he is to plant		30
the plants for Mother and		
that they are very delicate plants		40
that must be planted immediately. (Period)		
By this time the beautiful		50
summer evening has faded and		
the mosquitoes have come out. (Period)		3 min.

Reprinted with permission from Gregg Shorthand Simplified for Colleges, *Leslie, Zoubeck, and Hosler. 1958, Gregg Publishing Division, McGraw-Hill Book Co., Inc.*

The Transcript

Compare your notes with the transcript. Then select the correct word for each blank space and write the letter of your choice in the space.

Word List

Write *E* if the answer is NOT listed.

arbiter—B	hard—D	of—B
arbitrated—A	he's—B	office—C
are—B	hid—B	often—A
as—C	him—C	orbited—C
	his—D	our—D
boat—B	home—B	
both—A	horse—C	pair—C
	house—A	
came—B	hut—D	quakes—C
children's—C		quarrels—B
child's—B	if—D	
come—D	it—A	racing—B
	it's—D	running—D
dined—C		
	keep—D	said—D
	keeps—B	say—C
even—C		simmer—D
evening—A	light—A	stated—A
every—D	lit—C	summer—A
	lively—A	
farther—B	look—C	true—A
favorable—D	lovely—C	truth—B
favorite—B	luck—B	
fro—C		us—D
from—A	many—C	
	most—B	
	much—A	

Transcript

We _____ that _____ _____ the _____
         1   2   3   4

_____. Father _____ that the house keeps
 5   6

_____ running. Probably _____ _____
 7   8   9

_____ _____.
 10   11

Let _____ _____ at _____ in the _____
    12   13   14   15

_____ _____—the light _____ a _____
 16   17   18   19

_____ _____. Father has _____ _____
 20   21   22   23

_____ the _____, has _____ his _____,
 24   25   26   27

and has _____ _____ the _____
        28   29   30

_____. . . .
 31

Word List

Write *E* if the answer is NOT listed.

always—C	he—B	relapse—A
	him—D	relax—C
beautiful—D		
beauty—C	incubate—B	saddled—C
bountiful—A	incurable—C	same—C
	injure—A	sat—B
continent—D		scts—C
	knew—C	settled—B
done—A	know—B	share—B
down—D	known—D	sits—A
drag—C		some—D
drugs—A	life—B	someone—C
	live—C	something—B
either—A	living—A	
enjoy—D		than—C
ether—C	new—B	that—D
even—C		to relapse—D
evening—A	optometrist—A	to relax—B
ever—C	our—D	
every—D	out—B	us—A
farther—B	porch—A	we—C
Father—D	pouch—C	when—D
favorable—D		
favored—B		

Transcript (continued)

. . . He has _____ _____ in his _____
          32   33   34

chair on the _____ _____ and _____ the
             35   36   37

_____ _____. Right _____ _____ _____
38   39   40   41   42

that _____ is _____ _____ to _____
      43   44   45   46

_____ or _____ he is an _____ _____.
47   48   49   50

Every _____ summer evening _____ _____
      51   52   53

in that _____ _____ to _____, and _____
     54   55   56   57

_____ summer evening _____ _____
58   59   60

_____ _____ of the _____. . . .
61   62   63

Word List

Write *E* if the answer is NOT listed.

be—C	hers—A	offhand—B
being—D	herself—D	our—A
bell—C		out—C
bowl—A	if—A	
bricks—A	immediate—C	perchance—C
bride—B	immediately—B	perhaps—D
		plans—D
came—C	James—D	plants—B
come—B	Jones—C	purchase—A
comes—A		
	knew—A	ring—D
delighted—B		rings—A
deluded—D	Miss—B	
	mom—B	said—D
even—B	Mrs.—A	says—A
evening—A		sum—C
	neighbor—A	
get—C	new—D	telegraph—D
got—D	news—D	telephone—B
	night—C	their—B
hear—A	now—A	them—B
heard—C		they're—A
hears—D	of—C	those—A
her—C	offered—D	

Transcript (continued)

. . . This _____ _____ the _____ _____
        64   65   66   67

_____. Almost _____ Father _____ _____
 68   69   70   71

_____, "Of course, he will _____ _____.
 72   73   74

"Then Mother _____ _____ and _____ the
            75   76   77

_____ to Father that _____ _____, _____
 78   79   80   81

_____, has _____ _____ _____ _____
 82   83   84   85   86

_____ _____ Father will _____ _____
 87   88   89   90

_____. . . .
 91

Word List

Write *E* if the answer is NOT listed.

above—B	even—B	our—D
and—A	evening—C	over—C
are—A	ever—C	
	every—C	part—A
back—D		partial—C
bake—B	faded—B	planted—B
barge—D	faith—C	plants—B
bargain—B	Father—E	
beautiful—D	feted—D	solely—D
begin—A	found—A	soon—D
bountiful—C		
	immaterially—C	than—C
came—B	immediately—A	that—D
car—A	into—B	them—B
cart—D	is—E	they—A
climbs—C		time—B
climbed—D	masked—A	to find—B
come—C	most—B	to get—C
	must—C	to have—B
delicate—D		to plant—D
delicious—A	naturally—C	
driven—C	neutral—A	very—B
drives—D		
drove—D	one—A	
dug—A	only—C	

Transcript (continued)

So, ___92___ ___93___ ___94___ the ___95___ and
___96___ ___97___ ___98___ the ___99___ ___100___
___101___ ___102___, only to find, ___103___, that he
___104___ ___105___ the plants for Mother and
___106___ ___107___ ___108___ ___109___ ___110___ plants
that ___111___ be ___112___ ___113___. By this ___114___
the ___115___ ___116___ ___117___ has ___118___ and the
___119___ have ___120___ out.

Answers for Practice Set 5

1. **C**	16. **D**	31. **B**	46. **E**
2. **E**	17. **A**	32. **B**	47. **A**
3. **B**	18. **B**	33. **D**	48. **D**
4. **A**	19. **C**	34. **E**	49. **C**
5. **D**	20. **A**	35. **A**	50. **E**
6. **B**	21. **A**	36. **B**	51. **D**
7. **C**	22. **D**	37. **D**	52. **B**
8. **A**	23. **B**	38. **E**	53. **A**
9. **E**	24. **A**	39. **A**	54. **C**
10. **B**	25. **C**	40. **E**	55. **E**
11. **A**	26. **E**	41. **C**	56. **C**
12. **D**	27. **E**	42. **B**	57. **D**
13. **C**	28. **A**	43. **D**	58. **D**
14. **A**	29. **E**	44. **A**	59. **B**
15. **B**	30. **C**	45. **C**	60. **E**

61. D	76. C	91. A	106. D
62. B	77. E	92. E	107. A
63. E	78. D	93. C	108. A
64. A	79. A	94. B	109. B
65. D	80. C	95. A	110. D
66. B	81. B	96. D	111. C
67. C	82. A	97. C	112. B
68. A	83. D	98. C	113. A
69. B	84. E	99. B	114. B
70. D	85. C	100. A	115. D
71. E	86. E	101. D	116. E
72. E	87. B	102. D	117. C
73. C	88. A	103. C	118. B
74. B	89. C	104. E	119. E
75. A	90. B	105. D	120. C

PART V

THE OFFICE MACHINE OPERATOR SPECIAL TEST: THE SIMPLIFIED TYPING TEST

Introduction to the Simplified Typing Test: A Diagnostic Test

THE SIMPLIFIED TYPING TEST

Special tests are added when Office Machine Operator positions are covered by the examination. If the Office Assistant examination has not included a typing test, then a Simplified Typing Test is given for positions such as Data Transcriber, which may require knowledge of a typewriter-style keyboard.

If the examination for Office Machine Operator positions is announced separately, the Clerical Examination is given with the appropriate special tests. All applicants for Office Machine Operator positions are required to pass the Clerical Examination.

The simplified or short typing test is used by agencies at the agencies' discretion. Agencies may use the tests developed by the Office of Personnel Management or a different test.

Nature of the Test

Persons who have passed most Clerk-Typist examinations may be appointed as Composing Machine Operators. Otherwise, applicants for positions requiring knowledge of the typewriter-style keyboard must pass the 10-minute Simplified Typing Test. This test does not include any punctuation, and the interchangeable use of capital or small letters is permitted since the machines that appointees will operate have no shift key.

How the Test Is Administered and Scored

The Simplified Typing Test is administered in the same manner as the Typing Test. Each competitor will need a copy of the test and two sheets of typewriter paper. About 25 minutes will be needed for the Simplified Typing Test.

Five minutes will be allowed for reading the instructions on the face of the test. Ten minutes will be allowed for the practice exercise. After the practice typing, competitors put fresh paper in their machines, and turn the page over and begin the test. Ten minutes arc allowed for the test proper. As the test is scored by the number of correct lines, no erasures or corrections are allowed.

How to Determine the Test Score

For the Simplified Typing Test, the minimum passing score for entry-level positions is 25 correct lines.

A Diagnostic Test

The purpose of this diagnostic exam is to familiarize you with the Simplified Typing Test. This unique exam type requires a great deal of practice. Chapter 10 will give you seven full-length practice sets.

Directions

This is a test of your knowledge of the typewriter keyboard.

Type each line precisely as it is in the exercise.

Double space between lines; *single space* between words; use all *capitals.*

Type *one column down the center* of the sheet.

Leave about a 2½-inch *margin* on the left.

If you notice that you made an error, double space and begin the same line again. Do not *make any erasures or any other kinds* of *corrections.*

If you finish before time is called, begin typing the exercise again.

If you were copying from a list like the practice exercise at the top of the next page and you abandoned incorrect lines, you would be credited for having the first three lines of the exercise correctly typed if your paper looked like this—

NESBIT ED ELECTRICIAN TRANSIT BELMONT

FOLEY, DA

FOLEY DAVID SURVV

FOLEY DAVID SURVEYOR BAY COMPANY AVON

LEWIS DAN LINEMAN HYDROPOWER B

LEWIS DAN LINEMAN HYDRO POWER BEDFORD

Now copy the ten lines of the practice exercise below, in one column. If you finish before time is called, begin copying the exercise a second time. You will not be rated on this practice. The purpose of this practice is to let you exercise your fingers and to see that your machine is working properly.

Practice List

NESBIT ED ELECTRICIAN TRANSIT BELMONT

FOLEY DAVID SURVEYOR BAY COMPANY AVON

LEWIS DAN LINEMAN HYDRO POWER BEDFORD

BURKERT KARL MINER PENN COLLIERY GARY

NESBITT GUY WELDER UNITED STEEL AKRON

PRICE IRA DRYCLEANING SERVICE MANAGER

ADAM FRED ASSEMBLER AND BENCH GRINDER

BROWN MAX AUTOMOBILE MECHANIC SKILLED

WEST CORA DEMONSTRATOR OFFICE DEVICES

LOMAN LEO CALCULATING MACHINE REPAIRS

The Test

Time allotted—10 minutes

Type as many of these lines as you can in the time allowed. Double space. Type them in one column down the center of your sheet.

If you notice that you have made an error, double space and begin the same line again. Do NOT make any ERASURES or other corrections.

BABB FRIEDA AMESBURY MD BILTMORE BLVD

BACKUS EARL PONTIAC OREG RADCLIF APTS

BERRY ELMER CLAYTONA MINN ROSLYN ARMS

BEAUMONT WM SHERWOOD ILL GUNTHER CORP

LOIS GREENVILLE ALA HILL HOUSE

BUTCHER BOB BARPORT MISS ROSWELL STRT

CAPARELLO A GRANTLAND WIS FOREST LANE

DONAHUE EDW PORTLAND MO WHITELAW AVEN

ESSEX LOUIS HANOVER KANS HUNTERS APTS

FOWLER JOHN LOGANPORT LA ST PIERRE CT

HARTLEY GEO SUNCLIFFE LA CHESTER STRT

ISERMAN JOE HUNTSVILLE WY MARINE CLUB

JACOBS FRED FAIRPORT ILL GRENADA DRIV

KEMPER SAML PERDUE IND BEVERIDGE BLDG

KENNEDY LEO SEWARDS WASH TARBORO PARK

LAWRENSON W GASTONIA CONN SOCONY BLVD

LINDERMIAN F LEWISTOWN IND SEWELL AVEN

LONG GERALD GALESBURG KY NICHOLS REST

MARTIN BRAD SHAMROCK TEX FEDERAL BLDG

MORTON CHAS MEMPHIS GA CARSTAIRS VIEW

NAYLOR PAUL MANHATTAN TENN WOODY REST

NATHANSON L CLARENDON VT SEAVIEW PKWY

OBERG CAREY KNOXVILLE VA WINSTON HALL

PARKER HUGH GLENLEY WASH HOOVERS LANE

PINCKERTS M BLYFIELD ALA BURKARD BROS

POTTER ROBT WASHINGTON FLA CITRUS WAY

SKUPCEK JAS PULLMAN ME STOCKERLY BLDG

SNYDER WILL BLUERIDGE MINN OAKEN YARD

TREADWELL R GRISSBY MASS PIRATES PIKE

WALKER CARL KITTANING PA JOHNSON CORP

ACME ELECTRIC INC ADAIRSVILLE AERIALS

ARTHURS DRUG CORP EAST WILTON POWDERS

A SIMPSON TOOL CO RICHARDSTON HAMMERS

BRIGHTWOOD AND CO WALLA WALLA BASKETS

BROOKE PAINTS INC SIOUX FALLS SIZINGS

CARLTON AND BLOCK WINTON CITY GASKETS

CROWN TOOL CO INC MITCHELBURG SHOVELS

CRUCIBLE STEEL CO E SANDERTON ROLLERS

DANIEL V GENTZ CO WHITNYVILLE KETTLES

DUNN AND SONS INC BELLINGSHAIM BOILERS

ELI WYNN AND BROS YELLOWSTONE CUTTERS

E WYLAND AND SONS NORFORDTOWN HANDLES

CONTINUE WITH NEXT COLUMN.

EXPERT IRON WORKS CALLENSBURG ENGINES

F A GREGORY STORE STEUBENVINE CHISELS

FARMERS SUPPLY CO GREAT RIVER HALTERS

FREY GAS LIGHT CO FREYCHESTER BURNERS

GRECIAN MARBLE CO FAIRDEALING STATUES

HAMDEN MUSIC MART GREENCASTLE VIOLINS

I MASON TOOL SHOP CORTANNINGS GIMLETS

JOHN WEST AND SON HENSONVILE SPRINGS

JOHN W WILLIS INC GEORGESBURG BEAKERS

LA BANTA PRODUCTS GRAY ISLAND MATCHES

LEIGH IMPORTS INC LANDSVILLE WOOLENS

L PARKER GLASS CO SHREVESTOWN BOTTLES

MURRAY OPTICAL CO MILLERVILLE CLASSES

CONTINUE WITH NEXT COLUMN.

NEW YORK BAR CORP BARTHOLOMEW LANCETS

OFFICE SUPPLY INC NUTTALLBURG LEDGERS

PAPER PRODUCTS CO PAXTONVIILE TISSUES

P FRY ELECTRIC CO MONTGOMERFY MAGNETS

REO VARIETY STORE RUTERSVLLLE LADDERS

R J HOWARDS MILLS HYATTSVILLE TROWELS

S TODT AND COOPER SPRINGFIELD RIPSAWS

TREIK BROS AND CO LOGANSVILLE REAMERS

UTAH SUPPLY STORE CEDAR WOODS TRIPODS

V C CORNELL SHOPS FREEMANPORT WINCHES

IF YOU FINISH BEFORE TIME IS CALLED, BEGIN
COPYING THE LIST THE SECOND TIME.

Office Machine Simplified Typing Test

CHAPTER 10

Practice, Practice, Practice

This chapter gives you seven full-length practice tests, which should be taken under strict timed conditions. Allow only 10 minutes for each practice set.

Because this method of testing your knowledge of the typewriter keyboard is unique and probably unfamiliar to you, it is essential that you do additional practice. Repeating the practice sets can be helpful.

Remember, this test is scored by the number of *correct* lines; therefore, you must not erase or correct any errors.

Practice Set 1

Type as many of these lines as you can in the time allowed. Double space. Type them in one column down the center of your sheet.

If you notice that you have made an error, double space and begin the same line again. Do NOT make any ERASURES or other corrections.

ANGEL GRACE BRINKLEY AR SURFSIDE WALK

BERRY ALICE BRIGHTON AL TAMARIND LANE

MATTHEWS WM CULLMAN IL ROWLAND CIRCLE

MORELAND ED DAYVILLE CT VENTURA HOUSE

MULLIN MARK CORSSWELL MI VICTORIA AVE

OSTER HELEN CARBONDALE PA MOLINA CORP

PARISH KIRK CARROLLTON GA MANVIEW AVE

POPE MARCIA CEDARVILLE OH MANOR DRIVE

QUINN KELLY CHALMETTE LA COLOARDO WAY

RADER EDWIN BOULDER CO EASTLAKE HOUSE

REAGAN PAUL BUCHANAN MI DURANGO COURT

REID GEORGE MIDDLEBURY VT DOROTHY AVE

RUSSELL TAS TAMASQUA PA MANSFIELD STR

CONTINUE WITH NEXT COLUMN.

SANDERSON I WOODVILLE MS ISABEL DRIVE

SAVAGE CARL SYRACUSE NY MICHELLE PKWY

SHAPIRO BEA SWEETWATER ND MILLER CORP

SINCLAIR WM SYCAMORE IL RICHVIEW ARMS

SLATER CHAS TOWNSEND MT REDCLIFF LANE

SMALL STEVE TORRINGTON WY LINCOLN AVE

SPENCER JOE ZANESVILLE OH LOMBARD WAY

STOKES GARY WOODBINE IA LILLIAN HOUSE

TAYLOR STAN ONEONTA NY HEATHER CIRCLE

TOMLINSON P YERINGTON NV HUTCHINS CIR

TUCKER ENID OWENSBORO KY HAYWORTH WAY

VALDEZ PAUL MARINETTE WI HIGHLAND AVE

VAZQUEZ LON PROVIDENCE RI HAYFORD APT

WADE NORMAN MEDFIELD MA CLARIDGE LANE

WARREN LYNN DUCHESS UT COGSWELL HOUSE

WOODS DIANE DULUTH MN CORASSETT DRIVE

YOUNG VINCE BRADDOCK PA CENTINELA STR

ALARM SUPPLIES CO TAYLORVILLE BURGLAR

AMERICAN TILE INC E ROSSVILLE CERAMIC

B AND D AVIATIONS LOS ANGELES CHARTER

COMER AND FUENTES PUTNAM CITY CANDLES

DEWEY PLUMBING CO SANTA CLARA SHOWERS

FORTSONS WORD PRO MT PROSPECT RESUMES

GANTERS LUMBER CO EAGLE RIVER ROOFING

HAMILTON BROTHERS GREENCASTLE HAMMERS

JOANS UNIFORMS CO SHELBYVILLE CLOTHES

JOYCE AND MARTINI JOHNSONBURG LAWYERS

KIDS R US SERVICE TUNKHANNOCK CLOTHES

MAIN DISTRIBUTING MONROE PARK STATUES

MARINAS BIKE SHOP FOREST HILL BICYCLE

MEYERS AND DURHAM STURGIS BAY ROOFING

CONTINUE WITH NEXT COLUMN.

NAKAHARA BROTHERS GREAT FALLS ROOFING

PACIFIC BLINDS CO UPPER MILLS AWNINGS

PEDRINO WINDOW CO SANTA MARIA FRAMING

QMC SERVICES CORP MADISONBURG IMPORTS

ROSS AVIATION INC GRAND BANKS AIRLINE

SECURITY GATES CO EAST SEWARD CLOSERS

STONEWALL SHOE CO JOPLIN CITY BOOTERY

SUNRISE GIFT SHOP LENOIR CITY FLOWERS

TAUB AND THORNTON OLIVER HILL LAWYERS

THOMPSONS FABRICS HOLDENVILLE BATTING

TRIANGLE CLEANERS SPRINGFIELD LAUNDRY

VALLEY PORCELAINS LIVINGSTONE BATHTUB

WLM AIR CARGO INC MOUNT OLIVE FREIGHT

XENOS REFINISHING LITTLE ROCK SANDERS

YODERS FISHING CO MONDOVI BAY NETTING

ZIMMERMANS PHOTOS PORT ARTHUR CAMERAS

IF YOU FINISH BEFORE TIME IS CALLED, BEGIN
COPYING THE LIST THE SECOND TIME.

Practice Set 2

Type as many of these lines as you can in the time allowed. Double space. Type them in one column down the center of your sheet.

If you notice that you have made an error, double space and begin the same line again. Do NOT make any ERASURES or other corrections.

ABEL HORACE TAYLORVILLE IL JACKMAN ST

ARMSTRONG N TILLAMOOK OR IRONDALE AVE

AUSTIN DOUG WILTON ND PICKERING DRIVE

AYERS FRANK SHELBYVILLE IN JALAPAN WY

BARTON ROBT SHERIDAN OR PEARTREE BLVD

CADMAN THOS IOWA FALLS IA VANOWEN WAY

DIAMOND BEN JEFFERSON GA VERONICA AVE

FLOYD OSCAR GABRIEL TX MONTEZUMA GLEN

GAINES MARY PAYNESVILLE MN HERALD HWY

CONTINUE WITH NEXT COLUMN.

GRIMES BERT PASADENA CA MOUNTAIN ROAD

HARRISON WM FREDONIA KS LIBERTY HOUSE

HUELSMANN S FORT MEADE FL LOOKOUT AVE

ISHIKAWA LE BUSHNELL IL OAKLAWN COURT

MENDOZA MAX BYESVILLE OH NOVELDA CORP

METKOVICH R COATESVILLE PA WEBSTER ST

MYERS LARRY CODY WY CARMELITA LANE NE

OGONOWSKI A FRANKLIN LA BONSALLO LANE

POTTER FRED SCOTT CITY KS CALGROVE PL

PURCELL JAS PROVIDENCE RI BENFIELD ST

QUICK CRAIG ROSSVILLE GA HUNSAKER WAY

QUINN STEVE ST GEORGE UT BENJAMIN HWY

RADA HAROLD MARSHFIELD MO LIGGETT CTY

RAMIREZ TED DES MOINES IA LEADWELL CT

RASMUSSEN N EAST MEDFORD OK SHARON ST

RAY WILLARD MAYSVILLE KY BERMUDA ROAD

ROYAL SUSAN SAN BENITO CA GUNNISON ST

RUSCH KEVIN OSGOOD IN HALLWOOD LANE S

TAYLOR LEON OVERLAND MO PARK OAK ROAD

WHEATLEY ED ZEELAND MI QUEENSIDE CLUB

WISE ARTHUR SANTA MONICA CA PURDUE ST

ADRA SERVICES INC FORESTVILLE MAILING

AVALON MAILING CO BRIDGEVILLE PRINTER

AVION AIR FREIGHT BUNKER HILL EXPRESS

BOBS LOCK AND KEY WEST AUBURN LOCKERS

CHILDRENS BOOK CO EAGLE GROVE RECORDS

CROWNS APPLIANCES EATONE PARK FREEZER

DANAN ADVERTISING MT PLEASANT CONCERT

EMPIRE PROPERTIES NEW HOLLAND ESCROWS

FENNELL INSURANCE PORT HERALD LEASING

GROSSMAN AND HALL ITHACA CITY LAWYERS

CONTINUE WITH NEXT COLUMN.

HERTWOOD ANTIQUES MORAN BLUFF GALLERY

HUGHES TERMITE CO NORTH PEASE CONTROL

HUNTERS BOOKS INC JERSEYVILLE RECORDS

INFO MGMT SYSTEMS BRACEBRIDGE COPYING

KESON CAMERA SHOP CARLINVILLE LEDGERS

LAWNDALE BLOCK CO KENTON CITY CENTERS

MASTER TATTAN INC AYDEN RIVER BASKETS

NIPPON EXPRESS CO FREDERICTON FREIGHT

ORVAL ENTERPRISES MORNINGSIDE MAGNETS

PARAMOUNT RV CORP POWELL CITY CAMPERS

RAND MUFFLER CORP CENTERSBURG SPRINGS

RICKERTS CABINETS BUENA VISTA HANDLES

ROCKYS SANDWICHES GUNTERVILLE LUNCHES

SECURITY AVIATION CEDAR FALLS ENGINES

SMITH AND STAKINS AMBERG CITY LAWYERS

TRI CITY TITLE CO MOUNDSVILLE ESCROWS

UNIVERSAL FORWARD NORTH OGDEN FREIGHT

V L DECORATING CO ALCOVE CITY FIXTURE

WESTWOODS LEASING BELLA VISTA RENTALS

WIDE AREA PAGINGS ALMAN RIVER MESSAGE

IF YOU FINISH BEFORE TIME IS CALLED, BEGIN
COPYING THE LIST THE SECOND TIME.

Practice Set 3

Type as many of these lines as you can in the time allowed. Double space. Type them in one column down the center of your sheet.

If you notice that you have made an error, double space and begin the same line again. Do NOT make any ERASURES or other corrections.

ADCOCK MAYE AUSTIN TX SUNFLOWER DRIVE

BABB ANDREW INDEPENDENCE MO WILCOX CT

BEYER JAMES KNOXVILLE TN COUNTRY VIEW

CAIN SHARON CALVERTON NY ANNETTE APTS

DAVIS LARRY ALEXANDRIA VA WATSON REST

CONTINUE WITH NEXT COLUMN.

GRAY EDWINA PHOENIX AZ SOUTHERN DRIVE

JACKSON JAS FAIRBANKS AL DOUGLAS REST

KAUFMAN RON ASHDOWN AR VALENCIA DRIVE

KLEIN LYNNE SHAWNEE OK ROSECRANS APTS

LAMMERS SUE MARYVILLE MO CRESTVIEW CT

LAPIN FRANK PITTSBURGH PA CRESCENT ST

LOGAN HARRY DEARBORN MI HYACINTH CLUB

MELNICK VAL WINNFIELD LA MAYBROOK WAY

NEWMAN ALAN LAWRENCEVILLE GA PALM AVE

PEREZ GLENN NASHVILLE TN SIERRA HOUSE

PEYTONS VAL BELLEVILLE IL ZELZAH LANE

PLINER JEFF ROCHESTER NY ABBOTT DRIVE

RAMAGE LISA GREENSBORO NC GUNDRY VIEW

REEVES DAVE SHENANDOAH IA YUKON DRIVE

ROLFE SALLY JACKSONVILLE FL HALSEY CT

SHIBATA JAS WATERTOWN WI CENTRAL BLDG

SILVERMAN M MANCHESTER NH CHESTER STR

SINGLETON L WATERBURY CT CAMPUS DRIVE

SMITH PETER ELLENVILLE NY CANAL HOUSE

STANEK ROSE PORTLAND ME CAMPBELL APTS

TESDAHL RAY LANCASTER NY ADDISON CORP

THORPE JOHN LUNENBURG MD BLAKELY BLDG

VARNUM MIKE WILMINGTON PA BEVERLY WAY

WEBER ROBIN CARRIZOZO NM VIVIAN HOUSE

WILLIAMS ED COLDWATER KS WILLIAMS STR

A TO Z LEGAL SRVS LOS ANGELES LAWYERS

ALS WAVE MATE INC IMPERIALCTY CONSULT

BARRYS BAR SUPPLY GREEN RIVER BURNERS

BATEMM PEST CORP MIDDLERIDGE TERMITE

CALIFORNIA FINISH HADDONFIELD WINDOWS

CAREER SERVICE CO WILLOWBROOK RESUMES

CHRIS PIZZA STOPS EAGLE RIDGE PARTIES

CONTINUE WITH NEXT COLUMN.

DIANES AND ROCKYS HAPPY TRAIL LUNCHES

DIRECT A PAGE INC NORTH CLIFF BEEPERS

EVANS BABY SHOPPE KINGS RIDGE CLOTHES

FURMANTI AND SONS MAPLE WOODS LAWYERS

HONEYCUTT ASPHALT PARKWESTERN PATCHES

J OCEAN CLOTHIERS OCEAN RIDGE DRESSES

JAYS POODLE SALON HALLEYVILLE KENNELS

KELL PICTURES INC SIGNAL HILL FRAMING

LINNS CARD SHOPPE MULBERRY PK LEDGERS

LONGS ELECTRONICS GRAND LAKES RECORDS

MARKS WORKCLOTHES TRIDENT CTY CLOTHES

MORRISON ALUMINUM WAGON TRAIL PATCHES

NYLANDERS STUDIOS CULVER CITY PASTELS

PHILS ENTERPRISES BELLINGBURG LAWYERS

QUINN AND SON INC N HOLLYWOOD CONSULT

ROLFE ROLFE ROLFE SPRINGSTEIN CHISELS

ROSE POOL AND SPA GRAHAM CITY HEATERS

ROYS POOL SERVICE GOLDENFIELD FILTERS

S TOOM AND LINDEN LOGANSVILLE REAMERS

SLUMBER BABY SHOP EMERY LAKES CLOTHES

TIMOTHY BERG CORP PARKWESTERN STYLING

UTAH SUPPLIES INC NORTH WILEN KETTLES

VARGAS AND SON CO LOS ANGELES AERIALS

ZIPPERS AND STUFF WESTERN WAY FABRICS

ZOO ANIMALS TO GO LARRYSVILLE ANIMALS

IF YOU FINISH BEFORE TIME IS CALLED, BEGIN
COPYING THE LIST THE SECOND TIME.

Practice Set 4

Type as many of these lines as you can in the time allowed. Double space. Type them in one column down the center of your sheet.

If you notice that you have made an error, double space and begin the same line again. Do NOT make any ERASURES or other corrections.

ADLER DAVID CINCINNATI OH SUPERIOR CT

ATKINSON JO ROANOKE VA CAVALIER HOUSE

BAIRD MYRON PONTIAC MI BILTMORE HOUSE

BLACK DIANE SEATTLE WA RICHMOND DRIVE

ESSIE LOWEN ABERDEEN SD SHOEMAKER AVE

FOX ROBERT OGALLALA NE LOWEMONT ARMS

FREEMAN JIM CHEYENNE WY ASHWORTH BLVD

GARNER KENT LOVELAND CO HIGHDALE LANE

GASS DANIEL WATERLOO IA WHITAKER CORP

JOHNSON BOB SACRAMENTO CA WESTERN WAY

KLOOSTER ED MINNEAPOLIS MN CENTURY CT

LINN RANDAL PELLA IA PARAMOUNT COURTS

LITTLE ANDY BUFFALO NY IRONWOOD DRIVE

LONG ARTHUR BROWNSVILLE TX PARADE AVE

MARASCO EVE LOUISVILLE KY JAVELIN WAY

MARIS LOUIS CHICAGO IL FLORENCE HOUSE

MCPHERSON E OMAHA NE MANCHESTER HOUSE

MORTON DANE SAN DIEGO CA CARROLL LANE

MURPHY DEAN BRANCHVILLE SC PALERMO CT

NEAL GERALD HONOLULU HI PROSPECT APTS

ORTEGA RYAN LOGAN UT MORNINGSIDE PKWY

OSTERHOLT A AMARILLO TX GILBERT HOUSE

PARKER LYNN DALLAS TX QUEENSLAND BLVD

PATTERSON J BROOKHAVEN MI SIMMONS STR

RUSTAD JOHN MEMPHIS TN HOLLYWOOD CLUB

SHERLOCK WM DAYTON IA WESTCHESTER AVE

SIDMAN GREG SCRANTON PA HAWTHORNE AVE

VARGAS EARL PORTLAND OR WEBSTER HOUSE

WASSON JEFF INGLEWOOD CA OVERLAND AVE

YOUNG COREY FT DODGE WI GARDENIA BLVD

A TO Z SOUND CORP W GREENBELT PAGINGS

AGENCY RENT A CAR GLOVERTOWNE LEASING

CONTINUE WITH NEXT COLUMN.

AMERICAN PLUMBING MONTMORENCY HEATERS

AMY LAMINATING CO GLENS FALLS PLASTIC

ASHLEY ART CENTER CULVER CITY FRAMING

BURNS, TYPESETTING SANTAFE SPG GRAPHIC

C AND L TOWING CO CERISE CITY CARRIER

DIAL ONE PEST INC SOUTH HILLS TERMITE

EAGLE AUDIO VIDEO GREEN HILLS REPAIRS

GORDON INDUSTRIES MARLBOROUGH BEEPERS

HILL PET GROOMING HALLETTBURG KITTENS

JETTONS GALLERIES STUDIO CITY FRAMING

KENTWOOD CLEANERS FORESTVILLE LAUNDRY

KITCHENS AND MORE SAXTON CITY BASKETS

LAWRENCE JEWELERS MORRISVILLE WATCHES

LYNNES AUTOMOTIVE SHREVESPORT REPAIRS

M WILSON GLASS CO HAMLIN CITY BOTTLES

MARIES INDUSTRIES W HOLLYWOOD PILLOWS

MEDICAL ARTS LABS FOREST HILL TESTING

MILLER TELEVISION GRAND HAVEN REPAIRS

MURPHY STUDIO INC SIGNAL HILL PASTELS

NEW WATCH REPAIRS FRIEDLANDER JEWELRY

ORIGINAL PIZZA CO CANOGA PARK PARTIES

PIONEER VIDEO INC LOS ANGELES RENTALS

PROFESSIONAL WORD DAYTON CITY RESUMES

RANDALLS PHARMACY KINGS CREST POWDERS

SPARKLING LAUNDRY GAITHERBURG CLEANER

SUZANNES KITCHENS MAPLE GROVE BASKETS

TIDELINE IMPORTER SIOUX FALLS BOTTLES

VILLAGE DRUGS INC HIDDEN PINE POWDERS

WESTSIDE CAB CORP HEARTSHORNE TAXICAB

YOUNG AUTO REPAIR JACKSONBURG REPAIRS

IF YOU FINISH BEFORE TIME IS CALLED, BEGIN
COPYING THE LIST THE SECOND TIME.

Practice Set 5

Type as many of these lines as you can in the time allowed. Double space. Type them in one column down the center of your sheet.

If you notice that you have made an error, double space and begin the same line again. Do NOT make any ERASURES or other corrections.

BOOTH KELLY REEDSPORT OR RINDGE HOUSE

BROWN NORMA PENDLETON OR RAYMOND PKWY

CAMPBELL WM COOPERSTOWN ND SHAVER WAY

CARTER ALAN FARMINGTON UT GOTHIC REST

CLARRIDGE T SEWARD NH SEPULVEDA PLACE

COOK RODNEY CHAMPAIGN IL SEADLER BROS

CURREY FRED DARLINGTON WI TRAVIS PARK

DONALDSON C LORDSBURG NM THOMAS PLACE

GARCIA BILL GOLDFIELD NV TELFAIR YARD

GARDNER ROY MORNINGSIDE IA SWEET LANE

HANDEL SAML POCATELLO ID SERRANO BLVD

HODSON KENT ENGLEWOOD CO TRENTON PKWY

JOSEPH JOHN WATERLOO IA FRANKLIN ARMS

KAPLAN CARL SHELBY NC UNIVERSITY BLVD

KATZ DANIEL HUMBOLDT IA VALINDA DRIVE

LANDON BART OCEANSIDE CA SHADOW PLACE

LAWSON JACK PLACERVILLE CA UNION ROAD

MADISON ANN ROSEVILLE MN ARMY POST RD

MARTINEZ WM RUSSELL KS ALVERSTONE WAY

MOORE AARON APPLETON MN TYBURNE HOUSE

NASH GORDON OKANOGAN WA E VALLEY VIEW

OWEN DONALD LIVINGSTON MT MAYFAIR AVE

PATTON JUDY HURRICANE UT UPLAND PLACE

PETERSON ED MONTAGUE MI TUSCANY HOUSE

POWERS ANNE MOUNT AYR IA DELGANY CLUB

PULIDO ADAM COLUMBIA KY WATKINS DRIVE

RICE DENNIS REPUBLIC WA RELIANCE LANE

ROSE ARTHUR SPRINGFIELD IL HARVEY WAY

SULLIVAN ED MUSKEGON MI TRUXTON DRIVE

THOMAS ERIC MONTPELIER ID SEVILLE WAY

ALARM SYSTEMS INC BLUE ISLAND PATROLS

ARMANS VACUUM INC WERNERVILLE VACUUMS

BELLOTTO AUTO INC GRAND RIVER LININGS

BEST AND SONS INC PORTERVILLE SHOVELS

BILLS CAMERA SHOP LOS ANGELES PICTURE

CRES CLINICAL LAB FOREST CITY TESTING

DELIAN MUSIC CORP NORTONSBURG VIOLINS

DIAMONDS PLUMBING MONTEREY PK HEATERS

GOODS SHEET METAL VIKING CITY WELDING

HEALTH HABIT CLUB WEST OAKMAN WORKOUT

JAY OF CALIFORNIA N TARRYTOWN COPYING

MAGIC FIGURE CLUB PARTONVILLE WORKOUT

MCPHERSON AND SON GRANDEVILLE WOOLENS

MURPHY STUDIO INC VISTA FALLS PICTURE

NATIONAL TRAILERS DANTONSPORT RENTALS

NATIONWIDE CREDIT OTTERSVILLE FINANCE

RESTER INDUSTRIES GREENCASTLE PAGINGS

ROYS POOL SERVICE GOLDENFIELD FILTERS

RUSSELLS JEWELERS FRANKLIN PK WATCHES

SELF STORAGE CORP MINNEAPOLIS STORAGE

SMILEY ASSOCIATES GRAND FORKS PUMPERS

SPECIALTY WELDING HANSONVILLE SIZINGS

TUCKWOOD MUSIC CO E PARAMOUNT GUITARS

UNITED LEASING CO GREAT BLUFF LEASING

V A LAMINATING CO GLOVERVILLE PLASTIC

VIDEO FILMEX CORP CEDAR FALLS RENTALS

WESTERN MOVING CO N URBANDALE STORAGE

WESTSIDER LAUNDRY GALLATIN PK CLEANER

CONTINUE WITH NEXT COLUMN.

WHITMORE CLEANERS GAINESVILLE LAUNDRY

YALE MUSIC STUDIO MILTONVILLE VIOLINS

YOUNG SHAVER SHOP N URBANDALE SHAVERS

CONTINUE WITH NEXT COLUMN.

YUKON AVE NURSERY WESTCHESTER GARDENS

IF YOU FINISH BEFORE TIME IS CALLED, BEGIN
COPYING THE LIST THE SECOND TIME.

Practice Set 6

Type as many of these lines as you can in the time allowed. Double space. Type them in one column down the center of your sheet.

If you notice that you have made an error, double space and begin the same line again. Do NOT make any ERASURES or other corrections.

ADAMS MARIA KENNEWICK WA NATHENE CORP

ASHE MARTIN WHEATLAND WY NEWCOMB ARMS

BEATTY CHAD LENNOX CA NATHANSON CREST

BRYANT MARY STEVENSVILLE MT MEAD HALL

CARROLL JOE WELLSVILLE UT MAYNARD WAY

GREENE OWEN MIDVILLE NY HUBBARD COURT

HALEY KAREN HAMILTON VA BREMAND HOUSE

HALL THOMAS VILLISCA IA BRANDON HILLS

HARTMAN DON WARREN IN MACDONNELL APTS

JONES FRANK WATERVILLE WA STEWART AVE

JOSEPH JOHN WATERLOO IA FRANKLIN ARMS

KAPLAN JOAN SHELBY AK UNIVERSITY BLVD

LARSEN LYLE SIKESTON MO MADISON COURT

QUINN DAVID MONDOVI WI LONGTON SQUARE

REAVES DALE MORRISON IL HARVARD COURT

RUSSELL GUY MOUNT PLEASANT SC LUND ST

SAKAI ALVIN MADISON FL NORTH ILLINOIS

SCHULTZ RON GARRISON ND JASMINE HOUSE

SIMON JAMES GENEVA NY JEFFERSON COURT

STROCK GARY GILLETTE WY WASHINGTON WY

TAYLOR LYLE DENISON TX SOUTH JENNINGS

TURNER NINA DODGE CITY KS BEVERLY WAY

VANCE BRUCE DUBUQUE IA STANFORD CLUBS

WAKEFIELD S DUCKTOWN TN MARYLAND CORP

CONTINUE WITH NEXT COLUMN.

WARD EUGENE BOLLINGTON MT EUCLID BLVD

WELCH MARIA BOONTON NJ WELLESLEY LANE

WHITE JAMES BLOOMFIELD NE SEAFIELD ST

WILSON ANDY HARTWELL GA SHERBOURNE CT

WOOD JANICE HARTFORD CT NEARSIDE LANE

WYMAN SUSAN HAMILTON MO NEWBROOK APTS

ACE FREIGHT LINES ORANGEVILLE SENDERS

ADEC LABORATORIES E WATERTOWN POWDERS

AIRPORT STATIONER WESTCHESTER PENCILS

ALPHA DATA SYSTEM SPRINGSTEIN RIBBONS

AMERICAN PRODUCTS CHILLICOTHE MATCHES

BAY OFFICE SUPPLY OLMOSE PARK COPYING

BRITE RUGS CO INC CARTERVILLE CARPETS

CARAVAN MOTEL INC GROTON CITY ROOMING

COMPUTERS R US CO MOUNT PEALE RIBBONS

FABRICS AND STUFF MONTE VISTA FABRICS

FLAME CUTTERS INC BLUE ISLAND GRINDER

G AND L ENGINEERS GREAT FALLS HAMMERS

GARDEN SPOT HOTEL GREENEWOODS ROOMING

GOLD STAR NURSERY WESTCHESTER GARDENS

GRAND CHARTER INC W KERRVILLE CRUISES

H FRONER CONCRETE BRIDGEVILLE CEMENTS

HAIR IS US SHOPPE MURRYSVILLE STYLING

HOUSE OF STYLINGS ALBUQUERQUE SHAMPOO

JOHNSON AND ALROD EAST DAYTON LAWYERS

LANDSCAPE ARTISTS N COACHELLA FLOWERS

LEWIS ELECTRIC CO WEST SAMSON WIRINGS

LINDSEYS LIMOSINE N KNOXVILLE DRIVERS

RALFS PHOTOGRAPHY VENTUR CITY PICTURE

SANCTION SECURITY RICHARDTOWN PATROLS

SHERIDAN HARDWARE GREAT RIVER HAMMERS

SQUIRE TUXEDO INC CEDAR WOODS RENTALS

CONTINUE WITH NEXT COLUMN.

STEVES JANITORIAL BROWNSVILLE CLEANER

SUPREME GARDENING NEWTONVILLE SHOVELS

WESTWOOD BUILDING SANTA CLARA SIZINGS

WORLD TRAVEL CORP OVAR ISLAND CRUISES

YOUNG BROS MOVING FLOWER CITY STORAGE

YALE MUSIC STUDIO MILTONVILLE VIOLINS

IF YOU FINISH BEFORE TIME IS CALLED, BEGIN
COPYING THE LIST THE SECOND TIME.

Practice Set 7

Type as many of these lines as you can in the time allowed. Double space. Type them in one column down the center of your sheet.

If you notice that you have made an error, double space and begin the same line again. Do NOT make any ERASURES or other corrections.

ADKINS KATY HAMMONTON NJ HYPERION WAY

BALDWIN PAT LYNDONVILLE VT JACKSON CT

BECKER GENE LUMBERTON MS IMPERIAL AVE

BERG WALTER LOUISVILLE KY CRESTWAY ST

CHAN SANDRA MACKENZIE OR CROCKER ROAD

CLARK ALLEN MIDDLESBORO KY LOMITA WAY

COBB HAROLD NIOBRARA NE LINDBLADE AVE

CURTIS RUTH NORMAN OK MARAVILLA DRIVE

DECKER RICK NOBLETON IN MARIMBA COURT

DOUGLAS DEE OGDENSBURG NY MARKTON CIR

EDWARDS ART OAKDALE LA MULHOLLAND HWY

EVANS ALICE NORWICH CT MOONRIDGE ROAD

FELIX PETER RICE LAKE WI LINDLEY WALK

FONTANA ANN ROGERS CITY MI OAKLAWN DR

GELLER EARL SAN ANTONIO TX NORMAN WAY

GOODE CLARA SANDERSVILLE GA OAKLEY ST

GRAY GEORGE SANDPOINT ID REXFORD CLUB

GRIGGS PAUL SYLVANIA GA RINALDI DRIVE

HARRIS JOHN FULLERTON LA RAYMOND ARMS

CONTINUE WITH NEXT COLUMN.

HAYES CRAIG GIBSON CITY IL WAVERLY ST

HOLM DONALD FAIRVIEW OK WALGROVE BLVD

HUNTLEY BOB EVANSTON WY YARNELL COURT

JOHNSON JAN ESSEXVILLE MI HUSTON LANE

KING THOMAS ENTERPRISE AL ISABEL PKWY

KNIGHT DALE FAYETTEVILLE NC CLOVIS PK

KAMACHI SAM FALCONER NY CLIFTON VISTA

LOUFF BRIAN DES MOINES IA COLFAX ARMS

MANNING LEE DODGEVILLE WI AVALON BLVD

MATHIS DOUG DOUGLAS TN ATLANTIC DRIVE

MATSUMOTO F CUMBERLAND MD MORGAN ROAD

ANDRE BEAUTY MART E INGLEWOOD STYLING

ANNS CATERING INC W BIG SANDY LUNCHES

ASTROS CAR FINISH YELLOWSTONE WAXINGS

BELL HOTEL CO INC W GREYCOURT ROOMING

BROWN CORNELL LTD W KITTANING BEAKERS

COASTAL CLEANINGS WALLA WALLA CARPETS

CONN AND SONS INC E PRINCETON ENGINES

CURRY AND PICKARD GRANBY CITY LAWYERS

EXPOS TRAVEL SRVS PAINESVILLE CRUISES

FLOWERS BY ANDREW E MANHATTAN FLOWERS

JAMES AND BENNETT N SUMMERTON CUTTERS

JOES ITALIAN DELI WARRENSBURG LUNCHES

KENT AND SONS INC LEVERSVILLE SPRINGS

LEIGH FENCING INC MONROEVILLE STATUES

LINCOLN INTERIORS CAMPBELLTON CARPETS

MARK I CUTLER INC MORRISVILLE GASKETS

MAYOR BROS TRAVEL MOUNDSVILLE CRUISES

N E TIME PLUMBING S CLARINDON PLUMBER

OFFICE SUPPLY INC CLEARFIELDS LEDGERS

OPTICAL DISCOUNTS CIRCLE CITY GLASSES

PHILLIPS GLASS CO BISHOPVILLE BOTTLES

CONTINUE WITH NEXT COLUMN.

QUALITY WORK CORP NORTHBRIDGE BOTTLES

RAINBOW CARPET CO W LEXINGTON CARPETS

RELIABLE IRON INC NORTHBRIDGE ENGINES

RIVIERA FINANCIAL NEW HAMPTON LENDERS

ROBERTS BEAUTY CO LOS ANGELES SHAMPOO

ROYALTY TUX SHOPS SIOUX FALLS RENTALS

SILK SCREEN ASSOC W STOCKHOLM ROLLERS

SUNSET LUMBER INC MOUNDSVILLE SIZINGS

THE MESSENGER INC WALLINGFORD SENDERS

TITAN TOOL CO INC SHELBYVILLE SHOVELS

ZAIN TRADING CORP GRAND FALLS WOOLENS

IF YOU FINISH BEFORE TIME IS CALLED, BEGIN
COPYING THE LIST THE SECOND TIME.

PART VI

THE INTERVIEW

The Interview: Showing That You Fit the Job

CHAPTER 11

THE INTERVIEW

Lengthy books have been written about how to interview for a job. This section does not intend to provide the breadth and depth that a several-hundred-page book on the subject can provide. Rather, this chapter highlights the most important elements about job interviewing, especially for a civil service clerical position, and how to prepare for the interview in order to do your best.

Form of the Interview

Nearly every interview follows a typical form of four distinct parts:

1. **Getting comfortable.** First the interviewer begins informally, usually talking about something unrelated to the job (the weather, sports, a local event) to help make you comfortable and set the stage for the conversation. This is usually extremely short, just enough to create a relaxed atmosphere and give you time to settle in.

2. **Learning about the available position.** Then the interviewer may tell you about the position, its responsibilities, its location, its requirements, perhaps the package of benefits that comes with it. Here the interviewer will do nearly all the talking. Finally the interviewer may ask you if you have any questions about the position that weren't answered by his or her overview.

3. **Learning about you.** Or, instead, the interviewer will first review your work history, asking you questions about your skills and experience to see how well you and the position are a "good fit." This is the part where you do most of the talking. Although your answers should be thorough and address the questions asked, they should not be overly long. Each answer should typically be a minute or two. If the interviewer wants to know more, he or she will follow up to draw you out.

4. **Closing.** Finally, after both the job itself and your skills/experience have been explored, the interviewer will indicate a "closing," the end of the

interview. He or she may ask you for the date when you can start work if you are selected, so be prepared to answer with a solid date. He or she will probably ask if you have any other questions that haven't been answered, or may inform you of what the next steps are in the process and the timeline for notifying candidates about the position. If this information is not volunteered at this time, you may ask about them. The interviewer will stand to shake your hand, thank you and escort you to the door, and you should reciprocate as well.

Purpose of the Interview

The purpose of your Civil Service interview is to ascertain how well you and your prospective job are a "good fit." Typically two main elements determine whether or not you and the position are a good match: your **skills/experience** and your **persona**. The interviewer will be talking with you and asking questions to determine both these two elements. He or she will not be trying to trick you or make you slip up, but rather attempting to understand how your skills/experience and persona will mesh with the job responsibilities. For that reason you should be well prepared to discuss your work experience and your training for the job.

YOUR SKILLS/EXPERIENCE. Most of the questions posed to you will address your work experience and training and how they relate to the job opening for which you are being considered. You will likely be asked questions about your past job responsibilities, the kinds of tasks you were charged with accomplishing, your successes and perhaps even your failures in accomplishing them, the problems and difficulties you faced and had to overcome, and other elements of your work history. Knowing as much as possible about the job opening for which you are applying will help you to select your answers about your past experience so that your responses are appropriate to the responsibilities of the job opening you seek. You should be honest and open about your past experiences, but you should also shape your answers to be relevant to your desired position, if that's possible. If you are asked about a job accomplishment of which you are most proud, choose one as closely related as possible to the job for which you are applying.

Behavioral-based interviewing is becoming more and more popular, even for clerical jobs. In this type of interview, you are asked questions such as, "Tell me a time when you had a difficult problem on the job and overcame it," or "Tell me about a work achievement of which you are particularly proud," and so on. So spend time before the interview reflecting upon achievements, problems, interactions with peers and supervisors, and other significant events during your worklife. Develop answers that highlight your skills, especially those that are appropriate to the position.

It's important for you to be as familiar as you can with what the job opening requires. Get as much information as possible about its responsibilities from the civil service office or web site. If you can talk with someone who has at any time held the position or knows about it, that also will be extremely helpful. The more informed you can be about the job for which you are applying, the more you can provide honest answers that show how your experience and skills are a good fit for the job opening.

YOUR PERSONA. The other important element in any job interview is how you come across to the interviewer as a person. Even though the interviewer understands that you will likely be a bit nervous during the interview process—nearly everyone is—he or she will still be judging you on how you interact. For example:

> When you entered, did you smile and give the interviewer a firm handshake?
> Are you well groomed and dressed appropriately?
> Is your tone of voice strong yet cordial?
> Do you sit attentively, not slouched in the chair?
> Do you make comfortable eye contact throughout the interview?
> Do you take a few seconds to consider each question before answering?
> Is your language clear, appropriately business-like and not filled with slang?
> Are your answers complete but not overly long?

All of these—and more—give the interviewer a sense of your persona and if you will be a good fit with the others with whom you'll be working. Getting along and working well with co-workers is an important quality for a new hire. If your answers to questions can demonstrate this ability, you increase the chances of being hired. And certainly if your answers to questions are well considered and well expressed, this, too, will be important, as strong communication skills are needed in the workplace.

These two qualities—your skills/experience and your persona—are the big keys to a successful interview. But other elements will factor in as well.

Be on time. Better yet, be there slightly early (5 to 10 minutes) for the interview. If you are late to the interview, odds are that no matter how good your skills, you probably won't be offered the position. Why is that? Reliability and dependability are essential qualities for an employee. If you cannot be relied upon to be on time for the interview, it's likely your being on time for work each day will be problematic.

Before the day of your interview, make sure that you know how to get to the appointment and details such as parking, parking fees if any (if you are driving), weather conditions, and so on. Give yourself plenty of time to get there. You may even want to build in a few extra minutes so that before the interview you can visit a restroom to comb your hair, check your makeup, and so on, to ensure that you look your best.

Bring a copy of your resume in case the interviewer does not have one. Make sure you are familiar with everything on it and can discuss its details if asked.

You may be asked to discuss what you believe are your strengths and weaknesses for the position. If so, it's important to describe a weakness that won't disqualify you from consideration for the position, and even better if your "weakness" can be perceived as fitting well with the job. For example, if you said your weakness is that you are "far too detail oriented and often get too caught up in the small stuff," that would actually be an excellent quality if you were applying for a position as a proofreader.

Typically the interviewer will ask you at the end of the interview, "Do you have any questions?" Have some questions in mind to ask about the position. This shows that you've done your "homework" learning about the job opportunity and therefore you have some understanding that you are a good fit for its tasks and have interest about it. The best questions are usually about the challenges of the job that are not stated in the job description. Problematic questions are about its salary or benefits. In fact, asking too many questions about salary and benefits can give the impression that you care more about the money than the job itself, and anyway, civil service salary ranges for each job position are posted and available to the public. You can also ask when the hiring decision will be made, if additional interviews will be required, and prospective starting date.

Finally and not least of all, be a good listener. Employers say that excellent listening skills are an important requirement for just about any job position. Show that you can listen carefully by keeping eye contact with your interviewer, nodding if appropriate to show understanding, and asking clarifying questions if you did not completely understand something that was stated.

PRACTICE, PRACTICE, PRACTICE. The more you can practice being interviewed by friends or family about your past work experience, the better prepared you will be for the actual interview. Below are some, but not all, of the possible question types you could be asked. They can be either specific and narrow ("What kind of filing system . . .?") or broad and general ("What do you enjoy most about your work?"). If you practice answering these questions, by the time of your interview you should have an idea already in mind of what your answers will be. But take care not to have it sound as if your answer is so well practiced that it's been rehearsed. Taking a few seconds to organize your thoughts before answering may be helpful.

Describe a time when you worked with teammates on a project. What was your role and how did you help the team do its best?

What type of filing systems have you used in past jobs?

How do you ensure that filing is done accurately and completely?

Describe your clerical skills, especially those regarding financial and numeric processes.

What software programs (spreadsheets, databases, word processing) are you comfortable with?

What kinds of other software and processing forms are you familiar with?

What were your responsibilities on your last job? What was the most difficult?

Have you ever had a disagreement or conflict with a fellow employee? If so, how was it resolved?

What kind of supervision do you prefer having—lots of autonomy or lots of direction?

What kind of manager do you find difficult to work with?

How do you like to organize your work day?

What was the most complex assignment you've been tasked with? How did you accomplish it?

What do you enjoy most about your work?

What do you enjoy least about your work?

If you were to encounter problems on the job, how would you resolve them?

What has been your most technical task in any job? How did you accomplish it?

Have you ever had to learn a new skill in order to perform a required task? If so, what did you do?

Have you ever changed a procedure to get a task better accomplished? If so, please explain.

Have you ever had a deadline so tight you had trouble completing the work on time? If so, what happened? What did you do?

What kind of work is most challenging to you?

What has been your most difficult experience collaborating on a team? What did you do, if anything, to address the problem?

What are your specific work strengths? What are your specific work weaknesses?

How do you cope if work becomes too busy?

What are your career goals? Where would you like to be professionally in 5 years?

What do you do to update yourself about the latest developments in technology related to your work?

Tell me about a difficult time at work and what you did to address it.

Have you ever had too many tasks to do at once? How did you resolve that situation?

What's the biggest mistake you've made on a job? What did you learn from it?

Have you had work tasks requiring great detail? What were they and what did you do to accomplish them?

Have you ever been tasked with an assignment but were not given adequate direction? What did you do?

Occasionally we may need to temporarily alter work hours to meet a deadline, such as on weekends or evenings. Would this be an issue for you?

What Should You Bring to the Interview?

Bring a notebook and pen for you to take notes during the interview, if appropriate, and certainly afterward to jot down personal reflections you'll want to remember.

As indicated, bring at least one copy of your resume, more if you anticipate the likelihood of being interviewed by several individuals.

If you have a list of references, with phone numbers and/or email addresses, include these on a separate page to present, if requested.

Other materials (such as college transcripts, past work samples, or performance evaluations from previous employers) may be relevant, and if so, be prepared to give copies.

The materials listed above will likely be read *after* your interview, not during your session. If you leave copies of any of the above, assume that they will *not* be returned to you.

Appendix

The information and forms included in this appendix are available on the official website *www.usajobs.gov.*

443

Your Career in the U.S. Government Starts Here

USAJOBS WORK FOR AMERICA

Come work with us, the Federal Government.

The range of careers the Federal Government offers is virtually limitless. In addition to the variety to jobs, you can find no more rewarding work than providing vital services to the American people.

We are searching for individuals with a broad spectrum of educational and professional backgrounds. Opportunities are available in public policy and administration, domestic and international issues, information technology, human resources, engineering, health and medical sciences, law, financial management, and many other fields in support of public service programs.

Once you assume your Federal career, we give you tools to help you succeed and advance. We support you with training, development and personal guidance. Plus, we offer an array of generous benefits ranging from health care to retirement planning.

Check us out! It's easy. Just visit us at **www.usajobs.gov**, the Federal Government's official job website.

Working for America, your journey to success begins here!
Apply Today!

USAJOBS provides access to more than 30,000 job listings daily as well as applications, forms, and employment fact sheets. Job postings are updated daily and are available to job seekers in a variety of formats to ensure accessibility for those with differing physical and technological capabilities.

You can search for jobs by location, job category, and agency. Use the "Jobs in Demand" feature to identify positions that agencies are trying to fill quickly. These listings link directly to the announcements, which allow you to complete and submit your application online.

2

CREATE·SEARCH·APPLY USAJOBS

Take the following steps to conduct your Federal job search.

- **Create –** Set up your **My USAJOBS** account to:
  - Create & save résumés – (up to five different ones) specifically designed for applying for Federal jobs.
  - Attract employers – elect to have your résumé searchable by Federal agencies looking for job candidates; and,
  - Build a Job Search Agent – automatically receive e-mail notification for new job postings that meet your specific qualifications and interests.

- **Search Jobs –** Find the job that's right for you

  Enter your search requirements and explore the thousands of opportunities on **USAJOBS**. Once you've found a job announcement, read through the various tabs of the announcement: "Duties," "Qualifications & Evaluations," and "How to Apply" for that particular position. Questions about the job announcement or hiring agency should be directed to the point of contact listed at the bottom of the announcement or that agency's website.

  USAJOBS has an interactive voice response telephone system at (703) 724-1850. This line is for the visual impaired, or individuals without access to a computer or the Internet. The TDD line (978) 461-8404 is available for our hearing-impaired customers.

- **Apply –** Manage your career

  You can apply for most jobs using your **USAJOBS** online résumé. Check the "How to Apply" tab of current vacancy announcements for specific instructions for submiting your application by mail or fax. There you will find a list of any additional forms required and a contact name and phone number at the hiring agency. Use this contact information to check your application status or ask additional questions. Most importantly, read the announcement carefully and follow the instructions. Each agency has different requirements and application procedures.

- **TIP –** Be Diligent!

  The process of finding a job with the Federal Government requires diligence and persistence. Use **USAJOBS**: it's your one-stop source for Federal jobs and employment information.

USAJOBS®
"WORKING FOR AMERICA"

Federal Employment Information Fact Sheets   **EI-55**

HOW FEDERAL JOBS ARE FILLED

Many Federal agencies fill their jobs like private industry by allowing applicants to contact the agency directly for job information and application processing. Previously the Office of Personnel Management (OPM) maintained large standing registers of eligibles and required applicants to take standardized written tests. In addition, applicants completed a standard application form, the SF-171 to apply for all jobs. Today OPM no longer maintains registers of eligibles and only a few positions require a written test. The SF-171 is obsolete and no longer accepted by most Federal agencies. The new Federal application form is Optional Application for Federal Employment, OF-612, http://www.opm.gov/forms/pdf_fill/of612.pdf. In lieu of submitting an OF-612, applicants may submit a resume. Another change is that job seekers do not need a rating from OPM to enable them to apply for non-clerical vacancies. But, while the process is now very similar to that in private industry, there are still significant differences due to the many laws, executive orders, and regulations that govern Federal employment.

COMPETITIVE AND EXCEPTED SERVICE - There are two classes of jobs in the Federal Government: 1) those that are in the *competitive civil service*, and 2) those that are in the *excepted service*.

Competitive service jobs are under OPM's jurisdiction and subject to the civil service laws passed by Congress to ensure that applicants and employees receive fair and equal treatment in the hiring process. These laws give selecting officials broad authority to review more than one applicant source before determining the best-qualified candidate based on job-related criteria. A basic principle of Federal employment is that all candidates must meet the qualification requirements for the position for which they receive an appointment.

Excepted service agencies set their own qualification requirements and are not subject to the appointment, pay, and classification rules in title 5, United States Code. However, they are subject to veterans' preference. Some Federal agencies, the Federal Bureau of Investigations (FBI) and the Central Intelligence Agency (CIA) have only excepted service positions. In other instances, certain organizations within an agency or even specific jobs may be excepted from civil service procedures. Positions may be in the excepted service by law, by executive order, or by action of OPM.

SOURCES OF ELIGIBLES - In filling competitive service jobs, agencies can generally choose from among 3 groups of candidates:

1) A *competitive list of eligibles* administered by OPM or by an agency under OPM's direction. This list consists of applicants who have applied and met the qualification requirements for a specific vacancy announcement. It is the most common method of entry for new employees.

2) A list of eligibles who have *civil service status* consist of applicants who are eligible for

United States Office of Personnel Management

USAJOBS
"WORKING FOR AMERICA"

Federal Employment Information Fact Sheets   **EI-55**

noncompetitive movement within the competitive service because they either now are or were serving under career-type appointments in the competitive service. These individuals are selected under agency *merit promotion procedures and can receive an appointment* by promotion, reassignment, transfer, or reinstatement.

3) A list of eligibles that qualify for a *special noncompetitive appointing authority* established by law or executive order. Examples of special noncompetitive appointing authorities include the Veterans' Readjustment Appointment (VRA), http://www.opm.gov/Strategic Management of Human Capital/fhfrc/FLX02020.asp, the special authority for 30% or more disabled veterans, and the Peace Corps.

- Agencies in the competitive service are required by law and OPM regulation to post vacancies with OPM whenever they are seeking candidates from outside their own workforce for positions lasting more than 120 days. (*Agency*, in this context, means the parent agency -- i.e., Treasury, not the Internal Revenue Service.) These vacancies are posted on OPM's USAJOBS and posted with State Employment Service Offices.

USAJOBS, the Federal Government's Employment Information System, provides worldwide job vacancy information, employment information fact sheets, job applications and forms on-line. It has on-line resume development and electronic transmission capabilities. Job seekers can apply for some positions on-line. **USAJOBS** is updated every business day from a database of more than 20,000 worldwide job opportunities and is available to job seekers in a variety of formats to ensure access for customers with differing physical and technological capabilities. It is convenient, user friendly, accessible through the computer or telephone and available 24 hours a day, 7 days a week.

USAJOBS consists of: **INTERNET** - The official world-wide-web site for jobs and employment information is **http://www.USAJOBS.gov**.

The **Online Resume Builder** feature allows job seekers to create on-line resumes specifically designed for applying for Federal jobs. Applicants can use the resume builder to create, print, save, edit for future use, or send by fax or mail to employers. Many of the hiring agencies will accept electronic submissions of resumes created through **USAJOBS** for vacancies listed on the web site.

AUTOMATED TELEPHONE SYSTEM - An interactive voice response telephone system which can be reached at 1-703-724-1850 or TDD 1-978-461-8404. By telephone, job seekers can access current job vacancies, employment information fact sheets, applications, forms, and apply for some jobs.

A posted vacancy is an agency's decision to seek qualified candidates for a particular vacancy. The agency is under no obligation to make a selection. In some instances, an agency may cancel the

United States Office of Personnel Management

Federal Employment Information Fact Sheets   EI-55

posting and choose to reannounce the vacancy later.

AREA OF CONSIDERATION - The area of consideration is listed on the vacancy announcement and is the source from which the agency will consider candidates. The agency may designate whatever area of consideration it considers appropriate. A candidate who is outside the area of consideration will not be considered.

VETERANS' PREFERENCE - Veterans' preference recognizes the economic loss suffered by citizens who have served their country in uniform in times of strife, restores veterans to a favorable competitive position for Government employment, and acknowledges the larger obligation owed to disabled veterans.
Historically, Congress has reserved preference for those who were either disabled, who served in combat areas or during certain periods of time.

Veterans who qualify as preference eligibles (meaning they typically must have served on active duty for at least 2 years during a period of war or in a campaign or expedition for which a campaign badge is authorized, or be disabled) are entitled to an additional 5 or 10 points added onto their earned rating in a *competitive civil service examination*. In all other situations (for example, selection from a merit promotion list or other "internal" action such as reassignment, transfer, or reinstatement), veterans' preference is not a factor.

Veterans' preference was intended to give eligible veterans an extra assist in getting a job with the Government and in keeping it in the event of a reduction in force. Veterans' preference does not guarantee the veteran a job. Veterans' preference should not be confused with the special appointing authorities such as the VRA which allow eligible veterans to be appointed *noncompetitively* to the competitive service.

THE VETERANS EMPLOYMENT OPPORTUNITIES ACT (VEOA) - This act gave veterans who qualify as preference eligibles and veterans with 3 or more years of continuous active service access to jobs that might otherwise be closed to them. When an agency advertises for candidates outside its own workforce under merit promotion procedures, it must allow these veterans to apply. Of course, all applications are subject to any area of consideration that the agency has specified on the vacancy announcement. Thus, if the agency will only accept applications from status candidates within the local commuting area, veterans who are outside the commuting area are not eligible.

United States Office of Personnel Management

USAJOBS®
"WORKING FOR AMERICA"

Federal Employment Information Fact Sheets   **EI-63**

Applying for Clerical and Administrative Support Positions (Grades GS-2/3/4)

Applying for a clerical position just got easier! Taking the Clerical and Administrative Support Exam is no longer the only way to obtain a clerical position at the GS-2/3/4 grade levels with the Federal Government. Agencies can choose among several options to fill a position, (e.g., commercially developed test, work sample, etc.). This new procedure will help simplify the process of filling clerical positions.

The Office of Personnel Management (OPM) will no longer administer the Clerical and Administrative Support Exam on a regular basis. It will only be given if requested by the hiring agency to fill a position.

Question and Answers

In what ways can an agency fill a clerical position?

The hiring agency may use one or a combination of the options when filling a clerical position. The option the agency selects will be listed on the vacancy announcement for the position. These options may include, Commercially developed test; Rating Schedule/Crediting Plan; Work Sample, and Structured Interviews.

How can I find out what option an Agency is using to fill a position?

The hiring agency will state in the vacancy announcement the option it plans to use. Vacancy announcements can be found on the USAJOBS web site at **www.usajobs.gov**.

I have already taken the clerical exam and have a valid Notice of Results. Can I use it to apply for a clerical position?

The hiring agency will make the decision on whether to accept notices of ratings previously issued. The agency will post it's decision in the vacancy announcement for the position.

Must agencies use the same hiring option for all clerical positions?

No, typically an agency will decide on a hiring option when it announces a position. Agency decisions on which option to use may vary for each position. Likewise, there is no requirement to use the same hiring option each time an agency fills a specific position.

Experience and Education Requirements for Clerical Positions:

For grade GS-2, you are required to have a high school diploma (or equivalent) or 3 months of

United States Office of Personnel Management

Federal Employment Information Fact Sheets   EI-63

experience. For grades GS-3 and GS-4, additional education and/or experience are required.

Some positions may have special requirements in addition to the ones listed above. For example, clerk-typist, office automation clerk, and computer-related positions require typing or other skills. Requirements for the position will be listed in the vacancy announcement.

How to Apply for Clerical Positions

To apply for clerical positions, you must conduct your own job search. The U.S. Office of Personnel Management (OPM) has developed **USAJOBS** to assist you along the way. **USAJOBS** is available by Internet and phone. By using **USAJOBS,** you can access federal job listings, as well as, some state and local government, and private sector listings. **USAJOBS** provides current information, is updated daily, and is available 24 hours-a-day, 7 days-a-week.

STEP 1: USE ANY OF THE AUTOMATED COMPONENTS OF THE FEDERAL EMPLOYMENT INFORMATION SYSTEM

On the **USAJOBS web site** http://www.usajobs.gov, job seekers can access worldwide current job vacancies, employment information fact sheets, applications and forms, and in some instances, apply for jobs online. Complete job announcements can be retrieved from the web site. The **USAJOBS** web site has an **Online Resume** feature. Resumes created on **USAJOBS** can be printed, saved and edited for future use, or sent by Fax or mail to employers.

Many of the hiring agencies will accept electronic submissions of resumes created through USAJOBS for vacancies listed on this site.

AUTOMATED TELEPHONE SYSTEM - An interactive voice response telephone system can be reached at 1-703-724-1850 or TDD 1-978-461-8404.

Job seekers can access worldwide current job vacancies, employment information fact sheets, and applications and forms, and in some instances, apply for jobs by phone.

STEP 2: OBTAIN THE VACANCY ANNOUNCEMENT

Once you have found an opportunity that interests you, using **STEP 1**, you will need more information on the specific job and appropriate application forms. Use **USAJOBS** to obtain a copy of the vacancy announcement. The vacancy announcement is an important source of information. Be sure to read this closely. It will specify the information you need to know to apply for clerical positions. Most of the questions you may have will be answered as you read through the announcement. For example: closing/deadline dates for applications, specific duties of the position, whether or not a written test is required, educational requirements, duty location, salary, etc.

 United States Office of Personnel Management

Federal Employment Information Fact Sheets   EI-63

STEP 3: FOLLOW THE APPLICATION INSTRUCTIONS

You may apply for most jobs with a resume, or the Optional Application for Federal Employment (OF-612), or any written format you choose. For jobs that are filled through automated procedures, Federal agencies **may** require that you submit a resume and/or other specialized forms. Jobs with unique requirements may require special forms.

United States Office of Personnel Management

General Information
Optional Application for Federal Employment – OF 612

You may apply for most Federal jobs with a résumé, an Optional Application for Federal Employment (OF 612), or other written format. If your résumé or application does not provide all the information requested on this form and in the job vacancy announcement, you may lose consideration for a job. Type or print clearly in black ink. Help speed the selection process by keeping your application brief and sending only the requested information. If essential to attach additional pages, include your name and job announcement number on each page.

- Information on Federal employment and the latest information about educational and training provisions are available at www.usajobs.gov or via interactive voice response system: (703) 724-1850 or TDD (978) 461-8404.

- Upon request from the employing Federal agency, you must provide documentation or proof that your degree(s) is from a school accredited by an accrediting body recognized by the Secretary, U.S. Department of Education, or that your education meets the other provisions outlined in the OPM Operating Manual. It will be your responsibility to secure the documentation that verifies that you attended and earned your degree(s) from this accredited institution(s) (e.g., official transcript). Federal agencies will verify your documentation.

  For a list of postsecondary educational institutions and programs accredited by accrediting agencies and state approval agencies recognized by the U.S. Secretary of Education, refer to the U.S. Department of Education Office of Postsecondary Education website at http://www.ope.ed.gov/accreditation/.

  For information on Educational and Training Provisions or Requirements, refer to the OPM Operating Manual available at http://www.opm.gov/qualifications/SEC-II/s2-e4.asp.

- If you served on active duty in the United States Military and were discharged or released from active duty in the armed forces under honorable conditions, you may be eligible for veterans' preference. To receive preference, if your service began after October 15, 1976, you must have a Campaign Badge, Expeditionary Medal, or a service-connected disability. Veterans' preference is not a factor for Senior Executive Service jobs or when competition is limited to status candidates (current or former career or career-conditional Federal employees).

- Most Federal jobs require United States citizenship and also that males over age 18 born after December 31, 1959, have registered with the Selective Service System or have an exemption.

- The law generally prohibits public officials from appointing, promoting, or recommending their relatives.

- Federal annuitants (military and civilian) may have their salaries or annuities reduced. Every employee must pay any valid delinquent debt or the agency may garnish their salary.

- Send your application to the office announcing the vacancy. If you have questions, contact the office identified in the announcement.

How to Apply

1. **Review** the listing of current vacancies.
2. **Decide** which jobs, pay range, and locations interest you.
3. **Follow instructions** provided in the vacancy announcement including any additional forms that are required.

   - You may apply for most jobs with a resume, this form, or any other written format; **all applications must include the information requested in the vacancy announcement as well as information required for all applications for Federal employment** (see below):
   - The USAJOBS website features an online résumé builder. This is a free service that allows you to create a résumé, submit it electronically (for some vacancy announcements), and save it online for use in the future.

Certain information is required to evaluate your qualifications and determine if you meet legal requirements for Federal employment. If your resume or application does not include all the required information as specified below, the agency may not consider you for the vacancy. Help speed the selection process - submit a concise resume' or application and send only the required material.

Information required for all applications for Federal employment:

Job Vacancy Specifics

- Announcement number, title and grade(s) of the job you are applying for

Personal Information

- Full name, mailing address (with zip code) and day and evening phone numbers (with area code) and email address, if applicable
- Social Security Number
- Country of citizenship (most Federal jobs require U.S. citizenship)
- Veterans' preference
- Reinstatement eligibility (for former Federal employees)
- Highest Federal civilian grade held (including job series and dates held)
- Selective Service (if applicable)

Work Experience

- Provide the following information for your paid and volunteer work experience related to the job you are applying for:
  - ▶ job title (include job series and grade if Federal)
  - ▶ duties and accomplishments
  - ▶ employer's name and address
  - ▶ supervisor's name and telephone number - indicate if supervisor may be contacted
  - ▶ starting and ending dates (month and year)
  - ▶ hours per week
  - ▶ salary

U.S. Office of Personnel Management
Previous edition usable

NSN 7540-01-351-9178
50612-101

OF 612
Revised June 2006

Page 1 of 4

How to Apply (continued)

Education

- High School
  - ▶ Name, city, and State (Zip code if known)
  - ▶ Date of diploma or GED
- Colleges or universities
  - ▶ Name, city, and State (Zip code if known)
  - ▶ Majors
  - ▶ Type and year of degrees received. (If no degree, show total credits earned and indicate whether semester or quarter hours.)
- Do not attach a copy of your transcript unless requested
- Do not list degrees received based solely on life experience or obtained from schools with little or no academic standards

Upon request from the employing Federal agency, you must provide documentation or proof that your degree(s) is from a school accredited by an accrediting body recognized by the Secretary, U.S. Department of Education, or that your education meets the other provisions outlined in the OPM Operating Manual. It will be your responsibility to secure the documentation that verifies that you attended and earned your degree(s) from this accredited institution(s) (e.g., official transcript). Federal agencies will verify your documentation.

For a list of postsecondary educational institutions and programs accredited by accrediting agencies and state approval agencies recognized by the U.S. Secretary of Education, refer to the U.S. Department of Education Office of Postsecondary Education website at http://www.ope.ed.gov/accreditation/.

For information on Educational and Training Provisions or Requirements, refer to the OPM Operating Manual available at http://www.opm.gov/qualifications/SEC-II/s2-e4.asp.

Other Education Completed

- School name, city, and State (Zip code if known)
  - ▶ Credits earned and Majors
  - ▶ Type and year of degrees received. (If no degree, show total credits earned and indicate whether semester or quarter hours.)
- Do not list degrees received based solely on life experience or obtained from schools with little or no academic standards

Other Qualifications

- Job-related:
  - ▶ Training (title of course and year)
  - ▶ Skills (e.g., other languages, computer software/hardware, tools, machinery, typing speed, etc.)
  - ▶ Certificates or licenses (current only). Include type of license or certificate, date of latest license, and State or other licensing agency
  - ▶ Honors, awards, and special accomplishments, (e.g., publications, memberships in professional honor societies, leadership activities, public speaking and performance awards) (Give dates but do not send documents unless requested)

Any Other information Specified in the Vacancy Announcement

Privacy Act Statement

The U.S. Office of Personnel Management and other Federal agencies rate applicants for Federal jobs under the authority of sections 1104, 1302, 3301, 3304, 3320, 3361, 3393, and 3394 of title 5 of the United States Code. We need the information requested in this form and in the associated vacancy announcements to evaluate your qualifications. Other laws require us to ask about citizenship, military service, etc. In order to keep your records in order, we request your Social Security Number (SSN) under the authority of Executive Order 9397 which requires the SSN for the purpose of uniform, orderly administration of personnel records. Failure to furnish the requested information may delay or prevent action on your application. We use your SSN to seek information about you from employers, schools, banks, and others who know you. We may use your SSN in studies and computer matching with other Government files. If you do not give us your SSN or any other information requested, we cannot process your application. Also, incomplete addresses and ZIP Codes will slow processing. We may confirm information from your records with prospective nonfederal employers concerning tenure of employment, civil service status, length of service, and date and nature of action for separation as shown on personnel action forms of specifically identified individuals.

Public Burden Statement

We estimate the public reporting burden for this collection will vary from 20 to 240 minutes with an average of 90 minutes per response, including time for reviewing instructions, searching existing data sources, gathering data, and completing and reviewing the information. Send comments regarding the burden statement or any other aspect of the collection of information, including suggestions for reducing this burden to the U.S. Office of Personnel Management (OPM), OPM Forms Officer, Washington, DC 20415-7900. The OMB number, 3206-0219, is currently valid. OPM may not collect this information and you are not required to respond, unless this number is displayed. Do not send completed application forms to this address; follow directions provided in the vacancy announcement(s).

THE FEDERAL GOVERNMENT IS AN EQUAL OPPORTUNITY EMPLOYER

U.S. Office of Personnel Management
Previous edition usable

NSN 7540-01-351-9178
50612-101

OF 612
Revised June 2006

OPTIONAL APPLICATION FOR FEDERAL EMPLOYMENT - OF 612

Form Approved
OMB No. 3206-0219

Section A - Applicant Information

Use Standard State Postal Codes (abbreviations). If outside the United States of America, and you do not have a military address, type or print "OV" in the State field (Block 6c) and fill in the Country field (Block 6e) below, leaving the Zip Code field (Block 6d) blank.

1. Job title in announcement	2. Grade(s) applying for	3. Announcement number
4a. Last name	4b. First and middle names	5. Social Security Number

6a. Mailing address		7. Phone numbers (include area code if within the United States of America)
		7a. Daytime
6b. City	6c. State 6d. Zip Code	7b. Evening

6e. Country (if not within the United States of America)

8. Email address (if available)

Section B - Work Experience

Describe your paid and non-paid work experience related to the job for which you are applying. Do not attach job description.

1. Job title (if Federal, include series and grade)

2. From *(mm/yyyy)*	3. To *(mm/yyyy)*	4. Salary per $	5. Hours per week
6. Employer's name and address			7. Supervisor's name and phone number
			7a. Name
			7b. Phone

8. May we contact your current supervisor?   Yes ☐   No ☐
If we need to contact your current supervisor before making an offer, we will contact you first.

9. Describe your duties, accomplishments and related skills (if you need to attach additional pages, include your name, address, and job announcement number)

Section C - Additional Work Experience

1. Job title (if Federal, include series and grade)

2. From *(mm/yyyy)*	3. To *(mm/yyyy)*	4. Salary per $	5. Hours per week
6. Employer's name and address			7. Supervisor's name and phone number
			7a. Name
			7b. Phone

8. May we contact your current supervisor?   Yes ☐   No ☐
If we need to contact your current supervisor before making an offer, we will contact you first.

9. Describe your duties, accomplishments and related skills (if you need to attach additional pages, include your name, address, and job announcement number)

U.S. Office of Personnel Management
Previous edition usable

NSN 7540-01-351-9178
50612-10
Page 3 of 4

OF 612
Revised June 2006

Section D - Education

Upon request from the employing Federal agency, you must provide documentation or proof that your degree(s) is from a school accredited by an accrediting body recognized by the Secretary, U.S. Department of Education, or that your education meets the other provisions outlined in the OPM Operating Manual. It will be your responsibility to secure the documentation that verifies that you attended and earned your degree(s) from this accredited institution(s) (e.g., official transcript). Federal agencies will verify your documentation.

For a list of postsecondary educational institutions and programs accredited by accrediting agencies and state approval agencies recognized by the U.S. Secretary of Education, refer to the U.S. Department of Education Office of Postsecondary Education website at http://www.ope.ed.gov/accreditation/.

For information on Educational and Training Provisions or Requirements, refer to the OPM Operating Manual available at http://www.opm.gov/qualifications/SEC-II/s2-e4.asp.

Do not list degrees received based solely on life experience or obtained from schools with little or no academic standards.

1. Last High School (HS)/GED school. Give the school's name, city, state, ZIP Code (if known), and year diploma or GED received:

2. Mark highest level completed: Some HS ☐ HS/GED ☐ Associate ☐ Bachelor ☐ Master ☐ Doctoral ☐

3. Colleges and universities attended.
   Do not attach a copy of your transcript unless requested.

| | Total Credits Earned | | Major(s) | Degree (if any), Year Received |
| | Semester | Quarter | | |

3a. Name

| City | State | Zip Code |

3b. Name

| City | State | Zip Code |

3c. Name

| City | State | Zip Code |

Section E - Other Education Completed

Do not list degrees received based solely on life experience or obtained from schools with little or no academic standards.

Section F - Other Qualifications

License or Certificate	Date of Latest License or Certificate	State or Other Licensing Agency
1f.		
2f.		

Section G - Other Qualifications

Job-related training courses (give title and year). **Job-related** skills (other languages, computer software/hardware, tools, machinery, typing speed, etc.). **Job-related** honors, awards, and special accomplishments (publications, memberships in professional/honor societies, leadership activities, public speaking, and performance awards). Give dates, but do **not** send documents unless requested.

Section H - General

1a. Are you a U.S. citizen? Yes ☐ No ☐ → 1b. If no, give the Country of your citizenship

2a. Do you claim veterans' preference? Yes ☐ No ☐ → If yes, mark your claim of 5 or 10 points below.

2b. 5 points ☐ → Attach your *Report of Separation from Active Duty* (DD 214) or other proof.

2c. 10 points ☐ → Attach an *Application for 10-Point Veterans' Preference* (SF 15) and proof required.

3. Check this box if you are an adult male born on or after January 1st 1960, and you registered for Selective Service between the ages of 18 through 25 → ☐

4. Were you ever a Federal civilian employee? Yes ☐ No ☐ → If yes, list highest civilian grade for the following:

4a. Series	4b. Grade	4c. From *(mm/yyyy)*	4d. To *(mm/yyyy)*

5a. Are you eligible for reinstatement based on career or career-conditional Federal status? Yes ☐ No ☐
   If requested in the vacancy announcement, attach *Notification of Personnel Action* (SF 50), as proof.

5b. Are you eligible under the ICTAP*? Yes ☐ No ☐
   *ICTAP (Interagency Career Transition Assistance Plan): A participant in this plan is a current or former federal employee displaced from a Federal agency. To be eligible, you must have received a formal notice of separation such as a RIF separation notice. If you are an ICTAP eligible, normally you will be provided priority consideration for vacancies within your commuting area for which you apply and are well qualified.

Section I - Applicant Certification

I certify that, to the best of my knowledge and belief, all of the information on and attached to this application is true, correct, complete, and made in good faith. I understand that false or fraudulent information on or attached to this application may be grounds for not hiring me or for firing me after I begin work, and may be punishable by fine or imprisonment. I understand that any information I give may be investigated.

1a. Signature	1b. Date *(mm/dd/yyyy)*

Previous edition usable
U.S. Office of Personnel Management

NSN 7540-01-351-9178
50612-10
Page 4 of 4

OF 612
Revised June 2006

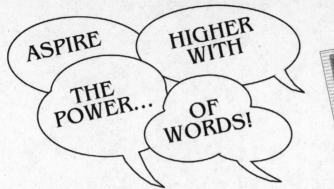

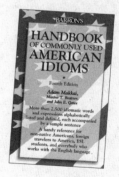